41: *Afro-American Poets Since 1955,* edited by Trudier Harris and Thadious M. Davis (1985)

42: *American Writers for Children Before 1900,* edited by Glenn E. Estes (1985)

43: *American Newspaper Journalists, 1690-1872,* edited by Perry J. Ashley (1986)

44: *American Screenwriters,* Second Series, edited by Randall Clark, Robert E. Morsberger, and Stephen O. Lesser (1986)

45: *American Poets, 1880-1945,* First Series, edited by Peter Quartermain (1986)

46: *American Literary Publishing Houses, 1900-1980: Trade and Paperback,* edited by Peter Dzwonkoski (1986)

47: *American Historians, 1866-1912,* edited by Clyde N. Wilson (1986)

48: *American Poets, 1880-1945,* Second Series, edited by Peter Quartermain (1986)

49: *American Literary Publishing Houses, 1638-1899,* 2 parts, edited by Peter Dzwonkoski (1986)

50: *Afro-American Writers Before the Harlem Renaissance,* edited by Trudier Harris (1986)

51: *Afro-American Writers from the Harlem Renaissance to 1940,* edited by Trudier Harris (1987)

52: *American Writers for Children Since 1960: Fiction,* edited by Glenn E. Estes (1986)

53: *Canadian Writers Since 1960,* First Series, edited by W. H. New (1986)

54: *American Poets, 1880-1945,* Third Series, 2 parts, edited by Peter Quartermain (1987)

55: *Victorian Prose Writers Before 1867,* edited by William B. Thesing (1987)

56: *German Fiction Writers, 1914-1945,* edited by James Hardin (1987)

57: *Victorian Prose Writers After 1867,* edited by William B. Thesing (1987)

58: *Jacobean and Caroline Dramatists,* edited by Fredson Bowers (1987)

59: *American Literary Critics and Scholars, 1800-1850,* edited by John W. Rathbun and Monica M. Grecu (1987)

60: *Canadian Writers Since 1960,* Second Series, edited by W. H. New (1987)

61: *American Writers for Children Since 1960: Poets, Illustrators, and Nonfiction Authors,* edited by Glenn E. Estes (1987)

62: *Elizabethan Dramatists,* edited by Fredson Bowers (1987)

63: *Modern American Critics, 1920-1955,* edited by Gregory S. Jay (1988)

64: *American Literary Critics and Scholars, 1850-1880,* edited by John W. Rathbun and Monica M. Grecu (1988)

65: *French Novelists, 1900-1930,* edited by Catharine Savage Brosman (1988)

66: *German Fiction Writers, 1885-1913,* 2 parts, edited by James Hardin (1988)

67: *Modern American Critics Since 1955,* edited by Gregory S. Jay (1988)

68: *Canadian Writers, 1920-1959,* First Series, edited by W. H. New (1988)

69: *Contemporary German Fiction Writers,* First Series, edited by Wolfgang D. Elfe and James Hardin (1988)

70: *British Mystery Writers, 1860-1919,* edited by Bernard Benstock and Thomas F. Staley (1988)

71: *American Literary Critics and Scholars, 1880-1900,* edited by John W. Rathbun and Monica M. Grecu (1988)

72: *French Novelists, 1930-1960,* edited by Catharine Savage Brosman (1988)

73: *American Magazine Journalists, 1741-1850,* edited by Sam G. Riley (1988)

74: *American Short-Story Writers Before 1880,* edited by Bobby Ellen Kimbel, with the assistance of William E. Grant (1988)

75: *Contemporary German Fiction Writers,* Second Series, edited by Wolfgang D. Elfe Hardin (1988)

76: *Afro-American Writers, 1940-1955,* edited by Trudier Harris (1988)

77: *British Mystery Writers, 1920-1939,* edited by Bernard Benstock and Thomas F. Sta

78: *American Short-Story Writers, 1880-1910,* edited by Bobby Ellen Kimbel, with the assi liam E. Grant (1988)

79: *American Magazine Journalists, 1850-1900,* edited by Sam G. Riley (1988)

(Continued on back endsheets)

Dictionary of Literary Biography • Volume One Hundred Nine

Eighteenth-Century British Poets

Second Series

Dictionary of Literary Biography • Volume One Hundred Nine

Eighteenth-Century British Poets
Second Series

Edited by
John Sitter
Emory University

A Bruccoli Clark Layman Book
Gale Research Inc.
Detroit, London

Matthew J. Bruccoli and Richard Layman, *Editorial Directors*
C. E. Frazer Clark, Jr., *Managing Editor*

Printed in the United States of America

Published simultaneously in the United Kingdom
by Gale Research International Limited
(An affiliated company of Gale Research Inc.)

The paper used in this publication meets the minimum requirements
of American National Standard for Information Sciences—Permanence
Paper for Printed Library Materials, ANSI Z39.48-1984. ∞™

ISBN 0-8103-4589-7
91-19801 CIP

Contents

Plan of the Series

... Almost the most prodigious asset of a country, and perhaps its most precious possession, is its native literary product–when that product is fine and noble and enduring.

Mark Twain*

The advisory board, the editors, and the publisher of the *Dictionary of Literary Biography* are joined in endorsing Mark Twain's declaration. The literature of a nation provides an inexhaustible resource of permanent worth. We intend to make literature and its creators better understood and more accessible to students and the reading public, while satisfying the standards of teachers and scholars.

To meet these requirements, *literary biography* has been construed in terms of the author's achievement. The most important thing about a writer is his writing. Accordingly, the entries in *DLB* are career biographies, tracing the development of the author's canon and the evolution of his reputation.

The purpose of *DLB* is not only to provide reliable information in a convenient format but also to place the figures in the larger perspective of literary history and to offer appraisals of their accomplishments by qualified scholars.

The publication plan for *DLB* resulted from two years of preparation. The project was proposed to Bruccoli Clark by Frederick G. Ruffner, president of the Gale Research Company, in November 1975. After specimen entries were prepared and typeset, an advisory board was formed to refine the entry format and develop the series rationale. In meetings held during 1976, the publisher, series editors, and advisory board approved the scheme for a comprehensive biographical dictionary of persons who contributed to North American literature. Editorial work on the first volume began in January 1977, and it was published in 1978. In order to make *DLB* more than a reference tool and to compile volumes that individually have claim to status as literary history, it was decided to organize volumes by topic, period, or genre. Each of these freestanding volumes provides a biographical-bibliographical guide and overview for a particular area of literature. We are convinced that this organization–as opposed to a single alphabet method–constitutes a valuable innovation in the presentation of reference material. The volume plan necessarily requires many decisions for the placement and treatment of authors who might properly be included in two or three volumes. In some instances a major figure will be included in separate volumes, but with different entries emphasizing the aspect of his career appropriate to each volume. Ernest Hemingway, for example, is represented in *American Writers in Paris, 1920-1939* by an entry focusing on his expatriate apprenticeship; he is also in *American Novelists, 1910-1945* with an entry surveying his entire career. Each volume includes a cumulative index of subject authors and articles. Comprehensive indexes to the entire series are planned.

With volume ten in 1982 it was decided to enlarge the scope of *DLB*. By the end of 1986 twenty-one volumes treating British literature had been published, and volumes for Commonwealth and Modern European literature were in progress. The series has been further augmented by the *DLB Yearbooks* (since 1981) which update published entries and add new entries to keep the *DLB* current with contemporary activity. There have also been *DLB Documentary Series* volumes which provide biographical and critical source materials for figures whose work is judged to have particular interest for students. One of these companion volumes is entirely devoted to Tennessee Williams.

We define literature as the *intellectual commerce of a nation:* not merely as belles lettres but as that ample and complex process by which ideas are generated, shaped, and transmitted. *DLB* entries are not limited to "creative writers" but extend to other figures who in their time and in their way influenced the mind of a people. Thus the series encompasses historians, journalists, publishers, and screenwriters. By this means readers of *DLB* may be aided to perceive litera-

*From an unpublished section of Mark Twain's autobiography, copyright © by the Mark Twain Company.

ture not as cult scripture in the keeping of intellectual high priests but firmly positioned at the center of a nation's life.

DLB includes the major writers appropriate to each volume and those standing in the ranks immediately behind them. Scholarly and critical counsel has been sought in deciding which minor figures to include and how full their entries should be. Wherever possible, useful references are made to figures who do not warrant separate entries.

Each *DLB* volume has a volume editor responsible for planning the volume, selecting the figures for inclusion, and assigning the entries. Volume editors are also responsible for preparing, where appropriate, appendices surveying the major periodicals and literary and intellectual movements for their volumes, as well as lists of further readings. Work on the series as a whole is coordinated at the Bruccoli Clark Layman editorial center in Columbia, South Carolina, where the editorial staff is responsible for accuracy of the published volumes.

One feature that distinguishes *DLB* is the illustration policy–its concern with the iconography of literature. Just as an author is influenced by his surroundings, so is the reader's understanding of the author enhanced by a knowledge of his environment. Therefore *DLB* volumes include not only drawings, paintings, and photographs of authors, often depicting them at various stages in their careers, but also illustrations of their families and places where they lived. Title pages are regularly reproduced in facsimile along with dust jackets for modern authors. The dust jackets are a special feature of *DLB* because they often document better than anything else the way in which an author's work was perceived in its own time. Specimens of the writers' manuscripts are included when feasible.

Samuel Johnson rightly decreed that "The chief glory of every people arises from its authors." The purpose of the *Dictionary of Literary Biography* is to compile literary history in the surest way available to us–by accurate and comprehensive treatment of the lives and work of those who contributed to it.

The *DLB* Advisory Board

Foreword

The poets discussed in this volume were all born after the death of Queen Anne in August 1714; their publishing careers range from the 1740s to the early years of the nineteenth century. It is not surprising that generalizations about such a long span should be difficult: being born after the end of the Stuart line and under George I, George II, or George III did not infuse English poets with an identifiable "post-Stuart," "Georgian," or "Hanoverian" spirit.

The later eighteenth century was both an era of rapid—even critical—change and one of political stagnation. The period was marked by great shifts in population, technological and agricultural advances, industrialization, and transformations of social organization and modes of daily life, but political institutions did not generally keep pace with these dramatic changes. The perception of living in a time of rapid movement in some areas and relative immobility in others seems to have led then, as it often does now, to anxious nostalgia as well as to eager experimentation in the arts.

Appeals to the past are common in the poetry of many periods and had rung throughout the early eighteenth century and the Restoration. But in place of the invocations of Augustan Rome and hopeful or rueful comparisons with "Augustan" England, poets of the later eighteenth century often express nostalgia through the mists of medievalism; through the legendary past of such unclassical lands as Scotland, Ireland, or Wales; and through folk traditions redolent of simpler times. William Collins's *An Ode on the Popular Superstitions of the Highlands of Scotland: Considered as the Subject of Poetry* (1788), written by 1750, and Robert Burns's earthy poetry at the close of the century have little in common in style or voice; but they share the confidence that some of poetry's richest mines may lie farthest from the urbanity of either London or Rome.

It is difficult to separate nostalgia from experimentation in some of the era's fascination with "primitive" oral poetry. Figures such as Thomas Gray's ancient Welsh poet, Christopher Smart's biblical David, and James Macpherson's gloomy, influential Ossian are all poets singing directly to their listeners. Poetry of many periods can be seen as suggestive of, or even scripted for, oral performance; but these examples hint at a particular historical longing for simple community and unmediated expression just as urbanization and increasing literacy were making authorship less direct and audiences more anonymous.

The desire to achieve oral and sometimes oracular immediacy in poetry surfaces in many of the experimental odes of the 1740s and in the general heightening of interest in lyric poetry throughout the period. Odes, especially those of Collins and Gray, may be more difficult, abstract, and abstruse than any verse epistle. But epistles and other kinds of topical or occasional poetry call attention, even at their most informal, to writing and reading, while the ode strives for the illusion of rapt speech. The wish to transcend the medium of print is at variance both with the poetry of Alexander Pope, whose careful annotation of his own work called attention to its printed existence, and with the great novelists of the era, whose documentary claims or comic asides call on the reader to recall that the text is very much a text.

But it is easy to exaggerate the differences between later eighteenth-century poetry and the Age of Pope. Satires continued to be written in the later decades, classical allusions did not suddenly vanish in Gothic darkness, and poetry remained a largely supple and social medium. Pope's striking domination of the first half of the century no doubt leads even most specialists to regard the poetry of the period as more homogeneous than it was. The later half of the century presents the opposite problem: there is no presiding poet for whom one is tempted to name it. Much of the period is frequently called the Age of Johnson; but it is principally Samuel Johnson's achievement as a prose writer and the sheer weight of his personality—not his distinctive voice as a poet—that has led to that designation.

Without the convenient designation (however misleading) of a part to stand for the whole, literary historians have tended to find the poetry of the later eighteenth century confusing in its variety and sometimes to impose unity on it under the banners of "Sentiment," "Sensibility," or "Pre-Romanticism." The limits of these labels are best recognized at once. If they keep a reader from catching the humor in even such ardent enthusiasts as Collins or Smart or from hearing anything in the disarming conversation of William Cowper's blank verse but occasional intimations of William Wordsworth, then generalization has impoverished experience.

It is the hope of the editor and contributors that this volume will provide information and guidance enough to direct readers back to the poets themselves and thus to the full variety of experience represented in and by later eighteenth-century poetry.

—John Sitter

Acknowledgments

This book was produced by Bruccoli Clark Layman, Inc. Karen L. Rood is senior editor for the *Dictionary of Literary Biography* series. Philip B. Dematteis was the in-house editor.

Production coordinator is James W. Hipp. Projects manager is Charles D. Brower. Photography editors are Edward Scott and Timothy C. Lundy. Permissions editor is Jean W. Ross. Layout and graphics supervisor is Penney L. Haughton. Copyediting supervisor is Bill Adams. Typesetting supervisor is Kathleen M. Flanagan. Systems manager is George F. Dodge. Charles Lee Egleston is editorial associate. The production staff includes Rowena Betts, Teresa Chaney, Patricia Coate, Gail Crouch, Margaret McGinty Cureton, Sarah A. Estes, Robert Fowler, Mary L. Goodwin, Cynthia Hallman, Ellen McCracken, Kathy Lawler Merlette, Catherine A. Murray, John Myrick, Pamela D. Norton, Cathy J. Reese, Laurrè Sinckler-Reeder, Maxine K. Smalls, and Betsy L. Weinberg.

Walter W. Ross and Timothy D. Tebalt did library research. They were assisted by the following librarians at the Thomas Cooper Library of the University of South Carolina: Jens Holley and the inter-library loan staff; Roger Mortimer and the staff of the Department of Rare Books and Special Collections; reference librarians Gwen Baxter, Daniel Boice, Faye Chadwell, Jo Cottingham, Cathy Eckman, Rhonda Felder, Gary Geer, Jackie Kinder, Laurie Preston, Jean Rhyne, Carol Tobin, Virginia Weathers, and Connie Widney; circulation-department head Thomas Marcil; and acquisitions-searching supervisor David Haggard.

Dictionary of Literary Biography • Volume One Hundred Nine

Eighteenth-Century British Poets
Second Series

Dictionary of Literary Biography

Mark Akenside

(9 November 1721 - 23 June 1770)

Robert Mahony
The Catholic University of America

BOOKS: *The British Philippic: A Poem, in Miltonic Verse. Occasion'd by the Insults of the Spaniards, and the Preparations for War,* as Britannicus (London: Printed by J. Chaney, for A. Dodd, 1738); also published as *The Voice of Liberty; or, A British Philippic: A Poem, in Miltonic Verse. Occasion'd by the Insults of the Spaniards, and the Preparations for War. To Which Is Prefix'd a Copper-plate, Representing the Sufferings of Our Captive Sailors in a Spanish Prison* (London: Printed by J. Chaney, for A. Dodd, 1738);

The Pleasures of Imagination: A Poem. In Three Books (London: Printed for R. Dodsley, 1744; revised, 1754); revised as *The Pleasures of Imagination. By Mark Akenside, M.D. To Which Is Prefixed a Critical Essay on the Poem, by Mrs. Barbauld* (London: Printed for T. Cadell, junior, and W. Davies, by R. Noble, 1794); republished as *The Pleasures of Imagination: A Poem, in Three Books. By Dr. Akenside. To Which Is Added The Art of Preserving Health: A Poem, in Three Books by Dr. Armstrong* (Exeter, N.H.: Printed by Thomas Odiorne, 1794);

An Epistle to the Rev. Mr. Warburton: Occasioned by His Treatment of the Author of The Pleasures of Imagination (London: Printed for R. Dodsley; and sold by M. Cooper, 1744);

An Epistle to Curio (London: Printed for R. Dodsley; and sold by M. Cooper, 1744);

Dissertatio Medica Inauguralis de Ortu et Incremento Fœtus Humani (Leiden: Potuliet, 1744);

Odes on Several Subjects (London: Printed for R. Dodsley, and sold by M. Cooper, 1745);

revised and enlarged edition (London: Printed for R. & J. Dodsley, 1760);

An Ode to the Right Honourable the Earl of Huntingdon (London: Printed for R. Dodsley, and sold by M. Cooper, 1748);

An Ode to the Country Gentlemen of England (London: Printed for R. & J. Dodsley; and sold by M. Cooper, 1758);

Notes on the Postscript to a Pamphlet Intitled, "Observations Anatomical and Physiological &c. by Alexander Monro, Junior, M.D. (London: Printed for R. & J. Dodsley, 1758);

Oratio Anniversaria, quam ex Harveii in Theatro Collegii Regalis Medicorum Londinensis die Octobris XVIII a. MDCCLIX Habuit Marcus Akenside (London: Printed for R. & J. Dodsley, 1760);

De Dysentaria Commentarius (London: Printed for R. & J. Dodsley, 1764); translated by John Ryan, M.D., as *A Commentary on the Dysentery; or, Bloody Flux* (London: Printed for F. Noble; and J. Noble, 1767);

An Ode to the Late Thomas Edwards, Esq.: Written in the Year M.DCC.LI. (London: Printed for J. Dodsley, 1766);

The Poems of Mark Akenside, M.D., edited by Jeremiah Dyson (London: Printed by W. Bowyer & J. Nichols; and sold by J. Dodsley, 1772);

The Poetical Works of Mark Akenside, with "Life" by Samuel Johnson, volume 55 of *The Works of the English Poets* (London: C. Bathurst, 1779); revised edition, edited, with "Life," by Alexander Dyce (London: Pickering, 1835; Boston: Little, Brown, 1854); republished, with "Memoir and Critical Dissertation" by George Gilfillan (Edinburgh: Nichol, 1857); revised again, edited by Charles Cowden Clarke, with Gilfillan's "Memoir" (Edinburgh: Nichol, 1863).

OTHER: "A Song," in *Friendship and Love: A Dialogue. Addressed to a Young Lady. To Which Is Added, a Song by Mr. Akinside, Author of The Pleasures of Imagination* (London: Printed for G. Steidel; and sold by M. Cooper, 1745);

The Museum; or, The Literary and Historical Register, 3 volumes, edited by Akenside (London: printed for J. Dodsley, 1746-1747);

Robert Dodsley, ed., *A Collection of Poems in Six Volumes: By Several Hands*, editorial assistance and contributions in volume 6 by Akenside (London: Printed by J. Hughs, for R. & J. Dodsley, 1748-1758);

William Harvey, *Guilielmi Harveii Opera Omnia: A Collegio Medicorum Londinensi Edita: MDCCLXVI*, edited, with a preface, by Akenside (London: Printed by William Bowyer, 1766);

John Almon, ed., *The New Foundling Hospital for Wit: Being a Collection of Curious Pieces in Verse and Prose, Several of Which Were Never Before Printed: Part the Sixth*, includes poems by Akenside (London: Printed for J. Almon, 1773), pp. 23-29.

SELECTED PERIODICAL PUBLICATION—UNCOLLECTED: R. M. Williams, "Two Unpublished Poems by Akenside," *Modern Language Notes*, 57 (December 1942): 626-631.

Shown the manuscript of Mark Akenside's first major work, *The Pleasures of Imagination* (1744), Alexander Pope is said to have commented to the bookseller Robert Dodsley that this was "no every-day writer." Pope was generous to younger poets, but in this case he was encouraging Dodsley to publish what would become one of the more popular poems of the eighteenth century. Akenside was only twenty-two when it appeared, and *The Pleasures of Imagination* dominated the rest of his literary career; ten years after its first publication he began a rewriting and expansion of it that was still unfinished at his death. This long verse essay was his most important work; but his shorter poems are valuable both as experiments in form and theme in their own right and as part of a body of lyric poetry produced in the 1740s and 1750s, the period of Akenside's most concentrated poetic activity. While poems by Thomas Gray and William Collins are the most enduring monuments to this period, Akenside's contribution to the venturesomeness that characterizes these decades is a significant one.

Mark Akinside (as the name was originally spelled) was born in Newcastle-upon-Tyne on 9 November 1721 to Mark Akinside, a butcher, and Mary Lumsden Akinside. The boy injured his foot in an accident with a cleaver in his father's shop when he was seven, leaving him with a limp for the rest of his life. He attended the Royal Free Grammar School in Newcastle and then a private academy operated by a Nonconformist minister. He began writing poems while still in school, and four poems in the *Gentleman's*

Magazine have been identified as his. The first, "The Virtuoso: in Imitation of Spenser's Style and Stanza" (April 1737), appeared with a brief note signed "Marcus" describing the piece as "The Performance of one in his sixteenth Year." A satire on indiscriminate collecting, the poem is one of the first examples of Spenserian imitation in the mid eighteenth century. It was followed by "Ambition and Content: A Fable" (May 1737), an allegory in heroic couplets also signed "Marcus." "Marcus" returned to satire with "The Poet: A Rhapsody" (July 1737), an exercise in deliberately overwrought self-mockery and his first attempt at blank verse. A year later, signing himself "Britannicus," he used that measure again in "A British Philippic: Occasioned by the Insults of the Spaniards and the Present Preparations for War" (August 1738), a jingoistic attack on the Robert Walpole government's pacific stance toward Spain. It was quickly published separately—Akenside's first independent appearance in print—in two editions, as *The British Philippic* and as *The Voice of Liberty*.

The congregation at Akenside's Dissenting church recognized his scholastic promise, and support for further study was arranged from a fund used to prepare Dissenters for the ministry at a Scottish or Continental university. He entered Edinburgh University, probably in autumn 1738; but he soon decided against becoming a minister and shifted to medical studies, though he continued to receive assistance from the Dissenters' fund. "Hymn to Science," which appeared unsigned but dated at Newcastle in the *Gentleman's Magazine* (October 1739), points to his academic transition, invoking science to dispel the "phantoms" of superstition and authority and penetrate to the sources of true knowledge. "An Ode," dated July 1740 in the manuscript at the Huntington Library but first published as "To Cordelia" in *The Works of Mark Akinside, M.D., in Verse and Prose* (1808), encourages Cordelia's love; whereas "Love, an Elegy" (said to have been privately printed, though no copy appears to survive) reflects in heroic couplets the speaker's disappointment in love and renounces the pursuit of it. Perhaps included with this poem in its apparently lost private edition was "For the Winter Solstice," dated 11 December 1740, the first version of an ode published in *Odes on Several Subjects* (1745). Here the approach of winter prompts musings on Providence and the poet's susceptibility to classical, patriotic, and academic influences.

Akenside joined the Medical Society of Edinburgh on 30 December 1740, but little else is known of his years as a student. By mid 1742 he had returned to Newcastle, where presumably he established himself sufficiently to begin repaying the Dissenters' fund. Three letters of 1742-1743 to David Fordyce, professor of moral philosophy at Marischal College in Edinburgh, indicate that Akenside was studying philosophy (he mentions both the Greek Stoics and the earl of Shaftesbury) and working on what became *The Pleasures of Imagination*. It was also in 1742 that he seems to have met Jeremiah Dyson, who then went to Leiden to study civil law. Akenside finished the first version of *The Pleasures of Imagination* in the summer of 1743, brought it to London, and offered it to Dodsley for £120. After showing it to Pope, Dodsley accepted the work. The poet stayed in London, probably seeing the work through the press. During the autumn of 1743 Dyson returned from Holland and their friendship grew stronger. *The Pleasures of Imagination* was published anonymously 14 January 1744 and was dedicated to Dyson.

The Pleasures of Imagination has roots in both ancient Greek and modern English philosophy, bringing ethics, aesthetics, and psychology into harmony by emphasizing the primacy of the individual poet. Akenside draws his title from Joseph Addison's "The Pleasures of The Imagination" in the *Spectator*, numbers 411-421 (1712). Addison had applied the psychological ideas of John Locke to aesthetics, noting the literary effects gained by appealing to the senses, particularly vision. He insisted that "a poet should take as much pains in forming his imagination as a philosopher in cultivating his understanding" (number 417) and that "The talent of affecting the imagination sets off all writing in general but is the very life and highest perfection of poetry" (number 421). Addison's papers on imagination had already inspired poetry; his contemporary Thomas Parnell's *Essay on the Different Stiles of Poetry* (1713) was an allegorical, vision-based poem. Akenside's project thirty years later was more ambitious, including Plato, the Stoics, Shaftesbury, and Francis Hutcheson as well as Locke and Addison among its philosophical influences. Moreover, Akenside's prose introduction, "Design," mentions Virgil's *Georgics* and Horace's epistles as his models for choosing the blank-verse familiar essay as his form (though his poem more closely resembles Lucretius's *De Rerum Natura*), and his

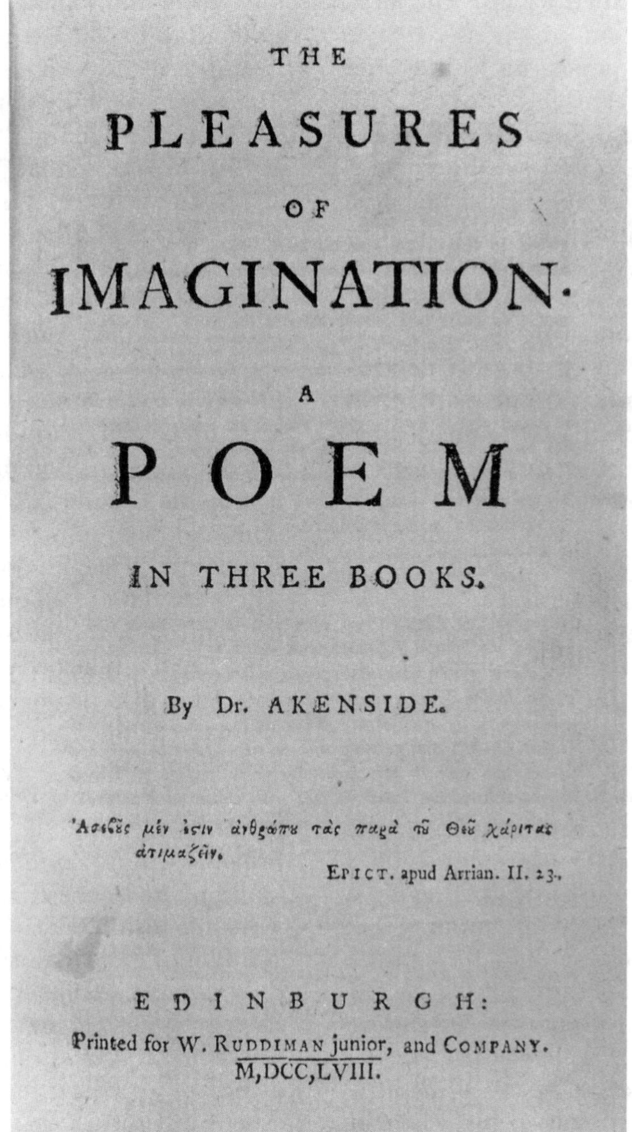

THE

PLEASURES

OF

IMAGINATION.

A

POEM

IN THREE BOOKS.

By Dr. AKENSIDE.

Ἀσεβοῦς μὲν ἐστιν ἀνθρώπου τὰς παρὰ τοῦ Θεοῦ χάριτας ἀτιμαζεῖν.

EPICT. apud Arrian. II. 23.

EDINBURGH:

Printed for W. RUDDIMAN junior, and COMPANY.

M,DCC,LVIII.

Title page for the 1758 edition of the long verse essay, first published in 1744, that was Akenside's most important work. He was still revising the poem at the time of his death.

style shows the influences of John Milton, James Thomson, and Pope.

This remarkably assimilative enterprise is an analysis and psychological history of imaginative pleasure. While it is a descriptive poem, mental processes rather than the beauties of nature are its subject. The natural world and its artistic representations evoke pleasure, of course, but Akenside treats this sort of pleasure without employing any descriptions of nature. According to "Design," the imaginative powers occupy the middle ground "between the organs of bodily sense and the faculties of moral perception"; they enable us to form delightful perceptions that we can recall independent of the objects provoking them. Such independent recollection makes possible the creation of poetry and other imaginative arts, which in turn arouse imaginative pleasure. Detailing these processes and the varieties of pleasure that imagination thus affords, Akenside maintains the relationship of ethics and psychology to aesthetics and ascribes to the poet the task of so harmonizing them as to guide humankind to an increased awareness of the world and of its own place in the world. This orientational function is the more necessary because art and philosophy have become separated since ancient times, and the more possible because the atmosphere of political freedom in modern England is conducive to their reunion. There is, however, more to nature than the external world. In the third book of *The Pleasures of Imagination* Akenside considers human character, especially as delineated in ridicule, which, upholding Shaftesbury, he regards as a means of destroying folly.

In *The Pleasures of Imagination* Akenside took upon himself the work of analyst and guide he attributes to the true poet; the task is impeded somewhat by long-windedness and obscurities of diction. Nevertheless, the poem appealed to contemporary readers, appearing in three more editions from Dodsley in London and one from Faulkner in Dublin in 1744; for Dodsley's third edition the poet revealed his name (still spelled "Akinside") on the title page, perhaps because the hack Richard Rolt was said to have claimed credit for the poem. Gray wrote ambivalently to his friend Thomas Warton on 26 April 1744 that the work "seems to me above the middleing [*sic*], and now and then (but for a little while) rises even to the best, particularly in Description. it [*sic*] is often obscure and even unintelligible." Akenside had more sharply offended William Warburton, who attacked two footnotes on the utility of ridicule in his *Remarks on Several Occasional Reflections* (1744).

Dodsley published the poet's anonymous rejoinder (sometimes attributed to Dyson), *An Epistle to the Rev. Mr. Warburton*, on 29 April 1744, while Akenside was completing his medical education. Having taken no degree at Edinburgh, he had proceeded to Leiden early in April 1744; obtaining the M.D. from Leiden required only an examination upon entry and the completion and defense of a thesis. He enrolled on 7 April and received the degree on 16 May. Obviously he had been preparing his thesis on the origin and growth of the human fetus well before arriving in Leiden, probably while writing *The Pleasures of the Imagination*. His work in embryology seems to have influenced the composition of the poem, in which images of fecundity abound. Concerning a long verse paragraph describing the poet at work, Robin Dix has argued that "Akenside was consciously drawing a parallel between the production of a work of art and the production of a living organism," thus anticipating the "fully fledged theory of creativity and organicism developed in Romantic aesthetics."

Akenside's thesis controverted the generally established embryological position advanced by Antonie van Leeuwenhoek, the Dutch scientist and inventor of the microscope, and in other respects Akenside shows that he had little love for Holland. His ode "On Leaving Holland," published in *Odes on Several Subjects*, contrasts the country's "marshy levels lank and bare," its people's "sober love of gain," and their rulers, "undignified by public choice," with the hills, groves, bright skies, and freedom of England, to which he quickly returned on receiving his degree. In June 1744 he settled in Northampton and began a medical practice. The anonymous *Epistle to Curio*, published by Dodsley in November 1744, renews the political stance of *The British Philippic* by satirizing William Pulteney's desertion of the "Patriot" Whig cause. Akenside then turned to lyrics: with *Friendship and Love*, a poem apparently written by someone else and published in London by G. Steidel in January 1745, there appeared the brief "Song" by "Mr. Akinside." On 26 March 1745 his anonymous collection *Odes on Several Subjects* was published by Dodsley.

Composed at intervals over the years since his juvenile *Gentleman's Magazine* pieces, these ten odes show greater diversity in subject, form, and meter than those early lyric experiments. Their aim, expressed in the introductory "Advertisement," is correctness, a matter of following the best—especially classical—models "in the beauty of words and the gracefulness of numbers." The collection alternates between odes dealing with poetry or with Akenside's sense of himself as a poet, and those offering friends advice or caution against love's passion. The first type is more noteworthy, moving from the tentativeness of "On the Winter Solstice" through the confidence of "On the Absence of the Poetic Inclination"—in which invoking "the soul of Milton" is sufficient to regain the absent muse—to the assertiveness of the final poem, "On Lyric Poetry." Here he catalogues the Greek lyric poets whose company he, though "so late," has joined by virtue of his sensitivity to natural beauty and the inspiration of English liberty. His achievement in the odes is uneven: he displays great metrical assurance and is occasionally forceful and elegant; he evokes nature and his classical influences, but he lacks a vision or voice, such as Gray or Collins could produce, that transcends the limits of those influences. Horace Walpole described Akenside to Horace Mann in a letter of 29 March 1745 as "another of these tame geniuses." *Odes on Several Subjects* was reprinted in 1745 in an apparent Edinburgh piracy, for the public was more generous; the work paved the way for other lyric collections, such as the odes of Joseph Warton and Collins, which were published soon afterward.

Akenside did not succeed in his medical practice in Northampton. Before the end of 1745 he moved to London, where he lived and began a practice in Dyson's house in Hampstead. Early in 1746 Dodsley engaged Akenside as editor of the *Museum,* a fortnightly literary magazine launched at the end of March. Akenside wrote essays, organized book reviews, and supervised the whole production, which ran until September 1747 and included poems by Collins, Joseph and Thomas Warton, and David Garrick. The *Museum* is an accurate index of the taste of the mid 1740s. Two of Akenside's own poems of 1746, not published until years later, also reflect the period in their very different embodiments of the supernatural within the natural world. "Hymn to the Naiads" celebrates the title creatures' dominion over nature in elegant blank verse; it is an exercise in classical correctness, indebted—Akenside remarks in a note—to the hymns of Callimachus for its "mythological passion." "To the Evening Star" more elegiacally invokes the power of evening to inspire the poet and soothe the afflictions of human life, anticipating poems by Collins, William Blake, William Wordsworth, and John Keats. While the trend it represents is, in retrospect, that of the most lasting poetry of the period, Akenside's lyrics for the next two decades take a different direction. They are mainly addressed to friends and acquaintances, and contain references to his political sympathies. They seem almost experiments in theme, developing from the slight odes of friendly advice in the 1745 collection to combine the classicism of his nearly republican politics with that of friendship poetry. Akenside's didacticism can be heavy-handed, and his emphasis on the poet's function as political voice and guide is stronger than his social feeling, so that these poems leave a chilly impression. Only one appeared at all quickly: *An Ode to the Right Honourable the Earl of Huntingdon,* an encomium fraught with classical allusions calling upon Huntingdon to join the cause of freedom, which Dodsley published 19 January 1748 (and reprinted in February) with notes and with Akenside's name on the title page.

Akenside's medical career fared little better in Hampstead than it had in Northampton, and about 1748 the generous Dyson, who had become clerk of the House of Commons, provided him with a house in Bloomsbury Square and three hundred pounds a year. Akenside then began to make headway in his profession. He became a licentiate of the Royal College of Physicians in 1751, obtained a medical degree mandamus from Cambridge in 1753, and advanced to fellow of the Royal College of Physicians in 1754. He delivered the Gulstonian Lectures in Anatomy at the college in 1755 and the Croonian Lectures in 1756; he repeated parts of the Gulstonian Lectures to the Royal Society in 1757. In January 1759 he was appointed assistant physician at St. Thomas's Hospital in Southwark and in March was promoted to physician. In the same year he was Harveian orator at the Royal College, and his address was published in 1760. Meanwhile, he continued to compose lyrics. In 1754, a decade after the first four editions of *The Pleasures of Imagination* had appeared, a fifth was published with significant revisions. He then em-

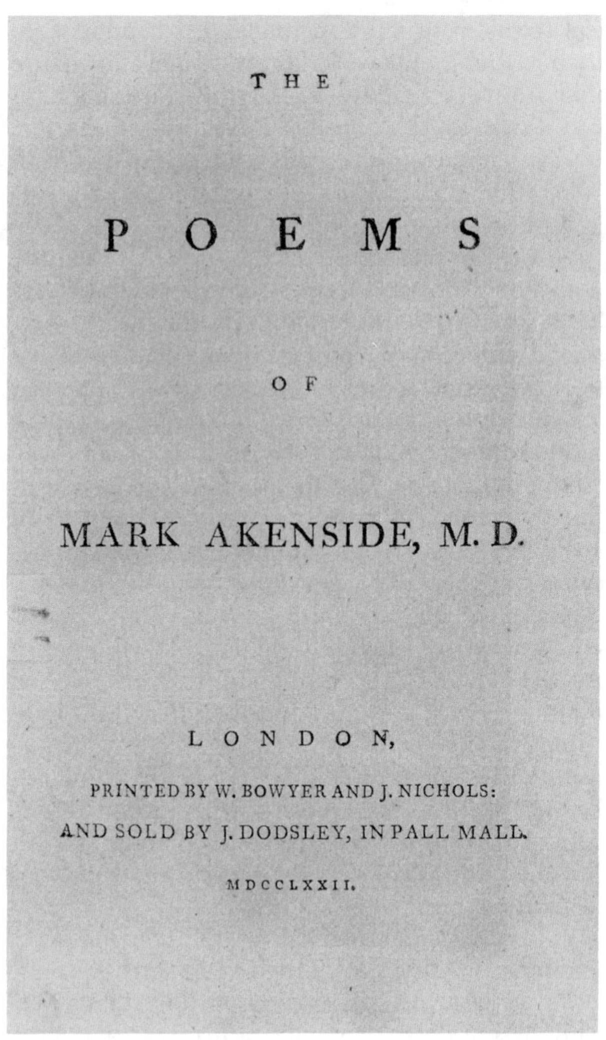
THE

POEMS

OF

MARK AKENSIDE, M. D.

LONDON,

PRINTED BY W. BOWYER AND J. NICHOLS:

AND SOLD BY J. DODSLEY, IN PALL MALL.

MDCCLXXII.

Title page for the posthumous collection of Akenside's poems edited by his friend Jeremiah Dyson

barked upon a complete rewriting of the poem as *The Pleasures of the Imagination*, finishing the first book in 1757; it was printed in a small private edition that has not survived. In 1758 Dodsley published two editions of *An Ode to the Country Gentlemen of England* (spelling the poet's name "Akenside"), a call to patriotism during the Seven Years' War. Akenside had assisted Dodsley in assembling *A Collection of Poems in Six Volumes: by Several Hands*, the great anthology of contemporary verse published between 1748 and 1758, and some of Akenside's poems were first printed in the final volume: its opening pages include "Hymn to the Naiads," the patriotic "Ode to the Bishop of Winchester" (composed in 1754), and six "Inscriptions," as well as *An Ode to the Right Honourable the Earl of Huntingdon*. Gray complained in a letter to Thomas Warton on 8 March 1758: "why should people learn Greek to lose their imagination, their ear, and their mother tongue [?]" Gray may have been provoked by the cool classicism of the "Hymn to the Naiads," but Akenside's "Inscriptions," apparently influenced by the *Greek Anthology*, inspired similar works by Samuel Taylor Coleridge and Robert Southey, and, according to Geoffrey H. Hartman, formed "a vital intermediary between the conventional lyric forms of the eighteenth century and the romantic poem"

Dodsley published a second edition of *Odes on Several Subjects* in 1760; it was much expanded from the ten odes of 1745, which were themselves somewhat revised and rearranged. This volume included a few poems of disappointed love, showing competence in a stock lyric form. The other poems in the collection, both those mixing friendly address and political comment and such patriotic pieces as the reprinted *Ode to the Country Gentlemen of England*, sound the political tone of much of his lyric writing after 1745. But Akenside's politics soon shifted. In 1760 he joined Dyson in supporting the government after the accession of George III. Perhaps in return, Dyson got a place in the royal household, and in 1761 Akenside became physician-in-ordinary to the queen. That same year an admirer presented him with the bed on which Milton had died, hoping to prompt a celebration of Milton and British liberty in verse; the poet did not oblige, though he was delighted with the gift. Indeed, he wrote little more poetry at all, except for continuing to rework *The Pleasures of the Imagination*. From Craven Street, where he had lived since 1759, he moved to Burlington Street and devoted himself almost entirely to medicine. A paper on the heart, read to the Royal Society in 1763, was published in its *Philosophical Transactions*, and the next year Robert and James Dodsley published his major medical work, *De Dysentaria Commentarius*. The reworked second book of *The Pleasures of the Imagination* was finished in 1765; it may, like the first, have been printed in a private edition that has not survived. In 1766 Akenside prepared the Royal College of Physicians' edition of the works of William Harvey for the press and wrote the preface. Also in 1766 James Dodsley published *An Ode to the Late Thomas Edwards, Esq.*, written fifteen years earlier to castigate Warburton's 1751 edition of Pope; its publication was provoked by Warburton's republishing in 1766 his critical comments of 1744 on a point raised in *The Pleasures of Imagination*. The 1766 ode was the last of Akenside's poems to appear in his lifetime; his final medical writings, three papers read before the Royal College of Physicians in 1767, were published in the first volume of its *Medical Transactions* in 1768.

On 23 June 1770 Akenside died on Milton's deathbed of a fever caused by a throat infection. He had written much of the third book of *The Pleasures of the Imagination* and a fragment of a fourth. Dyson, his executor, collected most of his verse in 1772 in *The Poems of Mark Akenside, M.D.*, including both *The Pleasures of Imagination* and its unfinished expansion; *Odes on Several Subjects*, with some additions; the "Hymn to the Naiads"; and the six "Inscriptions" of 1758, to which three were added. It appears from Dyson's introductory "General Argument" that *The Pleasures of the Imagination* was intended to be almost a completely new poem, expanding and clarifying the earlier version. But in the intervals of a busy professional life Akenside only had the opportunity to make the poem more sonorous than the original and add some illustrative matter, without significantly developing its theme. In fact, while the unfinished later version usually accompanied the earlier in successive editions of his poems, it was the original *Pleasures of Imagination* that maintained Akenside's popularity among readers of poetry for generations after his death. This success was assisted by a long critical essay on the poem by Anna Laetitia Barbauld which introduced the 1794 edition and was often reprinted. In 1832 Charles Bucke's admiring biographical and critical study of the poet and the poem appeared, and Alexander Dyce compiled an edition, with a useful biography, for the much-reprinted Aldine series in 1835. George Gilfillan supplied a biographical and critical introduction for an edition in 1857; Gilfillan's introduction was included with Charles Cowden Clarke's edition of the text in 1863. Charles Houpt's biographical and critical summary, published in 1944, has stood since as the standard source of information on the poet's life.

Akenside's other lyrics had less staying power. Even in the late eighteenth century he was thought inferior to such contemporaries as Gray, and though he exerted occasional influence on Romantic poets he came to represent an outmoded temper. Moreover, as popular taste in poetry shifted gradually in the nineteenth century, even his long verse essay was neglected. Akenside came to be known as, at best, a poet of historical rather than enduring significance, as commentators from the Victorian era through the first half of the twentieth century regarded him mainly as a "pre-Romantic." More recently his poetry has drawn sporadic attention for its own sake. Akenside did more than pave the way for other, finer poets; he caught the tenor of his time, especially in the 1740s, demonstrating the direction in poetry the public would accept. An accomplished metrist in a variety of forms, he was an exponent of a classical taste and of the conception of the poet as guide, whether in aesthetic or political matters. Nonetheless, he could not often establish in his poems an atmosphere of emotion or warmth, and he was—increasingly so after his death—a poet more respected than loved.

Bibliography:

I. A. Williams, "Mark Akenside," in his *Seven Eighteenth-Century Bibliographies* (London: Dulau, 1924), pp. 75-97.

Biographies:

Charles Bucke, *On the Life, Writings and Genius of Akenside: With Some Account of His Friends* (London: Cochrane, 1832);

Charles T. Houpt, *Mark Akenside: A Biographical and Critical Study* (Philadelphia: University of Pennsylvania, 1944).

References:

Alfred Owen Aldridge, "Akenside and Imagination," *Studies in Philology*, 42 (October 1945): 769-792;

Aldridge, "Akenside and the Hierarchy of Beauty," *Modern Language Quarterly*, 8 (March 1947): 65-67;

Aldridge, "The Eclecticism of *The Pleasures of Imagination*," *Journal of the History of Ideas*, 5 (June 1944): 292-314;

Aldridge, "Mark Akenside, Anna Seward and Colour," *Notes and Queries*, 193 (December 1948): 562-563;

Mark Box, "A Quotation in 'The Pleasures of Imagination' Identified," *Notes and Queries*, 229 (March 1984): 9-10;

Howard Buck, "Smollett and Dr. Akenside," *Journal of English and Germanic Philology*, 31 (January 1932): 10-26;

Otto Bundt, "Akenside's Leben and Werke," *Anglia*, 20 (1898): 1-44, 467-532; 21 (1898): 89-164;

Bundt, *Akensides Leben und Werke: Mit besonderer beruecksichtigung der "Pleasures of Imagination"* (Halle: Karras, 1897);

John Buxton, "Mark Akenside," in his *The Grecian Taste: Literature in the Age of Neoclassicism* (London: Macmillan / New York: Barnes & Noble, 1978), pp. 25-47;

R. W. Chapman, "A Note on the First Edition of The Pleasures of Imagination," *Review of English Studies*, 1 (July 1925): 346-348;

W. P. Courtney, *Dodsley's Collection of Poetry: Its Contents and Contributors* (London: Humphreys, 1910), p. 60;

Robin Dix, "Akenside's University Career: The Manuscript Evidence"; "Organic Theories of Art: The Importance of Embryology," *Notes and Queries*, 230 (June 1985): 212-218;

Dix, "The Composition of Akenside's *The Pleasures of the Imagination* (1772)," *Notes and Queries*, 231 (December 1986): 521-523.

Edward Dowden, "Mark Akenside," in *The English Poets*, edited by T. H. Ward (London: Macmillan, 1880), III: 341-344;

D. F. Foxon, "Akenside's *The Pleasures of Imagination*," *Book Collector*, 5 (Spring 1956): 77-78;

Edmund Gosse, "Mark Akenside, Poet and Physician," *Living Age*, 311, no. 4 (1921): 787-791;

Thomas Gray, *Correspondence of Thomas Gray*, edited by Paget Toynbee and Leonard Whibley, with corrections and additions by H. W. Starr (Oxford: Clarendon Press, 1971), I: 224; II: 566;

Jeffrey Hart, "Akenside's Revision of *The Pleasures of Imagination*," *Publications of the Modern Language Association*, 74 (March 1959): 67-74;

Geoffrey H. Hartman, "Reflections on the Evening Star: Akenside to Coleridge," in *New Perspectives on Wordsworth and Coleridge: Selected Papers from the English Institute,* edited by Hartman (New York: Columbia University Press, 1972), pp. 85-131;

Hartman, "Wordsworth, Inscriptions and Romantic Nature Poetry," in *From Sensibility to Romanticism,* edited by F. W. Hilles and Harold Bloom (New York: Oxford University Press, 1965), pp. 379-399;

G. J. ten Hoor, "Akenside's *The Pleasures of Imagination* in Germany," *Journal of English and Germanic Philology,* 38 (January 1939): 96-106.

Samuel Johnson, "Akenside," in his *Prefaces Biographical and Critical to the Works of the English Poets* (London: C. Bathurst, 1781), X: 1-18;

Johnson, "Akenside," in his *Lives of the English Poets,* edited by G. B. Hill (Oxford: Clarendon Press, 1905), III: 411-420;

Martin Kallich, "The Association of Ideas and Akenside's Pleasures of Imagination," *Modern Language Notes,* 62 (March 1947): 166-173;

W. S. Lewis, ed., *Correspondence of Horace Walpole,* volume 19 (New Haven: Yale University Press, 1954), p. 28;

John L. Mahoney, "Akenside and Shaftesbury: The Influence of Philosophy on English Romantic Poetry," *Discourse,* 4 (Autumn 1961): 241-247;

Robert Marsh, "Akenside and Addison: The Impact of Psychological Criticism on Early English Romantic Poetry," *British Journal of Aesthetics,* 6 (October 1966): 365-374;

Marsh, "Akenside and the Powers of Imagination," in his *Four Dialectical Theories of Poetry* (Chicago: University of Chicago Press, 1965), pp. 48-86;

John F. Norton, "Akenside's The Pleasures of Imagination: An Exercise in Poetics," *Eighteenth Century Studies,* 3 (Spring 1970): 366-383;

Arthur Pollard, "Keats and Akenside: A Borrowing in the 'Ode to a Nightingale,' " *Modern Language Review,* 51 (January 1956): 75-77;

George R. Potter, "Mark Akenside, Prophet of Evolution," *Modern Philology,* 24 (August 1926): 55-64;

W. L. Renwick, "Akenside and Others," *Durham University Journal,* new series 3 (1942): 94-102;

Renwick, "Notes on Some Lesser Poets of the Eighteenth Century," in *Essays on the Eighteenth Century Presented to David Nichol Smith* (Oxford: Clarendon Press, 1945), pp. 141-145;

C. Anderson Silber, "The Evolution of Akenside's *The Pleasures of the Imagination*: The Missing Link Established," *Papers of the Bibliographical Society of America,* 65 (October-December 1971): 357-363;

John E. Sitter, "Mother, Memory, Muse and Poetry after Pope," *English Literary History,* 44 (1977): 312-336;

Sitter, "Theodicy at Mid-Century: Young, Akenside and Hume," *Eighteenth-Century Studies,* 12 (Fall 1978): 90-106;

Sitter, "To the *Vanity of Human Wishes* through the 1740's," *Studies in Philology,* 74 (October 1977): 445-464;

Lyle E. Smith, "Akenside's A British Philippic: New Evidence," *Papers of the Bibliographical Society of America,* 68 (October-December 1974): 418-427;

William Warburton, *Remarks on Several Occasional Reflections* (London: Printed for J. & P. Knapton, 1744);

Richard Wendorf, "Poetical Character in the 1740's," in his *William Collins and Eighteenth Century English Poetry* (Minneapolis: University of Minnesota Press, 1981), pp. 33-41.

Anna Laetitia Barbauld

(20 June 1743 - 9 March 1825)

Elizabeth Kraft
University of Georgia

See also the Barbauld entry in *DLB 107: British Romantic Prose Writers, 1789-1832: First Series.*

BOOKS: *Poems*, as Anna Laetitia Aikin (London: Printed for Joseph Johnson, 1773); enlarged as *Poems: A New Edition, Corrected. To Which Is Added An Epistle to William Wilberforce, Esq.* (London: Printed for Joseph Johnson, 1792; Boston: Wells & Lilly, 1820);

Miscellaneous Pieces in Prose, by Aikin and John Aikin (London: Printed for J. Johnson, 1773);

Hymns in Prose for Children (London: Printed for J. Johnson, 1781; Norwich, Conn.: Printed by John Trumbull, 1786);

Lessons for Children, from Two to Three Years Old (London: Printed for J. Johnson, 1787);

Lessons for Children of Three Years Old: Part I (London: Printed for J. Johnson, 1788);

Lessons for Children of Three Years Old: Part II (London: Printed for J. Johnson, 1788);

Lessons for Children, from Three to Four Years Old (London: Printed for J. Johnson, 1788);

An Address to the Opposers of the Appeal of the Corporation and Test Acts (London: Printed for J. Johnson, 1790);

Epistle to William Wilberforce, Esq., on the Rejection of the Bill for Abolishing the Slave Trade (London: Printed for J. Johnson, 1791);

Evenings at Home; or, The Juvenile Budget Opened, 6 volumes, by Barbauld and John Aikin (London: Printed for J. Johnson, 1792-1796; 1 volume, Philadelphia: Printed by T. Dobson, 1797);

Civic Sermons to the People Number I: Nay, Why Even of Yourselves, Judge Ye Not What Is Right (London: Printed for J. Johnson, 1792);

Civic Sermons to the People Number II: From Mutual Wants Springs Mutual Happiness (London: Printed for J. Johnson, 1792);

Remarks on Mr. Gilbert Wakefield's Enquiry into the Expediency and Propriety of Public or Social Worship (London: Printed for J. Johnson, 1792);

Sins of the Government, Sins of the Nation; or, A Discourse for the Fast, Appointed on April 19, 1793 (London: Printed for J. Johnson, 1793);

Eighteen Hundred and Eleven: A Poem (London: Johnson, 1812; Boston: Bradford & Read, 1812; Philadelphia: Finley, 1812).

Editions: *The Works of Anna Laetitia Barbauld: With a Memoir by Lucy Aikin* (2 volumes, London: Longman, Hurst, Rees, Orme, Brown & Green, 1825; 3 volumes, Boston: Reed, 1826);

A Legacy for Young Ladies, Consisting of Miscellaneous Pieces, in Prose and Verse, edited by Lucy Aikin (London: Printed for Longman, Hurst, Rees, Orme & Green, 1826; Boston: Reed, 1826);

Things by Their Right Names, and Other Stories, Fables, and Moral Pieces, in Prose and Verse, Selected and Arranged from the Writing of Mrs. Barbauld: With a Sketch of Her Life by Mrs. S. J. Hale (Boston: Marsh, Capen, Lyon & Webb, 1840);

Tales, Poems, and Essays by Anna Laetitia Barbauld, with a Biographical Sketch by Grace A. Oliver (Boston: Roberts, 1884).

OTHER: Mark Akenside, *The Pleasures of the Imagination*, edited, with a critical essay, by Barbauld (London: Cadell & Davies, 1794);

The Poetical Works of Mr. William Collins: With a Prefatory Essay, edited by Barbauld (London: Cadell & Davies, 1797);

The Correspondence of Samuel Richardson, edited by Barbauld (London: Phillips, 1804);

Selections from the Spectator, Tatler, Guardian, and Freeholder, 3 volumes, edited by Barbauld (London: Johnson, 1804);

The British Novelists, 50 volumes, edited, with an essay and prefaces, by Barbauld (London: Printed for F. C. & J. Rivington, 1810);

The Female Speaker; or, Miscellaneous Pieces in Prose and Verse, Selected from the Best Writers, edited by Barbauld (London: Printed for Baldwin,

Medallion by Josiah Wedgwood; from Anna Letitia LeBreton, Memoir of Mrs. Barbauld Including Letters and Notices of Her Family and Friends, *1874)*

Cradock & Joy, 1816; Boston: Wells & Lilly, 1824).

With her first publication, a slender volume titled *Poems* (1773), Anna Laetitia Aikin became a figure of eminence in the world of letters; she would hold that position until her death—as Anna Laetitia Barbauld—well into the next century. While ultimately Barbauld was renowned as an educator and a literary critic as well as a poet, it was her early success with verse that laid the foundation for all her later work by revealing not only a poetic sensibility but also a principled and educated mind. Barbauld belongs, like many late-eighteenth- and early-nineteenth-century poets, almost equally to two generations. Like the poets who preceded her she evinces the Horatian principle *utile dulce* (the useful with the agreeable) and favors poetic diction over more ordinary speech; like the poets who followed her she celebrates the individual, the passionate, the natural, and the ordinary. She is more than simply a representative poetic voice, however; for in spite of the neglect of her work by twentieth-century critics, even a cursory acquaintance with her poetry and prose reveals that her talent was as unusual as it was real and that her fame in her own time was well deserved.

Born at Kibworth Harcourt, Leicester, into a family of Dissenters on 20 June 1743, Aikin was the elder of John and Jane Jennings Aikin's two children; her brother, John, was four years younger. Disabled by poor health from serving in the ministry for which he had taken orders, their father had opened a boys' school in Kibworth. By the time his children were born the school was well established and enjoyed a high reputation; Dissenters sent their boys to learn Latin, Greek, French, Italian, and other subjects taught by the Reverend Mr. Aikin, who was distinguished for an open, stimulating manner of instruction. Anna Aikin's early life was spent in this environment, an ideal setting for, as her mother described her later, "a little girl who was as eager to learn as her instructors could be to teach her, and who, at two years old, could read sentences and little stories in her *wise book*, roundly, without spelling, and in half a year more could read as well as most women." Her precocity led to a sound education first in modern and then in classical languages and literature.

When Aikin was fifteen her father accepted a position as classical tutor at Warrington Academy in Lancashire, a newly established Dissenting institution where she formed many lasting and important friendships. The society at Warrington, made up of John Aikin's colleagues and their families, included Joseph Priestley; his future wife, Mary Wilkinson; and a regular visitor, Josiah Wedgwood. According to Lucy Aikin, Anna Barbauld's niece and the editor of her works, part of the social idiom of the Warrington set included the exchange of complimentary or occasional poems: "both *bout rimes* and *vers de societe* were in fashion with the set," she reports. "Once it was their custom to slip anonymous pieces into Mrs. Priestley's workbag. One copy of verses, a very eloquent one, puzzled all guessers for a long time; at length it was traced to Dr. Priestley's self." The group considered privately putting on plays; the students favored the plan, but the tutors vehemently prohibited it.

In his *Memoirs*, Joseph Priestley speaks to the symbiotic nature of literary life at Warrington, with particular reference to Anna Aikin's own development of poetic skill: "Mrs. Barbauld has told me that it was the perusal of some verses of mine that first induced her to write anything in verse; so that this country is in some measure indebted to me for one of the best poets it can boast of. Several of her first poems were written while she was in my house, on occasions that occurred while she was there." One of these poems remained unpublished until after her death, but it bears the distinct lightness of touch amid allusive erudition that marked Barbauld's style throughout her career. "An Inventory of the Furniture in Dr. Priestley's study" reveals:

A map of every country known
With not a foot of land his own.
A list of folks that kicked a dust
On this poor globe from Ptol. the First;
. . . .
A Juvenal to hunt for mottos;
And Ovid's tales of nymphs and grottos.

Throughout her life at Warrington, Anna Aikin wrote poems that were passed around among the scholars to universal admiration. With the encouragement of her brother, who by this time had begun a medical practice, she had a collection of her poems published just before her thirtieth birthday. The volume went through four editions in one year and secured for Aikin the attention of the literary establishment.

The poems are lyrics and include odes, songs, hymns, verse epistles, and fables on a variety of subjects, many making specific reference, as Priestley suggests, to life at Warrington; but others reach beyond the academy to more universal themes. "Corsica," written in 1769, expresses admiration for the island's spirit of independence in the year its long struggle for freedom ended in surrender to France. The poem includes in its blank-verse lines a description of nature worthy of its sublime theme:

Thy swelling mountains, brown with solemn shade
Of various trees, that wave their giant arms
O'er the rough sons of freedom; lofty pines,
And hardy fir, and ilex ever green,
And spreading chesnut, with each humbler plant,
And shrub of fragrant leaf, that clothes their sides
With living verdure; whence the clustering bee
Extracts her golden dews: the shining box,
And sweet-leaved myrtle, aromatic thyme,
The prickly juniper, and the green leaf
Which feeds the spinning worm; while glowing
  bright
Beneath the various foliage, wildly spreads
The arbutus, and rears his scarlet fruit
Luxuriant, mantling o'er the craggy steeps;
And thy own native laurel crowns the scene.

Such a setting is emblematic of "Liberty, / The mountain Goddess" who "loves to range at large / Amid such scenes," and although Aikin laments "The iron fates" that have brought military defeat, she invokes another kind of freedom, "the freedom of the mind" which lies "Beyond the proud oppressor's cruel grasp / Seated secure, uninjured, undestroyed. / Worthy of Gods."

The exploration of freedom through the description of natural setting in "Corsica" is striking, both formally and thematically; for although

The house at Warrington, Lancashire, where Anna Laetitia Aikin lived from 1758 until her marriage to the Reverend Rochemont Barbauld in 1774 (after an engraving by H. J. Bellars)

nature is ubiquitous throughout Aikin's volume of poetry it generally appears in a much more limited and controlled context. "The Invitation," for example, is written in closed iambic pentameter couplets, replete with personification, poetic diction, decorum, and polish:

> The Muse invites; my Delia, haste away,
> And let us sweetly waste the careless day.
> Here gentle summits lift their airy brow;
> Down the green slope here winds the labouring
> plough;
> Here, bathed by frequent showers cool vales are
> seen,
> Clothed with fresh verdure and eternal green. . . .

Amid the natural setting, however, is evidence of human control—in the duke of Bridgewater's "smooth canals," which "across the extended plain / Stretch their long arms to join the distant main"—and human endeavor in Warrington itself:

> Mark where its simple front yon mansion rears,
> The nursery of men for future years!
> Here callow chiefs and embryo statesmen lie,
> And unfledged poets short excursions try.

Other poems depict a sentimental anthropomorphism, as in "To Mrs. P. . . . . with Some Drawings of Birds and Insects." In this poem the "tawny Eagle" "with cruel eye premeditates . . . war" while the butterflies "idly fluttering live their little hour; / Their life all pleasure, and their task all play." Still other poems celebrate nature's gentle presence in the scenes of domesticity: One of Aikin's "Characters," for example, describes a "happy old man" who is "stretched beneath the shade / Of large grown trees, or in the rustic porch / With woodbine canopied, where linger yet / The hospitable virtues," and who "calm enjoy'st / Nature's best blessings."

Aikin's religious training and sensibility are evident in "Address to the Diety," which expresses the personal and deeply felt reverence that characterizes Dissenting belief: "I feel that name my inmost thoughts controul, / And breathe an awful stillness through my soul." Other verses, probably her best, are more lighthearted and playful, attempting to entertain or tease the reader into moral awareness. "The Groans of the Tankard" reports the complaints of a goblet fallen into disuse:

Unblest the day, and luckless was the hour,
Which doomed me to a Presbyterian's power:
Fated to serve the Puritanic race,
Whose slender meal is shorter than their grace;
Whose moping sons no jovial orgies keep;
Where evening brings no summons—but to sleep;
No Carnival is even Christmas here,
And one long Lent involves the meagre year.

In "The Mouse's Petition," the trapped creature, being held for one of Dr. Priestley's experiments on the noxious effects of certain gases, pleads for mercy in Deistic terms: "The cheerful light, the vital air, / Are blessings widely given; / Let Nature's commoners enjoy / The common gifts of Heaven."

Finally, there are the poems wherein the rebellious voice of youthful vitality sounds the note of personal indignation that would characterize Barbauld's writings throughout her life. In "To Wisdom" the outcry is prompted by the Warrington tutors' objections to the proposal for private theatricals; later, graver social offenses would provoke similar arguments for independence:

Wisdom! thine empire I disclaim,
Thou empty boast of pompous name!
In gloomy shade of cloisters dwell,
But never haunt my cheerful cell:
Hail to Pleasure's frolic train!
Hail to Fancy's golden reign!
Festive Mirth, and Laughter wild,
Free and sportful as the child!
Hope with eager sparkling eyes,
And easy faith, and fond surprise!—
Let these, in fairy colours drest,
For ever share my careless breast:
Then, though wise I may not be,
The wise themselves shall envy me.

Critical response was overwhelmingly favorable. The *Monthly Review* (February 1773) wrote: "We congratulate the public on so great an accession to the literary world, as the genius and talents of Miss Aikin. We very seldom have an opportunity of bestowing praise with so much justice, and so much pleasure." Mary Scott's *The Female Advocate* (1774) paid tribute in verse:

Fir'd with the Music, Aikin, of thy lays,
To thee the Muse a joyful tribute pays;
Transported dwells on that harmonious line,
Where taste, and spirit, wit, and learning shine;
Where Fancy's hand her richest colourings lends,
And ev'ry shade in just proportion blends.
How fair, how beauteous to our gazing eyes
Thy vivid intellectual paintings rise!
We feel thy feelings, glow with all thy fires,
Adopt thy thoughts, and pant with thy desires.
Proceed, bright maid! and may thy polish'd page
Refine the manners of a trifling age.

The one point of adverse criticism came from the generally enthusiastic reviewer in the *Monthly Review* who wished "that she had marked, from her own feelings, the particular distresses of some female situations!"

In May 1774 she married Rochemont Barbauld, one of the Warrington Academy's former pupils and a clergyman six years her junior. Mr. Barbauld had accepted a position as minister to a congregation in Palgrave in Suffolk, where he planned to establish a boys' school. Mrs. Barbauld's recent fame as a poet helped to attract a large initial enrollment; the school prospered for eleven years. Barbauld's most popular writings came out of this experience: *Hymns in Prose for Children* (1781), considered by many her best work; and four volumes of *Lessons for Children* (1787-1788), written for her nephew Charles Rochemont Aikin, whom she and her husband adopted. Of this foray into children's literature Samuel Johnson, who had praised her prose style in her *Miscellaneous Pieces in Prose* (1773) as being nearest his own of any he had read, was, according to James Boswell, disdainfully severe:

> Miss Aikin was an instance of early cultivation, but in what did it terminate? In marrying a little Presbyterian parson, who keeps an infant boarding school, so that all her employment now is "To suckle fools, and chronicle small-beer." She tells the children, "This is a cat, and that is a dog, with four legs and a tail; see there! you are much better than a cat or a dog, for you can speak." If I had bestowed such an education on a daughter, and had discovered that she thought of marrying such a fellow, I would have sent her to the *Congress*.

Hester Lynch Piozzi, however, records Johnson's admiration for Barbauld's "voluntary descent from possible splendour to painful duty." Barbauld seems to have embraced such "duty" with an enthusiasm buttressed by a belief in and respect for the importance of early education in the forming of mind and character.

The more popular of Barbauld's children's works, *Hymns in Prose for Children*, went through thirty editions by 1849 and was translated into five languages. Designed, as Barbauld says in the preface, to impress the "idea of God" on the infant mind, each hymn guides the child into recognizing experience as an expression of the divine order. Hymn eight, for example, teaches that social organization, from the most private level to the most public, is a reflection of the mind of God:

> See where stands the cottage of the labourer, covered with a warm roof; the mother is spinning at the door; the young children sport before her on the grass; the elder ones learn to labour, and are obedient; the father worketh to provide them food.... Many kingdoms, and states, and countries full of people, and islands, and large continents, and different climates, make up this whole world. God governeth it.

Not that Barbauld would have the children think that God's governance prevents evil or sadness. On the contrary, her hymns teach that both exist, the one a result of human perfidy which goes against the will of God and the other simply a part of human life. Hymn eight concludes with an example of the first: "Negro Woman, who sitteth pining in captivity, and weepest over thy sick child; though no one seeth thee, God seeth thee; though no one pitieth thee, God pitieth thee: raise thy voice, forlorn and abandoned one; call upon him from amidst thy bonds, for assuredly he will hear thee." The hymns were widely known to children and adults alike, including, one might assume, the poet William Blake, who in his "Little Black Boy" (published in *Songs of Innocence* [1789]) seems to echo the "Negro Woman" passage and whose *Songs of Innocence* and *Songs of Experience* (1794) in general recall many of Barbauld's images and sentiments.

Barbauld gave careful thought to the practical aspects of children's books, insisting, for instance, on large type for the younger readers and choosing rhythmical prose for her hymns to aid in memorization and recitation; she avoided verse itself, she explained, for "It may well be doubted whether poetry ought to be lowered to the capacities of children, or whether they should not rather be kept from reading verse till they are able to relish good verse; for the very essence of poetry is an elevation in thought and style above the common standard; and if it wants this character, it wants all that renders it valuable." Her care and concern found reward in the distinguished careers of many of her students, including Lord Thomas Denman, who became the lord chief justice, and Sir William Gell, scholar of Troy and Pompeii.

In 1785 the Barbaulds gave up their school to spend a year traveling on the Continent. When they returned to England they settled in Hampstead, where Mr. Barbauld officiated at a small church. Mrs. Barbauld began writing again, producing children's stories and fables for her brother's *Evenings at Home* (1792-1796). She also wrote poetry, contributing occasionally to the *Monthly Magazine* poems that continued the general tenor of her 1773 collection—observations about contemporary events, classical pieces, religious odes or hymns, and domestic light verse such as "Washing Day" (December 1797). This poem begins in mock-epic form: "Come, Muse, and sing the dreaded Washing-Day." It continues with homely detail as striking for its realism as for its wit:

> The silent breakfast-meal is soon dispatch'd;
> Uninterrupted, save by anxious looks
> Cast at the lowering sky, if sky should lower.
> From that last evil, oh preserve us, heavens!
> For should the skies pour down, adieu to all
> Remains of quiet; then expect to hear
> Of sad disasters,—dirt and gravel stains
> Hard to efface, and loaded lines at once
> Snapped short,—and linen-horse by dog thrown down,
> And all the petty miseries of life.
> Saints have been calm while stretched upon the rack,
> And Guatimozin smiled on burning coals;
> But never yet did housewife notable
> Greet with a smile a rainy washing-day.

Later the poem takes an autobiographical turn as Barbauld depicts herself as a child denied on washing day the "usual indulgences" of "jelly," "creams," or "butter'd toast." Petulant, Barbauld recalls, she "would . . . sit me down, and ponder much / Why washings were." Another poem published in the *Monthly Magazine* (August 1799) reflects Barbauld's experience as an educator. "A School Eclogue" draws both on the many conversations Barbauld must have overheard among her boys and on the lessons she had them recite for her.

In Hampstead, also, Barbauld began her work as an editor and literary critic. She edited and wrote an introduction for Mark Akenside's

Barbauld's younger brother, John Aikin, circa 1823. Barbauld contributed children's stories to Aikin's Evenings at Home *in the late 1790s (engraving by Englehart).*

Pleasures of the Imagination in 1794, and in 1797 she prefaced her edition of the poems of William Collins with an essay which earned her the assessment of Collins's twentieth-century biographer, Edward Gay Ainsworth, as one of the poet's "most penetrating critics."

Barbauld's poem "To Mr. S. T. Coleridge," published in the *Monthly Magazine* in April 1799, speaks to her involvement in contemporary literature as well as in the literature of the preceding age; though her advice to Coleridge may strike one now as being wrongheaded, she offered the verse more in praise than in reproof: ". . . Youth beloved / Of Science—of the Muse beloved,—not here, / Not in the maze of metaphysic lore, / Build thou thy place of resting!" This poem brings to mind the well-known exchange between Barbauld and Coleridge about Coleridge's *The Rime of the Ancient Mariner* (1798). As Coleridge recounted the incident: "Mrs. Barbauld told me that the only faults she found with the Ancient Mariner were—that it was improbable, and had no moral. As for the probability—to be sure that might admit some question—but I told her that in my judgment the chief fault of the poem was that it had too much moral, and that too openly obtruded on the reader." This conversation is often cited to illustrate the gulf between eighteenth-century and Romantic sensibilities; but despite such differences, Coleridge entertained for quite some time as great an admiration for Barbauld's intelligence as she held for his talent. The relationship of mutual respect soured around 1804, when Coleridge began to take offense at harsh reviews in the *Annual Review* and the *Monthly Review* attributed—sometimes erroneously—to Barbauld.

Many of Barbauld's essays and poems during the Hampstead years addressed social themes, such as the Revolution in France, which she supported, and the Test Act, which she did not. Her *Epistle to William Wilberforce, Esq., on the Rejection of the Bill for Abolishing the Slave Trade* (1791) praises Wilberforce for his support of the defeated bill, although he "strove in vain." Her admiration for Wilberforce is evident throughout, as is her bitter disappointment at the fate of the bill: "For, not unmark'd in Heaven's impartial plan, / Shall man, proud worm, contemn his fellow-man!" Barbauld's outspokenness provoked the conservative Horace Walpole to write Hannah More (29 September 1791), "I cannot forgive the heart of a woman . . . that curses our clergy and feels for negroes."

The obvious productivity of this period notwithstanding, during most of the final decade of the eighteenth century and the initial decade of the nineteenth Barbauld was preoccupied with domestic problems: her husband's hereditary mental instability began to take on an abusive quality that more than once threatened her life. In 1802 the Barbaulds moved to Stoke Newington to be near John Aikin and his family. While there, Mrs. Barbauld edited a selection of essays from the *Spectator*, *Tatler*, *Guardian*, and *Freeholder* (1804) and a six-volume edition of the letters of Samuel Richardson (1804). In 1808 Mr. Barbauld drowned in the New River.

After her husband's death, which left her devastated, Barbauld seems to have thrown herself into her work, undertaking first a massive edition of *The British Novelists* (1810), including a long introductory essay, "On the Origin and Progress of Novel-Writing," and biographical and critical essays on each of the novelists. She then prepared an edition of poetry and prose suitable to young women, *The Female Speaker* (1816).

Barbauld was still drawn to the theme of independence. The poem *Eighteen Hundred and Eleven* (1812) is a comment on the condition of freedom in her own day and country. A satire, the work describes the experiences of a visitor from America who discovers in England "faded glories" and "desolated shores" as opposed to the possibility of freedom available in the New World. The few favorable reviews were overwhelmed by the cries of protest, the *Quarterly Review* (June 1812) being particularly severe: "we must take the liberty of warning [Mrs. Barbauld] to desist from satire, which indeed is satire on herself alone; and of entreating, with great earnestness, that she will not, for the sake of this ungrateful generation, put herself to the trouble of writing any more party pamphlets in verse." She did not; Barbauld was so discouraged by the attack that she ceased preparations for an edition of her collected works.

Barbauld had little work published after 1812 other than an occasional poem in the *Monthly Repository*, such as "Poetical Thought on Death" (1822) and "Lines Written at the Close of the Year" (1823). Yet she ended her life revered and honored, still the center of a literary circle. In spite of disappointment, she retained hope for the human condition and faced the end of her life with equanimity. The final stanza of her poem "Life," written when she was in her eighties, expresses what seems to have been her characteristic state of mind:

> Life! we've been long together,
> Through pleasant and through cloudy weather;
> 'Tis hard to part when friends are dear;
> Perhaps 'twill cost a sigh, a tear;
> Then steal away, give little warning,
> Choose thine own time;
> Say not Good night, but in some brighter clime
> Bid me Good morning.

This graceful verse touched a sympathetic chord in many readers. Fanny Burney, in her final years, is reported to have repeated it to herself every night before going to sleep; and, according to Henry Crabb Robinson, Wordsworth said of the stanza: "I am not in the habit of grudging other people their good things, but I wish I had written those lines." Barbauld died at Stoke Newington on 9 March 1825, a few months shy of her eighty-second birthday.

Any final assessment of Barbauld's work must recognize that her contribution to children's literature was innovative, her criticism was sound, and her poetry was pleasing in the highest sense of that word. Her reputation as a poet was justly won; only the customary undervaluing of late-eighteenth-century verse can explain her omission from twentieth-century anthologies, for her work adds to the simple elegance that characterizes the best of this period's poetry a quiet sincerity and a gentle wit all her own.

Biographies:

Jerom Murch, *Mrs. Barbauld and Her Contemporaries: Sketches of Some Eminent Literary and Scientific Englishwomen* (London: Longmans, Green, 1871);

Anna Letitia LeBreton, *Memoir of Mrs. Barbauld Including Letters and Notices of Her Family and Friends* (London: Bell, 1874);

Grace A. Oliver, *The Story of Anna Laetitia Barbauld*, second edition (Boston: Cupples, Upham, 1886);

Betsy Rodgers, *Georgian Chronicle: Mrs. Barbauld and Her Family* (London: Methuen, 1958).

References:

Edward Gay Ainsworth, *Poor Collins* (Ithaca, N.Y.: Cornell University Press, 1937), p. 115;

James Boswell, *Boswell's Life of Johnson, Together with Boswell's Journal of a Tour to the Hebrides and Johnson's Diary of a Journey into North Wales*, 6 volumes, edited by George Birkbeck Hill, revised and enlarged by L. F. Powell (Oxford: Clarendon Press, 1934-1964), II: 408-409;

W. S. Lewis, ed., *The Yale Edition of Horace Walpole's Correspondence*, 48 volumes (New Haven: Yale University Press, 1937-1983);

Catherine E. Moore, "Mrs. Barbauld's Criticism of Eighteenth-Century Women Novelists," in *Fetter'd or Free? British Women Novelists, 1670-1815*, edited by Mary Anne Schofield and Cecilia Macheski (Athens: Ohio University Press, 1982), pp. 383-397;

Samuel Pickering, "Mrs. Barbauld's Hymns in Prose: 'An Air-Blown Particle' of Romanticism?" *Southern Humanities Review*, 9 (Summer 1975): 259-268;

Hester Lynch Piozzi, *Anecdotes of Samuel Johnson*, edited by S. C. Roberts (Freeport, N.Y.: Books for Libraries Press, 1969), p. 14;

Joseph Priestley, *Memoirs of Dr. Joseph Priestley, to the Year 1795 ... With a Continuation, to the Time of His Decease, by His Son* (London: Printed for Joseph Johnson, 1806), p. 49;

Henry Crabb Robinson, *On Books and Their Writers*, 3 volumes, edited by Edith J. Morley (London: Dent, 1938), I: 8;

Porter Williams, "The Influence of Mrs. Barbauld's *Hymns in Prose for Children* upon Blake's *Songs of Innocence and Experience*," in *A Fair Day for the Affections*, edited by Jack Durant and Thomas Hester (Raleigh, N.C.: Winston Press, 1980), pp. 131-146;

Carl Woodring, ed., *The Collected Works of Samuel Taylor Coleridge*, 14 volumes (London: Routledge & Kegan Paul, 1971-1990), I: 272-273;

Paul M. Zall, "The Cool World of Samuel Taylor Coleridge: Mrs. Barbauld's Crew and the Building of a Mass Reading Class," *Wordsworth Circle*, 2 (Summer 1971): 74-79;

Zall, "Wordsworth's 'Ode' and Mrs. Barbauld's *Hymns*," *Wordsworth Circle*, 1 (Autumn 1970): 177-179.

James Beattie

(25 October 1735 - 18 August 1803)

Everard H. King
The Memorial University of Newfoundland

BOOKS: *Original Poems and Translations* (Aberdeen: Printed by F. Douglas; sold in London by A. Millar, 1761);

Verses Occasioned by the Death of the Revd Mr. Charles Churchill: Written by a Native of Britain (London, 1765);

The Judgment of Paris: A Poem (London: Printed for T. Becket & P. A. De Hondt; and J. Balfour, Edinburgh, 1765);

Poems on Several Subjects (London: Printed for W. Johnson, 1766);

An Essay on the Nature and Immutability of Truth, in Opposition to Sophistry and Scepticism (Edinburgh: Printed for A. Kincaid & J. Bell; sold at London by E. & C. Dilly, 1770; enlarged, 1771; revised edition, Edinburgh: Printed for William Creech; and for E. & C. Dilly, and T. Cadell, London, 1777);

The Minstrel; or, The Progress of Genius. A Poem. Book the First (London: Printed for E. & C. Dilly; and for A. Kincaid & J. Bell, Edinburgh, 1771);

The Minstrel; or, The Progress of Genius. A Poem. The Second Book (London: Printed for Edward & Charles Dilly; and William Creech, Edinburgh, 1774); first and second books republished as *The Minstrel; or, The Itinerant Poet, and Musician: A Descriptive Poem, on the Progress of Genius; in Two Books* (Philadelphia: Printed & sold by Robert Bell, 1784);

Poems on Several Occasions (Edinburgh: Printed for W. Creech, 1776; Philadelphia: Printed for Thomas Dobson, 1787);

Essays: On the Nature and Immutability of Truth, in Opposition to Sophistry and Scepticism; On Poetry and Music, as They Affect the Mind; On Laughter, and Ludicrous Composition; On the Utility of Classical Learning (Edinburgh: Printed for William Creech; and for E. and C. Dilly, London, 1776);

A Letter to the Rev. Hugh Blair . . . on the Improvement of Psalmody in Scotland (Aberdeen: J. Chalmers, 1778);

A List of Two Hundred Scoticisms: With Remarks (Aberdeen, 1779); republished as *Scoticisms: Arranged in Alphabetical Order Designed to Correct Improprieties of Speech and Writing* (Edinburgh: Printed for William Creech; and T. Cadell, London, 1787);

Dissertations Moral and Critical: Of Memory and Imagination; On Dreaming; The Theory of Language; On Fable and Romance; Illustrations on Sublimity (London: Printed for W. Strahan; and T. Cadell; and W. Creech at Edinburgh, 1783);

Evidences of the Christian Religion: Briefly and Plainly Stated (Edinburgh: Printed for A. Strahan & T. Cadell, London; and W. Creech, Edinburgh, 1786; Philadelphia: Printed for Thomas Dobson, 1787);

The Theory of Language: In Two Parts. Part I: Of the Origin and General Nature of Speech. Part II: Of Universal Grammar (London: Printed for A. Strahan; T. Cadell; and W. Creech, Edinburgh, 1788);

Elements of Moral Science, 2 volumes (Edinburgh: Printed for T. Cadell, London; and W. Creech, Edinburgh, 1790-1793; Philadelphia: Printed for Mathew Carey, 1792-1794);

Essays and Fragments in Prose and Verse: To Which Is Prefixed an Account of the Author's Life and Character (Edinburgh: Printed by J. Moir, 1794);

The Poetical Works of James Beattie, volume 37 of *The Works of the British Poets*, edited by Thomas Park (London: Whittingham, 1805);

Beauties Selected from the Writings of James Beattie (London: Printed for Longman, Hurst, Rees & Orme, 1809);

James Beattie's London Diary, 1773, edited by Ralph S. Walker (Aberdeen: Aberdeen University Press, 1946);

James Beattie's Day-Book, 1773-1798, edited by Walker (Aberdeen: Third Spalding Club, 1948).

James Beattie in 1774, holding his Essay on the Nature and Immutability of Truth *(1770) as Truth lashes Infidelity down to the bottomless pit (portrait by Sir Joshua Reynolds; Collection of the University of Aberdeen)*

OTHER: Thomas Gray, *Poems by Mr. Gray*, edited by Beattie (Glasgow: Printed for Robert & Andrew Foulis, 1768);

The Papers of Joseph Addison, Esq. in the Tatler, Spectator, Guardian, and Freeholder: Together with His Treatise on the Christian Religion. To Which Are Prefixed Tickell's Life of the Author, and Extracts from Dr. Johnson's Remarks on His Prose Writings. With Original Notes Never Before Published, edited by Beattie (Edinburgh: Printed for William Creech, 1790).

SELECTED PERIODICAL PUBLICATIONS—UNCOLLECTED: "Remarks on Some Passages of the Sixth Book of the Eneid," *Transactions of the Royal Society of Edinburgh*, 2 (1790): 33-54;

E. C. Mossner, ed., "Beattie's 'The Castle of Scepticism': An Unpublished Allegory against Hume, Voltaire, and Hobbes," *Texas University Studies in English*, 27 (June 1948): 108-145;

Mossner, ed., "Beattie on Voltaire: An Unpublished Parody," *Romantic Review*, 41 (February 1950): 26-32.

Before the publication of *An Essay on the Nature and Immutability of Truth, in Opposition to Sophistry and Scepticism* in 1770, James Beattie was an obscure poet and teacher in the north of Scotland; but by the time of his visit to London in the summer of 1771, when the second edition of his essay was published, the book had made him one of the most celebrated authors in Great Britain. The popularity of *An Essay on the Nature and Immutability of Truth* endured well beyond Beattie's lifetime, with at least twenty-six editions up to 1852. Meanwhile, with the publication of the first book of *The Minstrel; or, The Progress of Genius* during the summer of 1771, many readers in England, as well as in Scotland, expressed amazement that

Beattie as a young man (engraving by W. Ridley, 1801)

the brilliant young philosopher, who had recently demolished the arguments of David Hume, George Berkeley, and others, was also an exciting, original poet. This enthusiastic response to *The Minstrel* increased with the publication of the second book in 1774 and continued unabated well into the nineteenth century, resulting in at least thirty-nine editions of the poem up to 1858; it was also included in all editions of Beattie's collected poems after 1776. Beattie's fame as a poet and philosopher ensured the popularity of his literary essays when they were published in 1776 and 1783.

By the mid 1780s the controversy concerning *An Essay on the Nature and Immutability of Truth* as the defiant answer of the Christian philosopher to the agnostic metaphysician had died down; and for most readers Beattie's book had been decisive in settling the issue. As a consequence, Beattie wrote a new book as a sequel to *An Essay on the Nature and Immutability of Truth* which focuses entirely on the joy of the Christian life. This jubilant celebration of "true religion," *Evidences of the Christian Religion* (1786), went through six reprintings up to the author's death in 1803. Similarly, three editions of his last major publication, *Elements of Moral Science* (1790-1793), were published during the last ten years of his life. But perhaps the best indication of Beattie's great popularity is the fact that his major works were well known in pirated editions in North America in the eighteenth century and later.

These largely forgotten books contain valuable evidence of the literary tastes and philosophical, religious, and educational beliefs of their time. In addition, his literary essays and *The Minstrel* exercised an important influence on many writers of the Romantic period. Beattie was a minor, transitional figure; but to understand fully the compositions of such poets as William

Marischal College, Aberdeen, where Beattie was a student for five months each year from 1749 to 1753 (from an engraving by J. Swan in the library at Marischal College; based on a painting by G. Smith)

Wordsworth, Lord Byron, Percy Bysshe Shelley, and John Keats, one must assess their responses to Beattie's work.

Beattie was born on 25 October 1735 into the large family of a poor farmer and shopkeeper in the village of Laurencekirk near the eastern coast of Scotland; his parents were James Beattie, Sr., and Jean Watson Beattie. After his father died in 1742 and left the family destitute, Beattie experienced seven years of physical privations that affected him for the rest of his life. But he was removed from these trying circumstances at the age of fourteen when he won a bursary to study at Marischal College in Aberdeen.

Apart from the five months of each year from 1749 to 1753 when he was a student at Marischal College, Beattie spent the first twenty-three years of his life in the isolated villages of Laurencekirk and Fordoun. His bright, imaginative mind and studious attention to detail, as well as his early attempts at composition, prompted his classmates to name him "the poet Beattie." During his school years he read his favorite poet for the first time in John Ogilby's celebrated translation of Virgil. The study and writing of poetry became the early passion of Beattie's intellectual and imaginative life. While teaching at Fordoun from 1753 to 1758 he spent much of his time when not in the classroom reading poetry in English, Greek, Latin, French, and Italian. As respites from reading and study he played the violoncello and rambled around the surrounding countryside by day and by night.

He often visited a favorite glen near the mountains, where he wrote some of his early poems. It was, according to his biographer William Forbes, "his supreme delight to saunter in the fields the live-long night, contemplating the sky, and marking the approach of day"; and it was from the top of a high hill near Fordoun that he first saw the ocean, an experience which ever after exercised a mystical power on his imagination. His first published poem appeared in the *Scot's Magazine* in 1756. In 1760 he was appointed professor of moral philosophy and logic at Marischal College. His first book, *Original Poems and Translations*, was published in 1761.

Beattie devoted considerable attention in his classes to literary topics in general and poetry in particular. All of his prose works were originally lectures: *An Essay on the Nature and Immutability of Truth* was written to warn his students of the dangers of skepticism and atheism; and his literary essays were culled from his lecture notes when his fame as an author created a demand for more writings. *Elements of Moral Science* was a summation of

ORIGINAL POEMS

AND

TRANSLATIONS.

By *JAMES BEATTIE*, A. M.

ABERDEEN:

Printed by F. DOUGLAS; and fold by him for the Benefit of the Author, and in London by A. MILLAR, in the Strand.

M DCC LXI.

Title page for Beattie's first book

his thinking as it had evolved during his thirty years of teaching. All of these books show the teacher's concern for the moral health and intellectual stimulation of his students as he recommends and illustrates abundantly the best that has been written on each of his topics. His prose works are rarely original; but by that very fact they often present a full and accurate survey of a subject. Even *The Minstrel* exhibits to some extent this representative quality; by including every notion and image that seemed to him appropriate, Beattie made the poem into a record of the characteristic thought and poetic technique of the time. The lectures on history and philosophy that the hermit delivers to the minstrel in the second book correspond to Beattie's course in moral philosophy and logic.

The same year Beattie became a professor he was elected to the Philosophical Society of Aberdeen, a debating club of about ten professors from Marischal and King's Colleges who met every two weeks during the university year to read and discuss their essays. Beattie first read "An Essay on Poetry and Music" (1776) at a meeting in 1762 and drafts of *An Essay on the Nature and Immutability of Truth* at several meetings between 1766 and 1768, and he later read some of his other literary essays to the club. But he received more from the club than he contributed to it; his essays reveal the great extent to which he borrowed ideas and revised his thoughts in the light of the readings and discussions in the club.

Most of the compositions in *Original Poems and Translations* and in *Poems on Several Subjects*

(1766) show Beattie striving to progress beyond the imitation of favorite models. But five of these poems, the odes to hope and peace, "The Triumph of Melancholy," "Retirement," and "The Hermit," present scenes, characters, and themes which later became important in *The Minstrel.* Here and there within these poems are descriptions of his own experience of nature. Such scenes aid the poet's attempts to write about his own melancholic personality in the guise of various poetic personae who contemplate the melancholy aspects of nature.

"Retirement," for example, is about a "pensive youth" whose hopes and fears are imaged "in the crimson cloud of even" as "the lingering light decays." This character is Beattie's earliest attempt to find a place for himself in his poetic landscape. The poem exhibits a close observation of nature that evokes both joy and fear, the use of personal experience as an informing principle, the contrasting themes of man's vanity and nature's splendor, as well as the lingering over "the sad vicissitudes of life."

"The Hermit" improves on these characteristic features of "Retirement." The speaker is an old recluse who, through his contemplation of nature, has received a kind of visionary power and become the prophetic spokesman for the deepest hopes and fears of humanity. The hermit seems to represent a later stage of poetic development than the youth in "Retirement"; both characters recur in *The Minstrel* as the poetic hero and the hermit. But in the later poem the recluse possesses very little of the sympathetic insight into the poetic life that characterizes "The Hermit" because he is modeled much more closely on the stock figure of the hermit of earlier writers.

An Essay on the Nature and Immutability of Truth was entirely responsible for the propagation of the Philosophy of Common Sense throughout Great Britain, Europe, and North America. Common Sense was developed as a school of philosophical thought by the members of the Philosophical Society of Aberdeen, who were convinced that the vice, corruption, and decadence of the times were directly linked to the skeptical writings of Hume, Berkeley, and others. In *Inquiry into the Human Mind on the Principles of Common Sense* (1764) Thomas Reid demonstrated that the principles of Common Sense are ancient truths that have been obscured by modern skepticism.

But Reid's book was read by few, so Beattie was urged by his friends in the Philosophical Society to have his own thoughts on the subject published. The result, *An Essay on the Nature and Immutability of Truth,* was an emotionally charged, simplistic view of philosophical thought which was bitterly polemical in its intolerance and abhorrence of skeptical writings. In the place of the "dark and mysterious form" of modern skeptical thought, Beattie attempted to reestablish true philosophy as a useful and popular mode of intellectual inquiry. Those who bought the book expecting a polemical diatribe were not disappointed; but they discovered it to be so well argued and so well written that it seemed to refute skeptical reasoning and perhaps even to forecast a new era of enlightenment. As a consequence, Beattie earned the unique distinction of writing a book about metaphysics which achieved instant, widespread success.

Beattie's intention was to demonstrate that true philosophy has always adhered to the principles of Christianity. Common Sense is a natural gift from God which gives intimations of immortality to the true believer; *An Essay on the Nature and Immutability of Truth* is in effect a restatement of New Testament doctrines for the common reader in the guise of philosophical argument: "truth is something fixed and determinate, depending not upon man, but upon the Author of Nature." The book was read as a Christian answer to corrupt philosophical principles, and it became a kind of devotional work for many readers. Beattie's bold declaration that Common Sense was divinely inspired delighted so many Christian readers that he became the most celebrated Christian apologist of his time.

The model for *An Essay on the Nature and Immutability of Truth* was the Addisonian essay. In the tenth issue of the *Spectator* (12 March 1711) Joseph Addison informed his readers that he was aiming at their instruction and diversion by attempting "to enliven Morality with Wit, and to temper Wit with Morality" so as to rescue them from "that desperate State of Vice and Folly, into which the Age is fallen." He is determined to save the mind "that lies fallow but a single Day, for it sprouts up in Follies that are only to be killed by a constant and assiduous Culture." Addison's hope is to cure this moral decadence and intellectual indolence by becoming a popular, modern philosopher: "It was said of Socrates, that he brought Philosophy down from Heaven to inhabit among men; and I shall be ambitious to have it said of me, that I have brought Philosophy out of the Closets and Libraries, Schools and Colleges, to dwell in Clubs and Assem-

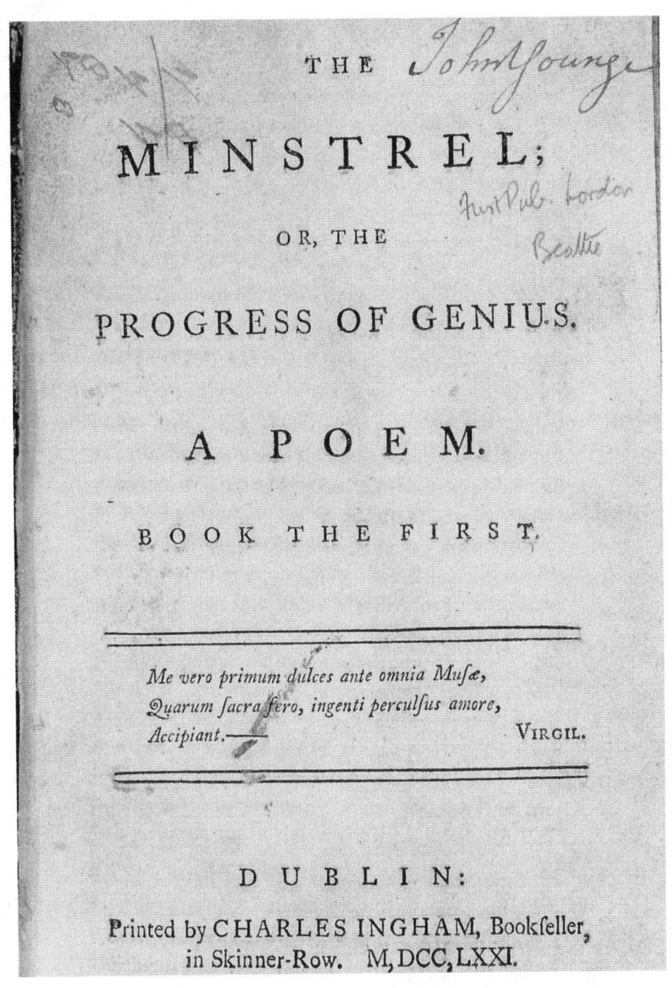
THE

MINSTREL;

OR, THE

PROGRESS OF GENIUS.

A POEM.

BOOK THE FIRST.

Me vero primum dulces ante omnia Musæ,
Quarum sacra fero, ingenti perculsus amore,
Accipiant.— VIRGIL.

DUBLIN:

Printed by CHARLES INGHAM, Bookseller, in Skinner-Row. M,DCC,LXXI.

Title page for the first book of Beattie's poem about a medieval bard

blies, at Tea-tables, and in Coffe-houses." *An Essay on the Nature and Immutability of Truth* is Beattie's attempt to achieve these Addisonian ambitions by making philosophy accessible to the common man. Beattie not only modeled his prose style on Addison's but also often used Addison's ideas in his lectures and continually recommended Addison's essays to his students and his readers. As the direct heir of the *Spectator, An Essay on the Nature and Immutability of Truth* is a fulfillment of Addison's wish that philosophy might be made popular as well as useful to mankind.

The hard work associated with researching and writing the book, as well as frequent headaches and stomach disorders, often drove Beattie to music and poetry, and he began to think more and more during the summer of 1766 about his early experiences with nature. Meanwhile, he read Thomas Percy's *Reliques of Ancient English Poetry* (1765) with its essay on the ancient minstrels in England and immediately perceived parallels between his own life as a poet and musician and Percy's evidence about earlier bards and musicians. Beattie was particularly interested in Percy's discovery that in old songs and ballads the minstrel is almost always Scottish; he formed the plan of writing about such an ancient minstrel, with the intention of reviving the tradition of these inspirational bards by becoming himself a modern Scottish minstrel.

The Minstrel is the story of a medieval bard and musician whose imagination is strongly affected by his rambles through nature. In the first book he begins to reflect on the extremes of joy and fear in his relationship with the natural world and to see such emotions in contrast to the unthinking, spontaneous pleasures of his boyhood. This newly perceived sense of danger in his life stimulates further exploration of the world around him:

. . . whate'er of beautiful or new,
Sublime, or dreadful, in earth, sea, or sky,

By chance or search, was offer'd to his view,
He scann'd with curious and romantic eye.

In the second book Edwin receives a great shock when he discovers in the wilderness an old recluse who tells him the grim truth about the horrors of the human condition. The hermit tries to divert the minstrel from the imaginative view of life into more practical, intellectual considerations. Edwin listens attentively to the hermit's lectures on history and philosophy; but as the poem ends, he persists in writing verse.

Beattie's admiration for Edmund Spenser's poetry and for James Thomson's imitation of the Spenserian mode led him to experiment with the Spenserian stanza as a possible means of dealing with the many disparate poetic concerns that filled his mind. As Beattie claimed in the preface to *The Minstrel*, the stanza was consistent with "the subject and spirit of the poem." He adapted the Spenserian mode to suit modern sensibilities; as a result, the poem seemed fresh and original to early readers. Beattie's skillful manipulation of language moved eighteenth-century readers so deeply that they perceived his use of the Spenserian stanza to be the proper means of combining and crystallizing so many diverse elements of the poetic life. Scattered throughout the poem are angry denunciations of Humean reason similar to the polemical statements in *An Essay on the Nature and Immutability of Truth*; they stand in stark contrast to the paradise regained that is imaged in the poet's descriptions of his adventures with nature. Many readers regarded *The Minstrel* as a kind of Christian apology; they perceived the young minstrel's joy in nature to be a means of judging philosophical and religious truth.

Edwin's fall from the world of childhood innocence of the first book into the adult world of experience of the second book is marked by his acceptance of the hermit's belief that the imagination of youth must be tempered and controlled by the philosophic reason of maturity:

And Reason now thro' number, time, and space,
Darts the keen lustre of her serious eye,
And learns, from facts compar'd, the laws to trace,
Whose long progression leads to Deity.
. . . lo' the shadows fly
From Nature's face; confusion disappears,
And order charms the eye, and harmony the ears.

The popularity of *The Minstrel* in the eighteenth century may be explained in large measure by its acceptable blending of intellectual enlightenment with imaginative sensibility.

The work was the first sustained attempt in English to write an autobiographical poem which traces the growth of the author's own mind and imagination. The resemblances between *The Minstrel* and such poems as Wordsworth's *The Excursion* (1814) and *The Prelude* (1850), Byron's *Childe Harold's Pilgrimage* (1812-1818), Shelley's *Alastor* (1816), and Keat's *Endymion* (1817), as well as the many other similarities to be found throughout Romantic poetry, indicate that the poem was used by later writers as a kind of commonplace book of ideas, images, attitudes, and poetic rhythms. There is hardly a thought or image in the poem which does not reappear in the poetry or prose of the Romantic poets. One of the main appeals of *The Minstrel* for the Romantic poets was its autobiographical nature.

Many early readers insisted on identifying the poet with his young minstrel; and Beattie readily admitted shortly after the publication of the first book in 1771 that he had re-created his own experiences in the adventures of Edwin. In addition, resemblances were often noted between his poetic hero and writers such as Oliver Goldsmith, John Thelwall, and Samuel Rogers; Dorothy Wordsworth declared in 1793 that "the whole character of Edwin resembles much" her brother William at age sixteen. Such striking similarities of character, attitude, and action between Edwin and the young Romantic poets were noted from time to time, and these affinities contributed to the poetic self-portraits of many of them. The Romantic poets seem to have been enthralled by Edwin's purity, innocence, trust in his instincts and emotions, and, above all, by his fascination with nature and imagination. They realized that for the first time in an English poem an author was presenting himself as his own hero. By placing himself in his own poetic landscape, Beattie adapted the traditional peregrination over the countryside as the means of creating and exploring images of his own mental landscape. Poetic self-revelation is achieved in *The Minstrel* largely by accurate descriptions of nature and by the strong expression of emotion.

It has always been acknowledged that Beattie emulated much from English poetry; but it has rarely been noted that he also used in *The Minstrel* a great deal of his knowledge of the life, landscape, and literature of Scotland. As a result, he achieved an impressive marriage of the Scottish and English poetic traditions. Ideas about the

Edwin, the hero of Beattie's The Minstrel, *as depicted in an oil painting (1777-1778) by Joseph Wright of Derby (private collection)*

poet's life scattered throughout earlier English nature poetry had been much more fully explored by Scottish poets such as Robert Henryson, King James I, William Dunbar, and Gavin Douglas. In their poems are many passages containing realistic descriptions of the natural world, as well as presentations of poetic self-revelation and of intense personal emotion, which are much closer to the atmosphere of the English Romantics than anything to be found in the eighteenth-century English nature poets. The most distinctive features of *The Minstrel*, as well as those most influential on Romantic poetry, were derived from these Scottish concerns which Beattie introduced into his imitations of various aspects of English verse.

The Minstrel was also a seminal work in the evolution of French Romanticism. François-Auguste-René de Chateaubriand lived in England from 1793 to 1800, and English poetry helped him to explore his own melancholic personality. His autobiographical novellas *René* (1801) and *Atala* (1802), which established him as a pioneer in the French Romantic movement, were modeled closely on *The Minstrel*. Chateaubriand acknowledged the influence of the poem on his books in an essay on Beattie in the *Mercuri* in June 1801, shortly after his return to France. Chateaubriand discovers striking originality in the melancholic personality and adventures of Beattie's imaginative bard and proclaims that the poem's publication began a new era of lyric poetry. This essay,

Beattie circa 1776

which is apparently unknown to English critics of Beattie, shows Chateaubriand to be one of the earliest and still one of the most astute commentators on *The Minstrel.*

Beattie's literary essays survey all of the major and many of the minor concerns of eighteenth-century criticism. His aim as a critic was to improve his readers' taste by using his considered judgments of the best literary works and opinions of the past as the basis for the study of contemporary writings. The essays present familiar, accepted beliefs and assumptions as the proper context for the exploration of new ideas and literary compositions. They are influenced by intellectual currents of the time such as the association of ideas and rationalism.

In "An Essay on Poetry and Music" (1776), for example, Beattie insists that true poetry is perfectly rational, that emotion should be controlled within rational limits, and that the poet should discard everything that does not conform to rational tests. He often challenges earlier critical judgments that seem to him not to be in tune with reason; this kind of re-evaluation prompted him to reexamine earlier works in the context of their time and place of writing. His long essay "On Fable and Romance" (1783) was a significant contribution to this growing sense of historical relativity. In this essay Beattie was one of the first not only to perceive the eighteenth-century novel to be a direct descendant of the old fable and romance but also to write at length about the novels of Miguel de Cervantes, Daniel Defoe, Samuel Richardson, Tobias Smollett, and Henry Fielding. In "An Essay on Laughter, and Ludicrous Composition" (1776) he claims that the English satirists —Geoffrey Chaucer, Samuel Butler, Alexander Pope, and Jonathan Swift—are superior to the ancients in wit and humor. His essays reflect the contemporary preoccupation with such concepts as primitivism, sublimity, sentimentalism, melancholy, didacticism, and medievalism. His remarks about poetry deal with such poetic forms as verse-satire and the Spenserian stanza, with poetic diction and composition, with such longstanding problems as the relationship between poetry and music and the use of natural description in poetry, with the doctrine of the inviolateness of the "kinds" and the "rules" of poetic composition, with the growing tendency to invent new poetic forms and subjects, with the sympathetic or emotional response to art, and with the need to establish durable standards of judgment in art. Beattie was a particularly fine critic of individual writers, such as John Dryden and Alexander Pope; he was at his best in writing close commentaries on selected literary passages.

Beattie's literary essays anticipate many aspects of the prose and poetry of the Romantic period. Like *The Minstrel,* the essays are transitional documents in the evolution of Romanticism; they demonstrate that many so-called Romantic concerns were in wide circulation long before Romantic poets and critics adopted and adapted them to their own purposes. Like *The Minstrel,* therefore, Beattie's essays contain a comprehensive survey of many of the important influences on the next generation of writers.

Beattie died on 18 August 1803. For the most part, he has been remembered solely for the fascination *The Minstrel* exerted on the young Romantic poets. A few modern critics use the poem to illustrate the poor judgment or weak taste sometimes found in the juvenile verse of the Romantic poets, who, it is implied, quickly surpassed and forgot Beattie's exploration of the poetic life. This view of the poem is in need of revision, and much may be learned about the times from his other neglected works as well: they provide a clear reflection of literary, philosophical, religious, and educational beliefs and practices of the late eighteenth century. One is impressed by Beattie's consistently high standard of judgment: everything that he recommends or emulates is invariably the best from earlier writers, and his strain of originality led him to explore and strengthen the most important aspects of developing trends. An appeal to proven principles, while the acceptance of new points of view is being recommended, is the main aim not only of his poetry and literary essays but also of his moral and educational essays and of his Christian apologetics.

Beattie's main value lies in the considerable extent to which he prepared his readers for later writers by teaching them to be receptive to new approaches. His books give not only the last popular expression to the Augustan Age but also early important intimations of inevitable change.

Letters:

James Beattie, "The Minstrel": Some Unpublished Letters, edited by Alexander Mackie (Aberdeen: Daily Journal Office, 1908);

The Letters of J. Beattie, Chronologically Arranged from Sir W. Forbes's Collection, 2 volumes (London: Sharpe, 1819-1821).

Biographies:

Alexander Bower, *An Account of the Life and Writings of James Beattie* (London: Baldwin, 1804);

William Forbes, *An Account of the Life and Writings of James Beattie, Including Many of His Original Letters*, 2 volumes (Edinburgh: Constable, 1806);

Alexander Chalmers, "Life of James Beattie," in volume 18 of *The Works of the British Poets* (London: Johnson, 1810), pp. 515-533;

Margaret Forbes, *Beattie and His Friends* (London: Constable, 1904; reprinted, Altrincham, U.K.: Stafford, 1990).

References:

Vincent M. Bevilacqua, "James Beattie's Theory of Rhetoric," *Speech Monographs*, no. 34 (1967): 109-124;

Aisso Bosker, *Literary Criticism in the Age of Johnson* (Groningen: Wolters, 1930; Folcroft, Pennsylvania: Folcroft Press, 1969);

François-Auguste-René de Chateaubriand, "Beattie," in his *Oevres Completes de Chateaubriand*, 12 volumes (Paris: Garnier, 1929-1938), II: 774-777;

Robert Eberwein, "James Beattie and David Hume on the Imagination and Truth," *Texas Studies in Literature and Language*, 12 (Winter 1971): 595-603;

James Gray, "Beattie and the Johnson Circle," *Queen's Quarterly*, 58 (Winter 1951-1952): 519-532;

Everard H. King, "Beattie and Byron: A Study in Augustan Satire and Romantic Vision," *Aberdeen University Review*, 48 (Autumn 1980): 404-418;

King, "Beattie and Coleridge: New Light on the Damaged Archangel," *Wordsworth Circle*, 7 (Spring 1976): 142-151;

King, "Beattie and Keats: The Progress of the Romantic Minstrel," *English Studies in Canada*, 3 (Summer 1977): 176-194;

King, "Beattie and Shelley: The Making of the Poet," *English Studies*, 61 (August 1980): 338-353;

King, "Beattie's *Minstrel* and Wordsworth's *Excursion*: What the Critics Overlook," *Bulletin of Research in the Humanities*, 83 (Autumn 1980): 339-359;

King, "Beattie's *The Minstrel* and the French Connection," *Scottish Literary Journal*, 11 (December 1984): 36-55;

King, "Beattie's *The Minstrel* and the Scottish Connection," *Wordsworth Circle*, 13 (Winter 1983): 20-26;

King, *James Beattie* (Boston: Hall, 1977);

King, "James Beattie and the Eighteenth-Century University," *Aberdeen University Review*, 44 (Autumn 1971): 174-185;

King, "James Beattie and the Growth of Romantic Melancholy," *Scottish Literary Journal*, 5 (May 1978): 23-38;

King, "James Beattie's 'Essay on the Sixth Book of Vergil's Aeneid . . . ,'" *Aberdeen University Review*, 47 (Autumn 1977): 173-185;

King, "James Beattie's 'Essay on Truth' (1770): An Eighteenth-Century 'Best-Seller,' " *Dalhousie Review*, 51 (Autumn 1971): 390-403;

King, "James Beattie's Literary Essays (1776, 1783): An Eighteenth-century 'Feast for an Epicure in Books,' " *Aberdeen University Review*, 45 (Autumn 1974): 389-401;

King, "James Beattie's Literary Essays (1776, 1783) and the Evolution of Romanticism," *Studies in Scottish Literature*, 11 (April 1974): 199-216;

King, "James Beattie's 'Remarks on the Utility of Classical Learning' (1776)," *Aberdeen University Review*, 49 (Spring 1981): 19-32;

King, "James Beattie's 'Retirement' and 'The Hermit': Two Early Romantic Poems," *South Atlantic Quarterly*, 72 (Autumn 1971): 174-185;

King, "James Beattie's 'The Castle of Scepticism' (1767): A Suppressed Satire on Eighteenth-Century Sceptical Philosophy," *Scottish Literary Journal*, 2 (December 1975): 18-35;

King, "James Beattie's *The Minstrel* and the Romantic Poets," *Aberdeen University Review*, 46 (Spring 1976): 273-287;

King, "James Beattie's *The Minstrel*: Its Influence on Wordsworth," *Studies in Scottish Literature*, 8 (July 1970): 3-29;

King, "James Beattie's Verses Occasioned by the Death of the Revd Mr. Charles Churchill and the Demise of Augustan Satire," *Studies in Scottish Literature*, 12 (April 1975): 234-249;

King, "Robert Burns and James Beattie, Minstrels 'Of the North Countrie,' " *Dalhousie Review*, 67 (Winter 1990): 45-53;

King, "Scott and Beattie's *Minstrel*: Autobiography or Fiction?" *Aberdeen University Review*, 50 (Autumn 1984): 406-415;

King, "A Scottish 'Philosophical' Club in the Eighteenth Century," *Dalhousie Review*, 50 (Summer 1970): 201-214;

King, "Wordsworth and Beattie's *Minstrel*: The Progress of Poetic Autobiography," *REAL: The Yearbook of Research in English and American Literature*, 3 (1985): 131-162;

James Kinsley, "The Music of the Heart," *Renaissance and Modern Studies*, 8 (1964): 5-52;

Karen Kloth and Bernhard Fabian, "James Beattie: Contributions Towards a Bibliography, *Bibliotheck*, 5, nos. 7-8 (1970): 232-245;

Stephen K. Land, "James Beattie on Language," *Philosophical Quarterly*, 51 (October 1972): 887-904;

Pierre Morere, *James Beattie's The Minstrel: Traduction de Chateaubriand et de J. B. Soulie* (Grenoble: Publications de l'Université des Langues et Lettres de Grenoble, 1981);

Morere, *L'oeuvre de James Beattie: Tradition et Perspectives Nouvelles*, 2 volumes (Paris: Librarie Honore Champion, 1980);

Joan Pittock, "James Beattie: A Friend to All," in *Literature of the North*, edited by David Hewit and Michael Spiller (Aberdeen: Aberdeen University Press, 1983), pp. 55-69;

Abbie F. Potts, *Wordsworth's Prelude: A Study of Its Literary Form* (Ithaca, N.Y.: Cornell University Press, 1953), pp. 63-76;

T. J. Roundtree, "Wordsworth and Beattie's Minstrel," *South Atlantic Quarterly*, 69 (Spring 1970): 257-263;

Ernest de Selincourt, ed., *The Early Letters of William and Dorothy Wordsworth* (Oxford: Clarendon Press, 1935), pp. 97-98;

William Sinclair, "The Bibliography of James Beattie," *Records of the Glasgow Bibliographical Society*, 7, (1923): 27-35;

R. P. Wolff, "Kant's Debt to Hume via Beattie," *Journal of the History of Ideas*, 21 (June 1961): 165-175.

Papers:

The Beattie Collection in the Aberdeen University Library contains more than four hundred letters and fragments by James Beattie and twice as many received by him, including letters to Beattie from Samuel Johnson and Thomas Gray. The Library of the University of Glasgow holds the manuscript of notes taken at Beattie's lectures by a student in 1767.

Robert Burns

(25 January 1759 - 21 July 1796)

Mary Ellen Brown
Indiana University

BOOKS: *Poems, Chiefly in the Scottish Dialect* (Kilmarnock: Printed by John Wilson, 1786; revised and enlarged edition, Edinburgh: Printed for the author, and sold by William Creech, 1787; Philadelphia: Printed for, and sold by Peter Stewart and George Hyde, 1788; enlarged edition, 2 volumes, Edinburgh: Printed for T. Cadell, London, and William Creech, Edinburgh, 1793).

Collections: *The Works of Robert Burns: With an Account of His Life, and a Criticism of His Writings. To Which Are Prefixed, Some Observations of the Character and Condition of the Scottish Peasantry*, 4 volumes, edited by James Currie (Liverpool: Printed by J. M'Creery; for T. Cadell, Jun. and W. Davies, London; and W. Creech, Edinburgh, 1800);

The Works of Robert Burns, 5 volumes, edited by James Hogg and William Motherwell (Glasgow: Fullarton, 1834-1836);

The Life and Works of Robert Burns, edited by P. Hateley Waddell (Glasgow: Wilson, 1867);

The Life and Works of Robert Burns, 4 volumes, edited by Robert Chambers, revised by William Wallace (Edinburgh: Chambers, 1896);

The Poetry of Robert Burns, 4 volumes, edited by W. E. Henley and T. F. Henderson (Edinburgh: Jack, 1896-1897);

The Songs of Robert Burns, edited by J. C. Dick (London & New York: Frowde, 1903); reprinted, with "Notes on Scottish Songs by Robert Burns" (Hatboro, Pa.: Folklore Associates, 1962);

Robert Burns's Commonplace Book 1783-1785, facsimile edition, edited by J. C. Ewing and Davidson Cook (Glasgow: Cowans & Gray, 1938);

The Poems and Songs of Robert Burns, 3 volumes, edited by James Kinsley (Oxford: Clarendon Press, 1968).

OTHER: *The Scots Musical Museum*, 6 volumes, edited by Burns and James Johnson, with contributions by Burns (Edinburgh: Printed and sold by James Johnson, 1787-1803);

A Select Collection of Original Scottish Airs for the Voice, 5 volumes, edited by George Thomson, with contributions by Burns (London: Preston & Son, 1793-1818);

The Merry Muses of Caledonia: A Collection of Favorite Scots Songs, attributed to Burns as editor and contributor (Edinburgh?: Peter Hill?, 1800?); republished as *The Merry Muses of Caledonia: Collected and in Part Written by Robert Burns*, edited by Gershon Legman (New Hyde Park, N.Y.: University Books, 1965).

Born on 25 January 1759 in Alloway, Scotland, to William and Agnes Brown Burnes, Robert Burns followed his father's example by becoming a tenant farmer. Unlike William Burnes, however, Burns was able to escape the vicissitudes and vagaries of the soil in two ways: toward the end of his life he became an excise collector in Dumfries, where he died in 1796; and throughout his life he was a practicing poet. As a poet he recorded and celebrated aspects of farm life, regional experience, traditional culture, class culture and distinctions, and religious practice and belief in such a way as to transcend the particularities of his inspiration, becoming finally the national poet of Scotland. Although he did not set out to achieve that designation, he clearly and repeatedly expressed his wish to be called a Scotch bard, to extol his native land in poetry and song, as he does in "The Answer":

Ev'n then a wish (I mind its power)
A wish, that to my latest hour
    Shall strongly heave my breast;
That I for poor auld Scotland's sake
Some useful plan, or book could make,
    Or sing a sang at least.

And perhaps he had an intimation that his "wish" had some basis in reality when he described his Edinburgh reception in a letter of 7 December 1786 to his friend Gavin Hamilton: "I am in a fair way of becoming as eminent as Thomas a Kempis or John Bunyan; and you may

Painting by Alexander Nasmyth (National Portrait Gallery, London)

expect henceforth to see my birthday inserted among the wonderful events, in the Poor Robin's and Aberdeen Almanacks. . . . and by all probability I shall soon be the tenth Worthy, and the eighth Wise Man, of the world."

That he retains the designations "Scotch bard" and "national poet of Scotland" today owes much to his position as the culmination of the Scottish literary tradition, a tradition stretching back to the court makars, to Robert Henryson and William Dunbar, to the seventeenth-century vernacular writers from James VI of Scotland to William Hamilton of Gilbertfield, to early-eighteenth-century forerunners such as Allan Ramsay and Robert Fergusson. Burns is often seen as the end of that literary line both because his brilliance and achievement could not be equaled and, more particularly, because the Scots vernacular in which he wrote some of his celebrated works was—even as he used it—becoming less and less intelligible to the majority of readers, who were already infected with English culture and language. The shift toward English cultural and linguistic hegemony had begun in 1603 with the Union of the Crowns when James VI of Scotland became James I of Great Britain; it had continued in 1707 with the merging of the Scottish and English Parliaments in London; and it was virtually a fait accompli by Burns's day save for pockets of regional culture and dialect. Thus, one might say that Burns remains the National Poet of Scotland because Scottish literature ceased with him, thereafter yielding poetry in English or in a pale Anglo-Scots or in inferior and slavish imitations of Burns.

Burns, however, has been viewed alternately as the beginning of another literary tradition: he is often called a pre-Romantic poet for his sensitivity to nature, his high valuation of feeling and emotion, his spontaneity, his fierce stance for freedom and against authority, his individualism, and his antiquarian interest in old songs and legends. The many backward glances of Romantic poets to Burns, as well as their critical comments and pilgrimages to the locales of Burns's life and work, suggest the validity of connecting Burns with that pervasive European cultural movement of the late eighteenth and early nineteenth centuries which shared with him a concern for creating a better world and for cultural renovation.

Nonetheless, the very qualities which seem to link Burns to the Romantics were logical responses to the eighteenth-century Scotland into which he was born. And his humble, agricultural background made him in some ways a spokesperson for every Scot, especially the poor and disenfranchised. He was aware of humanity's unequal condition and wrote of it and of his hope for a better world of equality throughout his life in epistle, poem, and song—perhaps most eloquently in the recurring comparison of rich and poor in the song "For A' That and A' That," which resoundingly affirms the humanity of the honest, hardworking, poor man: "The honest man, though e'er sae poor, / Is king o' men for a' that."

Burns is an important and complex literary personage for several reasons: his place in the Scottish literary tradition, his pre-Romantic proclivities, his position as a human being from the less-privileged classes imaging a better world. To these may be added his particular artistry, especially his ability to create encapsulating and synthesizing lines, phrases, and stanzas which continue to speak to and sum up the human condition. His recurring and poignant hymns to relationships are illustrative, as in the lines from the song beginning "Ae fond Kiss":

> Had we never lov'd sae kindly,
>   Had we never lov'd sae blindly!
>   Never met—or never parted,
>   We had ne'er been broken-hearted.

The Scotland in which Burns lived was a country in transition, sometimes in contradiction, on several fronts. The political scene was in flux, the result of the 1603 and 1707 unions which had stripped Scotland of its autonomy and finally all but muzzled the Scottish voice, as decisions and directives issued from London rather than from Edinburgh. A sense of loss led to questions and sometimes to actions, as in the Jacobite rebellions early in the eighteenth century. Was there a national identity? Should aspects of Scottish uniqueness be collected and enshrined? Should Scotland move ahead, adopting English manners, language, and cultural forms? No single answer was given to any of these questions. But change was afoot: Scots moved closer to an English norm, particularly as it was used by those in the professions, religion, and elite circles; "think in English, feel in Scots" seems to have been a widespread practice, which limited the communicative role, as well as the intelligibility, of Scots. For a time, however, remnants of the Scots dialect met with approbation among certain circles. A loose-knit movement to preserve evidences of Scottish culture embraced products that had the stamp of Scotland upon them, lauding Burns as a poet from the soil; assembling, editing, and collecting Scottish ballads and songs; sometimes accepting James Macpherson's Ossianic offerings; and lauding poetic Jacobitism. This movement was both nationalistic and antiquarian, recognizing Scottish identity through the past and thereby implicitly accepting contemporary assimilation.

Perhaps the most extraordinary transition occurring between 1780 and 1830 was the economic shift from agriculture to industry that radically altered social arrangements and increased social inequities. While industrialization finished the job, agricultural changes had set the transition in motion earlier in the eighteenth century. Agriculture in Scotland had typically followed a widespread European form known as runrig, wherein groups of farmers rented and worked a piece of land which was periodically re-subdivided to insure diachronic if not synchronic equity. Livestock was removed to the hills for grazing during the growing season since there were no enclosures. A subsistence arrangement, this form of agriculture dictated settlement patterns and life possibilities and was linked inextricably to the ebb and flow and unpredictable vicissitudes of the seasons. The agricultural revolution of the eighteenth century introduced new crops, such as sown grasses and turnips, which made wintering over of animals profitable; advocated enclosing fields to keep livestock out; developed new equipment—in particular the iron plow—and improved soil preparation; and generally suggested economies of scale. Large landowners, seeing profit in making "improvements," displaced runrig practices and their adherents, broadening the social and economic gap between landowner and former tenant; the latter frequently became a farm worker. Haves and have-nots became more clearly delineated; "improvements" depended on capital and access to descriptive literature. Many small tenant farmers foundered during the transition, including both Burnes and his father.

Along with the gradual change in agriculture and shift to industry there was a concomitant shift from rural to urban spheres of influence. The move from Scots to greater reliance on English was accelerated by the availability of cheap print made possible by the Industrial Revolution. Print became the medium of choice, lessening the power of oral culture's artistic forms and aesthetic structures; print, a visual medium, fostered linear structures and perceptual frameworks, replacing in part the circular patterns and preferences of the oral world.

Two forces, however, served to keep change from being a genuine revolution and made it more nearly a transformation by fits and starts: the Presbyterian church and traditional culture. Presbyterianism was established as the Kirk of Scotland in 1668. Although fostering education, the printed word, and, implicitly, English for specific religious ends, and thus seeming to support change, religion was largely a force for constraint and uniformity. Religion was aided but simultaneously undermined by traditional culture, the inherited ways of living, perceiving, and creating. Traditional culture was conservative, preferring the old ways—agricultural subsistence or near subsistence patterns and oral forms of information and artistry conveyed in customs, songs, and stories. But if both religion and traditional culture worked to maintain the status quo, traditional culture was finally more flexible: as inherited, largely oral knowledge and art always adapting to fit the times, traditional culture was less rigid. It was diverse and it celebrated freedom.

Scotland's upheavals were in many ways Burns's upheavals as well: he embraced cultural nationalism to celebrate Scotland in poem and song; he struggled as a tenant farmer without the requisite capital and know-how in the age of "improvement"; he combined the oral world of his childhood and region with the education his father arranged through an "adventure school"; he accepted, but resented, the moral judgments of the Kirk against himself and friends such as Gavin Hamilton; he knew the religious controversies which pitted moderate against conservative on matters of church control and belief; he reveled in traditional culture's balladry, song, proverbs, and customs. He was a man of his time, and his success as poet, songwriter, and human being owes much to the way he responded to the world around him. Some have called him *the* typical Scot, Everyman.

Burns began his career as a local poet writing for a local, known audience to whom he looked for immediate response, as do all artists in a traditional context. He wrote on topics of appeal both to himself and to his artistic constituency, often in a wonderfully appealing conversational style.

Burns's early life was spent in the southwest of Scotland, where his father worked as an estate gardener in Alloway, near Ayr. Subsequently William Burnes leased successively two farms in the region, Mount Oliphant nearby and Lochlie near Tarbolton. Between 1765 and 1768 Burns attended an "adventure" school established by his father and several neighbors with John Murdock as teacher, and in 1775 he attended a mathematics school in Kirkoswald. These formal and more or less institutionalized bouts of education were extended at home under the tutelage of his father. Burns was identified as odd because he always carried a book; a countrywoman in Dunscore, who had seen Burns riding slowly among the hills reading, once remarked, "That's surely no a good man, for he has aye a book in his hand!" The woman no doubt assumed an oral norm, the medium of traditional culture.

Life on a pre- or semi-improved farm was backbreaking and frequently heartbreaking, since bad weather might wipe out a year's effort. Bad seed would not prosper even in the best-prepared soil. Rain and damp, though necessary for crop growth, were often "too much of a good thing." Burns grew up knowing the vagaries of farming and understanding full well both mental preparation and long days of physical labor. His father had married late and was thus older than many men with a household of children; he was also less physically resilient and less able to endure the tenant farmer's lot. Bad seed and rising rents at various times spelled failure to his ventures. At the time of his approaching death and a disastrous end to the Lochlie lease, Burns and his brother secretly leased Mossgiel Farm near Mauchline. Burns was twenty-five.

The death of his father, the family's patriarchal force for constraint in religion, education, and morality, freed Burns. He quickly became recognized as a rhymer, sometimes signing himself after the farm as Rab Mossgiel. The midwife's prophecy at his birth—that he would be much attracted to the lasses—became a reality; in 1785 he fathered a daughter by Betty Paton, and in 1786 had twins by Jean Armour. His fornications and his thoughts about the Kirk, made public, opened him to church censure, which he bore but little accepted. It was almost as though the floodgates had burst: his poetic output between 1784 and 1786 includes many of those works on which his reputation stands—epistles, satires, manners-painting, and songs—many of which he circulated in the manner of the times: in manuscript or by reading aloud. Many works of this period, judiciously chosen to appeal to a wider audience, appeared in the first formal publication of his work, *Poems, Chiefly in the Scottish Dialect*, printed in Kilmarnock in 1786 and paid for by subscriptions.

The Kilmarnock edition might be seen as the result of two years or so of riotous living: much conviviality, much socializing with women in an era before birth control, much thinking about humanity without the "correcting" restraint of the paterfamilias, much poetry and song ostensibly about the immediate environment but encapsulating aspects of the human condition. All of this was certainly more interesting than the agricultural round, which offered a physical constraint to match the moral and mental constraint of religion. Both forms of constraint impeded the delight in life that many of Burns's finest works exhibit. Furthermore, he was in serious trouble with the Armour family, who destroyed a written and acceptable, if a bit unorthodox, marriage contract. He resolved to get out of town quickly and to leave behind something to prove his worth. He seems to have made plans to immigrate to the West Indies, and he brought to fruition his plan to publish some of his already well-received works. One of the 612 copies reached Edinburgh and was perceived to have merit. Informed of this casual endorsement, Burns abandoned his plans for immigration—if they had ever been serious—and left instead for Edinburgh.

The Kilmarnock edition shows Burns's penchant for self-presentation and his ability to choose variable poses to fit the expectations of the intended receiver. Burns presents himself as an untutored rhymer, who wrote to counteract life's woes; he feigns anxiety over the reception of his poems; he pays tribute to the genius of the "Scotch Poets" Ramsay and Fergusson; and he requests the reader's indulgence. In large measure, the material belies the tentativeness of the preface, revealing a poet aware of his literary tradition, capable of building on it, and deft in using a variety of voices—from "couthie" and colloquial, through sentimental and tender, to satiric and pointed. But the book also contains evidences of Burns as local poet, turning life to verse in slight, spur-of-the-moment pieces, occasional rhymes made on local personages, often to the gratification of their enemies. The Kilmarnock edition, however, is more revealing for its illustration of his place in a literary tradition: "The Cotter's Saturday Night," for example, echoes Fergusson's "The Farmer's Ingle" (1773); "The Holy Fair" is part of a long tradition of peasant brawls, drawing on a verse form, the Chrystis Kirk stanza, known by the name of a representative poem attributed to James I: "Chrystis Kirk of the Grene." Many of Burns's poems and verse epistles employ the six-line stanza, derived from the medieval tail-rhyme stanza which was used in Scotland by Sir David Lindsay in *Ane Satyre of the Thrie Estaitis* (1602) but was probably seen by Burns in James Watson's *Choice Collection* (1706-1711) in works by Hamilton of Gilbertfield and Robert Sempill of Beltrees; Sempill's "The Life and Death of Habbie Simpson" gave the form its accepted name, Standard Habbie. Quotations from and allusions to English literary figures and their works appear throughout his work: Thomas Gray in "The Cotter's Saturday Night," Alexander Pope in "Holy Willie's Prayer," John Milton in "Address to the Deil."

Poems, Chiefly in the Scottish Dialect (an undistinguished title used often before and after as a title of local poets' effusions) was a success. With all its obvious contradictions—untutored but clearly lettered; peasant but perspicacious; conscious national pride ("The Vision," "Scotch Drink") together with multiple references to other literatures—the Kilmarnock edition set the stage for Burns's success in Edinburgh and anticipated his conscious involvement in the cultural nationalistic movement. Such works as "Address to the Deil" anticipate this later concern:

O Thou, whatever title suit thee!
Auld Hornie, Satan, Nick, or Clootie,
Wha in yon cavern grim an' sooty
    Clos'd under hatches,
Spairges about the brunstane cootie,
    To scaud poor wretches!

Hear me, *auld Hangie*, for a wee,
    An' let poor, *damned bodies* bee;

APRIL 14th, 1786.

PROPOSALS,

FOR PUBLISHING BY SUBSCRIPTION,

SCOTCH POEMS,

BY ROBERT BURNS.

The Work to be elegantly Printed in One Volume, Octavo,
Price Stitched *Three Shillings*.

As the Author has not the most distant *Mercenary* view in Publishing, as soon as so many Subscribers appear as will defray the *necessary* Expence, the Work will be sent to the Press.

Set out the brunt side o' your shin,
For pride in *Poets* is nae sin;
Glory's the Prize for which *they* rin,
And *Fame's* their jo;
And wha blaws best the Horn shall win:
And wherefore no?

RAMSAY.

We, under Subscribers, engage to take the above mentioned Work on the Conditions Specified.

Subscription list for Burns's Poems, Chiefly in the Scottish Dialect (*#311,* Memorial Catalogue of the Burns Exhibition Held in the Galleries of The Royal Glasgow Institute of the Fine Arts, Glasgow, from 15th July till 31st October, 1896)

I'm sure sma' pleasure it can gie,
Ev'n to a *deil*,
To skelp an' scaud poor dogs like me,
An' hear us squeel!

These two stanzas provide evidence of the implicit tension between established religion and traditional culture rampant in Burns's early work. Burns takes his epigraph from Milton—

O Prince, O chief of many throned pow'rs,
That led th' embattl'd Seraphim to war—

conjuring up biblical ideas of Satan as fallen angel, hell as a place of fire and damnation, the devil as punisher of evil. But Burns's deil, familiarly addressed, is an almost comic, ever-present figure, tempting humanity but escapable. Burns allies him with traditional forces—spunkies, water-kelpies—and gives old Clootie no more force or power. Traditional notions of the devil are much less restraining than the formal religious concepts. By juxtaposing Satan and Auld Nickie, Burns conjures up metaphorically the two dominant cultural forces—one for constraint and the other for freedom. Here as elsewhere in Burns's work, freedom reigns.

Burns's affection for traditional culture is amply illustrated. In a well-known autobiographical letter to Dr. John Moore (2 August 1787) he pays tribute to its early influence when he says, "In my infant and boyish days too, I owed much to an old Maid of my Mother's, remarkable for her ignorance, credulity and superstition.—She had, I suppose, the largest collection in the county of tales and songs concerning devils, ghosts, fairies, brownies, witches, warlocks, spunkies, kelpies, elf-candles, dead-lights, wraiths, apparitions, cantraips, giants, inchanted towers, dragons and other trumpery.—This cultivated the latent seeds of Poesy. . . ."

Burns's first and last works were songs, reflecting his deep connection with oral ballad and song. The world of custom and belief is most particularly described in "Halloween," an ethnographic poem with footnotes elucidating rural customs. Many forms of prognostication are possible on this evening when this world and the other world or worlds hold converse, a time when unusual things are deemed possible—especially foretelling one's future mate and status. Burns's notes and prefatory material have often been used as evidence of his distance from and perhaps disdain for such practices. Yet the poem itself is peopled with a sympathetic cast of youths, chaperoned by an old woman, joined together for fun and fellowship. The youthful players try several prognosticatory rites in attempting to anticipate their future love relationships. In one stanza Burns alludes to a particular practice—"pou their *stalks o' corn*"—and explains in his note that "they go to the barn-yard, and pull each, at three several times, a stalk of Oats. If the third stalk wants the *top-pickle*, that is, the grain at the top of the stalk, the party in question will come to the marriage-bed any thing but a Maid." Burns concludes the stanza by saying that one Nelly almost lost her *top-pickle* that very night. Some of the activities in what is essentially a preliminary courtship ritual are frightening, requiring collective daring. Burns describes the antics, anticipation, and anxieties of the participants as they enjoy the communal event, which is concluded with food and drink:

Wi' merry sangs, an' friendly cracks,
    I wat they did na weary;
And unco tales, an' funnie jokes,
    Their sports were cheap an' cheary:
Till *buttr'd So'ns*, wi' fragrant lunt,
    Set a' their gabs a steerin;
Syne, wi' a social glass o' strunt,
    They parted aff careerin
    Fu' blythe that night.

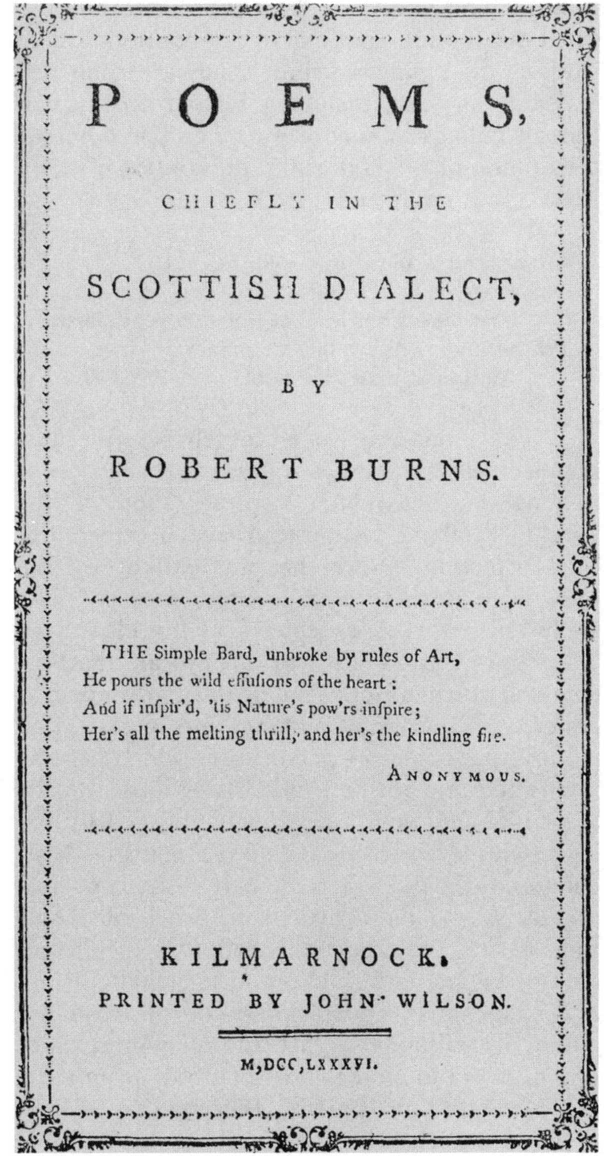
POEMS,

CHIEFLY IN THE

SCOTTISH DIALECT,

BY

ROBERT BURNS.

THE Simple Bard, unbroke by rules of Art,
He pours the wild effusions of the heart:
And if inspir'd, 'tis Nature's pow'rs inspire;
Her's all the melting thrill, and her's the kindling fire.

ANONYMOUS.

KILMARNOCK.
PRINTED BY JOHN WILSON.

M,DCC,LXXXVI.

Title page for the Kilmarnock edition, the first formal publication of Burns's work

"The Cotter's Saturday Night" is on one level a microcosmic description of the agricultural, social, and religious practices of the farm worker—albeit an idealized vision that reiterates Burns's absolute affection for traditional aspects of life, a fictive version of his own experience. The poem is a celebration of the family and of the lives of simple folk, sanitized of hardship, crop failure, sickness, and death. Burns achieves this vision by focusing on a moment of domestic repose of a family reunited in love and affection. The Master and Mistress are the architects of the family circle; Jenny and "a neebor lad" seem destined to provide continuity. The gathering concludes with family worship: songs are sung and Scripture is read, including biblical accounts of human failings by way of warning. The domestic celebration of religion within the context of traditional life is noble and good.

From Scenes like these, old SCOTIA'S grandeur springs,
That makes her lov'd at home, rever'd abroad:
Princes and lords are but the breath of kings,
'An honest man's the noble work of GOD.'

This poem was lauded largely because of its linguistic accessibility, as a pastoral expression of nationalism, a symbolic representation of the "soul of Scotland." Auguste Angellier offers critical affirmation: "Never has the existence of the poor been invested with so much dignity." The lowly farm worker is depicted as the ideal Scot. The cotter's good life was already an anachronism, so Burns's depiction in this early poem is antiquarian, backward-looking, and imbued with cultural nationalism—perspectives which became intensified and focused in his later work. But by 1784-1785 his work was already engaged in dialogue with larger cultural issues. The linguistic attributes of the poem become part of this conversation as Burns modulates from Scots into Scots English to English, poetically reflecting the dichotomy of feeling and thinking. The stability of life as described in this poem is a wonderful accommodation of traditional culture and religion; celebration of belief in God follows naturally from sharing a way of life. But the religion that is here applauded is domestic and familial. Institutional religion Burns saw as something quite other.

Institutional religion at its worst is excessively hierarchical, constraining, and above all unjust, damning some and saving others. As a child Burns was steeped in the doctrine of predestination and effectual calling, which asserts that some people are "elected" by God to be saved without any consideration of life and works; the unchosen are damned no matter what they do. Carried to an extreme, the doctrine would permit an individual who felt assured of election to do all manner of evil, a scenario developed in Burns's "Holy Willie's Prayer." Burns could not accept the orthodox position of the so-called Auld Lichts; he believed in the power of good works to determine salvation. His corner of Scotland was a bastion of conservative religious position and practice: the Kirk session served as a moral watchdog, summoning congregants who strayed from the "straight and narrow" and handing out censure and punishment.

Thus religion was a cultural force with which to contend. Burns participated in the debate through poetry, circulating his material orally and in manuscript. Chief among his works in this vein is the satire "Holy Willie's Prayer." Prompted by the defeat of the Auld Licht censure of his friend Hamilton for failure to participate in public worship, the poem, shaped like a prayer, is put into the mouth of the Auld Licht adherent Holy Willie. It begins with an effective invocation which articulates Willie's doctrinal stance on predestination in Standard Habbie:

O Thou that in the heavens does dwell!
Wha, as it pleases best thysel,
Sends ane to heaven an ten to h-ll,
A' for thy glory!
And no for ony gude or ill
They've done before thee.

The poem continues with Willie's thanks for his own "elected" status and reaches its highest moments in Willie's confession that "At times I'm fash'd wi' fleshly lust." Burns has Willie condemn himself by describing moments of fornication and justifying them as temptations visited on him by God. The concluding stanzas recount Willie's opinion of Hamilton—"He drinks, and swears, and plays at cartes"—and his chagrin that Minister Auld was defeated. The poem ends with the requisite petition, calling for divine vengeance on those who disagree with him and asking blessings for himself and his like. Burns condemns both the doctrine and the practice of institutional religion.

The tensions between religion and traditional culture are particularly obvious in "The Holy Fair." Burns's depiction of an open-air communion gathering, with multiple sermons and exhortations, includes an important subtext on the sociability of food, drink, chat, and perhaps love—attractions which will lead to behavior decried in sermons that very day. Again religious constraint and traditional license meet, with freedom clearly preferable:

How monie hearts this day converts,
O' Sinners and o' Lasses!
Their hearts o' stane, gin night are gane
As saft as ony flesh is.
There's some are fou o' *love divine*;
There's some are fou o' *brandy*;

The Cotter's Saturday night. Inscribed to R. A****, Esq.

Let not Ambition mock their useful toil,
Their homely joys, and destiny obscure;
Nor Grandeur hear, with a disdainful smile,
The short and simple annals of the Poor. Gray.

1

My lov'd, my honor'd, much respected friend,
No mercenary Bard his homage pays;
With honest pride, I scorn each selfish end,
My dearest meed, a friend's esteem and praise:
To you I sing, in simple Scottish lays,
The lowly train in life's sequester'd scene;
The native feelings strong, the guileless ways,
What A**** in a Cottage would have been;
Ah! tho' his worth unknown, far happier there I ween!

2

November chill blaws loud wi' angry sugh;
The short'ning winter-day is near a close;
The miry beasts retreating frae the pleugh;
The black'ning trains o' craws to their repose:
The toil-worn Cotter frae his labor goes,
This night his weekly moil is at an end,
Collects his spades, his mattocks and his hoes,
Hoping the morn in ease and rest to spend,
And weary, o'er the muir, his course does hameward bend.

3

At length his lonely Cot appears in view,
Beneath the shelter of an aged tree;
Th' expectant wee-things, toddlan, stacher thro'
To meet their Dad, wi' flichterin noise and glee.
His wee-bit ingle, blinkan bonilie,
His clean hearth-stane, his thrifty Wifie's smile,
The lisping infant, prattling on his knee,
Does a' his weary kiaugh and care beguile,
And makes him quite forget his labor and his toil.

Page from a manuscript for Burns's poem about simple farm workers (G. Ross Roy Scottish Poetry Collection, Thomas Cooper Library, University of South Carolina)

An' monie jobs that day begin,
May end in *Houghmagandie*
Some ither day.

"The Jolly Beggars; or, Love and Liberty: A Cantata" goes even further toward affirming freedom through traditional culture. Probably written in 1785 but not published until after Burns's death, this work combines poetry and song to describe a joyful gathering of society's rejects: the maimed and physically deformed, prostitutes, and thieves. The work alternates life histories with narrative passages describing the convivial interaction of the social outcasts. Despite their low status, the accounts they give of their lives reveal an unrivaled ebullience and joy. The texts are wedded to traditional and popular tunes. The choice of tunes is not random but underlines the characteristics and experiences described in the words: thus the tinker describes his occupation to the woman he has seduced away from a fiddler to the tune "Clout the Caudron," whose traditional text describes an itinerant fixer of pots and pans, that is, a seducer of women. The assembled company exhibits acceptance of their lots in life, an acceptance made possible because their positions are shared by all present and by the power of drink of soften hardships. Stripped of all the components of human decency, lacking religious or material riches, the beggars are jolly through drink and fellowship, rich in song and story—traditional pastimes. The cantata rushes to a riotous conclusion in which those assembled sing a rousing countercultural chorus that would certainly have received Holy Willie's harshest censure:

A fig for those by LAW protected,
LIBERTY's a glorious feast!
COURTS for Cowards were erected,
CHURCHES built to please the Priest.

"The Jolly Beggars" implicitly speaks to the economic situation of the time: more and more people were made jobless and homeless in the rush for "improvement," and the older pattern of taking care of the parish poor had broken down because of greater mobility and greater numbers of needy. Burns offers no solution, but he does illustrate the beggars' humanity and, above all, their capacity for Life with a capital L—a mode of behavior that is convivial; unites people in story, song, and drink; and exudes delight and joy: traditional culture wins again.

Burns worked out in poetry some of his responses to his own culture by showing opposing views of how life should be lived. Descriptions of his own experiences stimulated musings on constraint and freedom. Critical tradition says that John Richmond and Burns observed the beggars in Poosie Nansie's; "The Holy Fair" may be based on the Mauchline Annual Communion, which was held on the second Sunday of August in 1785; the gathering of the cotter's family may not describe a specific event but certainly depicts a generalized and typical picture. Thus Burns's own experiences became the base from which he responded to and considered larger cultural and human issues.

The Kilmarnock edition changed Burns's life: it sprang him away for a year and a half from the grind of agricultural routine, and it made him a public figure. Burns arrived in the capital city in the heyday of cultural nationalism, and his own person and works were hailed as evidences of a Scottish culture: the Scotsman as a peasant, close to the soil, possessing the "soul" of nature; the works as products of that peasant, in Scots, containing echoes of earlier written and oral Scottish literature.

Burns went to Edinburgh to arrange for a new edition of his poems and was immediately taken up by the literati and proclaimed a remarkable Scot. He procured the support of the Caledonian Hunt as sponsors of the Edinburgh edition and set to work with the publisher William Creech to arrange a slightly altered and expanded edition. He was wined and dined by the taste-setters, almost without exception persons from a different class and background from his. He was the "hit" of the season, and he knew full well what was going on: he intensified aspects of his rural persona to conform to expectations. He represented the creativity of the peasant Scot and was for a season "Exhibit A" for a distinct Scottish heritage.

Burns used this time for a variety of experiments, trying on several roles. He entered into what seems to have been a platonic dalliance with a woman of some social standing, Agnes McLehose, who was herself in an ambiguous social situation—her husband having been in Jamaica for some time. The relationship, whatever its true nature, stimulated a correspondence, in which Burns and Mrs. McLehose styled themselves Sylvander and Clarinda and wrote predictably elevated, formulaic, and seemingly insincere letters. Burns lacks conviction in this role; but he

Holy Willie's Prayer.

And send the godly in a pet to pray — Pope.

O Thou that in the heavens does dwell!
Wha, as it pleases best Thysel,
Sends ane to heaven and ten to h-ll,
A' for Thy glory;
And no for ony guid or ill
They've done before Thee.

I bless and praise Thy matchless might,
When thousands Thou has left in night,
That I am here before Thy sight,
For gifts and grace,
A burning and a shining light
To a' this place.

What was I, or my generation,
That I should get such exaltation?
I, who deserv'd most just damnation
For broken laws,
Sax thousand years ere my creation
Thro' Adam's cause.

Yet I am here, a chosen sample,
To show Thy grace is great and ample;
I'm here, a pillar o' Thy temple,
Strong as a rock;
A guide, a ruler and example
To a' Thy flock.

But yet, O L—d, confess I must,
At times I'm fash'd wi' fleshly lust;
And sometimes too in warldly trust
Vile Self gets in;

Page from a manuscript for Burns's poem about a hypocritical religious fanatic (#1093, Memorial Catalogue of the Burns Exhibition Held in the Galleries of The Royal Glasgow Institute of the Fine Arts, Glasgow, from 15th July till 31st October, 1896)

met more congenial persons: boon companions, males whom he joined in back-street howffs for lively talk, song, and bawdry.

If the Caledonian Hunt represented the late-eighteenth-century crème de la crème, the Crochallan Fencibles, one of the literary and convivial clubs of the day in which members took on assumed names and personae, represented the middle ranks of society where Burns felt more at home. In the egalitarian clubs and howffs Burns met more sympathetic individuals, among them James Johnson, an engraver in the initial stages of a project to print all the tunes of Scotland. That meeting shifted Burns's focus to song, which became his principal creative form for the rest of his life.

The Edinburgh period provided an interlude of potentiality and experimentation. Burns made several trips to the Borders and Highlands, often being received as a notable and renowned personage. Within a year and a half Burns moved from being a local poet to one with a national reputation and was well on his way to being the national poet, even though much of his writing during this period continued an earlier versifying strain of extemporaneous, occasional poetry. But the Edinburgh period set the groundwork for his subsequent creativity, stimulated his revealing correspondence, and provided him with a way of becoming an advocate for Scotland as anonymous bard.

If Burns were received in Edinburgh as a typical Scot and a producer of genuine Scottish products, that cultural nationalism in turn channeled his love of his country—already expressed in several poems in the Kilmarnock edition—into his songs. Burns's support for Johnson's project is infectious; in a letter to a friend, James Candlish, he wrote in November 1787: "I am engaged in assisting an honest Scots Enthusiast, a friend of mine, who is an Engraver, and has taken it into his head to publish a collection of all our songs set to music, of which the words and music are done by Scotsmen.—This, you will easily guess, is an undertaking exactly to my taste.—I have collected, begg'd, borrow'd and stolen all the songs I could meet with.—Pompey's Ghost, words and music, I beg from you immediately. . . ." Here was a chance to do what he had been doing all his life—wedding text and tune—but for Scotland. Thus Burns became a conscious participant in the antiquarian and cultural movement to gather and preserve evidences of Scottish identity before they were obliterated in the cultural drift toward English language and culture. Burns's clear preference for traditional culture, and particularly for the freedom it represented, shifted intensity and direction because of the Edinburgh experience. He narrowed his focus from all of traditional culture to one facet—song. Balladry and song were safe artifacts that could be captured on paper and sanitized for polite edification. This approach to traditional culture was distanced and conscious, while his earlier depiction of the larger whole of traditional culture had been immediate, intimate, and largely unconscious. Thus Edinburgh changed his artistic stance, making him more clearly aware of choices and directions as well as a conscious antiquarian.

In all, Burns had a hand in some 330 songs for Johnson's *The Scots Musical Museum* (1787-1803), a six-volume work, and for George Thomson's five-volume *A Select Collection of Original Scottish Airs for the Voice* (1793-1818). As a nationalistic work, *The Scots Musical Museum* was designed to reflect Scottish popular taste; like similar publications, it included traditional songs—texts and tunes—as well as songs and tunes by specific authors and composers. Burns developed a coded system of letters for identifying contributors, suggesting to all but the cognoscenti that the songs were traditional. It is often difficult to separate Burns's work from genuinely traditional texts; he may, for example, have edited and polished the old Scots ballad "Tam Lin," which tells of a man restored from fairyland to his human lover. Many collected texts received a helping hand—fragments were filled out, refrains and phrases were amalgamated to make a whole—and original songs in the manner of tradition were created anew. Burns's song output was enormous and uneven, and he knew it: "Here, once for all, let me apologise for many silly compositions of mine in this work. Many beautiful airs wanted words." Yet many of the songs are succinct masterpieces on love, on the brotherhood of man, and on the dignity of the common man—subjects which link Burns with oral and popular tradition on the one hand and on the other with the societal changes that were intensifying distinctions between people.

Perhaps the most remarkable thing about Burns's songs is their singability, the perspicacity with which words are joined to tune. "My Love she's but a lassie yet" provides a superb example: a sprightly tune holds together four loosely connected stanzas about a woman, courtship, drink, and sexual dalliance to create a whole much

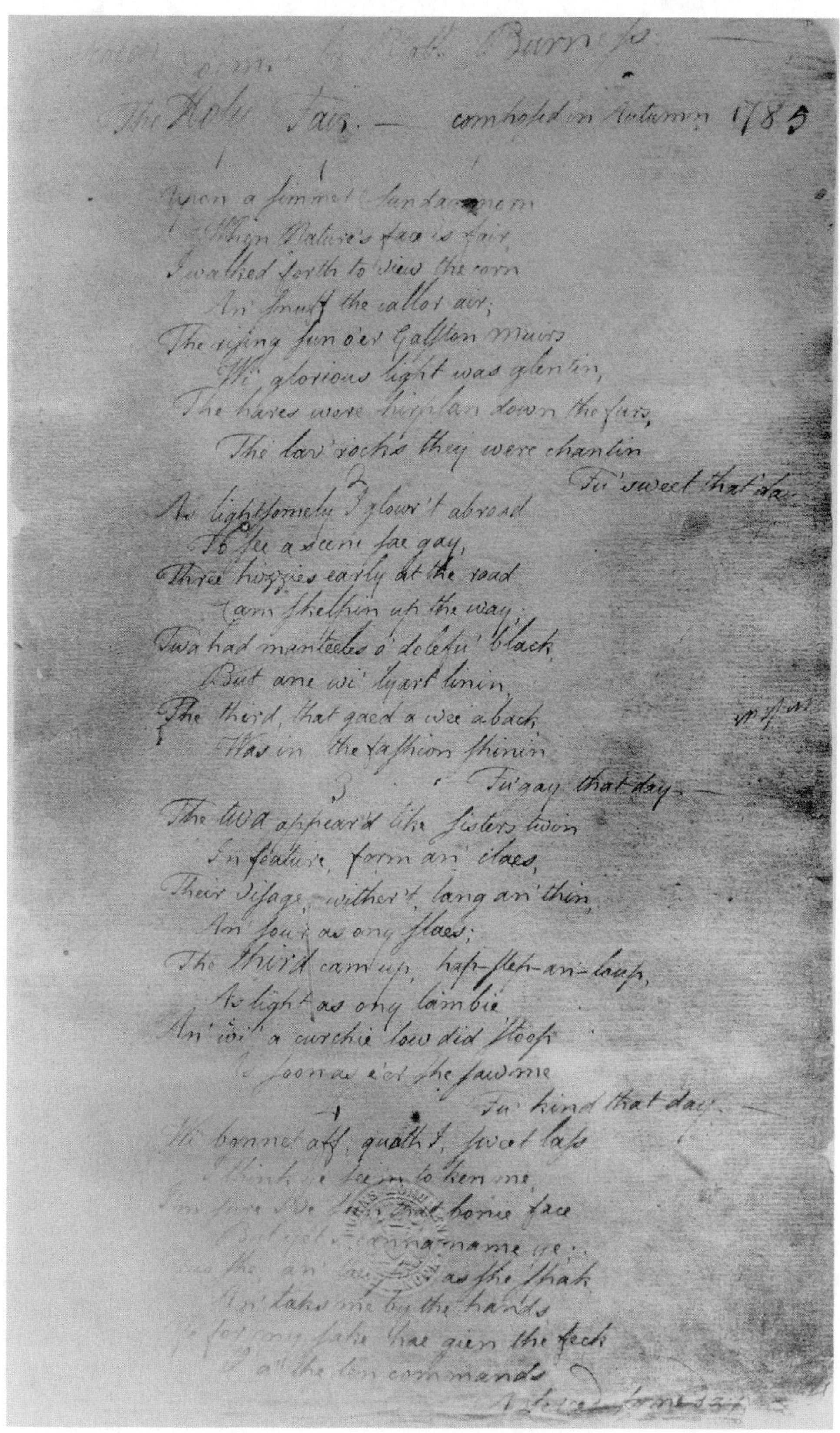

Poems by Robt. Burns

The Holy Fair. — composed in Autumn 1785

1

Upon a simmer Sunday morn
When Nature's face is fair,
I walked forth to view the corn
An' snuff the caller air;
The rising sun o'er Galston Muirs
Wi' glorious light was glentin,
The hares were hirplan down the furs,
The lav'rocks they were chantin
Fu' sweet that da[y]

2

As lightsomely I glowr'd abroad
To see a scene sae gay,
Three hizzies early at the road
Cam skelpin up the way;
Twa had manteeles o' dolefu' black,
But ane wi' lyart linin,
The third, that gaed a wee aback,
Was in the fashion shinin
Fu' gay that day.

3

The twa appear'd like sisters twin
In feature, form an' claes,
Their visage wither'd lang an' thin,
An' sour as ony slaes;
The third cam up, hap-step-an'-lowp,
As light as ony lambie
An' wi' a curchie low did stoop
As soon as e'er she saw me
Fu' kind that day.

4

Wi' bonnet aff, quoth I, sweet lass
I think ye seem to ken me,
I'm sure I've seen that bonie face
But yet I canna name ye:
Quo' she an' laughs as she spak
An' taks me by the hands
Ye for my sake hae gi'en the feck
O' a' the ten commands
A screed some day

Page from a manuscript for Burns's account of an open-air religious gathering (#1092, Memorial Catalogue of the Burns Exhibition Held in the Galleries of The Royal Glasgow Institute of the Fine Arts, Glasgow, from 15th July till 31st October, 1896)

greater than the sum of the parts. The song begins:

My love she's but a lassie yet,
My love she's but a lassie yet;
We'll let her stand a year or twa,
She'll no be half sae saucy yet.

It concludes, enigmatically:

We're a' dry wi' drinking o't,
We're a' dry wi' drinking o't:
The minister kisst the fidler's wife,
He could na preach for thinkin o't.—

The songs are at their best when sung, but there may be delight in text alone, for brilliant stanzas appear most unexpectedly. The chorus of "Auld Lang Syne" encapsulates the pleasure of reunion, of shared memory:

For auld lang syne, my jo,
For auld lang syne,
We'll tak a cup o' kindness yet
For auld lang syne.

The vignette of a couple aging together—"We clamb the hill the gither" in "John Anderson My Jo" suggests praise of continuity and shared lives. In a similar manner "A Red, Red Rose" depicts a love that is both fresh and lasting: "O my Luve's like a red, red rose, / That's newly sprung in June."

Burns's comment in a letter to Mrs. Dunlop of Dunlop in 1790—"Old Scots Songs are, you know, a favorite study and pursuit of mine"—accurately describes his absorption with song after Edinburgh. He not only collected, edited, and wrote songs but studied them, perusing the extant collections, commenting on provenance, gathering explanatory material, and speculating on the distinct qualities of Scottish song: "There is a certain something in the old Scotch songs, a wild happiness of thought and expression" and of Scottish music: "let our National Music preserve its native features.—They are, I own, frequently wild, & unreduceable to the more modern rules; but on that very eccentricity, perhaps, depends a great part of their effect." This nationalism did not stop with song but pervaded all Burns's work after Edinburgh. Certainly the most critically acclaimed product of this period is a work written for Francis Grose's *Antiquities of Scotland* (1789-1791). Burns suggested Alloway Kirk as a subject for the work and wrote "Tam o' Shanter" to assure its inclusion.

"Tam o' Shanter" is the culmination of Burns's delight in traditional culture and his selective elevation of parts of that culture in his antiquarian and nationalistic pursuit of Scottish distinctness. The poem retells a legend about a man who comes upon a witches' Sabbath and unwisely comments on it, alerting the participants to his presence and necessitating their revenge. Burns provides a frame for the legend, localizes it at Alloway Kirk, and peoples it with plausible characters—in particular, the feckless Tam, who takes every opportunity to imbibe with his buddies and avoid going home to wife and domestic responsibilities. Tam stops at a tavern for a drink and sociability and gets caught up in the flow of song, story, and laughter; the raging storm outside makes the conviviality inside the tavern doubly precious. But it is late and Tam must go home and "face the music," having yet again gotten drunk, no doubt having used money intended for less selfish and more basic purposes. On his way home Tam experiences the events which are central to the legend; the initial convivial scene has provided the context in which such legends might be told. After passing spots enshrined in other legends, he comes upon the witches' Sabbath revels at the ruins of Alloway Kirk, with the familiar and not quite malevolent devil, styled "auld Nick," in dog form playing bagpipe accompaniment to the witches' dance. Burns incorporates skeptical interpolations into the narrative—perhaps Tam is only drunk and "seeing things"—which replicate in poetic form aspects of an oral telling of legends. And the concluding occurrence of Tam's escapade, the loss of his horse's tail to the foremost witch's grasp, demands a response from the reader in much the same way a legend told in conversation elicits an

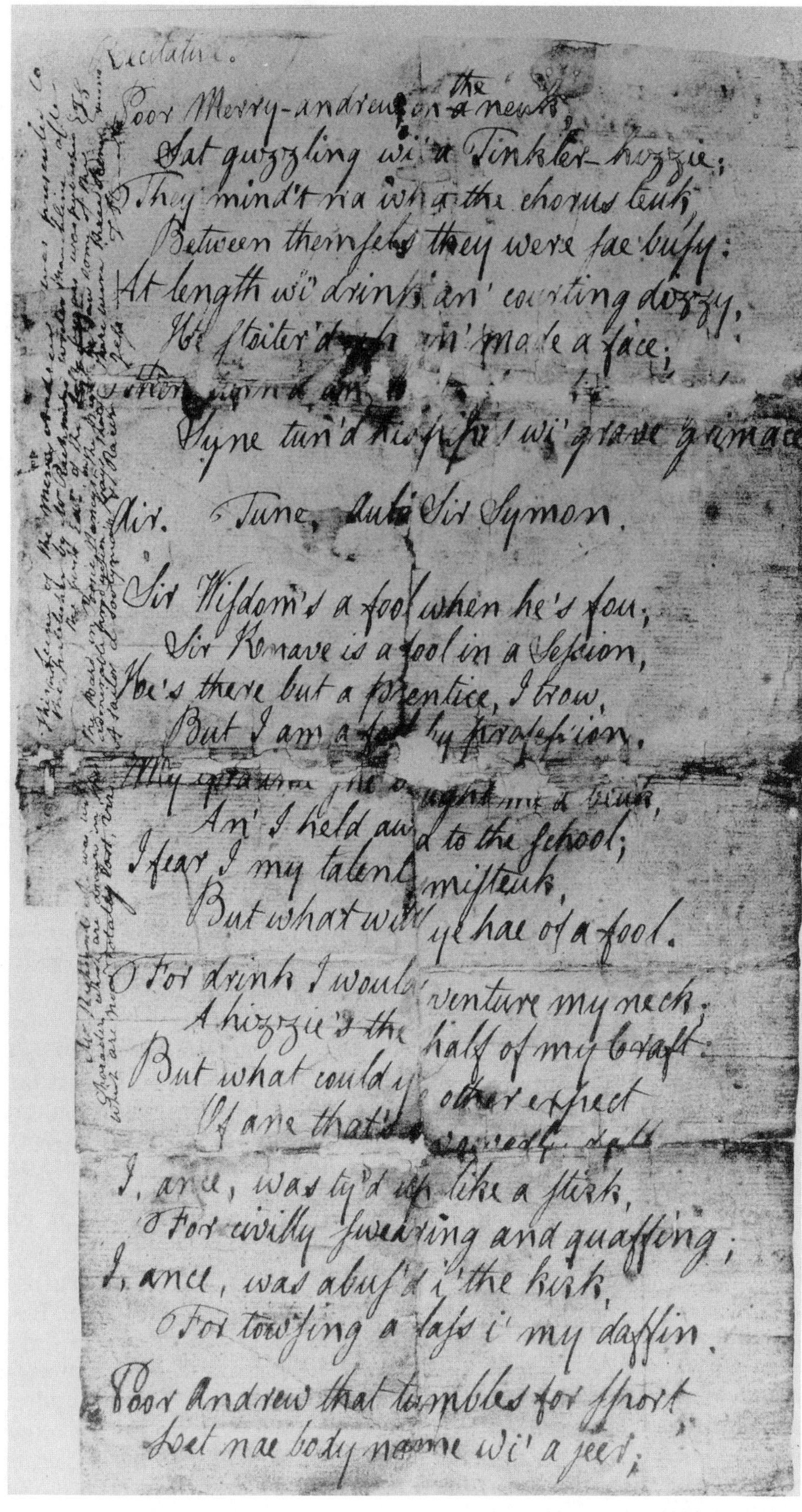
Recitativo.

Poor Merry-andrew in the neuk,
Sat guzzling wi' a Tinkler-hizzie;
They mind't na wha the chorus teuk,
Between themsels they were sae busy:
At length wi' drink an' courting dozzy,
He stoiter'd [illegible] an' made a face;
Then turn'd an' [illegible]
Syne tun'd his pipes wi' grave grimace

Air. Tune, Auld Sir Symon.

Sir Wisdom's a fool when he's fou,
Sir Knave is a fool in a Session,
He's there but a prentice, I trow,
But I am a fool by profession.
My [illegible] she [illegible] me a beuk,
An' I held awa to the school;
I fear I my talent misteuk,
But what will ye hae of a fool.
For drink I would venture my neck;
A hizzie's the half of my craft:
But what could ye other expect
Of ane that's [illegible] daft.
I, ance, was ty'd up like a stirk,
For civilly swearing and quaffing;
I, ance, was abus'd i' the kirk,
For towsing a lass i' my daffin.
Poor Andrew that tumbles for sport
Let nae body name wi' a jeer;

Page from a manuscript for Burns's "The Jolly Beggars; or, Love and Liberty: A Cantata" (#1117, Memorial Catalogue of the Burns Exhibition Held in the Galleries of The Royal Glasgow Institute of the Fine Arts, Glasgow, from 15th July till 31st October, 1896)

immediate response from the listener. Burns, then, has not only used a legend and provided a setting in which legends might be told but has replicated poetically aspects of a verbal recounting of a legend. And he has used a traditional form to celebrate Scotland's cultural past. "Tam o' Shanter" may be seen as Burns's most mature and complex celebration of Scottish cultural artifacts.

If there were a shift of emphasis and attitude toward traditional culture as a result of the Edinburgh experience, there was also continuity. Early and late Burns was a rhymer, a versifier, a local poet using traditional forms and themes in occasional and sometimes extemporaneous productions. These works are seldom noteworthy and are sometimes biting and satiric. He called them "little trifles" and frequently wrote them to "pay a debt." These pieces were not thought of as equal to his more deliberate endeavors; they were play, increasingly expected of him as a poet. He probably would have disavowed many now attributed to him, particularly some of the mean-spirited epigrams. Several occasional pieces, however, deserve a closer look for their ability to raise the commonplace to altogether different heights.

In 1786 Burns wrote "To a Haggis," a paean to the Scottish pudding of seasoned heart, liver, and lungs of a sheep or calf mixed with suet, onions, and oatmeal and boiled in an animal's stomach:

Fair fa' your honest, sonsie face,
Great Chieftan o' the Puddin-race!
Aboon them a' ye tak your place,
    Painch, tripe, or thairm:
Weel are ye wordy of a *grace*
    As lang's my arm.

Varying accounts claim that the poem was created extempore, more or less as a blessing, for a meal of haggis. Burns's praise has contributed to the elevation of the haggis to the status of national food and symbol of Scotland. Less well known and dealing with an even more pedestrian subject is "Address to the Tooth-Ache," prefaced "Written by the Author at a time when he was grievously tormented by that Disorder." The poem is a harangue, delightfully couched in Standard Habbie, beginning: "My curse on your envenom'd stang, / That shoots my tortur'd gums alang," a sentiment shared by all who have ever suffered from such a malady.

The many songs, the masterpiece "Tam o' Shanter," and the continuation and profusion of ephemeral occasional pieces of varying merit all stand as testimony to Burns's artistry after Edinburgh, albeit an artistry dominated by a selective, focused celebration of Scottish culture in song and legend. This narrowing of focus and direction of creativity suited his changed situation. Burns left Edinburgh in 1788 for Ellisland Farm, near Dumfries, to take up farming again; on 5 August he legally wed Jean Armour, with whom he had seven more children. For the first time in his life he had to become respectable and dependable. Suddenly the carefree life of a bachelor about town ended (although he still sired a daughter in 1791 by a woman named Anne Park), and the trials of life, sanitized in "The Cotter's Saturday Night," became a reality. A year later he also began to work for the Excise; by the fall of 1791 he had completely left farming for excise work and had moved to Dumfries. "The De'il's awa wi' th' Exciseman," probably written for Burns's fellow excise workers and shared with them at a dinner, is a felicitous union of text and tune, lively, rollicking, and affecting. The text plays on the negative view of tax collecting, delighting that the de'il—that couthie bad guy, not Milton's Satan—has rid the country of the blight.

The Ellisland/Dumfries phase must have been curiously disjointed for Burns. At first he found himself back where he had started—farming and with Jean Armour—as though nothing had changed. But much had changed: Burns was now widely recognized as a poet, as a personage of note, and things were expected of him because of that, such as willingness to share a meal, to stop and talk, or to exhibit his creativity publicly. But he was clearly in an ambiguous class position, working with his hands during the day and entertained for his mind during the evening. Perhaps the mental and physical tensions were just too much. He died on 21 July 1796, probably of endocarditis. He was thirty-seven.

His was a hard life, perhaps made both better and worse by his fame. His art catapulted him out of the routine and uncertainty of the agricultural world and gave him more options than most people of his background, enabling him to be trained for the Excise. His renown gave him access to persons and places he might otherwise not have known. He seems to have felt thoroughly at home in all-male society, whether formal, as in the Tarbolton Bachelor's Club and Crochallan Fencibles, or informal. The male shar-

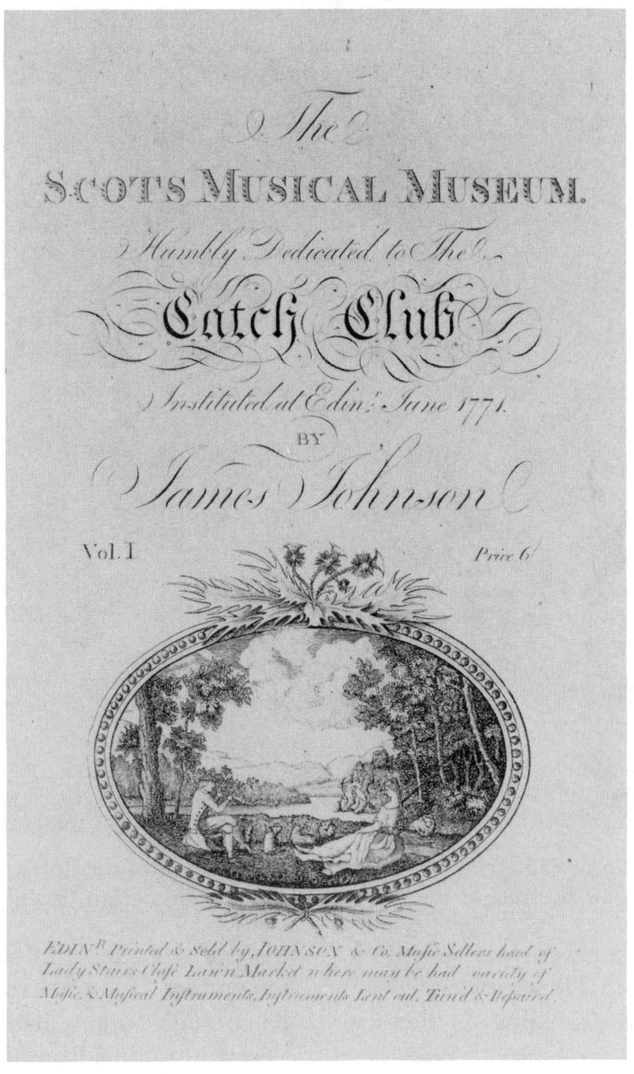

Title page for the first volume of the collection of Scottish traditional songs compiled by Burns and James Johnson

ing of bawdy song and story cut across class lines. Depicting women as objects, filled with sexual metaphors, bragging about sexual exploits, such bawdy material was a widespread and dynamic part of Scottish traditional culture. Because the sharing of the bawdy material was covert and largely oral, it is impossible to sort out definitively Burns's role in such works as the posthumously published and attributed volume, *The Merry Muses of Caledonia* (1799).

Burns's formal education was unusual for an individual in his situation; it was more like the education of the son of a small laird. His references to Scots, English, and Continental writers provide evidence of his awareness of literary tradition; he was remarkably knowledgeable. Lines quoted from Thomas Gray's "Elegy Written in a Country Churchyard" (1751) acknowledge the literary precursor of the "The Cotter's Saturday Night," while Fergusson's "Farmer's Ingle" was the direct, though unstated, model. Fergusson provides a less sentimental, more realistic, secular account of one evening's fireside activities. Fergusson and Ramsay were direct inspirations for Burns's vernacular works. He inherited particular genres and verse forms from the oral and written traditions, for example, the Spenserian stanza and English Augustan tone of "The Cotter's Saturday Night" or the comic elegy and vernacular informality drawn from such models in Standard Habbie as Sempill's "The Life and Death of Habbie Simpson," used in "The Death and Dying Words of Poor Mailie." His concern for feeling and sentiment would seem to connect him with the eighteenth-century cult of sensibility. Living in a time of extraordinary transition clearly en-

Red crayon drawing of Burns by Archibald Skirving (#562, Memorial Catalogue of the Burns Exhibition Held in the Galleries of The Royal Glasgow Institute of the Fine Arts, Glasgow, from 15th July till 31st October, 1896)

riched Burns's array of influences—oral and written, in Scots and English. These resources he molded and transmuted in extending the literary traditions he inherited.

Both critics and ordinary people have responded to Burns. Early critical response often placed more emphasis on the man than on his poetry and focused first on his inauspicious origins, later grappling with his character. Burns was seen by some as an ideal, as a model Scot for his revolutionary political, social, and sexual stances. By other critics his revolutionary behavior was viewed negatively: his morality, especially with reference to women and drink, was criticized, and his attitude toward the Kirk and to forms of authority and his use of obscure language were questioned.

Burns the man became central because he was at one and the same time typical and atypical—a struggling tenant farmer become tax collector and poet. If he could transcend his birthright, achieving recognition in his lifetime and posthumous fame thereafter, so might any Scot. Thus Burns became a symbol of every person's potentiality and even of Scotland's future as an independent country. To many, Burns became a hero; almost immediately after his death a process of traditionalizing his life began. People told one another about their personal experiences with him; repeated tellings formed a loose-knit legendary cycle which emphasizes his way with women, his impromptu poetic abilities, and his innate humanity. Many apocryphal accounts found their way into early works of criticism. But the legendary tradition has had a particularly dynamic life in a "calendar custom" called the Burns Supper.

Shortly after Burns's death, groups of friends and acquaintances began to gather in his memory. In 1859, the centenary of his birth, memorial events were held all over Scotland and among the Scottish diaspora, and 25 January virtually became a national holiday. The memorial events have taken on a particular structure: there is a meal, one ingredient of which must be the haggis, addressed with Burns's poem before serving. After the meal there are two speeches with fixed titles, but variable contents: "To the Immortal Memory" and "To the Lasses." "The Immortal Memory" offers a serious recollection of Burns, usually with emphasis on him as man rather than as poet, and often incorporates legendary instances of his humanity: he is said, for example, to have warned a woman selling ale without a license that the tax collectors would be by late in the day, thereby giving her the opportunity to destroy the evidence. The toast "To the Lasses" is usually short and humorous, paying tribute to Burns's way with women and to the many descriptive songs he wrote about them. Interspersed among these speeches and other toasts are performances of Burns's songs and poems. Typically, the event concludes with the singing of "Auld Lang Syne" by the assembled company, arrayed in a circle and clasping hands.

The legendary cycle about Burns and the calendar custom in his honor represent an incorporation of Burns into the developing body of oral tradition which inspired some of his own work. The Burns Suppers in particular, held by formal Burns clubs, social clubs, church groups, and gatherings throughout the world, keep Burns alive as symbol for Scotland. Yet this widespread cultural response to Burns is often denigrated by serious critics as "Burnomania."

Initially Burns's songs were dismissed by the critics as trivial; the bawdry was discounted; poems on sensitive topics were sometimes ignored; vernacular pieces were deemed unintelligible; aspects of his character and life were censured. Subsequent critics have responded to Burns out of altered personal and cultural environments. Wordsworth's admiration of Burns's depiction of real life is clearly a selective identification of a quality pertinent to his own poetic ideology. The initial perspective on the songs has changed completely; Burns's bawdry has been seriously analyzed and seen in the context of a long male tradition of scatological verse; his satires have been lauded for their identification of social inequities; his vernacular works have been praised as the very apogee of the Scottish literary tradition. Critical praise of Burns's songs and vernacular poetry curiously confirms a long Scottish popular tradition of preference for these works: no Burns Supper is complete without the singing of Burns's songs and recitation of such works as "To a Haggis" and "Tam o' Shanter." National concerns, then, are often implicit in the valuation of Burns: he remains the National Poet of Scotland.

Since Burns was Scottish, his artistic achievements seem outside the mainstream of eighteenth-century English literature. Nor does he fit neatly into the Romantic period. As a result he is often left out of literary histories and anthologies of those periods, the linguistic qualities of his best work providing an additional barrier. But language need not be a stumbling block, as translations of his work attest. Burns's roots among the people and his concern with social inequalities have made him particularly popular in Russia and China. While Burns and his literary products are firmly rooted in the societal environment from which he came, both continue to be powerful symbols of humanity's condition; and his utopian cry remains as elusive and appropriate today as when he wrote it:

That Man to Man the warld o'er,
    Shall brothers be for a' that.

Letters:

The Letters of Robert Burns, 2 volumes, edited by J. De Lancey Ferguson (Oxford: Clarendon Press, 1931); second edition, 2 volumes, edited by G. Ross Roy (Oxford: Clarendon Press, 1985).

Bibliography:

J. W. Egerer, *A Bibliography of Robert Burns* (Edinburgh: Oliver & Boyd, 1964).

Biographies:

J. G. Lockhart, *The Life of Robert Burns* (Edinburgh: Constable, 1828);

John MacIntosh, *Life of Robert Burns* (Paisley, U.K.: Gardner, 1906; reprinted, New York: AMS Press, 1975);

Franklin Bliss Snyder, *The Life of Robert Burns* (New York: Macmillan, 1932);

J. De Lancey Ferguson, *Pride and Passion* (New York: Oxford University Press, 1939);

R. T. Fitzhugh, ed., *Robert Burns: His Associates and Contemporaries* (Chapel Hill: University of North Carolina Press, 1943);

R. D. Thornton, *James Currie: The Entire Stranger and Robert Burns* (Edinburgh: Oliver & Boyd, 1963);

Maurice Lindsay, *The Burns Encyclopedia*, third edition (New York: St. Martin's Press, 1980).

References:

Auguste Angellier, *Etude sur la vie et les oeuvres de Robert Burns*, 2 volumes (Paris: Hachette, 1893);

Edinr. April, ninth 1787 — 1.

Printed vol 1 pa 157

As I have seen a good deal of human life in Edinr., a great many characters which are new to one bred up in the shades of life as I have been, I am determined to take down my remarks on the spot. — Gray observes in a letter of his to Mr. Palgrave that "Half a word fixed upon or near the spot, is worth a cart-load of recollection." — I don't know how it is with the world in general, but with me, making remarks is by no means a solitary pleasure. — I want some one to laugh with me, some one to be grave with me; some one to please me and help my discrimination with his or her own remark, and at times, no doubt, to admire my acuteness and penetration. — The World are so busied with selfish pursuits, ambition, vanity, interest or pleasure, that very few think it worth their while to make any observation on what passes around them; except where that observation is a sucker or branch of the darling plant they are rearing in their fancy. — Nor am I sure, notwithstanding all the sentimental flights of Novel-writers & the sage philosophy of Moralists, if we are capable of so intimate and cordial a coalition of friendship as that one of us may pour out his bosom, his every thought and floating fancy, his very inmost soul, with unreserved confidence, to another, without hazard of losing part of that respect man demands from man; or, from the unavoidable imperfections attending human nature, of one day repenting his confidence. — For these reasons, I am determined to make these

Page from Burns's commonplace book (#1094, Memorial Catalogue of the Burns Exhibition Held in the Galleries of The Royal Glasgow Institute of the Fine Arts, Glasgow, from 15th July till 31st October, 1896)

Mary Ellen Brown, *Burns and Tradition* (London: Macmillan, 1984);

David Buchan, *The Ballad and the Folk* (London: Routledge & Kegan Paul, 1972);

David Craig, *Scottish Literature and the Scottish People 1680-1830* (London: Chatto & Windus, 1961);

Thomas Crawford, *Burns: A Study of the Poems and Songs* (Edinburgh: Oliver & Boyd, 1960);

Crawford, *Society and the Lyric* (Edinburgh: Scottish Academic Press, 1979);

R. H. Cromek, ed., *Reliques of Robert Burns; Consisting of Original Letters, Poems, and Critical Observations on Scottish Songs* (London: McCreery, 1808);

David Daiches, *Robert Burns* (London: Bell, 1952);

Catarina Ericson-Roos, *The Songs of Robert Burns: A Study of the Unity of Poetry and Music* (Uppsala, Swed.: Acta Universitatis Upsaliensis, Studia Anglistica Upsaliensia, 1977);

Hans Hecht, *Robert Burns: The Man and His Work* (London: Hodge, 1936);

R. D. S. Jack and Andrew Noble, eds., *The Art of Robert Burns* (London: Vision, 1982; Totowa, N.J.: Barnes & Noble, 1982);

Maurice Lindsay, *Burns: The Man, His Work, the Legend* (London: MacGibbon & Kee, 1971);

Donald A. Low, ed., *Critical Essays on Robert Burns* (London: Routledge & Kegan Paul, 1975);

Low, ed., *The Critical Heritage* (London: Routledge & Kegan Paul, 1974);

Carol McGuirk, *Robert Burns and the Sentimental Era* (Athens: University of Georgia Press, 1985);

Kurt Wittig, *The Scottish Tradition in Literature* (Edinburgh: Oliver & Boyd, 1958).

Papers:

The main collections of manuscript materials by Robert Burns are in the Burns Cottage Collection, Alloway; the Pierpont Morgan Library, New York; the British Museum; the National Library of Scotland, Edinburgh; the Adam Collection of the Rosenbach Company, Philadelphia; the Kilmarnock Monument Museum; the Henry E. Huntington Library, San Marino, California; and the Edinburgh University Library.

Elizabeth Carter

(16 December 1717 - 19 February 1806)

Jennifer M. Keith
Emory University

BOOKS: *Poems upon Particular Occasions* (London, 1738);

Remarks on the Athanasian Creed: On a Sermon Preached at the Parish Church of Deal, October 15, 1752. In a Letter to the Rev. Mr. Randolph, Rector of Deal. By a Lady (London: Printed for R. Griffiths, 1752);

Poems on Several Occasions (London: Printed for John Rivington, 1762; enlarged edition, London: Printed for John, Francis & Charles Rivington, 1776);

Memoirs of the Life of Mrs. Elizabeth Carter, with a New Edition of Her Poems, Some of Which Have Never Appeared Before; To Which Are Added, Some Miscellaneous Essays in Prose, Together with Her Notes on the Bible, and Answers to Objections Concerning the Christian Religion. By the Rev. Montagu Pennington (London: Printed for F. C. & J. Rivington, 1807; Boston: Greenleaf, 1809).

OTHER: Jean Pierre de Crousaz, *An Examination of Mr. Pope's* Essay on Man, translated by Carter (London: Printed for A. Dodd, 1739);

Francesco Algarotti, *Sir Isaac Newton's Philosophy Explain'd for the Use of the Ladies: In Six Dialogues on Light and Colours*, 2 volumes, translated by Carter (London: Printed for E. Cave, 1739);

All the Works of Epictetus, Which Are Now Extant: Consisting of His Discourses, Preserved by Arrian, in Four Books, the Enchiridion, and Fragments, translated, with an introductory essay and notes, by Carter (London: Printed by S. Richardson; and sold by A. Millar; John Rivington; and R. & J. Dodsley, 1758);

The Works of the Late Mrs. Catherine Talbot: A New Edition, edited by Carter (London: Printed by John Rivington, Jun. for John, Francis & Charles Rivington, 1780).

Called "our British Minerva" by Samuel Richardson and "daughter to Plato" by Elizabeth Montagu, Elizabeth Carter was for her contemporaries a symbol of the ideal classicist. Her translation of works by the Greek Stoic philosopher Epictetus (1758), which went through three editions in her lifetime, was long the standard English text. In 1910 J. M. Dent and Sons published Carter's Epictetus in the Everyman's Library series; the firm reprinted the volume thirteen times, the last in 1966. In the eighteenth century Carter's reputation was such that Queen Charlotte requested an interview with the scholar-poet; and within the circles of the London intelligentsia, particularly at the salon gatherings of the Bluestockings, Carter held a place of honor for her vast knowledge of Greek and Latin classics. Her learning transcended traditional gender lines: a contemporary described her as "not only the most learned Woman of any age but one of the most learned Persons of that in which she lives." Carter's poetry is the product of a woman extraordinarily educated for her era—a woman with the intellectual power but without the political avenues of the eighteenth-century male elite. Carter's delicately crafted verses show a writer familiar with literature extending back to the ancient Greeks. Her attention to the Christian doctrine of the afterworld as well as to the Platonic view that reality exists apart from the visible world characterizes her poetry, which had, until the late 1980s, all but evaporated from twentieth-century accounts of eighteenth-century literary history.

Some of the eighteenth century's most respected figures regarded her work highly. Richardson said in a letter that he believed that Carter, unlike those women who were "little Poetical Dabblers," ranked among female writers of "real Genius." In his poem "On Reading Miss Carter's Poems in Manuscript," George Lord Lyttleton announced that her poems could "tame / The savage Heart of brutal Vice, and bend / At pure Religion's Shrine the stubborn Knees / Of bold Impiety." Carter was a conservative Anglican, and her piety was as well known as her poetry. The novelist Frances Burney remarked that

Elizabeth Carter, with her translation of the works of Epictetus; painted circa 1765 by Catherine Read (Dr. Johnson's House Trust, Gough Square, London)

Carter's "whole face" appeared to "beam with goodness, piety, and philanthropy." Her friends gave her character their highest praise: "of all human creatures" she comes "the nearest to perfection," in the opinion of the Bluestocking Hester Mulso Chapone. Montagu compared Carter's morality with that of the eighteenth century's quintessentially virtuous heroine: "I am sure Mr. Richardson knew you when you was a girl," wrote Montagu to Carter. "I believe at thirteen you was exactly Clarissa Harlowe."

As the eldest daughter of the clergyman Nicolas Carter and his first wife, Margaret Swayne Carter, Carter received an upbringing that cultivated her piety. Born in the coastal town of Deal in Kent on 16 December 1717, Carter was ten years old when her mother died; Margaret Carter's health had deteriorated after her husband lost her inheritance in the South Sea Bubble. Nicolas Carter served as the curate of Deal and as one of the six preachers of Canterbury Cathedral. Learned in Hebrew, Greek, Latin, and the sciences, he passed on a similarly demanding education to his sons and daughters. Elizabeth's difficulty with the ancient languages was so severe, however, that at first Dr. Carter implored the child to give up her goal of becoming a scholar. To overcome this initial lack of aptitude, the young Carter girded herself for hours at the study table by taking snuff, chewing green tea and coffee, and placing wet cloths around her head and on her stomach. Such perseverance was finally rewarded: she learned Latin, Greek, Hebrew, and French; taught herself Italian, Spanish, and German; and gained some competency in Portuguese and Arabic. Dr. Carter came to respect his daughter's accomplishments so much that he allowed her to prepare Henry Carter, her half-brother from Dr. Carter's second marriage, for his studies at Cambridge.

Carter's reading included the Bible, ancient and modern literature, philosophy, history, and astronomy. In a letter to her friend Catherine Talbot, Carter described the beginning of a typical day: between four and five in the morning she was awakened by a bell hanging over her bed, from which a string led through a crack in the window and down into the garden, where the sexton pulled on it. She went immediately to her studies; an hour or two later she took a vigorous walk; at breakfast she and her father sat down to "finish the discourse and the tea-kettle," a scene abandoned by the rest of the family when the conversation went "beyond Latin and French."

Although she is sometimes referred to as "Mrs. Elizabeth Carter," Carter never married and once wrote to a friend that marriage was a "very right scheme for every body but myself." At thirty-three, apparently after a series of domestic "commotions" at her father's house, she remarked: "it has been a great subject of consolation to me, that I never was tempted by any voluntary connexion to engage myself in the interests, passions, and tumults of the world. If I have suffered from the troubles of others, who have more sense, more understanding, and more virtues than I might reasonably have expected to find, what might I not have suffered from a husband! Perhaps be needlessly thwarted and contradicted in every innocent enjoyment of life: involved in all his schemes right or wrong, and perhaps not allowed the liberty of even silently seeming to disapprove them!" In rejecting marriage, Carter rejected much of what she considered "the world"; in her poetry she looked forward to an immaterial afterworld.

In 1734, when she was only seventeen, Carter first saw her poetry in print in the *Gentleman's Magazine*, edited by her father's friend Edward Cave. Cave also published *Poems upon Particular Occasions* (1738), an anonymous collection of verses Carter had written before she was twenty. In this volume of eight poems the poet inculcates moral and spiritual values through a variety of genres. The collection begins with "In Diem Natalem," a birthday poem of praise to God for her life and an appeal to Him for spiritual strength. *Poems upon Particular Occasions* also includes a translation of Anacreon's thirtieth ode; a translation of Horace's Ode IV.7 and an adaptation of his Ode I.22, in which Carter emphasizes the rewards of a virtuous life; a conventional satire on human vanity; and an original elegy for Queen Caroline. The volume ends with verses complimenting the thresher-poet Stephen Duck ("Occasioned by a Present of His Poems"), a compliment that begins, unpropitiously, "Accept, O Duck, the Muse's grateful lay, / Who owns a favour which she can't repay."

One of Carter's early poems that received Samuel Johnson's praise appeared in the *Gentleman's Magazine* in 1738 as well as in *Poems upon Particular Occasions*. This poem, "A Riddle"—whose answer is "a dream"—introduces a theme she addressed throughout her career, a theme strongly connected to her choice of scholarship over marriage: the powers of the mind. The definition of the dream also suggests the poetic process; the dream creates an unreal world that resembles an artist's creation of a fictive world, which can "Transfer the Thames where Ganges' waters roll, / Unite th'Equator to the frozen Pole." As the dream explains: "Nor form, nor substance in my being share, / I'm neither Fire nor Water, Earth, nor Air."

Carter's poems repeatedly show power transferred from physical and political domains to intellectual and spiritual terms. The dream riddle includes her recurrent source of artistic inspiration: the evening or nighttime setting in which sublime darkness transports her from diurnal objects to otherworldly ones. In an untitled poem, in the *Gentleman's Magazine* (June 1738) that explores the powers of the mind as seen in the science of astronomy, darkness empowers poetic vision: "While clear the Night, and ev'ry Thought serene, / Let Fancy wander o'er the solemn Scene." A nighttime survey of the sea inspires eloquent introspection in "Written Extempore on the Sea-Shore. 1741.—By Moon Light," published in *Poems on Several Occasions* (1762):

Thou restless fluctuating Deep,
  Expressive of the human Mind,
In thy for ever varying Form,
  My own inconstant Self I find.

Most of Carter's poems show a typically Christian transformation in either the speaker's or addressee's attitude—a turn away from despair over life's deceptions and toward thankfulness for them as they reveal the superiority of the world beyond. John Sena, one of her few recent critics, has noted that although she adopts the conventions of many eighteenth-century melancholy poems ("yew trees, hooting owls, tolling bells, graveyards, and scenes of decay and destruction"), melancholy for her is only a steppingstone in the intellectual perception of God's sublime presence. In a letter to Montagu, Carter

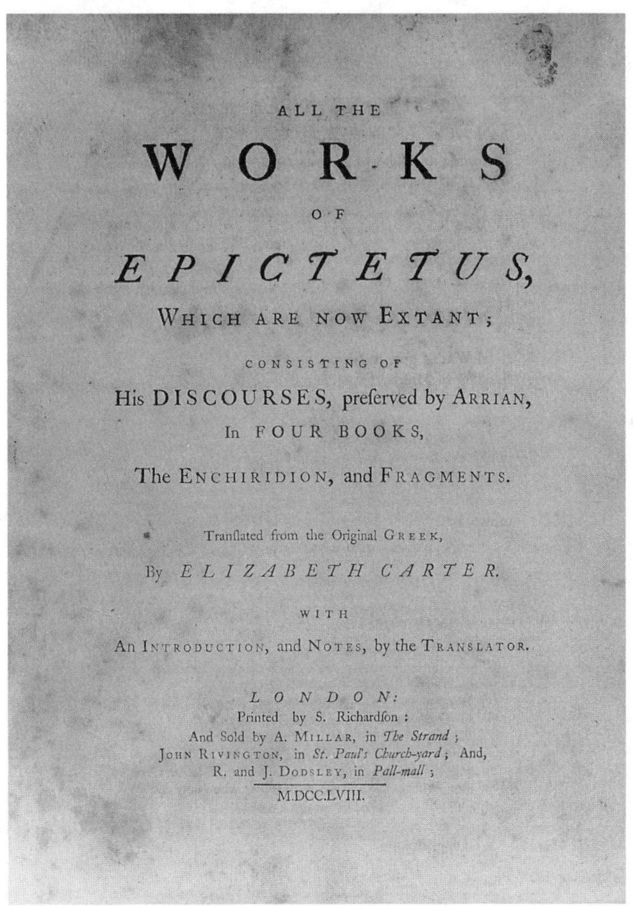

ALL THE

WORKS

OF

EPICTETUS,

WHICH ARE NOW EXTANT;

CONSISTING OF

His DISCOURSES, preſerved by ARRIAN,

In FOUR BOOKS,

The ENCHIRIDION, and FRAGMENTS.

Tranſlated from the Original GREEK,

By *ELIZABETH CARTER.*

WITH

An INTRODUCTION, and NOTES, by the TRANSLATOR.

LONDON:

Printed by S. Richardſon:

And Sold by A. MILLAR, in *The Strand*;

JOHN RIVINGTON, in *St. Paul's Church-yard*; And,

R. and J. DODSLEY, in *Pall-mall*;

M.DCC.LVIII.

Title page for Carter's translation of the works of the Greek Stoic philosopher

expresses such an attitude toward the sublime when she recounts one of her daily walks: "I rambled till I got to the top of a hill, from whence I surveyed a vast extent of variegated country all round me, and the immense ocean beneath. . . . The first impression it gave me, was a sense of my own littleness. . . . But I soon grew more important by the recollection that nothing which my eyes could survey, was of equal dignity with the human mind, at once the theatre and spectator of the wonders of Omnipotence. How vast are the capacities of the soul. . . ."

One of Carter's most artistically successful poems, circulated in manuscript in the early 1740s, elaborates the triumph of a life of the mind. Richardson so appreciated "Ode to Wisdom" that, without knowing who had written it, he appropriated it for *Clarissa* (1747-1748): his heroine explains to Miss Howe that the poem "does honour to our sex, as it was written by one of it." (Carter later had a correct version printed in the *Gentleman's Magazine* [December 1747].) Clarissa, a heroine so virtuous that she does not survive long in this world, honors the poem by setting the last three stanzas to music. The ode's graceful restraint combines with images of motion maintained by fast-flowing rhythm to convey the control and clarity of active intelligence:

The solitary Bird of Night
Thro' the pale Shades now wings his Flight,
  And quits the Time-shook Tow'r:
Where, shelter'd from the Blaze of Day,
In philosophic Gloom he lay,
  Beneath his Ivy Bow'r.

"Modest suppliant" at the shrine of Pallas Athena, the speaker asks for "better Gifts" than material ones: "Each moral Beauty of the Heart / By studious Thought refin'd." This poetic realm of wisdom replaces wealth with "the Smiles of glad Content" and power with "An Empire o'er my Mind."

In the two decades that followed the publication of *Poems upon Particular Occasions* Carter worked on several prose compositions, including essays that were published in Johnson's *Rambler*:

"Religion and Superstition: A Vision" (18 August 1750) and "Modish Pleasures" (2 March 1751). Her pen was busiest, however, with translations. In 1738 (although "1739" appears on the title page) her anonymous translation of Jean Pierre de Crousaz's *Examen de L'essay de Monsieur Pope sur l'homme* (1737) was published as *An Examination of Mr. Pope's* Essay on Man, and in 1739 appeared her anonymous translation of Francesco Algarotti's *Newtonianismo per le dame* (1737) as *Sir Isaac Newton's Philosophy Explain'd for the Use of the Ladies*. . . . In 1749, at the age of thirty-two, she began translating Epictetus's extant works at the request of her friends Talbot and Dr. Thomas Secker (bishop of Oxford and later archbishop of Canterbury). The translation, with notes and an introduction, was published in 1758. In addition to her literary activities, Carter dedicated much of her time to preparing her half-brother Henry for Cambridge, and, while she did not have the duties of wife and mother, she readily accepted the many other domestic obligations that fell to her in her father's house. "The insignificant occupations of vulgar life," she wrote to Montagu, "however disproportioned they may appear to the elevation of our intellectual faculties, are a necessary discipline to the irregularity of our passions, and to the perverseness of our will." Carter's proficiency in such labors prompted Samuel Johnson to claim, in what today might be read as an ambiguous compliment, that she "could make a pudding as well as translate Epictetus from the Greek and work a handkerchief as well as compose a poem."

Her translation was printed as a 539-page quarto volume and attracted more than one thousand subscribers at a guinea a copy. That a woman could translate Greek was itself sensational news, but Carter's expert translation astonished her contemporaries: her reputation among the literati traveled as far as Russia. But while many on the Continent admired the linguistic feat, several persons in her own country doubted the work was her own and insisted that either her father or Dr. Secker had done the translation.

Montagu, along with William Pulteney (the Earl of Bath) and Lyttleton, urged her to have a second collection of her poems published. Though always modest about her "trifles in rhyme," as she called them, Carter finally acquiesced. *Poems on Several Occasions* contains thirty-six poems, including translations of Pietro Metastasio's "Sonnetto Proemiale" and "Canzone"; elegies to the poet Elizabeth Rowe and to a young child, "Master -----"; odes to "Melancholy" and "Wisdom"; and twenty epistles (some vers de société), most of which scorn transitory shows and praise virtue's lasting rewards. *Poems on Several Occasions* was generally acclaimed, and later editions appeared in 1766, 1776, 1777, and 1789; the 1776 edition included additional poems. In 1796 the Count de Bedée translated twelve of the poems into French.

In her meditative epistles Carter presents a melancholy moralized landscape that recalls for the speaker the importance of faith in the afterlife, though not in an explicitly Christian one. A typical treatment appears in "To Mrs. Vesey" in the 1776 edition, which begins with the topic of the gloomy beauty of nature:

> Silent and cool the Dews of Ev'ning fall,
> Hush'd is the vernal Music of the Groves,
> From yon thick Boughs the Birds of Darkness call,
> And mark the Walk that Contemplation loves.

The view of a Gothic cathedral prompts the poet to consider the transience of human life, including the loss of friends, but friendship has a permanent place in the spiritual afterworld: "Where safe from Suff'ring, and from Frailty pure, / Unite the social Spirits of the Just."

Although many of her letters discuss contemporary political events and issues, in much of Carter's poetry politics is treated in terms of spiritual values rather than in terms of practical or partisan concerns. A political conservative, she explains in a letter to Montagu that "I have nothing to do with politics, but to resist as far as one properly can, every tendency to a spirit of faction." Thus in "On the Death of Her Sacred Majesty Queen Caroline" (in *Poems upon Particular Occasions*) Carter focuses on the queen's personal values—"Sure friend to virtue's and religion's cause"—and concludes that the queen, acting as a friend to the nation, "built her empire on a people's love." Carter pursues history and politics in "To Mrs. Montagu" (in the 1776 edition of *Poems on Several Occasions*) only to transmute historical episodes into spiritual transgressions and political issues into the single objective of peace. She invites Montagu to join her in an imaginative walk in Winchester Cathedral's graveyard in order to confront England's concerns: "By Fancy led thro' many a *British* Age, / O'er *Winton's* melancholy Walks we'll stray." But the event the poet refers to is the civil war of a century past, when Oliver

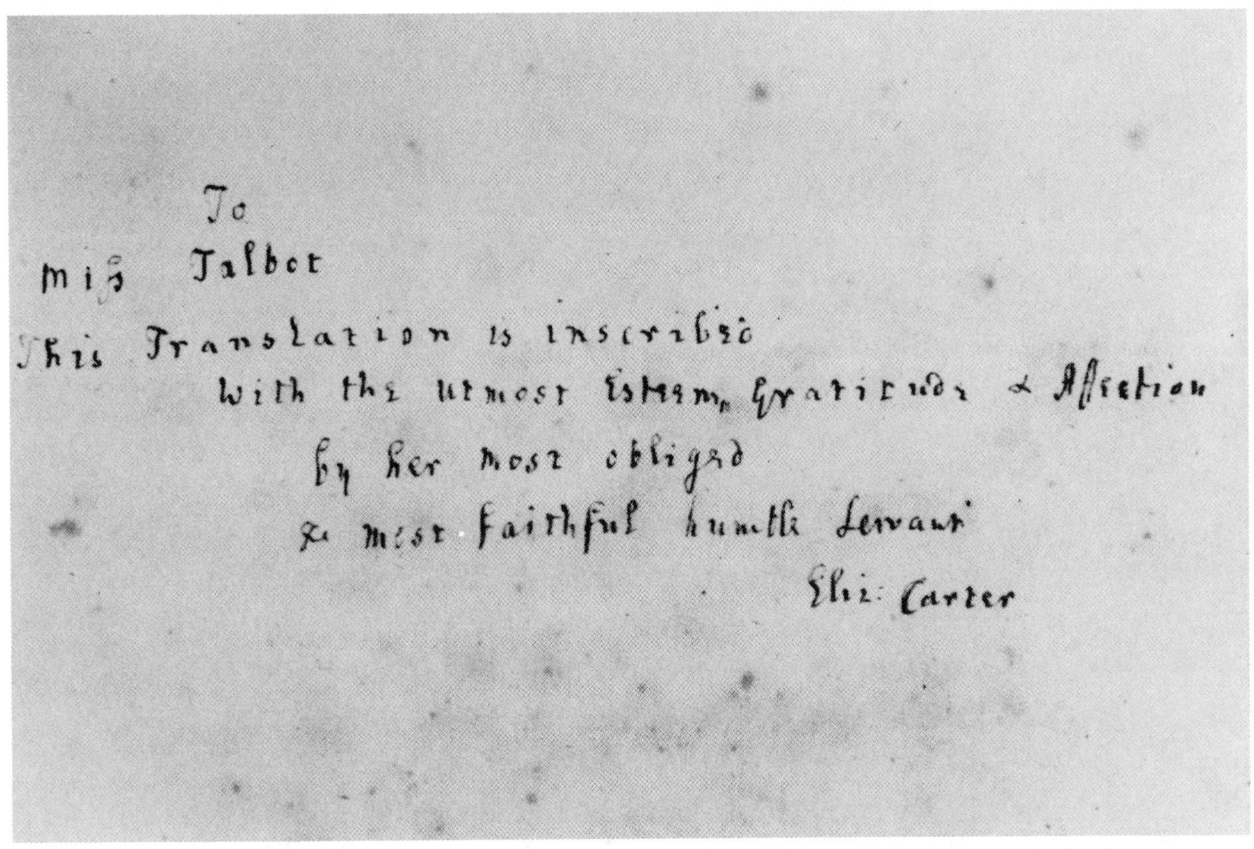

To
Miss Talbot
This Translation is inscribed
with the utmost Esteem, Gratitude & Affection
by her most obliged
& most faithful humble Servant
Eliz: Carter

Inscription in the copy of All the Works of Epictetus *that Carter gave to her friend Catherine Talbot. Carter began the translation in 1749 at the request of Talbot, who could not read Greek (Maggs Bros., catalogue 1038, 1983).*

Cromwell's soldiers marred the graves at Winchester Cathedral. Carter really attacks spiritual rather than social injustice when she condemns Cromwell's soldiers for disturbing the "peace" of the graveyard, an impious disturbance of the souls of the dead rather than a physical destruction of the bodies of the living.

Whereas the few ostensibly political poems emphasize spiritual issues, several of Carter's poems presenting relations between the sexes give more weight to issues of physical, and by extension political, power. In her translation of Anacreon's Ode XXX (first published in the *Gentleman's Magazine* in 1735) the female Muses playfully imprison Cupid: "With flow'ry Wreaths his Hands confin'd, / And bound to *Beauty* brought." A much more provocative power struggle between the sexes appears in her original poem "A Dialogue" (first published in the *Gentleman's Magazine* in 1741). There, Body and Mind quarrel over their differences: "As great Plagues to each other as Husband and Wife." Body acts the role of the husband careful to preserve the property to which he owns the rights: "[You] Encroach ev'ry Day on my lawful Possession. / The best Room in my House you have seiz'd for your own, / And turn'd the whole Tenement quite upside down." The "wife," "Poor *Mind*," suffers physical abuse from her spouse—"crampt and confin'd like a Slave in a Chain"—and is punished for attending to philosophical rather than physical concerns. Nothing short of death ends the struggles between masculine body and feminine mind:

I've a Friend, answers *Mind*, who, tho' slow, is yet sure,
And will rid me, at last, of your insolent Pow'r:
Will knock down your mud Walls, the whole Fabric demolish,
And at once your strong Holds and my Slav'ry abolish:
And while in the Dust your dull Ruins decay,
I shall snap off my Chains and fly freely away.

The contradictory needs of male body and female mind thus lead to a scene of prophetic denunciation—the wicked city destroyed, the righteous remnant delivered. It is noteworthy

Carter's friend, the Bluestocking Elizabeth Montagu (drawn by W. Evans and engraved by T. Cheesman, from a painting by Sir Joshua Reynolds)

that Mind's ally and the agent of destruction—death—bears the title "Friend," the most intense social relationship in Carter's poetry and life.

Carter's translation of Horace's Ode I.15, "The Prophecy of Nereus" (published in *The Works of Horace in English Verse*, edited by William and John Duncombe [1757]), shows the interrelation of military politics with conflicts between the sexes. Nereus foretells the punishment awaiting Paris for stealing the beautiful Helen, "Whom injur'd Greece shall soon reclaim." The female divinity associated with war, wisdom, and domestic handicrafts, Pallas Athena, inflicts the punishment: "She waves her Aegis, nods her plumes, / And all the pomp of war assumes" to combat a man who has kidnapped a woman. Revenge for the masculine usurpation of the feminine appears in historical and mythic terms at the close of the poem, when Nereus foresees that Troy will in "Grecian flames expire."

Carter expressed such vehemence obliquely: through the dialogue of dramatic poetry and through verse and prose translation she found indirect ways to express violence and rebellion, speaking through characters or other writers. Whether translating Horatian odes, Stoic ethics, or a "ladies' " version of Newtonian physics, she acquired the authority and protection of the male writers she translated. It may be pertinent to her gender and personality that her most praised and most financially rewarding publication was her translation of a classical male philosopher, Epictetus. "So feelingly alive to censure," as her biographer and nephew Montagu Pennington explained, Carter resisted opportunities to have her own work published, including her translations.

Painting of Carter by Joseph Highmore (Dover District Council)

She confided in a letter to a friend: "none but those who enjoy it, can have any idea of the comforts of insignificancy."

The severe headaches that plagued Carter since childhood became even more debilitating in her old age. After the third edition of *Poems on Several Occasions* she did not write for publication, although in 1780 she prepared an edition of the works of her friend Talbot, who had died in 1770. The thousand pounds Carter made from her translation of Epictetus and a few small annuities from friends afforded her the leisure in her middle and old age to continue her studies and to maintain her knowledge of several foreign languages by reading in each language for at least half an hour a day. She also enjoyed reading novels and romances, preferring works written by women (as long as the works and writers were sufficiently moral), especially those by Burney and Ann Radcliffe. In 1762 Carter bought a house in Deal from which she could view the countryside and the English Channel; she and her father lived there together until his death in 1774. In 1763 she traveled to the Continent with her friends Lord Bath and Montagu and her husband, a trip Carter recounts in detail in her letters. She spent some time in London every winter, staying in her own "small but neat" apartment on Clarges Street, Piccadilly. This situation gave her a privacy and independence she cherished. In a letter she claims that "My spirit of liberty is strangely untractable and wild" and insists on having "something like a home; somewhere to rest an aching head without giving any body any trouble; and some hours more absolutely at my own disposal than can be had in any other situation." In London she visited her more famous friends, including the presiding Bluestockings Montagu and Elizabeth Vesey; Johnson; Horace Walpole; and Frances Burney and her father Charles Burney. Personally as well as poetically, Carter replaced material with nonmaterial "goods": the affection of her friends she called her "treasure."

In a letter to Montagu, Carter reveals the inner world she prized: "any picture that furnishes agreeable reveries to the imagination, is a valuable reality, though it may never prove a matter of fact"; the "magic power" of the mind "can equally give life and energy to ideal forms and annihilate the objects of external sense." In her *Rambler* essay "Religion and Supersition: A Vision," which recounts "a very extraordinary dream"—a debate between personified Superstition and personified Religion—Carter explains in religious terms the importance of having internal rather than external goals. The true hero is the Christian who seeks a "View of obtaining Approbation from the Sovereign of the Universe." Her spiritual hero practices a "silent resignation" to Providence—"the most excellent sort of self-denial." On 19 February 1806, after a life resigned to Providence and with the silent fortitude of her Christian hero, she died in London, according to her nephew, "without a groan." She was eighty-eight.

When Carter was only twenty-one years old Johnson, who had seen her work in the *Gentleman's Magazine*, wrote to Cave that "I have compos'd a Greek Epigram to Eliza, and think she ought to be celebrated in as many different Languages as Lewis le Grand." Today Carter is little celebrated, but poetry like Carter's 1753 rendering of Metastasio's "Sonnetto Proemiale" still sounds the classic elegance and music of her voice as it addresses the subject of the gaps and intersections between an artist's life and art:

Fables and dreams my sportive genius feigns:
  Yet dreams and fables while I range with art,
Caught by their magic force, to serious pains
  Th'inventive head betrays the simple heart:
Imagin'd woes with real grief I mourn,
Imagin'd wrongs resent with real scorn.

Carter challenges readers in the twentieth century to understand that the unseen realms of Platonic ideas and Christian divinity might be more eventful and moving to an eighteenth-century woman excluded from political heroics, eschewing marriage to a husband who would have legal authority over her, and writing in a poetic tradition that comprised topoi, symbols, metaphors, and diction predominantly fashioned by male writers.

Letters:

A Series of Letters between Mrs. Elizabeth Carter and Miss Catherine Talbot, from the Year 1741 to 1770: To Which Are Added, Letters from Mrs. Elizabeth Carter to Mrs. Vesey, between the Years 1763 and 1787, 2 volumes, edited by Montagu Pennington (London: F. C. & J. Rivington, 1808);

Letters from Mrs. Elizabeth Carter, to Mrs. Montagu, between the years 1755 and 1800: Chiefly upon Literary and Moral Subjects, 3 volumes, edited by Pennington (London: F. C. & J. Rivington, 1817).

Biographies:

Montagu Pennington, *Memoirs of the Life of Mrs. Elizabeth Carter, with a New Edition of Her Poems, Some of Which Have Never Appeared Before; To Which Are Added, Some Miscellaneous Essays in Prose, Together with Her Notes on the Bible, and Answers to Objections Concernng the Christian Religion* (London: Printed for F. C. & J. Rivington, 1807; Boston: Greenleaf, 1809);

Samuel Egerton Brydges, "Mrs. Elizabeth Carter," in his *Censura Literaria*, volume 5 (London: Longman, Hurst, Rees & Orme, 1807), pp. 194-209;

John Clayton, "Elizabeth Carter," in his *Sketches in Biography, Designed to Show the Influence of Literature on Character and Happiness* (Edinburgh: Waugh & Innes, 1825), pp. 311-331;

Alice C. C. Gaussen, *A Woman of Wit and Wisdom: A Memoir of Elizabeth Carter, One of the "Bas Bleu" Society (1717-1806)* (New York: Dutton, 1906);

Austin Dobson, "The Learned Mrs. Carter," in his *Later Essays, 1917-1920* (London: Oxford University Press, 1921), pp. 97-123.

References:

John Carroll, ed., *Selected Letters of Samuel Richardson* (Oxford: Clarendon Press, 1964), p. 310;

Oliver Elton, *A Survey of English Literature, 1730-1780*, 2 volumes (London: Arnold, 1928), I: 73-77;

Leonore Helen Ewert, "Elizabeth Montagu to Elizabeth Carter: Literary Gossip and Critical Opinions from the Pen of the Queen of the Blues," Ph.D. dissertation, Claremont Graduate School, 1967;

Hoxie Neale Fairchild, *Religious Trends in English Poetry; Volume 2: 1740-1780, Religious Sentimentalism in the Age of Johnson* (New York: Columbia University Press, 1942), pp. 197-199, 231, 282;

G. Hampshire, "Johnson, Elizabeth Carter and Pope's Garden," *Notes and Queries*, 19 (June 1972): 221-222;

Roger Lonsdale, ed., *Eighteenth-Century Women Poets* (Oxford: Oxford University Press, 1989), pp. 165-171;

Reginald Martin, "Elizabeth Carter: 'Found' Poet of the 18th Century," *Publications of the Arkansas Philological Association*, 11 (Fall 1985): 49-64;

Sylvia Harestark Myers, *The Bluestocking Circle: Women, Friendship, and the Life of the Mind in Eighteenth-Century England* (Oxford: Clarendon Press, 1990);

Edward Ruhe, "Birch, Johnson, and Elizabeth Carter: An Episode of 1738-39," *PMLA*, 73 (December 1958): 491-500;

Barbara Brandon Schnorrenberg, "Elizabeth Carter," In *A Dictionary of British and American Women Writers: 1660-1800*, edited by Janet Todd (Totowa, N.J.: Rowman & Allanheld, 1985), pp. 75-76;

John F. Sena, "Melancholy in Anne Finch and Elizabeth Carter: The Ambivalence of an Idea," *Yearbook of English Studies*, 1 (1971): 108-119;

Patricia Meyer Spacks, "Female Rhetorics," In *The Private Self: Theory and Practice of Women's Autobiographical Writings*, edited by Shari Benstock (Chapel Hill: University of North Carolina Press, 1988), pp. 177-191;

Robert W. Uphaus and Gretchen M. Foster, eds., *The Other Eighteenth Century: English Women of Letters, 1660-1800* (East Lansing, Mich.: Colleagues Press, 1991), pp. 213-222.

Papers:

Some of Elizabeth Carter's letters and a few poems are in the Additional Manuscripts collection of the British Library.

Thomas Chatterton

(10 November 1752 - 24 August 1770)

Joan H. Pittock
University of Aberdeen

BOOKS: *The Auction a Poem: A Familiar Epistle to a Friend*, attributed to Chatterton (London: Printed for George Kearsly, 1770);

An Elegy on the Much Lamented Death of William Beckford, Esq. Late Lord-Mayor of, and Representative in Parliament for, the City of London (London: Printed for G. Kearsly, 1770);

The Execution of Sir Charles Bawdin: Dedicated to Her Grace the Dutchess of Northumberland, as Thomas Rowlie (London: Sold by W. Goldsmith, 1772);

Poems, Supposed to Have Been Written at Bristol, by Thomas Rowley, and Others, in the Fifteenth Century: The Greatest Part Now First Published from the Most Authentic Copies, edited by Thomas Tyrwhitt (London: Printed for T. Payne and Son, 1777); enlarged as *Poems, Supposed to Have Been Written at Bristol, in the Fifteenth Century, By Thomas Rowley, Priest, &c.: With a Commentary, in Which the Antiquity of Them is Considered, and Defended, Edited by Jeremiah Milles, D.D. Dean of Exeter* (London: Printed for T. Payne and Son, 1782);

Miscellanies in Prose and Verse: By Thomas Chatterton, the Supposed Author of the Poems Published under the Names of Rowley, Canning, &c. (London: Printed for Fielding & Walker, 1778);

Love and Madness: A Story Too True. In a Series of Letters between Parties, whose Names Would Perhaps Be Mentioned, Were They Less Known, or Less Lamented, edited by Herbert Croft (London: Printed for G. Kearsly, 1780);

A Supplement to the Miscellanies of Thomas Chatterton (London: Printed for T. Becket, 1784);

The History and Antiquities of the City of Bristol; Compiled from Original Records and Authentic Manuscripts, in public Offices or Private Hands; Illustrated with Copper-Plate Prints. By William Barrett, Surgeon, F.S.A. (Bristol: Printed by William Pine, 1789);

The Revenge: A Burletta. Acted at Marybone Gardens, MDCCLXX. with Additional Songs (London: Printed by C. Roworth for T. King, H. Chapman, and J. Egerton, 1795);

The Works of Thomas Chatterton, 3 volumes, edited by Robert Southey and Joseph Cottle (London: T. N. Longman & O. Rees, 1803);

The Poetical Works of Thomas Chatterton, with Notices of His Life, History of the Rowley Controversy, a Selection of His Letters, and Notes Critical and Explanatory, 2 volumes, edited by C. B. Willcox (Cambridge: Grant, 1842; enlarged edition, Boston: Little, Brown, 1857);

The Poetical Works of Thomas Chatterton with an Essay on the Rowley Poems, 2 volumes, edited by Walter W. Skeat (London: Bell & Daldy, 1871);

The Complete Works of Thomas Chatterton: A Bicentenary Edition, 2 volumes, edited by Donald S. Taylor and Benjamin B. Hoover (Oxford: Clarendon Press, 1971).

OTHER: John Dix, *The Life of Thomas Chatterton*, includes unpublished poems and correspondence of Chatterton (London: Hamilton, Adams, 1837).

Of all English poets, Thomas Chatterton seemed to his great Romantic successors most to typify a commitment to the life of imagination. His poverty and untimely suicide represented the martyrdom of the poet by the materialistic society of his time. William Wordsworth, listing in "Resolution and Independence" (1807) those poets to whom he owed most, describes Chatterton as

> the marvellous Boy,
> The sleepless Soul that perished in his pride.

Samuel Taylor Coleridge wrote a monody on Chatterton; Robert Southey edited his poems (1803); John Keats dedicated *Endymion* (1817) to him; in "Adonais" (1821) Percy Bysshe Shelley ranks Chatterton with Sir Philip Sidney as "inheritors of unfulfilled renown":

> Chatterton
> Rose pale,—his solemn agony had not

Thomas Chatterton

Yet faded from him . . .
Oblivion as they rose shrank like a thing reproved.

Alfred de Vigny, Robert Browning, Dante Gabriel Rossetti, and Francis Thompson wrote about him; George Meredith posed for Henry Wallis's painting of his death.

Chatterton, for a variety of reasons to a large extent relating to the state of letters in his time, achieved the status of a myth. This is not to discount his formidable influence on English, French, and German literature through his "Rowley" poems, which he attributed to a fifteenth-century Bristol priest, Thomas Rowley. His acknowledged satires and periodical essays were too scurrilous or too close to the work of fashionable contemporaries to attract much attention after his death. In literary history, Chatterton's invention of Rowley coincides with other famous "forgeries": James Macpherson's Ossian, which preceded him, and William Henry Ireland's Shakespeare, which followed.

Chatterton's suicide in a London garret at the age of seventeen, the victim of starvation and despair, enhanced his social and literary significance to an archetypal level. The life and death of Chatterton coincided with new awarenesses of political ideas, individual potentialities, class differences, and the stultifying narrowness of provincial life. In contrast to the ephemerality and shoddinesses of commercial practice and political maneuver, to an age suffused with a revolutionary spirit Chatterton's peculiar vigor of imagination and apparent martyrdom seemed purer and more spiritual. Thus he came to represent to the Romantics and their successors a kind of idealism in the face of the rationalizing materialism of the eighteenth century. William Blake's rejection of Isaac Newton and John Locke was anticipated by the Bristol youngster who plunged into the world of the fifteenth century to release his creative energy. The life of his own time provided him with a subject for satire; that of the past left him uninhibited, free to explore the possibilities of poetry.

Chatterton was born on 10 November 1752 in Bristol, the posthumous son of a schoolmaster—also named Thomas—of an eccentric disposition but with strong musical and antiquarian interests. The elder Thomas Chatterton's ancestors had been sextons of the church of Saint Mary in the

The church of Saint Mary Redcliff in Bristol, where Chatterton's ancestors had been sextons. The muniment room, on the left, contained documents relating to the history of Bristol that may have inspired Chatterton's forgeries.

parish of Redcliff for generations. His wife, Sarah Young Chatterton, was only seventeen and already the mother of their young daughter when they married in 1749. Chatterton grew up in a household of women (his father's mother lived with them) precariously maintained by his mother's work as a needlewoman. Stories of Chatterton's apparent early inability to learn to read and being in consequence judged stupid; his falling in love with an illuminated manuscript at the age of six, after which he did little but read and demonstrate his precocity; his haunting of bookshops; his passion for fame; and his sense that the loss of his father deprived both himself and his family of the standing they might have otherwise had in the community all add color and poignancy to his story. The constant proximity of the old and beautiful church, however, with whose fabric his ancestors had been so closely connected, nurtured his extraordinary sensibility and sheltered his strong ego from the rebuffs which a thriving commercial and maritime community dealt to the growth of his wayward temperament.

At the age of eight Chatterton was sent to Colston's charitable foundation, where his education was geared to the vocational requirements of his community—commerce and law—rather than to encouraging the development of his imagination through classical training. At the end of his schooling he was indentured to a local lawyer, John Lambert, as a scrivener or copy clerk. His employer beat him on finding out that he wrote poetry in his spare time, and, tearing up what he had written, forbade him to continue. There were like-minded young men with whom he gossiped and for whom he produced verse exercises of various kinds. Thomas Phillips, the usher at Colston's, had been regarded as a remarkable versifier, but Phillips died in 1769; Chatterton's three elegies to Phillips show he had been to some extent a fellow spirit.

Chatterton's earliest recollections were of the Gothic beauty of the church of Saint Mary Redcliff. It had been founded in the fifteenth century by William Canning, mayor of Bristol and a romantic figure of enormous wealth and property. Rather than obey King Edward's command to marry a second wife after the death of his first, he had entered a monastery. Among his contemporaries had been Thomas Rowley, at one time sheriff of Bristol; for Chatterton, Canning was to become enshrined in the role of patron to Rowley, who was cast by the boy as priest, poet, and chronicler. The strategic role of Bristol as gateway to the west country and the men who ventured from Bristol to fight in patriotic struggles against the invaders who threatened the independence of England and the liberty of its people were to be "Rowley's" themes.

Canning's name had been featured in leases, heraldry, buildings, grants of property, and bequests in documents housed in chests in the muniment room of Saint Mary Redcliff. Chatterton's father had used old parchments left in disorder to cover his pupils' books, and after his death his widow used strips of the parchments for thread papers. Chatterton collected all the remnants of parchment he could find and took them to a lumber room which he appropriated for his own use. There his solitary brooding, combined with the unsatisfactorinesses of his daily life, encouraged the surrealistic dreamlike quality of his narratives, the vigorous dramatic evocativeness of his poems, and the passionate outpourings of his heroes and heroines.

In his reading Chatterton encountered the Ossian fragments and epics of Macpherson, which had become the rage of the polite world in the 1760s. He also read Thomas Percy's three-volume *Reliques of Ancient English Poetry* (1765), with Percy's "Essay on the Ancient Minstrels," where differences between ancient and modern ballads were discussed. Equally important, as Bertrand Bronson has shown, was Elizabeth Cooper's *The Muses Library* (1737), a four-hundred-page account of such older English poets as Edward the Confessor, Samuel Daniel, William Langland, John Gower, Geoffrey Chaucer, Thomas Occleve, Alexander Barclay, and the earl of Surrey. If one adds to these the collection *Old Plays* (1744) by Robert Dodsley; the works of the antiquarians of the previous century; the dictionaries and encyclopedias of the eighteenth century; Thomas Speght's edition of the works of Chaucer (1598); and the poetry of Edmund Spenser, Thomas Gray, William Collins, and William Shakespeare, one can see that Chatterton's imaginative resources were rich indeed.

Bristol was the second largest city in England and was growing fast in commerce. Its historic role as a strategic gateway to the west country, and consequently in the warlike struggles of the remote past, enabled Chatterton to cast it in a mythical role. Its origin was swathed in legend; its fortunes were intertwined with the fate of the nation; it had played its part in the lives and deaths of the Saxon monarchs; its men had fought against foreign invaders; its citizens and poets had been munificent and learned. The present reality of the town for anyone who was poor and lacked social connections, however, was dire. If influential friends did not exist, they had to be made. The caliber of friends that might be made in Bristol did not seem promising, an irritating state of affairs for so proud and sensitive an adolescent as Chatterton.

Chatterton's first attempt to confront present-day Bristol with its past came with his successful submission to the local newspaper, *Felix Farley's Bristol Journal*, of a piece on the opening of the Old Bridge over the river Severn so that it might be compared with the opening of the new in 1768. Civic pride and a sense of occasion, pageantry, and history combine in Chatterton's piece, which re-creates ancient Bristol for the eighteenth-century reader. It attracted the attention of William Barrett, a surgeon and local antiquary, whose *History of Bristol* (1789) was to include much Rowley material as genuine and of George Catcott, a local pewterer, who questioned Chatterton on his sources for the fifteenth-century account (as it had been represented) of the Old Bridge. At this point the existence of the manuscripts in the muniment room and in Mrs. Chatterton's house became public. Barrett's own collection of such manuscripts was augmented by Rowleian productions handed to him by Chatterton. Following the publication of the Old Bridge piece on 1 October 1768 Chatterton gave Barrett Rowley's "Memoirs," "Epitaph on Robert Canynge," "Songe to Ælla," "Yellow Roll," "Bristow Tragedy," the first part of "The Battle of Hastings," "The Parliament of Sprytes," "Three Eclogues," and the "Tragedy of Godwynn," as well as a "History of Bristol," supposedly by the eleventh-century prior of Durham, Turgot, with Rowley's emendations (Chatterton cunningly offered material which would attract an antiquary and reinforced the forgery with pedantry, also forged, to enhance its supposed authenticity). So it was to impress the somewhat opaque intelligence of his Bristol acquaintances that Chatterton entrusted to them a great part of his richest and most spontaneously produced Rowley material.

Sir

Being versed a little in antiquitys I have met with several Curious Manuscripts among which the following may be of Service to you in any future Edition of your truly — entertaining Anecdotes of Painting — In correcting the mistakes (if any) in the Notes you will greatly oblige

Your most humble Servant.

Thomas Chatterton.

Bristol March 25th

Corn Street —

The Ryse of Peyncteynge, yn Englade, wroten bie [1]T. Rowleie. 1469 for Mastre Canynge.

[1]T. Rowleie was a Secular Priest of St. Johns, in this City. his Merit as a Biographer Historiographer is great, as a Poet still greater: some of his Pieces would do honor Pope; and the Person under whose Patronage they may appear to the World, will lay the Englishman, the Antiquary, and the Poet, under an eternal Obligation —

Chatterton's first letter to Horace Walpole, dated 25 March 1769, offering Walpole a work purportedly written in 1469 by Thomas Rowley (Radio Times Hulton Picture Library)

Consequently, not only was none of the Rowley poetry published during Chatterton's lifetime but his "friends" were among the most adamant after his death in asserting that the boy they had known could not possibly have written the Rowley poems.

If Chatterton compiled history to catch Barrett, he prepared a pedigree to catch Henry Burgum, Catcott's partner. The "Account of the De Berghams from the Norman Conquest to this time" was exposed when Burgum checked the fabrication with the College of Heralds and discovered the hoax. But in the meantime he had parted with a small sum of money which Chatterton might have scorned but certainly needed. It was clear that he must fly higher to catch a worthwhile patron. He wrote to James Dodsley, a London publisher, who may have given him moderate encouragement. His next target was suggested by success in the same field. Horace Walpole, who had acknowledged his authorship of *The Castle of Otranto* (1764) only in its second edition, having at first pretended he had found the manuscript in an old chest, had recently had a new edition of the first volume of his *Anecdotes of Painting in England* (1762) published. What better ploy than to have Canning send Rowley to catalogue the paintings of the fifteenth century in a journey around Britain in order to whet Walpole's appetite for unknown artists? Walpole had already been taken in by Macpherson and was inclined to be a little wary; at first, however, he was enthusiastic enough and welcomed Chatterton's opening gambit, a piece titled "The Rise of Peyncteynge yn Englande, wroten bie T. Rowleie, 1469 for Mastre Canynge." Walpole gave courteous encouragement: "Give me leave to ask you where Rowley's poems are to be found. I should not be sorry to print them, or at least a specimen of them, if they have never been printed."

Chatterton not only sent poems but disclosed the truth of his own situation—that he was the son of a poor widow and wished to be released from his drudgery as an attorney's apprentice. The obviously modern tone of the specimens Walpole received (particularly of the Pastorals) and his vulnerability to imposture and consequent ridicule resulted at first in neglect of the correspondence, then in the brusque dismissal of any hopes Chatterton might have had from this particular great man.

After Chatterton's suicide Walpole was cast in the role of persecutor of the indigent and youthful genius. For more than twenty years Walpole battled to rescue his reputation from this slur, but the neatness of the opposition between the rich dilettante and the poverty-stricken and tragic youth was too intriguing to be laid completely to rest. The immediate difficulty for Chatterton was Walpole's delay in returning the manuscripts. Walpole had pointed out that the harmoniousness of the verses was too modern, as well as the improbability of their surviving from Anglo-Saxon times. Chatterton rebuts this criticism in a letter to Walpole of 14 April 1769:

> The Harmony is not so extraordinary:—as Joseph Iscan is altogether as harmonious—
>
> The Stanza Rowley wrote in, instead of being introduc'd by Spencer was in use 300 Years before . . . by Rowley—tho' I have seen some Poetry of that Age—exceeding Alliterations without Rhyme—
>
> I shall not defend Rowleys Pastoral: its merit can stand its own defence—
>
> Rowley was employ'd by Canynge to go to the Principal Monasterys in the Kingdom to Collect drawings, Paintings & all MSS relating to Architecture—is it then so very extraordinary he should meet with the few remains of Saxon Learning—'Tis allow'd by evry Historian of Credit, that the Normans destroy'd all the Saxon MSS, Paintings &c that fell in their Way; endeavoring to suppress the very Language—the want of knowing what they were, is all the Foundation you can have for stiling them a barbarous Nation.

The last sentence asserts an older identity than that which had provided England with its civilized veneer since the Restoration. All invaders, whether French fashions or Norman soldiers, had been set on the obliteration of an indigenous culture. The first history of English poetry (1774-1781), by Thomas Warton, was to chart the same awareness of an older tradition. Warton's understanding of this tradition, however, was an academic one in comparison with that of Chatterton, whose Rowley poems he learned of too late. The episode with Walpole is clearly a clash between lord and low-born apprentice; it reveals the antagonism of cosmopolitan sophistication versus provincial authenticity. Chatterton's last letter to Walpole, on 24 July 1769, at last elicited the manuscripts: "I think myself injured, sir; and, did not you know my circumstances, you would not dare to treat me thus. I have sent twice for a copy of the MS.:—No answer from you. An explanation or excuse for your silence would oblige."

Although the situation, like the contention between Samuel Johnson and Lord Chesterfield over the patronage for Johnson's *Dictionary* (1755), sets low against high in true folk fashion, Chatterton, as his dedicated biographer, E. H. W. Meyerstein, points out, had merely not succeeded in imposing on Walpole. His verses that were not sent to Walpole because "my Sister persuaded me out of it" affirm his fixed purpose:

> Scorn I will repay with Scorn, & Pride with Pride.
> Still Walpole, still, thy Prosy Chapters write
> And twaddling Letters to some fair indite,
> Laud all above thee,—Fawn and Cringe to those
> Who, for thy fame, were better Friends than
>   Foes . . .
> Had I the Gifts of Wealth and Luxury shar'd
> Not poor & Mean—Walpole! thou hadst not dared
> Thus to insult. But I shall live and stand
> By Rowley's side—when *Thou* are dead and
>   damned.

The *Town and Country Magazine* published Rowley's "Elinor and Juga" in June 1769, but from this time Chatterton seems to have written in propria persona, producing only a few more pieces by Rowley in the remaining months of his life. Among the poems written in Chatterton's own name are several elegies, notably on Phillips, in which dramatic life is given to the evocation of his friend's poetic power. The stanza echoes Gray, the imagery Collins, yet the characteristic Chatterton registering of the impact of light and movement foreshadows Keats:

> When golden Autumn, wreathed in riped'd corn,
> From purple clusters prest the foamy wine,
> Thy genius did his sallow brows adorn,
> And made the beauties of the season thine.
>
> Pale rugged Winter bending o'er his tread,
> His grizzled hair bedropt with icy dew;
> His eyes, a dusky light congeal'd and dead,
> His robe, a tinge of bright ethereal blue;
>
> His train a motley'd sanguine sable cloud,
> He limps along the russet dreary moor;
> Whilst rising whirlwinds, blasting keen and loud,
> Roll the white surges to the sounding shore.

Eclogue the first.

Whanne Englonde smeetheynge frō her lethal Wounde,
Frō her gallod Necke dyd twytte the chayne awaie.
Kennynge her legeful Sonnes falle all arounde,
Myghtie theie fell 'twas honoure ledde the fraie.
Thanne inne a Dale bie Eve's dark Surcote graie,
Twayne lonelie Shepsterres dyd abrodden flie,
The rostlyng Liff doth theyr whyttehartes affraie,
And wythe the Owlette trembled and dyd crie;
Firste Roberte Neatherde hys sore Boesom stroke,
Then fellen on the Grounde and thus yspoke

Roberte.

Ah Raufe! gif thos the howres do comme alonge,
Gif thos wee flie in chase of farther Woe,
Oure Fote wylle fayle albeytte wee bee stronge,
Ne wylle oure Pace swefte as oure Danger goe.

---

a. smething – smoking – in some Copys blethoynge but in the orig as above b deadly . c pluck or pull.
d. Surcote a Cloke or mantle which hid all the other dress—
e. Shepheards — f abruptly so Chaucer
Syke he abrodden dyd attourne
g. Affright —

Chatterton's so-called fair copy of an eclogue by "Rowley" (British Museum, Add Ms 24890)

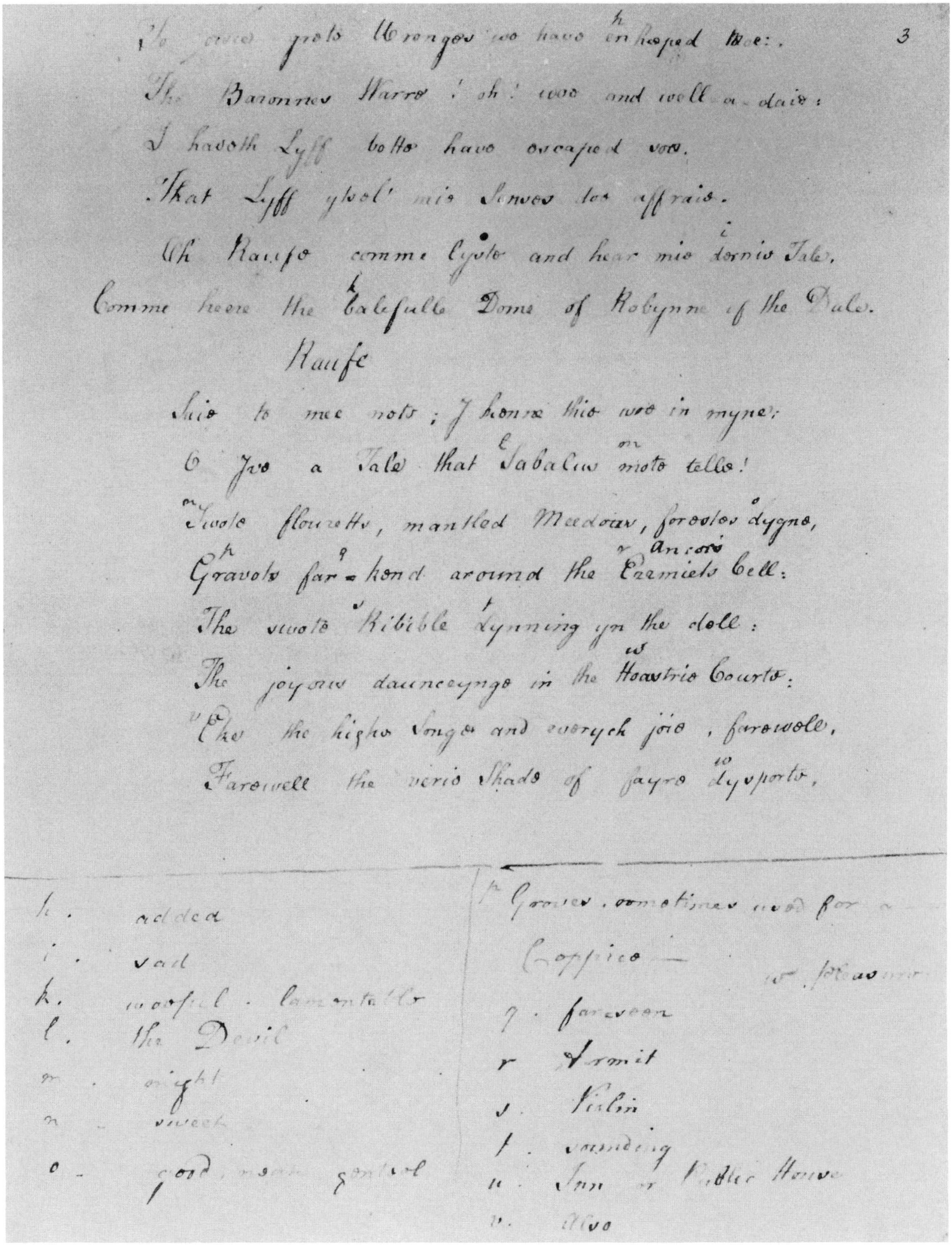

To yowe poote Wronges wee have en[h]heped bee:. 3

The Baronnes Warre ! oh! woe and well a daie:

I haveth Lyff botte have escaped soe.

That Lyff ythel' mie Senses doe affraie.

Oh Raufe comme lyste and hear mie d[i]ernie Tale.

Comme heere the [k]baleful Dome of Robynne of the Dale.

Raufe

Saie to mee nete; I kenne thie woe in myne:

O Ise a Tale that [l]Sabalus [m]mote telle!

[n]Swote flourettes, mantled Meedows, forestes [o]dygne,

Gr[p]avots far[q]-kend around the [r]Ermiets Cell:

The swote [s]Ribible [t]dynning yn the dell:

The joyous dauncyngs in the [u]Hoastrie Courte:

[v]Eke the highe Songe and everych joie, farewell,

Farewell the verie Shade of fayre [w]dysporte,

h. added
i. sad
k. woeful . lamentable
l. the Devil
m. might
n. sweet
o. good, near gentel

p Groves, sometimes used for a Coppice —
q. fareseen
r Armit
s. Violin
t. sounding
u. Inn or Publick House
v. Also
w. pleasure

Page from one of the forgeries on parchment that Chatterton passed off as medieval manuscripts (from Edmund Gosse, English Literature: An Illustrated Record, *1904)*

Chatterton's state of mind in his last autumn months suggests that of William Cowper. "Elegy II" concludes,

A dreary stillness broods o'er all the vale,
The clouded Moon emits a feeble glare;
Joyless I seek the darkling hill and dale,
Where'er I wander Sorrow still is there.

But a Promethean figure expresses a self-sustaining pride in the fragment the editors Donald S. Taylor and Benjamin B. Hoover title "Heroic Fragment" in *The Complete Works of Thomas Chatterton* (1971):

He fled
Eternal Vengeance flaming o'er his head
He clash'd the Clouds bade swelling Thunders sound
And rapid whirls the forky Lightnings round
A Triune Substance of etherial Smoke
The Godhead stood confest and thus he spoke.

The sheer variety of his output at this time exhibits both fluency and determination to succeed. From August to November he wrote burlesques; a burletta, *Amphitryon*; elegies; an antique piece, "The Hirlas"; satires on the themes of Interest, Happiness, and Conversation; a "Journal" in Hudibrastics; and "Epistle to Catcott." At this time, too, he wrote "Elegy, Written at Stanton Drew," on a Maria who had departed from him. Chatterton's female acquaintances were numerous: there is evidence of a Rochester-like dismissal of those who had served their turn. A letter from one Esther Saunders, written on 3 April 1770, offers to meet him "in the morning for . . . we shant be seen a bout 6 a Clock But we must wait with patient for there is a Time for all Things." Chatterton adds a note: "There is a time for all things—Except Marriage my Dear And so your hbl Servt. T. Chatterton, April 9th."

He freely satirized figures in the town, and his attacks on provincial life offer continuing evidence of the precocity and cynicism of his attitudes. In "Happiness" he declaims:

Conscience, the Soul-Camelion's varying hue
Reflects all Notions to no Notion true
The bloody Son of Jesse when he saw
The mystic Priesthood kept the Jews in awe
He made himself an Ephod to his Mind
And sought the Lord and always found him kind
In Murder, horrid Cruelty and Lust
The Lord was with him, and his Actions just. . . .
Content is Happiness as Sages say
But what's Content? The Trifle of a Day
Then Friend let Inclination be thy Guide
Nor be by Superstition led aside
The Saint and Sinner Fool and Wise attain
An equal Share of Easiness and Pain.

If in public he were to go from cynic to calumniator in his satires on the developing political crisis, his home life remained close and affectionate. "The Antiquity of Christmas Games," published in the *Town and Country Magazine* in December 1769, probably helped with the family finances. "The Copernican System," published in the same month, indicates a resolve to make his living by writing, as Richard Savage, a fellow Bristolian, had tried but failed to do. But he was bound to his master, Lambert, and could not get away to London and literary life. He had become a freethinker and wrote out his "Articles of Belief," which were not published until 1842 (in C. B. Willcox's edition of *The Poetical Works of Thomas Chatterton*): "That God being incomprehensible: it is not required of us, to know the mysterys of the Trinity &c. &c. &c. &c." He goes on:

That it matters not whether a Man is a pagan Turk Jew or Christian
if he acts according to the Religion he professes
That if a man leads a good moral Life he is a Christian
That the Stage is the best School of Morality
and
The Church of Rome (some Tricks of Priestcraft excepted) is
certainly the true Church."

Chatterton admired the satiric point and flair of Charles Churchill and the patriotic stance of John Wilkes against the party of the Dowager Princess of Wales and her reputed lover, Lord Bute. The manipulation of the king by the princess and Bute in the interests of the Scottish party drew Chatterton's fire. He addressed the duke of Grafton on the occasion of his resignation from the prime ministership: "your whole administration has been derogatory to the honour and dignity of the crown; for the honour of the crown is the liberty of the subject." This piece appeared in the *Monthly Journal* for 24 February 1770. His next major piece, "The Whore of Babylon"—the title refers to the Dowager Princess of Wales—remained unpublished until 1803 (in Robert Southey and Joseph Cottle's edition of *The Works of Thomas Chatterton*), "Resignation" ap-

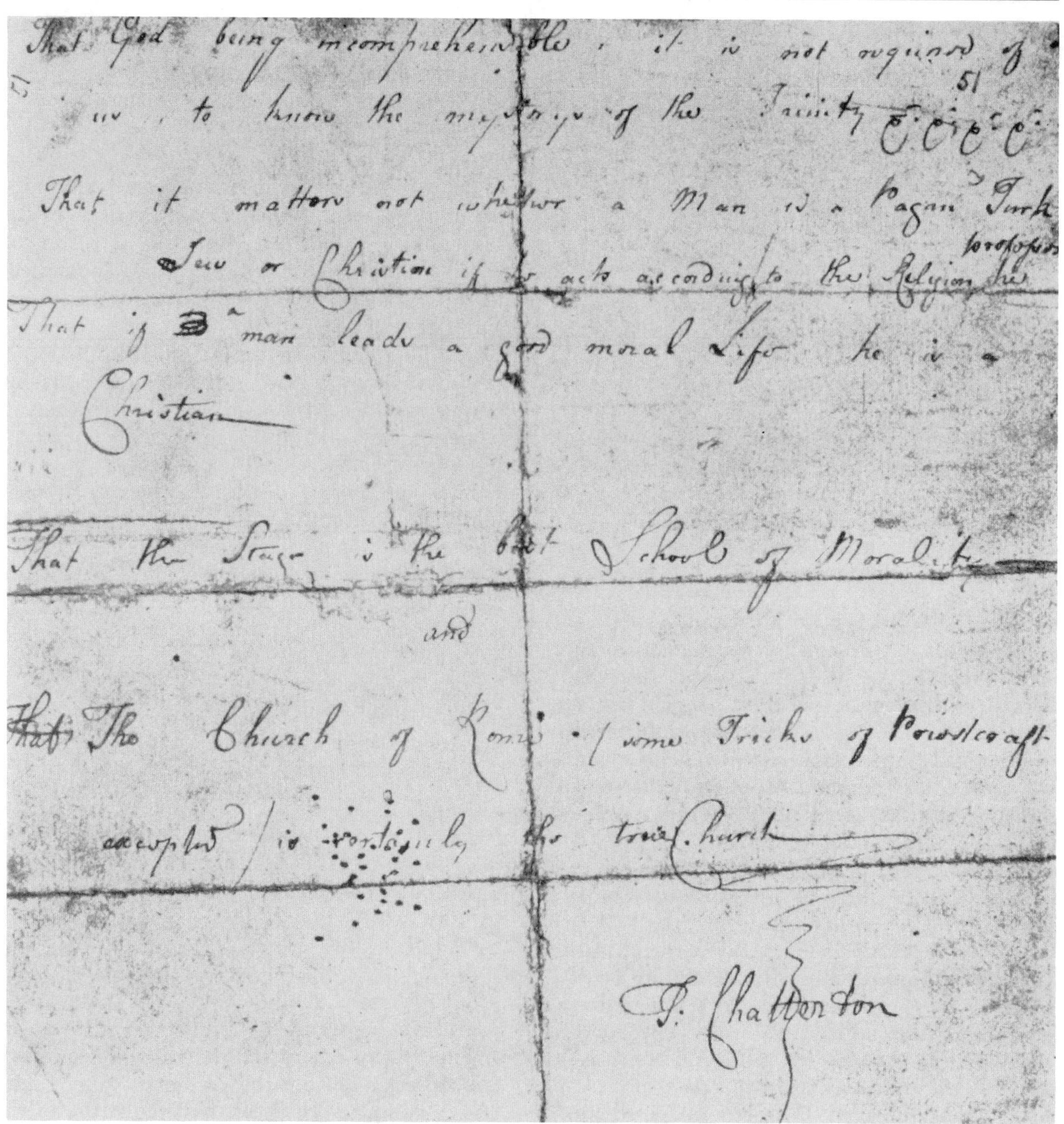

51

That God being incomprehensible, it is not required of us, to know the mysterys of the Trinity &c &c &c

That it matters not whether a Man is a Pagan Turk Jew or Christian if he acts according to the Religion he professes

That if a man leads a good moral Life he is a Christian

That the Stage is the best School of Morality

and

The Church of Rome (some Tricks of Priestcraft excepted) is certainly the true Church

T. Chatterton

Manuscript for Chatterton's "Articles of Belief," written on parchment around 1769 (British Library, Add. Ms. 5766 B f.51)

peared in the *Freeholder's Magazine* in April and May 1770; Bute is one of the targets:

Fir'd by Ambition he resolved to roam
Far from the famine of his native home . . .
Clad in his native many-colour'd Suit
Forth struts the walking Majesty of Bute . . .
A joy prophetic untill then unknown
Assur'd him all he view'd would be his own . . .
Fate beheld him as he trudg'd the Street
Bare was his buttocks and unshod his feet. . . .

The strains of John Dryden and Alexander Pope have collapsed into the burlesque mockery of Churchill.

With the Wilkes furor reaching its climax—Wilkes was again elected to the House of Commons and again expelled by the government—Chatterton had a fortune to seek through the press, where new periodicals such as the *Freeholder's Magazine* had been founded to voice the sentiments of those opposed to the government. So ripe must the time have seemed for his new life to begin that Chatterton found a way to extricate himself from his apprenticeship. On 14 April he devised a last will and testament which begins, "All this wrote bet 11 & 2 oclock Saturday in the utmost Distress of Mind." He addresses Burgum:

> If ever obligated to thy Purse
> Rowley discharges all; my first chief Curse
> For had I never known the antique Lore
> I ne'er had ventured from my peaceful Shore
> To be ye wreck of promises and hopes
> A Boy of Learning and a Bard of Tropes
> But happy in my humbler Sphere had mov'd
> Untroubled unrespected unbelov'd.

After specifying memorials to be placed on the tombs of his ancestors he devises his own:

> To the Memory of Thomas Chatterton. Reader Judge not;
> if thou art a Christian, believe that he shall be Judged by a
> Superior Power, to that Power only is he now answerable—

Listing his (ironic) bequests, he includes Moderation "to the Politicians on both Sides the Question" and Abstinence "to the Company at the Sheriffs annual feast in General more particularly to the Aldermen." He leaves his "Debts in the whole not five Pounds to the Payment of the Charitable and generous Chamber of Bristol"; he leaves his mother and sister to "the protection of my Friends if I have any," and ends with arrangements for the printing of the will. The clear delight in his own inventiveness and the satiric mischief in the document do not conceal the real desperation and wretchedness of his plight. His scheme succeeded: the largely factitious emotions were assumed to be authentic, and Lambert released him from his apprenticeship. Chatterton was free to go to London to make his fortune. He left Bristol on 17 April for the first and last time. He had already written to booksellers and publishers in London, and he visited them promptly on the evening of his arrival.

From then on the pace of his life and the hectic qualities of his letter writing increased. At first he took lodgings in a house in Shoreditch with one of his relatives. From there he wrote glowing accounts of his fashionable acquaintance and of his influence with London publishers. He had already established connections with the editors of the *Town and Country Magazine*, the *Middlesex Journal*, and the *Freeholder's Magazine*. For the most part his work was taken by editors who favored the populist causes of Wilkes, so that when the government clamped down on their activities and imprisoned the editor of the *Freeholder's Magazine* in July Chatterton's market became constricted. It was reduced, too, by the sudden death of a potential patron, William Beckford, Lord Mayor of London. The controversy over Wilkes's election to the House of Commons and his expulsion therefrom by the government raged throughout April and May; it was fanned on 23 May by the lord mayor's "humble remonstrance" to the king at his rejection of London's petition that Wilkes should be restored to his seat. Beckford had violated decorum and was hailed as a hero by the Wilkes party. Chatterton wrote his characteristically portentous letters to the lord mayor, addressing him as "Probus." He received some reward and hoped for more, but on 21 June Beckford died. A celebrated anecdote concerns a letter written to one of his Bristol friends giving an account of what he had gained through writing essays and elegies and lost in patronage by the lord mayor's death, ending with "am glad he is dead by [£]3 13 6."

Most of his works at this time—the long satire "Kew Gardens," referring to the establishment there of the Dowager Princess of Wales; "The Candidate"; and the contributions by "Decimus" and "Menemus" to the *Middlesex Journal*—are politically partisan. "An Exhibition of Sign Paintings" appeared on 26 May (the success of the Wilkes group had been connected with its anti-Hogarth Exhibition of Sign Paintings, in which the authors pilloried the government). He earned a little money from periodical stories such as "Letter of Maria Friendless," which was published in the *Town and Country Magazine* of 15 June 1770, and "Memoirs of a Sad Dog," published in the same magazine in July and August. Lyric pieces were published in the *London Magazine* in June 1770 and in the *Court and City Magazine* in July. These poems mark a new venture into exotic themes and images. The perspectives are cosmic in grandeur: the fiery imagination of Rowley is transposed into a world of more universalized mythology. The description of the river in "The Death of Nicou an African Eclogue" previews that by Coleridge in "Kubla Khan" (1797): "Fiercely propell'd the whiten'd billows rise / Break from the cavern and ascend the skies. . . ." The prowess of Nicou ex-

The Death of Chatterton, *engraved by Edward Orme in 1794*

ceeds in splendor and spaciousness the motions of Keats's Titans:

Strong were the warriors, as the ghost of Cawn,
Who threw the hill of archers to the lawn:
When the soft earth at his appearance fled;
And rising billows played around his head:
When a strong tempest rising from the main,
Dash'd the full clouds, unbroken, on the plain.
Nicou, immortal in the sacred song,
Held the red sword of war, and led the strong;
From his own tribe the sable warriors came,
Well try'd in battle, and well known in Fame.
Nicou, descended from the god of war,
Who liv'd coeval with the morning star. . . .

In the later piece "An African Song" a slighter vein of lyric luxury is still characteristic:

Haste, ye purple gleams of light,
    Haste and gild the spacious skies;
Haste, ye eagles, take your flight,
    Haste and bid the morning rise.

Now the eastern curtain draws;
    Now the red'ning splendor gleams;
Now the purple plum'd maccaws,
    Skim along the silver streams.

Now the fragrant-scented thorn,
    Trembles with the gummy dew;
Now the pleasures of the morn,
    Swell upon the eager view.

The musical units are still sure; the delicacy of sensation is remarkable, and the capacity to startle with a freshness of association is characteristically Chatterton's. Although his predominantly satiric work is similar to that of Lloyd and Churchill, there are signs that his temperament is seeking new and imaginative means of lyric expression.

In June Chatterton moved from Shoreditch to the house of Mrs. Angel, a sacque-maker in

Brooke Street. About this time he must have written, or more likely improved, his "Excelente Balade of Charitie," the only poem of this period written in the Rowleian style. It was not accepted for publication by the *Town and Country Magazine*, which merely printed an acknowledgment of its receipt. The poem describes how Charity and Love are not found "aminge highe elves" for "Knights and Barons live for pleasure and themselves." The poor man of the poem is assailed by bad weather:

> Liste! now the thunder's rattling clymminge [noisy] sound
> Cheves [moves] slowlie on, and then, embollen [swelled], clangs,
> Shakes the hie spyre, and losst, dispended, drown'd,
> Still on the gallard [frighted] eare of terroure hanges;
> The windes are up; the lofty elmen swanges;
> Againe the levynne and the thunder poures,
> And the full cloudes are braste [burst] attenes [at once] in stonen showers.

An abbot refuses to give alms; a priest takes pity on him. The poem ends:

> Virgynne and hallie Seyncte, who sitte yn gloure [glory],
> Or give the mittee [mighty, rich] will, or give the gode man power.

The sentiments of the poem have long been supposed those of Chatterton himself as his fortunes sank even lower. He wrote to his old Bristol acquaintance William Barrett for support in gaining a position as a ship's surgeon, but, since Chatterton had no medical training, Barrett could hardly do other than refuse. The openings for his work were reduced by the measures taken by the government against its opponents; in any case, the *Town and Country Magazine* had already accepted as much material as it could publish. The doldrums of August had descended on the town. In "Memoirs of a Sad Dog" Chatterton traces the decline in fortune of a wealthy young man poetically left at leisure to reflect on Ossianic landscapes: "The man who sits down to write his own history, has no very agreeable task to execute." Left five thousand pounds which he squanders on women, employed by a booby who is visited by a certain "Baron Otranto, who has spent his whole life in conjectures," and fooled by an inscription on a stone in much the same way as the Pickwickians in Dickens's novel, his fortunes are briefly rescued by luck in gambling; but the Sad Dog loses his money again in an unlucky love adventure and returns to London to work for the magazines: "as I know the art of Curlism pretty well, I make a tolerable hand of it. But, Mr Printer, the late prosecutions against the booksellers having frightened them all out of their patriotism, I am necessitated either to write for the entertainment of the public, or in defence of the ministry. As I have some little remains of conscience the latter is not very agreeable . . ."—nor, perhaps, at this juncture, very practicable. The story is close to Chatterton's own.

The last presents for home were sent with confident and affectionate letters to his mother and sister, the two women who remained the center of his emotional concern. He promised more gifts and future good fortune, but in fact he was being beset by the ironically named Mrs. Angel. On 20 July he wrote to his sister, "I have an universal acquaintance: my company is courted every where; and could I humble myself to go into a compter, could have had twenty places before me now; but I must be among the great: State matters suit me better than commercial. The ladies are not out of my acquaintance." The last statement, at least, was true. In a letter to George Catcott in Bristol, dated 12 August, he wrote: "Angels, according to the Orthodox Doctrine, are Creatures of the Epicene Gender, like the Temple Beaux: the Angel here, is of no such materials; for staggering home one Night from the Jellyhouse, I made bold to advance my hand under her covered way, and found her a very very Woman. She is not only an Angel, but an arch Angel; for finding I had Connection with one of her Assistants, she has advanced her demands from 6s to 8s 6 per Week, assured that I should rather comply than leave my Dulcinea, & her soft embraces." At this date he was still hoping that Barrett might help him to the post of ship's surgeon. The near 50 percent increase in his rent must have been the final blow to his finances. Chatterton's "A Hunter of Oddities," published in September in the *Town and Country Magazine*, includes an exchange in which a lodger asks his landlady what he may be given for dinner, and it concludes "Your score is now seven and thirty shillings; and I think it is time it should be cleared." Mrs. Angel told a neighbor that, knowing Chatterton had not eaten for two or three days, she begged him to take a meal with her on 24 August, but that he refused. The same day he was reputed to have tried to beg a loaf from a

The Death of Chatterton, *oil painting by Henry Wallis (1856). George Meredith served as the model for Chatterton (Tate Gallery).*

baker he knew. A neighboring chemist, Mr. Cross, suggested after Chatterton's death that he was using vitriol to cure himself of venereal disease, which seems a likely hazard of his life-style at this time. In the course of the night of 24 August he committed suicide by swallowing opium and then arsenic in water. At the time he died, an Oxford scholar, Dr. Thomas Fry, had started to inquire about the Rowley poems.

In terms of Chatterton's literary achievement there seemed to be a total opposition between the political and often scabrous satires comprising the bulk of his acknowledged work and the Rowley productions that had been left in Bristol. Catcott had amassed a large number of the Rowley poems, and Barrett possessed those apparently relating to the history of Bristol. Fascination with the Rowley material grew as doubts were expressed about its authenticity. In 1776 Thomas Tyrwhitt, the eminent scholar and editor of Chaucer, undertook to edit the Rowley poems, and his edition appeared in 1777. He became convinced they were Chatterton's forgeries. In 1778 Chatterton's *Miscellanies in Prose and Verse* appeared, and the debate raged, with voluminous attacks, rebuttals, and massive periodical coverage for the next fifteen years. The age of the parchments, Chatterton's lack of opportunity and knowledge, and his desire for the fame the poems might have brought him were the arguments of the Rowleians; that forgeries had previously been fabricated on edges and scraps of old parchment used for deeds and other documents, that most of the poems were transcripts, that they contained historical inaccuracies, and other evidence of modern composition were those of their opponents. In the third edition of the Rowley poems in 1778 Tyrwhitt included an appendix proving that their language showed them Chatterton's, and in the same year Warton reached the same conclusion in the second volume of his *History of English Poetry*. At this time other threads of the Chatterton web were being explored by men who were more interested in his life than in his poetry. Herbert Croft's *Love and Madness* (1780) printed Chatterton's letters to his mother and sis-

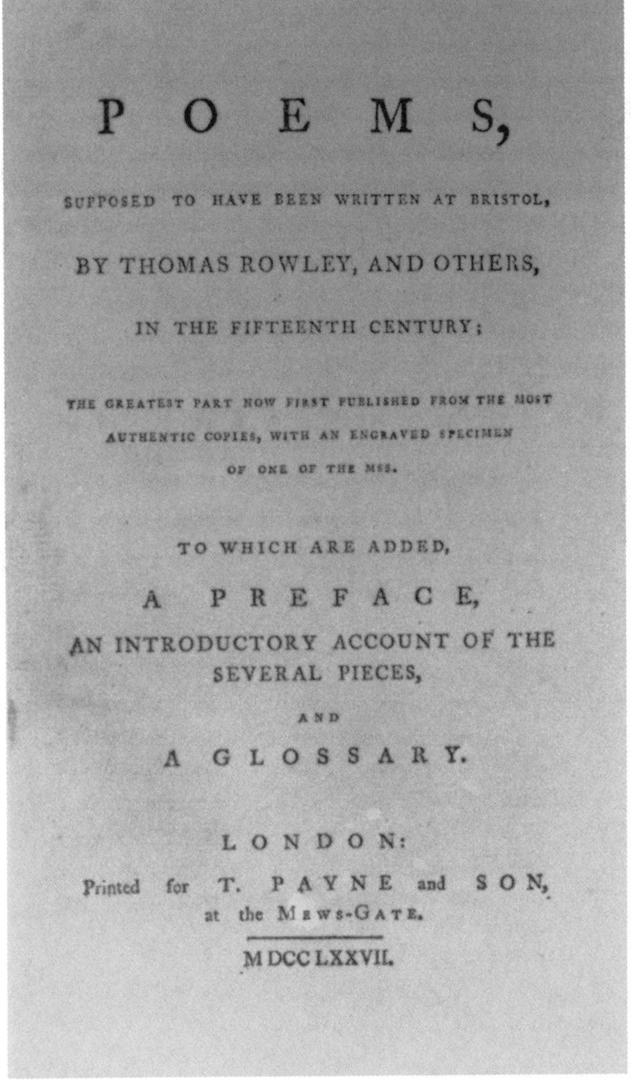

POEMS,

SUPPOSED TO HAVE BEEN WRITTEN AT BRISTOL,

BY THOMAS ROWLEY, AND OTHERS,

IN THE FIFTEENTH CENTURY;

THE GREATEST PART NOW FIRST PUBLISHED FROM THE MOST AUTHENTIC COPIES, WITH AN ENGRAVED SPECIMEN OF ONE OF THE MSS.

TO WHICH ARE ADDED,

A PREFACE,

AN INTRODUCTORY ACCOUNT OF THE SEVERAL PIECES,

AND

A GLOSSARY.

LONDON:

Printed for T. PAYNE and SON, at the MEWS-GATE.

MDCCLXXVII.

Title page for the first collected edition of Chatterton's Rowley poems, edited by Thomas Tyrwhitt and published seven years after Chatterton's death

ter (bought by Croft for a trifling sum) for the first time and also enhanced the sensational aspects of his death. What Meyerstein calls the "ponderous obscurantism" of Dean Jeremiah Milles of Exeter and of Dr. Robert Glynn of King's College, Cambridge, coincided with these developments, and the battle in periodicals and pamphlets raged from 1780 onward, with Warton, Edmund Malone, and even the queen's solicitor general, George Hardinge, joining in. And fresh Rowley and Chatterton material continued to be brought out of obscurity. In 1797, to alleviate the poverty of Chatterton's sister and niece, Southey and Joseph Cottle decided to edit Chatterton's works, including the Rowley material, and to publish them by subscription. This edition appeared in three volumes in 1803.

John Dix's *The Life of Thomas Chatterton* (1837) included the "Last Lines" for the first time. David Masson provided an exemplary account of the political maelstrom into which Chatterton entered in the novel *Chatterton: A Story of the Year 1770* (1874), which was emended and published as a biography in 1899. In France and Germany the revolutionary feelings of the early eighteenth century found affinities in the story of Chatterton; in Alfred de Vigny's drama *Chatterton* (1835) the poet's ghost saves the destitute Francis Thompson from a similar fate. His triumphs as a poet are the theme of Daniel Wilson's *Chatterton* (1869) and Charles Edward Russell's *Thomas Chatterton: The Marvellous Boy* (1908). His most

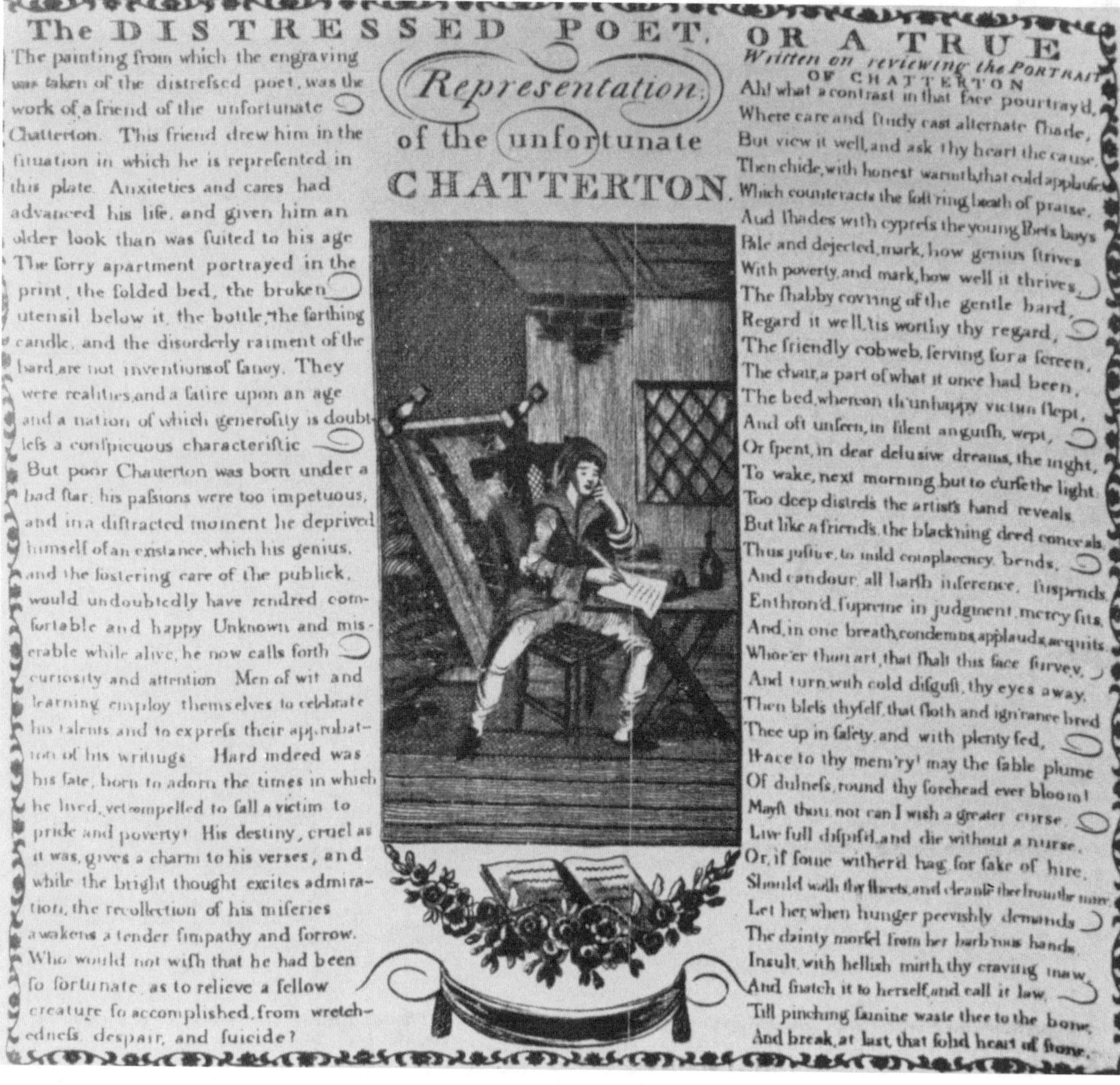

The DISTRESSED POET, OR A TRUE Representation of the unfortunate CHATTERTON.

The painting from which the engraving was taken of the diſtreſsed poet, was the work of a friend of the unfortunate Chatterton. This friend drew him in the ſituation in which he is repreſented in this plate. Anxiteties and cares had advanced his life, and given him an older look than was ſuited to his age. The ſorry apartment portrayed in the print, the folded bed, the broken utensil below it, the bottle, the farthing candle, and the disorderly raiment of the bard are not inventions of fancy. They were realities, and a ſatire upon an age and a nation of which generoſity is doubtleſs a conſpicuous characteriſtic. But poor Chatterton was born under a bad ſtar; his paſsions were too impetuous, and in a diſtracted moment he deprived himself of an existance, which his genius, and the fostering care of the publick, would undoubtedly have rendred comfortable and happy. Unknown and miserable while alive, he now calls forth curiosity and attention. Men of wit and learning employ themselves to celebrate his talents and to expreſs their approbation of his writings. Hard indeed was his fate, born to adorn the times in which he lived, yet compelled to fall a victim to pride and poverty! His destiny, cruel as it was, gives a charm to his verses, and while the bright thought excites admiration, the recollection of his miſeries awakens a tender ſimpathy and ſorrow. Who would not wiſh that he had been ſo fortunate, as to relieve a fellow creature ſo accomplished, from wretchedneſs, despair, and ſuicide?

Written on reviewing the PORTRAIT OF CHATTERTON

Ah! what a contrast in that face pourtray'd,
Where care and ſtudy cast alternate ſhade,
But view it well, and ask thy heart the cause,
Then chide, with honest warmth, that cold applauſe,
Which counteracts the falt'ring breath of praise,
And ſhades with cypreſs the young Poets bays.
Pale and dejected, mark, how genius ſtrives
With poverty, and mark, how well it thrives,
The ſhabby cov'ring of the gentle bard,
Regard it well, tis worthy thy regard,
The friendly cobweb, ſerving for a ſcreen,
The chair, a part of what it once had been,
The bed, whereon th'unhappy victim ſlept,
And oft unſeen, in ſilent anguiſh, wept,
Or ſpent, in dear delusive dreams, the night,
To wake, next morning, but to curſe the light.
Too deep distreſs the artist's hand reveals
But like a friend's, the black'ning deed conceals.
Thus juſtice, to mild complacency bends,
And candour, all harſh inference, ſuspends,
Enthron'd, ſupreme in judgment, mercy ſits,
And, in one breath, condemns, applauds, acquits.
Whoe'er thou art, that ſhalt this face ſurvey,
And turn, with cold diſguſt, thy eyes away,
Then bleſs thyſelf, that ſloth and ign'rance bred
Thee up in ſafety, and with plenty fed,
Peace to thy mem'ry! may the ſable plume
Of dulneſs, round thy forehead ever bloom!
May'ſt thou, not can I wish a greater curse,
Live full diſpis'd, and die without a nurse,
Or, if ſome wither'd hag, for ſake of hire,
Should wash thy ſheets, and cleanſe thee from the mire,
Let her, when hunger peevishly demands
The dainty morſel from her barb'rous hands,
Insult, with hellish mirth, thy craving maw,
And ſnatch it to herself, and call it law,
Till pinching famine waste thee to the bone,
And break, at last, that ſolid heart of ſtone.

One of the red and blue "Chatterton handkerchiefs" that were sold in 1781, during the height of the Rowley controversy (British Museum, C 39 h 20)

formidable biographer, Meyerstein, was surely haunted by him, as his lines written on Chatterton show. Peter Ackroyd's best-selling novel *Chatterton* (1987) is a contemporary witness to his magic. Linda Kelly describes him in *The Marvellous Boy* (1971) as a mythical figure evoking something beyond his achievement, a haunting reminder of the fascination and power of the imagination.

The admiration of the Romantic poets for Rowley extended from Coleridge through Browning to Rossetti, who assisted in the preparation of the next notable edition of the poems, that of the Reverend Walter W. Skeat in 1871. It is this edition which offered conclusive evidence of the forgery by identifying the sources of Chatterton's Rowleyese (chiefly the dictionaries of John Kersey [1708] and Nathan Bailey [1736]). Skeat also translated the Rowley poems into modern English. In this exercise he was assisted by the enthusiastic Rossetti, who wrote to Skeat on 13 May 1880: "I keep some archaisms to give colour, but not many." Rossetti was not unaware, however, of the "Rowley rhythm," and referred to Malone's suggestion that the true test to establish whether Rowley was written by Chatterton would be "to run the 3 'African Eclogues' (the only ones which are poetry proper among the 'acknowledged' class) into Rowleian idiom, and that the common and even equal parentage will then be at once apparent." Rossetti also points out that Christopher Smart's *Song to David* (1763) has "far more sterling English pith than anything else so early in that era"; both Smart and Chatterton, he says, were revivifying older native strains of poetry. For Rossetti, "Not to know Chatterton is to be ignorant of the *true* day-spring of modern romantic poetry." At arguably the most crucial stage in his poetic development, Keats wrote to John Hamilton Reynolds on 22 September 1819: "Chatterton . . . is the purest writer in the English Language . . . 'tis genuine English idiom in English words. I have given up Hyperion—there were too many Miltonic inversions in it." Skeat's translation of Rowley, whatever it did for the intelligibility of Chatterton's work, alerted readers to the musicality of his construction. However outlandish some of his coinages might seem, the sheer fluidity and versatility of his poetry induced a fresh awareness of the possibilities open to the poet.

Chatterton's Rowley uses language to convey a reality not of cognition but of the imagination. His verse, whether dramatic or lyric, excels in its sense of occasion, physicality, color, and incantation. There is the sense of the event, of the poetic utterance, to charm the reader—or, better still, the listener—as in "The Parlement of Sprytes":

Soon as the Morn but newlie wake,
Spyed Nyghte ystorven Lye;
On herre Corse dyd dewedroppes shake—
Then fore the Sonne upgotten was I—
The Rampynge lyon, felle tygere,
The bocke that skyppes from place to place;
The olyphaunt and rhynocere,
Before mee throughe the greene woode I dyd
chace—
Nymrodde as Scryptures hyght mie Name,
Baalle as jetted Stories saie.

Blake's comment is clearly apposite: "I believe both Macpherson and Chatterton that what they say is ancient, is so."

The displacement of reality as presented in history or social narrative is in the interests of a subtle modulation of tone and feeling, as in *Ælla: A Tragycal Enterlude*:

The soldyers stoode uponne the hillis side,
Lyke yonge enlefed trees whyche yn a forreste
byde.

Manhood's promise, described thus, holds a hint of its wasting by war. Birtha's much anthologized song, "O! synge untoe mie roundlaie / O! droppe the brynie teare wythe mee," not only echoes Ophelia; it is a plangently dramatized lament set in the shocks of a ruthless war in which the Danish enemy exhibits his own sense of physical force:

Whene swefte-fote tyme doe rolle the daie
alonge,
Some hamlette scalle onto oure fhuyrie brende;
Brastynge alyche a rocke, or mountayne stronge,
The talle chyrch-spyre apon the grene shalle
bende;
Wee wylle the walles, and auntyante tourettes
rende,
Pete everych tree whych golden fruyte doe beere,
Down to the goddes the ownerrs dhereof sende,
Besprengynge all abrode sadde warre and
bloddie weere.

In *Goddwyn: A Tragedie* the conceptualization of an ancient patriotism takes on a modern note in the personification of Freedom. It is a Freedom envisaged in the context of emotion, overpowering opposition, and warlike death in the face of insuperable odds. The courage, fluency, and spellbinding musicality of metaphor and stress insist on the physical force and energy of the confrontation:

Whan Freedom dreste, yn blodde steyned Veste,
To everie Knyghte her Warre Songe sunge;
Uponne her hedde, wylde Wedes were spredde,
A gorie Anlace bye her honge.
She daunced onne the Heathe,
She hearde the Voice of Deathe;

Pale-eyned Affryghte hys harte of Sylver hue,
In vayne assayled [endeavored] her bosomme to
acale [graze];
She hearde onflemed [undismayed] the shriekynge
Voice of Woe,
And Sadnesse ynne Owlette shake the Dale.

She shooke the burled [pointed] Speere,
On hie she jeste [hoisted] her Sheelde,
Her Foemen all appere,
And flizze [fly] alonge the feelde—
Power, wythe his Heafod [head] straughte
[stretched] ynto the Skyes,
His Speere a Sonne beame, and his Sheelde a
Starre;
Alyche twaie brendynge Gonfyres [two flaming
meteors] rolls hys Eyes,

Monument to Chatterton erected in 1783 by Philip Thicknesse on his estate near Bath (from Lady's Magazine, *February 1784)*

Chaftes [stamps] with hys Yronne feete, and
soundes to War—

She syttes upon a Rocke,
She bendes before hys Speere;
She ryses from the Shocke
Wieldynge her owne in Ayre.
Hard as the Thonder, dothe she drive ytte on,
Wytte scillye wympled gies [closely mantled guides]
ytte to hys Crowne,
Hys longe sharpe Speere, hys spreddynge Sheelde
ys gon
He falles and fallynge rolleth thousandes down—

War, goare faced War, bie Envie burld [armed],
arist [arose],
His feerie Heaulme [helmet] noddynge to the Ayre;
Tenne bloddie Arrowes ynne hys streynynge
fyste. . . .

The momentum, power, and—for all its dramatic action and charged atmosphere—the barren rhythms of Chatterton's vision are distinctive still. His antique world gave him a freedom denied him elsewhere; in its terms he experienced the emotions and creative energies of a doomed yearning for a fulfilment that conditions of the modern world inhibited. There is the promise of the primitive, the unspoiled, in his sweetest lyrical phrases, where a still golden world beckons. In isolation he can listen to the illuminations of past lives with their color, idealism, and fulfilment. In "The Course of a Particular" Wallace Stevens wrote:

I hear the motions of the spirit and the sound
Of what is secret becomes, for me, a voice
That is my own voice speaking in my ear.

It is still worth straining one's ears to listen to the voice of Chatterton.

Bibliographies:

E. R. Norris Matthews, *Thomas Chatterton: A Bibliography* (Bristol, 1916);

Francis Adams Hyett and John Bazeley, *Chattertonia* (Gloucester: Burleigh Press, 1930);

Murray Warren, *A Bibliography of Thomas Chatterton* (New York: Garland, 1977).

Biographies:

John Dix, *The Life of Thomas Chatterton* (London: Hamilton, Adams, 1837);

David Masson, *Chatterton: A Story of the Year 1770* (London: Macmillan, 1874; New York: Dodd, Mead, 1899); revised as *Chatterton: A Biography* (London: Hodder & Stoughton, 1899);

Charles Edward Russell, *Thomas Chatterton: The Marvellous Boy* (New York: Moffat, York, 1908);

J. H. Ingram, *The True Chatterton* (London: Unwin, 1910);

E. H. W. Meyerstein, *A Life of Thomas Chatterton* (London: Ingpen & Grant, 1930);

Linda Kelly, *The Marvellous Boy: The Life and Myth of Thomas Chatterton* (London: Weidenfield & Nicolson, 1971).

References:

Peter Ackroyd, *Chatterton* (London: Penguin, 1987);

G. E. Bentley, ed., *William Blake's Writings*, 2 volumes (Oxford: Clarendon Press, 1978), I: 1512;

Bertrand Bronson, "Chattertoniana," *Modern Language Quarterly*, 2 (1950): 417-424;

Sir Ernest Clarke, *New Lights on Chatterton* (London: Blades, East & Blades, 1916);

George Hardinge, *Rowley and Chatterton in the Shades*, edited by Joan H. Pittock, Augustan Reprint Society Publication no. 193 (Los Angeles: University of California Press, 1979);

Thomas Lockwood, *Post-Augustan Satire* (Seattle: University of Washington Press, 1979);

"The Original Correspondence on the Discovery of Rowley's Poems," *Gentleman's Magazine*, 56 (1786): 361-362, 460-464, 544-547, 1859-1860;

Donald S. Taylor, *Thomas Chatterton's Art* (Princeton: Princeton University Press, 1978);

Daniel Wilson, *Chatterton: A Biographical Study* (London: Macmillan, 1869).

Papers:

There are substantial holdings of Thomas Chatterton's manuscripts in the British Library; the Bristol Public Library Collection includes a large group of transcripts by George Catcott, particularly of the Rowleian material of 1768 and 1769. Manuscript memoranda on Chatterton's life by the Reverend Richard Hort are in the Bristol Library.

Charles Churchill

(February 1731 - 4 November 1764)

Lance Bertelsen
University of Texas at Austin

BOOKS: *The Rosciad* (London: Printed for the author and sold by W. Flexney, 1761; second through eighth editions, revised and enlarged, 1761-1763);

The Apology: Addressed to the Critical Reviewers (London: Printed for the author, and sold by W. Flexney, 1761; second through sixth editions, revised, 1761-1763);

Night: An Epistle to Robert Lloyd (London: Printed for the author, and sold by W. Flexney, 1761; second through fourth editions, revised, 1761-1763);

The Ghost (London: Printed for the author, and sold by W. Flexney, 1762);

The Ghost: Book III (London: Printed for the author, and sold by W. Flexney, 1762; enlarged, 1763);

The Prophecy of Famine: A Scots Pastoral (London: Printed for the author, and sold by G. Kearsly, 1763);

An Epistle to William Hogarth (London: Printed for the author, and sold by J. Coote, and by J. Gardiner, 1763);

The Ghost: Book IV (London: Printed for J. Coote; W. Flexney; G. Kearsly; T. Henderson; J. Gardiner; and J. Almon, 1763);

Poems: Containing The Rosciad; The Apology; Night; The Prophecy of Famine; An Epistle to William Hogarth; And The Ghost, in Four Books (London: Printed for the author, by Dryden Leach; and sold by W. Flexney; G. Kearsly; T. Henderson; J. Coote; J. Gardiner, Westminster; J. Almon; and E. Broughton, at Oxford, 1763);

The Conference: A Poem (London: Printed for G. Kearsly; J. Coote; W. Flexney; C. Henderson; J. Gardiner; and J. Almon, 1763);

The Author: A Poem (London: Printed for W. Flexney; G. Kearsly; J. Coote; C. Henderson; J. Gardiner; and J. Almon, 1763);

The Duellist: A Poem. In Three Books (London: Printed for the author; and sold by W. Flexney; J. Almon; J. Coote; C. Henderson; J. Gardiner; and C. Moran, 1764);

Gotham: A Poem. Book I (London: Printed for the author, and sold by W. Flexney; G. Kearsly; C. Henderson; J. Coote; J. Gardiner; and J. Almon, 1764);

Gotham: A Poem. Book II (London: Printed for the author, and sold by G. Kearsly; W. Flexney; C. Henderson; J. Coote; J. Gardiner; and J. Almon, 1764);

The Candidate: A Poem (London: Printed for the author, and sold by W. Flexney; G. Kearsly; C. Henderson; J. Coote; J. Gardiner; J. Almon; and A. Moran 1764);

Gotham: A Poem. Book III (London: Printed for the author, and sold by J. Almon; J. Coote; W. Flexney; C. Henderson; J. Gardiner; and C. Moran, 1764);

The Farewell: A Poem (London: Printed for the author, and sold by W. Flexney; G. Kearsly; C. Henderson; J. Coote; J. Gardiner; J. Almon; and C. Moran, 1764);

The Times: A Poem (London: Printed for the author, and sold by J. Coote; J. Almon; W. Flexney; C. Henderson; J. Gardiner; and C. Moran, 1764);

Independence: A Poem. Addressed to the Minority (London: Printed for the author, and sold by J. Almon; J. Coote; W. Flexney; C. Henderson; J. Gardiner; and C. Moran, 1764);

Sermons (London: Printed by W. Griffin; for John Churchill and William Flexney, 1765);

The Journey: A Fragment (London: Printed for John Churchill, and sold by William Flexney, 1765);

Poems: Containing The Conference; The Author; The Duellist; Gotham, in Three Books; The Candidate; The Farewell; The Times; Independence; and Fragment of Journey. Volume II (London: Printed for John Churchill and W. Flexney, 1765);

The Poetical Works of Charles Churchill: With Copious Notes and a Life of the Author, 3 volumes, edited by William Tooke (London: Pickering, 1844);

Portrait by J. S. C. Schaak; National Portrait Gallery, London

The Poetical Works of Charles Churchill, edited by Douglas Grant (Oxford: Clarendon Press, 1956).

OTHER: *North Briton*, edited by Churchill and John Wilkes (1762-1763).

Charles Churchill was the most important satiric poet between Alexander Pope and Lord Byron. Undisciplined and rebellious, he produced an extraordinary amount of verse at an extremely rapid rate between 1760 and 1764—years in which he dominated the English literary scene. With a typical mixture of self-satire and self-aggrandizement, he summarized his methods of composition in *Gotham: A Poem. Book II* (1764): "Nothing of Books, and little known of men, / When the mad fit comes on, I seize the pen, / Rough as they run, the rapid thoughts set down, / Rough as they run, discharge them on the Town." This irreverence toward establishment standards and this stress on spontaneity and independence pervaded not only Churchill's poetry but his life. Although a clergyman, he was notorious as a tippler, womanizer, "bruiser," and political rebel (although perhaps not a "radical" in the modern sense of the word). His political stance, which developed from his close friendship with John Wilkes, led to his writing for and editing the opposition periodical *North Briton* (1762-1763) and left an important mark on his most significant poetry.

Charles Churchill was born in February 1731 in Vine Street, Westminster, the second son of Ann Churchill and the Reverend Charles Churchill, curate and lecturer of St. John the Evangelist and vicar of Rainham, Essex. In May 1741 young Churchill entered Westminster School and began his most important formative experience. At the very center, geographically and ideologically, of the British establishment, Westminster School was designed to reproduce patrician values: classical languages and hierarchical thinking, deference to one's betters and superciliousness to one's inferiors. Yet the school reproduced much more than this. Surrounded by neighborhoods ranging from town houses to tenements and open to a massive literary stimulus in the form of the daily, weekly, and monthly productions of the London press, Westminster School represented a kind of crucible for the complex negotiations of eighteenth-century English society. A heterogeneous mixture of boys ranging from the sons of lords to the sons of apothecaries, Westminster students experienced with unique immediacy the rituals of power and the counter-rituals of irreverence, the paradoxes of birth and rank within the dominant ideology of liberty, and—particularly for boys of Churchill's "middling" rank—the confusing pressures of social aspiration and traditional deference in a society whose people were becoming more sophisticated as the circle of real power became more exclusive. These paradoxes of class and power would have a defining effect on the form and substance of Churchill's satiric poetry.

Churchill seems to have thrived at Westminster. There he met Robert Lloyd, George Colman, Bonnell Thornton, and William Cowper, who would become his closest friends and literary allies. In 1745 he earned the singular honor of being named captain of the King's Scholars, an elite group of students who won their room, board, and tuition through competitive examinations. But Churchill also displayed a rebellious streak, one that reached an early culmination in his abortive college career at St. John's College, Cambridge, in 1748. In 1749 he married Martha Scott and moved home to obscurity and near poverty.

During the next ten years Churchill moved around England, pursuing a highly unsatisfying career as a minor clergyman. In 1751 he was in Sunderland in the north of England, preparing to take holy orders, but during this period, according to William Tooke, he "devoted almost all of his time to his favourite poetical amusements." Churchill may have returned to London in 1753; in any case, he was ordained a deacon in 1754 and licensed to the curacy of South Cadbury and Sparkford in Somerset. In 1756 he was ordained a priest and licensed to be curate to his father at Rainham in Essex. On the death of his father in 1758 Churchill succeeded him as curate of St. John's, Westminster, and by 1759 he and his family had again taken up residence in London.

These must have been extremely frustrating years for a man of Churchill's ambitions and mercurial temperament. With three children and a wife to support, he found himself living in poverty and obscurity, condemned, as he would later write in *The Author* (1763), to "pray, and starve on forty pounds a year." By 1760 he had tried several expedients to supplement his income and had narrowly escaped debtors' prison. His friends from Westminster, Thornton and Colman, had already achieved modest literary fame and, with Lloyd and Cowper, had founded the Nonsense Club. Churchill must have felt himself on the periphery—undervalued, exploited, entrapped. An explosion was imminent, and in the early 1760s it came.

Perhaps spurred by the successes of Lloyd's poetical treatise *The Actor* (April 1760) and Colman's dramatic afterpiece *Polly Honeycombe* (December 1760), during the season of 1760-1761 Churchill began regularly attending the theater, where, according to Thomas Davies, "he bestowed incessant attention to stage representation; and, by close application, laboured to understand perfectly the subject which was the choice of his muse. His observatory was generally the first row of the pit, next to the orchestra." Davies, himself an actor, was in an excellent position to know; David Garrick wrote to him that "you were always *confus'd & unhappy* whenever you saw M[r] Churchill before You." And Davies had reason to be unhappy; he was to become the victim of the most famous line in Churchill's *The Rosciad* (1761)—"He mouths a sentence as curs mouth a bone"—a description which is said to have driven him from the stage.

Published on 14 March 1761, *The Rosciad* is a satirical poem devoted to the players of the London stage. Churchill's keen powers of observation coupled with his razor-sharp phrasing make the poem a vivid series of theatrical snapshots: actors and actresses are frozen in performance, their mannerisms and foibles ridiculously displayed.

The loose structure of *The Rosciad* (made considerably looser by the addition of more than three hundred lines through eight editions) is provided by the fiction of disputed succession as the players compete for the vacant chair of the great Roman actor Roscius. In the course of choosing Shakespeare and Ben Jonson as contest judges, Churchill manages to compliment his friends

Lloyd and Colman and attack several of his enemies, including John Hill and Arthur Murphy. Then the procession of competing actors advances, and Churchill begins his satiric snapshots. William Havard's lifelessness, Davies's delivery, Charles Holland's imitation of Garrick, Thomas King's overdone expressions—all are presented with great attention to detail. Churchill's central critical notion is the same as that of Lloyd's *The Actor*: a player must understand his own nature in order to choose his parts properly. This tenet, which critically and chronologically falls somewhere between the rigid formality of the ten dramatic "passions" and the emotional authenticity associated with the twentieth-century theorist Konstantin Stanislavsky, is the theoretical center of the *The Rosciad*. Not surprisingly, it is Garrick—whose talent comes from "Nature's pure and genuine source" and whose "strokes of Acting flow with gen'rous force"—who finally wins Roscius's chair.

The players and their allies responded to the anonymous *Rosciad* with a steady stream of publications attacking the author, his motives, and his friends. Tobias Smollett's *Critical Review* (March 1761) proclaimed that the author was Lloyd or "a new triumvirate of wits" (Lloyd, Colman, and Thornton) but soon retracted this allegation. The playwright Murphy attacked Churchill in both an *Ode to the Naiads of Fleet Ditch* (1761) and *The Examiner* (1761). Lloyd defended him in his *An Epistle to C. Churchill* (1761). The so-called battle of the players and poets eventually generated scores of publications and made Churchill a public figure. It also solved his financial problems: unable to find a publisher, he had had the poem printed and distributed at his own expense and thus kept all the profits—an estimated one thousand pounds.

Once established as a satiric poet and public personality, Churchill immediately undertook to aggrandize his position by publishing a stream of new poems, as well as revised editions of earlier poems, over the next three years. In May 1761 *The Apology: Addressed to the Critical Reviewers* continued the "battle" with further attacks on Murphy and Smollett, as well as containing, rather surprisingly, a satiric portrait of Garrick as a "Tyrant" of the greenroom. The poem is also notable for its introduction of Churchill's poetic principles—principles which caused him to prefer John Dryden's strength and spontaneity to Pope's refinement and polish. "Perish my Muse," he writes, "If e'er her labours weaken to refine / The gen'rous roughness of a nervous line." Critics have pointed out that in his actual poetic practice Churchill was perhaps closer to Pope than he would have liked to admit. Nevertheless, he certainly felt himself to be breaking from Pope's rather regular, closed couplet and reintroducing the more vigorous, enjambed couplet associated with Dryden.

The values expressed in *The Apology*—spontaneity, unconstrained expression, rebellion against establishment forms, individuality—directed Churchill's poetry as well as his life. In his next poem, *Night: An Epistle to Robert Lloyd* (November 1761), Churchill imagines himself and Lloyd sitting late in a tavern, railing against their detractors. Most critics of *Night* have been content to stress its overt themes: Kenneth Hopkins calls it a defence of libertinism; Raymond J. Smith emphasizes its praise of individualism and its attacks on establishment hypocrisy. But the poem has another, more dubious quality, one suggested by William Kenrick in 1776 when he wrote of Churchill and Lloyd's "suicide genius," which by "railing at others . . . thinks to excuse itself; imputing to ignorance or malevolence the cause of that ruin in which, against its own better knowledge, it is . . . unpardonably involved." Churchill's emphasis early in the poem on the "grief" and "care" he feels has the effect of qualifying the following attacks on the "important blanks" of the hypocritical "daylight world" and the institutions that they represent: government, business, the church. His stance is that of a social critic, but also of a bohemian, a hedonist, a night owl—"Misfortunes, like the Owl, avoid the light; / The sons of CARE are always sons of NIGHT." In attacking methodical men and establishment rules Churchill seeks, self-destructively, to replace daylight concerns with "joys, by fancy form'd" and to drown "in Oblivion's grateful cup . . . / The galling sneer, the supercilious frown, / The strange reserve, the proud affected state, / Of upstart knaves grown rich and fools grown great." *Night* is a defense of libertinism, a plea for personal liberty, and a satire on false propriety; but more than that, it is a portrait of Churchill in the midst of his rebellion; at once bold and doubtful, boisterous and self-destructive, cheerful and afraid.

Having gained a reputation as a libertine, Churchill began to flaunt it, separating from his wife in 1762 and resigning his curacy in January 1763. During this period his intimacy with Wilkes began. Seemingly drawn together by their love of pleasure, both men were members of the infamous Monks of Medmenham and attended the libertine celebrations and rituals at Medmenham Abbey. But more important, both were soon caught up in the political troubles surrounding William Pitt's resignation from the cabinet and George III's elevation of the Scottish Lord Bute (John Stuart) to first lord of the treasury (in essence, the prime minister). By June 1762 Churchill found himself editing Wilkes's political essay paper, the *North Briton* (he is also credited with writing numbers 7, 8, 10, 18, 21, 22, 26, 27, and 42) and writing increasingly sharp poetical attacks against the Bute administration. Two poems especially typify this period. *The Ghost* begins in Books I and II (March 1762) as something of a self-reflective jeu d'esprit but in Book III (October 1762) and Book IV (November 1763) becomes progressively more political. *The Prophecy of Famine* (January 1763) derives directly from Churchill's experience with the *North Briton* and the virulent anti-Scot satire that characterized the opposition's campaign against Bute.

The Ghost purports to satirize the celebrated episode of the Cock-Lane Ghost, in which reports of a ghost haunting a house in Cock-Lane became so widely believed that they were investigated by a committee that included Samuel Johnson. But the primary subject of poem—especially the last three books—is Churchill's own digressive, self-reflexive poetic process. Book I is a rewriting of Churchill's unpublished "The Fortune Teller" and amounts to a rather mundane attack on popular superstition. But Book II is a strikingly associational, process-oriented poem, called by the *Monthly Review* (1762) "a digressive, incoherent production ... which may not improperly be termed a kind of *Tristram Shandy* in *verse*." As Smith writes, "Churchill uses the ghost story in somewhat the same way that [Laurence] Sterne was using the life of Tristram Shandy—it is the nucleus for a virtual miscellany of parody and satire held together by a web of associations." The poem marks the extreme demonstration of a principle central to Churchill's poetry, one which might be called the "aesthetic of spontaneity." Deploring the "mechanic" or "methodized" technique and fantastic settings that he and his friends in the Nonsense Club associated with the writers of modern odes and elegies (the writers who today are called the "poets of sensibility"), Churchill attempted to practice a more truly unpremeditated style of composition which took as its subject the events and objects of everyday life as they occurred spontaneously to him during the process of poetic association. As T. E. Blom has pointed out, this "self-reflective process poetry," like the "oracular" poetry it decried, rejects the limiting effects of formal education and stresses the importance of uncontrolled association—what in the eighteenth century would have been thought of as the "flow of genius." While evident in all of Churchill's poetry after *The Rosciad*, this scorn of method and revision, this reliance on unpremediated association, is given extreme, almost parodic form in the *The Ghost*.

The Prophecy of Famine constitutes Churchill's definitive transition from satire concerned chiefly with aesthetic and personal issues to satire motivated primarily by political events. At the time of its writing Churchill's life was also in transition. His association with Wilkes and the *North Briton* had increased his already substantial notoriety as a poet and libertine: Murphy's proadministration *Auditor* attacked him on 22 July 1762, and the first satiric prints to picture him appeared in September. During this period Churchill contracted venereal disease, and he spent the fall of 1762 suffering and writing (with Wilkes's encouragement) *The Prophecy of Famine*. The poem opens with a typical attack on modern ode and elegy writers for discarding the "workings of the heart" and banishing nature for "mechanic art." Then, to close the literary section, Churchill names Nature as his "goddess," only to suddenly and deftly subvert his terminology in a brilliantly relativistic passage:

By Nature's charms (inglorious truth!) subdued,
However plain her dress, and 'haviour rude,
To *northern* climes my happier course I steer,
Climes where the Goddess reigns throughout the year;
Where, undisturb'd by Art's rebellious plan,
She rules the *loyal Laird*, and *faithful Clan*.

The passage begins with Churchill's usual aesthetic position—anti-"art," pro-"nature." But as the passage proceeds, the formula becomes ironic by association, as Churchill uses it to introduce a satire on Scotland—a land, even by his standards, *too* rude and plain. The reader begins by agreeing with something that is suddenly transformed into its opposite. As in *The Ghost*, Churchill moves through the connotations of a given word or concept without overtly taking sides. Meanings are not opposed as good or bad, true or corrupt, but merely used in the many ways

11

Jockey, whose manly high-bon'd cheeks to crown,
With freckles spotted flam'd the golden down,
With mickle art could on the Bagpipes play,
E'en from the rising to the setting day;
Sawney as long, without remorse, could bawl
Home's madrigals, and ditties from Fingal,
Oft at his strains, all natural tho' rude,
The Highland Lass forgot her want of food,
And, whilst she scratch'd her Lover into rest,
Sunk pleas'd, tho' hungry, on her Sawney's breast.

I have seen Hogarth's print; sure it is much unequal to the former productions of that master of Humour. I am happy to find that he hath at last declar'd himself, for there is no credit to be got by breaking flies upon a wheel, But Hogarths are Subjects worthy of an Englishman's pen.

Speedily will be published,

An Epistle to W. Hogarth by C. Churchill,

Pictoribus atq; Poetis,

Quidlibet audendi semper fuit aequa Potestas.

I was t'other day at Richmond, but lost much of the pleasure I had promis'd myself, being disappointed of seeing You. What is the use or meaning of the Pegoda — is it not improperly pronounced — it should certainly be Pego-da.

I long for the opening of the House on many accounts, but on none more than the opportunity it will give me of seeing that little Whimsical fellow Garrick, and that most agreeable of Women, to whom I am always proud of being remember'd, Mrs. Garrick. Hubert I hear has got a weakness in his eyes. I am, Dr Garrick,

Your's most sincerely,

Saturday Night, Charles Churchill,

Second page of letter from Churchill to the actor David Garrick, written circa September 1762, requesting a loan of forty or fifty pounds and offering as collateral an excerpt from The Prophecy of Famine: A Scots Pastoral *(1763), which Churchill was then writing (Pierpont Morgan Library). Churchill did not receive the loan.*

that society uses them. In essence, Churchill shows that, in Thomas Lockwood's words, "the true basis of the associations evoked by moral abstractions such as Virtue, Vice, Reason, and Nature, lies not in morals but in language." In Churchill's poetry, as in life, such abstractions must always be judged in context. And the context, in the hands of Churchill, is constantly changing, slipping away, reversing itself. The response of the reader is usually a form of confusion—a confusion too often attributed to the failure of Churchill's poetic expression. The disjunctions in his poems are caused in part by the speed with which he wrote them, but they are also conscious attempts to convey the disjunction of the times and the inherent ambiguity of aesthetic and ethical abstractions. Rather than being guilty of confused expression, Churchill is perhaps guilty only of expressed confusion.

In *The Prophecy of Famine* Churchill continues in this relativistic mode to "defend" the Scots in the ironic manner of the *North Briton*. His allusion to "*waggon-loads* of courage, wealth, and sense," for example, takes its context from the many popular prints showing caravans of Scots on their way south to take advantage of Bute's patronage, and Churchill's ambiguous apostrophe to Wilkes seems to praise him for condemning the "fierce *North-Briton*"—the paper which he was in fact writing along with Churchill. Following the defense and the apostrophe comes the "Scottish eclogue," in which the starving Scottish shepherds, Sawney and Jockey, parody the conventions of the pastoral eclogue. Here Churchill places his chief political concerns against a strongly imagined background of waste, loathsomeness, and disease. His description of Famine's cavern emphasizes hunger and debility: "half-starv'd spiders prey'd on half-starv'd flies"; and Famine herself is a horrific creation: "With double rows of useless teeth supplied, / Her mouth, from ear to ear, extended wide, / Which, when for want of food her entrails pin'd, / She op'd, and cursing swallow'd nought but wind." At the time he wrote this description Churchill was himself suffering from a form of starvation: the mercury-induced "salivation" treatment for venereal disease loosened the teeth and made it hard to eat. On 12 December 1762 Churchill wrote to Wilkes, "My teeth begin to loosen but yet I think they could bite a proud Scot."

Throughout the spring and summer of 1763 Churchill and his friends in the Nonsense Club, especially Lloyd, worked as allies of Wilkes. On 23 April Wilkes and Churchill published *North Briton* no. 45, Wilkes's famous attack on the king's speech from the throne. On 26 April the government issued warrants for their arrest on grounds of seditious libel. Churchill was possibly taken into custody and released, although there is also evidence that Wilkes helped him escape arrest. On 6 May Wilkes's case was heard in the Court of Common Pleas, and he was discharged amid great popular rejoicing. But during the proceedings William Hogarth, a disaffected friend of both Wilkes and Churchill, executed a sketch that would become the satirical portrait *John Wilkes, Esq.* (May 1763) and would inspire Churchill's next important political poem, *An Epistle to William Hogarth* (June 1763).

An Epistle to William Hogarth was a long time in the making. Churchill had originally contemplated an attack on Hogarth in September 1762 when Hogarth published the satirical print *The Times,* which includes caricatures of Churchill and Wilkes. Soon thereafter, Churchill wrote to Garrick, "I have seen Hogarth's print. . . . I am happy to find that he hath at last declar'd himself. . . . Speedily to be published, An Epistle to W. Hogarth by C. Churchill." But Wilkes answered first in *North Briton* number 17, and Churchill's promised satire did not materialize until Wilkes's arrest and Hogarth's second attack. This delay helps to explain the odd structure of the poem, the first half of which is given over to a long argument between Churchill and the personified abstraction "Candour" (in the eighteenth-century usage, meaning "freedom from malice"). As Candour attacks satire as a destructive art and counsels Churchill to be generous, one senses a replay of many of the arguments Churchill must have used on himself during the nine months he delayed attacking his old friend. In the key transitional passage, Candour dares Churchill to produce one person so degraded as to deserve satiric exposure. In answer, Churchill drags forth Hogarth to stand trial "in that great Court, where Conscience must preside." In the midst of the trial, Churchill as prosecutor executes an especially vicious satirical portrait of the aged Hogarth:

WITH all the symptoms of assur'd decay,
With age and sickness pinch'd, and worn away,
Pale quiv'ring lips, lank cheeks, and falt'ring
  tongue
The Spirits out of tune, the Nerves unstrung,
Thy Body shrivell'd up, thy dim eyes sunk
Within their sockets deep, thy weak hams shrunk

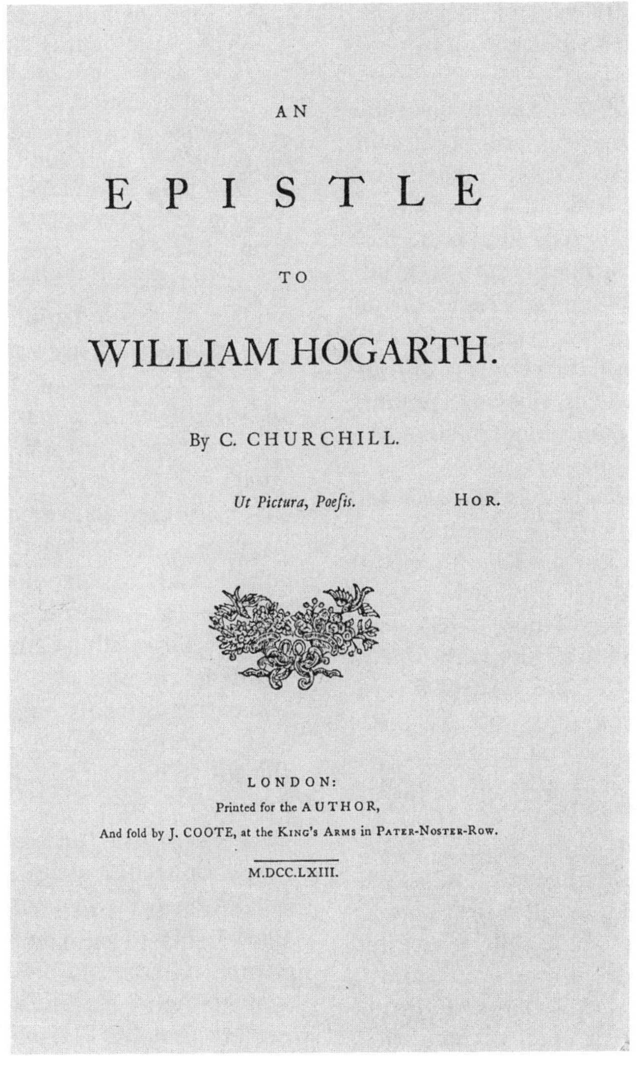

AN

EPISTLE

TO

WILLIAM HOGARTH.

By C. CHURCHILL.

Ut Pictura, Poeſis. HOR.

LONDON:
Printed for the AUTHOR,
And ſold by J. COOTE, at the KING'S ARMS in PATER-NOSTER-ROW.

M.DCC.LXIII.

Title page for Churchill's poetic attack on the artist Hogarth

> The body's weight unable to sustain,
> The stream of life scarce trembling thro' the vein,
> More than half-kill'd by honest truths, which fell,
> Thro' thy own fault, from men who wish'd thee well,
> Can thou, e'en thus, thy thoughts to vengeance give,
> And, dead to all things else, to Malice live?

In the event, Hogarth did give his thoughts to vengeance, publishing on 1 August *The Bruiser*, his great satirical portrait of Churchill as a drunken bear.

The fall of 1763 was not a good one for Churchill. In November he eloped with fifteen-year-old Elizabeth Carr, the daughter of a respected Westminster stonemason. He was warned of assassination threats and responded with typical bravado, "My Life I hold for the purposes of pleasure; those forbid, it is not worth my care." Eventually he returned Elizabeth to her home, but she ran away and was living at his house in Acton Common at the time of his death. Churchill's next poem, *The Conference* (November 1763), contains what amounts to an apology for these private actions coupled with a strong defense of his public life. Structured as a dialogue between Churchill and a corrupt lord, the poem addresses the various temptations faced by any honest man during depraved times and reiterates Churchill's dedication to his public—those independent, unpatronized men who, like himself, openly defy the hereditary power and corruption of the great. Indeed, by this time Churchill had made his openness something of a trademark: in an interesting innovation, he was not only named on the title page of his poems but he often hand-signed them.

Close on the heels of *The Conference* came *The Author* (December 1763), a minor poem contrasting the slavish authors of the present (especially John Kidgell, who had attacked Wilkes's morals) to the heroic writers of the past. The poem is noteworthy historically because it is one of two for which a draft contract between Churchill and his publishers exists: George Kearsly and William Flexney gave Churchill a £150 advance for *The Author* and *The Duellist* (January 1764), with a promise of an additional £300 on delivery.

On 15 November 1763 Wilkes was attacked in the House of Commons by Sir Fletcher Norton and Samuel Martin and in the House of Lords by the earl of Sandwich (John Montagu) and William Warburton, the bishop of Gloucester. Two days later he fought a duel with Martin and was badly wounded in the side. Later it was revealed that Martin had practiced with his pistol all summer, making the "duel" tantamount to attempted murder. Wilkes had already fought a duel with Earl Talbot in 1762 and had been challenged in August 1763 by a Scottish officer. In December another Scots officer attempted to assassinate him. When the beleaguered Wilkes fled to France on 24 December, Churchill converted these events into the basis for *The Duellist,* a poem devoted to telling in octosyllabics a kind of Gothic horror story about the plot of Sandwich, Warburton, and Norton to assassinate Wilkes, using Martin as their instrument. Churchill may himself have been in France in late December and early January: he was reported as having been seen there, and an extant letter of his from Calais is dated January 15 but with no year.

In the final year of his life Churchill produced an extraordinary amount of very uneven poetry. In the three books of *Gotham* (March-August 1764) he constructs an imaginary kingdom with himself as monarch. Drawing on the English popular tradition of the "wise fools of Gotham," the poem enacts a rather carnivalesque critique of English society and the English monarchy. In Book III, especially, Churchill uses his concerns as king of Gotham to highlight the failings of George III as king of Britain:

What, to myself and to my State unjust,
Shall I from ministers take things on trust,
And, sinking low the credit of my throne,
Depend upon dependants of my own? . . .
Shall I, true puppet-like, be mock'd with State,
Have nothing but the Name of being great,
Attend at Councils, which I must not weigh,
Do, what they bid, and what they dictate say,
Enrob'd, and hoisted up into my chair,
Only to be a royal Cypher there?

Counseling the monarch to become an independent "patriot king," Churchill somewhat disingenuously contended that George III was not himself evil but had been misled by evil counselors.

In *The Candidate* (May 1764) Churchill took on one of those evil ministers, his former friend the earl of Sandwich. The occasion was Sandwich's campaign for the position of high steward of Cambridge University, and the attack focused primarily on Sandwich's notoriously libertine behavior and his responsibility for what Churchill saw as the failures of the administration of George Grenville. Churchill draws a portrait of Sandwich as the vice-ridden "Lothario," only to contrast this figure, in a typically relativistic way, with another figure called "Sandwich." "Lothario" symbolizes a corrupt aristocracy, while "Sandwich" supposedly stands for a virtuous one. But since the Lothario-Sandwich equation is clear, Churchill achieves a kind of doubling effect when he writes that if two such lords as Lothario were to be found, "Man would rather be a worm, / Than be a Lord," only to conclude that Nature, to mend the "ills which Error caus'd . . . having brought LOTHARIO forth to view, / To save her credit, brought forth SANDWICH too."

The antiaristocratic bias so evident in *The Candidate* forms the negative counterpoint to the positive theme of independence in Churchill's work and is particularly evident in his next poem, *The Farewell* (June 1764). Here it takes the form of a sustained attack on "titled upstarts" who purportedly aspire to an all-powerful oligarchy on the Venetian model. Structured as a dialogue between the patriot poet and an anonymous friend on the occasion of the poet's departing for India, the poem explores Churchill's attitudes toward patriotism and political corruption, and warns the British, "Let not, whatever other ills assail, / A damned ARISTOCRACY prevail." Churchill's next poem (after *Gotham*, Book III) was *The Times* (September 1764), an attack on homosexuals which marks a brief hiatus in Churchill's political poetry. But the antiaristocratic, proindependence theme recurs with renewed forcefulness in *Independence* (October

A series of engravings chronicling the feud between Churchill and Hogarth; clockwise from top left: Hogarth's The Bruiser, *depicting Churchill as a drunken bear; the anonymous* Bruiser Triumphant: A Farce, *showing Hogarth—as an ass—creating* The Bruiser *while Churchill and Churchill's political ally John Wilkes laugh at him; the anonymous* Boot & the Block-Head, *in which Churchill whips an elderly Hogarth*

1764), Churchill's personal manifesto and the last poem published during his lifetime.

Set in a celestial courtroom, *Independence* pits the real worth of an independent, self-made "Bard" against the unearned privilege of a hereditary "Lord" (ostensibly Lord Lyttelton [George Lyttelton]). It is particularly notable for Churchill's brilliant self-portrait as the "Bard," a man whose lumbering figure symbolically incorporates the awkward but powerful characteristics of the lower spectrum of English society:

> Broad were his shoulders, and from blade to blade,
> A H------- might at full length have laid;
> Vast were his Bones, his Muscles twisted strong,
> His Face was short, but broader than 'twas long,
> His Features, tho' by Nature they were large,
> Contentment had contriv'd to over charge
> And bury meaning, save that we might spy
> Sense Low'ring on the penthouse of his eye;
> His Arms were two twin Oaks, his legs so stout
> That they might bear a Mansion House about,
> Nor were They, look but at his body there,
> Design'd by Fate a much less weight to bear.
> O'er a brown *Cassock*, which had once been black,
> Which hung in tatters on his brawny back,
> A sight most strange, and aukward to behold
> He threw a covering of *Blue* and *Gold*.
> Just at that time of life, when Man by rule,
> The Fop laid down takes up a graver fool,
> He started up a Fop, and fond of show,
> Look'd like another HERCULES, turn'd *Beau*.

As Fop and Bruiser, stout laborer and contented "cit" (an eighteenth-century abbreviation for *citizen*, meaning a denizen of the City of London as opposed to Westminster or the West End and connoting vulgar materialism), Churchill subsumes in this portrait the humorous but threatening contradictions of the classes for which he fought and with whom he identified.

Despite his stance against public corruption and aristocratic luxury, Churchill throughout 1764 continued his life as a well-heeled libertine. Grossly overweight and probably sick with venereal disease, he had repeatedly put off a trip to Boulogne to visit Wilkes. On 22 October 1764 he finally departed, only to be struck down by fever after a week in France. He died on Sunday, 4 November, and was buried in the churchyard of St. Martin-le-Grand, Dover, beneath a slab inscribed with a line from *The Candidate*: "Life to the last enjoy'd, *here* Churchill lies."

Churchill left behind two fragments of poetry. *The Journey* (1765) is memorable chiefly for the haunting aptness of one of its lines: "I on my Journey all Alone proceed." The ironic "Dedication" to Warburton, the bishop of Gloucester, was intended for Churchill's collected *Sermons*, published posthumously in February 1765. Generally considered Churchill's most complex satire, the "Dedication" is characterized by an incessantly shifting tone and point of view as Churchill, in the role of a "humble" clergyman, mockingly compliments Warburton while at the same time disclaiming any desire for his patronage:

> Think not, a Thought unworthy thy great soul,
> Which pomps of this world never could controul,
> Which never offer'd up at Pow'r's vain shrine,
> Think not that Pomp and Pow'r can work on mine.
> 'Tis not thy Name, though that indeed is great,
> 'Tis not the tinsel trumpery of state,
> 'Tis not thy Title, Doctor tho' thou art,
> 'Tis not thy Mitre, which hath won my heart.

As the clergyman peels back the veneer to expose the virtues of the "inward man," the very trappings he discounts are shown to be Warburton's only reason for existing. In the final lines he finds the bishop posed high on the ladder of power, far above the multitude:

> Let GLOSTER well remember, how he rose,
> Nor turn his back on men who made him great;
> Let Him not, gorg'd with pow'r, drunk with state,
> Forget what once he was, tho' now so high;
> How low, how mean, and full as poor as I.

Churchill ends his poetic career in typical fashion, lashing and threatening the great in the name of the struggling common man.

Churchill's poetry was greatly admired in his own time and indisputably had its effect on the reflexive process poetry of a later admirer, Lord Byron. But because of its extremely topical and rather scurrilous nature, it fell into neglect during the nineteenth century. In the 1950s Douglas Grant's outstanding edition of the poems (1956), Edward H. Weatherly's publication of the correspondence with Wilkes (1954), and Wallace Cable Brown's biography (1953) made Churchill's poetry and its background more available to scholars. In the 1970s and 1980s studies by Lockwood, Smith, Vincent Carretta, and Lance Bertelsen have firmly placed Churchill's work in its poetic, historical, and social contexts.

Letters:

The Correspondence of John Wilkes and Charles Churchill, edited by Edward H. Weatherly (New York: Columbia University Press, 1954).

Churchill's grave in the churchyard of St. Martin-le-Grand, Dover

Biography:

Wallace Cable Brown, *Charles Churchill: Poet, Rake, and Rebel* (Lawrence: University of Kansas Press, 1953).

References:

Joseph M. Beatty, Jr., "The Battle of the Players and Poets, 1761-1776," *Modern Language Notes*, 35 (December 1919): 449-462;

Beatty, "The Political Satires of Charles Churchill," *Studies in Philology*, 16 (October 1919): 303-333;

Lance Bertelsen, "The Crab: An Unpublished Poem by Charles Churchill," *Philological Quarterly*, 63 (Spring 1984): 255-265;

Bertelsen, *The Nonsense Club: Literature and Popular Culture, 1749-1764* (Oxford: Clarendon Press, 1986);

T. E. Blom, "Eighteenth-Century Reflexive Process Poetry," *Eighteenth Century Studies*, 10 (Fall 1976): 52-72;

Wallace Cable Brown, "Charles Churchill and Criticism in Transition," *Journal of English and Germanic Philology*, 43 (April 1944): 163-169;

Brown, *The Triumph of Form: A Study in the Later Masters of the Heroic Couplet* (Chapel Hill: University of North Carolina Press, 1948);

Walter Bliss Carnochan, "Satire, Sublimity, and Sentiment: Theory and Practice in Post-Augustan Satire." *PMLA*, 85 (March 1970): 260-267;

Vincent Carretta, *The Snarling Muse: Verbal and Visual Political Satire From Pope to Churchill* (Philadelphia: University of Pennsylvania Press, 1983);

Thomas Davies, *Memoirs of the Life of David Gar-*

rick, 2 volumes (London: Printed for the author, 1780);

Alan S. Fisher, "The Stretching of Augustan Satire: Charles Churchill's 'Dedication to Warburton,'" *Journal of English and Germanic Philology*, 72 (July 1973): 360-377;

Morris Golden, "Sterility and Eminence in the Poetry of Charles Churchill," *Journal of English and Germanic Philology*, 66 (July 1967): 333-346;

Kenneth Hopkins, *Portraits in Satire* (London: Barrie, 1958);

Robert Lloyd, *The Poetical Works of Robert Lloyd, A.M., to Which Is Prefixed an Account of the Life and Writings of the Author, by William Kenrick, LL.D.*, 2 volumes (London: Printed for T. Evans, 1774);

Thomas Lockwood, *Post-Augustan Satire: Charles Churchill and Satirical Poetry, 1750-1800* (Seattle: University of Washington Press, 1979);

George Nobbe, *The North Briton: A Study in Political Propaganda* (New York: Columbia University Press, 1939);

Raymond J. Smith, *Charles Churchill* (Boston: Twayne, 1977);

Arthur Waldhorn, *Charles Churchill: Conservative Rebel* (New York: New York University Press, 1955);

Edward H. Weatherly, "Churchill's Literary Indebtedness to Pope," *Studies in Philology*, 43 (January 1946): 59-69;

Yvor Winters, *Forms of Discovery: Critical and Historical Essays on the Forms of the Short Poem in English* (Denver: Swallow, 1967).

Papers:

Letters from Charles Churchill to John Wilkes are in the British Library and the Guildhall Library, London; letters from Churchill to David Garrick are at the Pierpont Morgan Library and at Harvard University. Some of these letters contain drafts of verse and prose works—or portions thereof—by Churchill. Other letters are at the Boston Public Library, the Essex Record Office, the Folger Library, and Princeton University.

William Collins

(25 December 1721 - 12 June 1759)

John Sitter
Emory University

BOOKS: *Persian Eclogues: Written Originally for the Entertainment of the Ladies of Tauris. And Now First Translated, &c.* (London: Printed for J. Roberts, 1742); revised as *Oriental Eclogues: Written Originally for the Entertainment of the Ladies of Tauris. And Now Translated* (London: Printed for J. Payne 1757);

Verses Humbly Address'd to Sir Thomas Hanmer: On His Edition of Shakespear's Works. By a Gentleman of Oxford (London: Printed for M. Cooper, 1743); revised as *An Epistle: Addrest to Sir Thomas Hanmer, on His Edition of Shakespear's Works. The Second Edition. To Which Is Added a Song from the Cymbeline of the Same Author* (London: Printed for R. Dodsley, and M. Cooper, 1744);

Odes on Several Descriptive and Allegoric Subjects (London: Printed for A. Millar, 1747 [i.e., 1746]);

Ode Occasion'd by the Death of Mr. Thomson (Printed for R. Manby and H. S. Cox, 1749);

The Passions: An Ode. Written by Mr. Collins. Set to Musick by Doctor Hayes (Oxford, 1750);

An Ode on the Popular Superstitions of the Highlands of Scotland: Considered as the Subject of Poetry (London: Printed by J. Bell, 1788).

Editions and Collections: *The Poetical Works of Mr. William Collins: With Memoirs of the Author; and Observations on His Genius and Writings,* edited by John Langhorne (London: Printed for T. Becket & P. A. Dehondt, 1765);

The Works of the English Poets: With Prefaces, Biographical and Critical, edited by Samuel Johnson, volume 49 (London: Printed by J. Nichols for C. Bathurst et al., 1779);

The Poetical Works of William Collins: Containing His Miscellanies, Oriental Eclogues, Odes Descriptive and Allegorical, &c. &c. &c. With the Author's Life, and Observations, by Dr. Langhorne (Philadelphia: Printed for Thomas Dobson, 1788);

The Poetical Works of Mr. William Collins: With a Prefatory Essay, edited by Anna Laetitia Barbauld (London: Printed for T. Cadell, jun. and W. Davies, 1797);

The Poetical Works of William Collins: Collated with the Best Editions, volume 30 of *Works of the British Poets,* edited by Thomas Park (London: Sharpe, 1805);

The Poetical Works of William Collins, edited by Alexander Dyce (London: Pickering, 1827);

The Poetical Works of Goldsmith, Collins, and T. Warton, edited by G. Gilfillan (Edinburgh: Nichol, 1854);

The Poetical Works of William Collins, edited by W. Moy Thomas (London: Bell & Daldy, 1858);

The Poems of William Collins, edited by W. C. Bronson (Boston: Ginn, 1898);

The Poetical Works of Gray and Collins, edited by Austin Lane Poole (London: Oxford University Press, 1917); revised as *Gray and Collins: Poetical Works,* edited by Roger Lonsdale (Oxford: Oxford University Press, 1977);

The Poems of William Collins, edited by Edmund Blunden (London: Etchells & Macdonald, 1929);

William Collins: Drafts and Fragments of Verse, edited by J. S. Cunningham (Oxford: Clarendon Press, 1956);

Selected Poems of Thomas Gray and William Collins, edited by Arthur Johnston (London: Arnold, 1967);

The Poems of Thomas Gray, William Collins, and Oliver Goldsmith, edited by Lonsdale (London: Longman, 1969);

The Works of William Collins, edited by Richard Wendorf and Charles Ryskamp (Oxford: Clarendon Press, 1979).

William Collins had his first poem published when he was seventeen, his first book at twenty, his major volume a few days before turning twenty-five, and seems to have stopped writing poetry altogether by the time he was twenty-eight. For more than two centuries Collins has been praised as a poet of limited greatness.

William Collins

While critics have differed over the proportions, most have agreed with Samuel Johnson in seeing in Collins moments of "sublimity and splendor" and at the same time evidence of a mind "obstructed," by fragility of temperament or by the supposed hostility of his era to his gifts. His status has wavered between that of the "minor" and "major" poet. His modern biographer has called him "a minor poet, though first perhaps, among the minor poets who abounded between the age of [John] Dryden and the age of [William] Wordsworth." If some recent critics have regarded Collins as "major," William Hazlitt's judgment of 1818 still catches the usual emphasis on Collins's promise: "He is the only one of the minor poets of whom, if he had lived, it cannot be said that he might not have done the greatest things. The germ is there." Usually grouped with Thomas Gray, Collins has sometimes been ranked as the greater writer. For Henry Crabb Robinson, Gray "is not the Tithe of Collins," and Hazlitt finds in Collins a "much greater poetical genius"—a view Samuel Taylor Coleridge reportedly shared. Near the end of the nineteenth century Algernon Charles Swinburne declared even more emphatically that "the Muse gave birth to Collins; she did but give suck to Gray" (quoted by Richard Wendorf). If Collins's "range of light was perhaps the narrowest," it was "assuredly the highest of his generation." Collins's reputation is all the more remarkable for resting almost entirely on a slender volume of odes and probably for most readers on as few as three or four of its poems.

Collins's middle-aged father, also named William, and his mother, Elizabeth Martin Collins, had daughters aged seventeen and sixteen when their third and last child was born on 25 December 1721 in Chichester, a small cathedral town in Sussex. The elder William Collins, a hatter, served twice as mayor of Chichester and seems to have been moderately prosperous. He died in 1733, his wife in 1744. Little is known of the family or of Collins's earliest years. He may have gone to the Prebendal (charity) School in

Chichester Cathedral in the eighteenth century

Chichester or may have been tutored by local clergymen. In any case, he was sufficiently prepared to be sent to the eminent public school, Winchester College, at the age of twelve, in February 1734.

If a second-hand reminiscence is accurate, Collins turned at once to English as well as Latin composition. In his first year at Winchester he is supposed to have written a satiric poem, "Battle of the School Books." In 1736 he met Joseph Warton, who entered the school in that year, and the two seem to have influenced each other almost immediately; they would continue to do so for at least a decade. Their careers in print may have been launched together. A poem "cautiously" attributed to Collins by Richard Wensdorf and Charles Ryskamp appeared in the *Gentleman's Magazine* for January 1739. In October of that year the more striking (and more definitely attributed) "Sonnet" beginning "When *Phœbe* form'd a wanton smile" was published in the same magazine along with poems by Warton and another Winchester student.

Poetic ambition, a dominant theme in Collins's mature poetry, seems to have haunted him at Westminster. According to Warton, *Persian Eclogues,* published in 1742, had been completed two or three years earlier, while Collins was still at school. In addition to these four pastorals and the poem or poems published in the *Gentleman's Magazine*, Collins while at Winchester may have written his "Song: The Sentiments Borrowed from Shakespeare," which was not published until 1788. In their final year at the school Collins and Warton had a marble monument erected to the memory of Thomas Otway, the Restoration dramatist who had also attended Winchester and whom Collins would later invoke as a master of pathos in his "Ode to Pity" (1746). The act was presumably one of hopeful identification as well as piety. But the most vivid and poignant evidence of Collins's early ambition comes from his schoolmate William Smith, who reported that when he saw Collins "twelve or fourteen years" after Winchester, Collins immediately asked if Smith remembered a dream Collins had told him while the two were still at school. Collins had appeared "particularly depressed and melancholy" one morning; when asked why, he had said that he had been disturbed by a dream in which he climbed a tree, got near the top, and fell as a branch broke under him. An amused schoolfellow had asked "how he could possibly be affected by this common consequence of a school-boy adventure, when he did not pretend, even in imagination and sleep, to have received any hurt." A somber Collins replied: "the Tree was the Tree of Poetry."

Persian Eclogues, retitled *Oriental Eclogues* in 1757, is not much read today; Collins himself seems later to have been chagrined that the eclogues were more popular than his odes and, remarking on their lack of orientalism, to have dismissed them as "Irish eclogues." But if they were indeed substantially complete when Collins was seventeen, they mark a beginning of nearly Popean precocity. Collins's versification is less musical and his diction less sure than Alexander Pope's, but his use of imagery and incident is fresh and evocative. In a brief preface the supposed translator of the poems emphasizes the "rich and figurative" style of "Arabian or Persian" poetry and its "Elegancy and Wildness of Thought," for which the English genius is "as much too cold . . . as our Climate is for their Fruit and Spices." Most of what Collins knew about "Arabian" events and poetry came from Thomas Salmon's *Modern History* (1724-1739), but accuracy is less important than Collins's feeling that his Persian pose allows him more license than the usual English modes, especially that of the thoroughly neoclassicized pastoral.

Like Pope, Collins sets his poems at different times of day but not (presumably because of their Arabian locale) in different seasons. They range from seventy to eighty-six lines in length; only the fourth follows the form of Virgilian dialogue. The first, "Selim; or, The Shepherd's Moral," is a monologue exhorting the Persian maids to prize virtue over beauty; the second is the soliloquy of Hassan the camel-driver as he struggles alone across the burning desert; and the third tells the story of the exemplary union of Abra and Abbas, "rural maid" and "royal lover," respectively.

The morality of the first eclogue is conventional enough, but the poem is interesting in its anticipation of the mixture of protective and erotic concern that characterizes Collins's manner of addressing females—literal or personified—in his odes. In the beginning this manner works at the expense of conceptual clarity: the opening lines cast Selim as a poet inspired by Truth and desiring no praise "but hers alone," while thirty

PERSIAN

ECLOGUES.

Written originally for the

ENTERTAINMENT

OF THE

Ladies of *TAURIS.*

And now firſt tranſlated, *&c.*

Quod ſi non hic tantas fructus oſtenderetur, & ſi ex his ſtudiis delectatis ſola peteretur; tamen, ut opinor, hanc animi remiſſionem humaniſſimam ac liberaliſſimam judicaretis.

Cic. pro Arch. Poeta.

LONDON:

Printed for J. Roberts, in *Warwick-Lane.* 1742.

(Price Six-pence.)

Title page for Collins's first book of poetry, written while Collins was a student at Winchester School

lines later Collins says of Wisdom, also feminine, that "With Truth she wedded in the secret grove, / The fair-eyed Truth, and daughters blessed their love." The error was corrected in the second edition; but it is consistent with Collins's tendency to address several females in his poems, expressing concern on the part of the male speaker for their welfare, chastity, triumphant marriage, and offspring, all at once.

"Hassan; or, The Camel-Driver" is the most original and haunting of the eclogues. The speaker's fear of death as he moves "in silent Horror o'er the boundless Waste" underscores both his isolation and the sultry sublimity of the sandscape. Since Hassan has left the "green Delights" of home for the sake of "far-fatiguing Trade," the "unrelenting Rage" of his present surroundings expresses the "Ruin" of greed and commerce. His eventual decision to return to his home and the "tender Zara" again suggests a pattern of the later poetry in which a worldly ambition is renounced in favor of something more poetically pure.

The potential conflict between political and poetic life surfaces in the fourth eclogue, "Agib and Secander; or, The Fugitives." Set at midnight on a Circassian mountain, the poem dramatizes the flight of two shepherds from an army of invading Tartars, while their own "*Persian* Lord" remains "far off in thoughtless Indolence," unsuited to the role of protector. The poem closes with the encroaching "shriller Shriek, and nearer Fires" of the enemy and the pastoral poets' departure from their "spicy Groves." This poem may have helped shape Joseph Warton's younger brother Thomas's *Five Pastoral Eclogues* (1745), the "Scenes of which are Suppos'd to lie among the Shepherds, oppress'd by the War in Germany," and it anticipates the clashing of poets and public power in midcentury poems such as Gray's "The Bard" (1757).

Whether Collins significantly revised *Persian Eclogues* during his first two years at Oxford is not known. He and Joseph Warton had gone there in 1740, though not to New College nor with the fellowships that they must have expected. Collins and Warton had been placed at the top of the list of students graduating from Winchester, but no vacancy occurred at New College in their year. Instead, Collins entered Queens College and Warton enrolled at Oriel College. In July 1741 Colllins was admitted as a Demy (a sort of half-pay fellow) to Magdalen. According to John Langhorne (who published the first real edition of Collins's work in 1765), during Collins's initial year at Oxford he was "at once distinguished for genius and indolence," his written exercises giving evidence of both traits, "when he could be prevailed upon to write." Langhorne speculates that Collins, high-minded and eager, was disillusioned by a university still wearing the "fetters of logic and Aristotle." Little record exists of Collins's life at Oxford, but one anecdote gives a portrait of a young man of learning, grace, and wit. An afternoon conversation in Collins's rooms was interrupted by the quarrelsome visit of another student, who soon kicked the tea table across the room. According to Gilbert White, "our poet, tho' of a warm temper, was so confounded at the unexpected downfall, and so astonished at the unmerited insult, that he took no notice of the aggressor, but getting up from his chair calmly, he began picking up the slices of bread and butter, and the fragments of his china, repeating very slowly, 'Invenias etiam disiecti membra poetae.' " The droll quotation from Horace—"even when he is dismembered, you would find the limbs of the poet"—suggests not only Collins's resourcefulness but, like the troubling dream earlier, his strong sense of literary identity.

The major new work written by Collins while at Oxford was *Verses Humbly Address'd to Sir Thomas Hanmer: On His Edition of Shakespear's Works,* published in December 1743. Like all of Collins's work to this point, the poem appeared anonymously. A second edition the following May, which also included "A Song from Shakespear's Cymbeline," was the first publication to bear the author's name. The second version also eliminates some of the praise of Hanmer, whose minor if handsome edition was published by the Clarendon Press, and of Oxford; probably by then Collins had given up hopes of support by either. The 148-line epistle surveys the "progress" of drama from ancient Athens to Elizabethan England. Collins's critical account is competent rather than original; two emphases, however, are striking. He immediately characterizes pity as the primary power of drama, just as he would give it first place later in his book of odes. For Collins, Euripides sums up Greek drama; watching his plays, "With kind Concern our pitying Eyes o'erflow, / Trace the sad Tale and own another's Woe." Secondly, in his praise of Shakespearean sympathy Collins is soon led to stress the visual "fancy" of the playwright; Collins imagines, and to some extent renders, a series of "wond'rous Draughts" of pictures based on William Shakespeare's scenes.

Collins's responsiveness to Shakespearean moments as well as to his style informs "A Song from Shakespear's 'Cymbeline" (identified in the subtitle as "Sung by Guider[i]us and Arviragus over Fidele, suppos'd to be Dead"). Like the later odes that allude to Edmund Spenser, Shakespeare, and John Milton, this song is both an act of piety toward one of the great poetic masters and a gesture of ambition, even competition. Collins's poem asks to be read alongside Shakespeare's "Fear no more the heat o' th' sun," and remarkably it does not wither in that light. It contains no lines so memorable as "Golden lads and girls all must, / As chimney-sweepers, turn to dust," but Collins attains sureness in the final stanza: "Each lonely Scene shall thee restore, / For thee the Tear be duly shed: / Belov'd, till

Life could charm no more; / And mourn'd till Pity's self be dead." Laconic simplicity is not a common virtue of eighteenth-century elegiac writing; Collins's successful Shakespearean imitation anticipates the striking understatement of one of his best-known poems, the "Ode, Written in the Beginning of the Year 1746" ("How sleep the Brave").

Collins was awarded the B.A. degree in November 1743 and probably left Oxford in the early months of the next year. He went to London, according to Samuel Johnson, as a "literary adventurer with many projects in his head, and very little money in his pocket." A London acquaintance, John Ragsdale, recalled that shortly after arriving in London Collins called on an older (and wealthier) cousin, George Payne. Collins was "gaily dresst, and with a feather in his hat." The graver relative "told him his appearance was by no means that of a young man who had not a single guinea to call his own." Since he at any rate had not many guineas to call his own, Collins is said to have concealed his resentment from Payne but to have let others know that "he thought him a d----d fellow." As Ragsdale tells it, Collins's "frequent demands for a supply obliged Mr. Payne to tell him he must pursue some other line of life.... This resourse being stopped, forced him to set about some work of which his 'History of the Revival of Learning' was the first."

As Johnson says, Collins "designed many works; but his great fault was irresolution, or the frequent calls of immediate necessity broke his schemes and suffered him to pursue no settled interest." Of the intellectual history of the Renaissance that Collins planned—and published proposals for—Johnson supposes that "probably not a page" of it "was ever written." Word of Collins's project seems to have spread quickly and optimistically enough for an Irish journal to announce in December 1744 that "A Review of the Advancement of Learning from 1300 to 1521 by Wm. Collins" had been published in London. Johnson's guess seems to have been closer to the truth. Collins's interest in the project continued for at least the rest of the decade, however, and he may have made some progress on it.

Although his poverty is sometimes exaggerated, London must have been as difficult for Collins as Johnson suggests in speaking of "immediate necessity" as a hindrance to his many projects: "A man doubtful of his dinner, or trembling at a creditor, is not much disposed to abstracted meditation, or remote inquiries." When his mother died in 1744 Collins was left one-third of the family property, but the will was not executed until the following year and there was little clear inheritance. Writing from London in July 1744, John Mulso (a classmate of Collins's at Winchester) tells a mutual friend that Collins is "entirely an Author, & hardly speaks out of Rule." If the latter phrase suggests amusement at Collins's literary manner, the former implies that Collins had declared his intention to live by his pen. But it appears that before the summer was out he thought of entering the clergy. He petitioned Charles Lennox, Duke of Richmond, for a curacy, apparently obtained it, and then declined the position. Whether the decision was based on his views of religion or of rustication is not known, but it does appear that Collins thought again, in the upheaval of 1745, of joining the Church, this time as an army chaplain. By that point he had been arrested at least once for a debt owed to the landlady of his Soho residence; while this was not an unusual event in the career of a young gentleman, Collins must have become increasingly aware that neither history nor poetry would yield quick rewards.

Like many aspiring authors, Collins seems to have hoped for success as a playwright. Johnson, who probably knew Collins by 1745 and who had dramatic ambitions of his own, remarked that Collins "planned several tragedies but he only planned them." Langhorne says that Collins "turned his thoughts to the drama, and proceeded so far towards a tragedy—as to become acquainted with the manager." While he did little if any actual dramatic writing, he seems to have acquired something of a theatrical reputation. "He was an acceptable companion everywhere," Ragsdale recalled, "and among the gentlemen who loved him for a genius, I may reckon the Doctors Armstrong, Barrowby, and Hill, Messrs. Quin, Garrick, and Foote, who frequently took his opinion on their pieces before they were seen by the public.... From his knowledge of Garrick, he had liberty of the scenes and green-room, where he made diverting observations on the vanity and false consequence of that class of people; and his manner of relating them to his particular friends was extremely entertaining." Whether his association with David Garrick might also have helped him have a play performed was never put to the test.

Collins's interest in the theater, as the verse epistle to Hanmer indicates, was consistently historical and poetic as well as practical. Another of his projects at this time, a translation and edition of Aristotle's *Poetics,* seems to have progressed beyond pure abstraction. Johnson seems to be referring to late 1745 or early 1746 when he recalls finding Collins "immured by a bailiff that was prowling in the street." Perhaps with Johnson himself as intermediary, "recourse was had to the booksellers, who, on the credit of a translation of Aristotle's *Poetics,* which he engaged to write with a large commentary, advanced as much money as enabled him to escape into the country." (In the preface to Robert Dodsley's *The Preceptor,* published in 1748, Johnson referred to the work as "soon to be published.") Twice during this period Collins traveled to Flanders to seek the help of his uncle, Colonel Edmund Martin, who is reported not to have encouraged Collins to the soldier's life.

As they did for Henry Fielding's Tom Jones, the events of 1745 seem to have quickened Collins's interest in the army. The first of his odes to be published was "Ode, to a Lady on the Death of Colonel Ross in the Action of Fontenoy"; dated May 1745, it appeared the next year in Mark Akenside's *Museum.* The other explicitly martial poem, "Ode, Written in the Beginning of the Year 1746" ("How sleep the Brave"), apparently commemorates those who had died that January at the Battle of Falkirk. In light of the complexity of attitude in what are commonly referred to as Collins's "patriotic odes," it would be interesting to know more about the proportions of expediency and desire in his consideration of the army and Church as possible careers. Indeed, one would like to find out much more than is now discoverable about Collins's day-today life during his great creative period, the year or year and a half in which he wrote the dozen poems that comprise *Odes on Several Descriptive and Allegoric Subjects* (1746).

It is known that he was, if not poor, financially insecure and at least occasionally embarrassed. It is known that he started or planned a history, a translation, and some plays, but that the young man who was said two years earlier to be "entirely an author" was casting about as late as the summer of 1746 for more reliable employment. Only a single event of this year suggests that before its end the author of eclogues, an epistle, and some occasional poems would have an ambitious volume of lyrics published. Collins met his friend from Winchester and Oxford, Joseph Warton, in late May at the Guildford Races in Surrey. Soon after, Joseph wrote to Thomas Warton that he and Collins had exchanged odes there (presumably while other young men were trading wagers), and "being both in very high spirits we took courage, resolved to join our forces, and to publish them immediately." This collaborative volume was to have included one of Thomas's odes as well. Apparently Collins was to approach the bookseller, for Joseph reports that "Collins is not to publish the Odes unless he gets ten guineas for them."

The collaborative volume never came into being. Instead, Joseph Warton's *Odes on Various Subjects* was published on 4 December 1746 and Collins's *Odes on Several Descriptive and Allegoric Subjects* on 20 December, five days before his twenty-fifth birthday. (Presumably because of its late December publication, the edition is dated 1747.) It is one of the familiar ironies of literary history that the now nearly forgotten odes of Warton were published in quarto by the leading bookseller, Robert Dodsley, who brought out a second edition just a month later, while those of Collins appeared in octavo under the less prestigious imprint of Andrew Millar and nearly disappeared. "It dropped, a still-born immortal, from the press," in Swinburne's high phrase, and evidently without arousing the slightest suspicion of a special destiny. One of the few early—indeed immediate—readers was Gray, who told a correspondent on 27 December 1746 that "it is odd enough, but each is the half of a considerable Man, & one the Counter-Part of the other. The first [Warton] has but little Invention, very poetical choice of Expression, & a good Ear. The second, a fine Fancy, model'd upon the Antique, a bad Ear, great variety of Words, & Images with no Choice at all. They both deserve to last some Years, but will not." For the next two decades Collins's volume would go virtually unnoticed.

With the exception of two commemorative poems, all of the odes in the book are addressed to personified abstractions. The sequence of the poems has usually been felt to be significant, although no critical consensus has been reached. The order of the poems in the volume—"Ode to Pity," "Ode to Fear," "Ode to Simplicity," "Ode on the Poetical Character," "Ode, Written in the Beginning of the Year 1746," "Ode to Mercy," "Ode to Liberty," "Ode, to a Lady on the Death of Colonel Ross in Action of Fontenoy," "Ode to Evening," "Ode to Peace," "The Manners. An Ode," "The Passions. An Ode for Music"—is not the order of composition. The ode on the death

Recto and verso of a draft for Collins's verse epistle to the publisher Jacob Tonson, probably written between spring 1744 and December 1746 (Trinity College, Oxford). This manuscript was discovered among Joseph Warton's papers in the Trinity College Library; the poem was first published in 1956.

Dealt from thy press the ~~Distant Lovers~~ Maid of Elder days ~~ages~~
Lisp'd the soft lines to Sacharissa's praise
Or the gay Youth for livelier Spirits known
By Cowleys pointed thought improv'd his own
Ev'n all the Easy Sons of Song who gain'd
a Poets Name when Charles and Pleasure reign'd
~~All~~ All from thy Race a lasting praise denied
Not ~~from~~ by ~~themselves~~ their toil the careless Bards surviv'd
You wisely sav'd the Race who gay
But sought to wear the Myrtles of a day
~~Ah Soft~~ Bare Elms (Let Song Contra join)
You more than all Enjoy Each flowing line
Your's is the prize whate'er their merit claim
Heir of their Verse and guardian of their Fame!

moor
Luxury and Love

of Ross was dated May 1745 in its original subtitle and was first published in the summer of 1746, and there is no reason not to assume that the poem that begins "How sleep the Brave" was written, as its title declares, in the "beginning" of 1746. These two occasional poems may well be the earliest of Collins's odes. (In May, Collins showed Joseph Warton "some of " his odes, but Warton specifically mentions only the ode on the death of Ross.) If they were written before a volume was in the works, it appears that the idea of a book of odes as abstractly "allegoric" as the rest of the poems are did not begin to form until sometime after January 1746. Thus the difficulty critics have in discovering a comprehensive scheme for the volume might simply derive from the fact that Collins included the earlier poems not because they were part of his plan but because they were his. On the other hand, a closer consideration of the volume may suggest a plausible case for their thematic and sequential relevance to the whole.

The presence of the odes to Pity and Fear at the beginning of the volume links *Odes on Several Descriptive and Allegoric Subjects* to Collins's interest in Aristotle's *Poetics,* where the arousal of those two emotions is at the heart of the tragedy, and to Collins's own ambition of writing tragedy. The two poems also allude, like many others of his and his contemporaries, to Milton's *L'Allegro* (1632) and *Il Penseroso* (1632). Like Milton's poems to mirth and melancholy, they address personified states of feeling, declare the speaker's allegiance to each in turn, provide an occasion for a display of incidents or icons associated with the feeling, and end with a resolution or wish to dwell henceforth with the feminine personification as "her" votary and chosen poet. The "Ode to Pity" also looks forward to John Keats's "Ode to Psyche" (1820) in its self-conscious construction of a temple to the newly promoted deity, a shrine which stands for the poem itself. Several of Collins's odes are "metapoetic" in the double sense that they are *about* poetry—specifying its conditions and qualities—and that they call attention to the act of fiction-making or mythopoesis. The third poem in the volume, "Ode to Simplicity," is about poetry primarily in the first sense, especially about the need for apparent naturalness in writing. But the fourth poem, "Ode on the Poetical Character," is both a statement and a powerful enactment of the powers of imagination. It is Collins's most difficult, most discussed, and certainly most ambitious work.

Its difficulty and ambition were acknowledged in the eighteenth century by admiring and skeptical readers. Langhorne considered it "so infinitely abstracted" that it would appeal only to the "few readers" able to "penetrate the high mysteries of inspired fancy, and to pursue the loftiest flights of enthusiastic imagination." But Collins's editor of 1797, Anna Laetitia Aikin Barbauld, found the poem's mingling of "fancy" and religious "mystery" shocking; the section of the poem in which God is imagined as having retired "alone" with Fancy and "placed her on his Saphire Throne" was a "strange and by no means reverential fiction concerning the Divine Being." Modern readers do not usually like to sound so easily shocked, but Mrs. Barbauld is essentially right. Collins is not very reverential toward the male deity, nor even very much concerned with him. Instead, he extends reverence and concern to the poem's new female deity, Fancy, who becomes God's inspiration, quasi-sexual partner, and cocreator.

Perhaps the main critical controversy concerns the identity of the offspring of this "abstracted" union: from it, "Thou, Thou rich-haired Youth of Morn, / And all thy subject Life was born!" A majority of critics identify the Youth as the sun, but several have argued that he is the Poet (as archetypal figure). There is good reason to regard the Youth as both sun and poet, however, since allusions to Apollo suggest both and since the poem consistently fuses ideas of poetic and cosmic creation. Both sun and poet bring a "subject Life" into being, just as Milton later in the poem is imagined as the Godlike creator of another Eden. The tone of the final section, in which Milton's "Scene" is imagined now as "curtain'd close . . . from ev'ry future View," is a second source of ambiguity. Many readers find the conclusion deeply pessimistic, an assertion that the great heights of poetic sublimity can no longer be attained. But one can also read the poem as a more playful and confident appropriation of the poetic tradition and of the "poetical character" by its latest heir, Collins himself. Whatever the poem suggests about the future of English poetry, or of its author's place, it dramatizes a daring conception of imagination and implies that the true "poetical character" leads to a highly demanding voice and vision.

The next four odes are often regarded as a "patriotic" group of poems on political topics, contrasting with the four more privately "poetic" odes that open the volume. In this view the fifth and eighth poems, "Ode, Written in the Beginning of the Year 1746" and "Ode, to a Lady on the Death of Colonel Ross in the Action of Fontenoy," are explicitly public and occasional poems framing two others, "Ode to Mercy" and "Ode to Liberty," that are also directly connected, despite their reliance on personifications, to the military and political anxieties of 1745 and 1746. This view is somewhat plausible, but it would be more compelling if there were agreement about the last four poems comprising a third unified group. The ninth poem, however, the lovely and unrhymed "Ode to Evening," is one of Collins's most intensely private apostrophes, while the tenth, "Ode to Peace," returns to national concerns and a more oratorical style. Oliver Sigworth sensibly warns against seeking perfect unity in the volume with the reminder that *Odes on Several Descriptive and Allegoric Subjects* "is a book of poems, not a poem." But perhaps the volume is unified around the implied ideal figure of the poet, who moves from the role of primarily private aspirant in the first group of poems to that of public celebrant in the second group, and then shows in the third group that the visionary solitude courted by Evening's votary also nurtures the imagination of the prophet of British peace. In any case, the eleventh poem, "The Manners. An Ode," and the last, "The Passions. An Ode for Music" return to the subject of requisites for art but at the same time assert the need for a more worldly theater for the poet and a less subjective view of the passions than the opening poems suggested.

Collins may have placed "The Passions" last because he thought it not only thematically conclusive but also his best work. Langhorne declared it "the finest ode in the English language." With its parade of painterly personifications, celebration of musical power, and several shifts of rhythm and mood, the poem is a tour de force and was indeed set to music in 1750 and at least twice more in the eighteenth century. It was popular as a set piece for declamation into the nineteenth century; in Charles Dickens's *Great Expectations* (1860-1861) Mr. Wopsle impresses the schoolboys every term with his harrowing recitations of Marc Antony's oration and Collins's ode. Declamatory sublimity seems somewhat too self-conscious today, however, and accordingly two of Collins's quieter poems, "Ode to Evening" and "Ode, Written in the Beginning of the Year 1746" ("How sleep the Brave") are modern favorites. Collins is not Keats, but "Ode to Evening" is one of the few poems that it makes sense to regard as a significant predecessor of the great ode "To Autumn" (1820).

Collins wrote two important poems after the publication of *Odes on Several Descriptive and Allegoric Subjects*. "Ode Occasion'd by the Death of Mr. Thomson" (which begins "In yonder Grave a Druid lies") was published in June 1749. The second was left incomplete in manuscript, where it is headed simply "Ode to a Friend on his Return &c"; it is better known today by the title assigned to it when it was published in 1788, long after Collins's death, as *An Ode on the Popular Superstitions of the Highlands of Scotland: Considered as the Subject of Poetry*. Both works were prompted by literary friendships. Collins became acquainted with James Thomson in 1747 (if not earlier), when he moved the short distance from London to Richmond, where Thomson resided from 1736 until his death in August 1748. How well the two poets knew each other is unclear; three stanzas from Thomson's *Castle of Indolence* (1748) describing a dreamy poet whose "glorious systems" and "great ideas" were never written down were once believed to describe Collins but are now taken to refer to a lesser writer. Whatever their degree of intimacy, Collins's respect for Thomson as "Meek Nature's Child" sustains the poem's eleven understated quatrains. William Wordsworth would recall one of these stanzas—"REMEMBRANCE oft shall haunt the Shore / When THAMES in Summer-wreaths is drest, / And oft suspend the dashing Oar / To bid his gentle Spirit rest!"—with allusive piety in his early "Remembrance of Collins, Composed upon the Thames near Richmond" (1798):

> Now let us, as we float along,
> For *him* suspend the dashing oar;
> And pray that never child of song
> May know that Poet's sorrows more.

Ode on the Popular Superstitions of the Highlands of Scotland was also "occasioned," this time by the departure of a new friend, John Home, the aspiring Scottish playwright whose successful *Douglas* (1756) was still a few years in the future. Collins was introduced to Home by Thomas Barrow, a fellow native of Chichester, probably in November 1749. The poem is usually dated from December of that year to January 1750. Although unfinished, it is Collins's longest work, consisting of 194 lines with apparently 25 lines missing

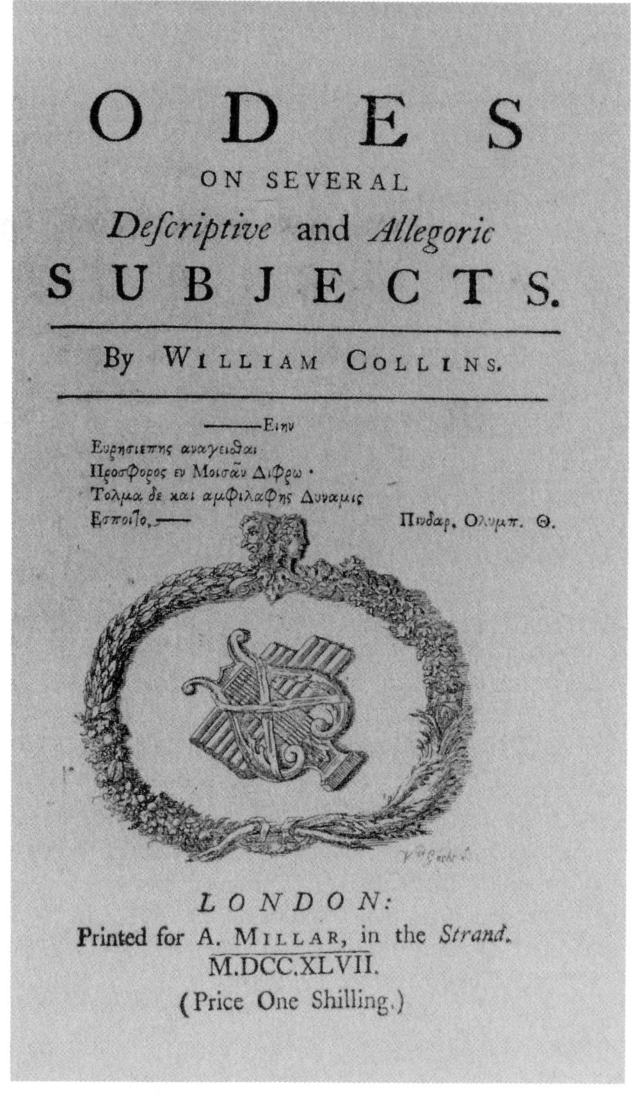

ODES
ON SEVERAL
Descriptive and *Allegoric*
SUBJECTS.

By WILLIAM COLLINS.

——Ειην
Ευρησιεπης αναγειωθαι
Προσφορος εν Μοισᾶν Διφρω·
Τολμα δε και αμφιλαφης Δυναμις
Εσποιτο.—— Πινδαρ. Ολυμπ. Θ.

LONDON:
Printed for A. MILLAR, in the *Strand*.
M.DCC.XLVII.
(Price One Shilling.)

Title page for Collins's collection of lyric poems, originally planned as a collaboration with Joseph Warton

from the middle stanzas. Whether the poem was motivated more by friendship or by reading is debatable. Collins had read two works by Martin Martin describing the "primitive" life in the remoter parts of Scotland, *A Description of the Western Islands of Scotland* (1703) and *A Voyage to St. Kilda* (1749; originally published in 1698 as *A Late Voyage to St. Kilda*), and he uses both works for many of the poem's details.

Collins addresses Home as a writer who has an enviably vital folk tradition to draw upon:

> Fresh to that soil thou turn'st, whose every Vale
> Shall prompt the Poet, and his Song demand;
> To Thee thy copious Subjects ne'er shall fail
> Thou need'st but take the Pencil to thy Hand
> And paint what all believe who own thy Genial Land.

The word *believe* seems to get special emphasis: because the "rural faith" in such things as fairies, "kelpies" (water spirits), and the clairvoyant premonitions known as "second sight" remains intact in the Scottish countryside, Home can use this material as more than decorative fiction. Living in a simpler society than England, Home may be able to recapture the power of a Renaissance poet like Torquato Tasso, "whose undoubting Mind / Believ'd the Magic Wonders which He sung!"

Despite being unfinished, Collins's last ode attains a mature "finish" and easy range surpassing most of the poems of three years earlier. His late success in combining urbanity and ardor again suggests a Keatsian parallel, in this case with the new narrative voice of *Lamia* (1820). Collins's productivity was much less than Keats's and his development less dramatic. But real growth is just unmistakable enough to underscore Hazlitt's at least tentative belief in Collins's rare capacity, the conviction that "if he had lived, it cannot be said that he might not have done the greatest things." In a sense, however, Collins the poet did not live after this point. One of his two surviving letters dates from November 1750, and a fragment of verse mentioned in it, "Music of the Grecian Theatre," may also have been composed that late. Otherwise, Collins seems to have written little or nothing during his final decade, which was characterized by physical and mental debility.

Collins's illness or illnesses from 1751 on would be irrelevant to the study of his poetry were it not that a myth of the "mad poet" has influenced Collins criticism ever since his day. The most judicious discussion of the sparse facts and the history of fanciful speculation wrought upon them is Richard Wendorf's chapter " 'Poor Collins' Reconsidered" in his *William Collins and Eighteenth-Century English Poets* (1981). All that is known is that Collins was in poor physical health in the early 1750s, traveled to Bath and to France sometime between 1751 and 1754 in quest of improvement, was confined in a private madhouse in Chelsea for part of 1754, and then was taken to Chichester by his sister Anne, who cared for him until his death on 12 June 1759. Johnson's last glimpse of Collins, probably in 1754, survives as one of the most evocative sketches in *The Lives of the Most Eminent English Poets* (1781). "After his return from France, the writer of this character paid him a visit at Islington, where he was waiting for his sister, whom he had directed to meet him: there was then nothing of disorder discernible in his mind by any but himself; but he had withdrawn from study, and travelled with no other book than an English Testament, such as children carry to the school: when his friend took it into his hand, out of curiosity to see what companion a man of letters had chosen, 'I have but one book,' said Collins, 'but that is the best.' "

In considering the confusing array of speculation since the eighteenth century concerning the nature of Collins's mental illness, Johnson's careful summary should be kept in mind: "His disorder was not alienation of mind, but general laxity and feebleness, a deficiency rather of his vital than intellectual powers. What he spoke wanted neither judgment nor spirit; but a few minutes exhausted him, so that he was forced to rest upon the couch, till a short cessation restored his powers, and he was again able to talk with his former vigour." Given the chronology of Collins's illness and its nature according to the few extant descriptions of it, it makes little sense to continue to read his achievement of the 1740s as tinctured by his debility in the 1750s; but Romantic notions of tragic or "doomed" artists have allowed this critical habit to yield only slowly to less stereotypic readings of the poems.

Collins left fewer than two thousand lines of poetry behind, including unfinished works, and probably only a few hundred lines are reread by most students of his poetry today. Nonetheless, his achievement and distinction are unmistakable. In an era when personification was sometimes a mechanical habit, Collins's poetry of apostrophe attains visionary authenticity. Whether addressing Evening with fine solicitude or Liberty with patriotic concern, Collins draws the reader into a shared invocation and act of creation. His odes imply in the eighteenth century a program for modern poetic imagination that is similar to Wallace Stevens's requisites for it in *Notes toward a Supreme Fiction* (1942): it must be abstract, it must change, it must give pleasure. Happily, for many more than the "some years" Gray thought Collins's *Odes on Several Descriptive and Allegoric Subjects* deserved; readers have greeted the call of his abstractly sensuous poetry.

Bibliographies:

The Poems of William Collins, edited by W. C. Bronson (Boston: Ginn, 1898), pp. lxxix-lxxxv;

Iolo A. Williams, *Seven Eighteenth-Century Bibliographies* (London: Dulau, 1924).

Biography:

P. L. Carver, *The Life of a Poet: A Biographical Sketch of William Collins* (London: Sidgwick & Jackson, 1967).

References:

Harold Bloom, "From Topos to Trope, from Sensibility to Romanticism: Collins's 'Ode to Fear,' " in *Studies in Eighteenth-Century British Art and Aesthetics,* edited by Ralph Cohen (Berkeley: University of California Press, 1985), pp. 182-203;

Paul H. Fry, *The Poet's Calling in the English Ode* (New Haven: Yale University Press, 1980);

H. W. Garrod, *Collins* (Oxford: Clarendon Press, 1928);

Jean H. Hagstrum, *The Sister Arts: The Tradition of Literary Pictorialism from Dryden to Gray* (Chicago: University of Chicago Press, 1958), pp. 268-286;

Janice Haney-Peritz, " 'In Quest of Mistaken Beauties': Allegorical Indeterminacy in Collins' Poetry," *ELH,* 48 (Winter 1981): 732-756;

William Hazlitt, *Lectures on the English Poets* (London: Taylor & Hessey, 1818);

R. Holt-White, ed., *The Letters to Gilbert White of Selbourne from His Intimate Friend and Contemporary the Rev. John Mulso* (London: Porter, 1907), p. 3;

Wallace Jackson, *The Probable and the Marvelous: Blake, Wordsworth, and the Eighteenth-Century Critical Tradition* (Athens: University of Georgia Press, 1978);

Samuel Johnson, "Collins," in his *The Lives of the Most Eminent English Poets,* 4 volumes (London: Printed for C. Bathurst and others, 1781), IV: 321-331;

Alan D. McKillop, "Collins's *Ode to Evening*—Background and Structure," *Tennessee Studies in Literature,* 5 (1960): 73-83;

McKillop, "The Romanticism of William Collins," *Studies in Philology,* 20 (January 1923): 1-16;

Edith Morely, ed., *The Correspondence of Henry Crabb Robinson with the Wordsworth Circle,* 2 volumes (Oxford: Clarendon Press, 1927), I: 45;

Ricardo Quintana, "The Scheme of Collins's *Odes on Several . . . Subjects,*" in *Restoration and Eighteenth-Century Literature: Essays in Honor of Alan Dugald McKillop,* edited by Carroll Camden (Chicago: University of Chicago Press, 1963), pp. 371-380;

Paul S. Sherwin, *Precious Bane: Collins and the Miltonic Legacy* (Austin: University of Texas Press, 1977);

G. N. Shuster, *The English Ode from Milton to Keats* (New York: Columbia University Press, 1940);

Oliver F. Sigworth, *William Collins* (New York: Twayne, 1965);

John Sitter, *Literary Loneliness in Mid-Eighteenth-Century England* (Ithaca, N.Y.: Cornell University Press, 1982);

Patricia Meyer Spacks, "The Eighteenth-Century Collins," *Modern Language Quarterly,* 44 (March 1983): 3-22;

Spacks, *The Insistence of Horror: Aspects of the Supernatural in Eighteenth-Century Poetry* (Cambridge, Mass.: Harvard University Press, 1962);

Spacks, *The Poetry of Vision: Five Eighteenth-Century Poets* (Cambridge, Mass.: Harvard University Press, 1967);

Earl R. Wasserman, "Collins' 'Ode on the Poetical Character,' " *ELH,* 34 (March 1967): 92-115;

Richard Wendorf, *William Collins and Eighteenth-Century English Poetry* (Minneapolis: University of Minnesota Press, 1981);

A. S. P. Woodhouse, "The Poetry of Collins Reconsidered," in *From Sensibility to Romanticism: Essays Presented to Frederick A. Pottle,* edited by F. W. Hilles and Harold Bloom (New York: Oxford University Press, 1965), pp. 93-137.

Papers:

Few of William Collins's manuscripts survive. Those edited by J. S. Cunningham in *William Collins: Drafts and Fragments of Verse* (1956) are part of the Trinity College Warton papers, now housed in the Bodleian Library, Oxford University. A manuscript for *An Ode on the Popular Superstitions of the Highlands of Scotland: Considered as the Subject of Poetry* (1788), discovered in 1967, is also in the Bodleian. The single known copy of a letter by Collins (to John Gilbert Cooper) is in the British Library.

William Cowper

(15 November 1731 - 25 April 1800)

Vincent Newey
University of Leicester

See also the Cowper entry in *DLB 104: British Prose Writers, 1660-1800*.

BOOKS: *Olney Hymns, in Three Books*, by Cowper and John Newton (London: Printed and sold by W. Oliver, sold also by J. Buckland and J. Johnson, 1779; New York, 1787);

Anti-Thelyphthora: A Tale, in Verse (London: Printed for J. Johnson, 1781);

Poems by William Cowper, of the Inner Temple, Esq. (London: Printed for J. Johnson, 1782);

The Task: A Poem, in Six Books. By William Cowper, of the Inner Temple, Esq.... To Which Are Added, by the Same Author, An Epistle to Joseph Hill, Esq. Tirocinium, or a Review of Schools, and the History of John Gilpin (London: Printed for J. Johnson, 1785);

Poems by William Cowper, 2 volumes (London: Printed for J. Johnson, 1786; enlarged, 1794-1795; enlarged, 1798; enlarged, 1800);

The Task: A Poem. In Six Books. To Which Is Added, Tirocinium: Or, A Review of Schools. A New Edition (Philadelphia: Printed for Thomas Dobson, 1787);

Proposals for Printing, by Subscription, a New Translation of the Iliad and Odyssey of Homer into Blank Verse (London: Printed for J. Johnson, J. Walter, and J. Debrett, 1791);

Poems (Salem, Mass.: Printed by Thomas C. Cushing, for D. West, Marlborough-Street, and E. Larkin Jun., Cornhill, Boston, 1792);

Poems: I. On the Receipt of My Mother's Picture. II. The Dog and the Water-Lily (London: Printed for J. Johnson, 1798);

Adelphi: A Sketch of the Character, and an Account of the Last Illness, of the Late Rev. John Cowper ... Written by His Brother (London: Printed by C. Whittingham, sold by T. Williams, 1802; Andover, Mass.: Printed by Flagg and Gould for the New England Tract Society, 1814);

Memoir of the Early Life of William Cowper, Esq. Written by Himself (London: Printed for R. Edwards, 1816; Philadelphia: Published by Edward Earle, printed by T. H. Palmer, 1816); also published as *Memoirs of the Most Remarkable and Interesting Parts of the Life of William Cowper, Esq. of the Inner Temple* (London: Printed for the editor and sold by E. Cox and Son, 1816).

Editions and Collections: *The Life, and Posthumous Writings, of William Cowper, Esqr.*, 4 volumes, edited by William Hayley (Chichester: Printed by J. Seagrave for J. Johnson, London, 1803-1806);

Poems, by William Cowper, 3 volumes, edited by John Johnson (volumes 1-2, London: Stereotyped and printed by A. Wilson for J. Johnson and Co., 1815; volume 3, London: Printed for F. C. and J. Rivington and others, 1815; Philadelphia: Published by Benjamin Johnson, 1816);

Poems: The Early Productions of William Cowper, edited by James Croft (London: Printed for Baldwin, Cradock, and Joy, 1825);

The Life and Works of William Cowper, 15 volumes, edited by Robert Southey (London: Baldwin & Cradock, 1835-1837);

The Poetical Works of William Cowper, edited by H. S. Milford, fourth edition, with corrections and additions by Norma Russell (London & New York: Oxford University Press, 1967);

The Poems of William Cowper, volume 1, 1748-1782, edited by John D. Baird and Charles Ryskamp (Oxford & New York: Clarendon Press/Oxford University Press, 1980).

OTHER: William Duncombe, ed., *The Works of Horace in English Verse*, volume 2, includes translations by Cowper of Satire V and Satire IX of Book I (London: Printed for R. and J. Dodsley, 1759);

Tobias Smollett, Thomas Francklin and others, trans., *The Works of M. de Voltaire: Translated from the French. With Notes, Historical and Critical*, volume 24, includes translation by Cow-

Crayon drawing by George Romney; National Portrait Gallery, London

per of Books V-VIII of the *Henriade* (London: Printed for J. Newbury and others, 1762);

The Iliad and Odyssey of Homer, 2 volumes, translated by Cowper, with preface (London: Printed for J. Johnson, 1791; revised edition, with new preface, London: Printed for J. Johnson by Bunney and Gold, 1802);

Helperus Ritzema van Lier, *The Power of Grace Illustrated, in Six Letters, from a Minister of the Reformed Church to John Newton*, translated by Cowper (London: Printed for J. Johnson, 1792; Philadelphia: Printed by Neale and Kammerer, Jun., 1796);

Frances Maria Cowper (attributed), *Original Poems by a Lady*, revised by Cowper (London: Printed for J. Deighton, J. Mathews, and R. Faulder, 1792; Philadelphia: Printed by William Young, 1793);

Jeanne Marie Guyon (Bouvier de La Motte), *Poems Translated from the French of Madame de la Mothe Guion*, translated by Cowper (Newport Pagnell: Printed and sold by J. Wakefield, 1801; Philadelphia: Printed and sold by Kimber, Conrad & Co., 1804);

Cowper's Milton, 4 volumes, edited by William Hayley (Chichester: Printed by W. Mason for J. Johnson and Co., London, 1810).

SELECTED PERIODICAL PUBLICATION—UNCOLLECTED: "New Poems by William Cowper," edited by Charles Ryskamp, *Book Collector*, 22 (1973): 443-478.

William Cowper was the foremost poet of the generation between Alexander Pope and William Wordsworth and for several decades had probably the largest readership of any English poet. From 1782, when his first major volume appeared, to 1837, the year in which Robert Southey completed the monumental *Life and Works of Cowper*, more than a hundred editions of his poems were published in Britain and almost fifty in America.

Cowper's immense popularity owed much to his advocacy of religious and humanitarian ideals at a time of widespread Evangelical sentiment, manifest as much in the moral zeal of the antislavery movement, which he fervently supported, as in the tide of spiritual enthusiasm issuing directly from the great Revival. But his importance goes far deeper. Echoing the opinion of many early reviewers, Samuel Taylor Coleridge called him "the best modern poet"; and, though his practice reflects in some ways a commitment to Neoclassical, or so-called Augustan, precepts, his innovations in the treatment of nature and common life, in meditative and conversational techniques, and in the foregrounding of autobiography and confession constitute a crucial legacy to the first generation of Romantics. His various achievements in satire, didactic-descriptive verse, narrative, hymnody, and the lyric show an often spectacular command of the potentialities of inherited forms, but the distinctive force of his poetry derives above all from its expression of complex psychological currents and concerns. Cowper's melancholia, exile, and fears of damnation—the sufferings of the "stricken deer"—are among the best-known facts of literary biography: his writing is both their embodiment and the site of their transcendence. As they are formulated within his works, however, the trials and the triumphs of the self assume a significance beyond any purely private context and beyond the tradition of Puritan soul-struggle which influenced their shape. Viewed historically, they mark the rise of the modern existentialist hero who must continuously create value and stability for himself against a background of cultural dissolution and the threat of chaos within. More generally, they have their counterparts in the subterranean lives of all human beings.

Cowper was born on 15 November 1731 at the rectory in Great Berkhamstead (now Berkhamsted), Hertfordshire, the first surviving child of the Reverend John Cowper and Ann Donne Cowper, the daughter of Roger Donne of Ludham Hall, Norfolk. His family was well connected on both sides: his father's great-uncle had been the first Earl Cowper and twice lord chancellor of England, while the Donnes claimed descent from Henry III as well as from the Elizabethan poet John Donne. After short periods at dame school and under the Reverend William Davis at Aldbury, Cowper went, from about 1737 to 1739, to Dr. Pittman's boarding school at Markyate Street on the Hertfordshire and Bedfordshire border, where, as he recalled thirty years later in his *Memoir of the Early Life of William Cowper, Esq.* (1816), he was so severely bullied that he knew his tormentor "by his shoe-buckles better than any other part of his dress." This experience seems to have been second only to the death of his mother when he was not quite six in promoting the mental problems that were to determine the course of his life. The child's traumatic bereavement was to be seen by the aging poet himself, in the powerful verses of 1790 on his mother's portrait, as the primal scene in a relentless drama of affliction and arduous survival. He was "Wretch even then, life's journey just begun."

Some of Cowper's happiest boyhood memories were of visits to his cousins in Norfolk, and it was there that he acquired two books which predict a salient polarity in his own future writing—the light moral verse of John Gay's *Fables* (1727-1738) and the Calvinistic vision of John Bunyan's *The Pilgrim's Progress* (1678-1684). Mrs. Disney, the oculist with whom he lodged in London around 1740 to 1742 because of eye trouble, made little recorded impression upon him, though his short judgment on her house as a place "where Christianity was neither known nor practised" gives leave for speculation that here may be the harsh regimen which his later fantasies and his self-deprecating behavior in relationships with women indicate somewhere in his history. In 1742 he entered Westminster School, imbibing the classics and the strong Whig principles for which the school was renowned and forming notable friendships with the writers-to-be Robert Lloyd, Charles Churchill, and George Colman the Elder, and with the fifth-form usher Vincent Bourne, whose animal fables he translated from the Latin at intervals throughout his life. Intended for the law, he was enrolled in the Middle Temple in 1748. Membership of the Inns of Court, however, was more a formality than a training and, following the usual custom, Cowper took up articles under a solicitor, Mr. Chapman of Greville Street, Holborn, with whom he remained from 1750 to 1753. Although he was called to the bar in 1754 and transferred residence to the Inner Temple in 1757, the legal profession was one to which he admitted he "was never much inclined." The routine of Chapman's office was regularly exchanged for the pleasure of being "employed from Morning to Night in giggling and making giggle" with his cousins Theadora and Harriot at the house of his uncle, Ashley Cowper, in Southampton Row.

So far Cowper's poetic writing had been mostly talented adaptations of John Milton, Abraham Cowley, and "Mat Prior's easy jingle," the best of them exercises in the epistolary art of which he was always an instinctive master. An ill-fated affair with Theadora, which began in 1752 and ended at her father's insistence in 1755, prompted his first substantial body of verse. In this remarkable sequence of poems to "Delia," which was withheld from publication until 1825, Prior's colloquial wit and the raffishness of the Cavalier lyric are the starting point of a highly original chronicle of love, a movement progressively inwards from compliment and playful self-observation to oneiric landscapes of frustrated desire which introduce Cowper's characteristic image of himself as the object of a terrible doom, the outcast who "vainly strives to shun the threat'ning death." Ashley Cowper's exact reasons for opposing the match are not known, and it is unclear whether Cowper's bout of depression in 1753, serious enough to require a trip to Southampton with Harriot and her fiancé Thomas Hesketh, was a cause or effect of the objections that shadowed the relationship. By all accounts Theadora never recovered from the broken romance. Cowper, it seems, soon did, for the surviving letters of the seven years up to 1762 are amply spiced with the bravado of the man about town. The young barrister found ready access to fashionable social and literary circles in the metropolis, especially the Nonsense Club of former Westminster friends whose members included Colman and Bonnell Thornton, editors of the *Connoisseur*, to which he started to contribute satirical papers in 1756. The "several halfpenny ballads" Cowper remembered writing at this time, dealing with current politics from the Whig point of view, have been lost, together perhaps with much else of a topical cast. The death of his friend Sir William Russell in 1757 gave rise to the introspective elegy "Doom'd as I am in solitude to waste," but the other extant verse consists almost entirely of commissioned translations from Horace's *Satires* and Voltaire's *La Henriade* (1728), published respectively in 1759 and 1762.

Events took a dramatic turn in 1763. Family connections had already gained Cowper the sinecure of commissioner of bankrupts; he now accepted from Ashley Cowper the lucrative clerkship of the Journals in the House of Lords, but when his uncle's right of appointment was challenged by a rival faction, he found himself summoned to undergo a test of suitability at the Bar of the House. The suicidal derangement brought on by the prospect of this public ordeal drove him to Nathaniel Cotton's Collegium Insanorum at St. Albans, where he was gradually restored and converted to Evangelicalism in 1764. He left St. Albans in June 1765 but lived thenceforth in retirement, at first on his own and then, from November 1765, in the household of the Reverend Morley Unwin at Huntingdon. After Unwin's death from a riding accident in 1767 Cowper took up residence with Unwin's widow, Mary, and her daughter, moving with them to Orchard Side at Olney in Buckinghamshire in February 1768. At Olney he came at once under the influence of the Reverend John Newton, the one-time slave trader who was then a prominent Evangelical of strictly Calvinist persuasion.

The immediate upshot of these changed circumstances was the memoir which Cowper completed for private circulation in 1767, a late and compelling example of the Puritan conversion narrative in the manner of Bunyan's *Grace Abounding to the Chief of Sinners* (1666). At one point it describes how his attendance at the offices of the journals had been like a repeated journey to a "place of execution," so great were his dread and his inability to derive meaning from the books: "A finger raised against me was more than I could stand. . . . I expected no assistance from anybody there, all the inferior clerks being under the influence of my opponent, and accordingly I received none. The journal books were indeed thrown open to me—a thing which could not be refused, and from which perhaps a man in health and with a head turned to business might have gained all the information he wanted—but it was not so with me." For Cowper's former self the word is inaccessible. For the tough-minded author of the memoir, however, it is the medium of comprehension and order as he revisits the past, often in harrowing detail ("I placed it upright under my left breast, leaning all my weight upon it, but the point was broken off and would not pen-

Mrs. Mary Unwin, age twenty-six (engraving based on a painting by Davis). Cowper lived with Mrs. Unwin and her husband, the Reverend Morley Unwin, from November 1765 until Mr. Unwin's death in 1767. He then remained with Mrs. Unwin until her death in 1796.

etrate"), to affirm the workings of "the blessed providence of God" in his life, the breaking of the old man and the making of the new.

Religion brought Cowper both an outlet for his feelings and a means of organizing them, and also incidentally shaped his last contact with his brother John, fellow of Corpus Christi, Cambridge, whose deathbed acceptance of Evangelical truths under William's guidance in 1770 is narrated in *Adelphi* (1802), a didactic continuation of the autodidactic memoir. His sixty-seven contributions to the *Olney Hymns*, composed chiefly in 1771-1772 as a collaboration with Newton (who saw to the volume's publication in 1779), place him in the first rank of English hymnodists. Many of these hymns, including "Oh for a closer Walk with God," "God moves in a mysterious way" and "Hark, my soul! it is the Lord," remain in regular congregational use. The whole set is distinguished by a mastery of corporate symbolism (the cross, the fountain, the lamb, the worm and the thorn, the divine majesty) and the recognized stages of the ebb and flow of faith, resourcefully cast in the chaste diction and lucid stanzaic form pioneered by Isaac Watts but seasoned with an epigrammatic piquancy reminiscent of John Donne and George Herbert. Yet there is in the final analysis a patent dark underside to the hymns, in that the weight of authenticity lies ultimately not with the "sweet bounty" of the believer but with his conflicts, longings, and insecurity. "The Contrite Heart," for example, movingly realizes the state of being outside the company of God's elect:

Thy saints are comforted I know
  And love thy house of pray'r;
I therefore go where others go,
  But find no comfort there.

This hymn was shortly to prove prophetic, for in January 1773 Cowper had a dream in which he heard the words "Actum est de te, periisti" (It is all over with thee, thou hast perished). "God moves in a mysterious way" had made magnificently present the Calvinist God who is "his own Interpreter" and "will make it plain"; but what He made plain to Cowper in this vision was that his soul was eternally damned. Cowper continued to hold staunchly to his religious beliefs, but he never again entered a church or said a prayer.

In the nightmarish sapphics of 1774 entitled "Hatred and vengeance, my eternal portion" Cowper conceives himself as one "Damn'd below Judas," clearly attributing his sentence to his having sometime committed what was considered in Calvinist dogma to be the "unpardonable sin" of rejecting Christ. Thoughts of an altogether different transgression, however, may have been a subconscious factor in the obscure origins of the breakdown that had led to the dream of damnation and, in the autumn of 1773, his fourth attempt at suicide. Worried about the gossip that might arise after Miss Unwin's expected departure from the household at Orchard Side, Cowper's friends had successfully urged him in 1772 to announce his betrothal to Mrs. Unwin—the woman whom, as Harriot Hesketh affirmed, "he had always consider'd . . . as a *Mother*." The engagement was broken off by his illness, and the patient was placed under Newton's care at the vicarage. He nevertheless went back to Orchard Side when his health improved during 1774, seeking diversion in carpentry, gardening, keeping animals (the pet hares Puss, Tiney, and Bess, whom he memorialized in verse and prose), drawing, and in time a return to poetry.

In his blacker moods Cowper thought of Olney as a "sepulchre," but it was also a place of "blest seclusion from a jarring world," a demiparadise. His equally ambivalent image of "the loop-holes of retreat" suggests not only immurement but vantage point, and the shorter poems that began to flow from his pen in 1779 and 1780 were frequently alert, combative responses to great events—the controversy over Admiral Augustus Keppel's inconclusive engagement with the French fleet, George Rodney's relief of Gibraltar, and other episodes in the war with the Americans and their European allies—or else observant forays into the ritual oddities of provincial life, such as the verse cartoon "The Yearly Distress, or Tything Time at Stock." By a paradox that runs throughout his career, the potentially deadly assault of the words of reprobation thus generated a lively engagement with the external world, and an outgoing verbal dexterity whose range is further exemplified in poems such as the fable of "The Nightingale and Glow-worm" and the patriotic ode "Boadicea."

The impetus to active publication came, however, from a curious contemporary source. The Reverend Martin Madan, a relative of Cowper, was moved by his experiences in the chaplainship of the Lock Hospital, an institution for fallen women, to write a defense of polygamy as a remedy for the evils of prostitution. The appearance of Madan's treatise, *Thelyphthora*, in May 1780 gave rise to bitter public debate during which Cowper was persuaded by Newton, by then removed to the living of St. Mary Woolnoth in London, and by Samuel Badcock's sprightly criticism in the *Monthly Review* to compose his own anonymous rejoinder. Newton's publisher, Joseph Johnson, agreed to bring out the poem of more than two hundred lines early in 1781. *Anti-Thelyphthora*, a mock-Spenserian romance in which Madan, the Quixotic "Sir Airy," is bested by Badcock, alias "Sir Marmardan," was deservedly praised by Badcock himself for its vein of "elegant fancy," but in the broader view it shows Cowper learning to forge an adroit alliance between conflicting demands upon his genius—religio-moral duty and a robust comic impulse.

It was the skillful blend of profit and pleasure, along with the vigor of the rhymed couplets, that most impressed the reviewers of the eight long essays that formed the bulk of Cowper's first independent volume, *Poems by William Cowper, of the Inner Temple, Esq.* (1782). Edmund Cartwright in the *Monthly Review*, for example, discovered in the volume a poet sui generis whose "very religion has a smile that is arch, and his sallies of humour an air that is religious," and whose muscular, flexible versification set him apart from the pack of Pope's latter-day imitators who went "jingling along in uninterrupted unison."

Begun late in 1780, this series of verse discourses, which became generally known by readers as the "Moral Satires," had been completed in October 1781. It represents a comprehensive and hard-hitting proclamation of Evangelical attitudes and doctrine. "The Progress of Error" and "Truth" establish the two extremes of Cowper's moral position in an attack on the subversion of Christianity by rationalism and science and a complementary charting of Scripture's "easy, artless,

You know that I kept two hares. I have written nothing since I saw you but an Epitaph on one of them which died last week. I send you the *first* impression of it.

Here lies, whom hound did ne'er pursue,
Nor swifter greyhound follow,
Whose foot ne'er tainted morning dew,
Nor ear heard Huntsman's hallo',

Tiney, the surliest of his kind,
Who, nurs'd with tender care,
And to domestic bounds confin'd,
Was still a wild *Jack* Hare.

Though duly from my hand he took
His pittance ev'ry night,
He did it with a jealous look,
And when he could, *would* bite.

His diet was of wheaten bread,
And milk and oats and straw,
Thistles, or lettuces instead,
With sand to scour *his* maw.

On twigs of hawthorn he regal'd,
Or pippins russet peel,
And when his juicy sallads faild,
Sliced carrot pleas'd him well.

A Turkey carpet was his lawn,
Whereon he lov'd to bound,
To skip and gambol like a fawn,
And swing his rump *around*.

His frisking was at evening hours,
For then he lost his fear,

Page from a letter from Cowper to his friend the Reverend William Bull, including part of Cowper's epitaph for his pet hare, Tiney (auctioned by Sotheby's, London, 27 September 1988)

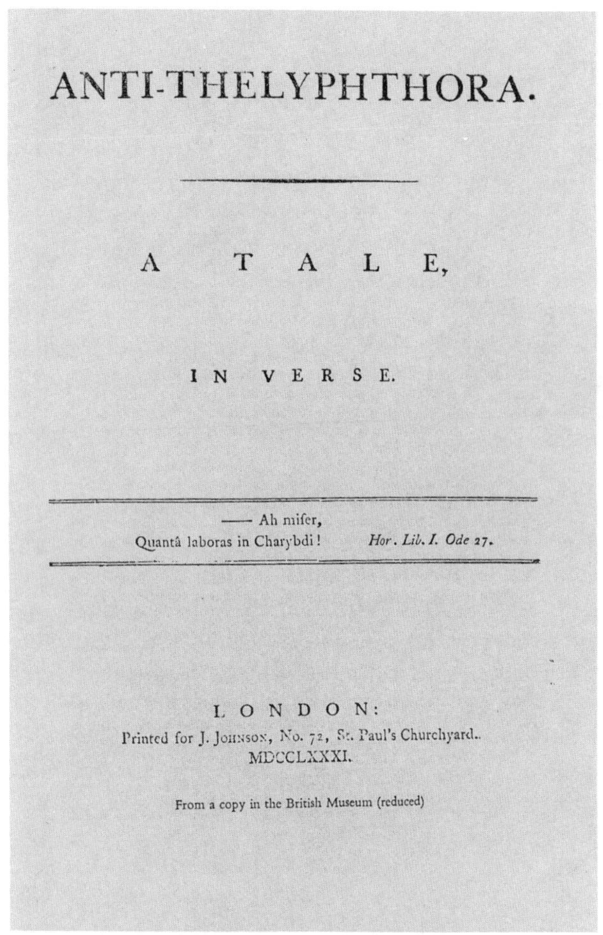

ANTI-THELYPHTHORA.

A TALE,

IN VERSE.

—— Ah mifer,
Quantâ laboras in Charybdi! *Hor. Lib. I. Ode 27.*

LONDON:
Printed for J. JOHNSON, No. 72, St. Paul's Churchyard.
MDCCLXXXI.

From a copy in the British Museum (reduced)

Title page for Cowper's rejoinder to the Reverend Martin Madan's Thelyphthora *(1780). Madan had advocated polygamy as a remedy for the evils of prostitution.*

unincumber'd plan." In "Table Talk" the dialogue form is used to argue the need for righteousness in all endeavors, including literature. The prophetic voice of "Expostulation" compares the history of England with that of Israel and laments the nation's moral decline, "Hope" contrasts the wonders of spiritual awakening with the drab futility of worldly existence, and "Charity" explores the greatest of the Christian virtues. "Conversation" and "Retirement," lighter and more intimate in tone, carry the religious standpoint into an appraisal of the sociable and sequestered spheres that were by this time Cowper's familiar domain.

Though the simple "opportunity to be amused" in composing verse is a frequent theme in Cowper's letters of the early 1780s, the author of the Moral Satires took his muse seriously, not only for reasons of self-esteem, signaled by his constant irritation at delays in reaching the press, but as a means of reclaiming an enfeebled age. "Table Talk," which is placed first in the volume, contains an aggressive manifesto deploring the "whipt-cream" and "push-pin play" of contemporary writing and pleading for a return to worthy purposes and the standards of "genius, sense, and wit." Pope's example had, for Cowper, made poetry "a mere mechanic art," but his own critical principles are here adapted from the *Essay on Criticism* (1711). Like those expressed in the correspondence, these principles align him with the late-Neoclassical school of Lord Kames, Hugh Blair, and Samuel Johnson, which stressed the writer's legislative function, his responsibility to communicate clearly but with imaginative and intellectual force on matters of general human concern. Cowper shared with the poets of Sensibility—William Collins, Thomas Gray, and Joseph and Thomas Warton—a sense of a laggard present; but whereas they sought to exorcise the spirit of Neoclassicism by emulating the Invention and Fancy of Greece, the Middle Ages, and the English Renaissance, he set himself the task of purifying and redirecting the energies of Neoclassicism in the service of God and the Christian ethos.

In pursuing this project Cowper sometimes brings all tellurian art under uneasy scrutiny as a potential source of error or a devising "far too mean for him that rules the skies." Yet the art of the Moral Satires possesses its own kind of assurance and versatility. The humorous vein that pleased Cartwright shows with particular brilliance in the inimitable satiric portraiture, more Hogarthian than Popian, where the interest lies as much in the unfolding reactions of the quizzical observer as in the configuration of vice itself: "Yon ancient prude, whose wither'd features show / She might be young some forty years ago. . . . " In *Hours in a Library* (1879) Leslie Stephen designated Cowper "a thinker too far apart from the great world to apply the lash effectually"; but detachment can seem a definite advantage when compared to the unfocused, if fiery, stance of Cowper's former schoolfellow, the profligate parson Churchill, who, immersed in a welter of metropolitan corruptness, flails out indiscriminately at everything in sight. Cowper's gaze is steady and trained on things of consequence, not only the individual soul and man's folly but the soul of a nation in crisis, torn by the catastrophic course of the American war, the Gordon Riots, and the effects of the armed neutrality of five European states:

Poor England! thou art a devoted deer,
Beset with ev'ry ill but that of fear.
The nations hunt; all mark thee for a prey,
They swarm around thee, and thou standst at bay.
Undaunted still, though wearied and perplex'd. . . .

These topical areas of the Moral Satires establish Cowper as at once journalist, patriot, and a confirmed ideologist for whom style itself is an index of value. The "manly, rough line" which he saw as a way of breaking the hegemony of Pope's emasculating musical finesse mirrors the very virtues of "sober zeal" and "integrity," strength without "wild excess," which he upholds and recommends to his bereft countrymen.

Modern readers, however, are likely to find most to engage them in the personal themes that sound beneath and sometimes on the surface of the Moral Satires. There are points throughout where Cowper draws on his own past, among them an objectification at the climax of "Hope" of his former maniacal despair and conversion, in which he sees heightened perception of the Creation as the primary manifestation of a new-found state of grace. This passage is a propitious moment in Cowper's interior progress. His present condition was far from the joyous assurance it describes; contemporaneous letters insist that there is "no remedy" for the "unprofitableness" of his life. Yet in identifying the appreciation of nature as a sign and source of spiritual well-being he found a way forward both as poet and as a man in search of an anchor for his feelings.

"Retirement," the last of the Moral Satires, registers a definite advance in confidence and in the use of contemplation to bring stability to the individual's own life. Didacticism merges with the strategies of the poet assessing his situation and its possibilities. Memorable, trenchant satire on the incipient bourgeois craze for country living—"Suburban villas, highway-side retreats"—and other abuses of retirement resides within a larger framework in which Cowper makes himself the exemplar of the sincere, virtuous, enlightened, and contented retiree of classical and recent tradition, "the happy man" of Virgil's *Georgics*, Horace, Cowley, and James Thomson's *The Seasons* (1726-1730). Building a positive identity for himself and offering his credentials to the world, he transforms exile into a welcome calling of which the greatest privilege is intercourse with the living organic reality of nature "in all the various shapes she wears." The detailed descriptions of that reality in "Retirement" have a double yield, foreshadowing the richer fruits of his masterpiece, *The Task* (1785). The harmonies of "forest where the deer securely roves" and the minute perfection of "Muscle and nerve miraculously spun" tell of the Artificer Divine as Cowper fulfills the anti-Deistic thrust of the Moral Satires by arguing from the evidence of design in the universe to the existence of the Christian God with a verve unrivaled until William Paley's *Natural Theology* (1802). Simultaneously, however, he finds his "heart enrich'd by what it pays." Interaction between self and nature brings immediate stimulation but is also proof of a capacity which has already been seen as the special possession of the reborn soul. A close reading of the poetry radically modifies the received image of Cowper the passive "stricken deer" and benighted "castaway," for much of it is an answer to his darker emotions and even a quest for evidences of election. He created two selves in his writings, the damned and the saved, and only in the final phase did he decide between them.

Cowper's maturation as a writer of comic, occasional, and narrative verse is attributable in large measure to psychological pressures. Among the best of the pieces in the 1782 volume, the lines on the marooned Alexander Selkirk and the taut little fable on a goldfinch starved in his cage both take a singular edge from his private experience. The former is a vivid drama of mind in which the polar images of island-paradise ("I am monarch of all I survey") and island-prison ("horrible place") are reconciled in a sober acceptance of affliction; the latter is a chillingly gleeful celebration of death as an escape from a cruel confinement. Cowper told Newton that "the mind long wearied with . . . a dull, dreary prospect will gladly fix its eyes on any thing that may make a little variety in its contemplations, though it were but a kitten playing with her tail"; but when he turns his gaze on three kittens and a full-grown cat one day in 1782 he discovers that nothing is predictable, for a viper "long as Count de Grasse's queue" brings terror to the garden and must be dispatched with "out-stretch'd hoe." The calculated swagger of "The Colubriad," the poem in which this incident is related, at once releases and controls Cowper's apprehension of the fearful truth that "We are never more in danger than when we think ourselves most secure." And it is precisely this irony that seizes his imagination in the stanzas on the loss of the *Royal George* in 1782: the crew of eight hundred go down not in tempest or battle but when they are seemingly

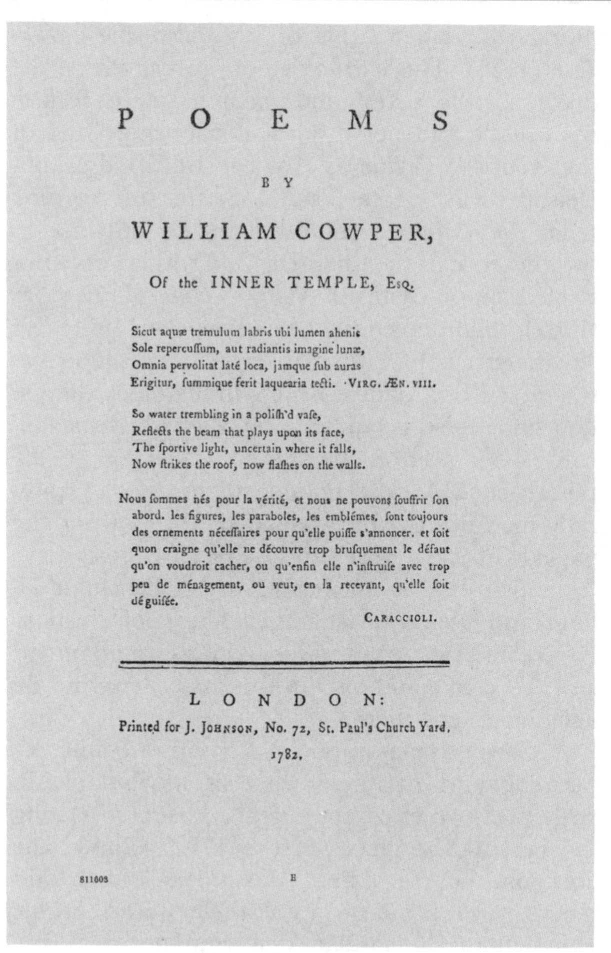

P O E M S

B Y

WILLIAM COWPER,

Of the INNER TEMPLE, Esq.

Sicut aquæ tremulum labris ubi lumen ahenis
Sole repercuſſum, aut radiantis imagine lunæ,
Omnia pervolitat laté loca, jamque ſub auras
Erigitur, ſummique ferit laquearia tecti. ·Virg. Æn. viii.

So water trembling in a poliſh'd vaſe,
Reflects the beam that plays upon its face,
The ſportive light, uncertain where it falls,
Now ſtrikes the roof, now flaſhes on the walls.

Nous ſommes nés pour la vérité, et nous ne pouvons ſouffrir ſon abord. les figures, les paraboles, les emblémes, ſont toujours des ornements néceſſaires pour qu'elle puiſſe s'annoncer. et ſoit quon craigne qu'elle ne découvre trop bruſquement le défaut qu'on voudroit cacher, ou qu'enfin elle n'inſtruiſe avec trop peu de ménagement, ou veut, en la recevant, qu'elle ſoit déguiſée.

Caraccioli.

L O N D O N:
Printed for J. Johnson, No. 72, St. Paul's Church Yard.
1782.

811603 B

Title page for Cowper's series of Evangelical verse discourses, which became known as the "Moral Satires"

safe in harbor. The commander of the *Royal George*, visited by fate while his fingers hold the pen, is, like the caged bird and the harmless old cat, one of Cowper's many doubles. The latter, however, are the more telling self-projections. Their vulnerability is oddly intermixed with a saving resilience as the one has the last laugh on his sadistic captor by speaking from beyond the grave and the other paws the invading snake out of curiosity to learn what the phenomenon might mean, just as Cowper wrests wisdom and shrewd artistic capital from the enigma of violence and threat that threw its shadow over his own life.

At this time Cowper developed several significant friendships: with William Bull, Independent minister of Newport Pagnell, whose encouragement led to Cowper's fine translations of the poems of the French Quietist Madame Guion (begun in 1782, published in 1801); with William Unwin, who replaced Newton as literary go-between once *Poems* had been seen through the press; and, most importantly, with Lady Austen, whom he met in 1781 just before she took up residence at Olney vicarage. Relations between Cowper and Lady Austen, until Cowper broke them off in 1784, were plagued by mutual irritation. She was domineering, he was subject to his habitual difficulties over intimacy with the fair sex. A chance remark suggests that he saw in her the threat of woman's destructive power, his Delilah, and in 1782 they quarreled bitterly when he rejected what he presumed was a veiled proposal of romantic attachment and marriage. Yet of all his muses she was the one who made the most difference. Her vivacity undoubtedly lay behind both the freer creativity of "Retirement" and the inception of *The Task* in the autumn of 1783, and it was her idea for a narrative poem that inspired "The Diverting History of John Gilpin," which Cowper drafted during a single night in October 1782 and which was published anonymously soon after in the *Public Advertiser*.

Spectacularly successful from the start ("hackney'd in ev'ry Magazine, in every News paper and in every street," as Cowper put it in 1785), the tale of citizen Gilpin's thwarted plans for a day out and his furious nonstop ride through an amazed metropolis has appealed to successive generations as sheer farce and inoffensive caricature, and may be read too as subtle parody of the genre of the street ballad and of romance conventions, with more than a hint of conscious rivalry with the burlesque of Geoffrey Chaucer's "Sir Thopas." Yet this jeu d'esprit was written in "the saddest mood," and concentrates in its hero's predicament a whole cluster of the poet's bleakest obsessions: the meaningless violence of the world, the aloneness of being beyond self-help or the help of others, the individual's insecurity within a field of unaccountable force. John Calvin gave rise to John Gilpin no less than to Cowper's periodic reports from the "fleshly tomb" where he was "buried above ground"; humor was not a thing apart from the inner nightmare but a visitant like "harlequin . . . intrud[ing] himself into the gloomy chamber where a corpse is deposited in state," not so much lightheartedness as an antic exuberance performed on the very edge of horror.

Cowper's vision of the world and being-in-the-world found fullest expression in *The Task*, which, originating inauspiciously in Lady Austen's playful request for a blank-verse poem on "the sofa," grew over a period of twelve months into a magnum opus of six books and around

Drawing of Cowper by W. Harvey, after L. Abbott (National Portrait Gallery, London)

five thousand lines. Poor sales of the 1782 volume of poems were of little consequence to Cowper; the reviews had been encouraging, if mixed, and this response, together with the popularity of "John Gilpin," pushed him into eager negotiations with Joseph Johnson for publication of a new volume. *The Task* appeared in July 1785 to universal acclaim. In composing it Cowper had behind him the example of Thomson's *The Seasons* and other works in the "georgic" tradition but evolved a wholly independent bent, texture, and range of subject matter. He produced a large-scale investigation of Man, Nature, and Society which was also the first extended autobiographical poem in English.

"God made the country, and man made the town," Cowper says in Book I, "The Sofa." The moral scheme of the work is at once apparent and is carried forward not only in denunciations of "gain-devoted cities" but in more particularized responses to such contemporary issues as the slave trade ("human nature's broadest, foulest blot"), the modishness of the Church and the universities, and the weakness of a postwar government shamelessly winking at what Cowper calls in Book II, "The Time Piece," "the perfidy of France, / That pick'd the jewel out of England's crown." Cowper is the conscience and monitor of the age, tracing the faults of the England he loves to a general want of those standards, grounded as much in the classical ideals of *humanitas* and *gravitas* as in the Christian ethic, to which he customarily subscribes, and speaking for many at a time of anxious soul-searching after the loss of empire. The scope of its satiric and patriotic interests, alongside its explorations of rural and domestic life, make *The Task* a truly national poem.

From the beginning, however, the public aspects of the poem are interwoven with or usurped by distinctly personal ones. Confessional passages like that on the "stricken deer, that left

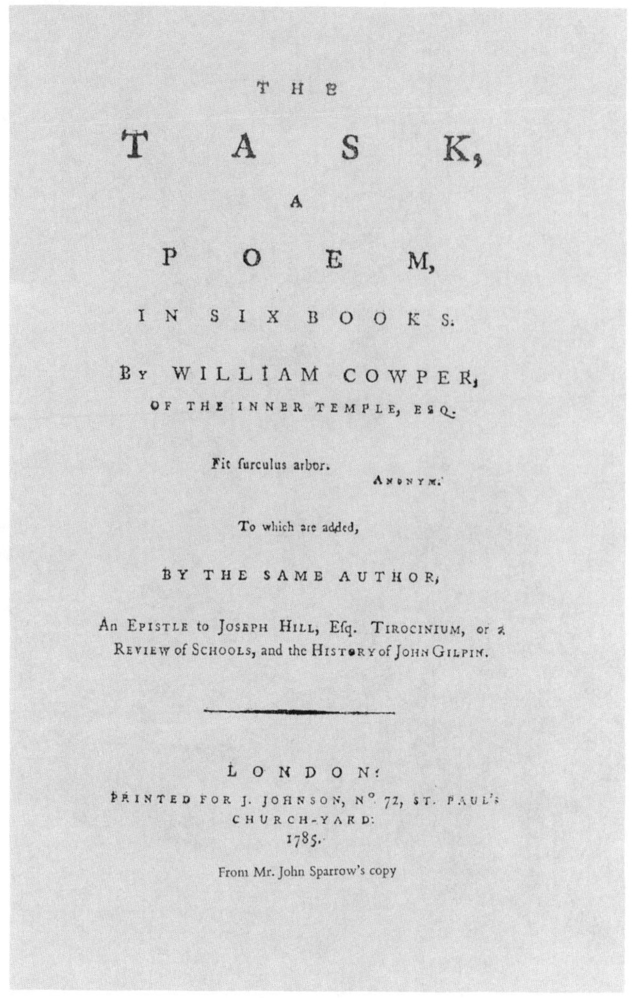

THE

TASK,

A

POEM,

IN SIX BOOKS.

By WILLIAM COWPER,

OF THE INNER TEMPLE, ESQ.

Fit ſurculus arbor.

ANONYM.

To which are added,

BY THE SAME AUTHOR,

An EPISTLE to JOSEPH HILL, Eſq. TIROCINIUM, or a REVIEW of SCHOOLS, and the HISTORY of JOHN GILPIN.

LONDON:

PRINTED FOR J. JOHNSON, N° 72, ST. PAUL'S CHURCH-YARD:

1785.

From Mr. John Sparrow's copy

Title page for the first extended autobiographical poem in English

the herd / Long since" in Book III, "The Garden," are the overt face of a process of self-revelation that persists elsewhere in repeated image patterns and preoccupations involving such oppositions as imprisonment and freedom, disease and health, chaos and order. The figure of the paralytic in Book I, who "can hold her cards, / But cannot play them" and "sits, / Spectatress both and spectacle, a sad / And silent cypher," is introduced as an exemplum of the debilitating effects of frivolous social pleasure but grows into a stark symbolic representation of the death-in-life of irrevocable isolation and desperate survival at the outer limits of normality. This passage, like the nearby piece on "crazy Kate," is the surfacing of the dark side of Cowper's imagination, his hard-won knowledge of the prison house of the self. But in the Ouse Valley episode (on which Wordsworth based his "Lines Composed a Few Miles above Tintern Abbey") one discovers a countervailing impulse as Cowper, taking a cue from "Retirement," reaffirms his gift for finding peace and joy in the presence of nature. First he uses retrospection to establish the lifelong continuity of his love of "fair prospect" and nature's service to that love; then he enacts this same reciprocity in a characteristically dense landscape description where mental activity, the poet "*feeding* at the eye," combines with the welcoming flow of the autonomous life without, the spirit of place that "*Conducts* the eye." *The Task* thus moves between tragic and epiphanic or therapeutic vision, projecting that perpetual oscillation between thoughts of "a happy eternity" and of being "thrust down to Hell" which Cowper reported to Newton as his inveterate condition. The topos of country versus town becomes a topography of psychic tension, the contemplation of nature the locus of emotional stability.

Books III and IV, "The Winter Evening,"

deal more particularly with the poet's life of retirement. The routine and objects of home and garden—cucumbers, stercoraceous heap, and all—offer the occasion for some of Cowper's most adept exploitation of the disparity between high style and ordinary subjects, that humorous magnification of Olney minutiae which is one means by which he elevates and shares his experience with the reader. He weaves from his materials both parables of how human beings should function in the world and microcosmic visions of how the world should ideally be. He does so in spite of a powerful awareness of an actual "civilization" restructuring itself on the basis of advancing manufacture, consumerism, and commercial enterprise, so that merchants "Incorporated . . . / Build factories with blood" and the "Midas finger of the state" reaches even into the countryside, making debauchery bleed gold for the exchequer. Unlike John Dyer in *The Fleece* (1757), or sometimes Thomson (who, for example, celebrates "gay Drudgery"), Cowper can reach no accommodation with industrialization and the other accompaniments of an expansionist economic system reflecting the popular doctrine, elaborated in Bernard de Mandeville's *Fable of the Bees* (1714 and 1728), that "private vices" make "publick benefits": he registers only a perverse harmony of dehumanizing excess and a corrupt polity. Alienated from the collective present, in a posture that emphatically signalizes the Romantic and post-Romantic split between value and the practical sphere, he fashions in his accounts of the innocent and fruitful pursuits of the sequestered man a sustaining myth of optimal existence which revivifies all the traditional motifs—friendship, books, cultivation of the mind—but stresses most the fertile cooperation and "glad espousals" of Art and Nature.

Human skill and nature are both viewed ambiguously elsewhere in *The Task*: the gentle savage Omai in Book I, for instance, is envied for his paradisal home and pitied because he is deprived of the "manners and the arts of civil life." But in Cowper's garden skill and nature are seen in a perfectly balanced and creative union that represents the apogee of man's relationship with his environment, a union operating in the work not only of the sensitive laborer but of the true poet, who ultimately traces in his surroundings the model of a goodly social order:

Few self-supported flow'rs endure the wind
Uninjur'd, but expect th' upholding aid
Of the smooth-shaven prop, and, neatly tied,
Are wedded thus, like beauty to old age,
For int'rest sake, the living to the dead.
Some clothe the soil that feeds them, far diffus'd
And lowly creeping, modest and yet fair,
Like virtue . . .
All hate the rank society of weeds,
Noisome, and ever greedy to exhaust
Th' impov'rish'd earth. . . .

Such moments of visionary insight underline one of the major messages of the poem—that imagination, which gives access to the ideal and the beautiful, is superior to every other form of production. The task of the writer, which the world might consider mere idleness, is presented in the end as the most important "business" of all, for it keeps people alive to "wisdom" and the best they may aim for.

Books V, "The Winter Morning Walk," and VI, "The Winter Walk at Noon," move back from a mythopoeic to a more contemplative register and bring to a climax Cowper's experiential and religio-philosophic interest in the natural world. One notable feature is their buoyant expansion of the anti-Deist arguments of "Retirement," this time with Pope's *Essay on Man* (1733-1734) an evident object of criticism. For Cowper, there is "A soul in all things, and that soul is God"—the God of divine revelation rather than mechanical causes. Yet he insists that this God is not only the end of inspired perception but also its source ("Acquaint thyself with God, if thou would'st taste / His works"), so that responsiveness to nature is made more forcibly than ever the touchstone of spiritual wholeness. The give and take between the energies of self and nature in *The Task* generates an incredible range of moods and perspectives, from the set-piece prospects of Book I through the reverie amid the frost on the "variegated show" and hidden stirrings of the fields in Book IV (which inspired Coleridge's "Frost at Midnight" [1798]) to the vast kaleidoscope of ever-changing engagements with the sentient and nonsentient life of the Creation in the later books. The desire to worship and the longing for grace are satisfied in the temple of the universe, Cowper's substitute church, but leave room still for humbler, yet necessary, dispensations of harmony and repose:

The roof, though moveable through all its length
As the wind sways it, has yet well suffic'd,
And, intercepting in their silent fall

William Unwin, Cowper's friend and literary go-between (engraving by John Henry Robinson after a drawing by William Harvey from Thomas Gainesborough's 1764 portrait)

The frequent flakes, has kept a path for me . . .
The redbreast warbles still, but is content
With slender notes, and more than half suppress'd:
Pleas'd with his solitude, and flitting light
From spray to spray, where'er he rests he shakes
From many a twig the pendent drops of ice.

Here the poet's double is the redbreast happy in his solitude and at home in a closed recess of beauteous forms. Yet Cowper finds in meditation not only entry to a private earthly paradise but a medium of enlightenment for all: in one of the poem's most influential statements he offers a philosophy elevating wise passiveness, where "the heart" gives lessons to "the head," above the "spells" and "unprofitable mass" of intellectual knowledge and learning from books.

The Task closes, however, in irresolution. Cowper's enjoyment of a second Eden fades before renewed thoughts of postlapsarian conflict and depravity, oddly but strikingly communicated in unsparing diagnoses of the cruelty of blood sports and the pseudoreligious ritualism of the recent George Frideric Handel and David Garrick festivals ("Man praises man"). These thoughts bring on a wishful prophecy of the Last Day, when all will be swept away and the greater Paradise restored. But Cowper was no mystic: his heart is not in the distant hope, and the reality pressed upon the reader in a final return to the theme of the sequestered life is the struggle of the individual to glean what consolation he can in the here and now of a fallen world. The poet's last review of his life in *The Task* is assertive but not glorious: to his sense of his uselessness in people's eyes he opposes the "fair example" of his patient privacy and humble strains. He concedes that he was "doom'd" to obscurity but sees it as a fate to be chosen for its rewards; he knows that "in contemplation is his bliss" but recognizes a continuing "warfare . . . within." The classical "happy man" and the Puritan introspective saint shade perceptibly into the Romantic solitary, trying yet vulnerable, armed with the powers of creation and self-creation but endlessly threatened by uncertainty and despair.

Cowper's own pride in *The Task* is summed up by his flourish in a letter of 10 October 1784 to William Unwin: "My descriptions are all from Nature. Not one of them second-handed. My delineations of the heart are from my own experience. Not one of them borrowed. . . . In my numbers . . . I have imitated nobody." The reviews, rising in degrees of favorableness to the near-ecstasy of the contributor to the *Monthly Review* (June 1786) who had "got on fairy ground," read like expansions of these claims, recommending Cowper for his depth of feeling, fluency, descriptive realism, and the interest of his character. Coleridge later put this reaction in a nutshell when emphasizing Cowper's originality in uniting "natural thoughts with natural diction" and "the heart with the head."

Coleridge must have been thinking mainly of the unprecedented use of blank verse as a vehicle for the flow of consciousness, of Cowper as the progenitor of an "interior" mode in which the poetry is a continual outgrowth of the mind. This inwardness is an outstanding feature of Cowper's influence, although subsequent criticism tended to stress his more obvious contribution in furthering accurate observation of the countryside. Moreover, he brought to humanity's relationship with nature a religious and philosophic dimension that proved central, in the "natural faith" and "One Life" theory of Coleridge and Wordsworth, to the Romantic quest for models of well-being and numinous design in a world rendered potentially void of meaning by Newtonian science and John Locke's mechanistic psychology, which indicated particles of matter as the only reality and made the objects of perception a mere illusion. As recent interpretations have shown, *The Task* constitutes a psychodrama in which the troubled Cowper seeks a bliss peculiar to his needs but in so doing sets new bearings for the corporate imagination involving belief in the mind's access to the prodigies of "pow'r divine" (wonderfully exemplified in Book IV when the poet, in a positively "unthinking" mood, receives an unmediated vision of the universal *discordia concors* as well as the throbbing life of the single "tender blade" protected by the snow's warm veil) and belief in a liberty of soul surpassing even the political rights he so strenuously espouses (wings that nothing can cripple or confine, "No nook so narrow but he spreads them there / With ease, and is at large"). The poem made the self, though cast out to the periphery of an antipathetic society and inhabiting a small corner of an infinite universe, not only an abiding center of attention in its own right but the bastion of moral, spiritual, and aesthetic value. What the concluding movement then brings into focus, however, is the less comforting seam of the same post-Enlightenment subjectivity: the promise of ceaseless mental struggle and incompleteness of which the closest analogue is the existentialism of Soren Kierkegaard and Byron's *Childe Harold's Pilgrimage* (1812-1818).

While *The Task* was in the press Cowper had gone back to an old project in couplets recommending private tuition in preference to school education. "Tirocinium" ("first training") eventually found a place alongside "John Gilpin" in the same volume as *The Task.* Cowper feared that his objections to the public schools would procure him enemies, but the poem caused no stir in spite of the agile reasoning which still makes it a worthwhile quarry for attitudes to the system before the period of nineteenth-century reforms. His major undertaking at this time, however, was the translation of the *Iliad*, begun toward the end of 1784. In *The Task* Cowper had unwittingly produced a revolutionary work, a personalization of the Miltonic sublime from which Wordsworth's *The Prelude* (1850) and a whole poetry of nature and the private realm soon flowed. Yet the task that exercised him most during his career was deliberately conservative and painstakingly objective—the faithful rendering into his own tongue of the harmony and energy of Homeric epic.

The encounter with Homer lasted on and off for the rest of Cowper's life, first in the prolonged preparation of *The Iliad and Odyssey of Homer* (1791) and afterwards in regular spates of revision. It was in some ways a heroic enterprise: ambitious, scrupulous, and driven by an unshakable antagonism toward Pope, whose standard version in rhyme he had set out to supplant on the grounds that—as he argued in a manifesto submitted to the *Gentleman's Magazine* in 1785—blank verse would do greater justice to both the unaffected grandeur and the detail of the original. Though Cowper loved Homer and wanted fame, his motivation was in part (like Pope's before him) undoubtedly financial. The long-lost Theadora settled a small annuity on the poet in 1785 in support of Lady Hesketh's plans to provide him with assistance. Publication of the Homer translation through the old-fashioned subscription method earned him one thousand pounds and the copyright; but it was a daunting affair, carried forward only by the indefatigable efforts of Lady Hesketh and Cowper's friend Walter Bagot. The watchful attentions of the publisher's reader, Henry Fuseli, were hardly less burdensome, despite Cowper's gratitude for help with a "long and arduous task" which he came to think might discredit him. His doubts were not altogether ill founded. Even among his contemporaries the translation achieved only a modicum of critical success. The basically literal approach helped to ensure a readership for the work well into the twentieth century; but as Fuseli and others were quick to suggest, while Cowper may be praised in theory for a respectful perspicuity, he avoided in practice neither dullness nor the awkwardness likely to arise from the use of Miltonic syntax. The opinion of informed posterity finds neat expression in Matthew Arnold's view in *On Translating Homer* (1861-1862) that "between Cowper and Homer . . . there is interposed the mist of Cowper's elaborate Miltonic manner, entirely alien to the flowing rapidity of Homer."

The studied competence of the Homer stands in marked contrast to the sprightliness of the vignettes on local events in the letters of the Olney years, such as the elegant farce of the visit of the "kissing candidate" at election time or the *essais* on the ballooning craze. In the spring of 1784 Cowper went to see a balloon go up at neighboring Weston Underwood on the estate of the Throckmortons, a distinguished Catholic family of "goodnature, complaisance, and innocent cheerfulness" with whom Mrs. Unwin and he soon became friends. At the Throckmortons' invitation he rented the Lodge at Weston Hall in November 1786. This change in residence was a removal to symbolic Parnassian splendor, as well as to the actual locality of the landscapes most warmly praised in *The Task*: in a 9 August 1791 letter to James Hurdis, imitator of *The Task*, Cowper was to describe how he had exchanged the life of a recluse at Orchard Side for that of a comfortable celebrity at Weston, exposed to "all manner of inroads" and "visited by all around." Cultivated and pleasant surroundings, however, could do nothing to prevent a fourth bout of extreme depression from setting in during 1787 after the sudden death of William Unwin. Mrs. Unwin herself cut the rope by which the poet once again tried to kill himself.

It was death in other quarters that gave Cowper his next chance to show a face to the world. One day in November he received a visit from the clerk of the parish of All Saints, Northampton, with a request for verses to affix to the forthcoming Bill of Mortality (the annual public list and analysis of deaths in the parish). He wrote Lady Hesketh on 27 November: "To this I replied—Mr. Cox, you have several men of Genius in your town. . . . There is a namesake of yours in particular, Cox, the Statuary, who, everybody knows, is a first-rate Maker of Verses. He is surely the man of all the world for your purpose. Alas Sir! I have heretofore borrowed help from him, but he is a Gentleman of so much reading that the people of our town cannot understand him." This wry anecdote brims with Cowper's confidence in his own powers as a man of genius and much reading who can, when he likes, write to be readily understood. He was never at a loss for an appropriate voice, and in the event supplied stanzas in "the Mortuary stile" six times between 1787 and 1793, using such shrewd devices as the disconcertingly grotesque idea of a predictive rather than retrospective Bill to bring a cutting edge to the genre's customary appeals for reformation, and recognition that no one can escape the fatal, often unexpected hour: "No med'cine, though it often cure, / Can always balk the tomb."

Cowper knew what a "sentence" was in more than one sense, and the aura of his private desert places undoubtedly contributed to the vivification of functional objectives in these poems, as it did also in the dramatic monologue of "The Negro's Complaint" and other lyrics commissioned in 1788 for the Committee for the Abolition of the Slave Trade, which were widely circulated and served as an effective guide to popular protest for Southey and later exponents of the cause. Nearer home, the residue of the psychotic disturbance of 1787 explains the return to nightmare at the heart of his uncanniest poem:

Just then, by adverse fate impress'd,
A dream disturb'd poor Bully's rest:
    In sleep he seem'd to view
A rat, fast-clinging to the cage,
And, screaming at the sage presage,
    Awoke and found it true.

Abstractly considered, "On the Death of Mrs. Throckmorton's Bulfinch" is the perfect example of the special mixture of conscious artistry and subjective impulse in Cowper that prefigures the modern poetry of tragicomical happenstance and the surreal. Yet nothing is faked. On one level a brilliant performance in mock elegy and the art of cementing friendship, the poem is invaded by Cowper's instinctive vision of how the end can come at any moment, for caged birds and secluded bards alike. The moral of Bully's demise seems to be that pets had better be kept in wire cages, not pretty wooden ones; but Cowper takes a secret delight in Mrs. Throckmorton's improvidence, for to be broken in upon is also to be freed from the suspense of a world where sinister forces wait ever ready to strike. His response to the image of his own long-awaited destruction is poised between terror and exhilarated relief, foretelling the deathbed utterance of "The Castaway."

The last decade of Cowper's life began promisingly. There were attempts to get him the laureateship left vacant by the death of Thomas Warton, the translation of Homer was lodged with the publisher, and a surprise appearance by John Johnson, the grandson of his uncle Roger Donne, put him in touch with his mother's family after a break of twenty-seven years. Cowper felt an immediate bond with "wild boy Johnson," in whom he saw "a shred of my own mother," and a few weeks into 1790 he received from his cousin, Anne Bodham, the portrait of his mother which, in an atmosphere of spontaneous "trepidation of nerves and spirits," inspired one of the most unusual, and finest, poems of self-revelation in the language.

The critic Hazlitt valued "On the Receipt of My Mother's Picture out of Norfolk" for its extraordinary pathos. But one is struck no less by the way Cowper's wide-awake intelligence refines and directs the unguarded feelings that emerge as he looks back in intimate detail to the security of infancy and then to the desolate bewilderment that descended when his mother died in his sixth year. Biographers have used the poem to describe what Cowper's early childhood was like. Though it certainly unearths the main material fact behind his lifelong sense of adversity, and though the recollections of a previous bliss—the "fragrant waters" or "confectionary plum," the smile that met his efforts to prick into paper the patterns of the "tissued flow'rs" on his mother's dress—are no doubt authentic, he is patently involved in a process of construction, sorting his life into a history so as to be able better to comprehend it. Yet whereas the Puritan autobiographers customarily traced in their past the consoling patterns of a journey to salvation, Cowper here confirms, and faces up to, a tragic destiny: the child wretchedly bereaved, "dupe of *to-morrow*" in his disappointed hopes that his mother will return, is father of the man denied all promise of reaching the heavenly shore, "always distress'd":

> Me howling winds drive devious, tempest-toss'd,
> Sails ript, seams op'ning wide, and compass lost,
> And day by day some current's thwarting force
> Sets me more distant from a prosp'rous course.

The poet comes to terms with his predicament, which he climactically objectifies in the sea imagery that was a habitual component of his private iconography. But the triumph of the poem is not only that of acceptance; for, building on the idea of art being able to baffle time, he uses memory, the recovery of spots of time, to bring solace in the present: "By contemplation's help, not sought in vain, / I seem t'have lived my childhood o'er again; / To have renewed the joys that once were mine. . . . " In a finely balanced ending he keeps faith with the "wings of fancy," with wishes and the answering charms of illusion, while admitting that they are only a provisional escape from harsh reality. "On the Receipt of My Mother's Picture" is related to eighteenth-century elegy but represents a new species of reflective meditation, the dialogue of the mind with itself commonly known as the "greater Romantic lyric." It was published in 1798 and at once entered the canon of essential English poetry.

The rediscovery and mapping out of a lost past was a liberating experience for Cowper. Another good chance came his way in 1791 when Joseph Johnson offered him the editorship of the works of Milton in a major publishing venture for which Fuseli was to design the engravings. This novel engagement, which Cowper welcomed as adding the rank of "Critic" to his other accomplishments, had an important offshoot in his friendship with William Hayley, who had agreed to write a life of Milton for a rival de luxe edition planned by the publishers John Boydell and George Nicol. Hayley's "handsome" and "affectionate" approach to a potential competitor, and his subsequent loyalty, are highlights of the later stages of Cowper's life. It was largely through his exertions that Cowper was granted a Crown pen-

John Johnson, the grandson of Cowper's maternal uncle Roger Donne (engraving by H. Robinson, from a drawing by W. Harvey, after the original by L. F. Abbott). Johnson's surprise appearance in 1790 put Cowper in touch with his mother's family for the first time in twenty-seven years.

sion in 1794 (an event made possible by the fact that, despite his Whig sympathies, Cowper had always been an outspoken monarchist and had publicly commemorated the king's recovery from madness in the panegyric "Annus Memorabilis 1789"); and it was in Hayley's *Life of Milton*, published in the same year, that Cowper's translations of Milton's Italian and Latin poems first appeared. These pieces and some fragmentary annotation on *Paradise Lost* (1667) and on Dr. Johnson's *Life of Milton* (1779), however, were the only elements of the Milton project ever to see the light of day. Enthusiasm had soon given way to frustration as domestic anxieties began to impinge mercilessly on Cowper's labors. In late 1791 Mrs. Unwin had suffered a paralytic stroke; the walls had started to close in again.

Mrs. Unwin lingered, through several further attacks, until 1796. To the poet who had undergone his own bouts of horrific stultification, the daily sight of his helpmate's living death must have seemed the cruelest visitation of all. Yet, as so often before, achievement was born of affliction. In "To Mary," written in 1793, he both subdues the fires and keeps the wraith of feeling alive. It is a marvelously poised and relentlessly painful love poem, altogether redeemed from sentimentality by an honest cleaving to the hard facts of the situation—Cowper's dependence on Mary; her incapacity; her blindness; and her "indistinct expressions"—and by the integrity of their artistic treatment:

Thy needles, once a shining store,
For my sake restless heretofore,
Now rust disus'd, and shine no more,
My Mary! . . .

My Boy, I long to see thee again. It has happen'd
some way or other that Mrs Unwin and I have con-
-ceived a great affection for thee. That I should, is
the less to be wonder'd at because thou art a shred
of my own mother; neither is the wonder great that
she should fall into the same predicament, for she
loves every thing that I love. You will observe
that your own personal right to be beloved
makes no part of the consideration. There is
nothing that I touch with so much tenderness as the
vanity of a young man, because I know how extremely
susceptible he is of impressions that might hurt him,
in that particular part of his composition. If you
should ever prove a coxcomb, from which character
you stand just now at a greater distance than any
young man I know, it shall never be said that I have
made you one. No—you will gain nothing by me

Third page of Cowper's 23 March 1790 letter to John Johnson (Princeton University Library)

But well thou play'd'st the housewife's part,
And all thy threads with magic art
Have wound themselves about this heart,
My Mary!

Familiar objects have become forceful symbols of a desolation Cowper cannot evade, but which he can oppose by the magic of his own worthiest art, the sincere affection that transforms atrophy into beauty, Mary's "silver locks" into "orient beams," her lifeless hands into a "richer store" than gold.

Cowper's imagination was more often gripped in these years, however, by the old nightmare of worthlessness and damnation. He again saw himself being led to execution, and he dreamed of his "everlasting martyrdom in fire." Samuel Teedon, the Olney schoolmaster to whom he sent his visions for analysis, has gone down in biographical tradition as a sham who duped the ailing poet of his money; but he brought some comfort as a confidant, even after Cowper came to consider his promising notices from God about Mary's health and his own salvation to be a divine joke, the Almighty's "deadliest arrows." Less helpful to Cowper's condition was the dissension that broke out at Weston following his return from a visit in 1792 to Hayley's estate at Eartham in Sussex, where Mrs. Unwin's temporary improvement and the company of the painter George Romney and other celebrities had put him in a better frame of mind. Lady Hesketh grew increasingly antagonistic toward Mrs. Unwin, attacking her on a variety of issues, including the flirtatious behavior of her ward, Hannah Wilson. One gets the impression sometimes of jealous dislike and sometimes of well-meaning but counterproductive concern to prise Cowper free from an obvious burden. Whatever Harriot Hesketh's motives and hopes in taking personal charge of her cousin during 1793 and 1794, by 1795 there seemed little left to save: according to a 19 June 1795 letter from John Johnson to Catharine Johnson, Cowper looked like "a Ghost"—"nothing but skin and bone."

It was decided that Johnson should take Cowper and Mrs. Unwin into his care in Norfolk. After short stays at North Tuddenham, Mundesley, and Dunham Lodge, the three settled in 1796 at East Dereham. Mrs. Unwin's death in December had little effect on Cowper, for his health was already deteriorating rapidly. He heard voices both night and day and suffered hallucinations, recorded in Johnson's diary, of drinking "rankest poison," being "disjointed by the Rack," and being "taken up in his bed by strange women," which suggest complicated and disturbingly specific infantile repressions. The only person from whom he sought help was the housekeeper, Margaret Perowne, a middle-aged woman who followed Mrs. Unwin in stationing herself in the corner of his bedroom. The vigilant Johnson nevertheless tried out the ingenious, but hopeless, stratagem of sending encouraging suggestions down a speaking tube secreted behind the bed.

At intervals, however, another Cowper emerges from this eerie, claustrophobic picture of introversion and inexorable decline. On leaving Weston he had written a "farewell" to God "with a hand that is not permitted to tremble," and near Mundesley he had seen as an exact emblem of himself "a solitary pillar of rock" awaiting the lashing of the storm. A conviction of uniqueness had always run through his life and writings: "I am of a very singular temper, and very unlike all the men I have ever conversed with," he told Harriot Hesketh as early as 1763. But there is something newly decisive and heroic in these later self-projections. This is the Cowper who at last stood beyond both aid and despair, who hugged his fate to him and drew stature expressly from it—the lucid, unflinching Cowper of "The Castaway."

A similar shift of sensibility can be seen in a hardening compulsion toward the primitive, the oracular, and the demonic during this phase of Cowper's career. In "Yardley Oak," written in 1791, he had brooded in cramped, angular Miltonic verse on a terrible autonomous beauty and on the shattered oak as a form companionate with his own monumental persistence and decay, but he had also consented to the rationalizing constraints of a Christian view of nature and human history. "Montes Glaciales," composed immediately before "The Castaway" in March 1799, has an entirely pagan landscape of wondrous "portents." Cowper associates himself with the ice-islands whose true abode is primeval "Cimmerian darkness," and in ordering them back from the light and softer air of the Apollonian world into which they have ventured allegorizes his embrace of an imaginative destination, Godless and forbidding, that is the obverse of the paradise of contemplative seclusion in which he had once laid claim to spiritual ease and renovation. When he recapitulates to Lady Hesketh in 1798 the "rapture" to be gained from "delightful scenes" it is only to complain of a present "blindness" that makes them "an universal blank"; the radiance of inspiration is past and gone, "an almost forgotten dream." Yet with the approach of death came not autistic dereliction but power of a different order.

The immediate trigger for "The Castaway" was a passage in George Anson's *Voyage round the World* (1748) recording the "unhappy fate" of a seaman swept overboard in a violent storm. Cowper briefly identifies with the "destin'd wretch" at the outset, but then withholds precise definition of the interrelationship for eight narrative stanzas which delve into the particulars of the mariner's struggle yet express with piercing clarity that whole bleak view of human life and destiny that underlies so many of his works. The opening personifications—"Obscurest night involv'd the sky . . . "—evoke a setting of actively hostile, conspiratorial forces. And everything that happens to the protagonist in this grim universe is full of incredible irony: his courage is admirable but futile, "supported by despair of life"; his comrades try to help him but, "pitiless perforce," must race

William Cowper (engraving by Francesco Bartolozzi after a portrait by Sir Thomas Lawrence, 1793)

away to save themselves on the very wind that carries his cries for help toward them; he understands their haste, yet "bitter felt it still to die / Deserted, and his friends so nigh." The climax exemplifies the immense figurative depth that Cowper brings to the plain, logical style he inherited, along with the pulsating metre of "sixes" and "eights," from hymnodic practice: "For then, by toil subdued, he drank / The stifling wave, and then he sank." We drink to stay alive, but here the act of imbibing is a dreadful communion with death as the mariner, by the greatest irony of all, is exhausted through his own efforts to survive and voluntarily participates in the preordained ritual of his destruction.

In this uncompromising vision Cowper is clearly writing out of and reviewing his own experience, his lasting strife in a world of rigid predestination. Yet the poem overall is more a cathartic assertion of strength than a lament for helplessness and suffering. When he comes to specify his interest in Anson's bereft mariner it is pleasure, not pain, that he stresses:

But misery still delights to trace
Its 'semblance in another's case.

No voice divine the storm allay'd,
  No light propitious shone;
When, snatch'd from all effectual aid,
  We perish'd, each alone:
But I beneath a rougher sea,
And whelm'd in deeper gulphs than he.

There is no self-pity here, but rather equanimity and gain. Cowper's "delight" is not simply the commonplace consolation of finding a fellow in affliction: on the contrary, he finally emphasizes " 'semblance" as *difference*, taking status from the greater extremity of his lot in the "deeper gulphs" of inner turmoil. The end of "The Castaway" is his most audacious act of writing the self uniquely and positively into being. When talking of the absence of divine aid he is thinking of the episode from Pope's *Odyssey* (1725-1726) where Odysseus is rescued from the torments of the sea by an interposition that decrees "thy miseries shall end"; he is feeding on the idea that his life is a somber latter-day version of the trials of the archetypal hero-sufferer whose adventures were in his mind from his continuing revision of his own translation of Homer. But the "voice divine" also signifies the God who had abandoned him. With utter self-possession, Cowper inscribes his acceptance of the fact that his world is literally Godforsaken; and, more defiantly still, he turns the tables on providential authority, displacing it to the margins of a drama in which he and his destiny are made the enduring attraction. Paradoxically, at the point of death he authors for himself an immortal voice and presence, snatching affirmation from the jaws of the Calvinist "plot" which had darkened his existence. The favored Christian in *The Pilgrim's Progress* had inherited eternal life by passing through the River of Death to salvation; the rejected Cowper achieved it through his art, never more impressively than when going under.

Cowper died of dropsy on 25 April 1800 and was buried in the parish church at East Dereham. His *Poems* had already passed its tenth edition; four years earlier the critic and theologian Alexander Knox had published in the Dublin *Flapper* (14 May 1796) the first sustained appraisal of his genius, which set him emphatically above Pope in acclaiming his democratization of the art and function of poetry. Thinking "with the wise" in a language "intelligible even to the vulgar," Cowper had carried a sense of the sublime into the familiar world so as to counter the "opiates of luxury" and nourish in his readers an awareness of the miracles of the commonplace. Knox's evaluation, which looks principally to *The Task*, anticipates many of the arguments of Wordsworth's preface to the second edition of his and Coleridge's *Lyrical Ballads* (1800) and is a forceful reminder of Cowper's importance to the coming generation as an example of the poet who is a man speaking to men but with insight sufficient to restore the mind from the lethargy of custom, the cult of sensationalism, and the growing torpor of urban and industrialized existence. Jane Austen—as is shown by references to Cowper in her letters and novels—admired him for comparable reasons, but in terms that declare the more conservative side of his early and later appeal. She found in him not the dawning of a Romantic valorization of redemptive feeling but a guardian of the traditional virtues of moral discipline and social stability.

Cowper's reputation suffered to some extent with the advent of the second, headier wave of Romanticism; Hazlitt thought him "a genuine poet" but complained of a certain "effeminacy," while Byron reacted ferociously, in a controversy with W. L. Bowles, to the prevailing preference for (in the latter's words) Cowper's "affecting pictures from the most common circumstances" over Pope's depiction of "artificial life." Yet Cowper's general standing and popularity stayed more or less intact throughout the nineteenth century and well into the twentieth, albeit on grounds that seem thin in comparison with Knox's account of a major innovator. Walter Bagehot's influential essay of 1855 reveals that he was a household name but puts this status down to his adoption by the middle, and particularly the religious, classes, and to his relatively modest talents in "delicate . . . and appreciative delineation of the simple essential English country" and "the petty detail of quiet relaxation" dressed in a "sober suit of well-fitting expressions." This notion of a cup that cheers but does not inebriate supplied the dominant critical view of Cowper's poetry for the next hundred years, although there was also continuing appreciation of the comic and patriotic poems and, aided by the dissemination of the unpublished verse and letters, an expanding interest in that strain of intense self-reference which had reached its climax in "The Castaway." This side of Cowper was one with which the Brontë sisters, Alfred Tennyson, Elizabeth Barrett Browning, and Charles Augustin Sainte-Beuve all felt special sympathy.

It became widely felt indeed that Cowper's life offered more of an adventure in understanding than his work. Biography flourished from the days of Hayley and Southey onwards, given impetus by polemic over the effects of his exposure to Evangelicalism but reflecting everywhere the fascination of his singular experiences and their well-documented milieu. That fascination remains, as does the unusually palpable consonance in Cowper between the life and the texts. Recent decades, however, have seen committed revaluation of the poetry itself on several fronts. The assumption that Cowper is a simple writer has given way both to a proper sense of his craftsmanship in social genres—that use of wit, cultured sobriety, or (as in the hymns) shared symbolic language which makes him a poet of community—and to investigation of his subjective and introspective modes, that densely textured poetry of experience and the inner recesses of the mind in which his modernity substantially lies.

Cowper has always been linked with other

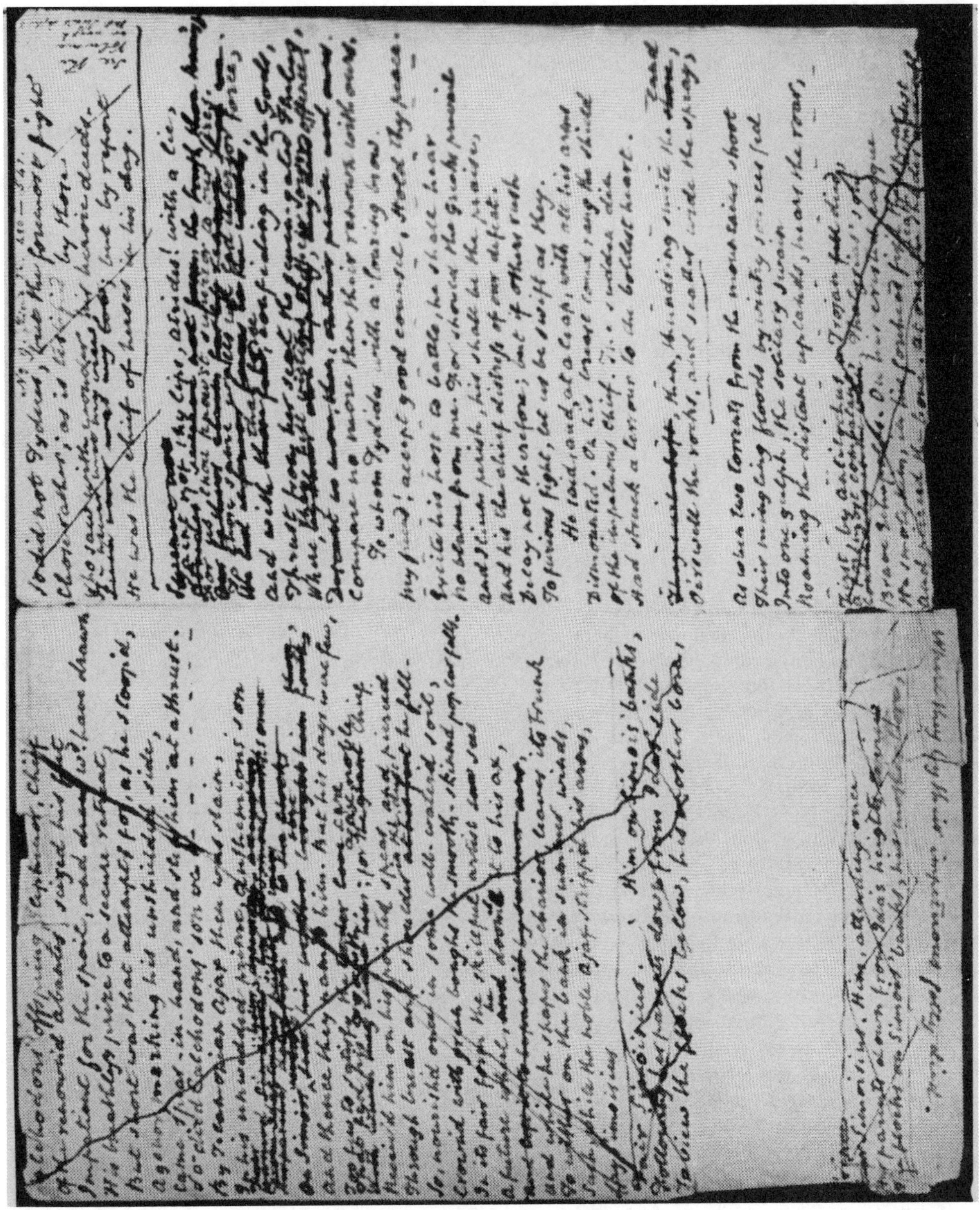

Part of a draft for Cowper's never-completed translation of the Iliad. *This draft is written on the back of a letter Cowper wrote to his cousin and patron Lady Harriot Hesketh on 30 May 1796. Apparently dissatisfied with the letter, Cowper rewrote it and mailed the second version (Pickering & Chatto, Catalogue 673, 1989).*

"pre-Romantics," such as Oliver Goldsmith, William Collins, and Thomas Gray, in a shift from the urban and satirical vision of Pope to a reflective and rural one; but he took the journey within—what Northrop Frye terms the poetry of "process" as opposed to rhetorical "product"—much further than any of his contemporaries and did so, especially in *The Task*, in ways that register historical change on a much larger scale. No poet perceived more acutely the unsettlement that came with the emplacement of progressive materialist ideology in the socioeconomic sphere and with the groundswell of rationalist thought where Deism, which transferred God to the reaches of space, was a natural concomitant of the Lockean concept of mind as screened off from metaphysical reality. As an advocate of revealed religion, Cowper fought a rearguard action in favor of an orthodox closed world bounded by Divinity; but in giving practical access to a value system and ontology grounded variously in the artist's imaginative idealism, interchange between self and nature, and the making of identity, he trod a path to the future. It has been effectively argued that the permanence of his poems and correspondence, and their overarching unity, rest above all on their portrayal of the basic conflicts of the human psyche; his preoccupations with fatality and revolt, freedom and the shut-in state, harmony and confusion, salvation and despair, Morris Golden has written, "are hugely powerful—so powerful that they constituted his madness—but they are preoccupations which, to a greater or lesser degree, we all share." Yet this timeless relevance is at one with Cowper's broader prediction of our condition in time. He was the first poet to articulate in depth and in his own character the anxieties and aspirations of the individual thrown back upon himself and his resources in the felt absence of a coherent living culture and inviolable framework of belief: the prototype not only (in W. B. Yeats's phrase) of the poet "walking naked" but (as the twentieth-century sociologist Philip Rieff puts it in *The Triumph of the Therapeutic* [1966]) of "psychological man" in whom "the new center, which can be held even as communities disintegrate, is the self."

Letters:

The Letters and Prose Writings of William Cowper, 5 volumes, edited by James King and Charles Ryskamp (Oxford & New York: Clarendon Press/Oxford University Press, 1979-1986).

Bibliographies:

Lodwick Hartley, *William Cowper: The Continuing Revaluation. An Essay and a Bibliography of Cowperian Studies from 1895 to 1960* (Chapel Hill: University of North Carolina Press, 1960);

Norma Russell, *A Bibliography of William Cowper to 1837* (Oxford: Oxford Bibliographical Society and Oxford University Press, 1963);

Biographies:

Samuel Greatheed, *Memoirs of the Life and Writings of William Cowper* (London: Printed for T. Williams, 1803; revised edition, London: Printed for Whittingham and Arliss, 1814);

Thomas Taylor, *The Life of William Cowper* (London: Smith, Elder, 1833; enlarged edition, London: Seeley & Burnside, 1833);

Thomas Wright, *The Life of William Cowper* (London: Unwin, 1892; revised and enlarged edition, London: Farncombe, 1921);

Hugh I'Anson Fausset, *William Cowper* (London: Cape, 1928);

Lord David Cecil, *The Stricken Deer; or, The Life of Cowper* (London: Constable, 1929; Indianapolis: Bobbs-Merrill, 1930);

Gilbert Thomas, *William Cowper and the Eighteenth Century* (London: Nicholson & Watson, 1935; revised edition, London: Allen & Unwin, 1948);

Maurice J. Quinlan, *William Cowper: A Critical Life* (Minneapolis: University of Minnesota Press, 1953);

Charles Ryskamp, *William Cowper of the Inner Temple, Esq. A Study of His Life and Works to the Year 1768* (Cambridge: Cambridge University Press, 1959);

James King, *William Cowper: A Biography* (Durham, N. C.: Duke University Press, 1986).

References:

Walter Bagehot, "William Cowper," *National Review*, 1 (July 1855): 31-72; reprinted in *Literary Studies by the Late Walter Bagehot*, edited by R. H. Hutton (London: Longmans, Green, 1898), I: 87-143;

T. E. Blom, "Eighteenth-Century Reflexive Process Poetry," *Eighteenth-Century Studies*, 10 (Fall 1976): 52-72;

David Boyd, "Satire and Pastoral in *The Task*," *Papers on Language and Literature*, 10 (Fall 1974): 363-377;

Wallace C. Brown, *The Triumph of Form: A Study of the Later Masters of the Heroic Couplet* (Chapel Hill: University of North Caronlia Press, 1948), pp. 132-141;

Dorothy H. Craven, "Cowper's Use of 'Slight Connection' in 'The Task': A Study in Structure and Style," Ph.D. dissertation, University of Colorado, 1953;

Donald Davie, "The Critical Principles of William Cowper," *Cambridge Journal*, 7 (December 1953); 182-188;

Davie, *Purity of Diction in English Verse* (London: Chatto & Windus, 1952), pp. 52-61;

D. J. Enright, "William Cowper," *The Pelican Guide to English Literature: From Dryden to Johnson*, edited by Boris Ford (Harmondsworth, U.K.: Penguin, 1957), IV: 387-398;

Richard Feingold, *Nature and Society: Later Eighteenth-Century Uses of the Pastoral and Georgic* (Hassocks, U.K.: Harvester Press, 1978; New Brunswick, N.J.: Rutgers University Press, 1978), pp. 121-192;

William Norris Free, *William Cowper* (New York: Twayne, 1970);

Northrop Frye, "Towards Defining an Age of Sensibility," *Journal of English Literary History*, 23 (June 1956): 144-152;

Morris Golden, *In Search of Stability: The Poetry of William Cowper* (New York: Bookman Associates, 1960);

Hoosag K. Gregory, "The Prisoner and His Crimes: A Psychological Approach to William Cowper's Life and Writings," Ph.D. dissertation, Harvard University, 1951;

Dustin Griffin, "Cowper, Milton and the Recovery of Paradise," *Essays in Criticism*, 31 (January 1981): 15-26;

Lodwick Hartley, " 'The Stricken Deer' and His Contemporary Reputation," *Studies in Philology*, 36 (October 1939): 637-650;

Hartley, *William Cowper, Humanitarian* (Chapel Hill: University of North Carolina Press, 1938);

William Hazlitt, "On Thomson and Cowper," in his *Lectures on the English Poets* (London: Dent, 1964; New York: Dutton, 1964), pp. 85-104;

Roderick Huang, *William Cowper: Nature Poet* (London: Oxford University Press, 1957);

Bill Hutchings, *The Poetry of William Cowper* (London & Canberra, Australia: Croom Helm, 1983);

Hutchings, "William Cowper and 1789," in *The Yearbook of English Studies*, volume 19: *The French Revolution in English Literature and Art*, edited by J. R. Watson (London: Modern Humanities Research Association, 1989), pp. 71-93;

Alexander Knox, "Cowper," *Flapper*, 30 (14 May 1796): 116-119; 34 (28 May 1796): 133-136; 38 (11 June 1796); 149-152; reprinted in *Eighteenth Century Critical Essays*, edited by S. Elledge (Ithaca, N.Y.: Cornell University Press, 1961), II: 1104-1121;

Kenneth MacLean, "William Cowper," in *The Age of Johnson: Essays Presented to Chauncey Brewster Tinker*, edited by Frederick W. Hilles (New Haven & London: Yale University Press, 1949), pp. 257-267;

Madeleine Forell Marshall and Janet Todd, *English Congregational Hymns in the Eighteenth Century* (Lexington: University Press of Kentucky, 1982), pp. 119-146;

Ann Matheson, "The Influence of Cowper's *The Task* on Coleridge's Conversation Poems," in *New Approaches to Coleridge*, edited by Donald Sultana (London: Vision, 1981; Totowa, N.J.: Barnes & Noble, 1981), pp. 137-150;

Joseph F. Musser, "William Cowper's Rhetoric: The Picturesque and the Personal," *Studies in English Literature*, 19 (Summer 1979): 515-531;

John Neve, *A Concordance to the Poetical Works of William Cowper* (London: Sampson Low, 1887);

Vincent Newey, *Cowper's Poetry: A Critical Study and Reassessment* (Liverpool: Liverpool University Press, 1982; Totowa, N.J.: Barnes & Noble, 1982);

Newey, "William Cowper and the Condition of England," in *Literature and Nationalism*, edited by Newey and Ann Thompson (Liverpool: Liverpool University Press, 1991; Totowa, N.J.: Barnes & Noble, 1991), pp. 120-139;

Norman Nicholson, *William Cowper* (London: Lehmann, 1951);

Martin Priestman, *Cowper's "Task": Structure and Influence* (Cambridge & New York: Cambridge University Press, 1983);

Maurice J. Quinlan, "Cowper's Imagery," *Journal of English and Germanic Philology*, 47 (July 1948): 276-285;

Bruce Redford, *The Converse of the Pen: Acts of Intimacy in the Eighteenth-Century Familiar Letter* (Chicago & London: University of Chicago Press, 1986), pp. 49-92;

Patricia Meyer Spacks, *The Poetry of Vision: Five Eighteenth-Century Poets* (Cambridge, Mass.: Harvard University Press, 1967), pp. 165-206;

Spacks, "The Soul's Imaginings: Daniel Defoe, William Cowper," *PMLA*, 91 (May 1976): 420-435;

J. S. Storer and John Greig, *Cowper, Illustrated by a Series of Views In or Near the Park of Weston-Underwood, Bucks* (London: Vernor & Hood, 1803);

J. R. Watson, "Cowper's Olney Hymns," *Essays and Studies*, n.s. 38 (1985): 45-65.

Papers:

Cowper manuscripts and associated materials are widely distributed in institutions and in private hands. Major holdings have been established at Princeton University Library (the Hannay and Povey Collections); the Henry E. Huntington Library, San Marino, California (including Cowper's record book of his poems); the British Library (notably letters and the Ash manuscripts of holograph poems); and the Cowper and Newton Museum, Olney, Bucks. Among other important collections and items are those at the Pierpont Morgan Library, New York; the Fitzwilliam Museum, Cambridge; Coughton Court, Warwickshire (Throckmorton Manuscripts); Hertford County Record Office (Panshanger Collection of correspondence); the Bodleian Library, Oxford; and those owned by the Marquess of Salisbury at Hatfield House, Hertfordshire (Chase Price's Commonplace Book of Cowper poems) and by the Misses C. and A. Cowper Johnson (archive of letters from 1755 to 1793).

Robert Fergusson

(5 September 1750 - 17 October 1774)

Alan T. McKenzie
Purdue University

BOOKS: *Poems by Robert Fergusson* (Edinburgh: Printed by Walter & Thomas Ruddiman, 1773);

Auld Reikie: A Poem (Edinburgh: Printed for the author, 1773);

A Poem to the Memory of John Cunningham (Edinburgh: Printed by Alexr. Kincaid, and sold at Ossian's Head, 1773);

Poems on Various Subjects, by Robert Fergusson: Part II (Edinburgh: Printed by Walter and Thomas Ruddiman, 1779);

The Poetical Works of Robert Fergusson: With the Life of the Author, edited by David Irving (Glasgow: Printed by and for Chapman and Lang, 1800);

The Works of Robert Fergusson: To Which Is Prefixed, a Sketch of the Author's Life [by Alexander Peterkin] (London: Printed for S. A. and H. Oddy, 1807);

The Works of Robert Fergusson, edited by A. B. Grosart (London: Fullarton, 1851);

The Poetical Works of Robert Fergusson, edited by Robert Ford (Paisley: Gardner, 1905);

The Poems of Robert Fergusson, 2 volumes, edited by Matthew P. McDiarmid, The Scottish Text Society, series 3, volumes 21 and 24 (Edinburgh: Blackwood, 1954-1956);

The Unpublished Poems of Robert Fergusson, edited by William E. Gillis (Edinburgh: McDonald, 1955);

Poems by Allan Ramsay and Robert Fergusson, edited by Alexander M. Kinghorn and Alexander Law, The Association for Scottish Literary Studies, No. 4 (Edinburgh: Scottish Academic Press, 1974).

Robert Fergusson was born in Edinburgh on 5 September 1750, the fourth child of William and Elizabeth Forbes Fergusson, who had moved to that city from rural Aberdeen a few years earlier. His father, an educated, restless, and somewhat disappointed man, earned a meager living as a "writer" or clerk-copyist, first in a law office and later in the linen trade. A sickly child, Fergusson was educated by his parents and then by a tutor. In 1758 he enrolled in the Edinburgh High School, where he received a strong classical education. In 1762 he transferred to the Grammar School of Dundee to take up a bursary (scholarship) limited to members of the Fergusson clan. The scholarship also entitled him to four years of support at the University of St. Andrews at ten pounds a year, so in December 1764 Fergusson entered the United Colleges of St. Leonard and St. Salvator. He continued his studies in the classics, excelled in mathematics, and acquired a reputation as a songster, a prankster, and a satirist. He was befriended and encouraged by William Wilkie, a highly eccentric scholar, poet, naturalist, and farmer, who employed Fergusson to copy some of his lectures and poems. Fergusson later looked back on his undergraduate years with some fondness in his "Elegy on John Hogg, late Porter to the University of St. Andrews" (published in the *Weekly Magazine,* 23 September 1773).

Toward the end of his first year at St. Andrews, Fergusson wrote "Elegy, on the Death of Mr. David Gregory, Late Professor of Mathematics in the University of St. Andrews," which was not published until 1773. The poem is full of undergraduate high spirits and mock solemnity, with just the right amount of dignity and respect for learning. Scots words such as *skaith* (loss) and phrases such as "skelpin at the ba' " (kicking a soccer ball) fall elegantly, but playfully, into both meter and context, while the reference to Newtonian fluxions ("A ganging point compos'd a line") and surd roots reminds the reader that Fergusson was reputed to be an excellent mathematics student. Alexander Grosart, who claimed to have inspected some of the books belonging to Fergusson when he was a student, thought they revealed a nice eye for fine copies, a decided bent for religious texts (he was studying for the ministry), and good taste in poetry.

While he was still a student Fergusson abandoned a patriotic play he had been writing about

Robert Fergusson (photogravure by W. Drummond Young, from a painting by Alexander Runciman)

the Scots hero William Wallace when he learned that there was already a work under way on the same subject. He wanted, he told a friend, only to publish what was "original." His father having died in May 1767, Fergusson left St. Andrews in May 1768 without taking a degree—a by-no-means unusual practice.

He had hoped that his mother's comparatively wealthy brother might offer him support or work on his farm near Aberdeen. He visited the farm but quarreled with his uncle and followed up his hasty departure with an indignant, biting, and imprudent letter. That prospect having failed, Fergusson returned to Edinburgh and took a job in the Commissary Office copying legal documents for a penny a page. He captured the drudgery of this work feelingly in a poem on the holidays from it, "The Rising of the Session":

Writers, your finger-nebbs unbend,
  And quatt the pen,
Till *Time* wi' lyart pow [hoary head] shall send
  Blythe June again.

He sought relief from the tedium of this job in social evenings at Edinburgh pubs, in the theater, and in occasional outings into the countryside. He employed his good ear for music to compose some pastoral songs, which his friend the singer Giusto Ferdinando Tenducci introduced into his Edinburgh performances of *Artaxerxes* in 1769. Fergusson also became a close friend of William Woods, the most prominent actor in eighteenth-century Edinburgh, and spent many evenings in the theater as his guest.

In February 1771 Fergusson's first published poetry, a series of three pastorals, appeared in Walter Ruddiman's *Weekly Magazine, or Edinburgh Amusement.* They are voguish imitations of William Shenstone that betray neither Fergusson's real familiarity with the Scottish countryside nor his genius with its language; they certainly do not reveal the "originality" he had in-

Fergusson as a member of the Cape Club, an Edinburgh literary and drinking society. Each member was given a title; Fergusson's was "Sir Precentor." This lithograph is based on a sketch by another member, Alexander Runciman ("Sir Brimstone").

sisted on when he discarded his work on Wallace. The glimpses of "Edina's lofty turrets" and the flooding Tay and the references to hard work and harsh conditions are not enough to root this poetry in the Scottish landscape nor to rescue it from neglect.

It is customary to depreciate Fergusson's English poetry, and Scottish critics are especially harsh on it. His achievement is unquestionably greater in his Scottish verse, but one of the three pastorals in the *Weekly Magazine*, "A Saturday's Expedition: In Mock Heroics," offers some vigorous blank verse, witty mock-heroics, and the feel and sounds of the sea. The young poet has mastered the line and the verse paragraph and does surprisingly well with the diction:

> Now o'er the convex surface of the flood
> Precipitate we fly—our foaming prow
> Divides the saline stream—on either side
> Ridges of yesty [yeasty] surge dilate apace. . . .

Fergusson is still listening to an English muse here, but his response to it is far from negligible. The poem goes on to treat Scottish nationalism, commerce, and the Fife shoreline, as well as the local dishes and cheering glasses that fill so many of his better poems.

Of his other English poems (there are some sixty in all), "Fashion" (published in the *Weekly Magazine*, 27 February 1772) is noteworthy for its cultural nationalism and "The Rivers of Scotland" (published in *Poems by Robert Fergusson* [1773]) for its moderately successful subordination of the vigorous Scottish landscape to the flaccid diction of Arcadia. In "The Town and Country Contrasted" (published in *Poems by Robert Fergusson*) he manages to transplant the "furzy heath," "blooming broom," and "thorny whins" of the local vegetation into the depleted soil of the pastoral. But there is more humor, more dialogue, and better poetry in the Scots "An Eclogue" (first published in 1773), in which Sandie

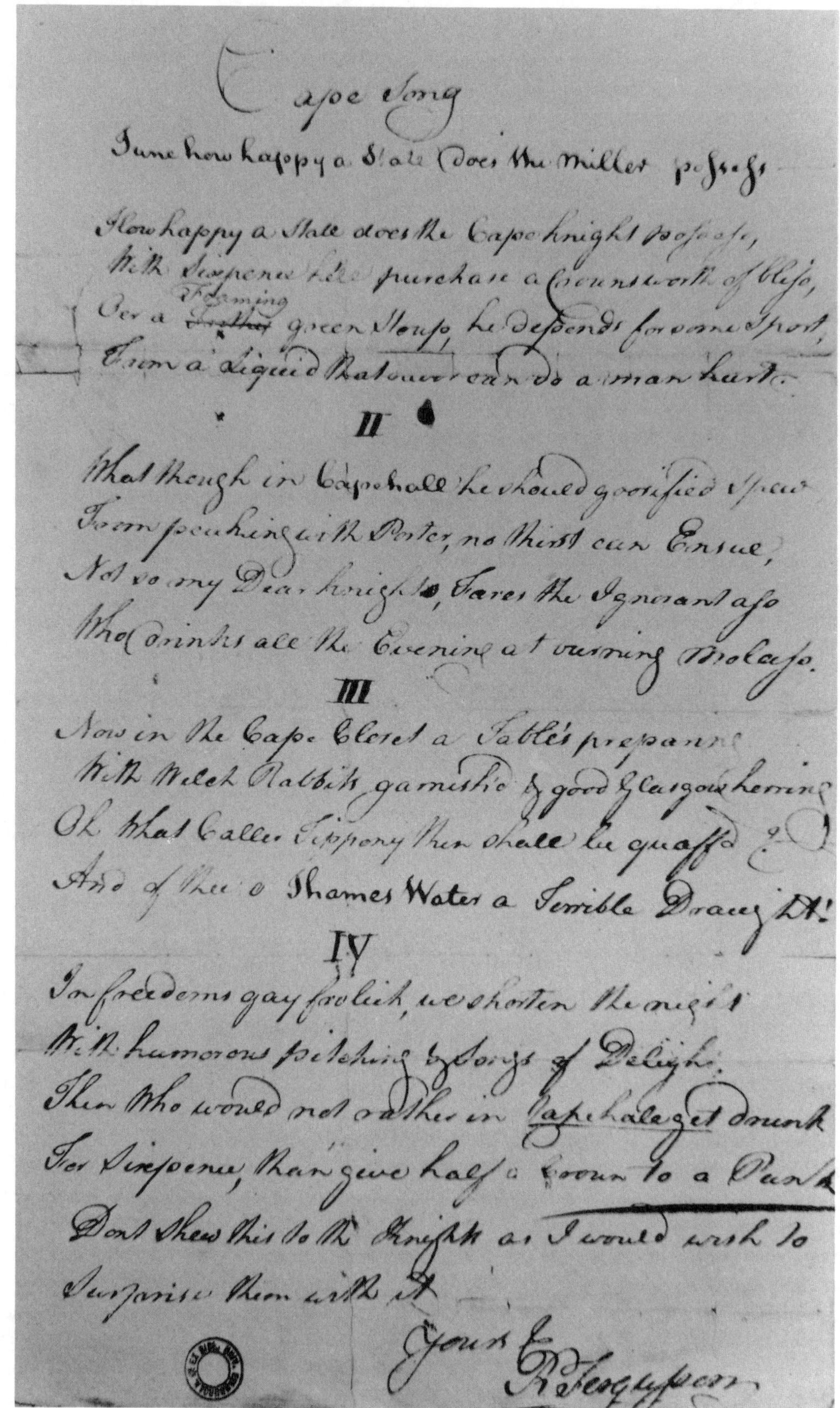

Cape Song

Tune how happy a State does the miller possess

How happy a State does the Cape knight possess,
With Sixpence [like] purchase a Crownsworth of bliss,
Oer a Foaming green House, he depends for some Sport,
From a Liquid that never can do a man hurt.

II

What though in Capehall he should goosified spew
From peuking with Porter, no thirst can Ensue,
Not so my Dear knights, Fares the Ignorant ass
Who Drinks all the Evening at burning Molass.

III

Now in the Cape Closet a Table's preparing
With Welch Rabbits garnish'd & good Glasgow herring
Oh what Caller tippony then shall be quaff'd
And of thee o Thames Water a Terrible Draught!

IV

In freedoms gay frolick, we shorten the night
With humorous pitching & Songs of Delight
Then who would not rather in Capehall get drunk
For Sixpence, than give half a Crown to a Punk

Dont Shew this to the Knights as I would wish to
Surprise them with it

Yours &c
R Fergusson

Manuscript for a song Fergusson wrote for a meeting of the Cape Club (Edinburgh University Library, MS Laing II 334/1)

Title page for Fergusson's first collection of poetry

complains of his wife, a "flyting [scolding] fury of a woman." Here the two speakers genuinely reply to one another, in language and of experiences that are made to seem vividly their own. This poem offers the modern reader, as it offered the eighteenth-century Edinburghian, a friendly but unsentimental glimpse of a rural farm with its crops, its chores, its furnishings, its luxuries and pretensions (tea!), and its own, rather than Virgil's, "cares." The *Weekly Magazine* published five more of Fergusson's English poems in 1771. "The Complaint: A Pastoral" records what must have been an actual disappointment in love; in November and December 1774 and March and April 1775 the *Weekly Magazine* published "Stella's" side of the story in even feebler verse. (The author of the poems written by "Stella" has never been identified; the poems grieve for the loss of Fergusson as both lover and tutor.)

In January 1772 the *Weekly Magazine* published "The Daft Days," the first of Fergusson's poems in the Scottish vernacular. A new note was sounded and a new voice heard in Scottish poetry. This poem is occasional, convivial, public, and playful, but enriched with an air of seriousness and a linguistic facility remarkable in so young a writer. It celebrates the holidays between Christmas and New Year and describes the effects of the December weather on Edinburgh, the surrounding fields, and the citizens who seek refuge from the cold, as in so much Scottish poetry, in the fireside and the bottle. Fergusson exploits the vernacular in words such as *mirk* (dark) and *canty* (cheerful) and employs his learning in technical terms such as *minimum* ("While, thro' his *minimum* of space, / The bleer-ey'd sun . . .). He addresses the city directly, familiarly, and fondly as "Auld Reikie"—a borrowing from Allan Ramsay and a reference to the smoking chimneys from all those convivial fires.

Before the end of 1772 the *Weekly Magazine* published nine more of Fergusson's Scots poems. One of these, "Caller [fresh, cool, invigorating] Oysters" (27 August), celebrates a quite different season and occasion, the return of fall and fresh oysters. Good for socializing and health, whether consumed at one of the taverns in the city or on a jaunt into the surrounding countryside, and the perfect accompaniment to any liquor, in any amount, the oyster becomes an occasion, a delicacy, and a treat.

The week after "Caller Oysters" appeared, the *Weekly Magazine* published the first of several tributes to its new poet from readers around the country. "To Mr Robert Fergusson," from one "J. S." in Berwick, imitates Fergusson's form and language and names him Ramsay's successor, while recognizing his hunger, his thirst, and the merit of his "sonsy [good-humoured], canty strain." A week later Fergusson reciprocated with a poem full of good humor, mild embarrassment in the face of such praise, a counteroffer of hospitality, and a playful defense of the beauty of Edinburgh women.

All four of these poems, "The Daft Days," "Caller Oysters," "J. S.'s" epistle, and Fergusson's "Answer to Mr J. S.'s Epistle" were written in "Standard Habbie," the six-line stanza form (*aaabab*) that Fergusson took over from Robert Sempill and Ramsay and polished into a quite supple medium. The fourth and sixth lines are half as long as the other four, providing a comic brevity. (That air is increased in those poems which repeat the last line as a refrain to every stanza.)

In the next poem to appear in Standard Habbie, "Braid Claith" (published in the *Weekly Magazine*, 15 October 1772), all of Fergusson's urbanity is at play, abetted by his humanism and his genius. The refrain, "gude Braid Claith," satirizes the superficial sophistication of those citizens of the city who estimate the worth of others by the cut of the clothes they wear, or who hope that others will estimate their worth by their attire.

While much of his best work is in Standard Habbie, and much of it fondly mocks the city of which he was rapidly becoming the laureate, Fergusson worked well in other forms and on other themes. "An Eclogue, to the Memory of Dr. William Wilkie, late Professor of Natural Philosophy in the University of St. Andrews" (published in the *Weekly Magazine*, 22 October 1772) is in heroic couplets. It purports to be a dialogue between two shepherds who, like all their pastoral predecessors and successors, talk as much about the making of poetry as about the lamented subject of their dirge:

> Blaw saft, my reed, and kindly to my maen [moan],
> Weel may ye thole [allow] a saft and dowie [gloomy] strain. . . .

The fond memories of Dr. Wilkie mix with an earthy vernacular and recognizably Scottish landscape ("yon broom-thackit brae"), complete with collie, ghosts, and a detailed account of Wilkie's good husbandry on the farm where Fergusson used to visit him. The poem closes with a fine tribute to his former teacher, promising him rest and fame and comparing him to Virgil.

Two more Scots poems from that first fruitful year are "Hallow Fair" (published in the *Weekly Magazine*, 12 November 1772) and "To the Tron-kirk Bell" (published in the *Weekly Magazine*, 26 November 1772). The first is in the "Christis Kirk" tradition and form—a celebration of a public festival and a nine-line stanza. The poem is full of courting couples, local fare, con men, pranks, drinking (of course), and local dialects—the informed ear can hear Aberdonian in stanza 5 and a Highland accent in stanza 10.

In October 1772 Fergusson was elected a member of the Cape Club, a selective group of bons vivants who met several evenings a week in a tavern for ceremonies, conversation, singing, and drinking. Among the members were antiquaries, printers, poets, painters, and musicians. Each member had a title; Fergusson's was "Sir Precentor," which reflected his fine voice and alluded to one of his pranks at St. Andrews. He lent his hand to the club as well as his voice, serving for a while as secretary (some of his notes and drawings survive in the club's "Sederunt Book" in the National Library of Scotland) and mentioning it in several of his poems. The club's convivial

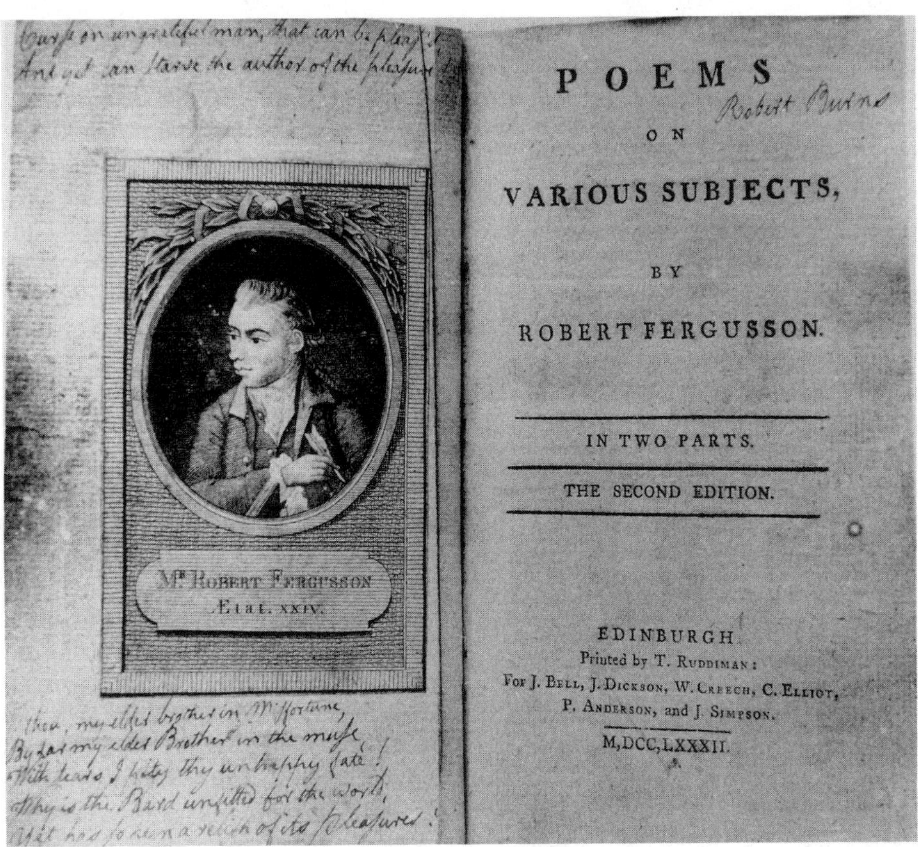
Mr. ROBERT FERGUSSON
Ætat. XXIV.

POEMS
ON
VARIOUS SUBJECTS,
BY
ROBERT FERGUSSON.

IN TWO PARTS.

THE SECOND EDITION.

EDINBURGH:
Printed by T. RUDDIMAN:
For J. BELL, J. DICKSON, W. CREECH, C. ELLIOT,
P. ANDERSON, and J. SIMPSON.
M,DCC,LXXXII.

Frontispiece and title page for the second edition of Fergusson's second collection of poems. This copy belonged to Robert Burns and is inscribed by him to "Miss R. Carmichael, Poetess"; above and below the frontispiece portrait are seven lines on Fergusson in Burns's handwriting (from Memorial Catalogue of the Burns Exhibition Held in the Galleries of the Royal Glasgow Institute of the Fine Arts, Glasgow, from 15th July till 31st October, 1896).

spirit of wit, alcohol, and bonhomie informs most of his verse.

In January 1773 the small volume *Poems by Robert Fergusson* appeared, containing twenty-seven English and nine Scots poems. The book was anticipated in several periodicals but apparently not reviewed by any. Nevertheless, it sold some five hundred copies and earned Fergusson fifty pounds—not a negligible sum for a volume of poetry, and a great deal more than he made in a year as a copyist. Several presentation copies survive, including one inscribed "To James Boswell, Esq., the Friend of Liberty and Patron of Science; the following Efforts of a Scottish youth are respectfully presented by his most obedient and very humble servt. R. Fergusson." Boswell does not seem to have recorded his reaction to this tribute.

Soon thereafter Fergusson again appeared in print outside the pages of the *Weekly Magazine,* this time in a single poem, published separately: *Auld Reikie: A Poem* (1773). The 328 lines were supposed to have been the beginning of a much longer work, but only 40 more lines were written; these were added in *Poems on Various Subjects: Part II* (1779). *Auld Reikie* follows the city through an early winter's day, moving rapidly from its "Lands" (tenement buildings) to its shops, markets, taverns, and clubs (especially the Cape Club). At the same time, it celebrates the city's smells and sounds and laments its whores, "Macaronies" (dandies), "Bruisers," and politicians. It moves easily up and down the social scale from "servant lasses," "cadies" (messengers), and sedan-chair men to traders, lawyers, and "some daft Birky [fellow], ranting fu'." It progresses through the week to give the reader a glimpse of over-sober kirkgoers, a funeral, strollers in the parks and surrounding countryside, and debtors seeking sanctuary in Holyrood Abbey. *Auld Reikie* is a brilliant urban amalgam, based on John Gay's *Trivia; or, The Art of Walking the Streets of London* (1716), but celebrating the Northern City in a Northern tongue. Even in its foreshortened version it is Fergusson's longest poem and one of his best. It shows how well he could handle the octosyllabic couplet as well as the layout (both geographic and social) and language of the city.

Two resoundingly Edinburghian poems appeared in the *Weekly Magazine* in March 1773. The first, "Mutual Complaint of Plainstanes and Causey, in their Mother-tongue" (4 March), consists of a nocturnal "crack" (chat) between Plainstanes, the class-conscious sidewalk who complains of the working-class boots that tramp over him, and the causeway, which bemoans the wagons, horses, and carriages that he must bear. Plainstanes pleads a dainty nature and a preference for ladies' feet, while Causey boasts of having been quarried from Arthur's Seat (the long extinct volcano that looms over the city of Edinburgh) and of the lawyers who gather on his stones out of habit. The second, "The Rising of the Session," (18 March) reverts to Standard Habbie. An occasional poem, it celebrates and laments the recent end of the winter legal term (12 November to 12 March), the departing of attorneys and judges, the relief of the clerks (including Fergusson), and the emptiness of the taverns. When the winter session resumed the next fall, Fergusson greeted it with "The Sitting of the Session." In this somewhat more satiric companion piece the money and the liquor flow freely, and the clerks go back to their drudgery very early in the day: "At five-hour's bell scribes shaw their faces, / And rake their ein [eyes]." Winter casts a chill over all, and the law takes on a grim, Dickensian aspect.

Fergusson did not immure himself in the city. In August 1773 he paid a long visit to the estate of a friend at North Belton, near Dunbar. Several poems, "Tea," "Ode to the Gowdspink," and "An Expedition to Fife . . . " (published in the *Weekly Magazine*, 5, 12, and 26 August 1773, respectively), emanated from this visit and serve as a reminder that his urbanity never cut him off from the surrounding countryside. Another expedition a month or so later took him to Dumfries, and that, too, resulted in a poem, a noticeably less serious piece of work. "Dumfries" was published in the *Dumfries Weekly Magazine* (28 September 1773), further evidence of how widely read and how much in demand Fergusson's works had already become (and also an indication of how widespread reading and poetry were in Scotland in this period). But it is not a very good poem. Perhaps by this time he needed the stimulus and the challenge of an Edinburgh outlet and a national audience.

Between the "Rising" and the "Sitting" of the session, that is, between the middle of March and the beginning of November 1773, Fergusson had twenty poems published in addition to the four expedition poems, all in the *Weekly Magazine*. These include "To the Principal and Professors of the University of St. Andrews, on their superb treat to Dr. Samuel Johnson" (2 September), which reproaches Fergusson's old college for the extravagant hospitality it had recently bestowed on that polysyllabic anti-Scot. Among the others was an English poem of some significance: "The Sow of Feeling" (8 April), a satiric declamation by a distressed pig, written to ridicule the fashionably excessive sentimentalism inspired by Henry Mackenzie's novel *The Man of Feeling* (1771) and many overly passionate speeches in recent plays, including Mackenzie's *The Prince of Tunis* (1773), performed at the Theatre Royal two weeks before the poem appeared. A clever blending of the barnyard and the library, the poem has several bookish models as well as a bookish target. The sow recounts a pigpen courtship and then breaks into a lament for her butchered husband and brother—with a wicked pun on "tender": "A tender husband, and a brother slain!" She concludes with a warning that no creature, warm- or cold-blooded, is safe from the threat of a banquet.

The other poems published between the "Rising" and "Sitting" of the session included several quite good moralizing odes addressed to such instructive animals as a bee (29 April), a butterfly (24 June), and a "gowdspink" (goldfinch, 12 August). The butterfly has wandered into Edinburgh from the countryside and suffers for it, while the goldfinch has been seen by Allan H. MacLaine as an emblem of the plight of the poet himself. These poems were much admired by Fergusson's contemporaries.

One of the two most important poems from this period is the Scots "The Farmer's Ingle" (published in the *Weekly Magazine*, 13 May 1773), which, many critics agree, surpasses Robert Burns's imitation of it, "The Cotter's Saturday Night" (1786). Fergusson sings in somewhat more "hamely strain" than usual, and in a nine-line Spenserian stanza he had not used before. The smoke in this poem emanates from a poor but clean and noble hut, the menu is modest (bannocks and kail), the conversation is rural (" 'Bout *kirk* and *market* eke their tales gae on"), and, this being rural Scotland, the supernatural appears in the "gudame's" tales about warlocks and "gaists."

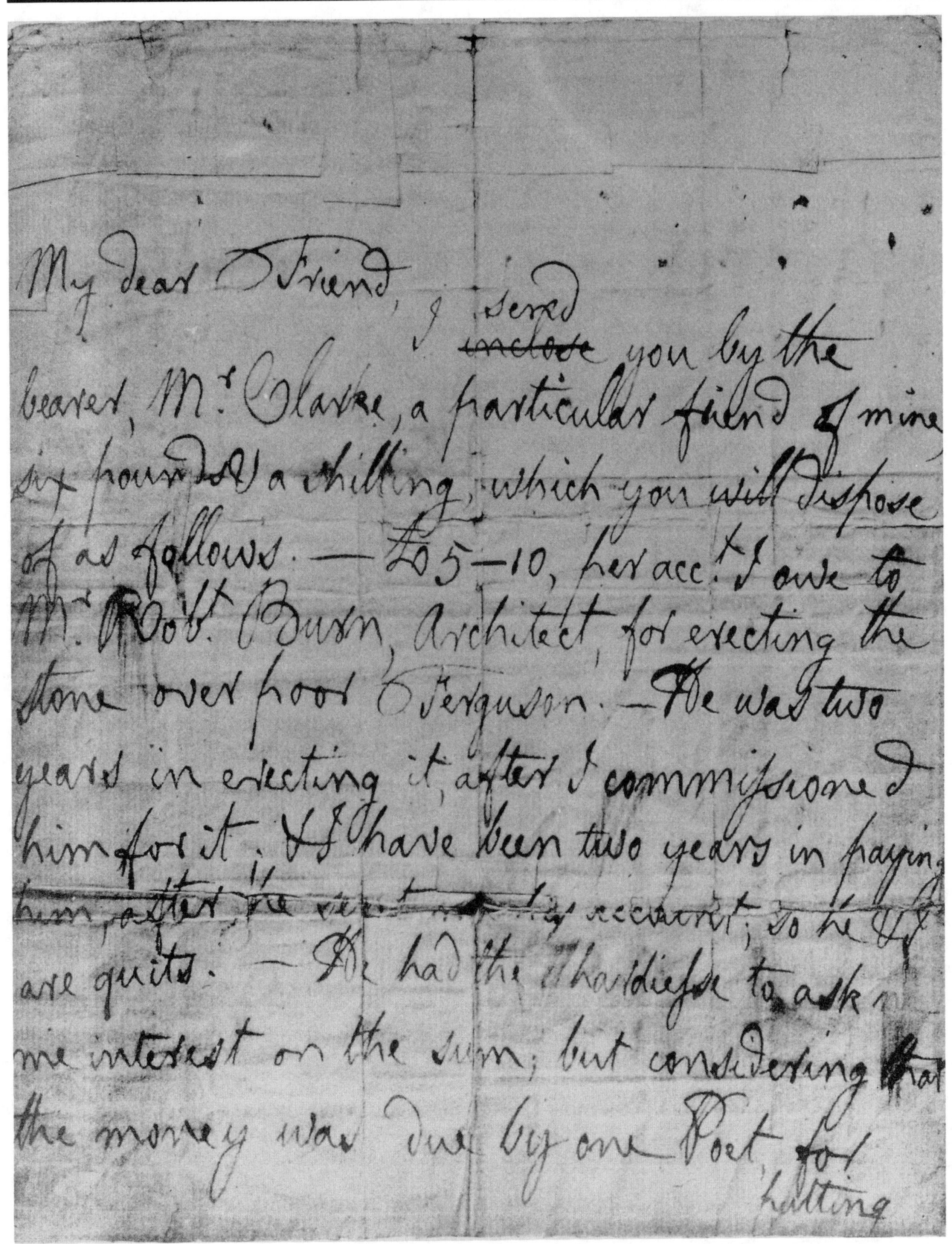

My dear Friend,

I ~~inclose~~ send you by the
bearer, Mr Clarke, a particular friend of mine
six pounds & a shilling, which you will dispose
of as follows. — £5–10, per acct I owe to
Mr Robt Burn, Architect, for erecting the
stone over poor Ferguson. — He was two
years in erecting it, after I commissioned
him for it; & I have been two years in paying
~~him, after he sent me his account~~; so he & I
are quits. — He had the hardiesse to ask me
me interest on the sum; but considering that
the money was due by one Poet, for
putting

First page of Robert Burns's 5 February 1792 letter to Edinburgh bookseller Peter Hill, in which Burns enclosed money to pay architect Robert Burn "for erecting the stone over poor Fergusson" (from Memorial Catalogue of the Burns Exhibition Held in the Galleries of the Royal Glasgow Institute of the Fine Arts, Glasgow, from 15th July to 31st October, 1896)

The poem provides a vivid, slightly sentimental glimpse into the workings and economies of a small farm household, from the spinning and cheese making within to the tilling and marketing without. There is no condescension of tone or language. On the contrary, the poem lifts the life and the language of the countryside up into the verse with grace, wit, and ease. Recent attempts by John MacQueen and F. W. Freeman to read political meanings into the old-fashioned methods of farming described in it have at least served to emphasize Fergusson's sharp eye for rural detail.

The other important Scots poem of this period, "Leith Races" (published in the *Weekly Magazine*, 22 July 1773), both celebrates and satirizes its occasion. A summery "Hallow Fair," this poem sets the abstraction "Mirth" (drawn from William Dunbar, John Milton, William Collins, and a handful of ballads) walking through the countryside around Edinburgh and speaking the local vernacular:

> I dwall amang the caller springs
>   That weet the LAND O' CAKES,
> And aften tune my canty strings
>   At BRIDALS and LATE-WAKES.

Very much a holiday poem, it mingles costumes and courting and boasts a recruiting officer, more accents and dialects, gambling, orations, drinking, and, in one quick line, the horse races that occasioned the festivities. The poem contains one unmistakeably political line, directed at the disorderly Whigs. "The Election," published two months later, devotes much more space to drinking and adultery than to the politics one might expect from its title.

On 23 October 1773 the *Weekly Magazine* praised Fergusson's elegy for a minor poet who had died in a madhouse: "Mr. Fergusson is already well known in the Poetical Department. His pieces wrote in the Scots language are perhaps equal to any of the kind this country has produced; and it is with no small surprise we see him, who has almost dedicated his talents to *humour* alone, shine in the *tender elegiac.*"

Several dozen other pieces from this period—songs, extemporaneous poems, epigrams, and the like—celebrate various companions and drinks. These poems are too brief and ephemeral to reflect the decline in health and spirits that Fergusson was undergoing. The *Weekly Magazine* of 25 November, however, contains two valedictory poems, both in octosyllabic couplets. "To My Auld Breeks" is a humorous dismissal of the worn-out breeches in which Fergusson had often "speel'd the braes [climbed the hills] o' rime." That playful phrase, which actually refers to Fergusson sitting in his garret struggling over poems, might well stand as a symbol of his best work. It brings together the Scottish landscape and language, incorporates an allusion to Parnassus, and toys with the topos of the inspired poet. Fergusson takes this occasion to remind himself of his poverty, his humility, and his contentment. In envisioning further uses for his discarded breeches, both as clothing and as a warning of humility to others, Fergusson returned to two of his favorite themes—textiles and self-importance. The poem is thick with Scots vernacular, mingled with Latin tags and a closing illustration from Philip of Macedon. In "Rob. Fergusson's Last Will" the poet repeats his satisfaction with his circumstances and bequeaths half a dozen friends something to remember him by—his snuffbox, his manuscripts, his debts, and his copy of Shakespeare (to the actor William Woods). The poem invokes the legal language Fergusson had been drudging away at for several years, and because of the tremor in the poet's hand it is signed by a notary public. A month later the *Weekly Magazine* published "Codicile to Rob. Fergusson's Last Will." This poem adds several bequests, including a picture of himself to Walter Ruddiman, evidently for an edition of his poetry. Three English poems, probably written in these final months, survive, a paraphrase of Job and odes to "Horror" and "Disappointment." While they indicate a grim state of mind, they also, according to Matthew P. McDiarmid, "have a compelling quality absent from most of his English verse."

By January 1774 Fergusson had left his job and fallen into fits of religious depression and melancholia which he termed the "Blue Devils." His chronic poor health, worsened by the effects of alcohol and perhaps syphilis, was exacerbated by a fall down a flight of stairs, and in July he was confined to the "Schelles" (cells), the Edinburgh Asylum on the grounds of Darien House, where he died on 17 October 1774. He was twenty-four years old. He was buried in the Canongate Churchyard; his grave is marked by a stone erected in 1787 by one of his greatest admirers, Robert Burns.

The obituary notice in the *Weekly Magazine* (20 October 1774) offered a judiciously laudatory estimate of Fergusson's poetic achievement: "His

Fergusson's grave in the Canongate Churchyard in Edinburgh. Robert Burns commissioned the tombstone and composed the epitaph: "No sculptur'd marble here, nor pompous lay / 'No story'd urn nor animated bust;' / This simple stone directs pale SCOTIA's way / To pour her sorrows o'er her POET's dust."

talent of versification in the Scots dialect has been exceeded by none, equalled by few. The subjects he chose were generally uncommon, often temporary. His images and sentiments were lively and striking, which he had a knack in cloathing with the most agreeable and natural expression. Had he enjoyed life and health to a maturer age, it is probable he would have revived our antient Caledonian poetry, of late so much neglected or despised." The obituary goes on to praise his powers of song and conversation. Subsequent critics have similarly acknowledged the excellence of his language, images, and sentiments and lamented the brevity of his poetic career. They have praised Fergusson for his daring (MacLaine), gravitas (David Daiches), humanism (Freeman), and the strong intellectual and satiric cast of his mind (McDiarmid). To these qualities might well be added several terms from Fergusson's own language: "braw" (fine, brave), "caller," "canty," and "pauky" (cunning, roguish, lively).

Bibliographies:

John A. Fairley, *A Bibliography of Robert Fergusson* (Glasgow: Maclehose, 1915);

Matthew A. McDiarmid, "Bibliography of Works Consulted," in *The Poems of Robert Fergusson,* edited by McDiarmid, volume 2 (Edinburgh: Blackwood, 1956), pp. xv-xxiii;

Tom Scott, "Robert Fergusson: A Bibliographical Review to 1966," *Scotia Review,* 7 (1974): 5-18.

Biographies:

David Irving, *The Life of Robert Fergusson* (Glasgow: Chapman & Lang, 1799);

Thomas Sommers, *The Life of Robert Fergusson, the Scottish Poet* (Edinburgh: Stewart, 1803);

Alexander B. Grosart, *Robert Fergusson,* Famous Scots Series (Edinburgh: Oliphant, 1898);

Matthew P. McDiarmid, "The Poet's Life," in *The Poems of Robert Fergusson,* edited by McDiarmid, volume 1 (Edinburgh: Blackwood, 1954), pp. 1-117.

References:

Frank Beaumont, "Fergusson and Burns: The Shaping of a Poet," *Proceedings of the Royal Philosophical Society of Glasgow,* 42 (1911): 71-92;

Thomas Crawford, "The Vernacular Revival and the Poetic Thrill: A Hedonist Approach," in *Scotland and the Lowland Tongue: Studies in the Language and Literature of Lowland Scotland in Honour of David Murison,* edited by J. Derrick McClure (Aberdeen: Aberdeen University Press, 1983), pp. 79-99;

David Daiches, "Eighteenth-Century Vernacular Poetry," in *Scottish Poetry: A Critical Survey,* edited by James Kinsley (London: Cassell, 1955), pp. 150-184;

Daiches, *Robert Fergusson,* Scottish Writers Series (Edinburgh: Scottish Academic Press, 1982);

Sir George Douglas, "Robert Fergusson," in his *Scottish Poetry: Drummond of Hawthornden to Fergusson* (Glasgow: Maclehose, 1911), pp. 159-193;

F. W. Freeman, *Robert Fergusson and the Scots Humanist Compromise* (Edinburgh: University Press, 1984);

Frederick C. Green, *Robert Fergussons Anteil an der Literatur Schottlands* (Heidelberg: Winter, 1923);

Daniel T. Holmes, "Robert Fergusson et son Influence," in his *French Essays on British Poets* (Glasgow: Bauermeister, 1902), pp. 1-95;

James Inverarity, "Strictures on Irving's Life of Fergusson," *Scots Magazine,* 63 (October 1801): 697-701; 63 (November 1801): 763-767;

Allan H. MacLaine, *Robert Fergusson* (New York: Twayne, 1965);

John MacQueen, "Unenlightened and Early Darkened: Alexander Ross and Robert Fergusson," in his *The Enlightenment and Scottish Literature, Volume One: Progress and Poetry* (Edinburgh: Scottish Academic Press, 1982), pp. 117-131;

Matthew P. McDiarmid, "A Study of the Poetry of Robert Fergusson," in *The Poems of Robert Fergusson,* edited by McDiarmid, volume 1 (Edinburgh: Blackwood, 1954), pp. 118-198;

Alan T. McKenzie, "*Two* 'Heads Weel Pang'd Wi' Lear': Robert Fergusson, Samuel Johnson, and St. Andrews," *Scottish Literary Journal,* 11 (December 1984): 25-35;

Jerry O'Brien, "The Sonsie Muse: The Satiric Use of Neoclassical Diction in the Poems of Robert Fergusson," *Studies in Scottish Literature,* 19 (1984): 165-176;

John W. Oliver, "Fergusson the Writer Chiel," in his *Essays in Literature* (Edinburgh: Oliver & Boyd, 1936);

William Roughead, "A Note on Robert Fergusson," *Juridical Review,* 30, 2 (1918): 99-126;

James A. Roy, "Robert Fergusson and Eighteenth-Century Scotland," *University of Toronto Quarterly,* 17 (January 1948): 179-189;

Sydney Goodsir Smith, ed., *Robert Fergusson, 1750-1774: Essays by Various Hands to Commemorate the Bicentenary of his Birth* (Edinburgh: Nelson, 1952);

John Speirs, "Robert Fergusson," in his *The Scots Literary Tradition: An Essay in Criticism* (London: Chatto & Windus, 1940), pp. 114-123.

Papers:

Robert Fergusson destroyed his papers just before he died. There are inscribed copies of his 1773 *Poems* (to Boswell and Gavin Wilson) in the National Library of Scotland, Edinburgh. Alexander B. Grosart claimed to have inspected some of the Commissary records that Fergusson copied and to have seen some letters and family documents; no trace of these has been found—see Alexander Law, "The Bibliography of Fergusson," in the 1952 collection by Sydney Goodsir Smith, pp. 157-158. A few scraps may be found in the Cape Records, MSS 2041-2044 in the National Library of Scotland; see Hans Hecht, *Songs from David Herd's Manuscripts* (Edinburgh: Hay, 1904), pp. 45-52. For the Cape Club "Summons" see Laing MS. II 334/2 in the Edinburgh University Library, and McDiarmid, volume 2, p. 295. The Edinburgh Room of the Edinburgh Central Library maintains a volume of newspaper clippings on Fergusson.

Oliver Goldsmith

(10 November 1730 or 1731 - 4 April 1774)

Oliver W. Ferguson
Duke University

See also the Goldsmith entries in *DLB 39: British Novelists, 1660-1800, DLB 89: Restoration and Eighteenth-Century Dramatists: Third Series,* and *DLB 104: British Prose Writers, 1660-1800: Second Series.*

BOOKS: *An Enquiry into the Present State of Polite Learning in Europe*, anonymous (London: Printed for R. & J. Dodsley, 1759);

The Bee, nos. 1-8 (London, 6 October - 24 November 1759); republished as *The Bee: Being Essays on the Most Interesting Subjects* (London: Printed for J. Wilkie, 1759);

The Mystery Revealed: Containing a Series of Transactions and Authentic Testimonials Respecting the Supposed Cock-Lane Ghost, anonymous (London: Printed for W. Bristow, 1762);

The Citizen of the World; or, Letters from a Chinese Philosopher, Residing in London, to His Friends in the East, anonymous, 2 volumes (London: Printed for the author & sold by J. Newbery & W. Bristow, J. Leake & W. Frederick, Bath; B. Collins, Salisbury; and A. M. Smart & Co., Reading, 1762; Albany, N.Y.: Reprinted by Barber & Southwick for Thomas Spencer, 1794);

The Life of Richard Nash, of Bath, Esq., Extracted Principally from His Original Papers, anonymous (London: Printed for J. Newbery & W. Frederick, Bath, 1762);

An History of England in a Series of Letters from a Nobleman to His Son, anonymous, 2 volumes (London: Printed for J. Newbery, 1764);

The Traveller; or, A Prospect of Society (London: Printed for J. Newbery, 1764; enlarged, 1765; Philadelphia: Printed for Robert Bell, 1768);

Essays: By Mr. Goldsmith (London: Printed for W. Griffin, 1765; enlarged, 1766);

Edwin and Angelina: A Ballad by Mr. Goldsmith, Printed for the Amusement of the Countess of Northumberland (London: Privately printed, 1765);

The Vicar of Wakefield: A Tale, 2 volumes (London: Printed by B. Collins for F. Newbery, London, 1766; revised edition, London: Printed for F. Newbery, 1766; Philadelphia: Printed for William Mentz, 1772);

The Good Natur'd Man: A Comedy (London: Printed for W. Griffin, 1768);

The Roman History, from the Foundation of the City of Rome, to the Destruction of the Western Empire, 2 volumes (London: Printed for S. Baker & G. Leigh, T. Davies & L. Davis, 1769);

The Deserted Village: A Poem (London: Printed for W. Griffin, 1770; Philadelphia: Reprinted by William & Thomas Bradford, 1771);

The Life of Thomas Parnell, D.D. (London: Printed for T. Davies, 1770);

The Life of Henry St. John, Lord Viscount Bolingbroke, anonymous (London: Printed for T. Davies, 1770);

The History of England, from the Earliest Times to the Death of George II, 4 volumes (London: Printed for T. Davies, Becket & De Hondt & T. Cadell, 1771);

Threnodia Augustalis: Sacred to the Memory of the Princess Dowager of Wales, anonymous (London: Printed for W. Woodfall, 1772);

Dr. Goldsmith's Roman History, Abridged by Himself for the Use of Schools (London: Printed for S. Baker and G. Leitch, T. Davies & L. Davis, 1772; Philadelphia: Printed for Robert Campbell, 1795);

She Stoops to Conquer; or, The Mistakes of a Night: A Comedy (London: Printed for F. Newbery, 1773; Philadelphia: Reprinted & sold by John Dunlap, 1773);

Retaliation: A Poem (London: Printed for G. Kearsly, 1774);

The Grecian History, from the Earliest State to the Death of Alexander the Great (2 volumes, London: Printed for J. & F. Rivington, T. Longman, G. Kearsly, W. Griffin, G. Robinson, R. Baldwin, W. Goldsmith, T. Cadell & T. Evans, 1774; 1 volume, Philadelphia: Printed for Mathew Carey, 1800);

Oliver Goldsmith (copy, probably by Sir Joshua Reynolds or one of his students, of an original portrait by Reynolds; National Portrait Gallery, London)

An History of the Earth, and Animated Nature (8 volumes, London: Printed for J. Nourse, 1774; 4 volumes, Philadelphia: Printed for Mathew Carey, 1795);

An Abridgement of the History of England from the Invasion of Julius Caesar to the Death of George II (London: Printed for B. Law, G. Robinson, G. Kearsly, T. Davies, T. Becket, T. Cadell & T. Evans, 1774; Philadelphia: Printed for R. Campbell, 1795);

The Haunch of Venison: A Poetical Epistle to Lord Clare (London: Printed for J. Ridley & G. Kearsly, 1776);

A Survey of Experimental Philosophy, Considered in Its Present State of Improvement, 2 volumes (London: Printed for T. Carnan & F. Newbery jun., 1776).

Editions and Collections: *The Miscellaneous Works of Oliver Goldsmith, M.B.: Containing All His Essays and Poems* (London: Printed for W. Griffin, 1775);

Poems and Plays: By Oliver Goldsmith, M.B. to Which Is Prefixed the Life of the Author (London: Printed for B. Newbery & T. Johnson, 1780);

The Miscellaneous Works of Oliver Goldsmith: Consisting of His Essays, Poems, Plays &c. &c., 2 volumes (Edinburgh: Printed for R. Morison & Son, Perth, 1791);

The Miscellaneous Works of Dr. Goldsmith: Containing All His Essays and Poems (Boston: Printed by P. Edes for Thomas & Andrews, 1793);

The Miscellaneous Works of Oliver Goldsmith, M.B.: A New Edition. . . . To Which Is Prefixed, Some Account of His Life and Writings [by Thomas Percy], 4 volumes, edited by Samuel Rose (London: Printed for J. Johnson and others, 1801; enlarged edition, London: Printed for

F. C. and J. Rivington by S. and R. Bentley, 1820)—includes *The Captivity: An Oratorio*;

The Miscellaneous Works of Oliver Goldsmith, 4 volumes, edited by James Prior (London: Murray, 1837; New York: Putnam's, 1850);

The Works of Oliver Goldsmith, 4 volumes, edited by Peter Cunningham (New York: Harper, 1881);

The Works of Oliver Goldsmith: A New Edition, Containing Pieces Hitherto Uncollected, and a Life of the Author, 5 volumes, edited by J. W. M. Gibbs (London: Bell, 1885-1886);

Complete Poetical Works of Oliver Goldsmith, edited by Austin Dobson (London: Frowde, 1906);

Collected Works of Oliver Goldsmith, 5 volumes, edited by Arthur Friedman (Oxford: Clarendon Press, 1966);

The Poems of Thomas Gray, William Collins, Oliver Goldsmith, edited by Roger Lonsdale (London & Harlow: Longmans, 1969).

PLAY PRODUCTIONS: *The Good-Natured Man*, London, Theatre Royal in Covent Garden, 29 January 1768;

She Stoops to Conquer, London, Theatre Royal, Covent Garden, 15 March 1773;

The Grumbler, London, Theatre Royal, Covent Garden, 8 May 1773.

OTHER: Jean Marteilhe, *The Memoirs of a Protestant, Condemned to the Galleys of France for His Religion*, translated by Goldsmith as James Willington, 2 volumes (London: Printed for R. Griffiths & E. Dilly, 1758);

Plutarch's Lives, Abridged from the Original Greek, Illustrated with Notes and Reflections, 7 volumes (London: Printed for J. Newbery, 1762);

Richard Brookes, *A New and Accurate System of Natural History*, preface and introductions to volumes 1-4 by Goldsmith, 6 volumes (London: Printed for J. Newbery, 1763-1764);

William Guthrie, John Gray, and others, *A General History of the World from the Creation to the Present Time*, preface to volume 1 by Goldsmith, 13 volumes (London: Printed for J. Newbery, R. Baldwin, S. Crowder, J. Coote, R. Withy, J. Wilkie, J. Wilson & J. Fell, W. Nicoll, B. Collins & R. Raikes, 1764);

C. Wiseman, *A Complete English Grammar on a New Plan*, preface by Goldsmith (London: Printed for W. Nicoll, 1764);

M. Formey, *A Concise History of Philosophy and Philosophers*, translated anonymously by Goldsmith (London: Printed for F. Newbery, 1766);

Poems for Young Ladies: In Three Parts. Devotional, Moral, and Entertaining, edited anonymously by Goldsmith (London: Printed for J. Payne, 1767);

The Beauties of English Poesy, 2 volumes, edited by Goldsmith (London: Printed for William Griffin, 1767);

Charlotte Lennox, *The Sister: A Comedy*, epilogue by Goldsmith (London: Printed for J. Dodsley & T. Davies, 1769);

Thomas Parnell, *Poems on Several Occasions*, with life of Parnell by Goldsmith (London: Printed for T. Davies, 1770);

Henry St. John, Lord Viscount Bolingbroke, *A Dissertation upon Parties*, with life of Bolingbroke by Goldsmith (London: Printed for T. Davies, 1770);

Joseph Cradock, *Zobeide: A Tragedy*, prologue by Goldsmith (London: Printed for T. Cadell, 1771);

The Comic Romance of Monsieur Scarron, 2 volumes, translated by Goldsmith (London: Printed for W. Griffin, 1775);

The Grumbler: A Farce, adapted by Goldsmith from Sir Charles Sedley's translation of David Augustin de Brueys' *Le Grondeur*, edited by Alice I. Perry Wood (Cambridge: Harvard University Press, 1931).

"Nullum fere scribendi genus non tetigit, nullum quod tetigit non ornavit." ("There was scarcely any kind of writing that he did not touch, none that he touched that he did not adorn.") Samuel Johnson's epitaph to Oliver Goldsmith is displayed on the monument in the Poets' Corner in Westminster Abbey; the list of Goldsmith's titles justifies the first clause in the epitaph. Essays, poems, plays, a novel, biographies, histories, memoirs, translations and compilations on such nonliterary subjects as natural history and philosophy, anthologies and prefaces to other writers' works—these diverse "kinds" are evidence of a crowded and varied literary career. They are also typical of the canon of a hack, "a man whose trade is writing," as Goldsmith once characterized himself. What distinguishes them from the vast bulk of eighteenth-century hackwork is that, as Johnson asserts in the epitaph, Goldsmith "adorned" the miscellaneous species of writing that he attempted. The monument in the Poets' Corner is a tangible sign of the esteem in which his writings were held by his contemporaries. Even before he attained widespread popularity, his abilities as a writer were appreciated by knowledgeable members of the London literary world. Along with Joshua Reynolds, Johnson, and Edmund Burke, he was a founding member of the Club, the most famous association of men of letters, the arts, and public affairs the English-speaking world has ever known. At the time of his death Goldsmith's reputation was second only to Johnson's; and Johnson himself said of his friend in 1773, the year of *She Stoops to Conquer*, "Whether ... we take him as a poet,—as a comick writer,—or as an historian, he stands in the first class."

The circumstances of Goldsmith's birth, education, and early career gave no promise of such distinction. Born in Ireland, probably at Pallas, County Longford (or possibly at his grandmother's house near Elphin), on 10 November 1730 or 1731, Goldsmith was the younger son of Ann Jones Goldsmith and an obscure Anglican clergyman, Charles Goldsmith. Soon after the child's birth his father succeeded to the parish of Kilkenny West, and the family moved to the neighboring village of Lissoy.

From his earliest schooldays throughout his college years, Goldsmith was a mediocre student. At the age of three he attended the school of a relative, Mrs. Elizabeth Delap, who, according to a local clergyman, regarded him as "impenetrably stupid." Later he went to the village school in Lissoy, and from about 1737 until 1745 he was a pupil in the diocesan school at Elphin and schools at Athlone and Edgeworthstown. Although during this period he showed a budding talent for poetry, he was not a remarkable student. Similarly at Trinity College, Dublin, where he matriculated on 11 June 1745, "he exhibited," in the words of a classmate, "no specimens of that genius which in his maturer years raised his character." He was awarded the Bachelor of Arts degree in February 1750.

Because of Charles Goldsmith's straitened circumstances, the expenses of Oliver's education at Trinity were borne by Thomas Contarine, who had married Charles's sister and was at this time prebend of Oran. It was the beneficence of this uncle—supplemented by contributions from other members of the family—that supported Goldsmith during an unsettled period in which, successively, he was rejected for candidacy for the priesthood, was briefly employed as a private tutor, made an ineffectual attempt to immigrate to America, and considered going to London to study law, before finally determining on a career in medicine. In 1752 he entered the University of Edinburgh, where he attended lectures on anatomy. Two years later he traveled to Holland to complete his medical education at Leyden University.

Although in later life he was routinely referred to as "Dr. Goldsmith," and although he did practice medicine for a brief time in London, there is no record of Goldsmith's ever having received the degree of Bachelor of Medicine. But whether or not he acquired the degree during his Continental sojourn, the two years Goldsmith spent in Europe played a significant part in his career as a writer. After a year at Leyden he set out on his version of the Grand Tour, traveling on foot to Paris and thence to Germany, Switzerland, and Italy. It was at this time, in the summer of 1755, that he began writing what would be his first major poem and a milestone in his literary career, *The Traveller* (1764). The verse portraits of Italy, Switzerland, France, and Holland that make up a good part of the poem are the product of observations Goldsmith made during his residence at Leyden and during the *Wanderjahr* of 1755.

Leaving the Continent early in 1756, Goldsmith arrived in London without money or prospects. He worked at various employments before securing a teaching position at a boys' school at Peckham. Onerous as this situation was, the appointment proved to be Goldsmith's introduction to the life of a professional writer. In 1757, through the headmaster, Dr. John Milner, he met Ralph Griffiths, the proprietor of the influential *Monthly Review*, and accepted Griffiths's offer of a job as a reviewer. For the next six years he wrote reviews for the *Monthly* and for Tobias Smollett's *Critical Review*, as well as essays for his own short-lived periodical, the *Bee* (6 October - 24 November 1759), and for various other magazines and newspapers. Also during this period appeared his *An Enquiry into the Present State of Polite Learning in Europe* (1759), an overly ambitious project that failed to bring him the renown he had hoped for. But though he was still unknown to the public, he was gaining professional standing with the booksellers and other writers. By 1761 he numbered among his acquaintances Smollett, Burke, Reynolds, Johnson, and Thomas Percy.

A more significant undertaking than *An Enquiry into the Present State of Polite Learning in Europe* was the series of letters that appeared serially in John Newbery's *Public Ledger* in 1760 and

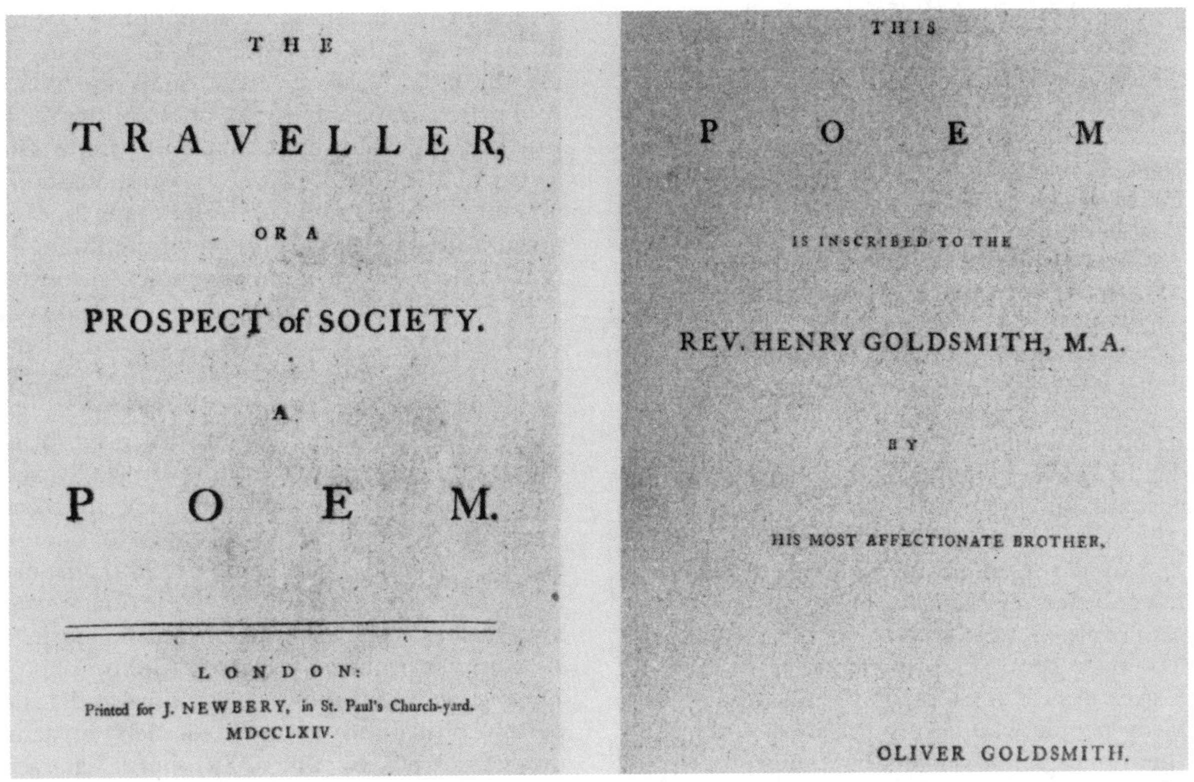
THE

TRAVELLER,

OR A

PROSPECT of SOCIETY.

A

POEM.

LONDON:

Printed for J. NEWBERY, in St. Paul's Church-yard.

MDCCLXIV.

THIS

POEM

IS INSCRIBED TO THE

REV. HENRY GOLDSMITH, M. A.

BY

HIS MOST AFFECTIONATE BROTHER,

OLIVER GOLDSMITH.

Title and dedication pages for Goldsmith's poem about the national characteristics of Italy, Switzerland, France, Holland, and England

1761 and that was published in 1762 as *The Citizen of the World; or, Letters from a Chinese Philosopher, Residing in London, to His Friends in the East.* The association with Newbery marked the beginning of the most important professional relationship of Goldsmith's career. Realizing that his impracticality in money matters required drastic measures, Goldsmith in 1762 agreed to let Newbery manage his domestic and financial affairs, in return for which he would undertake the literary tasks Newbery assigned him. At this time he moved to Canonbury House, Newbery's residence at Islington, not far from London, where he lived with the Newberys for almost two years. There is abundant contemporary testimony to John Newbery's benevolence and decency; Goldsmith paid a graceful tribute to his employer in chapter 18 of *The Vicar of Wakefield* (1766). Nevertheless, the arrangement with the publisher (and later with John's nephew Francis Newbery) enlisted Goldsmith in the ranks of hired writers, whose occupation he described as "a long habitude of writing for bread."

While he was living at Canonbury House Goldsmith resumed work on *The Traveller*, the poem he had begun during his Continental journey. He had already had some poetic trifles published in various of the periodicals with which he was involved; the best are the mock "Elegy on that Glory of her Sex, Mrs. Mary Blaize" (in the *Bee*, 1759), a parody of insipid verse elegies, and "The Double Transformation" (in the *Weekly Magazine*, 1760), a mildly Swiftian treatment of the stereotyped ideal of romantic love and marriage. And a January 1759 letter to his older brother Henry, a parish priest in Ireland, contained an early version of the poem later published in one of the Chinese letters as "The Description of an Author's Bedchamber," details from which Goldsmith would later incorporate into *The Deserted Village* (1770). *The Traveller; or, A Prospect of Society* was brought out in a quarto edition by Newbery on 19 December 1764. It was the first of Goldsmith's works to be printed with his name on the title page. Public reaction was immediate and almost uniformly favorable. Within the month commendatory notices appeared in the *London Chronicle*, the *Gentleman's Magazine*, and the *Critical Review*, the last written by Johnson (who may have contributed as many as eighteen lines to the poem).

The thesis of *The Traveller* is that Providence has bestowed on each nation a characteristic blessing that inevitably results in a characteristic flaw:

Hence every state, to one loved blessing prone,
Conforms and models life to that alone.
Each to the favourite happiness attends,
And spurns the plan that aims at other ends;
Till, carried to excess in each domain,
This favourite good begets peculiar pain.

This truth the Traveller arrives at as, from his vantage point on a peak in the Swiss Alps, he reflects on the national characteristics of Italy, Switzerland, France, Holland (the four countries Goldsmith had visited in 1754 and 1755), and England.

Italy has been blessed with nature's bounty; but, enervated by "sensual bliss" in such abundance, her sons have grown soft and contentedly accept their country's present decline from former greatness. The Swiss, on the other hand, are a hardy people who have persevered in the face of their inhospitable climate; but though they possess the admirable attributes of courage, hardihood, and independence of spirit, they lack the refinement and sensitivity that come from the arts nurtured in a civilized culture. The national temper of France is milder than that of Switzerland; but in this land where the social graces reign supreme, the lust to achieve "honour"—that is, public esteem—is so insatiable that solider virtues have given way to flattery and ostentation. Like the Swiss, the Dutch struggle successfully against a hostile environment; but the industry that reclaimed fertile lands from the sea has resulted in an inordinate love of material prosperity, and public and private virtues have been prostituted to "gold's superior charms."

Finally, the Traveller turns his analytical view toward England. There he perceives that the spirit of independence that is the nation's characteristic and most prized blessing has hardened into a self-dependence that "breaks the social tie." The initial result is faction; and now that the legitimate bonds of society—duty, honor, and social love—have been weakened, the social order is artificially held together by the force of wealth and arbitrary power. With the newfound awareness resulting from these reflections, the Traveller comes to understand that real happiness resides not within any particular nation but within the individual: "Our own felicity we make or find."

This resolution is a commonplace. Johnson in *The Vanity of Human Wishes* (1749) had invoked the "Celestial Wisdom [that] calms the mind, / And makes the happiness she does not find." Likewise, the appeal to the principle of compensation to explain Providence's unequal dispensation of blessings among various peoples was unexceptional. Alexander Pope's theory of the Ruling Passion to account for complementary virtues and vices in individuals could easily be applied collectively to nations. Johnson's translation of Father Jerome Lobo's *Voyage to Abyssinia* (1735) expresses the belief that "the Creator doth not appear partial in his distributions, but has balanced in most countries their particular inconveniences by particular favours." Equally familiar to Goldsmith's contemporaries was his characterization of countries in terms of national stereotypes. Although such a notion may seem simplistic to modern readers, the sketches of the five nations examined in *The Traveller* are brilliantly executed. Goldsmith's precise diction and apposite metaphors and his expertly constructed rhymed couplets revitalized the stereotypes by which Europeans characterized one another.

Not only were the theme, approach, and conclusions of *The Traveller* reassuringly familiar to readers confused by or weary of the "new" poetry of the mid century and beyond; it exhibited other traditional aspects as well. The subtitle, *A Prospect of Society*, revealed the poem's kinship with the topographical poem, a genre that reached back to John Denham's *Cooper's Hill* (1642). Dedicated and addressed to Goldsmith's brother Henry, it is also in the tradition of the Horatian verse-epistle. And the blending of philosophical or political reflection with the description of landscape was appealing to readers familiar with Pope's *Windsor Forest* (1713). These traditional elements in *The Traveller* are acknowledged in Johnson's review: "Such is the poem, on which we now congratulate the public, as on a production to which, since the death of Pope, it will not be easy to find any thing equal."

The presence of the familiar, however, was only partially responsible for the extraordinary popularity of Goldsmith's poem. Contemporary readers were also impressed with something new. The bulk of *The Traveller* comprises almost four hundred lines in which Goldsmith explores the problem the poem addresses and arrives at its resolution. The approach is objective, the tone impersonal. This thematic center is, however, framed by opening and closing passages that describe the emotional state of the speaker. These passages, especially the opening sixty-two lines, are highly subjective, with autobiographical overtones. The dedication to Henry Goldsmith, with its acknowledgment that "a part of this poem was formerly written to you from Switzerland"; the points in the poem itself at which the poet directly addresses his brother; and, especially, the moving lines in which he invokes blessings on Henry's simple home and manner of living and then contrasts his own melancholy life of solitary wandering are direct reflections of Goldsmith's reaction to events in his own experience and to his situation at the time he was composing the poem. This is not to say that it should be read as a direct autobiographical statement, that the "I" should be literally identified with Oliver Goldsmith. Rather, *The Traveller* provides an early example of Goldsmith's habit of translating, as Richard Helgerson has described it, "private experience into the public forms of neoclassical literature."

Goldsmith had concluded his letter of 1759 to Henry by saying, "Poetry is much an easier and more agreeable species of composition than prose, and could a man live by it, it were no unpleasant employment to be a Poet." Given the success of *The Traveller*, it is somewhat surprising that he next turned again to prose. In 1765, in a move to exploit his celebrity as the author of *The Traveller*, he brought out a collection of his essays; and the following year Francis Newbery published *The Vicar of Wakefield.*

Goldsmith's novel contains three poems, none of them central to the plot but each in its way an effective example of his easy competence in verse. Two of them seem to have been included primarily to express his opinion of much of the poetry of his day. "An Elegy on the Death of a Mad Dog," like the earlier elegy on Mrs. Blaize, parodies contemporary elegies; and the ballad "Edwin and Angelina" is offered as a corrective to the current taste for "luxuriant images, without plot or connexion." The third poem is the song sung by the vicar's daughter Olivia after her seduction and betrayal by her false lover:

When lovely woman stoops to folly,
  And finds too late that men betray,
What charm can soothe her melancholy,
  What art can wash her guilt away?
The only art her guilt to cover,
  To hide her shame from every eye,
To give repentance to her lover,
  And wring his bosom—is to die.

Olivia's lament is probably best known today because of its ironic echo in T. S. Eliot's *The Waste Land* (1922). In the sterile world of Eliot's poem, neither the plaintive lyricism nor the moral certainty of Goldsmith's poem has survived. After the lovely woman of the twentieth century stoops to folly, she mechanically smooths her hair and puts a record on the gramophone.

Although the reception given *The Vicar of Wakefield* was far less enthusiastic than had been accorded *The Traveller*, the novel did not diminish Goldsmith's reputation. The author of *The Traveller*, the essays collected in 1765, and *The Vicar of Wakefield* was acknowledged as one of the leading literary figures of the day. Furthermore, Goldsmith was beginning to achieve a certain financial success. Even though his comedy *The Good Natur'd Man*, produced and published in 1768, was only moderately well received, his profits from the production amounted to four hundred pounds. He had by this time quit his lodgings at Islington and returned to London; and he also had a second residence, a rented farmhouse some eight miles from the city, to which he could retreat when the demands of his publishers required uninterrupted solitude. It was in this rural setting, in the summer of 1768, that Goldsmith began writing what would become his greatest poem. *The Deserted Village* was published almost exactly two years later, on 26 May 1770, in an elegant quarto edition dedicated to his closest friend, Sir Joshua Reynolds.

Like Goldsmith's first major poem, *The Deserted Village* grew out of long observation and reflection. It is also similar to *The Traveller* in that it combines with an objective argument a subjective, intensely emotional element. The poem was written, Goldsmith explained in the dedication to Reynolds, in protest against the increasing number of wealthy men who, to gratify their love of luxury and ostentation, were purchasing extensive areas of rural land and turning the former inhabitants from their homes. Not only did this practice cause personal tragedy to the dispossessed but it also deprived the nation of the industry of a hardy native stock that was either being driven to an unproductive life of poverty in the city or was immigrating to the New World. Goldsmith had touched on this theme in *The Traveller*, where in the verse portrait of England he deplored the "solitary pomp" that had supplanted established hamlets and exiled the nation's "useful sons." In *The Deserted Village* this socioeconomic argument is presented by a speaker who is also the

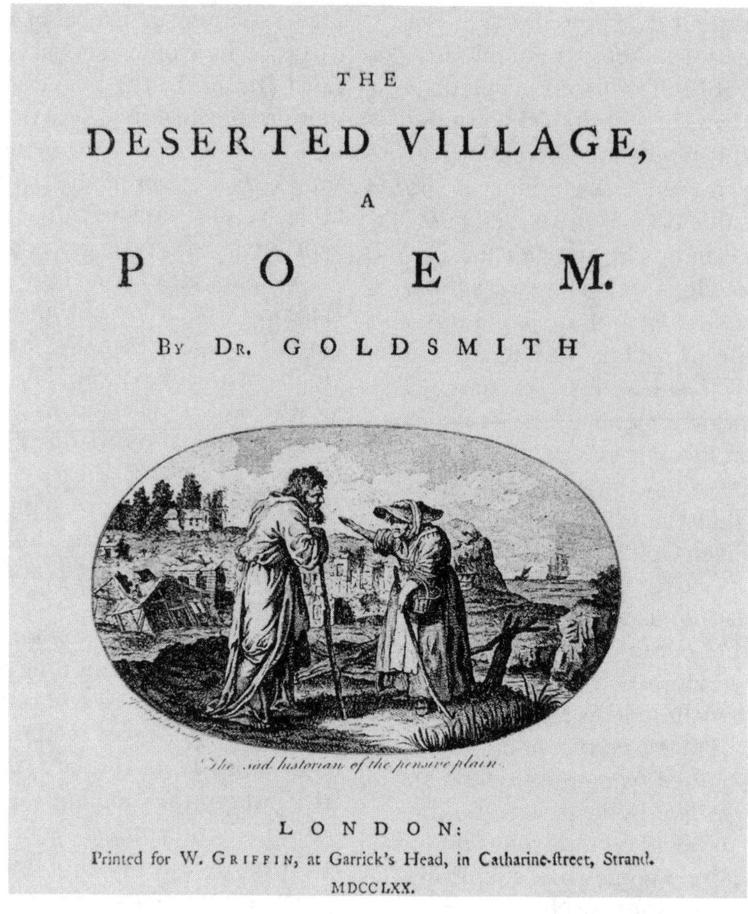
THE

DESERTED VILLAGE,

A

P O E M.

By Dr. GOLDSMITH

The sad historian of the pensive plain.

LONDON:

Printed for W. Griffin, at Garrick's Head, in Catharine-ſtreet, Strand.

MDCCLXX.

Title page for Goldsmith's poetic protest against the displacement of England's small farmers by wealthy landowners

source of the subjective element in the poem. A solitary wanderer (like his counterpart in *The Traveller*), he has for years dreamed of returning to Auburn, the village of his happy childhood. Now that he has done so, he finds the site deserted, its inhabitants forced from their homes by a single wealthy landowner. As he reflects on the contrast between the desolate landscape and the village of his youth, his mood swings between a poignant nostalgia and an indignant denunciation of luxury. Thematically, the focal point of the poem is the deserted village of the present; emotionally, it is the "sweet Auburn" of the speaker's memory.

Goldsmith was able to accommodate two such seemingly uncongenial components in the same poem by means of the speaker's powerful images of present and past and his moving vision of a future England deprived of the virtues embodied in and symbolized by the dispossessed villagers. He states his thesis with the succinctness and force of a proverb: "Ill fares the land, to hastening ills a prey, / Where wealth accumulates and men decay." He establishes its emotional validity in his affectionate recollections of the schoolmaster, the preacher, and the village inn and in his anguished reaction to the blasted idyll that was Auburn: "Remembrance wakes with all her busy train, / Swells at my breast and turns the past to pain." Thus in the passage beginning "Sweet was the sound, when oft at evening's close / Up yonder hill the village murmur rose," Auburn is recalled in terms of auditory imagery. "But now," the speaker laments, "the sounds of population fail"; and in the ensuing lines the silent landscape is dominated by a single visual image, a solitary woman who is emblematic of the present desolation: "She only left of all the harmless train, / The sad historian of the pensive plain." Like the solitary woman, the speaker is Auburn's historian. And he is also a prophet. After describing imagined scenes of the displaced villagers in the indifferent city and in the savage environment of wild America, he transforms the emigrants into abstractions, the "rural virtues" that England is exchanging for ostentatious luxury:

Downward they move, a melancholy band,
Pass from the shore and darken all the strand.
Contented toil and hospitable care,
And kind connubial tenderness are there;
And piety, with wishes placed above,
And steady loyalty and faithful love.

The public reaction to Goldsmith's poem was overwhelmingly favorable. Within five months of its appearance it had run to six editions, and it was praised by critics as well as by the general reader. This popularity was not owing to its thesis. Although many of the first readers believed that its account of depopulation was exaggerated, they responded to the poem's powerful emotional appeal, an appeal that derives its authority from the skill with which Goldsmith transmuted his own mood and experiences into poetry.

From his day to the present, readers have been aware of how much of Goldsmith's life and personality went into his writing. The affective quality of *The Traveller* was the result of his nostalgic yearning for the fireside and family circle of his brother. Henry Goldsmith, who had died in May 1768, was also in the poet's thoughts as he composed *The Deserted Village*. In the dedication Goldsmith explained why he chose Reynolds as his dedicatee: "The only dedication I ever made was to my brother, because I loved him better than most other men. He is since dead. Permit me to inscribe this Poem to you." The emotional tone of this simple, moving statement establishes an unmistakable link between Goldsmith and the speaker in the poem. Auburn is a composite of various remembered elements from Goldsmith's distant and recent past. As he says in the dedication, his "country excursions [to English villages], for these four or five years past" supplied him with evidence of the miseries of depopulation. Some of the details of Auburn in happier times, however, have their origin in Goldsmith's Irish boyhood. An example is the "hollow-sounding bittern," one of the few living creatures at the site of the desolate village. In *An History of the Earth, and Animated Nature* (1774), his book on natural history, Goldsmith would write of the bittern's call, "there is none so dismally hollow as the booming of the bittern. . . . I remember in the place where I was a boy with what terror this bird's note affected the whole village; they considered it as the presage of some sad event."

But *The Deserted Village* is autobiographical only in the sense that *The Traveller* is. Although specific details of the speaker's recollections and certain qualities of his character can be identified as pertaining to Goldsmith's life and personality, the "I" is not directly and consistently Goldsmith. Like the idealized scenes and characters evoked by the speaker, he himself is the creation of the poet, who is no more the historical Oliver Goldsmith than Auburn is the historical Lissoy. The locale of the poem is, as Roger Lonsdale has termed it, "the landscape of memory"; and it is every reader's landscape. As the speaker muses amid the ruins of the deserted Auburn, it becomes simultaneously the mournful illustration of the effects of luxury and pride and the symbol of Everyman's idealized past. Goldsmith's elegy for the "lovely bowers of innocence and ease" is likewise the reader's lament for a lost yesterday.

Goldsmith's two major poems grew out of the poet's deepest personal feelings about his past; and they were his last words on that subject. He may have felt that there was nothing more to be said, especially after *The Deserted Village*, which is in a sense a memorial to Henry. In any event, in the few years remaining to him he produced no other poems of the scope or quality of *The Traveller* and *The Deserted Village*. His next important work was *She Stoops to Conquer*, which was produced and published in 1773, the year before his death.

During the 1760s and 1770s Goldsmith wrote various occasional poems. Some, such as *The Captivity: An Oratorio* (written circa 1764 but not published until 1820) and *Threnodia Augustalis* (1772), were pedestrian hackwork. More successful were his efforts with the verse epistle. The best is *The Haunch of Venison* (1776), a rollicking account to a friend of how the friend's gift of venison to Goldsmith was spirited away by a parasitic acquaintance of the poet. He also wrote prologues and epilogues for his own and others' plays, as well as Tony Lumpkin's boisterous song in *She Stoops to Conquer* ("The Three Jolly Pigeons") and the charming air, "Ah, me! when shall I marry me?" intended for that play but discarded because the actress who played Kate Hardcastle could not sing. (It was first published by James Boswell in the *London Magazine*, June 1774.) His epilogue for Charlotte Lennox's play, *The Sister* (1769), is an especially good example of his facility in this minor but popular eighteenth-century genre. Counseling the playwright to transform her comedy into "a speaking masquerade," he points the way with a satiric view of genteel society that attests to his admiration for Restoration comedy:

Israelitish Woman (15)

Air

As panting flies the hunted hind
Where brooks refreshing stray
And ~~Where~~ rivers through the valley wind
That stops the hunter's way

Thus we O Lord alike ~~oppress'd deprest~~ distrest
For streams of mercy long
Those streams which cheer the sore opprest
And overwhelm the strong.

1st Prophet. Recit.

But whence that shout! Good heavens! Amazement all
See yonder tower just nodding to the fall
Behold, an army covers all the ground
'Tis Cyrus here that ~~They sap the wall, and~~ pours destruction round
And now behold the battlements recline
O God of Hosts the victory is thine.

Chorus of Captives.

Down with them Lord to lick the dust
Thy vengeance be begun
Serve them as they have serv'd the just
And let ~~behold~~ thy will be done.

1st Priest Recit.

All all is Lost. The Syrian army fails ~~O whither shall we fly~~
Cyrus the conqueror of the world prevails

Page from one of two known surviving manuscripts for Goldsmith's The Captivity: An Oratorio *(MA 162, Pierpont Morgan Library). The work was never performed and was not published until 1820.*

THE

HAUNCH OF VENISON,

A

POETICAL EPISTLE

TO

LORD CLARE.

By the late Dr. GOLDSMITH.

With a HEAD of the AUTHOR,
Drawn by HENRY BUNBURY, Efq; and Etched by BRETHERTON.

LONDON:
Printed for G. KEARSLY, in Fleet Street; and J. RIDLEY, in St. James's Street.

MDCCLXXVI.

Title page for Goldsmith's verse epistle about a purloined gift of meat

The world's a masquerade, the maskers, you, you, you.
[*To Boxes, Pit, and Gallery.*

Lud! what a group the motley scene discloses!
False wits, false wives, false virgins and false spouses:
There Hebes, turned of fifty, try once more
To raise a flame in Cupids of threescore.
These in their turn, with appetites as keen,
Deserting fifty, fasten on fifteen.
Miss, not yet full fifteen, with fire uncommon,
Flings down her sampler, and takes up the woman:
The little urchin smiles and spreads her lure,
And tries to kill ere she's got power to cure.

Goldsmith's own comedy *She Stoops to Conquer* was greeted with acclaim. The playwright, however, was distracted from fully enjoying this success because of his increasing financial problems. At some time in 1765 he had apparently no longer felt the need to place his affairs under Newbery's management. Without the bookseller's benevolent restraint, Goldsmith had resumed his prodigal ways and soon found himself deeply in debt. In an effort to resolve his difficulties he turned again to his pen. In 1773 he was at work on *The Grecian History, from the Earliest State to the Death of Alexander the Great* and *An History of the Earth, and Animated Nature*, both published the following year. "A long habitude of writing for bread," as he had put it at the outset of his literary career, could not be broken.

In addition to his worries over money, Goldsmith was plagued by ill health. For some time he had suffered from a chronic bladder or kidney or bladder ailment. A friend who visited him in 1773 reported that he "found him much altered and at times very low." There were happier intervals, however. He occasionally met for dinner and conversation with a group of friends, including at various times Burke, Reynolds, Johnson, and David Garrick. One of these gatherings in

My Dear Friend. Paris July 29th

I began a long letter to you from Lisle giving a description of all that we had done and seen but finding it very dull and knowing that you would shew it again I threw it aside and it was lost. You see by the top of this letter that we are at Paris, and (as I have often heard you say) we have brought our own amusement with us for the Ladies do not seem to be very fond of what we have yet seen. With regard to myself I find that travelling at twenty and at forty are very different things, I set out with all my confirmd habits about me and can find nothing on the continent so good as when I formerly left it. One of our chief amusements here is scolding at every thing we meet with and praising every thing and every person we left at home. You may judge therefore whether your name is not frequently bandied at table among us. To tell you the truth I never thought I could regret your absence so much as our various mortifications on the road have often taught me to do. I could tell you of disasters and adventures without number, of our lying in barns, and of my being half poisoned with a dish of green peas, of our quarelling with postillions, and being cheated by Landladies, but I reserve all this for an happy hour which I expect to share with you upon my return. I have very little to tell you more but that we are at present all well, and expect returning when we have staid out our month, which I did not care tho it were over this very day. I long to hear from you all, how you yourself do, how Johnson, Burke, Dyer, Chamier, Colman, and every one of the club do. I wish I could send you some amusement in this letter but I protest I am so stupefied by the air of this country (for I am sure it can-

Letter from Goldsmith to Reynolds, written during Goldsmith's six-week visit to France in 1770 (from J. Isaacs [Temple Scott], Oliver Goldsmith Bibliographically and Biographically Considered, *1928)*

never be natural) that I have not a word to say. I have been thinking of the plot of a comedy which shall be entitled a journey to Paris, in which a family shall be introduced with a full intention of going to France to save money. You know there is not a place in the world more promising for that purpose. As for the meat of this country I can scarce eat it, and tho we pay two good shillings an head for our dinner I find it all so tough that I have spent less time with my knife than my pick tooth. I said this as a good thing at table but it was not understood. I believe it to be a good thing. As for our intended journey to Devonshire I find it out of my power to perform it; for as soon as I arrive at Dover I intend to let the ladies go on, and I will take a country lodging for a couple of months somewhere near that place in order to do some business. I have so out run the constable that I must mortify a little to bring it up again. For God sake the night you receive this take your pen in your hand and tell me some thing about yourself, and myself if you know any thing that has happened. About Miss Reynolds, about Mr Bickerstaff, my nephew, or any body that you regard. I beg you will send to Griffin the bookseller to know if there be any letters left for me and be so good as to send them to me at Paris. They may perhaps be left for me at the Porters Lodge opposite the Pump in Temple lane. The same messenger will do. I expect one from Lord Clare from Ireland. As for others I am not much uneasy about. Is there any thing I can do for you at Paris, I wish you would tell me. The whole of my own purchases here is one silk coat which I have put on and which makes me look like a fool. But no more of that.

I find that Colman has gaind his law suit. I am glad of it. I suppose you often meet. I will soon be among you, better pleasd with my situation at home than I ever was before. And yet I must say that if any thing could make France pleasant the very good women with whom I am at present would certainly do it. I could say more about that but I intend shewing them this letter before I send it away. What signifies teizing you longer with moral observations when the business of my writing is over, I have one thing only more to say, and of that I think every hour in the day namely that I am your most

sincere and most affectionate
friend

Oliver Goldsmith

Direct to me at the Hotel de Denemarc
Rue Jacob. Fauxbourg St Germains.

March 1774 gave rise to the last poem he ever wrote, *Retaliation* (1774).

A sketch of Goldsmith written by Reynolds after his friend's death analyzes an aspect of the poet's character that directly bears on this poem. Goldsmith, Reynolds remarked, "was of a sociable disposition," and he was eager to be admired, a desire all the more intense because of his feelings of social inferiority over his Irish background and his unprepossessing appearance. Consequently, "he always took care to stand forward and draw the attention of the company upon himself. He talked without knowledge, [from] an impatience of neglect by being left out of the conversation." This compulsion "to shine" (the phrase is James Boswell's) was undoubtedly the reason that at one of those convivial dinners early in 1774 he offered to match wits with Garrick to see which could produce the best epitaph on the other. Garrick, far more skilled at extempore repartee than his opponent, immediately responded with Goldsmith's epitaph:

> Here lies NOLLY Goldsmith, for shortness call'd Noll,
> Who wrote like an angel, but talk'd like poor Poll.

According to Garrick's account of the incident, as quoted by Peter Cunningham in *The Works of Oliver Goldsmith* (1881), "Goldsmith, upon the company's laughing very heartily, grew very thoughtful, and either would not, or could not, write anything at that time: however, he went to work, and some weeks after produced the ... poem called *Retaliation*."

It was fortunate that Goldsmith was unable to make a spontaneous response in kind, for when he did reply, it was with something of more substance than Garrick's witty distich. Instead of answering Garrick alone, he also provided epitaphs for eight other members of the group that had been present on the occasion of the contest; and instead of confining the epitaphs to the limits of a couplet, he expanded them to full-length verse portraits. Some of the sketches—that of Reynolds, for example—are unequivocally complimentary; most strike a nice balance between panegyric and satire. In none is this balance better illustrated than in the one of Garrick: "Here lies David Garrick, describe me who can, / An abridgment of all that was pleasant in man." "On the stage he was natural, simple, affecting; / 'Twas only that when he was off he was acting." "Of praise a mere glutton, he swallow'd what came, / And the puff of a dunce, he mistook it for fame." Such remarks are more than witty; they are perceptive insights into Garrick's character. The concluding lines of the portrait show Goldsmith's ability to temper his understanding of Garrick's weaknesses with affection: "But peace to his spirit wherever it flies, / To act as an angel and mix with the skies."

Retaliation is attractive not only for its characterizations of Goldsmith's friends but also for its engaging, if largely implicit, self-portrait of the poet. The various epitaphs in the poem are introduced by a witty conceit that recalls the occasion of Goldsmith's challenge to Garrick, a gathering of friends for dinner. The menu for this metaphoric feast comprises the guests themselves. Thus Garrick, whose sharp epitaph provoked Goldsmith's retaliation, is a salad, "for in him we see / Oil, vinegar, sugar, and saltness agree"; Burke, the member of Parliament, is tongue; Richard Cumberland, a writer of sentimental comedies, is sweetbread; the amiable Reynolds is lamb; and "Magnanimous Goldsmith a gooseberry fool." This self-characterization is accurate. The relaxed tone of *Retaliation* and the affectionate tolerance of the character sketches belie the discomfort that the wounding sobriquet "poor Poll" caused Goldsmith. But if the graceful portrayals of his friends reveal his magnanimity, they also demonstrate the appropriateness of the dish he chose to represent himself: "gooseberry fool" is more than Goldsmith's wry acknowledgment of his social ineptitude; the dish is a tart custard, the perfect metaphor for the subtle mixture of satire and compliment in Goldsmith's epitaphs.

Retaliation is 146 lines in length, ending with the epitaph for Reynolds. Goldsmith probably intended to write further, for the portrait of Reynolds seems unfinished, and there is no sketch of Johnson. But though it is a fragment, the poem was sufficiently complete for Goldsmith to read it to the group at a second dinner meeting in March. He did not, however, add to it subsequently. The kidney or bladder complaint from which he had suffered for some time suddenly worsened, and the poet died on 4 April 1774. Fifteen days later *Retaliation* was published.

The *Monthly Review* published a brief laudatory notice of Goldsmith's last poem, commending its wit and good humor and singling out for particular praise the verse portrait of Garrick. Before the month was out, various tributes in prose and verse to the author's memory appeared. Reynolds, in his memoir of Goldsmith (first published

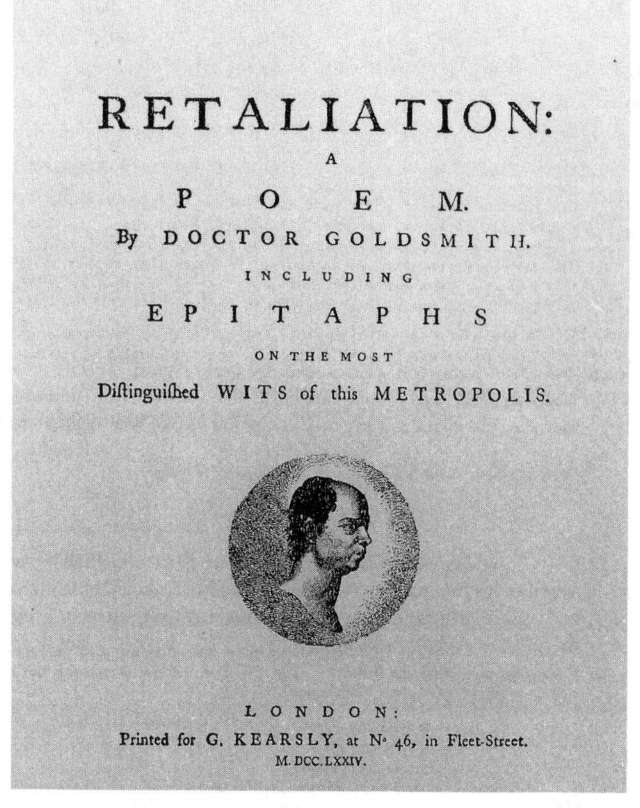
RETALIATION:

A

POEM.

By DOCTOR GOLDSMITH.

INCLUDING

EPITAPHS

ON THE MOST

Diſtinguiſhed WITS of this METROPOLIS.

LONDON:

Printed for G. KEARSLY, at Nº 46, in Fleet-Street.

M.DCC.LXXIV.

Title page for Goldsmith's last poem, which includes satirical "epitaphs" on nine of his eminent friends

in 1952), remarked on the flood of "epigrams, epitaphs and monodies to his memory." In addition, there were collections of anecdotes emphasizing his eccentricities. The Goldsmith legend—the portrayal of the writer as a blundering, uncouth clown, an "idiot inspired"—had already become firmly established during his lifetime; these posthumous addenda assured that it would survive into the next two centuries. The definitive response to all such stories—authentic as well as apocryphal—is Johnson's: "Let not his frailties be remembered; he was a very great man."

In 1758, writing from an obscurity that was almost total, Goldsmith had whimsically predicted in a letter to a friend that the time would come ("I beg you may live a couple of hundred years longer only to see the day") when scholars and critics would honor his works and his name. For all its facetiousness, this prophecy would seem to have been fulfilled. In the two centuries following Goldsmith's death his literary career has been the subject of important biographies, editions, and critical studies. Despite this scholarly and critical attention, however, and though his reputation remained secure throughout most of the nineteenth century, it has now diminished significantly. Popular editions of *The Vicar of Wakefield* are readily available, and the two major poems can still be found in anthologies; but the only really vital work in the Goldsmith canon today is *She Stoops to Conquer*.

One reason for this comparative neglect is implicit in the epitaph that Johnson wrote (in Latin) for Goldsmith's memorial in Westminster Abbey: "There was scarcely any kind of writing that he did not touch." Driven as he was by economic necessity, Goldsmith wrote too much too rapidly, a fault that Reynolds commented on in his memoir of his friend: "The literary world seemed to deplore his death more than could be expected, when it is considered how small a part of his works were wrote for fame." This judgment is especially true of his contribution to poetry. The only poems that Goldsmith "wrote for fame" are *The Traveller* and *The Deserted Village*. As admirable in their various ways as the others are, none of them—not even *Retaliation*—is the stuff that lasting poetic reputations are made on. "His name as a poet," Reynolds acknowledged, "must depend upon the quality, not the quantity of his works."

Goldsmith's memorial in Westminster Abbey

There is also the consideration that *The Traveller* and *The Deserted Village* were written in a poetic mode that no longer has the appeal it once had. Leaving aside the subject matter of the two poems, which many readers today regard as outmoded or as restrictively topical, twentieth-century sensibilities simply do not respond to Goldsmith's idiom in the way eighteenth- and nineteenth-century ones did. As late as 1930, T. S. Eliot could write of Goldsmith's poetry that its "melting sentiment [is] just saved by the precision of his language." But what another critic has called the "new sensibility" in *The Traveller* and *The Deserted Village* is likely to impress readers today as sentimentality.

These changes in taste notwithstanding, the qualities that first established Goldsmith's poetic reputation are readily discernible. Virtually all of the poems—the two major ones as well as the lesser efforts—demonstrate a high degree of metrical competence. From the beginning of his career to the end, from the jaunty rhythms of the alternating tetrameter and trimeter lines of the mock elegies on Mary Blaize and the mad dog to the cantering anapests of *The Haunch of Venison* and *Retaliation*, Goldsmith seems to have possessed an instinctive talent for light verse. His handling of metrics in the serious poems is equally assured. Both *The Traveller* and *The Deserted Village* are remarkable for the flowing, lyric quality of their closed couplets. "He judged," Reynolds wrote of Goldsmith, "by his ear, whether the verse was musical, without caring or perhaps knowing whether it would bear examination by the rules of the *prosodia*."

Clearly, Goldsmith also depended on his ear in his use of diction. The precision that Eliot noted is everywhere evident in the poetry. A sin-

Statue of Goldsmith by Foley at Trinity College, Dublin

gle line in *The Traveller* perfectly exemplifies the national character of France: "Gay sprightly land of mirth and social ease." A couplet in *The Deserted Village* fixes the wealthy landowner with the exactness and intensity of Popean satire: "The robe that wraps his limbs in silken sloth, / Has robbed the neighboring fields of half their growth." And in the same poem Goldsmith portrays the tragic, ironic contrast of England's plenty and poverty with a striking paradox: "The country blooms—a garden, and a grave."

Goldsmith's reputation as a poet has suffered both from reasons of his own making and from the winnowing process of changing tastes and times. Nevertheless, his poetry contains virtues of abiding merit.

Letters:

The Collected Letters of Oliver Goldsmith, edited by Katharine C. Balderston (Cambridge: Cambridge University Press, 1928);

Balderston, "New Goldsmith Letters," *Yale University Gazette*, 39 (October 1964): 67-72.

Bibliographies:

Iola A. Williams, *Seven XVIIIth Century Bibliographies* (London: Dulau, 1924), pp. 116-177;

J. Isaacs [Temple Scott], *Oliver Goldsmith Bibliographically and Biographically Considered* (New York: Bowling Green Press, 1928; London: Maggs Bros., 1928);

Samuel H. Woods, Jr., *Oliver Goldsmith: A Reference Guide* (Boston: G. K. Hall, 1982).

Biographies:

Thomas Percy, Memoir of Goldsmith in volume 1 of *The Miscellaneous Works of Oliver Goldsmith, M.B.* (London: Printed for J. Johnson by H. Baldwin & Sons, 1801); republished as *Thomas Percy's Life of Dr. Oliver Goldsmith*, edited by Richard L. Harp (Salzburg: Institut für Englische Sprache und Literatur, 1976);

James Prior, *The Life of Oliver Goldsmith, M.B., from a Variety of Original Sources*, 2 volumes (London: Murray, 1837);

John Forster, *The Life and Adventures of Oliver Goldsmith* (London: Bradbury & Evans, Chapman & Hall, 1848; revised and enlarged, 2 volumes, 1854);

Austin Dobson, *Life of Oliver Goldsmith* (London: Scott, 1888);

J. Isaacs [Temple Scott], *Oliver Goldsmith Bibliographically and Biographically Considered* (New York: Bowling Green Press, 1928; London: Maggs Bros., 1928);

Ralph M. Wardle, *Oliver Goldsmith* (Lawrence: University of Kansas Press, 1957);

John Ginger, *The Notable Man: The Life and Times of Oliver Goldsmith* (London: Hamilton, 1977).

References:

Howard Bell, Jr., "*The Deserted Village* and Goldsmith's Social Doctrines," *PMLA*, 59 (September 1944): 747-772;

Donald Davie, "*The Deserted Village*: Poem as Virtual History," *Twentieth Century*, 156 (August 1954): 161-174;

T. S. Eliot, "Eighteenth-Century Poetry," in *T. S. Eliot: Selected Prose*, edited by John Hayward (London: Penguin, 1953), pp. 163-169;

Oliver W. Ferguson, "Goldsmith's *Retaliation*," *South Atlantic Quarterly*, 70 (Spring 1971): 234-241;

Morris Golden, "Goldsmith's Reputation in His Day," *Papers on Language and Literature*, 16 (Spring 1980): 213-238;

Richard Helgerson, "The Two Worlds of Oliver Goldsmith," *Studies in English Literature*, 13 (Summer 1973): 516-534;

Robert H. Hopkins, *The True Genius of Oliver Goldsmith* (Baltimore: Johns Hopkins Press, 1969);

Richard J. Jaarsma, "Ethics in the Wasteland: Image and Structure in *The Deserted Village*," *Texas Studies in Language and Literature*, 13 (Fall 1971): 446-459;

Jaarsma, "Satire, Theme, and Structure in *The Traveller*," *Tennessee Studies in Literature*, 6 (1971): 46-66;

Clara M. Kirk, *Oliver Goldsmith* (New York: Twayne, 1967);

Roger Lonsdale, " 'A Garden and a Grave': The Poetry of Oliver Goldsmith," in *The Author in His Work: Essays on a Problem in Criticism*, edited by Louis L. Martz and Aubrey Williams (New Haven & London: Yale University Press, 1978), pp. 3-30;

Earl Miner, "The Making of *The Deserted Village*," *Huntington Library Quarterly*, 22 (February 1959): 125-141;

John Montague, "The Sentimental Prophecy: A Study of *The Deserted Village*," *Dolmen Miscellany*, 1 (1962): 72-79;

William D. Paden and Clyde Kenneth Hyder, *A Concordance to the Poems of Oliver Goldsmith* (Lawrence: University of Kansas Press, 1940);

Ricardo Quintana, "Logical and Rhetorical Elements in *The Deserted Village*," *College English*, 26 (December 1965): 204-214;

Quintana, *Oliver Goldsmith: A Georgian Study* (New York: Macmillan, 1967);

Joshua Reynolds, *Portraits by Sir Joshua Reynolds: Character Sketches of Oliver Goldsmith, Samuel Johnson, and David Garrick, Together with Other Manuscripts of Reynolds Discovered among the Boswell Papers and Now First Published*, edited by Frederick W. Hilles (New York: McGraw-Hill, 1952), pp. 44-59;

G. S. Rousseau, ed., *Goldsmith: The Critical Heritage* (London & Boston: Routledge & Kegan Paul, 1974);

Leo F. Storm, "Conventional Ethics in Goldsmith's *The Traveller*," *Studies in English Literature*, 17 (Summer 1977): 463-476;

Storm, "Literary Convention in Goldsmith's *Deserted Village*," *Huntington Library Quarterly*, 33 (May 1970): 243-256;

Andrew Swarbrick, ed., *The Art of Oliver Goldsmith* (London: Vision Press, 1984; Totowa, N.J.: Barnes & Noble, 1984).

Papers:

Aside from a small number in private hands, the few surviving holographs of Oliver Goldsmith's poems are in the New York Public Library; the Pierpont Morgan Library, New York; the Yale University Library; the Free Library of Philadelphia; and the British Library. For a full account, see Katharine C. Balderston, *A Census of the Manuscripts of Oliver Goldsmith* (New York: Hackett, 1926) and Roger Lonsdale, ed., *The Poems of Thomas Gray, William Collins, Oliver Goldsmith* (London & Harlow: Longmans, Green, 1969).

Thomas Gray

(26 December 1716 - 30 July 1771)

Wallace Jackson
Duke University

BOOKS: *An Ode on a Distant Prospect of Eton College* (London: Printed for R. Dodsley and sold by M. Cooper, 1747);

An Elegy Wrote in a Country Church Yard (London: Printed for R. Dodsley and sold by M. Cooper, 1751);

Designs by Mr. R. Bentley, for Six Poems by Mr. T. Gray (London: Printed for R. Dodsley, 1753);

Odes, by Mr. Gray (London: Printed at Strawberry-Hill, for R. and J. Dodsley, 1757);

Poems by Mr. Gray (London: Printed for J. Dodsley, 1768);

The Poems of Mr. Gray: To Which Are Prefixed Memoirs of His Life and Writings by W. Mason, M.A. (York: Printed by A. Ward; and sold by J. Dodsley, London; and J. Todd, York, 1775);

The Works of Thomas Gray, in Prose and Verse, 4 volumes, edited by Edmund Gosse (London: Macmillan, 1884);

Gray's English Poems, Original, and Translated from the Norse and Welsh, edited by D. C. Tovey (Cambridge: University Press, 1898);

The Complete Poems of Thomas Gray: English, Latin and Greek, edited by H. W. Starr and J. R. Hendrickson (Oxford: Clarendon Press, 1966);

The Poems of Thomas Gray, William Collins, Oliver Goldsmith, edited by Roger Lonsdale (London & Harlow: Longmans, Green, 1969).

OTHER: Robert Dodsley, ed., *A Collection of Poems: By Several Hands,* volume 2, includes Gray's "Ode on the Spring," "Ode on the Death of a Favourite Cat," and "Ode on a Distant Prospect of Eton College" (London: Printed for R. Dodsley, 1748).

Thomas Gray is generally considered the second most important poet of the eighteenth century (following the dominant figure of Alexander Pope) and the most disappointing. It was generally assumed by friends and readers that he was the most talented poet of his generation, but the relatively small and even reluctantly published body of his works has left generations of scholars puzzling over the reasons for his limited production and meditating on the general reclusiveness and timidity that characterized his life. Samuel Johnson was the first of many critics to put forward the view that Gray spoke in two languages, one public and the other private, and that the private language—that of his best-known and most-loved poem, "Elegy Written in a Country Churchyard" (published in 1751 as *An Elegy Wrote in a Country Church Yard*)—was too seldom heard. William Wordsworth decided in his preface to *Lyrical Ballads* (1798), using Gray's "Sonnet on the Death of Richard West" (1775) as his example, that Gray, governed by a false idea of poetic diction, spoke in the wrong language; and Matthew Arnold, in an equally well-known judgment, remarked that the age was wrong for a poetry of high seriousness, that Gray was blighted by his age and never spoke out at all. Such judgments sum up the major critical history of Gray's reception and reputation as a poet. He has always attracted attentive critics precisely because of the extraordinary continuing importance of the "Elegy," which, measured against his other performances, has seemed indisputably superior.

Born in Cornhill on 26 December 1716, Gray was the fifth of twelve children of Philip and Dorothy Antrobus Gray and the only one to survive infancy. His father, a scrivener given to fits of insanity, abused his wife. She left him at one point; but Philip Gray threatened to pursue her and wreak vengeance on her, and she returned to him. From 1725 to 1734 Thomas Gray attended Eton, where he met Richard West and Horace Walpole, son of the powerful Whig minister, Sir Robert Walpole.

In 1734 Gray entered Peterhouse College, Cambridge University. Four years later he left Cambridge without a degree, intending to read law at the Inner Temple in London. Instead, he and Horace Walpole sailed from Dover on 29

Thomas Gray (portrait by John Giles Eccardt, 1747-1748; National Portrait Gallery, London)

March 1739 for a Continental tour. The two quarreled at Reggio, Italy, in May 1741; Gray continued the tour alone, returning to London in September. In November 1741 Gray's father died; Gray's extant letters contain no mention of this event.

Except for his mother, West was the person most dear to Gray; and his death from consumption on 1 June 1742 was a grievous loss to the poet. West died in the year of Gray's greatest productivity, though not all of the work of that year was inspired either by West's death or by Gray's anticipation of it.

West's death did inspire the well-known (largely because of Wordsworth's use of it) "Sonnet on the Death of Richard West," yet it is the shortest and least significant work of the year. The "Ode on the Spring" (1748) owes something to an ode West sent Gray on 5 May, and *An Ode on a Distant Prospect of Eton College* (1747) may owe something to West's "Ode to Mary Magdelene." The "Hymn to Adversity" (1753) and the unfinished "Hymn to Ignorance" (1768) complete the work of the year, which, together with 1741, may comprise Gray's most critical emotional period.

Gray's poetry is concerned with the rejection of sexual desire. The figure of the poet in his poems is often a lonely, alienated, and marginal one, and various muses or surrogate-mother figures are invoked—in a manner somewhat anticipatory of John Keats's employment of similar figures—for aid or guidance. The typical "plot" of the four longer poems of 1742 has to do with engaging some figure of desire to repudiate it, as in the "Ode on the Spring," or, as in the Eton College ode, to lament lost innocence. Sometimes, as in the "Hymn to Adversity," a harsh

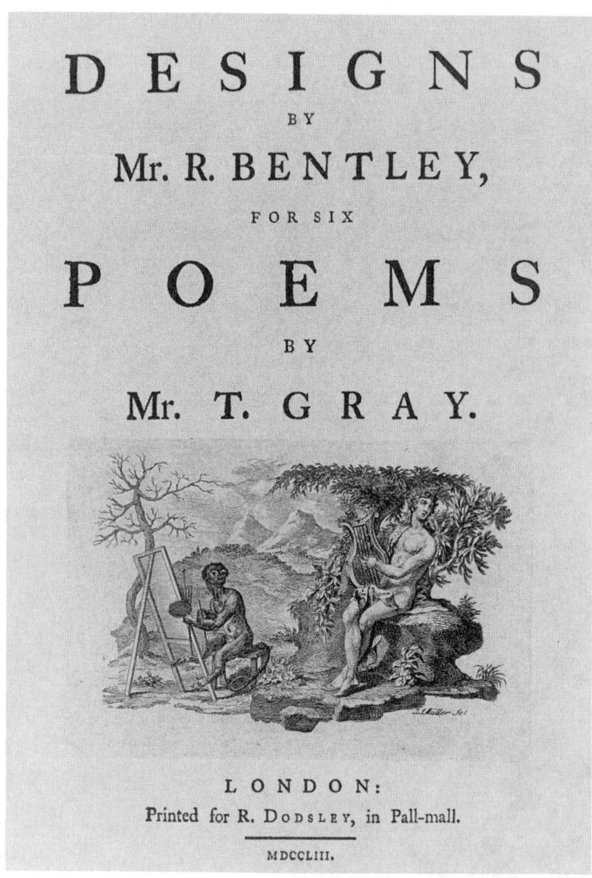
DESIGNS BY Mr. R. BENTLEY, FOR SIX POEMS BY Mr. T. GRAY.

LONDON: Printed for R. DODSLEY, in Pall-mall. MDCCLIII.

Title page for the volume in which Gray's "Hymn to Adversity" was first published

and repressive figure is conjured to rebuke excessive desire and to aid in the formation of a modest and humane fellowship, the transposed and social form of sexual desire. In the "Hymn to Ignorance" a goddess clearly modeled on Pope's Dulness in *The Dunciad* (1728) is used to rebuke the "I" who longs for the maternal and demonic presence. In different but related ways these four poems enact the poet's quest for his tutelary spirit, for the muse who will preside over the making of poetic and personal identity.

The "Ode on the Spring" was written while West was still alive and is to some extent a response to the ode he sent Gray on 5 May. In West's poem "the tardy May" is asked, as "fairest nymph," to resume her reign, to "Bring all the Graces in [her] train" and preside over a seasonally reviving world. Gray's "Ode on the Spring" was sent to West at just about the time of his death and was returned unopened ("Sent to Fav: not knowing he was then Dead," Gray noted on the manuscript in his commonplace book; Favonius was Gray's affectionate name for West). The ode takes the implicit form of elegy, displacing spring from the context of renewal to that of death, and is consistent with a 27 May 1742 letter to West in which Gray explains that he is the frequent victim of "a white Melancholy, or rather Leucocholy" but is also occasionally host to "another sort, black indeed, which I have now and then felt, that has somewhat in it like Tertullian's rule of faith, Credo quia impossible est [I believe because it is impossible]; for it believes, nay, is sure of every thing that is unlikely, so it be but frightful; and, on the other hand, excludes and shuts its eyes to the most possible hopes." Already characteristic of Gray is the view advocated in the "Ode on the Spring" by a tutelary figure:

> Beside some water's rushy brink
> With me the Muse shall sit, and think
> (At ease reclin'd in rustic state)
> How vain the ardour of the Crowd,
> How low, how little are the Proud,
> How indigent the Great!

The lines preview Gray's appreciation in the "Elegy" of rustic simplicity against the claims of the proud and the great and reveal the inception of a poetic persona that will be adapted and modified during the coming years. The poem therefore offers a model for reading Gray's early poetry, in which the various rejections of desire are the major adventure of the speaker of the poems.

In *An Ode on a Distant Prospect of Eton College,* which is "about" the return of a disillusioned adult to the site of his schoolboy years, desire is represented by "grateful Science [who] still adores / Her HENRY'S holy Shade" (Henry VI was the founder of the college). The ode's opening implies the persistence of desire within the trope of loss and mourning. Science and Henry are icons of desire and loss that signify the import of the speaker's return to Eton: the apprehension of yearning and loss. What arises from the Etonian landscape are more shades, prefiguring future loss: "Ministers of human fate," Anger, Fear, Shame, images of desire defeated: "Or pineing Love shall waste their youth, / Or Jealousy with rankling tooth. . . ." Father Thames authorizes the speaker's vision; he is a silent confirmatory figure, another version of the tutelary muse.

Muse, Contemplation (in the "Ode on the Spring"), and Father Thames are evoked for the prophetic wisdom they possess. One function of prophecy is to transform desire into "pineing Love" or the "fury Passions." The imagination's

On the Death of a favourite Cat
drown'd in a China-Tub of
Gold-Fishes.

'Twas on a lofty Vase's Side,
Where China's gayest Art had dyed
The azure Flow'rs that blow,
Demurest of the tabby Kind,
The pensive Selima reclined
Gazed on the Lake below.
Her conscious Tail her Joy declared,
Her fair round Face, her snowy Beard,
The Velvet of her Paws,
Her Coat, that with the Tortoise vies
Her Ears of Jet, & Emerald Eyes,
She saw & purr'd Applause.
Still had she gazed, but midst the Tide
Two angel Forms were seen to glide,
The Genii of the Stream:
Their scaly Armour's Tyrian Hue
Thro' richest Purple to the View
Betray'd a golden Gleam.
The hapless Nymph with Wonder saw;
A Whisker first, & then a Claw,
With many an ardent Wish,
She stretch'd in vain to reach the Prize:
What Female-Heart can Gold despise?
What Cat's averse to Fish?
Presumptuous Maid! with Eyes intent
Again she stretch'd, again she bent,
Nor knew the Gulph between.
Malignant Fate sat by, & smiled.
The slippery Verge her Feet beguiled:
She tumbled headlong in.
Eight times emerging from the Flood
She mew'd to ev'ry watry God
Some speedy Aid to send.
No Dolphin came, no Nereid stir'd,
Nor cruel John, nor Susan heard;
A Fav'rite has no Friend!
Volti sub.

First page of one of three known manuscripts for Gray's playful tribute to Walpole's cat, Selima, who drowned in a goldfish bowl in February 1747 (Pierpont Morgan Library)

Stanzas wrote in a Country Church-Yard.

The Curfeu tolls the Knell of parting Day,
The lowing Herd wind slowly o'er the Lea,
The Plowman homeward plods his weary Way,
And leaves the World to Darkness & to me.

Now fades the glimmering Landscape on the Sight,
And now the Air a solemn Stillness holds;
Save where the Beetle wheels his droning Flight,
Or drowsy Tinklings lull the distant Folds.

Save that from yonder ivy-mantled Tower
The mopeing Owl does to the Moon complain
Of such as stray too wand'ring near her secret Bower
Molest & pry into her ancient solitary Reign.

Beneath those rugged Elms, that Yewtree's Shade,
Where heaves the Turf in many a mouldring Heap,
Each in his narrow Cell for ever laid
The rude Forefathers of the Hamlet sleep.

For ever sleep, the breezy Call of Morn,
Or Swallow twitt'ring from the strawbuilt Shed,
Or Chaunticleer so shrill or ecchoing Horn,
No more shall rouse them from their lowly Bed.

For them no more the blazeing Hearth shall burn,
Or busy Huswife ply her Evening Care;
No Children run to lisp their Sire's Return,
Nor climb his Knees the envied coming Kiss to share.

Oft did the Harvest to their Sickle yield;
Their Furrow oft the stubborn Glebe has broke;
How jocund did they drive their Team a-field!
How bow'd the Woods beneath their sturdy Stroke!

Let not Ambition mock their useful Toil
Their rustic Joys & Destiny obscure:
Nor Grandeur hear with a disdainful Smile
The short & simple Annals of the Poor.

First page of one of three known drafts of Gray's An Elegy Wrote in a Country Church Yard *(Eton College)*

AN

ELEGY

WROTE IN A

Country Church Yard.

LONDON:
Printed for R. DODSLEY in *Pall-mall*;
And sold by M. COOPER in *Pater-noster-Row*. 1751.
[Price Six-pence.]

Title page for the first edition of Gray's "Elegy"

habit of personification exposes the debased forms assumed by desire ("Envy wan, and faded Care"), just as the "race of man" in the "Ode on the Spring" is revealed as insect life to "Contemplation's sober eye." Vision always serves to reveal form, and in Gray what is revealed is diminished, repudiated, or forbidden. The strategy of reductive acknowledgment in the "Ode on the Spring" dismisses the dream of desire; the strategy of creating giant spectral forms in the Eton College ode encourages bad dreams, translating desire into the demonic. Northrop Frye describes something similar to this action in his discussion of quest-romance: "Translated into dream terms, the quest-romance is the search of the libido or desiring self for a fulfillment that will deliver it from the anxieties of reality but still contain that reality." Fulfillment may require, as with Gray, that a protective maternal figure displace a threatening female judicial figure; guilt is thereby dissipated in the approval received by the obedient actor who has rejected desire. This summary also describes the "Hymn to Adversity."

Adversity and Virtue are both daughters of Jove; the former is older than and tutor to the latter. Adversity is equipped with "iron scourge and torturing hour" but also has an alternative "form benign," a "milder influence." Virtue needs Adversity "to form her [Virtue's] infant mind"; the function of the tutelary spirit here is to engender pity ("she learn'd to melt at others' woe"). The instruction is absorbed by Virtue (the "rigid lore / With patience many a year she bore"). Virtue, subdued by Adversity, is enabled to recognize grief ("What sorrow was, thou bad'st her know") and is preserved from desire ("Scared at thy frown terrific, fly / Self-pleasing Folly's idle brood, / Wild Laughter, Noise, and thoughtless Joy, / And leave us leisure to be good"). Adversity, implored to "lay thy chast'ning hand" on her "Suppliant's head" and to appear "Not in thy Gorgon terrors clad, / Nor circled with the vengeful band / (As by the Impious thou art seen)," suggests the threatening form of Adversity seen by those who are not "good." Desire is converted into the antithetical form of horror. The speaker who experiences Adversity's "milder influence," her "philosophic Train," undergoes a transformation in which guilt is changed into the generous emotions of love and forgiveness. Adversity here joins Muse, Contemplation, and Thames as figures authorizing the rejection of desire. At the end of the Eton College ode the reader is reminded that the suffering "all are men." At the end of the "Hymn to Adversity" the speaker asks to be taught "to love and to forgive," to be led to "know myself a Man."

Gray's poems indicate a radical sexual distress. In the "Hymn to Adversity" Gray has arrived at the first clear castrative symbolism in the progress of his imagination (though one might argue that the reduction of humanity to insect life in the "Ode on the Spring" is a significant form of sexual loss), the replacement of Virtue by the poet. The threat of castration is transposed into an acceptance of it. The threatening figure of Adversity is pacified but requires a surrender of sexual identity.

In the "Hymn to Ignorance" Gray returns to Cambridge, invoking its "gothic fanes, and antiquated towers" as he had Eton's "distant spires" and "antique towers." Whereas in the Eton College ode "ignorance [small *i*] is bliss," in the "Hymn to Ignorance" Ignorance [large *I*] is a "soft salutary power." Ignorance is a maternal presence ("Prostrate with filial reverence I adore") possessed of a "peaceful shade"; its "influence breathed from high / Augments the native darkness of the sky." Ignorance is ambivalently represented as undesirable within the terms of desire ("Thrice hath Hyperion rolled his annual race, / Since weeping I forsook thy fond embrace"). The oedipal actors include mother/muse (Ignorance), father (Hyperion), and the returning son/poet, Gray.

On 15 October 1742 Gray returned to Peterhouse as a fellow-commoner to read for a law degree. After 1742 he wrote poetry only sporadically. He received an LL.B. degree in November 1743. He and Walpole were reconciled in 1745, though the friendship was never again quite as intimate.

When Gray returned to writing poetry, he composed two poems that rebuke desire in different ways. Selima, Walpole's cat in "Ode on the Death of a Favourite Cat, Drowned in a Tub of Gold Fishes" (1748), is tempted beyond "lawful prize" into a watery grave. The "Ode on the Death of a Favourite Cat" is a cautionary tale; its purpose is to deaden desire by revealing its effect on the "Presumptuous Maid!" Selima's desire to apprehend "Two angel forms . . . / The Genii of the stream," is an investment in death. Implicit in the scene of desire are the unattainability of the object and the abandonment of the desiring figure to her fate: "Eight times emerging from the flood / She mew'd to ev'ry watery god." Selima's fate appears in the concluding stanza as if to Contemplation's sober eye. Her plunge into the goldfish bowl is another vain dream of the desiring self. Selmia wishes to possess what is taboo; it requires her engagement with a medium in which she cannot survive. Her fate is a variation on the fate of those who would appropriate that which is beyond their proper sphere. The poem might be read as pertinent to Gray's sense of his poetic vocation: his poetic output was small, and his poems were generally short and often unfinished.

In "A Long Story" (1753), composed in 1750, the Peeress whose judgment the poet fears invites him to dinner instead of rebuking him. Brought before her authority the poet disavows himself:

> "He once or twice had pen'd a sonnet;
> "Yet hoped, that he might save his bacon:
> "Numbers would give their oaths upon it,
> "He ne'er was for a conj'rer taken.["]

"A Long Story" involves a flight from the figures of desire, the "heroines" who attempt to lure the poet into polite country pleasures, leaving a note ("a spell") on the table. This self-representation points toward the poet of the "Elegy": the poet who is there heard by the hoary-headed swain, " 'Muttering his wayward fancies,' " is here "something . . . heard to mutter, / 'How in the park beneath an old-tree / '(Without design to hurt the butter, / 'Or any malice to the poultry,). . . .' " The old tree of "A Long Story" is the transplanted "nodding beech" of the "Elegy," under which the poet " 'His listless length at noontide would . . . stretch.' " The poet of "A Long Story" is the parodic form of the poet of the "Elegy." The shift in the "Elegy" from "I" to "thee" is prefigured in "A Long Story" in an unidentified voice which suddenly breaks in to rebuke the speaker for his tedium: "Your Hist'ry whither you are spinning? / Can you do nothing but de-

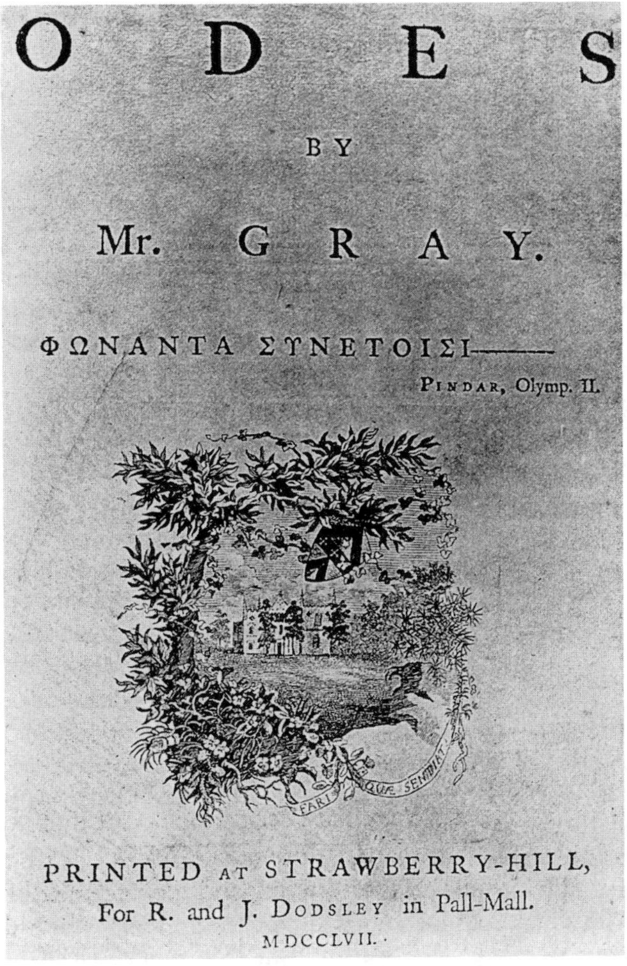

ODES

BY

Mr. GRAY.

ΦΩΝΑΝΤΑ ΣΥΝΕΤΟΙΣΙ——

PINDAR, Olymp. II.

PRINTED AT STRAWBERRY-HILL,

For R. and J. DODSLEY in Pall-Mall.

MDCCLVII.

Title page for the collection that includes Gray's Pindaric odes, "The Progress of Poesy" and "The Bard." The volume was the first book published by Horace Walpole's press at Strawberry Hill.

scribe?" "A Long Story" is actually a short one (145 lines) of identity mocked, function abused ("Whither are you spinning?"), and voice lost. What here dominates Gray's imagination is a vision of prophecy reduced to absurdity, of the seer as merely a bothersome miscreant

> Who prowl'd the country far and near,
> Bewitch'd the children of the peasants,
> Dried up the cows and lam'd the deer,
> And suck'd the eggs, and kill'd the pheasants.

If it were only for the "Elegy" Gray's reputation would endure, for it is surely the finest elegiac poem of the age and one of the half-dozen or so great English elegies. As was usual with Gray the poem's progress was hesitant and delayed (two distinctly different versions of the poem exist), and its publication was imposed on him when the poem was pirated from privately circulated copies and printed by the *Magazine of Magazines*. Its publication in 1751 places it more than halfway in Gray's poetic career, between the highly productive year of 1742 and the publication of the two Pindaric odes in 1757.

Almost everyone who reads poetry is familiar with the opening of the poem: "The curfew tolls the knell of parting day, / The lowing herd wind slowly o'er the lea, / The plowman homeward plods his weary way, / And leaves the world to darkness and to me." It echoes lines from John Milton and William Shakespeare (and is echoed later by James Beattie and Wordsworth); it reflects a melancholic evening mood that has probably never found better expression. The eye of the speaker moves along the periphery of vision and returns to its center, the churchyard where "The rude Forefathers of the hamlet sleep." As the legacy of day is the night, the legacy of the past is death, an inheritance of mortality bequeathed equally by the rich and by the poor.

Everyone awaits the inevitable hour. Within the poem the brooding churchyard stands as an abiding memento mori, a powerful eschatological symbol appropriately heralded by the "droning" beetle, the "mopeing owl," the "yew-tree's shade." Against such an initial vision, as its contrary, are set the emblems of Christian eschatology: the "incense-breathing Morn," "the swallow," "the cock's shrill clarion," "the echoing horn"—none of which shall ever again rouse the slumberers. The vast negative absolute of death informs the poem, and Gray confronts the omnipresent fact of mortality, letting the confrontation arise implicitly from the opposition of the two major symbols within the poem: the chronicle and the grave, the epitaph and the churchyard.

One of the abiding paradoxes of the poem resides in the idea of satisfactory unfulfillment: village-Hampdens; mute, inglorious Miltons; guiltless Cromwells of the rural life. The paradox is spawned by Gray's vision of human life as dominated by the only inevitability it contains, that of death. Before this inevitability the triumphs of man pass into insignificance, for "The paths of glory," like all paths, "lead but to the grave." Against the grave is posed the chronicle or epitaph, and the latter is of considerable complexity in the poem. It develops through various modalities before it emerges finally as the poet's own epitaph, with which the work concludes. The specific manifestations of the chronicle include the "annals of the poor," the "storied urn," the "boast of heraldry," the "animated bust," the "frail memorial." In each case the objects of remembrance are diminished by the qualifying context: the annals of the poor are "short and simple," the boast of heraldry "awaits ... th' inevitable hour," the storied urn and animated bust cannot "Back to its mansion call the fleeting breath," the memorial is "frail." Such images bespeak futility. Yet what emerges as truly valuable is human relationship. Gray's reading of epitaphs is a coming-to-know: he did not know these people as they lived; he knows them by the imaginative re-creation of their lives through a meditation on the surviving memorials.

So, too, the reader is given to understand, will the "kindred Spirit" know the narrator through his own epitaph. If in the end everyone is alone, solitude is qualified by shared mortality, and further qualified by the presence of a kindred sensibility. Mortality is not submitted to some scheme of personal salvation or redemption. The "Elegy" is not in this respect a conventional pastoral elegy; it does not provide the consolation of, say, Milton's *Lycidas* (1637). Gray's poem suggests that the elegist is himself powerless in the face of death, unable to refer it to a religious belief by which it can be made comprehensible. What are justified are the unrealized lives, of which the poet's life is one example. The "Elegy" is perhaps most of all an exercise in the varieties of feeling: the speaker feels for the unhonored dead and for the honored dead; he imagines particular persons for whom he can feel; he employs the pathetic fallacy to feel for the flower "born to blush unseen"; he feels for "mankind"; and through the "kindred Spirit" he feels for himself. The poem is an exercise in sensibility. The darkness in which the narrator stands is the night of mortality illuminated only by varieties of feeling. This common denominator of sympathy, as everything in the poem evidences, is all that binds man to man, and, along with the fact of death that occasions this sympathy, is the single principle of unity within life perceived by the poet.

The inception of "The Progress of Poesy: A Pindaric Ode" followed directly on the publication of the "Elegy." It presents a further, yet concealed, rendering of the self-image found especially at the end of the "Elegy." "The Progress of Poesy" associates the solitary poet with his mother-muse, the female goddess to whom he owes his capacity to perceive "forms" illuminated by "the Muse's ray," a light that is "unborrow'd of the Sun." Ceres ("Ceres' golden reign") embodies the generative power of nature. "Helicon's harmonious springs" are associated with generation ("The laughing flowers . . . / Drink life and fragrance as they flow"). The lyre is the "Parent of sweet and solemn-breathing airs." These three elements dominate the opening of the poem. The first ternary closes with Aphrodite ("Cytherea's day"), a figure of generative force mingling the union of water and music ("brisk notes in cadence beating"; "arms sublime, that float upon the air"). She is the reemergent Venus of the "Ode on the Spring," attended, as was Venus in that poem, by a train of celebrants: "O'er her warm cheek, and rising bosom, move / The bloom of young Desire, and purple light of Love." In the "Ode on the Spring," the "rosy-bosom'd Hours, / . . . Disclose the long-expected flowers, / And wake the purple year!"

The familiar Etonian demons recur in this poem: "Man's feeble race what Ills await, / Labour, and Penury, the racks of Pain." In the second ternary the recognition of loss rises against

Pembroke College at Cambridge University, Gray's principal residence from March 1756 until his death in 1771

the figures of desire, opposing them with "Night, and all her sickly dews." Night, a "mighty Mother" of sorts, will hold sway "Till down the eastern cliffs afar / Hyperion's march they spy, and glitt'ring shafts of war." Hyperion is an idealized figure associated through the "eastern cliffs" with Milton's Raphael, and more vaguely with Christ as he disposes half his might against Satan's legions. But the ode relegates his progress to an indefinite future, to an apocalyptic dawn that will "justify the laws of Jove." Hyperion departs from the poem at the close of the first strophe of the second ternary. Thus the defeat of Night, the graveyard goddess whose "Spectres wan, and Birds of boding cry" are the antithesis to the "rosy-crowned Loves" attending Aphrodite, is deferred.

The "Muse" who appears at this point is a variation on the pastoral-maternal female, one who "deigns to hear the savage Youth repeat / In loose numbers wildly sweet / Their feather-cinctured Chiefs, and dusky Loves." She is a "soft salutary power" ("Hymn to Ignorance"), "form benign" ("Hymn to Adversity").

The oedipal fantasy is played out in pastoral surroundings: "In thy green lap was Nature's Darling [Shakespeare] laid, / What time, where lucid Avon Stray'd, / To Him the mighty Mother did unveil / Her aweful face. . . ." The anticipation of unveiling led the voyeur Milton to ride "sublime / Upon the seraph-wings of Extasy, / The secrets of th' Abyss to spy." Yet the laws of Jove are preserved: the primal scene is never viewed. The Hyperionic march is rendered irrelevant by "Such forms, as glitter in the Muse's ray"; these forms that tease Gray's own "infant eyes," bringing him into proximity to Shakespeare, the "immortal Boy." The "orient hues" that dazzled the child Gray were "unborrow'd of the sun"—another rejection of the sublime poetic (Hyperionic) principle. Between oedipal desire (the desire for the "mighty Mother") and the lonely sublime passion of the middle poet there is no adequate middle ground (though Gray hopes to find one). The "distant way" chosen by the poet at the end of the poem is necessitated by the refusal to be the poet of sublime vision (Milton) and by the impossibility of possessing the mother-muse who appears to the child of nature (Shakespeare). Much of the ode is occupied with the scene of desire—Milton's and Shakespeare's—and is thus concerned, however covertly, with the relation between sexual power and poetic vision. Gray's modest announcement at the end of the poem shows a recognition of his distance from the great figures of English literature and from the power

Dear Mason

Of all loves come to Cambridge out of hand, for here is Mr Dillival & a charming set of glasses, that sing like nightingales, & we have concerts every other night, & shall stay here this month or two, & a vast deal of good company, & a Whale in pickle just come from Ipswich, & the Man won't die, & Mr Wood is gone to Chatsworth, & there is no body but you, & Tom, & the curl'd Dog, and don't talk of the charge, for we will make a subscription: besides we know, you always come, when you have a mind.

Dec: 8. 1761.
Pemb: Hall.

TGray.

Letter from Gray to his friend William Mason (collection of A. T. Lloyd, Esq., of Lockinge)

with which their visions were informed: he is "Beneath the Good . . . but far above the Great"—in any event, alone.

"The Bard: A Pindaric Ode" (1757) is a companion piece to "The Progress of Poesy." It presents another identity, a solitary prophet who can more readily justify the laws of Jove than can any agent in the "The Progress of Poesy." At the beginning of the ode he is "Robed in the sable garb of woe," the insignia of his office. At the end he "plung[es] to endless night," another entrance into darkness. The plunge into the abyss seems to be a wish-fulfillment fantasy; the mighty Mother is darkness itself, the unshaped figure of desire. The poet who strikes "the deep sorrows of his lyre" in "The Bard" produces not the "sweet and solemn-breathing airs" of "The Progress of Poesy" but the harmonies of loss and consolation.

The Eton College ode identifies the progress of human life in terms of absolute separation between youth and age. The "Ode on the Pleasure Arising from Vicissitude," written around 1754-1755 and published in 1775, recreates, through the language of kindredness, the law of succession and cycle: "Still, where rosy Pleasure leads, / See a kindred Grief pursue." "Rosy Pleasure" is joined here to an opposite that follows it in an endless alternation. The "blended form" composed by the two figures unifies the figures of desire and authority in what is apparently Gray's version of the marriage of heaven and hell. The principle of authority (and desire) is found in Vicissitude, a figure who imposes an Adversity-like "chastening":

> The hues of Bliss more brightly glow,
> Chastised by sabler tints of woe. . . .

The ode negates its initial figure of desire, "the golden Morn aloft" who

> . . . woo's the tardy spring:
> Till April starts, and calls around
> The sleeping fragrance from the ground;

And lightly o'er the living scene
Scatters his freshest, tenderest green.

Morn and April give way to tableaux in which the kindred activities of mourning and consolation are enacted: "Smiles on past Misfortune's brow / Soft Reflection's hand can trace; / And o'er the cheek of Sorrow throw / A melancholy grace." The initial act of wooing becomes another sort of engagement, Grief pursuing rosy Pleasure, Comfort approaching Misery. The "blended form" is a sublimation of the sexual ardor between Morn and April, transformed into a depersonalized aesthetic in which "artful strife" and "strength and harmony" displace the seductive Morn who "With vermeil cheek and whisper soft / . . . woo's the tardy spring." Courtship is metamorphosed into consolation, and Vicissitude becomes another figure like Contemplation or Adversity, under whose aegis desire is eliminated. Vicissitude, unlike Adversity, is a genderless figure, representing no threatening sexual image The ode revisits another place, as Eton is revisited by the disillusioned speaker in *An Ode on a Distant Prospect of Eton College* or as Gray returns to Cambridge in the "Hymn to Ignorance." Here the return is to the beginning of the "Elegy," to "darkness" and to the landscape over which the "plowman homeward plods his weary way." All of Gray's poems are poems of progress, journeys in which the challenge lies in discovering something other than the circularity of ends that are constituted of beginnings ("And they that creep, and they that fly, / Shall end where they began" ["Ode on the Spring"]).

Gray's mother died on 11 March 1753. On 5 March 1756 he moved from Peterhouse College across the street to Pembroke College, reportedly as a consequence of a prank played on him by some students who, knowing of his fear of fire, raised a false alarm. When the master of Peterhouse, Dr. Law, failed to take Gray's complaint about the prank seriously, Gray "migrated" to Pembroke. When the poet laureate, Colley Cibber, died in 1757, Gray was offered the position; but he declined it. In July 1759 he moved to London to study at the British Museum, which had been opened to the public in January. In December 1761 he returned to Cambridge; except for frequent trips to London, other parts of England, Scotland, and Wales, he remained in Cambridge for the rest of his life.

Poems by Mr. Gray (1768) includes two translations from the Norse. "The Fatal Sisters" and "The Descent of Odin" are poems of prophecy. The first is dominated by what Gray in the preface calls "twelve gigantic figures resembling women" whose purpose is to weave the web of futurity and whose way leads through another field of the dead ("As the paths of fate we tread, / Wading thro' th' ensanguin'd field. . . ." The easily identifiable figure of desire in the early verse has been replaced by vast terrifying forms, "*Mista* black, terrific Maid, / *Sangrida,* and *Hilda,*" "*Gondula,* and *Geira.*" Such women appeared first as Contemplation or Adversity. They represent the combined identities of muse-mother-death, the unified form of desire and authority toward which Gray's imagination has been traveling.

"The Descent of Odin" concerns Odin's visit to the underworld—the kingdom of Hela, Goddess of Death—to discover his son Balder's fate; he learns from the prophetess that Hoder will murder Balder and that Vali, the son of Odin and Rinda, will avenge the crime. The " prophetic Maid" is revealed as the "Mother of the giant-brood." Odin wakes her with "runic rhyme; / Thrice pronounc'd, in accents dread." The poem with the maid denying prophetic knowledge to any future "enquirer . . . / . . . till substantial Night / Has reassum'd her ancient right." The maid's last oracular utterance is a vision of ultimate closure, when "wrap'd in flames, in ruin hurl'd, / Sinks the fabric of the world."

In July 1768 Gray was made professor of modern history at Cambridge, though he never lectured or published on the subject. The most significant personal event of his last years was a brief, intense friendship with a young Swiss student, Karl Victor von Bonstetten. The friendship was apparently complicated by physical desire on Gray's part, though no sexual relation is believed to have occurred between them. In July 1771 Gray became ill while dining at Pembroke College; a week later, on 30 July, he died. In his *Souvenirs* (1832) Bonstetten reflected on the poet: "Je crois que Gray n'avait jamais aimé, c'était le mot de l'énigme, il en était résulté une misère de coeur qui faisait contraste avec son imagination, ardente et profond qui, au lieu de faire le bonheur de sa vie, n'en était que le tourment" (I think the key to the mystery is that Gray never loved; the result was a poverty of heart contrasting with his ardent and profound imagination, which, instead of comprising the happiness of his life, was only its torment).

Gray remains an important poet in the context of generally disappointing poets in the sec-

Gray's tomb in the churchyard at Stoke Pogis

ond half of the eighteenth century. In this sense he is one of a group, including William Collins, James Macpherson, Thomas Chatterton, William Cowper, Christopher Smart, and Joseph and Thomas Warton, who largely failed to provide English poetry with any especially distinctive period identity and whose achievements were shortly to be overshadowed by the emergence in the 1780s and 1790s of Wordsworth, Coleridge, and the quickly succeeding second generation of Romantic writers.

Three aspects of Gray's prose remain of value to modern students of the later eighteenth century. His extensive correspondence reveals his various interests and displays his intelligence and character in ways that the poetry cannot. Gray was an amateur entomologist, an enthusiastic traveler, and a discerning admirer of the sublime in nature. A well-known passage in his correspondence (16 November 1739) describes his journey to the Grande Chartreuse during his Continental tour: "Not a precipice, not a torrent, not a cliff, but is pregnant with religion and poetry. There are certain scenes that would awe an atheist into belief, without the help of other argument. One need not have a very fantastic imagination to see spirits there at noonday. You have death perpetually before your eyes, only so far removed, as to compose the mind without frightening it." His journal of his tour of the English Lakes was published in *The Poems of Mr. Gray* (1775); it is the work by him that most favorably influenced Wordsworth and is said to be the best of his prose compositions. Finally, Gray proposed a history of English literature which came to little more than some sketches and a few literary essays revealing his interest in meter, rhyme, unity of poetic effect, and older English poets. With the important exception of the correspondence, the prose remains largely unread today and occupies the sort of place in his oeuvre accorded the Latin compositions in prose and verse that he occa-

Detail of the monument to Gray, by John Bacon the Elder, in Westminster Abbey

sionally produced. Much of his career is marked by an unsettling tendency toward the occasional, the random, and the unsustained; his poetry may be the best indication of the difficulties in writing a new public poetry in the age following Alexander Pope.

Letters:

The Correspondence of Thomas Gray, 3 volumes, edited by Paget Toynbee and Leonard Whibley (Oxford: Clarendon Press, 1935; reprinted, with additions and corrections by Herbert W. Starr, Oxford: Clarendon Press, 1971).

Bibliographies:

Clark S. Northrup, *A Bibliography of Thomas Gray* (New Haven: Yale University Press, 1917);

Herbert W. Starr, *A Bibliography of Thomas Gray, 1917-1951* (Philadelphia: University of Pennsylvania Press, 1953);

Alan T. McKenzie, *Thomas Gray: A Reference Guide* (Boston: Hall, 1982);

Donald C. Mell, Jr., *English Poetry, 1660-1800* (Detroit: Gale Research, 1982), pp. 238-251.

Biographies:

Roger Martin, *Essai sur Thomas Gray* (London: Oxford University Press / Paris: Les Presses Universitaires de France, 1934);

William Powell Jones, *Thomas Gray, Scholar: The True Tragedy of an Eighteenth-Century Gentleman* (Cambridge, Mass.: Harvard University Press, 1937);

Robert W. Ketton-Cremer, *Thomas Gray: A Biography* (Cambridge: Cambridge University Press, 1955).

References:

Matthew Arnold, "Thomas Gray," in his *Essays in Criticism: Second Series* (London: Macmillan, 1889), pp. 69-99;

Karl Victor von Bonstetten, *Souvenirs de Ch. Victor de Bonstetten, écrits en 1831* (Paris: Cherbuliez, 1832);

Frank Brady, "Structure and Meaning in Gray's *Elegy*," in *From Sensibility to Romanticism: Essays Presented to Frederick A. Pottle,* edited by Frederick W. Hilles and Harold Bloom (New York: Oxford University Press, 1965), pp. 177-189;

Lord David Cecil, "The Poetry of Thomas Gray," in *Eighteenth Century English Literature: Modern Essays in Criticism,* edited by James L. Clifford (New York: Oxford University Press, 1959), pp. 233-250;

Albert S. Cook, *Concordance to the English Poems of Thomas Gray* (Boston & New York: Houghton, Mifflin, 1908; reprinted, Gloucester, Mass.: Smith, 1967);

Francis Doherty, "The Two Voices of Gray," *Essays in Criticism,* 13 (July 1963): 222-230;

Frank H. Ellis, "Gray's *Elegy:* The Biographical Problem in Literary Criticism," *PMLA,* 66 (December 1951): 971-1008;

Northrop Frye, *Anatomy of Criticism* (Princeton: Princeton University Press, 1957), p. 193;

Morris Golden, *Thomas Gray* (New York: Twayne, 1964);

Donald Green, "The Proper Language of Poetry: Gray, Johnson, and Others," in *Fearful Joy: Papers from the Thomas Gray Bicentenary Conference at Carleton University,* edited by James Downey and Ben Jones (Montreal: McGill-Queen's University Press, 1974), pp. 85-102;

Leon Guilhamet, "Imitation and Originality in the Poems of Thomas Gray," in *Proceedings of the Modern Language Association: Neoclassicism Conferences, 1967-1968,* edited by Paul J. Korshin (New York: AMS, 1970), pp. 33-52;

Wallace Jackson, "Thomas Gray and the Dedicatory Muse," *ELH,* 54 (Summer 1987): 277-298;

Jackson, "Thomas Gray: Drowning in Human Voices," *Criticism,* 28 (Fall 1986): 361-379;

Jackson and Paul Yoder, "Wordsworth Reimagines Thomas Gray: Notations on Begetting a Kindred Spirit," *Criticism,* 31 (Summer 1989): 287-301;

Samuel Johnson, "Life of Thomas Gray," in his *The Lives of the English Poets,* 3 volumes, edited by George Birkbeck Hill (London: Clarendon Press, 1905), III: 421-445;

Roger Lonsdale, "The Poetry of Thomas Gray: Versions of Self," *Proceedings of the British Academy,* 59 (1973): 105-123;

Patricia Meyer Spacks, " 'Artful Strife': Conflict in Gray's Poetry," *PMLA,* 81 (March 1966): 63-69;

Spacks, "Statement and Artifice in Thomas Gray," *Studies in English Literature,* 5 (Summer 1965): 519-532;

Howard D. Weinbrot, "Gray's *Elegy:* A Poem of Moral Choice and Resolution," *Studies in English Literature,* 18 (Summer 1978): 537-551;

Henry Weinfeld, *The Poet without a Name: Gray's* Elegy *and the Problem of History,* (Carbondale & Edwardsville: Southern Illinois University Press, 1991);

William Wordsworth, Preface to *Lyrical Ballads, with a Few Other Poems,* second edition, 2 volumes, by Wordsworth and Samuel Taylor Coleridge (London: Printed for T. N. Longman and O. Rees by Briggs & Co., Bristol, 1800; Philadelphia: Printed and sold by James Humphreys, 1802).

Papers:

A commonplace book, in three volumes, at Pembroke College, Cambridge, contains Thomas Gray's transcripts of many of his poems and transcripts of other of Gray's poems made by William Mason after Gray's death.

Sir William Jones

(23 September 1746 - 27 April 1794)

Garland Cannon
Texas A&M University

BOOKS: *A Grammar of the Persian Language* (London: Printed by W. and J. Richardson, 1771);

*Lettre à Monsieur A*** du P**** (London: P. Elmsly, 1771);

Dissertation sur la littérature orientale (London: P. Elmsly, and Richardson & Urquhart, 1771);

Poems, Consisting Chiefly of Translations from the Asiatick Languages: To Which Are Added Two Essays (Oxford: Clarendon Press, 1772);

An Oration Intended to Have Been Spoken in the Theatre at Oxford, on the 9th of July 1773, by a Member of the University (London: Privately printed, 1773);

Poeseos Asiaticæ Commentariorum Libri sex, cum Appendice: Subjicitur Limon, Seu Miscellaneorum Liber (London: Printed by Richardson and sold by T. Cadell, 1774);

Julii Melesigoni ad Libertatum Carmen (London: Printed by J. Nichols, 1780);

An Inquiry into the Legal Mode of Suppressing Riots, with a Constitutional Plan of Future Defence (London: Printed for C. Dilly, 1780; enlarged, 1782);

A Speech on the Nomination of Candidates to Represent the County of Middlesex, IX September, MDCCLXXX (London: Privately printed, 1780);

The Muse Recalled: An Ode, Occasioned by the Nuptials of Lord Viscount Althorp and Miss Lavinia Bingham (Strawberry Hill: Printed by Thomas Kirgate, 1781);

An Ode in Imitation of Alcæus (London, 1781);

An Essay on the Law of Bailments (London: Printed by J. Nichols for Charles Dilly, 1781; Philadelphia: Hogan & Thompson, 1836);

An Ode in Imitation of Callistratus (London: Privately printed, 1782);

A Speech of William Jones, Esq. to the Assembled Inhabitants of the Counties of Middlesex and Surry [sic], the Cities of London and Westminster, and the Borough of Southwark (London: Printed for C. Dilly, 1782);

The Principles of Government, in a Dialogue between a Scholar and a Peasant: Written by a Member of the Society for Constitutional Information (London: Printed and distributed gratis by the Society for Constitutional Information, 1782); enlarged as *The Principles of Government, in a Dialogue, between a Gentleman & a Farmer*, edited by T. S. Norgate (Norwich: Printed by J. March, for Lee and Hurst, London, 1797);

A Letter to a Patriot Senator, Including the Heads of a Bill for a Constitutional Representation of the People (London, 1783);

The Enchanted Fruit; or, The Hindu Wife: An Antediluvian Tale. Written in the Province of Bahar (Calcutta, 1784);

A Discourse on the Institution of a Society for Enquiring into the History, the Antiquities, Arts, Sciences, and Literature of Asia, Delivered at Calcutta, January 15th 1784; A Charge to the Grand Jury at Calcutta; and a Hymn to Camdeo (London: Printed for T. Payne and Son, 1784);

Sir William Jones's Charge to the Grand Jury, at Calcutta, X June, MDCCLXXXV (Calcutta, 1785);

A Discourse to the Society for Inquiring into the History, Civil and Natural, the Antiquities, Arts, Sciences, and Literature of Asia: Delivered 24 February, 1785, by the President (Calcutta, 1785);

Sir William Jones's Charge to the Grand Jury, at Calcutta, X June, MDCCLXXXVII (Calcutta, 1787);

A Discourse to the Society for Inquiring into the History, Civil and Natural, the Antiquities, Arts, Sciences, and Literature of Asia: Delivered 15 February, 1787. By the President (Calcutta, 1787);

Sir William Jones's Charge to the Grand Jury, at Calcutta, June 10, 1790 (Calcutta: Printed by Manuel Cantopher, 1790);

Two Hymns to Pracriti, and the First Nemean Ode of Pindar (Calcutta, 1790);

A Hymn to Gangá (Calcutta, 1790);

A Hymn to Náráyena (Calcutta, 1790);

A Hymn to Lacshmí (Calcutta, 1790);

A Hymn to Indra (Calcutta, 1790);

Sir William Jones (portrait by A. W. Devis; collection of Earl Spencer, Althorp Park, Northampton)

Britain Discovered: An Heroick Poem (Calcutta, 1790);

Sir William Jones's Charge to the Grand Jury at Calcutta, Delivered IX June M.DCC.XCII (Calcutta, 1792);

Dissertations and Miscellaneous Pieces Relating to the History and Antiquities, the Arts, Sciences, and Literature, of Asia, by Jones and others, 2 volumes (London: Printed for G. Nicol, J. Walter, and J. Sewell, 1792);

An Ode by Sir William Jones: What Constitutes a State? (London, 1795).

Collections: *The Works of Sir William Jones*, 6 volumes, edited by Anna Maria Jones (London: Printed for G. G. and J. Robinson and R. H. Evans, 1799);

The Works of Sir William Jones, 13 volumes, edited by Anna Maria Jones (London: Stockdale & Walker, 1807).

OTHER: Mahdī Khān of Astarābādī, *Histoire de Nader Chah*, 2 volumes, translated by Jones (London: P. Elmsly, 1770); translated into English by Jones as *The History of the Life of Nader Shah, King of Persia: Extracted from an Eastern Manuscript* (London: Printed by J. Richardson for T. Cadell, 1773);

The Speeches of Isæus in Causes Concerning the Law of Succession to Property at Athens, translated by Jones (London: Printed by J. Nichols for E. & C. Dilly, 1779);

Muhammad Ibn-al-Mulaqqin, *The Mahomedan Law of Succession to the Property of Intestates, in Arabick,* translated by Jones (London: Printed by J. Nichols for C. Dilly, 1782);

Al-Mu'allaqāt, *The Moallakát; or, Seven Arabian Poems,* translated by Jones (London: Printed by J. Nichols for P. Elmsly, 1782);

Lailà Majnún: A Persian Poem of Hátifí, translated by Jones (Calcutta: Manuel Cantopher, 1788);

Asiatick Researches; or, Transactions of the Society, Instituted in Bengal, for Inquiring into the History, the Antiquities, the Arts and Sciences, and Literature of Asia, volumes 1-4, edited by Jones (Calcutta: Manuel Cantopher, 1788-1794);

Kālidāsa, *Sacontalā; or, The Fatal Ring: An Indian Drama by Cālidās,* translated by Jones (Calcutta: Joseph Cooper, 1789);

Sirāj al-Dīn, *Al Sirajiyyah; or, The Mohammedan Law of Inheritance,* translated by Jones (Calcutta: J. Cooper, 1792);

The Seasons: A Descriptive Poem in the Original Sanscrit, edited by Jones (Calcutta: Calcutta Gazette, 1792; facsimile, edited by Herman Kreyenborg, Hannover: H. Lafaire, 1924);

Institutes of Hindu Law; or, The Ordinances of Menu, according to the Gloss of Cullūca, translated by Jones (Calcutta: Government of West Bengal, 1794).

Bicentennial reappraisals of Sir William Jones's Asiatic Society in various disciplines in the 1980s concluded that his fame and influence have not returned to the exalted worldwide levels reached just prior to the Victorian cultural and literary reappraisals of Asia, and that they may never do so. They also determined that his scholarship in anthropology, botany, history, and religion is chiefly of historical interest, and that it was not ultimately as lasting as was once anticipated. But the reappraisals verified that three of his poems are minor classics in Oriental Romanticism; that the quality of his literary translations and Asiatic scholarship permanently changed the whole Middle Eastern and Indian image in Western eyes; that he inspired an Indian renaissance that is still valued in India, especially through his Asiatic Society; and that his language-family theory is one of the enduring contributions to the history of ideas.

He was born on 23 September 1746, the son of William Jones, a mathematician and friend of Sir Isaac Newton. His father's death in 1749 left his mother, Mary Nix Jones, with modest assets, which she used in a relentless encouragement of the boy's studies. At Harrow, which he entered in 1753, he distinguished himself in classical scholarship and displayed his photographic memory, as when he wrote out the text of Shakespeare's *The Tempest* so that the boys could stage the play. Among his classmates were Samuel Parr, Joseph Banks, and Richard Brinsley Sheridan. To his school studies Jones added Hebrew and Arabic, as well as French and Italian.

By the time he was admitted to University College, Oxford, as a commoner in 1764, he was being called "the Great Scholar." But his colleagues there lacked his literary zeal, the school Latin used in the lectures was barbarous, and the intellectual pace was so slow that he was excused from lectures and allowed to progress at his own speed in philosophy, literature, and Middle Eastern studies. In 1765, to eliminate the financial burden on his mother, he became a tutor in the elegant Spencer household. George John, Viscount Althorp, the future second Earl Spencer, became his lifelong friend and stimulated urbane, illuminating letters modeled on Cicero's letters to Atticus. The Spencers permitted Jones to absent himself when necessary to complete his studies for the B.A., which he received in 1768, and he used their fine library to further his studies in law and to begin a Latin commentary on Persian and Arabic literature. He left the tutorship in a heated but minor spat to begin law studies in the Middle Temple in London in 1770.

A request by King Christian VII of Denmark that a difficult Persian biography be translated into French led to governmental pressure that culminated in a reluctant Jones neglecting his studies for a year to produce *Histoire de Nader Chah* (1770). The king's Latin testimonial to George III, which appeared in the London newspapers, helped to establish Jones as a major translator and language scholar from this first book. Four other Oriental works from 1771 to 1774 gave him the epithets of Persian Jones, Oriental Jones, and Linguist Jones, as well as the reputation of perhaps the world's greatest orientalist.

Jones's *A Grammar of the Persian Language* (1771), one of the best grammars ever written of an exotic language in English, went through several editions and translations. It inspired later scholars to follow his model, which used extensive literary quotations so that language study could simultaneously entertain, instruct, and morally uplift. It includes "A Persian Song of Hafiz," which still tantalizes readers with its Romantic dreamworld. The other three books had less impact. *Lettre à Monsieur A*** du P**** (1771), a

کتاب
شکرستان
در نحوی زبان پارسی
تصنیف
یونس اوکسفردی

A

GRAMMAR

OF THE

PERSIAN LANGUAGE.

BY WILLIAM JONES, ESQUIRE,

FELLOW OF UNIVERSITY COLLEGE, OXFORD.

چو عندلیب فصاحت فروشد ای حافظ
تو قدر او بسخن گفتن دری بشکن

LONDON:
PRINTED BY W. AND J. RICHARDSON, SALISBURY COURT,
FLEET STREET.
MDCCLXXI.

Title page for Jones's Persian grammar, which includes "A Persian Song of Hafiz"

harsh polemic against Anquetil Duperron's pioneering translation of the *Zend-Avesta* (1771), misdirected Avestan studies for fifty years. *Dissertation sur la littérature orientale* (1771) is filled with sensuous examples extolling the intellectual and artistic quality of Arabic and Persian writings. The 542-page *Poeseos Asiaticæ Commentariorum* (1774) is a brilliant, if somewhat incomplete, study of Asiatic poetic form, subject matter, diction, and individual poets; Jones thought that such a study might lead to needed innovations in Neoclassical European poetry.

All through his London years he was imbued with intense literary spirit, outlining and drafting a few stanzas of his never-composed epic "Britain Discovered." He selected and carefully revised nine of his early poems, which friends such as Sir Joshua Reynolds criticized for him. *Poems, Consisting Chiefly of Translations from the Asiatick Languages* (1772) is a successful fusion of classical conventions with Middle Eastern themes and images. It went through several editions and was as innovational in its limited way as Samuel Taylor Coleridge and William Wordsworth's *Lyrical Ballads* (1798) would be on a larger scale later. The reprinting in *Poems* of "A Persian Song of Hafiz" moved it toward acceptance as a standard British poem, which influenced Robert Southey and William Beckford. It became one of the most famous English renderings from Persian, surpassed only by Matthew Arnold's creative translation *Sohrab and Rustum* (1853) and by Edward FitzGerald's *The Rubáiyát of Omar Khayyám* (1859). "The Seven Fountains" was inspired by *The Arabian Nights Entertainments.* "Caissa; or, The Game of Chess" was an extremely popular poem stimulated by Girolamo Vida's *De Ludo Sacchorum* (The Game of Chess, 1527). Two concluding literary essays boldly challenged Neoclassical conventions with a poetic theory appealing for a simple style reflecting human passions and new subject matter, themes, and meters.

This combined literary and Oriental output, together with an engaging personality, brought Jones the desired professional and social status, although he was distinguished by his modesty. He became a fellow of the Royal Society and of the Society of Antiquaries and was elected to Samuel Johnson's literary group, the Club, in 1773. He received his M.A. from Oxford on 18 June 1773 and was asked to deliver an oration at the university, but he withdrew when there was pressure for him to alter his conservative discussion of scholarship and freedom of inquiry to include adulation of Lord North (Frederick North) and the ministers, whose American policies he was increasingly opposing. The speech was published as *An Oration Intended to Have Been Spoken in the Theatre at Oxford* (1773). Among his many friends were the young William Pitt, the American Arthur Lee, and Johnson's circle, especially Jones's Harrow classmate Banks, Edmund Burke, Anthony Chamier, David Garrick, Edward Gibbon, Thomas Percy, and Adam Smith. He sometimes visited Johnson's chambers, but his Whig prejudices prevented a close relationship. His friends embraced the whole literary and intellectual world of London, where he was a frequent guest at Elizabeth Montagu's parties as well as at gatherings at the homes of Fanny Burney and the duchess of Devonshire (Georgiana Spencer).

Admitted to the bar in 1774, Jones supported himself modestly as a barrister, attorney on the Oxford and Welsh circuits, and Oxford fellow. By 1778 it was obvious that his law practice could not adequately support him in his anticipated marriage to Anna Maria Shipley. When he learned of a lucrative Supreme Court justiceship in the Bengal presidency in 1778, he immediately began enlisting his friends' influence, with the thought that he could return home with thirty thousand pounds at the end of six years and could then pursue a parliamentary career.

He was also motivated by the injustice that he saw on every hand and that he believed he might help to alleviate through law rather than by revolution. Particularly disquieting were the reports from India, where alien British laws governed Hindus and Muslims. He assisted Burke and others on Indian legislation. His book *The Speeches of Isæus* (1779) consisted of the translation, his own summary of relevant Attic laws, notes, and an elegant commentary that permanently elevated Isæus's stature in Attic oratory and that sought to raise law to the status of a science. *An Essay on the Law of Bailments* (1781) is a perspicuous study of English bailments, enriched by wide comparisons with other legal systems. It went through several editions, was the standard source for British and American lawyers for fifty years, and guaranteed his place in legal scholarship. *The Mahomedan Law of Succession to the Property of Intestates* (1782), a translation of the Shafiite law of inheritance, had the central purpose of giving British lawyers an important source to implement the new Indian Judicature Act. It impressed Burke and Benjamin Franklin.

All of Jones's legal scholarship had an ultimately republican slant. Nor did his helping Burke on opposition legislation and his joining of Major John Cartwright's Society for Constitutional Information endear him to the Tory administration, especially Lord Chancellor Edward Thurlow. Seeking to show that a literary person could also be a superior politician, he made a spirited, unsuccessful effort for a university seat in Parliament in 1780; but the Tory power structure thwarted him and associated his name with firebrands such as Cartwright and John Wilkes. He had four political tracts published from 1780 to 1783, of which only *An Inquiry into the Legal Mode of Suppressing Riots, with a Constitutional Plan of Future Defence* (1780) was influential. The others were *A Speech on the Nomination of Candidates to Represent the County of Middlesex* (1780), *A Speech to the Assembled Inhabitants of the Counties of Middlesex and Surry* [*sic*] (1782), and *A Letter to a Patriot Senator* (1783). His "Plan of National Defence," which sought to augment the national forces by raising local militias, was never published.

His four political poems of 1780 to 1782 were better. *Julii Melesigoni ad Libertatum Carmen* (1780), a 172-line Alcaic ode, condemned Britain's war against America. *The Muse Recalled* (1781), an often-anthologized political epithalamium influenced by John Milton, also defended the American cause and was first printed by Horace Walpole's press at Strawberry Hill. *An Ode in Imitation of Alcæus* (1781), his greatest political poem, develops his ideas on government and morality in answering his opening question, "What constitutes a state?," and was later reprinted by Franklin in Passy, France. *An Ode in Imitation of*

70 Preparation for eternity.
Perfection of Earthly happiness.
65 Consciousness of a virtuous life.
Universal respect.
An amiable family.
A glorious retirement. Otium cum dignitate.
Fruits of his labours enjoyed.
60
Continuation of former Pursuits.
55 Mathematical Works.
Political Works.
Philosophical Works.
Oratorical Works.
Historical Works.
50 Virtue as a citizen.
Firmness as a patriot.
Vigilance as a legislator.
Education of his children.
Government of his family.
45 Fine arts patronized.
Laws enacted and supported.
Parliamentary affairs.
Science improved.
Compositions published.
40 The virtuous assisted.
The learned protected.
National rights defended.
Eloquence perfect.
Civil knowledge mature.

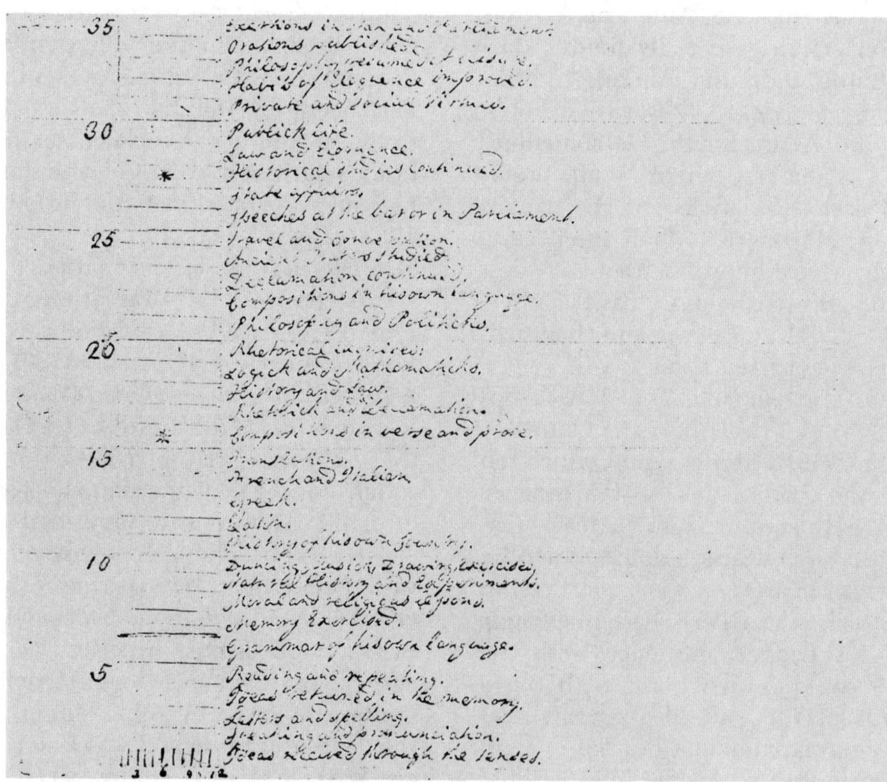
35 Exertions in Law and Parliament.
Orations published.
Philosophy resumed at leisure.
Habits of Eloquence improved.
Private and social virtues.
30 Publick Life.
Law and Eloquence.
Historical studies continued.
State affairs.
Speeches at the bar or in Parliament.
25 Travel and conversation.
Ancient Orators studied.
Declamation continued.
Compositions in his own language.
Philosophy and Politicks.
20 Rhetorical inquiries.
Logick and Mathematicks.
History and Law.
Rhetorick and Declamation.
Compositions in verse and prose.
15 Translations.
French and Italian.
Greek.
Latin.
History of his own Country.
10 Dancing, Musick, Drawing, Exercises.
Natural History and Experiments.
Moral and religious Lessons.
Memory exercised.
Grammar of his own language.
5 Reading and repeating.
Ideas retained in the memory.
Letters and spelling.
Speaking and pronunciation.
Ideas received through the senses.
3 6 9 12

Jones's "Andrometer," enclosed in a letter to George John, Viscount Althorp (26 December 1774). Jones explains in the letter: "I call it my Andrometer, *because it will enable you to measure* every man's merit *by looking for his* age *in the scale, and then comparing it with the other side, and seeing to what* degree *he has written in arts, sciences and ornamental qualifications" (Althorp Park).*

Callistratus (1782) celebrated the accession of a Whig ministry under the marquis of Rockingham (Charles Watson-Wentworth) and, later, Lord Shelburne (William Petty). These poems, plus three somewhat mysterious trips to Paris to see Franklin during the peak of the American war, further raised Tory doubts about Jones's suitability for the Indian judgeship; they also led to the suspicion (for which there was some basis in fact) that he was considering offers from Henry Laurens and others to migrate to America to help write the new American Constitution and laws. A friendly argument in Passy with the comte de Vergennes (Charles Gravier) and Franklin about whether basic governmental principles could be made intelligible to uneducated readers led Jones to compose a Socratic dialogue in French that sought to do so. Franklin ruled that Jones had won the argument, and Jones's translation of the dialogue was published anonymously by Cartwright's society as *The Principles of Government* (1782). When it was prosecuted as libelous, Jones had the pamphlet reprinted and proclaimed his authorship. The case culminated in Charles James Fox's Libel Act of 1792 that advanced the cause of freedom of the press. The dialogue went through several editions.

Jones's translation of *The Moallakát* (1782) was a departure from his usual political themes. One of his most artistic works, it gave the West the kismet motif and has haunted readers for two centuries with lines such as "shorten a cloudy day, a day astonishingly dark, by toying with a lovely delicate girl under a tent supported by pillars." It stimulated Alfred Tennyson's "Locksley Hall" (1842) and enjoyed long popularity and influence on later poets.

Jones's brilliant scholarship, determination, and assistance from powerful friends such as Shelburne and John Lord Ashburton finally led to his judicial appointment on 4 March 1783. Knighthood followed on 20 March and marriage to Anna Maria Shipley on 8 April. The last Club meeting he attended was on 25 March, when he saw Reynolds, Gibbon, and James Boswell for the last time. At the meeting he gave Burke his suggestions for legal changes in India, but a later disagreement led Burke to store away Jones's "Best Practicable System of Judicature for India" and never implement his excellent suggestions. Thus ended Jones's association with the Club, though he never resigned.

His ten years in India were fantastically crowded and productive. His six charges to the Calcutta Grand Jury from 1783 to 1794, which set the course of future Indian jurisprudence and reflected a veneration of British laws, stressed preserving Indians' rights to a trial by jury. Such democratic principles motivated all his judicial decisions, in which he considered Indians legally equal with Europeans.

He quickly fell in love with India's peoples and cultures. His greatest contribution to India was the founding of the Asiatic Society of Bengal in 1784. He envisioned the society as a vehicle for cooperative international scientific and humanistic projects cutting across social, ethnic, religious, and political lines. Indian prime minister Indira Gandhi understood his vision and, until her murder in 1984, intended to implement it to resolve territorial and other disputes among nations in her presidency of the Third World Nations' organization. She praised Jones's hatred of nationalism, war, territorial expansion, and oppression and sought to use the Asiatic Society to purvey that message. Few literary people have had such effects on posterity.

In his eleven anniversary discourses to the society he stressed the importance of learning Eastern languages as the key to the knowledge buried in ancient writings. Ancient Sanskrit botanical works might aid modern diet and medicine; ancient Indian architectural writings might foster beauty and sublimity in the modern world. In his third discourse, in 1786, he made his greatest contribution to the history of ideas by explaining language similarities on the basis of worldwide families of languages, with each family deriving from a common source. In later discourses he expanded his thesis by postulating branches within a family (such as Celtic, Indic, Germanic, Hellenic, and Iranian) and by sketching other language families. This explanation marked the end of the conception that God gave Hebrew to Adam and that language differences arose as the result of God's destruction of the Tower of Babel, replacing it with the modern view that language changes and that individual languages can die. It initiated the separation of religion from linguistics, discarding mythology and moving the discipline toward a scientific approach. He wrote other scholarly essays that further startled the West, for example, identifying Sandrocottus as the Greek Chandragupta Maurya I. His dramatic revelations about ancient India led to a renaissance among the Indian peoples themselves. He printed the *Ritusamhāra* in the original Sanskrit in 1792, under the English title *The Seasons*, to stim-

Relief from Jones's monument in the chapel of University College, Oxford, depicting Jones as "the Justinian of India"

ulate the Indians' love of their Sanskrit literary heritage. All of this information poured back to Europe in the much-reprinted and internationally popular *Asiatick Researches,* the first four volumes of which (1788-1794) Jones edited before he died.

The impetus that he gave to comparative literature through his Sanskrit translations and scholarship can hardly be exaggerated. Marco Polo had brought back tantalizing odds and ends; but Jones and his Asiatic Society gathered, integrated, and transmitted a synthesized body of objective data. Cultural pluralism was at hand. The writings of FitzGerald, Arnold, Rudyard Kipling, Ralph Waldo Emerson, Walt Whitman, Johann Gottfried von Herder, Johann Wolfgang von Goethe, and T. S. Eliot reveal the effects of Jones's work. Jones would not have been unhappy with this impact of his writings, for he viewed literature as a major source of information about the people who spoke the language in which a particular literary work was composed. His collection of phonetically and semantically similar words, which formed the basis of his revolutionary theory of common linguistic origins, was derived from literary—not oral—sources. His own poetry was generally motivated not by aesthetic but by scholarly purposes. He remains a minor poet, remembered chiefly for "A Persian Song of Hafiz" and *An Ode in Imitation of Alcæus.* His oriental influences on later poets is his major literary accomplishment.

A volume could be written on the history of Kālidāsa's fifth-century drama *Sacontalā* after Jones translated it into English in 1789 as *The Fatal Ring*; it has since been rendered many times into English and other languages. Also influential were his translations of the collection of Indian fables *Hitōpadēsa* and Jayadeva's lyric drama *Gīta Govinda,* both published posthumously in the 1807 edition of his works. He translated various stanzas in a projected rendering of the Vedas, the *Mahābhārata,* and the *Ramayana.* Other translations that he planned were of the Persian *Shahnamah,* the Arabic *Hamása,* and the Chinese *Shih Ching.*

Jones's work was not abstruse and impractical; he was a modern activist in every sense. His Jonesian System to transliterate Oriental writing into Roman orthography was a precursor to the International Phonetic Alphabet. He studied botanical records and plants to help Banks to acclimatize Oriental plants to the new Kew Gardens in London and St. Vincent in the West Indies, and he encouraged the naturalization of Kashmir goats for a Western wool industry. He encouraged European doctors to find a cure for elephantiasis. He urged the improvement by hybridization of the ketaka tree, mentioned in Sanskrit texts as a source of food during famines, characteristically without apologizing for bypassing the old doctrine of the fixity of species since the Creation. As all such knowledge needed to be cooperatively collected, refined, and disseminated through journals, he developed the whole concept of Orientalism and sought to develop a worldwide network of Oriental societies.

Jones demonstrated that literature cannot be separated from other disciplines and that it provides ideas, methods, images, and attitudes that can be moved back and forth across cultures to better the lot of human beings. He popularized the excitement, values, and even material gain that could result from the study of languages. He envisioned many of the tenets of modern sociolinguistics. Probably his greatest contribution to posterity has been the modern idea that languages are genealogically connected and are as mutable as biota. In its ultimate implications this notion may be comparable to Galileo's and Copernicus's breakthrough into scientific astronomy and Charles Darwin's integrated explanation of change in organisms.

The health of both Jones and his wife had deteriorated in the Indian climate. Anna Maria Jones returned to England in November 1793; Jones remained in India to try to complete his translation of a digest of the Hindu legal code, which would allow the Indian people to be governed by their own laws. He estimated that the task would take two more years. The only part to appear in print during his lifetime was *Institutes of Hindu Law; or, The Ordinances of Menu, according to the Gloss of Cullūca* (1794).

Jones died from an inflammation of the liver on 27 April 1794, a condition worsened by massive overwork and ignored in keeping with the Stoic view that the mind can rise above pain. He left a rich legacy. His writings and life are permeated with a spirit of peace and cooperative advancement and show an alternative to a world of savage high-tech war, Third World debt, and human exploitation.

Letters:

Memoirs of the Life, Writings and Correspondence of Sir William Jones, edited by John Shore, Lord Teignmouth (London: Hatchard, 1804);

The Letters of Sir William Jones, 2 volumes, edited by Garland Cannon (Oxford: Clarendon Press, 1970).

Bibliographies:

Garland Cannon, *Sir William Jones, Orientalist: An Annotated Bibliography of His Works* (Honolulu: University of Hawaii Press, 1952);

Cannon, *Sir William Jones: A Bibliography of Primary and Secondary Sources*, volume 7 of Library and Information Sources in Linguistics (Amsterdam: Benjamins, 1979).

Biographies:

John Shore, Lord Teignmouth, *Memoirs of the Life, Writings and Correspondence of Sir William Jones*, 2 volumes (London: Hatchard, 1804);

Henry Morris, *Sir William Jones, the Learned Oriental Scholar* (London: Christian Literary Society for India, 1901);

Arthur John Arberry, *Asiatic Jones: The Life and Influence of Sir William Jones* (London: Longmans, Green, 1946);

Garland Cannon, *Oriental Jones* (London: Indian Council for Cultural Relations, 1964);

S. N. Mukherjee, *Sir William Jones: A Study in Eighteenth-Century British Attitudes to India* (Cambridge: Cambridge University Press, 1968);

Cannon, *The Life and Mind of Oriental Jones: Sir William Jones, the Father of Modern Linguistics* (Cambridge & New York: Cambridge University Press, 1990).

References:

Garland Cannon, "The Construction of the European Image of the Orient: a Bicentennial Reappraisal of Sir William Jones as Poet and Translator," *Comparative Criticism*, 8 (1986): 166-188;

Cannon, "Foundations of Oriental and Comparative Studies: Correspondence of Sir William Jones," *Comparative Criticism*, 3 (1981): 157-178;

Cannon, "Jones's Founding and Directing of the Asiatic Society," *India Office Library and Records Report for 1984-85* (London: British Library, 1985), pp. 11-24;

Cannon, "Jones's 'sprung from some common source': 1786-1986," in *Sprung from Some Common Source*, edited by Sydney Lamb and Douglas Mitchell (Stanford: Stanford University Press, 1991), pp. 23-47;

Cannon, "Letters of Sir William Jones and His Correspondents," *Comparative Criticism*, 3 (1981): 179-196;

Cannon, "Sir William Jones and Anglo-American Relations during the American Revolution," *Modern Philology*, 76 (August 1978): 29-45;

Cannon, "Sir William Jones and Applied Linguistics," in *Papers in the History of Linguistics*, volume 38, edited by Hans Aarsleff and others (Amsterdam: Benjamins, 1987), pp. 379-389;

Cannon, "Sir William Jones and British Public Opinion toward Sanskrit Culture," *Journal of the Asiatic Society*, 23 (1980): 1-14;

Cannon, "Sir William Jones and Sanskrit Epigraphy," *Journal of the Oriental Society of Australia*, 13 (1978): 3-8;

Cannon, "Sir William Jones and the British Discovery of Ancient Sanskrit Culture," *Mankind Quarterly*, 22 (Spring 1982): 209-225;

Cannon, "Sir William Jones, Persian, Sanskrit and the Asiatic Society," *Histoire Épistémologie Langage*, 6, no. 2 (1984): 83-94;

Klaus and Krister Karttunen, Review of Cannon's *Sir William Jones: A Bibliography* (1979), *Acta Orientalia*, 44 (1983): 275-277;

Abu Taher Mojumder, "Three New Letters by Sir William Jones," *India Office Library and Records Report for 1981* (London: British Library, 1982), pp. 24-35;

R. H. Robins, "The Life and Work of Sir William Jones," *Transactions of the Philological Society*, 85 (1987): 1-23;

B. T. Styles, "Sir William Jones' Names of Indian Plants," *Taxon*, 25 (November 1976): 671-674.

Papers:

Sir William Jones's papers are held by the Asiatic Society, Calcutta; the British Library (Department of Western Manuscripts); University College, Oxford University; the Spencer Muniment Room, Althorp Park, Northampton (Jones's letters to the Spencers); and the Beinecke Library, Yale University (James Osborn Collection).

John Langhorne

(March 1735 - 1 April 1779)

Elizabeth Kraft
University of Georgia

BOOKS: *The Tears of Music: A Poem, to the Memory of Mr. Handel. With an Ode to the River Eden* (London: Printed for R. Griffiths, 1760);

Poems on Several Occasions (Lincoln: Printed by W. Wood for R. Griffiths, London, 1760);

A Hymn to Hope (London: Printed for R. Griffiths, 1761);

The Visions of Fancy: In Four Elegies (London: Printed for H. Payne and W. Cropley, 1762);

The Viceroy: A Poem. Addressed to the Earl of Halifax (London: Printed for H. Payne and W. Cropley, 1762);

Letters on Religious Retirement, Melancholy, and Enthusiasm (London: Printed for H. Payne and W. Cropley, 1762);

Solyman and Almena: An Oriental Tale (London: Printed for H. Payne and W. Cropley, 1762);

The Enlargement of the Mind: Epistle I (London: Printed for T. Becket and P. A. De Hondt, 1763);

The Effusions of Friendship and Fancy: In Several Letters to and from Select Friends, 2 volumes (London: Printed for T. Becket and P. A. De Hondt, 1763; enlarged, 1766);

Genius and Valour: A Scotch Pastoral (London: Printed for T. Becket and P. A. De Hondt, 1763);

The Letters That Passed between Theodosius and Constantia; after She Had Taken the Veil: Now First Published from the Original Manuscripts (London: Printed for T. Becket and P. A. De Hondt, 1763);

The Correspondence of Theodosius and Constantia, from Their First Acquaintance to the Departure of Theodosius: Now First Published from the Original Manuscripts (London: Printed for T. Becket and P. A. De Hondt, 1764);

Sermons by the Editor of the Letters between Theodosius and Constantia (London: Printed for T. Becket and P. A. De Hondt, 1764);

Letters on the Eloquence of the Pulpit: By the Editor of the Letters between Theodosius and Constantia (London: Printed for T. Becket and P. A. De Hondt, 1765);

The Enlargement of the Mind: Epistle II. To William Langhorne, M. A. (London: Printed for T. Becket and P. A. De Hondt, 1765);

The Poetical Works of John Langhorne, 2 volumes (London: Printed for T. Becket and P. A. De Hondt, 1766);

Precepts of Conjugal Happiness: Addressed to a Lady on Her Marriage (London: Printed for T. Becket and P. A. De Hondt, 1767);

Sermons Preached before the Honourable Society of Lincolns-Inn, 2 volumes (London: Printed for T. Becket and P. A. De Hondt, 1767);

Verses in Memory of a Lady written at Sangate Castle, anonymous (London: Printed for T. Becket and P. A. De Hondt, 1768);

Letters Supposed to Have Passed between M. de St. Evremond and Mr. Waller: Collected and Published by the Editor of the Letters between Theodosius and Constantia, 2 volumes (London: Printed for T. Becket and P. A. De Hondt, 1769);

Frederic and Pharamond; or, The Consolations of Human Life (London: Printed for T. Becket and P. A. De Hondt, 1769);

Letters to Eleonora, 2 volumes (London: Printed for T. Becket and P. A. De Hondt, 1770-1771);

The Fables of Flora (London: Printed for J. Murray, 1771);

The Origin of the Veil: A Poem (London: Printed for T. Becket, 1773);

The Country Justice: A Poem. By One of His Majesty's Justices of the Peace for the County of Somerset, 3 volumes (London: Printed for T. Becket, 1774-1777);

The Proper Happiness of the Ecclesiastic Life, in a Public and Private Sphere: A Sermon Preached before . . . the Lord Bishop of Bath and Wells, at His Primary Visitation at Axbridge, July 4, 1776 (Bristol: Printed by Bonner & Middleton, and sold by T. Cadell, in Wine Street; and T. Cadell, in the Strand, London, 1776);

John Langhorne

The Love of Mankind the Fundamental Principle of the Christian Religion: A Sermon Preached before the Gentlemen Natives of the County of Somerset, at Their Annual Meeting; in the Church of St. Mary Redcliff, Bristol, September 16, 1776 (London: Printed for T. Becket, 1777);

Owen of Carron: A Poem (London: Printed for Edward and Charles Dilly, 1778);

The Story of Abbas (Manchester: Printed by G. Nicholson and Co.; sold by T. Knott; and Champante & Whitrow, London, 1793);

The Superiority of Religious Views, by Dr. Langhorne. The Choice and Criterion of Religion; The Pleasures and Advantages of Religion; A Humble Station Superior to Grandeur and Riches, by the Rev. J. Moir. On Religion, Life, and Futurity, by Dr. Goldsmith (Manchester: Printed by G. Nicholson and Co., sold by T. Knott; and Champante & Whitrow, London, 1794);

The Poetical Works of J. Langhorne, D.D. With the Life of the Author (London: Printed for C. Cooke and sold by all the booksellers in Great Britain and Ireland, 1798);

The Poetical Works of John Langhorne, D.D., 2 volumes, edited by John Theodosius Langhorne (London: Printed for J. Mawman, 1804).

OTHER: *The Death of Adonis: A Pastoral Elegy From the Greek of Bion,* translated by Langhorne (London: Printed for R. Griffiths, 1759);

The Poetical Works of Mr. William Collins: With Memoirs of the Author; and Observations on His Genius and Writings, edited by Langhorne (London: Printed for T. Becket and P. A. De Hondt, 1765);

Plutarch's Lives, translated from the original Greek with Notes Critical and Historical, and a New Life of Plutarch, 6 volumes, translated by Langhorne and William Langhorne (London: Printed for Edward and Charles Dilly, 1770);

A Dissertation, Historical and Political, on the Ancient Republics of Italy: From the Italian of Carlo Denina, translated by Langhorne (London: Printed for T. Becket & Co., 1773);

Milton's Italian Poems Translated, and Addressed to a Gentleman of Italy, translated by Langhorne (London: Printed for T. Becket, 1776);

In an 1837 letter to Samuel Carter Hall, William Wordsworth praised John Langhorne's *The Country Justice* (1774-1777) as one of the first poems "to bring the Muse into the Company of Common Life." Langhorne's poetry, with its sincere piety, its gentle sentimentalism, and its freshness of expression was popular in its own day largely because the poet seems to have developed early a sure sense of his audience—a talent that certainly lies behind his fame as a lively pulpit orator. Langhorne succeeded in various poetic modes, including the elegy, the philosophical poem, the verse epistle, the topographical poem, and the dramatic poem. He had much prose published as well: an oriental tale, several volumes of sermons, and three popular works of epistolary fiction. He also produced translations from the Italian and, with his brother William, a still highly regarded translation of *Plutarch's Lives* (1770). His popularity in his own time suggests that his readers recognized and responded to his versatile talent even as he recognized and responded to what Donald Davie calls "the strain of historical change."

Langhorne was born in March 1735 in Kirkby Stephen, a parish in the county of Westmoreland. His father, Joseph Langhorne, was a clergyman who died when Langhorne was four. Isabel Langhorne was left to supervise the early education of her son, as Langhorne himself documents in the "Monody" he wrote on her death in 1759 (published in *Poems on Several Occasions* [1760]):

> For her these filial sorrows flow,
> Source of my life, that led my tender years,
> With all a parent's pious fears,
> That nurs'd my infant thought, and taught my mind to grow.

His education was begun at the village school in Winton and continued at Appleby, where by the age of thirteen he had distinguished himself as a Greek scholar.

At eighteen Langhorne left school for a position as a tutor in a family near Ripon. There he began to write poetry, apparently—if the earliest surviving piece from this period can be taken as representative—with the view of attracting the attention of some wealthy patron of the arts. "Studley Park" is a topographical poem in the manner of Sir John Denham's *Cooper's Hill* (1642) and Alexander Pope's *Windsor-Forest* (1713) and is addressed to the Reverend John Farrer. It celebrates in iambic-pentameter closed couplets the beauty of the Edenic estate as well as the "elegance" and "ease" of its owner. Although the poem did not elicit the desired response, its attention to chiastic balance, decorous language, and devices such as onomatopoeia and personification reveals Langhorne's poetic apprenticeship to classical and contemporary masters. During this period he occasionally contributed poetry to the *Grand Magazine* and the *Universal Magazine*. In September 1756 a poem entitled "To the Memory of Mr. John Farrer of York" appeared in the *Universal Magazine* over the initials J. L.

After leaving Ripon around 1758, Langhorne became an assistant in the school at Wakefield and continued tutoring as well; one of his private pupils was Edmund Cartwright, who became a poet himself and invented the power loom. It was in Wakefield that Langhorne began his clerical career, taking deacon's orders and achieving local renown for his energetic preaching style. By 1759 he had moved to Hackthorn to become tutor to the nine sons of Robert Cracroft. While there, he began to have his poetry published in earnest: a translation of Bion's *Death of Adonis* (1759), although lukewarmly received, began to establish Langhorne's reputation as a Greek scholar.

In 1760 Langhorne matriculated at Clarehall, Cambridge, with the apparent intention of taking a bachelor of divinity degree; there is no record that he completed his course of study. He continued to write poetry during his brief residence as a student. A poem on the royal marriage—which he later incorporated into his oriental tale *Solyman and Almena* (1762)—was written in 1760; and *The Tears of Music: A Poem, to the Memory of Mr. Handel. With an Ode to the River Eden* and *Poems on Several Occasions* were published during that year.

At Hackthorn, Langhorne had developed an interest which was to give direction to his poetry for some time. In addition to his large family of sons Cracroft had daughters as well, one of whom Langhorne instructed in the study of Italian. Langhorne proposed to Ann Cracroft in 1761; upon her refusal on the grounds of disproportionate fortunes, he left Cambridge for a curateship in Dagenham, Essex, expressing in his *A Hymn to Hope* (1761) his inability to resign himself to her decision:

Sun of the soul! whose cheerful ray
  Darts o'er this gloom of life a smile;
Sweet Hope, yet further gild my way,
  Yet light my weary steps awhile,
Till thy fair lamp dissolve in endless day.

A Hymn to Hope elicited the praise of George, Lord Lyttelton, and in 1762 Langhorne continued to explore the theme in *The Visions of Fancy*, four elegies that express, in contrast to the earlier poem, not the desire for continued delusion but the inevitability of disappointment: "Fancy dreams, . . . but Fancy's dreams are vain." Langhorne gives an example:

Wasted and weary on the mountain's side,
  His way unknown, the hapless pilgrim lies,
Or takes some ruthless robber for his guide,
  And prone beneath his cruel sabre lies.

Although Langhorne invokes "Insensibility" as an answer to "the fond anxieties of fame," the next quatrain betrays his own continued hope for exactly that as he praises Lyttelton's "generous praise," "sweet magic," and charm.

In general, Langhorne's efforts in 1762 were directed to the powerful. *The Viceroy*, an occasional poem, celebrates the virtues of Lord Halifax (George Montagu Dunk) as lord lieutenant to Ireland; Langhorne's "humble Muse" commemorates Halifax's refusal of personal enrichment at the expense of a country already under economic duress. As generous as Halifax was to Ireland, however, his largess did not extend to the poet who praised him on that account. As far as Halifax seems to have been concerned, Langhorne's muse could continue "a stranger to the world."

A prose work published the same year, *Letters on Religious Retirement, Melancholy, and Enthusiasm*, which Langhorne dedicated to Bishop William Warburton, fared rather better. Warburton encouraged Langhorne to undertake another work on a religious subject, a suggestion which produced in 1763 *The Letters That Passed between Theodosius and Constantia; after She Had Taken the Veil*. The popularity of the book—it went into its fourth edition in 1766—prompted a sequel, *The Correspondence of Theodosius and Constantia, from Their First Acquaintance to the Departure of Theodosius* (1764).

For the most part Langhorne's early literary success was in the realm of prose, but during the years 1763 to 1767 he continued to write poetry. The first "epistle" of the philosophical poem *The Enlargement of the Mind* was published in 1763 and the second "epistle" in 1765. In the latter year he also produced an edition of the poems of William Collins, with critical comments and a memoir. In 1766 appeared the collection *The Poetical Works of John Langhorne*, which included his "dramatic poem" *The Fatal Prophecy*. These years were most notably distinguished, however, by his success as a preacher and his growing involvement in London literary life. After serving as curate in Dagenham for three years Langhorne secured a position as curate and lecturer at St. John's, Clerkenwell; and in 1764, through Warburton's influence, he became assistant preacher at Lincolns-Inn under Richard Hurd.

Langhorne's clerical advancement was punctuated by the publication of *Sermons* in 1764, *Letters on the Eloquence of the Pulpit* in 1765, and *Sermons Preached before the Honourable Society of Lincolns-Inn* in 1767. Meanwhile, he had been writing for the *Monthly Review* since 1764, and he continued to do so at least until 1769. Through his work with the *Review* he began to attain the kind of prominence which procures both advantage and risk. He formed one enmity of significance during this time—with Charles Churchill, whose aspersions on the Scots in *The Prophecy of Famine* (1763) Langhorne answered in his *Genius and Valour: A Scotch Pastoral* (1763), "written in honour of a sister kingdom." The poem includes, among other portraits of great Scotsmen, a tribute to "The child of Nature, gentle [James] Thomson," who is described in an apostrophe to the River Tweed:

Young as he wander'd on thy flowery side,
With simple joy to see thy bright waves glide,
Thither, in all thy native charms array'd,
From climes remote the sister Seasons stray'd.

Although Langhorne earned the rancor of Churchill, he garnered the appreciation of Dr. William Robertson, the principal of Edinburgh University, who reportedly offered him an honorary doctor of divinity degree from that institution in 1766. (Another account has the title conferred two years later through the influence of the Archbishop of Canterbury.)

In 1767 Langhorne's long courtship of Ann Cracroft was happily concluded. Shortly after the marriage Langhorne assumed the rectorship of Blagdon, Somersetshire. His *Precepts of Conjugal Happiness* (1767), addressed to his sister-in-law on her marriage, recommended the temperate thoughts and behavior that ensure the "bliss beyond what lonely life can know, / The soul-felt sympathy of joy and woe." After his wife's death during the birth of their son in May 1768 he published, in accordance with a desire she had expressed, the letters he wrote her during their courtship: *Letters to Eleonora* appeared in two volumes in 1770-1771. In 1769 he paid further tribute in "A Monody," addressed to John Scott, who had experienced a similar loss. Langhorne addresses Scott as "Friend of my genius! partner of my fate! / To equal sense of painful suffering born!" His depiction of his own grief is poignant:

> She comes, by truth, by fair affection led,
> The long lov'd mistress of my faithful heart!
> The mistress of my soul, no more to part,
> And all my hopes and all my vows are sped.
> Vain, vain delusions! dreams for ever fled!
> Ere twice the spring had wak'd the genial hour,
> The lovely parent bore one beauteous flower,
> And droop'd her gentle head,
> And sunk, for ever sunk, into her silent bed.

In 1768 Langhorne moved to Folkestone, Kent, where his elder brother, William, held a curacy. The Langhornes' translation of *Plutarch's Lives* went through nine editions by 1805; it stood as the definitive translation until 1859, when Arthur Hugh Clough's revision of the hasty but lively "Dryden" translation (1683-1686) supplanted the turgid but correct work of the Langhornes.

During his three years at Folkestone Langhorne wrote *Letters Supposed to Have Passed between M. de St. Evremond and Mr. Waller* (1769) and *Frederic and Pharamond; or, The Consolations of Human Life* (1769). In 1771 appeared the only volume of poetry which equaled his success in prose: *The Fables of Flora*. The book employs pastoral imagery to illustrate "moral lessons." The evening primrose, for example, is an emblem of the solitary secluded life, and her fable is reminiscent of Thomas Gray's "Elegy Written in a Country Churchyard" (1751) in its celebration of the private and the unremarked:

> . . . far from Envy's lurid eye
> The fairest fruits of genius rear,
> Content to see them bloom and die,
> In Friendship's small but kindly sphere.

The violet's modest virtue is to be preferred to the alluring but destructive beauty of the pansy:

> This modest flower of humbler hue,
> That boasts no depth of glowing dyes,
> Array'd in unbespangled blue,
> The simple clothing of the skies—
> This flower, with balmy sweetness blest,
> May yet thy languid life renew.

Despite some critical animadversions, *The Fables of Flora* went into its fifth edition in 1773 and continued to be popular until the end of the century. In 1787 it was published in Philadelphia as an appendage to Edward Moore's *Fables for the Ladies*. Recognizing that the success of *The Fables of Flora* was due to his female readership, Langhorne paid tribute to the "feminine virtue" of modesty and the feminine "power" of "weakness" in *The Origin of the Veil*, written in 1771 and published in 1773. In this poem he attributes the success of *The Fables of Flora* to Charlotte Sophia, George III's queen:

> Kind to the lay that all unlabour'd flow'd
> What Fancy caught, where Nature's pencil glow'd
> She saw the path to new, tho' humble fame,
> Gave me her praise, and left the fools to blame.

Langhorne married a Miss Thompson in 1772. After a trip to France and Flanders he returned with his new wife to Blagdon, where he took the office of magistrate. He drew on this experience for his often-anthologized poem *The Country Justice*, published in three parts in 1774, 1775, and 1777. The satirical poem is in iambic pentameter couplets and is organized under such headings as "Apology for Vagrants," "Protection of the Poor," and "Prisons," the aspects of a magistrate's duty. "[F]or a score of lines at a time," Davie observes, Langhorne can "challenge and sustain comparison with his great predecessors in this genre, [Alexander] Pope and [Samuel] Johnson." On the subject of absentee landlords, for example, Langhorne's allusion to Gray's "Elegy" highlights his biting sarcasm:

> Forgone the social, hospitable Days,
> When wide Vales echoed with their Owner's Praise,
> Of all that *ancient Consequence* bereft,
> What has the *modern Man of Fashion left*?
> Does He, perchance, to rural Scenes repair
> And 'waste his Sweetness' on the essenc'd Air?

Ah! gently lave the feeble Frame He brings,
Ye scouring Seas! and ye sulphurous Springs!

These and other lines indicate a sympathetic attitude toward the indigent that suggests that Langhorne himself was the kind of judge he describes in "Character of a Country Justice," one who "in the rigid paths of law / Would still some drops from Pity's fountain draw."

In 1776 Langhorne's second wife died giving birth to a daughter. That year his translations of John Milton's Italian poems were published, and the next year he received his final clerical appointment as prebendary in the Cathedral of Wells. His final poem, the ballad *Owen of Carron*, is the story of an ill-fated love set in Scotland. It was published in 1778 and dedicated to a lady of "amiable sensibility" and "unaffected friendship."

Langhorne died in 1779 at the age of forty-four. He is generally understood to have been rather intemperate toward the end of his life, and his death is usually blamed on excessive sociability. His popularity, which has not been enduring, supports the notion that the late eighteenth century had a taste for the didactic, the sentimental, and the religious and gave public prominence to those who explored the lives of those who were retired, obscure, and unknown. His poetry and prose resound with echoes of Gray, Johnson, Joseph Addison, Laurence Sterne, and, in *Owen of Carron*, James Macpherson; yet he does not so much write in imitation as he partakes of a similar worldview: one which everywhere reveals the challenge of a difficult life, the inevitability of vain hope, and the emptiness of coveted fame. Langhorne's own words in the second elegy of *The Visions of Fancy* provide a poignant and fitting summary:

And were they vain, those soothing lays ye sung?
Children of Fancy! yes, your song was vain;
On each soft air though rapt Attention hung,
And Silence listen'd on the sleeping plain.

The strains yet vibrate on my ravish'd ear,
And still to smile the mimic beauties seem,
Though now the visionary scenes appear
Like the faint traces of a vanish'd dream.

Biographies:

John Theodosius Langhorne, "Memoirs of the Author," in *The Poetical Works of John Langhorne, D.D.* (London: Printed for J. Mawman, 1804), pp. 5-25;

"The Life of the Author," in Langhorne's *The Correspondence of Theodosius and Constantia: Before and after Her Taking the Veil* (London: Jones, 1807);

Alexander Chalmers, "The Life of Langhorne," in volume 16 of *The Works of the English Poets from Chaucer to Cowper*, edited by Chalmers (London: Printed for Johnson and others, 1810), pp. 407-413.

References:

Donald Davie, Introduction to *The Late Augustans*, edited by Davie (London: Heinemann, 1958), pp. xxviii-xxxi;

William Wordsworth, Letter to Samuel Carter Hall, 15 January 1837, in *The Letters of William and Dorothy Wordsworth: The Later Years*, volume 2, edited by Ernest De Selincourt (Oxford: Clarendon Press, 1939), pp. 828-830.

Mary Leapor

(26 February 1722 - 14 November 1746)

Donna Landry
University of Southern California

BOOK: *Poems upon Several Occasions*, 2 volumes (volume 1, London: Printed by John Watts and sold by J. Roberts, 1748; volume 2, edited by Isaac Hawkins Browne, London: Printed by Samuel Richardson and sold by J. Roberts, 1751).

Mary Leapor is distinguished by her capacity for being discovered again and again. The daughter of a Northamptonshire gardener, Leapor first went into service as a scullery maid and then kept house for her father after her mother's death; she had little formal education and was repeatedly described by eighteenth-century readers, who knew only of her obscurity, as representative of that prized poetic character of the period, the plebeian prodigy. Her works were collected and published posthumously by subscription in 1748 and 1751. There were notices or selected republications of her poems by Christopher Smart in the *Midwife* (1750), by the *Monthly Review* (1749 and 1751), by George Colman and Bonnell Thornton in *Poems by Eminent Ladies* (1755), by the *Lady's Poetical Magazine* (1782), by the *Gentleman's Magazine* (1784), by Alexander Dyce in *Specimens of British Poetesses* (1827), by *Blackwood's Magazine* (1837), by Frederic Rowton in *The Female Poets of Great Britain* (1848), and by Roger Lonsdale in *The New Oxford Book of Eighteenth Century Verse* (1984). In 1784 the *Gentleman's Magazine* quoted a line from "Colinetta" as particularly evocative, and in 1791 William Cowper cited Leapor's poems as exceptional examples of "strong natural genius." Dead at twenty-four, Leapor was remembered well into the nineteenth century as a touchstone of "natural" or "unlettered" poetic ability. She is more likely to be read by late-twentieth-century readers as a wonderfully arch and ironic poet who skillfully parodies traditional forms, often in the service of social and protofeminist protest.

Mary Leapor was born on 26 February 1722 at Marston St. Lawrence in Northamptonshire while her father, Philip Leapor, was gardener to Sir John Blencowe, former member of Parliament for Brackley, baron of the Exchequer, justice of Common Pleas, and justice of the King's Bench. Five years later, after Blencowe's death, Philip Leapor moved to nearby Brackley with his wife and daughter and established a nursery. It is not known whether Leapor attended the village school or was taught to read and write by her father and mother, who appear to have been literate. Her verses were at least initially encouraged by her mother, who was pleased with her ten- or eleven-year-old daughter's rhymes but tried to urge her toward some more profitable employment as she grew older. Leapor went into service as a maid not far from Brackley at Weston Hall, the house of Blencowe's daughter, Susannah Jennens; a copy of the first volume of Leapor's poems, still in the library at Weston, is inscribed "Once Kitchen maid at Weston." Her poetry bears traces of an embarrassing dismissal from service, followed by a return to Brackley to keep house for her widowed father. Leapor's mother died about five years before the poet's burial on 14 November 1746. Only her father lived to see the publication of her work and gain something from the subscriptions.

As the daughter of a nurseryman, Leapor employs precise and evocative horticultural language to describe rural plenitude. One of her most often anthologized poems, "The Month of August," makes good use of her father's fruit trees:

> In vain you tempt me while our Orchard bears
> Long-keeping Russets, lovely Cath'rine Pears,
> Pearmains and Codlings, wheaten Plumbs enough,
> And the black Damsons load the bending Bough.

Leapor's two volumes of verse represent a substantial oeuvre for one who died in her mid twenties. The books also include a play, *The Unhappy Father*; some letters; and a biographical sketch by her chief patron, Bridget Freemantle, which describes Leapor's obscurity; her small library of "sixteen or seventeen" volumes, including "Part of Mr. *Pope*'s Works, *Dryden*'s Fables, some Volumes of Plays, &c."; and the hardships, including parental disapproval of poetry as a frivolous occupation, from which she forged her poems. Like some other biographical prefaces of the period, Freemantle's stresses the extraordinary naturalness of the talent she has discovered and rescued for posterity, downplaying the wide reading that can be glimpsed in the sheer literariness of Leapor's poems. Leapor characterizes herself in her work most often as "Mira," a humble, rustic versifier "mired" in the mud and privation of a laboring life; but her command of genres such as the country-house poem suggests that one should not put too much stock in Freemantle's conception of a natural prodigy. Leapor's "Mira" is both an artful construction and an ironic undercutting of fashionable eighteenth-century notions about "unlettered" poets.

Readers of Leapor have tended to agree that she succeeds most brilliantly in aesthetic terms by subverting and transforming such popular eighteenth-century genres as the pastoral dialogue and the country-house poem, as in "The Month of August" and "Crumble-Hall," respectively. In "The Month of August," a dialogue between a courtier and a country maid, Phillis rejects Sylvanus's offer of rank and genteel comforts in favor of the rustic tastes her father's farm and the swain Corydon can satisfy. Few pastoral females answer back their elevated suitors as confidently and richly as Phillis: Leapor constructs for both farmers and plants a relatively democratic freedom to be found in agricultural gardening (gardening for use); Phillis's replies give working farm life a definite edge over the constraints of aristocratic ornamentation (gardening for show), with its implications of feudal mastery and subjugation:

No Pruning-knives our fertile Branches teeze,
While yours must grow but as their Masters please.
The grateful Trees our Mercy well repay,
And rain us Bushels at the rising Day.

Edenic plenitude outdoes mere wealth and rank. Sylvanus is silenced by Phillis's refusal of his desire to provide handsomely for her, so Phillis has the last word:

Let *Phillis* ne'er, ah never let her rove
From her first Virtue and her humble Grove.
Go seek some Nymph that equals your Degree,
And leave Content and *Corydon* for me.

This may seem a quintessentially "pastoral" move in the sense that country life represents a "simple" contentment not to be found at court; but unlike many pastoral poems, "The Month of August" maintains the superiority of a life of humble tenantry on its own terms instead of absorbing it into upper-class gentility through the discovery of high birth or the making of an elevating marriage.

Similarly, if on a more ambitious scale, "Crumble-Hall" subverts certain conventions of the traditional country-house poem. "Crumble-Hall" is a class-conscious plebeian country-house poem that mocks and seeks to demystify the values of the gentry, whose social power in large part depends upon the deference—the exploitable subservience—of servants and laborers. Leapor opens up long-closed doors and back stairways, lets light into the servants' hall, and shakes things up in a literary genre that traditionally works by assuring the reader that the world is best organized according to ancient custom and ceremony. Alexander Pope had mocked the owners of particular country houses for failing to fulfill their pact with England's glorious agrarian past, but even Pope had nevertheless sought to preserve the country-house ideal. Leapor leaves the modern reader wondering how a literary audience could have tolerated such evidently self-serving exaggeration for so long.

Traditionally, the country-house poem serves as a panegyric to the house's owners and their way of life. The flippant tone of "Crumble-Hall" thus represents a significant departure within the genre (with the exception of Andrew Marvell's *Upon Appleton House* and particular passages in Pope's *Epistle to Burlington* [1731]) that is not repeated at least until Thomas Gray's "On Lord Holland's Seat near Margate" of 1768. "Crumble-Hall" sets out at once to mock the pretensions to grandeur of a gentry class scarcely removed from its servants and laborers in terms of education and culture, and to mock the poetic sycophancy that would write a traditional panegyric in spite of these incongruities. Throughout the poem there is an ironical movement between the old tropes of country-house praise and less exalted disclosures: the venison is tainted, the vulnerable hare has been hunted to death to provide meat for an already groaning table, the guests gorge themselves until they are grossly bloated and nearly sick. Of such an establishment, the poet writes, it *might* be possible to sing for at least three or four months—a bathetic deflation.

Leapor's imitation of Pope's style in the service of quite different values, apparent elsewhere in her oeuvre, is particularly concentrated and effective in "Crumble-Hall"; she seizes upon the *Epistle to Burlington*, Pope's most sustained effort in the country-house mode, but goes beyond his criticisms of landowners' wastefulness and conspicuous consumption. For Pope confines himself to criticizing only the wealthiest and highest-ranking landlords. The middling sort of gentry and the select few "good stewards" among the aristocracy, such as Pope's friends Burlington and Bathurst, are redeemed, and the country-house ideal upheld. Leapor, while echoing Pope and frequently reminding the reader of his satirical outbursts in the *Epistle to Burlington* against such figures of excess as Timon, forces one to reread Pope's poem through the lens of her own, and so to reread it in a more democratic and gender-conscious way. With Pope one must toil up Timon's monumental garden terraces to greet the host:

My Lord advances with majestic mien,
Smit with the mighty pleasure, to be seen:
But soft—by regular approach—not yet—
First thro' the length of yon hot Terrace sweat,
And when up ten steep slopes you've dragged your thighs,
Just at his Study-door he'll bless your Eyes. . . .

With Leapor, on the other hand, a sense of cramped quarters and inconvenient architecture predominates; the gentry and squirearchy may dominate their parish and neighborhood, even appear to rule them without question, but their homes are far removed from the opulence of Timon's Villa:

Shall we proceed?—Yes, if you'll break the Wall:
If not, return, and tread once more the Hall.
Up ten Stone Steps now please to drag your Toes,
And a brick Passage will succeed to those.
Here the strong Doors were aptly fram'd to hold
Sir *Wary*'s Person, and Sir *Wary*'s Gold.

In the light of Leapor's poem, Pope's condemnation of aristocratic consumption and self-display on a Timonesque scale seems a limited protest.

Mira's proper sphere is the network of kitchens, pantries, sculleries, outbuildings, cottages, and kitchen gardens that supply Crumble-Hall with produce and labor. "Crumble-Hall" has forty-two lines of description of the lower orders that populate this "nether World," including the devastatingly satiric couple, Ursula and Roger; no one can accuse Leapor of sentimentality about her own class or about women's complicity in their own oppression. Ursula, the prosperous cottager's wife—so apparently fortunate beside other portrayals of cottager families in the period living on the verge of poverty and hunger—represents, however comically, the bankruptcy of romantic gender ideology and the wretchedness of the dependent "helpmate." While her exhausted husband, "o'erstuff'd" with beef, cabbage, and dumplings, sleeps at the table, and the dogs bark and howl, Ursula laments her fate until the kettle boils:

"Ah! *Roger*, Ah!" the mournful Maiden cries:
"Is wretched *Urs'la* then your Care no more,
"That, while I sigh, thus you can sleep and snore?
"Ingrateful *Roger*! wilt thou leave me now?
"For you these Furrows mark my fading Brow:
"For you my Pigs resign their Morning Due:
"My hungry Chickens lose their Meat for you:
"And, was it not, Ah! was it not for thee,
"No goodly Pottage would be dress'd by me.
"For thee these Hands wind up the whirling Jack,
"Or place the Spit across the sloping Rack."

There is a diffusion throughout the text of the perspective of the female servant, responsible for cleanliness and good order in the household. Even if Timon's Villa possessed spiders, mice, and decorative artifacts that require constant tending, a male guest like Pope would not likely to remark upon them. And more elevated members of the household at Crumble-Hall would dwell not on these "menial" questions of domestic maintenance but on objects of absorbing interest to gentry families, such as the genealogical significance of heraldic insignia and the provenance of china, wall hangings, and oil paintings—features of the house which Mira neglects entirely.

The poem concludes with a long-deferred escape into those pastoral groves surrounding Crumble-Hall—a briefly glimpsed alternative, even utopian, domain of leisure and freedom. But even here the landscape exists primarily as a site of conflict; the green world of the grove is no sooner escaped into than it is rent by shrieks. Like so many landlords bent on the "improvement" of an estate, Crumble-Hall's owners are felling their timber, in this case for the minor ostentation of a new parlor. Leapor reverses the praise that Pope had offered Burlington for his use of the forest in the service of building, commerce, and imperial exploits. For Pope, those who follow Burlington's example as improving stewards of their land are those

Whose rising Forests, not for pride or show,
But future Buildings, future Navies grow:

Let his plantations stretch from down to down,
First shade a Country, and then raise a Town.

But for Leapor the grove should not be sacrificed for mere aggrandizement of the country house:

And shall those Shades, where *Philomela*'s Strain
Has oft to Slumber lull'd the hapless Swain;
Where Turtles us'd to clasp their silken Wings;
Whose rev'rend Oaks have known a hundred Springs;
Shall these ignobly from their Roots be torn,
And perish shameful, as the abject Thorn;
While the slow Carr bears off their aged Limbs,
To clear the way for Slopes, and modern Whims;
Where banish'd Nature leaves a barren Gloom,
And aukward Art supplies the vacant Room?

"Improvement" and "progress" are thus subjected to ironical scrutiny, and an ecological consciousness and a more natural economy than the present "improving" one are recommended. "Crumble-Hall" is a country-house poem that advocates the containment, not the expansion, of the country house; its removal from the scene may be as yet unthinkable, but its demystification is complete.

If Leapor's readers have tended to agree about her skill as a parodist and innovative transformer of traditional forms, there has been less general recognition of her poetry as important for its mounting of protofeminist protest. More sharply and thoroughly than any other plebeian poet of the period, Leapor mounts a critique of the manifold injustices perpetuated by men against women. Filial and familial affections seem strained to their utmost in such poems as "The Cruel Parent" and in her play, *The Unhappy Father*. In Leapor's work, not only does marriage begin to seem an impossible institution from a woman's point of view but women's historical situation is regretted so roundly that the bounds of good-humored "mere" satire seem stretched, to say the least.

Leapor's most often anthologized poems, such as "The Month of August," come from her first volume; the most explicitly protofeminist poems appear in her second, from which few poems have been reprinted. And those few do not include the second "Mira to Octavia," more obviously hostile toward marriage than the first volume's poem of that title; the proudly separatist "Complaining Daphne: A Pastoral"; or such acerbic ripostes to the whole tradition of misogynist verse as "An Essay on Woman" and "Man the Monarch." In "An Essay on Woman" Leapor borrows Popean cadences, parallelism, and antithesis in the interests of a very un-Popean demystification of what it means to be Pope's idealized "softer man":

WOMAN—a pleasing but a short-liv'd Flow'r,
Too soft for Business, and too weak for Pow'r:
A Wife in Bondage, or neglected Maid;
Despis'd, if ugly; if she's fair—betray'd.
'Tis Wealth alone inspires ev'ry Grace,
And calls the Raptures to her plenteous Face.
What Numbers for those charming Features pine,
If blooming Acres round her Temples twine?
. . . .
Tho' Nature arm'd us for the growing Ill,
With fraudful Cunning, and a headstrong Will;
Yet, with ten thousand Follies to her Charge,
Unhappy Woman's but a Slave at large.

Abruptly, Belinda's dressing table from the first canto of *The Rape of the Lock* (1714) is stripped of its glamor and mystery, and the crude material base of Belinda's power of attraction is exposed: the "Magic" wrought by the sylphs is merely the desirability of wealth, politely disguised. An heiress's plenty will be read in her face; indeed, lovers may not be able to see her features for the superimposed topographical map of her estates. The feminized landscape of so much English verse literally *becomes* the beauty in question.

Leapor is worthy of critical attention not only for the considerations of class and gender in her texts but also for purely aesthetic reasons. The beauty of Leapor's verse lies often in its rich linguistic textures, its lively rhythms, and its specificity of natural detail. Though she sometimes sounds like Pope and other eighteenth-century poets in her descriptions, she often slips in words from quite different idioms than they use and notices things that they do not. "On Winter," for example, contains both a vivid evocation of the physical sensations of outdoor labor in cold weather and some arch reflection on the relation between neoclassical concepts of poetic inspiration and the realities of the English climate to which those concepts remain alien even after generations of "domestication":

Poor daggled *Urs'la* stalks from Cow to Cow,
Who to her Sighs return a mournful Low;
While their full Udders her broad Hands assail,
And her sharp Nose hangs dropping o'er the Pail.

With Garments trickling like a shallow Spring,
And his wet Locks all twisted in a String,
Afflicted *Cymon* waddles through the Mire,
And rails at *Win'fred* creeping o'er the Fire.
  Say gentle Muses, say, is this a Time
To sport with Poesy and laugh in Rhyme;
While the chill'd Blood, that hath forgot to glide,
Steals through its Channels in a lazy Tide:
And how can *Phoebus*, who the Muse refines,
Smooth the dull Numbers when he seldom shines.

Ironically, it is the same "unrefined" Muse of the rural plebeian poet who provides such a fresh portrait of "daggled" Ursula among her cows. Thus Mira makes skillful aesthetic use of her vantage point, which is rather closer to the mire of georgic and pastoral materials than most eighteenth-century poets were accustomed to getting.

That Mary Leapor, a gardener's daughter and a domestic servant, should have had her work published at all, even posthumously, may seem little short of miraculous, though—given her clearly literary inspiration—one should be skeptical regarding contemporary categorizations of her as an uneducated prodigy. That her work was published, read, remembered, forgotten, and repeatedly rediscovered reveals something about the appeal of the unlikely, the curious, and the marginal in the late eighteenth and early nineteenth centuries, a period of expanding literary markets. Current interest in her work is being fueled by feminist and other forms of revisionist literary history.

References:

Margaret Anne Doody, "Swift among the Women," *Yearbook of English Studies*, 18 (1988): 79-83;

Richard Greene, "Mary Leapor: A Problem of Literary History," Ph.D. thesis, Oxford University, 1989;

Bridget Hill, *Women, Work, and Sexual Politics in Eighteenth-Century England* (Oxford: Blackwell, 1989), pp. 109-110, 186;

Roger Lonsdale, ed., *The New Oxford Book of Eighteenth Century Verse* (Oxford & New York: Oxford University Press, 1984), pp. 408-412;

Betty Rizzo, "Christopher Smart, the 'C. S.' Poems, and Molly Leapor's Epitaph," *Library*, sixth series 5 (March 1983): 22-31;

Morag Shiach, *Discourse on Popular Culture: Class, Gender and History in the Analysis of Popular Culture* (Oxford: Polity Press, 1989), pp. 54-56.

James Macpherson

(27 October 1736 - 17 February 1796)

Elizabeth Kraft
University of Georgia

BOOKS: *The Highlander: A Poem In Six Cantos* (Edinburgh: Printed by Wal. Ruddiman Jun. and Company, 1758);

Fragments of Ancient Poetry, Collected in the Highlands of Scotland, and Translated from the Galic or Erse Language (Edinburgh: Printed for G. Hamilton and J. Balfour, 1760);

Fingal, an Ancient Epic Poem in Six Books: Together with Several Other Poems, Composed by Ossian, the Son of Fingal. Translated from the Galic Language, by James Macpherson (London: Printed for T. Becket and P. A. De Hondt, 1762 [i.e., 1761]);

Temora, an Ancient Epic Poem, in Eight Books: Together with Several Other Poems, Composed by Ossian, the Son of Fingal. Translated from the Galic Language, by J. Macpherson (London: Printed for T. Becket and P. A. De Hondt, 1763);

The Works of Ossian, the Son of Fingal: In Two Volumes. Translated from the Galic Language by James Macpherson. The Third Edition, 2 volumes (London: Printed for T. Becket and P. A. De Hondt, 1765); republished, with new preface, as *The Poems of Ossian: Translated by James Macpherson*, 2 volumes (London: Printed for W. Strahan and T. Becket, 1773); republished as *The Poems of Ossian, the Son of Fingal: Translated by James Macpherson, Esq.* (Philadelphia: Printed by Thomas Lang, 1790);

An Introduction to the History of Great Britain and Ireland (London: Printed for T. Becket and P. A. De Hondt, 1771); revised and enlarged as *An Introduction to the History of Great Britain and Ireland; or, An Inquiry into the Origin, Religion, Future State, Character, Manners, Morality, Amusements, Persons, Manner of Life, Houses, Navigation, Commerce, Language, Government, Kings, General Assemblies, Courts of Justice, and Juries, of the Britons, Scots, Irish and Anglo-Saxons* (London: Printed for T. Becket and P. A. De Hondt, 1772; revised and enlarged, 1773);

The History of Great Britain from the Restoration to the Accession of the House of Hannover, 2 volumes (London: Printed for W. Strahan and T. Cadell, 1775);

Original Papers: Containing the Secret History of Great Britain, from the Restoration, to the Accession of the House of Hannover. To Which Are Prefixed, Extracts from the Life of James II, as Written by Himself, 2 volumes (London: Printed for W. Strahan and T. Cadell, 1775);

The Rights of Great Britain Asserted against the Claims of America: Being an Answer to the Declaration of the General Congress (London: Printed for T. Cadell, 1776 [i.e., 1775]; Philadelphia: Reprinted and sold by R. Bell, 1776; enlarged edition, London: Printed for T. Cadell, 1776; enlarged, 1776; enlarged, 1776); enlarged as *The Rights of Great Britain Asserted against the Claims of America: Being an Answer to the Declaration of the General Congress. The Sixth Edition. To Which Is Now Added, a Refutation of Dr. Price's State of the National Debt* (London: Printed for T. Cadell, 1776); revised as *The Rights of Great Britain Asserted against the Claims of America: Being an Answer to the Declaration of the General Congress. The Ninth Edition. To Which Is Now Added, a Further Refutation of Dr. Price's State of the National Debt* (London: Printed for T. Cadell, 1776);

Original Papers relative to Tanjore: Containing All the Letters Which Passed, and the Conferences Which Were Held, between . . . the Nabob of Arcot and Lord Pigot, on the Subject of the Restoration of Tanjore together with the Material Part of Lord Pigot's Last Dispatch to the East India Company, possibly written by Macpherson and John Macpherson (London: Printed for T. Cadell, 1777);

A Short History of the Opposition during the Last Session of Parliament (London: Printed for T. Cadell, 1779);

The History and Management of the East-India Company, from its Origin in 1600 to the Present

James Macpherson (engraving after a portrait by Sir Joshua Reynolds)

Times, possibly written with John Macpherson (London: Printed for T. Cadell, 1779).

OTHER: *The Iliad of Homer*, 2 volumes, translated by Macpherson (London: Printed for T. Becket and P. A. De Hondt, 1773).

SELECTED PERIODICAL PUBLICATIONS—UNCOLLECTED: "Verses on the Death of Marshal Keith," *Scots Magazine* (October 1758): 550-551;

"On the Death of a Young Lady, *Scots Magazine* (May 1759): 255;

"To the Memory of an Officer Killed before Quebec," *Scots Magazine* (October 1759): 527;

"An Ode, Attempted in the Manner of Pindar," *Scots Magazine* (September 1760): 459-460.

James Macpherson is best remembered for the controversy surrounding his "translations" of the poet Ossian—a controversy yet to be resolved to universal satisfaction. One of several infamous "forgers" of the late eighteenth century, he has seemed to modern scholars to represent—along with, most notably, Thomas Chatterton—the need to escape the restrictions that defined the poetry of the immediate past in a search for the alternate forms and materials available in less polished, more "primitive" verse. Central to Macpherson's work, however, is a sentiment he shared with Alexander Pope: a veneration of the epic form and a recognition of the cultural longing for a national heroic tradition. Macpherson claimed to have discovered the ancient British epics *Fingal* (1761) and *Temora* (1763) entire and in Gaelic. At the heart of the controversy that erupted almost immediately was the issue of nationalism: the English were reluctant to credit the "discovery" as significant in any way; the Scots were too eager to see it as significant in every way. While Macpherson's place in the history of British poetry, then, is indisputable, it is a place in essence conferred by dispute. It might be true, as one scholar had claimed, that the Ossianic controversy spurred by Macpherson's poems has obscured his true contribution to Gaelic studies, but it is also true that had he not been at the center of controversy he might have remained an obscure and not very accomplished Gaelic scholar. As it is, he has a rather prominent place in the British poetic tradition, and through him poetry has a prominent place in the history of English-Scottish relations.

Macpherson was born in the village of Ruthven in the parish of Kingussie, Inverness-shire, on 27 October 1736. His father was Andrew Macpherson, a poor farmer. His mother, whose maiden name was Ellen Macpherson, was a member of another branch of the same clan. Following his early education at home, Macpherson was sent to the district school in Badendoch; his success there convinced his father to educate him for the ministry. At sixteen he entered King's College, Aberdeen, where he remained until 1754, when two months were added to the annual session. Because Macpherson, like other students from the poorer classes, employed the summer months making money to attend school during the winter, the new policy drove him to nearby Marischal College, which retained the shorter schedule.

Macpherson seems not to have shared his father's dream of a clerical career. He read widely in both classical and modern literature, and he seems to have had literary aspirations early. Yet from the beginning his efforts met with little acclaim. At Marischal he engaged in a battle of wits with a fellow Greek student named Machardy. Macpherson mocked his rival in Hudibrastic verse, prompting a response in heroics which provoked Macpherson to express further poetic ire. The skirmish continued until the principal of the college, Dr. Thomas Blackwell, collected the verses, read them with much solemnity to the class, and—much to Macpherson's indignation—pointed out at length the literary shortcomings on both sides.

In the winter of 1755-1756 Macpherson attended the University of Edinburgh, probably as a divinity student. He took no degree, nor does it appear that he ever took holy orders.

His early failure as a poet does not seem to have discouraged Macpherson; he continued to write, composing more than four thousand verses between 1753 and 1759. On leaving Edinburgh, Macpherson took a position as schoolmaster of the charity school at Ruthven, where he had taught during vacations from the university. Two poems written during this period eventually found their way into print in 1805. "Death" and the editorially titled "The Hunter" are imitative and awkward, as much student verse tends to be, but they are interesting as the earliest extant examples of Macpherson's poetry. "Death" displays his penchant for melancholy in tone and image: "Solemnly slow, along the mournful plain, / The melancholy croud support the corse / Of young Philaetes, snatched, in early bloom / Of youth, from life, and all its fading joys." "The Hunter" reveals a nationalistic pride. The poet deplores the "English'd whores" of Edin, "Once the proud seat of royalty and state," and celebrates the traditional tales and the countryside of Scotland: ". . . there smiles the vivid grass; / There timid deers, and shaggy goats abound; / There tripping fairies dance the fleeting round."

In 1758 appeared *The Highlander*, a heroic poem in six cantos on the Danish invasion of Scotland in the reign of Malcolm II. The poem is conceived in the epic style and centers on Alpin, a young man of an undistinguished family whose courage and skill in battle result in his becoming king. Idealization of the past, nationalistic fervor, and fondness for battle scenes are the main characteristics of the poem, but it is executed with a plodding determination that so thoroughly denies life to the epic theme that the poem's failure was inevitable. Other of Macpherson's early poems were published in the *Scots Magazine*, from which Thomas Blacklock retrieved them for his *A Collection of Original Poems*, published in Edinburgh in 1760-1762. These poems, signed at their original periodical publication "J. Mc." or "J. M.," include "Verses on the Death of Marshal Keith" (1758) "On the Death of a Young Lady" (1759), "To the Memory of an Officer Killed before Quebec" (1759), and "An Ode, Attempted in the Manner of Pindar" (1760). Other poems signed "M." in Blacklock's collection are of more doubtful attribution.

While the *Scots Magazine* was important as a repository for Macpherson's early efforts, it may have played a much more significant role in his poetic career. In 1755 the magazine published Jerome Stone's free translation of a Gaelic ballad. Macpherson probably saw this translation; he certainly began collecting Gaelic verses himself during the late 1750s. He was responding, it would seem, to the interest stirred by Stone and by others, including John Farquharson and Alexander

FRAGMENTS

OF

ANCIENT POETRY,

Collected in the Highlands of Scotland,

AND

Tranſlated from the Galic or Erſe Language.

Vos quoque qui fortes animas, belloque peremtas
Laudibus in longum vates dimittitis ævum,
Plurima ſecuri fudiſtis carmina Bardi.
LUCAN.

EDINBURGH:
Printed for G. HAMILTON and J. BALFOUR.
MDCCLX.

Title page for Macpherson's first collection of poems that he claimed to have translated from Gaelic verses (G. Ross Roy Collection, Thomas Cooper Library, University of South Carolina)

Macdonald, who collected Gaelic materials but did not attempt to render them into modern English.

In 1758 Macpherson left the school at Ruthven and secured a position as private tutor to the son of Mr. Graham of Balgowan. In the summer or early autumn of 1759 he accompanied young Graham to Moffat, a fashionable spa, where he met John Home, author of the popular tragedy *Douglas* (1756). In the course of conversation about Highland verse, Home requested that Macpherson translate some Gaelic poetry in Home's possession. The story goes that Macpherson, no Gaelic scholar, demurred at first but in a day or two produced a rough translation of "The Death of Oscar" and some other fragments.

"The Death of Oscar," as Macpherson presented it to Home, is the story of two friends, Oscar and Dermid, who both love the daughter of Dargo. Dermid, finding the young woman (who is "fair as the morn; mild as the beam of night") in love with "Oscur [*sic*]," beseeches his friend to kill him: "send me with honour to the grave, and let my death be renowned." Oscar reluctantly does so and then goes, grief-stricken, to the girl, whom he tricks into killing him in a display of her skill as an archer: "I fall resolved on death," he says, "and who but the daughter of Dargo was worthy to slay me?" She then kills herself, and the work concludes: "Often on their green earthen tombs the branchy sons of the mountains feed, when mid-day is all in flames, and silence is over all the hills."

Macpherson's "translations" did not attempt to be poetic renderings, and their great appeal might be attributed to the quaint charm of his "measured prose." Home took the fragments to Edinburgh, where they were received enthusiastically by Hugh Blair and others of the Edinburgh literary circle. Blair in particular encouraged their publication, and in 1760 they were printed in Edinburgh under the title *Fragments of Ancient Poetry, Collected in the Highlands of Scotland, and Translated from the Galic or Erse Language.*

Blair supervised the publication of the book and wrote a preface in which he maintained three points of significance to the later controversy surrounding Macpherson. First, he argued the antiquity of the poems: although, he says, "The date of their composition cannot be exactly ascertained," they were certainly written when "Christianity was not as yet established in the country." Second, he speculated as to the existence of a heroic epic to which some of the fragments seemed to belong: "This poem is held to be of greater antiquity than any of the rest that are preserved. . . . If the whole were recovered, it might serve to throw considerable light upon the Scottish and Irish antiquities." And finally, he maintained that "the translation is extremely literal. Even the arrangement of the words in the original has been imitated; to which must be imputed some inversions in the style, that otherwise would not have been chosen."

Fragments of Ancient Poetry was a great success, requiring a second edition almost immediately and quickly finding an audience in England. Yet from the beginning, discussion

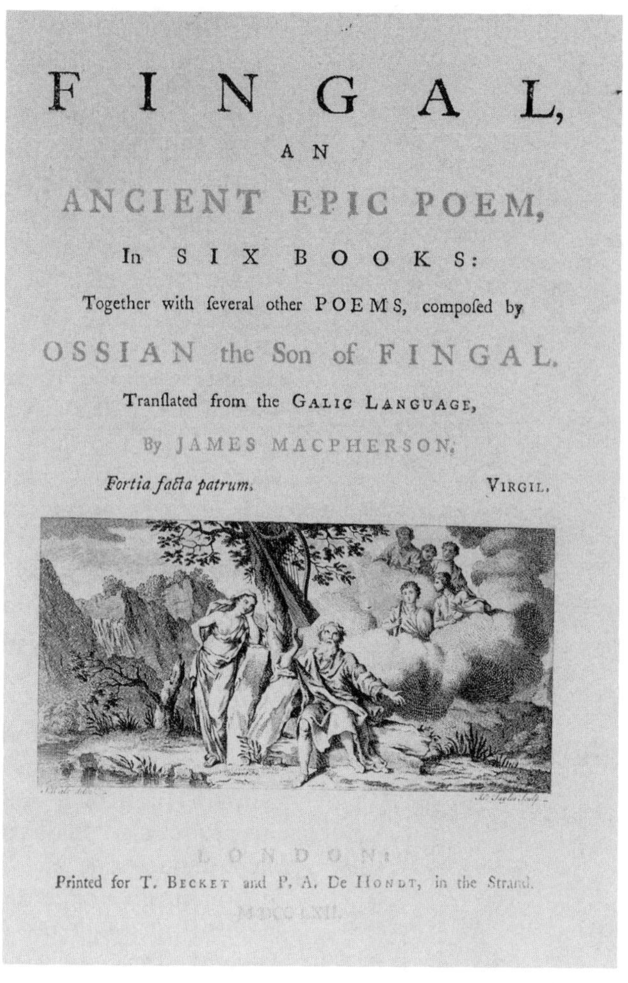

FINGAL,

AN

ANCIENT EPIC POEM,

In SIX BOOKS:

Together with ſeveral other POEMS, compoſed by

OSSIAN the Son of FINGAL.

Tranſlated from the GALIC LANGUAGE,

By JAMES MACPHERSON.

Fortia facta patrum. VIRGIL.

LONDON:

Printed for T. BECKET and P. A. DE HONDT, in the Strand.

MDCCLXII.

Title page for Macpherson's "translation" of the first part of an epic poem he claimed to have found on an expedition to the Scottish Highlands in 1760-1761 (G. Ross Roy Collection, Thomas Cooper Library, University of South Carolina)

focused on the question of authenticity. The philosopher and historian David Hume was skeptical "at the regular plan which appears in some of these pieces, and which seems to be the work of a more cultivated age"; but he did not dispute the authenticity of the subject matter, offering a rather whimsical corroboration: "the names of the heroes, Fingal, Oscar, Osur, Oscan, Dermid, are still given in the Highlands to large mastiffs, in the same manner as we affix to them the names of Caesar, Pompey, Hector, or the French that of Marlborough." Thomas Gray had his doubts but found the poems so charming, and Macpherson's answers to his inquiries so *un*charming, that on the whole he was "resolved to believe them genuine, spite of the Devil and the Kirk." Lord Lyttelton (George Lyttleton) refused to believe in their authenticity, and Mrs. Elizabeth Montagu refused to disbelieve in it. In other words, opinion was fairly evenly divided, with enough uncertainty even among the skeptics to make further investigation seem profitable.

The Edinburgh literati became so interested in the possibility that an epic existed in the Highlands that they raised funds to support Macpherson in a search for the longer poem. In addition to Blair, Macpherson's sponsors included Hume, Lord Elibank (Patrick Murray), William Robertson, Adam Ferguson, Lord Hailes (Sir David Dalrymple), and James Boswell. The project began to take on a highly nationalistic theme: Blair referred to "our epic" and encouraged its recovery on the grounds that the Anglicizing of Scotland was threatening the country's heritage. Macpherson, purportedly reluctant to undertake the project, was persuaded by Blair and the others. Macpherson, it was agreed, should resign his tutorship and devote himself to the search. He received one hundred pounds toward the journey.

Macpherson conducted his research in the course of two journeys into the Highlands, first to Iverness-shire, Skye, Uist, and Benbecula, and later to Argyleshire and Mull. The expedition occupied about four months, from the end of August or the beginning of September 1760 to early in January 1761, when he returned to Edinburgh. On 16 January he wrote to the Reverend James Maclagan, "I have been lucky enough to lay my hands on a pretty complete poem, and truly epic, concerning Fingal. The antiquity of it is easily ascertained, and it is not only superior to anything in that language, but reckoned not inferior to the more polite performances of other nations in that way." In February he went to London to supervise the printing of his translation of this epic.

London, rather than Edinburgh, was chosen as the place of publication largely because of the interest and influence of Lord Bute (John Stuart), the Scotsman who had been raised to a position of power as secretary of state by George III in 1761. The first part of the translation, *Fingal*, was published in December 1761 (dated 1762 on the title page) with an introduction in which Macpherson claimed the Celtic epic's superiority to the Greek. Immediately, enthusiasm was widespread. The *Critical Review*, under the direction of fellow Scotsman Tobias Smollett, was extravagantly favorable, and the *Annual Register*, in a review possibly written by Edmund Burke, was admiring. In general the English response was favorable, though a bit astonished at the refinement of the sentiments depicted in such passages as: "Joy rises in Oscar's face. His cheek is red. His eye sheds tears. The sword is a beam of fire in his hand. He came, and smiling, spoke to Ossian. 'O ruler of the fight of steel! my father, hear thy son! Retire with Morven's mighty chief. Give me the fame of Ossian. If here I fall: O chief, remember that breast of snow, the lonely sun-beam of my love, the white-handed daughter of Toscar! For, with red cheek from the rock, bending over the stream, her soft hair flies about her bosom, as she pours the sigh for Oscar. Tell her I am on my hills, a lightly-bounding son of the wind; tell her, that in a cloud, I may meet the lovely maid of Toscar.' " Gray's assessment was in some ways the common one: "The epic poem is foolishly so called; yet there is a sort of plan and unity in it very strange for a barbarous age." The Irish met the initial publication with unqualified hostility, feeling that their national heroes had been usurped by the Scottish impostor, and they were not alone in the belief that the issue was becoming a matter of politics as much as one of art.

The year 1761 was marked by English-Scots animosity of a more than usual degree of intensity. Bute had become prime minister with the fall of the Pitt ministry in October, and his unpopularity, which would become legendary, was already fairly widespread by December. Macpherson's fortune was linked to Bute's; as Bute's protégé if not his dependent, he came in for his share of the opposition's satire, expounded particularly in John Wilkes's periodical the *North Briton*. Bute's support, however, gave Macpherson the means by which to continue to present his "discovery" to the public. In 1763 *Temora* was published at the prime minister's personal expense, and this sponsorship probably contributed to Macpherson's increasingly offensive arrogance. In the preface to the second part of the "epic" Macpherson is quite disparaging toward the Irish and others who had expressed doubts about the authenticity of *Fingal*, and his attitude did not soften when *Temora* was greeted with ridicule by the London critics.

With the publication of the second poem, the public began to reassess *Fingal*, and soon both works came to be regarded, in Hume's words, as "impudent forgery." Although Macpherson had deposited manuscripts with his publishers, T. Becket and P. A. De Hondt, to answer doubts about the authenticity of the poems, he soon started refusing to answer queries with a stubborn air of superiority and disdain that firmly established for many the fact of the forgery. Even Blair, who had no doubts as to the authenticity of the poems, began to wax shy of Macpherson's touchiness on the subject, telling Hume, whose skepticism was never quite satisfied, that inquiries which seemed to be "tracing him out" would not please him.

Macpherson's most powerful detractor was Samuel Johnson, whose contempt for Macpherson and the poems prompted him to do some rudimentary research of his own on his trip through the Hebrides in the 1770s to prove Macpherson's Ossian to be Macpherson himself. When word reached Macpherson that Johnson planned to publish his findings in his *A Journey to the Western Islands of Scotland* (1775), the poet became incensed and sent a challenge to Johnson. In an act that quickly passed into literary legend, Johnson purchased an oak cudgel six feet long and wrote Macpherson:

T E M O R A,

A N

ANCIENT EPIC POEM,

In EIGHT BOOKS:

Together with ſeveral other POEMS, compoſed by

OSSIAN, the Son of FINGAL.

Tranſlated from the GALIC LANGUAGE,

By JAMES MACPHERSON.

Vultis et his mecum pariter conſidere regnis?
Urbem quam ſtatuo, veſtra eſt. VIRGIL.

LONDON:

Printed for T. BECKET and P. A. DE HONDT, in the Strand.

[illegible]

Title page for the continuation of Fingal. *Publication of this work led to widespread accusations of forgery against Macpherson (G. Ross Roy Collection, Thomas Cooper Library, University of South Carolina).*

> I received your foolish and impudent note. Whatever insult is offered me, I will do my best to repel, and what I cannot do for myself, the law shall do for me. I will not desist from detecting what I think a cheat, from any fear of the menaces of a Ruffian.
>
> What would you have me retract? I thought your book an imposture; I think it an imposture still. For this opinion I have given my reasons to the public, which I here dare you to refute. Your rage I defy.

Johnson's distaste for the Scots is well known, and while his opinion has been justified by posterity, national prejudice probably figured in. Macpherson came to attribute most of the negative response to such prejudice. In the 1773 edition of the Ossian poems, his prefatory remarks noted the work's continued worldwide popularity in spite of "the coldness with which a few have affected to treat them at home." He went on: "When rivers define the limits of abilities, as well as the boundaries of countries, a writer may measure his success by the latitude under which he was born. It was to avoid a part of this inconvenience that the author is said by some to have ascribed his own productions to another name. If this was the case, he was but young in the art of deception. When he placed the poet in antiquity, the translator should have been born on this side of the Tweed."

For the remainder of the eighteenth century national prejudice continued to cloud the issue of the authenticity of *Fingal* and *Temora*. It was not until after Macpherson's death that the nature and extent of his truthfulness was determined. Beginning with the Highland Society's 1805 report of the findings of a committee appointed in 1797 to look into the matter and culminating in Deric S. Thomson's *Gaelic Sources of Macpherson's "Ossian"* (1952), the matter has been fairly safely concluded. Macpherson did find materials pertain-

Portrait of Macpherson by George Romney (from Isodoro Montiel, Ossián en España, *1974)*

ing to the legends of Fingal and Ossian. He did see manuscripts and record recitations of poems dating from as far back as the fifteenth century and based on heroic cycles of the first and third centuries. He did *not* find an epic from the third century or from any other time. His translation was neither literal nor truly reflective of the original material. He composed transitions and left out what he could not construe. The language is based more on the Bible, classical works, and John Milton than on Gaelic sources. Further, the emphases derived not from the original ballads but from Macpherson's preoccupations with battle, melancholy, and the scenery of Badendoch. Some flavor of the originals remains, however, in monotony of tone and in certain characteristic phrasings, particularly in the use of parentheses.

Macpherson's original impetus to refine the materials he found seems to have come from a concern that "they would be very ill relished by the public, as so very different from the strain of modern ideas and of modern, connected, and polished poetry," a concern he expressed in his prefixed dissertation on *Fingal.* It says something about his ability to accurately "read" his audience that, controversy notwithstanding, the poems as he presented them had profound and long-lasting appeal. In Romantic poetry, in particular, can be heard the mournful echo of Macpherson's Ossian; for hardly a poet of the next generation does not somewhere pay homage to the dark passion, remote charm, and evocative simplicity of such passages as this one: "As the dark shades of autumn fly over hills of grass; so gloomy, dark, successive came the chiefs of Lochlin's echoing woods. Tall as the stag of Morven, moved stately before them the king. His shining shield is on his side, like a flame on the heath at night; when the world is silent and dark, and the traveller sees some ghost sporting in the beam! Dimly gleam the hills around, and show indistinctly their oaks! A blast from the troubled ocean removed the settled mist. The sons of Erin appear, like a ridge of rocks on the coast; when mariners, on shores unknown, are trembling at veering winds!"

Macpherson's fortune was made through the political advantage he accrued as a Scottish bard subject to English insult. His literary output was limited to one further attempt in the field of translation: his 1773 rendering of the *Iliad* into "measured prose" was roundly ridiculed by all but his staunchest Scottish supporters.

The remainder of Macpherson's career was a political one. From 1764 until 1766 he was in America as secretary to the governor of West Florida; while in Pensacola he also served as clerk of the Governor's Council and as justice of the peace. In 1766 he settled in London, employed as a writer for the government. He wrote *An Introduction to the History of Great Britain and Ireland* (1771), *The History of Great Britain from the Restoration to the Accession of the House of Hannover* (1775) and *Original Papers: Containing the Secret History of Great Britain, from the Restoration to the Accession of the House of Hannover* (1775), all of which betray the predictable Celtic patriotism and Jacobitism. From 1776 to 1781 he was employed by Lord North (Frederick North) as a writer to defend American policy, and he supervised the ministerial newspapers during this period as well. Macpherson was also appointed minister in London to the nabob of Arcot, a position which fell his way through his kinsman John Macpherson, who had made his career in India as a servant of the nabob; John Macpherson had come to London with papers and letters supporting the nabob against the East India Company and had asked James Macpherson to edit the material. In 1780, Macpherson obtained a seat in Parliament which he held until his death.

His service on behalf of the nabob, which after 1783 he held jointly with Sir Nathaniel Wraxall, gave him wealth, some of which he employed in building a mansion in Badendoch which he named Belville. He died there on 17 February 1796, leaving three hundred pounds for a monument to himself at Belville and instructions for burial in Poets' Corner at Westminister Abbey. He bequeathed one thousand pounds to John Mackensie toward the publication of Ossian in the original. He also left four or five illegitimate children: James, who inherited his estate; Charles, who met an early death in India; perhaps a third son; a daughter, Anne; and another daughter, Juliet. Macpherson provided for the children, and each of their mothers received an annuity by the terms of his will.

It is as the Ossian poet that Macpherson is remembered. Nineteenth-century poets, in particular, from Russia to Germany to England, France, and Ireland cared less for strict veracity than for the fragmentary suggestiveness, the noble primitivism, the strangely personal melancholy that infuse Macpherson's poems. As the "translator" of Ossian, Macpherson touched a chord; and whether he is regarded as a calculating deceiver or a well-meaning bumbler, his impact on the sensibility of his and the following age was widespread and significant.

Bibliographies:

George F. Black, "Macpherson's Ossian and the Ossianic Controversy," *Bulletin of the New York Public Library*, 30 (June 1926): 424-439, 508-524;

John J. Dunn, "Macpherson's Ossian and the Ossianic Controversy: A Supplementary Bibliography," *Bulletin of the New York Public Library*, 75 (November 1971): 465-473.

Biography:

Bailey Saunders, *The Life and Letters of James Macpherson* (London: Swann Sonnenschein, 1894).

References:

Hugh Blair, *A Critical Dissertation on the Poems of Ossian, the Son of Fingal*, second edition (London: Printed for T. Becket and P. A. De Hondt, 1765);

Josef Bysveen, *Epic Tradition and Innovation in James Macpherson's "Fingal"* (Stockholm: Uppsala, 1982);

Robert Hay Carnie, "Macpherson's *Fragments of Ancient Poetry* and Lord Hailes," *English Studies*, 41 (January 1960): 17-26;

Madeleine Pelner Cosman, "Mannered Passion: W. B. Yeats and the Ossianic Myths," *Western Humanities Review*, 14 (Spring 1960): 163-171;

John J. Dunn, "Coleridge's Debt to Macpherson's Ossian," *Studies in Scottish Literature*, 7 (July-October 1969): 76-89;

Dunn, "James Macpherson's First Epic," *Studies in Scottish Literature*, 9 (July 1971): 48-54;

Robert Fitzgerald, "The Style of Ossian," *Studies in Romanticism*, 6 (Autumn 1966): 22-33;

Robert Folkenflik, "Macpherson, Chatterton, Blake and the Great Age of Literary Forgery," *Centennial Review*, 18 (Fall 1974): 378-391;

John L. Greenway, "The Gateway to Innocence: Ossian and the Nordic Bard as Myth," in *Studies in Eighteenth-Century Culture*, volume 4, edited by Harold E. Pagliaro (Madison: University of Wisconsin Press, 1975), pp. 161-70;

Highland Society of Scotland, *Report of the Committee of the Highland Society of Scotland, Appointed to Inquire into the Nature and Authenticity of the Poems of Ossian* (Edinburgh: University Press, 1805);

Adrian H. Jaffe, "Chateaubriand's Use of Ossianic Language," *Comparative Literature Studies*, 5 (June 1968), 157-166;

Malcolm Laing, Preface and notes to Macpherson's *The Poems of Ossian*, 2 volumes, edited by Laing (Edinburgh: Printed by J. Ballantyne for A. Constable, 1805);

Iu. D. Levin, "Russian Responses to the Poetry of Ossian," in *Great Britain and Russia in the Eighteenth Century: Contacts and Comparisons*, edited by A. G. Cross (Newtonville, Mass.: Oriental Research Partners, 1979), pp. 49-64;

James S. Malek, "Eighteenth-Century British Dramatic Adaptations of Macpherson's Ossian," *Restoration and Eighteenth-Century Theatre Research*, 14, no. 1 (1975): 36-41, 52;

Arthur E. McGuinness, "Lord Kames on the Ossian Poems: Anthropology and Criticism," *Texas Studies in Literature and Language*, 10, (Spring 1968): 65-75;

Robert F. Metzdorf, "M'Nicol, Macpherson, and Johnson," *Eighteenth-Century Studies in Honor of Donald F. Hyde*, edited by W. H. Bond (New York: Grolier Club, 1970), pp. 45-61;

Isodoro Montiel, *Ossián en España* (Barcelona: Editorial Planeta, 1974);

Alfred Nutt, *Ossian and the Ossianic Literature* (London: Nutt, 1899; reprinted, New York: AMS Press, 1972);

Richard Sher, " 'Those Scotch Imposters and Their Cabal': Ossian and the Scottish Enlightenment," in *Man and Nature: Proceedings of the Canadian Society for Eighteenth-Century Literature*, edited by Roger L. Emerson and others (London, Ont.: University of Western Ontario, 1982), pp. 55-63;

J. S. Smart, *James Macpherson: An Episode in Literature* (London: Nutt, 1905);

Larry L. Stewart, "Ossian, Burke, and the 'Joy of Grief,' " *English Language Notes*, 15 (September 1977): 29-32;

Derick S. Thomson, *The Gaelic Sources of Macpherson's "Ossian"* (Edinburgh: Published for the University of Aberdeen by Oliver & Boyd, 1952; reprinted, Edinburgh: Oliver & Boyd, 1969);

P. Van Tiegham, *Ossian en France*, 2 volumes (Paris: Rieder, 1917).

Papers:

James Macpherson's journal, in the possession of his descendants after his death, disappeared in 1868. A 1760 letter to Hugh Blair is in the National Library of Scotland, Edinburgh.

Hannah More

(2 February 1745 - 7 September 1833)

Patricia Meyer Spacks
University of Virginia

See also the More entry in *DLB 107: British Romantic Prose Writers, 1789-1832: First Series.*

BOOKS: *The Search after Happiness: A Pastoral Drama* (Bristol: Printed & sold by S. Farley, 1773; Philadelphia: Printed by James Humphreys, Jr., 1774);

The Inflexible Captive: A Tragedy (Bristol: Printed & sold by S. Farley, 1774; Philadelphia: Printed for John Sparhawk by James Humphreys, Jr., 1774);

Sir Eldred of the Bower, and the Bleeding Rock: Two Legendary Tales (London: Printed for T. Cadell, 1776);

Essays on Various Subjects, Principally Designed for Young Ladies (London: Printed for J. Wilkie & T. Cadell, 1777; Philadelphia: Printed & sold by Young, Stewart & M'Culloch, 1786);

Ode to Dragon, Mr. Garrick's House-Dog, at Hampton (London: Printed for T. Cadell, 1777);

Percy, a Tragedy (London: Printed for T. Cadell, 1778);

The Works of Miss Hannah More in Prose and Verse (Cork: Printed by Thomas White, 1778);

The Fatal Falsehood: A Tragedy (London: Printed for T. Cadell, 1779);

Sacred Dramas: Chiefly Intended for Young Persons: the Subjects Taken from the Bible. To Which Is Added, Sensibility, a Poem (London: Printed for T. Cadell, 1782; Philadelphia: Printed for Thomas Dobson, 1787);

Florio: A Tale, for Fine Gentlemen and Fine Ladies: and, The Bas Bleu; or, Conversation: Two Poems (London: Printed for T. Cadell, 1786);

Slavery, a Poem (London: Printed for T. Cadell, 1788; Philadelphia: Printed by Joseph James, 1788; New York: Printed by J. & A. M'Lean, 1788);

Thoughts on the Importance of the Manners of the Great to General Society (London: Printed for T. Cadell, 1788; Philadelphia: Printed for Thomas Dobson, 1788);

Bishop Bonner's Ghost, as "A good old papist" (Strawberry Hill: Printed by Thomas Kirgate, 1789);

An Estimate of the Religion of the Fashionable World: By One of the Laity (London: Printed for T. Cadell, 1791; Philadelphia: Printed for & sold by M. L. Weems & H. Willis, 1793);

Village Politics, Addressed to All the Mechanics, Journeymen, and Day Labourers in Great Britain, as "Will Chip, a country carpenter" (London: Printed & sold by F. & C. Rivington, 1792);

Remarks on the Speech of M. Dupont, Made in the National Convention of France, on the Subjects of Religion and Public Education (London: Printed for T. Cadell, 1793); republished in *Considerations on Religion and Public Education, with Remarks on the Speech of M. Dupont, Delivered in the National Convention of France* (Boston: Printed by Weld & Greenough, 1794);

The Cottage Cook; or, Mrs. Jones's Cheap Dishes (London: Sold by J. Evans & J. Hatchard and S. Hazard, Bath, 1795);

The Sunday School (London: Sold by J. Evans & J. Hatchard and S. Hazard, Bath, 1795);

The Apprentice's Monitor; or, Indentures in Verse (Bath: Sold by S. Hazard and J. Marshall & R. White, London, 1795);

The Carpenter; or, The Danger of Evil Company (Bath: Sold by S. Hazard and J. Marshall & R. White, London, 1795);

The Gin-Shop; or, A Peep into a Prison (Bath: Sold by S. Hazard and J. Marshall & R. White, London, 1795);

The History of Tom White the Postilion (Bath: Sold by S. Hazard and J. Marshall & R. White, London, 1795; Philadelphia: Published by B. Johnson, 1798);

The Market Woman: A True Tale; or, Honesty Is the Best Policy (Bath: Sold by S. Hazard and J. Marshall & R. White, London, 1795);

The Roguish Miller; or, Nothing Got by Cheating (Bath: Sold by S. Hazard and J. Marshall & R. White, London, 1795);

H More

The Shepherd of Salisbury Plain (Bath: Sold by S. Hazard and J. Marshall & R. White, London, 1795; Philadelphia: Printed by B. & J. Johnson, 1800);

The Two Shoemakers (Bath: Sold by S. Hazard and J. Marshall & R. White, London, 1795); republished as *The History of the Two Shoemakers. Part I* (Philadelphia: Printed by B. & J. Johnson, 1800);

The Shepherd of Salisbury Plain. Part II (Bath: Sold by S. Hazard and J. Marshall & R. White, London, 1795; Philadelphia: Printed by B. & J. Johnson, 1800);

Patient Joe; or, The Newcastle Collier (Bath: Sold by S. Hazard and J. Marshall & R. White, London, 1795; Philadelphia: Printed & sold by J. Rakeshaw, 1808);

The Riot; or, Half a Loaf Is Better Than No Bread (London: Sold by J. Marshall & R. White and S. Hazard, Bath, 1795);

The Way to Plenty; or, The Second Part of Tom White (London: Sold by J. Marshall & R. White and S. Hazard, Bath, 1795; Philadelphia: Printed by B. & J. Johnson, 1800);

The Honest Miller of Glocestershire (London: Sold by J. Marshall & R. White and S. Hazard, Bath, 1795);

The Two Wealthy Farmers; or, The History of Mr. Bragwell. Part I (London: Sold by J. Marshall & R. White and S. Hazard, Bath, 1795; Philadelphia: Printed by B. & J. Johnson, 1800);

Robert and Richard; or, The Ghost of Poor Molly, Who Was Drowned in Richard's Mill Pond (London: Sold by J. Marshall & R. White and S. Hazard, Bath, 1796);

The Apprentice Turned Master; or, The Second Part of the Two Shoemakers (London: Sold by J. Marshall & R. White and S. Hazard, Bath, 1796); republished as *The History of the Two Shoemakers. Part II* (Philadelphia: Printed by B. & J. Johnson, 1800);

The History of Idle Jack Brown . . . Being the Third Part of the Two Shoemakers (London: Sold by J. Marshall & R. White and S. Hazard, Bath, 1796); republished as *The History of the Two Shoemakers. Part III* (Philadelphia: Printed by B. & J. Johnson, 1800);

The Shopkeeper Turned Sailor . . . Part I (London: Sold by J. Marshall & R. White and S. Hazard, Bath, 1796; Philadelphia: Printed by B. & J. Johnson, 1800);

Jack Brown in Prison . . . Being the Fourth Part of the History of the Two Shoemakers (London: Sold by J. Marshall & R. White and S. Hazard, Bath, 1796); republished as *The History of the Two Shoemakers. Part IV* (Philadelphia: Printed by B. & J. Johnson, 1800);

The Hackney Coachman; or, The Way to Get a Good Fare (London: Sold by J. Marshall & R. White and S. Hazard, Bath, 1796);

Sunday Reading: On Carrying Religion into the Common Business of Life. A Dialogue between James Stock and Will Simpson, the Shoemakers (London: Sold by J. Marshall & R. White, 1796);

Turn the Carpet; or, The Two Weavers: A New Song, in a Dialogue between Dick and John (London: Sold by J. Marshall & R. White and S. Hazard, Bath, 1796);

Betty Brown, the St. Giles's Orange Girl (London: Sold by J. Marshall & R. White and S. Hazard, Bath, 1796; Philadelphia: Printed by B. & J. Johnson, 1800);

Sunday Reading: The Grand Assizes; or, General Gaol Delivery (London: Sold by J. Marshall & R. White and S. Hazard, Bath, 1796);

The History of Mr. Bragwell; or, The Two Wealthy Farmers. Part III (London: Sold by J. Marshall & R. White, S. Hazard, Bath; J. Elder, Edinburgh, 1796); republished as *The Two Wealthy Farmers; or, The History of Mr. Bragwell: Part III* (Philadelphia: Printed by B. & J. Johnson, 1800);

A Hymn of Praise for the Abundant Harvest of 1796 (London: Sold by J. Marshall & R. White and S. Hazard, Bath, 1796);

Sunday Reading: The History of the Two Wealthy Farmers . . . Part IV (London: Sold by J. Marshall & R. White and S. Hazard, Bath, 1796); republished as *The Two Wealthy Farmers; or, The History of Mr. Bragwell: Part IV* (Philadelphia: Printed by B. & J. Johnson, 1800);

The Two Wealthy Farmers, with the Sad Adventures of Miss Bragwell: Part V (London: Sold by J. Marshall & R. White and S. Hazard, Bath, 1796); republished as *The Two Wealthy Farmers; or, The History of Mr. Bragwell: Part V* (Philadelphia: Printed by B. & J. Johnson, 1800);

Black Giles the Poacher . . . Part I (London: Sold by J. Marshall & R. White and S. Hazard, Bath, 1796; Philadelphia: Printed by B. & J. Johnson, 1800);

Sunday Reading: Bear ye one another's Burthens; or, The Valley of Tears: A Vision (London: Sold by J. Marshall & R. White; S. Hazard, Bath; and J. Elder, Edinburgh, 1796; Philadelphia: Benjamin Johnson, 1813);

Black Giles the Poacher: With the History of Widow Brown's Apple-tree. Part II (London: Sold by J. Marshall and S. Hazard, Bath, 1796; Philadelphia: Printed by B. & J. Johnson, 1800);

The Good Militiaman . . . Being a New Song by Honest Dan the Ploughboy Turned Soldier (London: Sold by J. Marshall & R. White and S. Hazard, Bath, 1797);

Tawny Rachel; or, The Fortune Teller (London: Sold by J. Marshall & R. White; S. Hazard, Bath; J. Elder, Edinburgh, 1797); republished as *The Fortune Teller* (Philadelphia: Published by B. Johnson, 1798);

The Two Gardeners (London: Sold by J. Marshall & R. White; S. Hazard, Bath; and J. Elder, Edinburgh, 1797);

The History of Hester Wilmot; or, The Second Part of The Sunday School (London: Sold by J. Marshall & R. White; S. Hazard, Bath; and J. Elder, Edinburgh, 1797; Philadelphia: Sunday and Adult School Union, 1818);

Sunday Reading: The Servant Man Turned Soldier; or, The Fair weather Christian (London: Sold by J. Marshall & R. White; S. Hazard, Bath; J. Elder, Edinburgh, 1797);

The History of Hester Wilmot; or, The New Gown: Part II. Being a Continuation of The Sunday School (London: Sold by J. Marshall; S. Hazard, Bath; J. Elder, Edinburgh, 1797);

The Lady and the Pye; or, Know Thyself (London: Sold by J. Marshall & R. White; S. Hazard, Bath; J. Elder, Edinburgh, 1797);

Sunday Reading: The Strait Gate and the Broad Way, Being the Second Part of the Valley of Tears (London: Sold by J. Marshall & R. White; S. Hazard, Bath; and J. Elder, Edinburgh, 1797);

The History of Mr. Fantom, the New Fashioned Philosopher and His Man William (London: Sold by J. Marshall; S. Hazard, Bath; J. Elder, Edinburgh, 1797; Philadelphia: Printed by B. & J. Johnson, 1800);

Sunday Reading: The Pilgrims. An Allegory (London: Sold by J. Marshall; S. Hazard, Bath;

and J. Elder, Edinburgh, 1797; Philadelphia: Printed & sold by Kimber, Conrad, 1808);

Dan and Jane; or, Faith and Works: A Tale (London: Sold by J. Marshall; S. Hazard, Bath; and J. Elder, Edinburgh, 1797);

The Two Wealthy Farmers; or, The Sixth Part of the History of Mr. Bragwell and His Two Daughters (London: Sold by J. Marshall; S. Hazard, Bath; and J. Elder, Edinburgh, 1797);

The Two Wealthy Farmers; or, The Seventh and Last Part of the History of Mr. Bragwell and His Two Daughters (London: Sold by J. Marshall; S. Hazard, Bath; and J. Elder, Edinburgh, 1797);

The Plum-Cakes; or, The Farmer and His Three Sons (London: Sold by J. Marshall and S. Hazard, Bath, 1797);

Strictures on the Modern System of Female Education: With a View of the Principles and Conduct Prevalent among Women of Rank and Fortune, 2 volumes (London: Printed by A. Strahan for T. Cadell Jun. & W. Davies, 1799; Philadelphia: Printed by Bunn & Bartram for Thomas Dobson, 1800);

The Works of Hannah More, Including Several Pieces Never Before Published (8 volumes, London: T. Cadell & W. Davies, 1801; enlarged, 19 volumes, 1818; enlarged, 11 volumes, London: T. Cadell, 1830; enlarged, with a memoir and notes, 6 volumes, London: H. Fisher, R. Fisher & P. Jackson, 1834; 2 volumes, New York: Harper & Brothers, 1837);

Hints towards Forming the Character of a Young Princess, 2 volumes (London: Printed for T. Cadell & W. Davies, 1805);

Coelebs in Search of a Wife: Comprehending Observations on Domestic Habits and Manners, Religion and Morals, as "Coelebs" (2 volumes, London: Printed for T. Cadell and W. Davies, 1808; 1 volume, New York: Published by David Carlisle, 1809);

Practical Piety; or, The Influence of the Religion of the Heart on the Conduct of Life, 2 volumes (London: Printed for T. Cadell, 1811; Albany: Websters & Skinners, 1811; Boston: Munroe & Francis, 1811; Burlington, N.J.: D. Allinson, 1811);

Christian Morals, 2 volumes (London: Printed for T. Cadell & W. Davies, 1813; New York: Eastburn, Kirk / Boston: Bradford & Read, 1813; New York: Published by D. Huntington, 1813);

An Essay on the Character and Practical Writings of Saint Paul, 2 volumes (London: Printed for T. Cadell & W. Davies, 1815; Boston: Wells, 1815; Philadelphia: Edward Earle / New York: Eastburn, Kirk, 1815);

Poems (London: Printed for T. Cadell & W. Davies, 1816; Boston: Wells & Lilly, 1817; enlarged edition, London: Cadell, 1829);

Moral Sketches of Prevailing Opinions and Manners, Foreign and Domestic; with Reflections on Prayer (London: Cadell & Davies, 1819; Boston: Wells & Lilly, 1819); sixth edition, with a new preface (London: Cadell & Davies, 1820);

The Twelfth of August; or, The Feast of Freedom (London: J. & T. Clarke, 1819); republished as *The Feast of Freedom; or, The Abolition of Domestic Slavery in Ceylon: The Vocal Parts Adapted to Music by C. Wesley* (London: T. Cadell, 1827);

Bible Rhymes on the Names of All the Books of the Old and New Testament: With Allusions to Some of the Principal Incidents and Characters (London: T. Cadell, 1821; Boston: Wells & Lilly, 1821);

The Spirit of Prayer: Selected and Compiled by Herself, from Various Portions Exclusively on that Subject, in Her Published Volumes (London: T. Cadell, 1825; Boston: Cummings, Hilliard, 1826);

Miscellaneous Works, 2 volumes (London: Printed for T. Tegg, 1840).

Collections: *Cheap Repository,* 3 volumes (London: Sold by J. Marshall and S. Hazard, Bath, 1795-1798);

The Entertaining, Moral, and Religious Repository, 2 volumes (Elizabethtown, N.J.: Printed by Shepard Kollock for Cornelius Davis, New York, 1798-1799);

Cheap Repository, 3 volumes (Philadelphia: Printed by B. & J. Johnson, 1800-1803).

PLAY PRODUCTIONS: *The Inflexible Captive,* Bath, Theatre Royal, 19 April 1775;

Percy, London, Theatre Royal, Covent Garden, 10 December 1777;

The Fatal Falsehood, London, Theatre Royal, Covent Garden, 6 May 1779.

OTHER: Ann Yearsley, *Poems, on Several Occasions,* edited, with a preface, by More (London: Printed for T. Cadell, 1785).

~~I Moore~~ (?)
Hannah More December 1 1818

Amelia Carissima! I thank, & love you for scolding me; since, had you not scolded a little after my singularly long silence, I should have apprehended some diminution of your regard for me, a kind of Loss, that I hope I shall never have to sustain! — My silence indeed is more deserving of pity, than of Reproof, as it has been owing to various afflicting circumstances 1st incessant & extreme anxiety for the Life of that amiable Mortal, the younger Brother of our beloved Captn of Purfleet — The long-suffering Invalide has endured much from inscrutable internal Malady, supposed to originate in the Liver! — our kind Captn has recently escorted Him to that singular Man of medical Eminence, Abernethy, who honestly confesses, He can afford them no Light in their distressing Darkness; and Time (the great Doctor of all) can alone

Letter from More to Amelia Opie, containing two poems (HM 25784, Henry E. Huntington Library and Art Gallery)

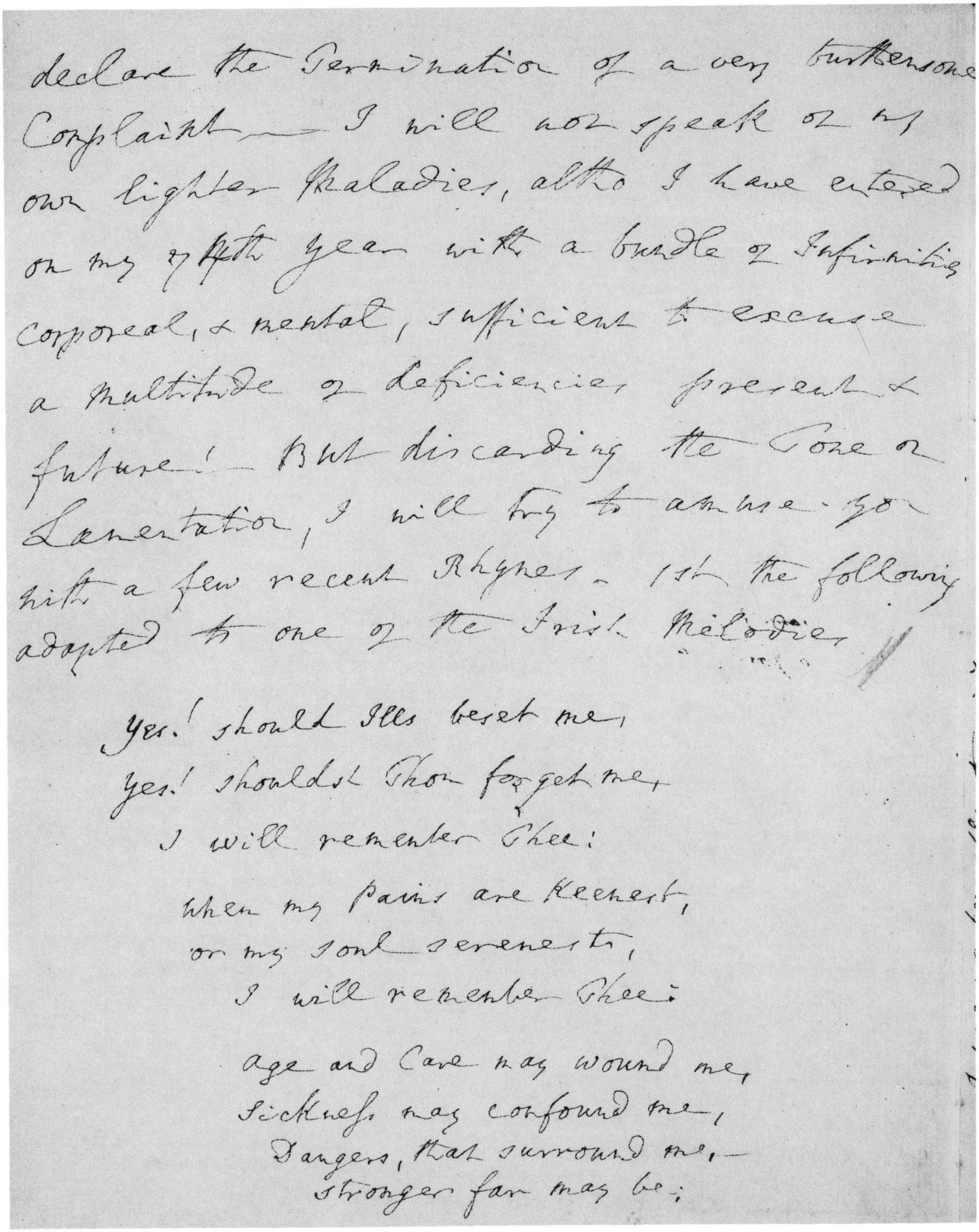

declare the Termination of a very burthensome Complaint — I will not speak of my own lighter Maladies, altho I have entered on my 77th year with a bundle of Infirmities corporeal, & mental, sufficient to excuse a multitude of deficiencies present & future! — But discarding the Tone of Lamentation, I will try to amuse you with a few recent Rhymes — 1st the following adapted to one of the Irish Melodies

Yes! should Ills beset me,
Yes! shouldst Thou forget me,
I will remember Thee:
When my pains are keenest,
or my soul sereneste,
I will remember Thee:

Age and Care may wound me,
Sickness may confound me,
Dangers, that surround me,—
stronger far may be;

But tho Life be waning,
While I've sense remaining,
I will remember Thee.

Let me now hope to make you smile by a little Gallantry of your superannuated Bard towards a Lady advanced in Life with extraordinary undiminished Beauty, & looking younger than her Daughter

To the Lady Elizabeth Monk

I hear; but say, dear Lady, is it true?
The name of Grand Mamma belongs to you:
If so you can direct me to a scene
Superior to the Fount of Hippocrene.

There is a Fountain, magically clear,
and to the Wife of Jove supremely dear,
For when she bath'd in it (as Bards declare)
She rose a Nymph with Youth's most graceful air.

Tell me, dear Lady! where this wonder flows,
Fron by the Light, that in your aspect glows,
You to this Fountain must well know the Path,
Your Beauty tells us 'tis your daily Bath.

I have not been able to visit our dear Lady of Lawant in all her long confinement from her tragic severe accident — Adieu. God bless you.

These dearest Amelia I hope this motley scrawl will make amends for my involuntary long silence. I trust your Kind Father continues to enjoy his rare evergreen old age & the Talents & Renown of his dear admirable Tale-telling Daughter. White Lies & the sweet little concluding story of Mariah Trelawny are my Favorites — the last above all — My Love to your Queen of ... I long to hear of her Levee

Accepted by many of her contemporaries as the ultimate authority on the moral life and how to achieve it, Hannah More wrote fiction, poetry, drama, treatises on education, and didactic essays. She concerned herself with the welfare of children, the poor, the middle classes, and the aristocracy, exerting immense influence by her passionate determination to communicate intense religious conviction and to lead others to incorporate such conviction in their lives. To instruct rather than to delight was her primary purpose, in poetry as in prose. But Samuel Johnson (and multitudes of the less illustrious) considered her an accomplished poet, and her best work remains appealing even now for its emotional authenticity and psychological imagination.

The fourth of five daughters of Jacob More, a Gloucestershire schoolmaster, and Mary Grace More, Hannah More was born at Stapleton, near Bristol, on 2 February 1745. She proved a precocious learner, teaching herself to read before the age of four by listening to her sisters' lessons. Her father told her stories from the classics and taught her Latin and mathematics; she learned French from a sister who had been sent to school at Bristol, and she improved her skill in the language by talking with French officers living in the neighborhood. When her eldest sister established a boarding school in Bristol about 1757, Hannah and the other girls joined her there; Hannah learned Italian, Spanish, and more advanced Latin from masters at the school. When she was sixteen she wrote a play, *The Search after Happiness: A Pastoral Drama;* it was published in 1773. At the age of twenty-two or twenty-three she accepted a proposal of marriage from Edward Turner, twenty years her senior. For six years Turner kept agreeing to successive wedding days and then postponing the event. Finally the engagement was broken off. Although More declined the annuity Turner offered her, her sisters and her friend and adviser James Stonehouse accepted for her—without her knowledge—two hundred pounds a year. More resolved, according to her biographer William Roberts, to avoid any "similar entanglement"; soon afterward she refused another offer. She never married.

Visits to London in the early 1770s stimulated More's literary ambitions. She became friendly with eminent literary women, including Elizabeth Montagu, Hester Chapone, Elizabeth Carter, and Frances Boscawen, as well as with such giants as Johnson, David Garrick, and Sir Joshua Reynolds. Challenged to new literary endeavor, she wrote in two weeks the ballad "Sir Eldred of the Bower," which Thomas Cadell published in 1776 together with an earlier poem of hers, "The Bleeding Rock." "Sir Eldred of the Bower" adapts a conventional tragic plot: gallant knight loves beautiful maiden, who agrees to marry him; he finds her embracing a handsome youth; in a jealous rage he kills the other man, who turns out to be his beloved's long-lost brother; his fiancée expires from a broken heart, and he dies of unspecified causes. More interests herself, however, less in lurid action than in psychological and moral implications. Sir Eldred's heroism derives not from "gallant deeds" of the military sort apparently pursued by his father, but from active benevolence:

When merit raised the sufferer's name,
  He showered his bounty then;
And those who could not prove that claim
  He succored still as men.

The hero's weakness, as the poem early specifies, is his susceptibility to passion. The ballad concludes with four stanzas of moralizing, pointing out that "Man's *mercies* from God's hands proceed, / His *miseries* from his *own.*" This doctrine of moral responsibility would focus, in one way or another, all of More's subsequent important work.

For the moment, however, she did not attempt "important work." Instead, she wrote *Ode to Dragon, Mr. Garrick's House-Dog, at Hampton* (1777), a fantasy of changing places with the dog. Although the poem has no serious pretensions, it reveals the author's anxiety about her talents:

Are those who cannot write, to blame
To draw their hopes of future fame,
From those who cannot read?

In the guise of a compliment to Garrick (how wonderful, she says, it would be to belong to his hospitable and happy household), she considers the problem of her proper role in the world.

Garrick, who had become a close friend, urged her to solve this problem by writing for the stage. Although she felt doubts about the morality of theatrical entertainment, she wrote one spectacularly successful secular drama, *Percy, a Tragedy* (1778) and a less widely acclaimed work, *The Fatal Falsehood* (1779). Both organize themselves around melodramatic plots of love, with emphasis on the sufferings and the virtue of good women. In *Percy* (a play much admired by the

Percy family) the virtuous heroine, in love with the gallant young Percy and pledged to marry him, is forced by her father to marry instead Percy's archrival, Douglas. Despite Elwina's absolute fidelity to a husband she cannot love, Douglas's jealousy eventuates in Percy's death, his wife's, and his own. A sense of what Mary Wollstonecraft would call "the wrongs of woman" infuses and invigorates the drama, although its blank verse often verges on the mechanical.

Shortly after Garrick's death in 1779 More retreated from London society and decided to employ her talents only in the service of her religion—that of the Church of England, but with a highly Evangelical flavor. (Most people considered her a Methodist.) When *Percy* was revived on the stage in 1784, she refused to attend: she had given up the theater. Her *Sacred Dramas* (1782)—intended, she said, to be read by the young and not for stage presentation—versified and dramatized the Old Testament stories of Moses in the bulrushes, David and Goliath, Belshazzar, and Daniel. As poetry and as narrative, they hold considerable interest. The story of Moses, for instance, concentrates on the psychological situation of a mother who accepts the misery of uncertainty, abandoning her child to avoid his certain death by the pharaoh's decree. Her anguish at her infant's unknown fate generates the work's emotional force. "I rather aspired after moral instruction than the purity of dramatic composition," More wrote in the "Advertisement" to the dramas. Her introduction calls attention to the moral problem of fictionality: "Shall fiction only raise poetic flame, / And shall no altars blaze, O Truth, to thee?" Yet much of the plays' interest depends on her fictionizing imagination, which uses biblical narratives as starting points for psychological elaboration. "A mother's sorrows cannot be conceived / But by a mother," Moses' mother cries, adding poignantly, "Would I were not one!" David's conflict between filial piety and yearning for military achievement finds vivid realization in the drama about the shepherd youth and the Philistine giant, which centers on the inner forces impelling the young man's participation in the conflict. More writes at her best in these unpretentious works, producing fluent blank verse (on occasion obviously Miltonic in origin) in which she evokes situations of high emotional tension.

"Sensibility, a Poem," published in the same volume as *Sacred Dramas,* offers a straightforward statement of conviction that places More squarely in central literary and moral traditions of her time. The poem praises those able "The rule of holy sympathy to keep, / Joy for the joyful, tears for them that weep," going on to insist that "To these the virtuous half their pleasures owe." In praising the capacity to feel for others and to act benevolently on the basis of such feeling, More allies herself with such philosophers as Anthony Ashley Cooper, third Earl of Shaftesbury, and Adam Smith and with the novelistic line most familiar to modern readers in Laurence Sterne's highly self-conscious fictions, which exploit sentiment despite their prevailing tone of mockery. The poem praises sensibility both for the ethical achievement it facilitates and for the pleasure it gives: "Sweet Sensibility! thou keen delight! / Unprompted moral! sudden sense of right!" It distinguishes between sentimentality as fashionable pose and the capacity for profound feeling that characterizes those possessed of genuine sensibility. Maintaining that divine love constitutes the source for such capacity, More argues that human feeling can either foster virtue or intensify vice. She thus articulates in more theoretical terms the implications of the biblical dramas, with their stress on the emotional conflicts that underlie and generate significant action. To twentieth-century readers, such a theoretical statement may seem less persuasive than the embodiment of ideas in dramatic form. More's contemporaries, however, found "Sensibility" both moving and provocative, hailing it as an important contribution to the cause of virtue.

During the period in the early 1780s when More apparently thought of herself mainly as a poet, she met and befriended a poor Bristol milkmaid, Ann Yearsley, whom she considered a poetic genius. For more than a year she occupied herself in editing Yearsley's poems, which were published in 1785, and raising money on her behalf. The project, however, ended in disaster when Yearsley decided that More envied her talents and was trying to steal her money. The approximately £350 More obtained had been put in trust for Yearsley's benefit. Yearsley wished to have the capital at her own disposal; More and Montagu, the other trustee, thought she would use it for immoral purposes (probably for drink). Eventually they turned the money over to a Bristol merchant, who apparently passed it on to the "milkmaid poet." More found the experience profoundly disillusioning.

Nonetheless, she continued her own poetic career. With "Florio" and "The Bas Bleu," pub-

Barley Wood, the house near Bristol where More lived from 1804 until 1828 (from a watercolor by Captain John Johnson; British Museum)

lished together in 1786, she returned to secular subjects. Both long poems, written in the tetrameter couplets usually reserved for light verse and employing frequent feminine rhymes, also associated with the comic, reveal serious feeling only faintly disguised by the humorous tone. Both also hold autobiographical interest.

"Florio" tells the story of a fashionable young man destined by his dead father to marry a country girl, the daughter of the father's good friend. Although Celia proves to be beautiful, virtuous, pious, intelligent, and affectionate, Florio is horrified by the monotony of rural existence and rural food (he has a passionate interest in the pleasures of the table). He flees as quickly as possible to the metropolis, where the worldly Flavia flirts with him, enticing him with Parisian cooking. Florio, however, finds his emotions strangely occupied by Celia, to whom he eventually returns. The contrast between Celia and Flavia is constructed as one between nature and artifice; the choice of nature, in the poem's logic, guarantees lasting happiness. On the same day that Celia and Florio marry, to live happily ever after, Flavia is divorced by her husband.

It is not hard to see in this slight fable allusions to a prolonged conflict in More's life. She enjoyed the company of London literary circles (the subject of praise in "The Bas Bleu") and aristocrats but felt drawn also to a life of rural retirement in which, she thought, she might examine her conscience and improve her character. Increasingly devout, she worried ever more about her moral obligations. For part of every year she retreated to the country, only to find, she reports in her letters, that time slipped away, interruptions accumulated, and her efforts at self-improvement always felt inadequate. Nonetheless, she gradually separated herself more and more from London and the ordinary forms of social exchange. "Florio," for all its apparent frivolity, discovers a form for expressing this crucial conflict of value.

"The Bas Bleu; or, Conversation" engages more directly the issues of its author's immediate life. Its title refers to the designation ("Bluestockings") of a distinguished group of learned women who had become important in the London social scene. Its subtitle more accurately evokes the poem, which is dedicated to the well-known Bluestocking Elizabeth Vesey and in which More considers seriously the nature and the value of good conversation as a social and as a moral force. Poetically uneven, the work strains in its classical allusions—particularly at the beginning, where the poet seems self-conscious. But as

More warms to her theme she displays both wit and passion. Here, as in "Florio," the contrast between nature and artifice organizes a substantial section of the poem, as More opposes the falsities of aristocratic society and the artificialities of French drawing rooms to the authentic human exchange that takes place among the Bluestockings. She praises Vesey as a hostess skilled both in "geometry" (the arrangement of people in small groups that facilitate conversation) and in "chemistry" (the mixture of disparate sorts of people). Both gifts, More argues, truly matter: to enable men and women to talk seriously and revealingly to one another is an important achievement. In a striking metaphor, the poem characterizes conversation as "That noblest commerce of mankind, / Whose precious merchandise is Mind!"

The freedom to use the mind openly would, of course, have seemed particularly meaningful to a woman, as women were traditionally relegated to decorative and trivial functions in the social world. Earlier in "The Bas Bleu" More praises ladies who prove as skilled as Martial in forming epigrams, adding that they "Yet in all female worth succeed / As well as those who cannot read." The point is crucial for someone who, like More, aspires to the most orthodox forms of female virtues yet takes pleasure in the life of the intellect. The poem suggests that neither kind of achievement need be sacrificed in a woman's life.

But it became increasingly rare for More to deal directly with the situation of women in her poetry. Writing to Horace Walpole in 1793, she complained: "I have been much pestered to read [Wollstonecraft's] Rights of Women, but am invincibly resolved not to do it. . . . there is something fantastic and absurd in the very title. How many ways there are of being ridiculous! I am sure I have as much liberty as I can make a good use of, now I am an old maid, and when I was a young one, I had, I dare say, more than was good for me. . . . there is perhaps no animal so much indebted to subordination for its behaviour, as woman." Less and less did she make claims for female liberty or complain about the situation of women; indeed, she typically advocated willing compliance with the severest forms of social restriction. Like Dr. Johnson a firm believer in the social and moral value of subordination, she accepted her condition as a socially inferior being.

In the same letter to Walpole, as part of the same discussion of woman's rights, More expresses her belief that women are fond of government specifically because they are unfit for it. By the time she wrote these words, she had done a good deal of "governing" herself. After her sisters retired from their school in 1789 they divided their time between their house in Bath and More's rural retreat at Cowslip Green, near Bristol. Together with the reformer William Wilberforce, More and her sisters visited Cheddar and were shocked by the ignorance, poverty, and reprehensible behavior of the villagers. As a direct consequence of this visit, More and her sisters established a series of Sunday schools (the first one was set up in Cheddar) and gradually reorganized the habits of many hundreds of men, women, and children. The schools taught people to read, introduced them to the Bible, promulgated precepts of conduct, and rewarded good behavior with gifts of respectable clothing and with eagerly anticipated annual feasts. It was characteristic of More that she never acknowledged that organizing and supervising the schools amounted to a considerable administrative achievement.

Slavery (1788), a poem that attracted considerable popular attention, resulted from More's association with Wilberforce: it also reveals the strong poetic influence of William Cowper, who wrote on similar subjects in a similar mode. A fierce denunciation of the trade in human beings, it ardently claims the universality of soul and of emotion. "Does then the immortal principle within / Change with the casual color of a skin?" To accept such a hypothesis would imply the supremacy of matter over spirit, an intolerable belief for a Christian society. The poem develops rhetorical force as it pursues its argument with both rational and emotional logic. It specifies the sufferings of African slaves, appeals to the philanthropy and the "sensibility" of the English, calls attention to the traditional British allegiance to the idea of liberty, and insists steadily on the incompatibility between the principles of slavery and all other principles of civilized life.

In its overt and relentless moral purpose, *Slavery* marks a point of change in More's life. For the next several years she wrote mainly didactic prose, dedicated to improving standards of conduct at all social levels. Her poetry, too, became purely didactic. Between 1794 and 1797 she composed fifty pamphlets for the cheap Repository Series, intended for a working-class audience: they include ballads of moralistic intent, inveighing against sexual indulgence, evil company, and drink. Her *A Hymn of Praise for the Abundant Har-*

Silhouette of More by Edouart, 1827 (National Portrait Gallery, London)

vest of 1796 (1796) suggests that the famine preceding the lavish harvest signaled God's disapproval:

He mark'd our angry spirits rise,
  Domestic hate increase;
And for a time withheld supplies,
  To teach us love and peace.

The advent of plenty in the land, the poem argues, should "Rekindle peace and love."

More's own existence became increasingly disciplined, and she made no secret of her views: for instance, she refused to accept any engagements on Sunday, and she denounced the growing practice of involving children in social events comparable to those of their elders. In a 1792 letter to Wilberforce she reported on "a true story recently transacted in London. A lady gave a very great children's ball: at the upper end of the room, in an elevated place, was dressed out a figure to represent *me,* with a large rod in my hand prepared to punish such naughty doings." More makes no comment on this anecdote. The image of herself as severe governor, perhaps, could not really penetrate the consciousness of someone committed to the view that women have no gift for government.

Despite her popularity, More suffered some opprobrium for her activities. The so-called Blagdon Controversy of 1800 to 1803 epitomized the difficulties she faced. Originating in a quarrel between the curate of Blagdon and the schoolmaster of More's Sunday school there, the controversy developed into a pamphlet war and involved the important London journals. The conflict was centered on two main issues: More's putative "Methodism" (a designation of no fixed meaning at the period but one implying deviation from the doctrine of the Church of England) and the belief on the part of conservative thinkers that educating the poor would lead to insubordination. More steadfastly refused to reply to her critics, although she did remove the schoolmaster. The furor eventually died away.

In 1804 More's sisters came to live with her in Barley Wood, a house near Cowslip Green where she had lived since 1802. More suffered increasingly from ill health, which had plagued her all her life. Nonetheless, she outlived her four sisters, continuing to write when her ailments allowed her to. In 1821, after all her sisters had died, she had her charming versifications of books of the Bible published for the benefit of children. Delightful in the speed, economy, and energy with which they summarize complicated narratives, they provide memorable accounts of biblical events. The first ten lines of "The Pentateuch" tell of the Creation, the Fall of Man, Cain's slaying of Abel, the Flood, and the destruction of Sodom and Gomorrah. The couplet "You ask, perhaps, 'Who slew all these?' / 'T was sin, the original disease!" typifies the confident tone and direct diction of the whole. In a preface More confesses to having had more difficulty with the New Testament than the Old, partly because it consists more of doctrine and less of narrative. But she manages with extraordinary dexterity the difficult task of narrating, for instance, the Crucifixion of Christ: "Things contrary, opposing creatures / Struck at the sight, forget their natures." The directness and authenticity of her faith emerge nowhere more compellingly.

More died on 7 September 1833, apparently of old age, in Clifton, where she had moved in 1828. Her enormous professional and personal popularity continued until the end; to the last days of her life, she remained surrounded by friends.

Letters:

Letters of Hannah More to Zachary Macaulay Esq., Containing Notices of Lord Macaulay's Youth, edited by Arthur Roberts (London: Nisbet, 1860);

Letters of Hannah More, edited by R. Brimley Johnson (London: Lane, 1925);

Charles H. Bennett, "The Text of Horace Walpole's Correspondence with Hannah More," *Review of English Studies,* new series 3 (October 1952): 341-345.

Bibliographies:

Emanuel Green, *Bibliotheca Somersetensis,* 3 volumes (Taunton: Barnicott & Pearce, 1902);

G. H. Spinney, "Cheap Repository Tracts: Hazard and Marshall Edition," *Library,* fourth series 20 (December 1939): 295-340;

Harry B. Weiss, "Hannah More's Cheap Repository Tracts in America," *Bulletin of the New York Public Library,* 50 (July 1946): 539-549; 50 (August 1946): 634-641.

Biographies:

William Shaw, *The Life of Hannah More, with a Critical Review of Her Writings* (London: Hurst, 1802);

William Roberts, *Memoirs of the Life and Correspondence of Mrs. Hannah More,* 4 volumes (London: Seeley & Burnside, 1834);

Henry Thompson, *Life of Hannah More, with Notices of Her Sisters* (London: Cadell, 1838);

Martha More, *Mendip Annals; or, A Narrative of the Charitable Labours of Hannah More and Martha More: Being the Journal of Martha More,* edited by Arthur Roberts (London: J. Nisbet, 1859);

Helen C. Knight, *Hannah More; or, Life in Hall and Cottage* (New York: American Tract Society, 1862);

Charlotte Mary Yonge, *Hannah More* (Boston: Roberts, 1888);

Mary Virginia Hawes Terhune [Marion Harland], *Hannah More* (New York & London: Putnam's, 1900);

Annette M. B. Meakin, *Hannah More, a Biographical Study* (London: Smith, Elder, 1911);

George Lacey May, *Some Eighteenth Century Churchmen: Glimpses of English Church Life in the Eighteenth Century* (London: Society for Promoting Christian Knowledge / New York: Macmillan, 1920);

Margaret Emma Tabor, *Pioneer Women,* second series (London: Sheldon Press / New York & Toronto: Macmillan, 1927);

Mary Alden Hopkins, *Hannah More and Her Circle* (New York & Toronto: Longmans, Green, 1947);

M. G. Jones, *Hannah More* (Cambridge: Cambridge University Press, 1952; New York: Greenwood Press, 1968).

References:

Betsy Aikin-Sneath, "Hannah More (1745-1833)," *London Mercury,* 28 (October 1933): 528-535;

Alfred Owen Aldridge, "Madame de Staël and Hannah More on Society," *Romantic Review,* 38 (December 1947): 330-339;

Thomas Bere, *The Controversy between Mrs. Hannah More, and the Curate of Blagdon* (London: W. Hughes for J. S. Jordan, 1801);

Ford K. Brown, *Fathers of the Victorians: The Age of Wilberforce* (Cambridge: Cambridge University Press, 1961);

Philip Child, "Portrait of a Woman of Affairs—Old Style," *University of Toronto Quarterly,* 3 (October 1933): 87-102;

Luther Weeks Courtney, *Hannah More's Interest in Education and Government* (Waco, Tex.: Baylor University Press, 1929);

Robin Reed Davis, "Anglican Evangelicalism and the Feminine Literary Tradition: From Hannah More to Charlotte Brontë," Ph.D. dissertation, Duke University, 1982;

E. M. Forster, "Mrs. Hannah More," *Nation* (London), 2 (January 1926): 493-494; republished in his *Abinger Harvest* (New York: Harcourt, Brace, 1936), pp. 241-248;

Gary Kelly, "Revolution, Reaction, and the Expropriation of Popular Culture: Hannah More's *Cheap Repository*." in *Man and Nature / l'Homme et la nature,* Proceedings of the Canadian Society for Eighteenth-Century Studies, edited by Kenneth W. Graham and Neal Johnson (Edmonton: Academic Printing & Publishing, 1987), pp. 147-159;

E. V. Knox, "Percy (The Tale of a Dramatic Success)," *London Mercury,* 13 (March 1926): 509-515;

Beth Kowaleski-Wallace, "Milton's Daughters: The Education of Eighteenth-Century Women Writers," *Feminist Studies,* 12 (Summer 1986): 275-293;

Eloise Lownsberry, "Hannah More," in her *Saints & Rebels* (New York & Toronto: Longmans, Green, 1937), pp. 171-206;

M. C. Malim, "Hannah More," *Contemporary Review,* 144 (September 1933): 329-336;

Mitzi Myers, "Hannah More's Tracts for the Times: Social Fiction and Female Ideology," in *Fetter'd or Free? British Women Novelists, 1670-1815,* edited by Mary Anne Schofield and Cecilia Macheski (Athens & London: Ohio University Press, 1986), pp. 264-284;

Myers, "Reform or Ruin: 'A Revolution in Female Manners,' " *Studies in Eighteenth-Century Culture,* 11 (1982): 199-216;

Susan Pedersen, "Hannah More Meets Simple Simon: Tracts, Chapbooks, and Popular Culture in late Eighteenth-Century England," *Journal of British Studies,* 25 (January 1986): 84-113;

Paule Penigault-Duhet, "Les femmes et l'église en France et en Angleterre à la fin du 18eme siecle; Actes du colloque tenu à Paris, les 24 et 25 octobre 1975," in *La femme en Angleterre et dans les colonies américaines aux XVIIe et XVIIIe siècles,* Pub. de l'Universite de Lille III (Lille, 1976), pp. 129-138;

Sam Pickering, "*The Cheap Repository Tracts* and the Short Story," *Studies in Short Fiction,* 12 (Winter 1975): 15-21;

E. W. Pitcher, Letter to *William and Mary Quarterly: A Magazine of Early American History and Culture,* 43 (April 1986): 327;

James Pitt, "Hannah More and the Blagdon Controversy," *Notes and Queries,* third series 8 (26 August 1865): 168-169;

C. L. Shaver, "The Publication of Hannah More's First Play," *Modern Language Notes,* 62 (May 1947): 343.

Papers:

Unpublished letters by Hannah More are at the Folger Shakespeare Library, the Henry E. Huntington Library, the University of Rochester, the Historical Society of Pennsylvania, the Massachusetts Historical Society, Harvard University, Yale University, the Pierpont Morgan Library, the New York Public Library, the John Rylands Library, the Bodleian Library, and the British Library.

Christopher Smart

(11 April 1722 - 20 May 1771)

Karina Williamson
St. Hilda's College, Oxford, and University of Edinburgh

BOOKS: *On the Eternity of the Supreme Being: A Poetical Essay* (Cambridge: Printed by J. Bentham; sold by W. Thurlbourn in Cambridge; C. Bathurst, R. Dodsley, London; and J. Hildyard at York, 1750);

The Horatian Canons of Friendship: Being the Third Satire of the First Book of Horace Imitated, as Ebenezer Pentweazle (London: Printed for the author and sold by J. Newbery, 1750);

An Occasional Prologue and Epilogue to Othello, As it was acted at the Theatre-Royal in Drury-Lane, on Thursday the 7th of March 1751, by Persons of Distinction for their Diversion (London: Printed for the author and sold by Thomas Carnan, at Mr. Newbery's, 1751);

A Solemn Dirge, Sacred to the Memory of His Royal Highness Frederic Prince of Wales, As it was Sung by Mr. Lowe, Miss Burchell, and others, at Vaux-hall. Written by Mr. Smart. The Music compos'd by Mr. Worgan, M.B. (London: Printed for T. Carnan, at Mr. Newbery's, 1751);

On the Immensity of the Supreme Being: A Poetical Essay (Cambridge: Printed by J. Bentham; sold by W. Thurlbourn in Cambridge; C. Bathurst, J. Newbery, London; and J. Hildyard at York, 1751);

Poems on Several Occasions (London: Printed for the author by W. Strahan; and sold by J. Newbery, 1752);

On the Omniscience of the Supreme Being: A Poetical Essay (Cambridge: Printed by J. Bentham; sold by W. Thurlbourn in Cambridge; C. Bathurst, J. Newbery, R. Dodsley, London; and J. Hildyard at York, 1752);

The Hilliad: An Epic Poem (London: Sold by J. Newbery and M. Cooper, 1753);

On the Power of the Supreme Being: A Poetical Essay (Cambridge: Printed by J. Bentham; sold by W. Thurlbourn in Cambridge; C. Bathurst, J. Newbery, London; and J. Hildyard at York, 1754);

On the Goodness of the Supreme Being: A Poetical Essay (Cambridge: Printed by J. Bentham; sold by W. Thurlbourn and T. Merrill in Cambridge; J. Newbery and T. Gardner, London, 1756);

Hymn to the Supreme Being, on Recovery from a dangerous Fit of Illness (London: Printed for J. Newbery, 1756);

A Song to David (London: Printed for the author and sold by Mr. Fletcher, and by all the booksellers in town and country, 1763);

Poems by Mr. Smart. Viz. Reason and Imagination a Fable. Ode to Admiral Sir George Pocock. Ode to General Draper. An Epistle to John Sherratt, Esq. (London: Printed for the author and sold by Mr. Fletcher and Co.; and Mr. Laurence, 1763);

Poems On several Occasions. Viz. Munificence and Modesty. Female Dignity. To Lady Hussey Delaval. Verses from Catullus, after Dining with Mr. Murray. Epitaphs. On the Dutchess of Cleveland. On Henry Fielding, Esq. On the Rev. James Sheeles. Epitaph from Demosthenes (London: Printed for the author and sold by Mr. Fletcher and Co.; Mr. Davies; Mr. Flexney; Mr. Laurence; and Mr. Almon, 1763);

Proposals for Printing, by Subscription, a New Translation of the Psalms of David: To Which Will Be Added, a Set of Hymns (London, 1763);

Hannah. An Oratorio. Written by Mr. Smart. The Musick composed by Mr. Worgan. As Perform'd at the King's Theatre in the Hay-Market (London: Printed for J. and R. Tonson, 1764);

Ode to the Right Honourable the Earl of Northumberland, on his being appointed Lord Lieutenant of Ireland. Presented on the Birth-Day of Lord Warkworth. With some other Pieces (London: Printed for R. and J. Dodsley and sold by J. Wilkie, 1764);

Abimelech, an Oratorio. As It Is Performed at the Theatre Royal in the Hay-Market (London: Sold at the Theatre only, 1768);

The Parables of Our Lord and Saviour Jesus Christ: Done into Familiar Verse, with Occasional Applications, for the Use and Improvement of Younger

Christopher Smart (artist unknown; Pembroke College, Cambridge)

Minds (London: Printed for W. Owen, 1768);

Hymns, for the Amusement of Children (London: Printed for T. Carnan, 1771).

Editions and Collections:

The Poems, of the Late Christopher Smart, M.A., Fellow of Pembroke College, Cambridge. Consisting of His Prize Poems, Odes, Sonnets, and Fables, Latin and English Translations; Together with Many Original Compositions, Not included in the Quarto Edition. To Which Is Prefixed, An Account of his Life and Writings, Never before published, 2 volumes (Reading: Printed and sold by Smart and Cowslade; and sold by F. Power and Co., London, 1791);

A Song to David with other Poems, edited by Edmund Blunden (London: Cobden-Sanderson, 1924);

Rejoice in the Lamb, edited by William Force Stead (London: Cape, 1939; New York: Holt, 1939); reedited from the original manuscript by W. H. Bond as *Jubilate Agno* (Cambridge, Mass.: Harvard University Press, 1954; London: Hart-Davis, 1954);

The Collected Poems of Christopher Smart, 2 volumes, edited, with an introduction and critical comments, by Norman Callan (London: Routledge & Kegan Paul, 1949);

Poems by Christopher Smart, edited, with an introduction and notes, by Robert Brittain (Princeton: Princeton University Press, 1950);

Christopher Smart: Selected Poems, edited by Marcus Walsh (Manchester, U.K.: Carcanet Press, 1979);

The Poetical Works of Christopher Smart, 5 volumes projected, 4 volumes to date, edited, with introductions and commentaries, by Walsh and Karina Williamson (Oxford: Clarendon Press, 1980-).

OTHER: *Carmen Cl. Alexandri Pope in S. Caeciliam Latine redditum*, translated by Smart (Cambridge: Printed for the author by J. Bentham, 1743); enlarged as *Carmen Cl. Alexandri Pope in S. Caeciliam Latine redditum: Editio Altera. To Which Is Added Ode for Musick on Saint Cecilia's Day* (Cambridge: Printed by J. Bentham and sold by R. Dodsley, London, 1746);

"To Miss A—n," in *Lyra Britannica: Book I. Being a Collection of Songs, Duets, and Cantatas, on Various Subjects. Compos'd by Mr. Boyce* (London: Printed for and sold by J. Walsh, 1747), pp. 18-21;

The Student; or, The Oxford and Cambridge Monthly Miscellany, edited by Smart and Bonnell Thornton, 1-2 (June 1750 - July 1751);

The Midwife; or, The Old Woman's Magazine, edited by Smart as Mary Midnight, 1-3 (October 1750 - June 1753); published in book form, 3 volumes (volume 1, London: Printed for Mary Midnight and sold by T. Carnan, 1751; volumes 2-3, London: Printed for Thomas Carnan, at J. Newbery's, 1751-1753);

An Index to Mankind; or, Maxims Selected from the Wits of All Nations, for the Benefit of the Present Age, and of Posterity; by Mrs. Mary Midnight, Author of The Midwife, or Old Woman's Magazine. Intermix'd with Some Curious Reflections by That Lady, and a Preface by Her Good Friend, the Late Mr. Pope, editorship attributed to Smart (London: Printed for T. Carnan, at Mr. Newbery's, 1751);

The Nut-cracker: Containing an Agreeable Variety of Well-Season'd Jests, Epigrams, Epitaphs, &c. Collected from the Most Sprightly Wits of the Present Age. . . . by Ferdinando Foot, Esq., 2 volumes, editorship attributed to Smart (London: Printed for J. Newbery, B. Collins in Salisbury; and sold by the booksellers in Great Britain and Ireland, 1751);

The Works of Horace, Translated Literally into English Prose; For the Use of those who are desirous of acquiring or recovering a competent Knowledge of the Latin Language, 2 volumes, translated by Smart (London: Printed for J. Newbery, 1756);

The Nonpareil; or, The Quintessence of Wit and Humour: Being a Choice Selection of Those Pieces That Were Most Admired in the Ever-to-Be Remember'd Midwife; or, Old Woman's Magazine. . . . To Which Is Added An Index to Mankind, editorship attributed to Smart as Mary Midnight (London: Printed for T. Carnan, 1757);

A Poetical Translation of the Fables of Phaedrus, with the Appendix of Gudius, And an accurate Edition of the Original on the opposite Page. To which is added, A Parsing Index for the Use of Learners, translated and edited by Smart (London: Printed for J. Dodsley and sold by J. Wilkie, and T. Merrill at Cambridge, 1765);

A Translation of the Psalms of David, Attempted in the Spirit of Christianity, and Adapted to the Divine Service, translated by Smart (London: Printed by Dryden Leach, for the author; and sold by C. Bathurst and W. Flexney, and T. Merril [*sic*] at Cambridge, 1765)—includes Smart's "Gloria Patri," "Hymns and Spiritual Songs for the Fasts and Festivals of the Church of England," and "A Song to David";

The Works of Horace, Translated into Verse: With a Prose Interpretation, for the Help of Students. And Occasional Notes, 4 volumes, translated and edited by Smart (London: Printed for W. Flexney, Mess. Johnson and Co., and T. Caslon, 1767); translation of odes republished as *Christopher Smart's Verse Translation of Horace's Odes: Text and Introduction*, edited by Arthur Sherbo (Victoria, B.C.: University of Victoria, 1979).

It is notable that beginning with Robert Browning, it has been poets rather than critics who have been the warmest and most perceptive admirers of the poetry of Christopher Smart. In a 1975 radio broadcast in Australia, Peter Porter spoke of Smart as "the purest case of man's vision prevailing over the spirit of his times." While it would be facile and unilluminating to characterize Smart as a proto-Romantic, there can be no doubt that the combination of visionary power, Christian ardor, and lyrical virtuosity in his finest poetry was unappreciated and unmatched in his own age.

Smart was born on 11 April 1722 at Shipbourne in Kent, the youngest of three children of Peter and Winifred Griffiths Smart. He was proud of having Welsh ancestry through his mother, who belonged to a family from Radnorshire; his boast in *Jubilate Agno* (first published in 1939 as *Rejoice in the Lamb*), "For I am of the seed of the WELCH WOMAN and speak the truth from my heart," is one of several references to his Welsh descent. Peter Smart had moved to Kent from Durham to take over the stewardship of Fairlawn, an estate belonging to the Vane family, whose principal seat was Raby Castle in Durham. Peter Smart himself belonged in a modest way to the landowning gentry, but "having been originally intended for Holy Orders, had a better taste for literature than is commonly found in country gentlemen" (so writes Christopher Hunter, Christopher Smart's nephew, whose 1791 account of Smart's life is the primary source of biographical information). If, as seems likely, this Peter Smart was the same one whose signature appears on the translation of an important Rosicrucian document dated 1714, Christopher Smart's interest in the supernatural and occult may have begun early. His earlier forebears included another Peter Smart—a prominent Puritan divine, prebendary of Durham Cathedral in the reign of Charles I, and one-time headmaster of Durham School who was jailed for ten years for publishing a fierce antiprelatical sermon in 1628. Another ancestor through his father was the sixteenth-century preacher Bernard Gilpin, the "Apostle of the North," renowned on the opposite side for his steadfast adherence to Catholic principles. Christopher Smart's religious preoccupations thus had mixed origins in his family history.

The Medway valley where he spent his earliest years became Smart's Arcadia; references in his poetry to the Kentish countryside around Shipbourne are always suffused with nostalgia. "For I bless God in SHIPBOURNE FAIRLAWN the meadows the brooks and the hills," he wrote in *Jubilate Agno*, twenty-five years after leaving them. This phase of his life came to an abrupt end in 1733 with the death of his father. Left in straitened circumstances, Winifred Smart returned with the children to Durham, where the eleven-year-old Christopher was taken under the wing of Lord Barnard (Henry Vane) and his family at Raby Castle and sent to Durham School. This period, too, however, he remembered as a happy one, in which he had the run of Raby's "blissful bowers" and his poetic gifts were fostered by noble patrons, as he recorded in "To the Rt. the Hon. Lord Barnard on His accession to that Title" (published in the *Gentleman's Magazine*, December 1754). According to a story related by Smart's daughter, Elizabeth Le Noir, in a letter to E. H. Barker (circa 1825), and corroborated by allusions in *Jubilate Agno*, he had a youthful love affair with the daughter of Lord Barnard, Anne Vane; she is said to have been the subject of an amorous poem that Smart claimed to have written at the age of thirteen: "To Ethelinda, on her doing my verses the honour of wearing them in her bosom" (first published in *Poems on Several Occasions* [1752]). Le Noir relates that "this very spirited ode had taken such effect that these young lovers had actually set off on a runaway match together; they were however timely prevented and saved." Whatever the truth of this colorful story, Smart never forgot Anne Vane, who is recalled by name or other reference with loving frequency in *Jubilate Agno*.

After distinguishing himself in his classical studies at school Smart went up to Pembroke Hall, Cambridge, at the age of seventeen, with the help of an annual allowance from Anne Vane's aunt, the duchess of Cleveland (Henrietta Fitzroy). As an undergraduate he earned acclaim both for his classical learning and for his abilities as a poet, which were considerable enough to win for him for three years in succession the honor of composing the Latin verses to accompany the tripos lists. In 1742 he was awarded the coveted Craven scholarship. He graduated the following year, celebrating the occasion with an ode, "On Taking a Bachelor's Degree" (published in the *Student*, 16 September 1750). Two years later he was elected to a fellowship at Pembroke.

All was set, it might have seemed, for the comfort, security, and modest distinction of an academic career, but Smart's desires and ambitions were pulling him in other directions. Already he had sought the attention of Alexander Pope by sending him *Carmen Cl. Alexandri Pope in S. Caeciliam Latine redditum* (1743), a Latin version of Pope's *Ode for Musick* (1713), to which Pope responded with a typically courteous and encouraging letter. By 1744 he had begun to frequent London; soon he was spending more time in town than in college, competing for recognition as a poet, enjoying the pleasures of the city, and running up tailor's bills. At Cambridge he showed little inclination to settle down to the tranquil seclusion of college life. His ode "On an Eagle confined in a College-Court," written sometime between 1744 and 1746 and published in the *Student* for 20 June 1751, is an eloquent expression of his discontent: though ostensibly concerned with the oppressive domination of mathematics and pedantic scholarship at the expense of humane letters, the poem clearly voices a more personal sense of frustration. Like the caged eagle, "Thou type of wit and sense confin'd," the poet cramped in his "servile cell" can find no outlet for his "daring fire."

Nevertheless, it was during this period that Smart's first original publication appeared: to the second edition of his Latin version of Pope's ode was added his own "Ode for Musick on St. Cecilia's Day." This poem was Smart's first major essay in the "sublime" mode. The interest of the work, however, lies more in its intentions than in its achievement. Smart asserts in a preface that his models, the Pindaric odes of John Dryden (1687) and Pope on the same subject, were, paradoxically, blemished by their beauty: in achieving "exact unity of design" they forfeited some of the "enthusiastic fire and wildness" of Pindar, which derives from the "vehemence of sudden and unlook'd for transitions." Smart's own ode is determinedly vehement and abrupt, but he does not succeed (as he was to do later in *A Song to David* [1763]) in substituting any other structural principle for logical or narrative coordination.

Smart at this time was breaking out in other, more material ways: drinking and entertaining prodigally, running up colossal debts from which only the hasty intervention of friends and colleagues rescued him, and producing and acting in a farce of his own composition, *The Grateful Fair; or, A Trip to Cambridge*. Thomas Gray, then at Peterhouse, gives an amusing account of this venture in a letter to William Mason written in March 1747, commenting with grim prescience that Smart's drunkenness, extravagance, and wild behavior would inevitably lead him to jail or to Bedlam. While he was a Cambridge fellow Smart had his second love affair, pursuing, as Hunter records, "a long and unsuccessful passion" for Harriote Pratt, sister of undergraduate friends of Smart and daughter of a Norfolk landowner. Smart visited her in Norfolk and listened to her playing on the spinet and organ, as he told Charles Burney in a letter of 29 July 1749. He addressed several poems to her and remembered her kindly in *Jubilate Agno*, but the affair may have been more literary than passionate; these poems lack the overheated sensuality of poems such as "To Ethelinda" and "To Miss A—n" (published in the collection *Lyra Britannica* [1747]).

Smart's career at Cambridge effectively ended in 1749 when he was granted a leave of absence from college and moved to London, though he retained his fellowship until his marriage. By 1751 "Harriote" had been replaced by "Nancy," Anna Maria Carnan, stepdaughter of the publisher John Newbery. According to Robert Surtees's history of Durham (1840), Smart came to know her when the Newberys were living at Canonbury House, Islington, where he was "a constant visitor." Intimacy soon "ripened into affection," and a "clandestine marriage" followed, "without the consent of Mr. Newbery, whose favour however was soon conciliated, and Smart was immediately established at Canonbury House, where he pursued his literary labours for several years." Documentation is lacking, but Anna Maria told her daughters that the marriage took place in 1752 at St. Bride's in Fleet Street. The reason for the secrecy of the marriage and for Newbery's disapproval was probably the precariousness of Smart's prospects: as a married man he could not retain his fellowship at Pembroke, and Newbery must have known about his improvident habits. Moreover, Anna Maria, like her mother, was a Roman Catholic, and Newbery would have been aware of the difficulties besetting a mixed alliance. Initially, however, the marriage seems to have been happy. Smart's poem "On my Wife's Birth Day" (published in the *Gentleman's Magazine*, February 1754) strikes a note of unaffected ardor, and in *Jubilate Agno* he remembered his life at Canonbury House with gratitude: "I bless God for my retreat at CANBURY, as it was the place of the nativity of my children." His daughters, Marianne and Elizabeth, were born there in 1753 and 1754, respectively.

After leaving Cambridge, Smart attempted to earn his living by writing. In practice this endeavor meant becoming a literary jack-of-all-trades: editing and supplying copy for magazines, including the *Student* (1750-1751), the *Midwife* (1750-1753), and other publishing ventures promoted by Newbery; translating Horace into prose for the use of students (1756); composing songs and other pieces for the theaters and pleasure gardens; and providing material for a series of popular entertainments, called "Mrs. Midnight's Oratory," sponsored by the tireless Newbery. These entertainments were something between a music-hall show and a circus, with songs, recitations, dances, performing animals, and other acts. Smart himself is said to have taken the part of "Mrs. Midnight" on some occasions. Although there is no evidence that he found this kind of activity uncongenial—indeed, he seems to have engaged in it with zest—he never lost sight of his serious ambitions as a poet in these busy years from 1749 to 1756.

Poems on Several Occasions represents his first major bid for public recognition. Published by subscription and handsomely printed, with full-page plates by Francis Hayman and Thomas Worlidge, the volume contained a careful selection of writings from the juvenile ode "To Ethelinda" onwards. The work of his Cambridge years was extensively quarried: more than a quarter of the space was occupied by his Latin version, written between 1743 and 1746, of Pope's *An Essay on Criticism* (1711) alone. Even at the time this translation must have seemed a sterile academic exercise: Hunter notes that it was received "with much praise from the learned, but without either profit or popularity." The collection was arranged by kind, beginning with a series of fifteen odes, followed by longer poems (Latin translations of Pope and John Milton; the three sets of tripos verses, with English translations by Smart's friend Francis Fawkes; and *The Hop-Garden*); a section titled "Ballads, Fables and other Miscellaneous Pieces," containing two epigrams, a prologue, and an epilogue; and finally a masque, *The Judgment of Midas*.

The shorter pieces, many of which had already appeared in print, show Smart to be an accomplished but not notably original performer in most of the popular modes of the day. The most ambitious work in the volume was *The Hop-Garden*, a georgic in two books running to well over seven hundred lines of Miltonic blank verse. The first part was written while Smart was an undergraduate and conscious of his status as apprentice poet. He explains in the opening paragraphs that he has chosen the georgic mode because of its lowliness in the hierarchy of genres, and its suitability therefore for the "infant bard," with the clear implication that Smart, the "young rustic," is cutting his teeth on country matters in preparation for "far nobler themes" in riper years. Like Smart's immediate model for an English georgic, John Philips's *Cyder* (1708), *The Hop-Garden* is written in the shadow of Virgil. Nevertheless, it is an "imitation" in the eighteenth-century creative sense: an attempt to anglicize a highly sophisticated form, with its own conventions of subject matter, organization, and diction. A conspicuous feature of the poem is its mixture of styles, ranging from polysyllabic Latinate coinages and Spenserian archaisms to blunt colloquialisms. As John Chalker points out, the interplay of styles enables Smart to express contrasting viewpoints; but his handling of this sophisticated weaponry is not altogether assured, and there is some justice in John Butt's comment that Smart's depreciation of the georgic as a genre represents a radical failure in sympathy for the Virgilian impulse. The poem attracted some modest attention in the eighteenth century. James Grainger referred flatteringly to Smart as an illustrious predecessor in his own georgic, *The Sugar Cane* (1764), and John Hill in the *Monthly Review* (August 1752) granted it "Many poetical strokes" and "whole pages that abound in beauty"; but Hill added that these were "only a few fine flowers, appearing here and there in an uncultivated field, over-run with nettles and briars." His main objection was to the choice of blank verse, which he called "a very unfortunate error," disregarding the precedent set by Philips's *Cyder*.

The reception of *Poems on Several Occasions* was lukewarm, in spite of a flattering prepublication notice in the *Westminster Journal* (10 August 1751) by Smart's friend Richard Rolt, in which parts of the volume were said to show "all the glowing fire . . . that can enrapture the Soul of Poetry, and enliven the Heart of the Reader." Hill cared even less for the Latin poems and translations than for *The Hop-Garden* and complained of many "glaring inaccuracies" in other poems; but he found some of the odes spirited and expressive and *The Judgment of Midas* "masterly" in execution and elegant in versification. An anonymous writer in *The General Review* (1752) grumbled about the inclusion of too many frivolous pieces from the *Student*, saying Smart would have earned more credit by reprinting his poems *On the Eternity of the Supreme Being* (1750) and *On the Immensity of the Supreme Being* (1751).

The reviewer's judgment was shrewd. These poems were the first and second of Smart's five Cambridge prize poems, published between 1750 and 1755, which later-eighteenth-century and early-nineteenth-century opinion rated the peak of his achievement; this assessment was reflected in the frequency with which they were quoted from and reprinted. They were written for the newly inaugurated Seatonian Prize, offered annually for the best poem by a Cambridge Master of Arts on "one or other of the perfections or attributes of the Supreme Being "; Smart won the prize every time he entered for it. Though outwardly conforming in theme and style to well-established eighteenth-century conventions for this kind of religious-didactic verse, Smart's Seatonian poems are important milestones in his development; they show him trying out a new conception of the role of the poet and groping toward a more powerful rhetoric. Blank verse is again his chosen medium, but it is employed this time with more assurance and flexibility: Miltonic elevation is now combined with discursive and argumentative fluency learned from Pope. The result is stylistically uneven, but the gaucheries are not the mere posturings of a minor versifier; they are signs of a new kind of imaginative energy uneasily harnessed to an older rhetoric. The structure of the poems is linear, consisting in a simple progression of ideas developed in successive paragraphs and often illustrated by lists of examples drawn from such natural objects as birds, trees, and rocks. As Robert Brittain observes, these catalogues anticipate some of the grandest effects Smart would achieve later in his religious poetry; they provide a foretaste of what Geoffrey Grigson calls Smart's "baroque vision" of nature in all its joyful plenitude, variety, and specificity.

Modern critics have been generally less enthusiastic than Smart's contemporaries about the Seatonian poems, but the importance of the poems as landmarks in his career has been widely recognized. As Christopher Devlin remarks, they show that he had "a natural bent for metaphysical religious verse long before he developed religious mania" and that he had "a remarkable gift for putting theological truths into vivid and sometimes beautiful language." Although Milton is Smart's most obvious literary father in these poems, a new and more significant source begins to emerge: David the Psalmist, who is invoked as "model, muse and pattern of the poet's career," in Allan J. Gedalof's succinct phrase. Smart opens the second Seatonian poem, *On the Immensity of the Supreme Being*, by appropriating David's words; in the fourth, *On the Power of the Supreme Being* (1754), he begins by boldly paraphrasing Psalm 114; and in the last poem of the series, *On the Goodness of the Supreme Being* (1756), he daringly equates David with Orpheus, whose power to enthrall nature by the magic of his song Smart had envied in some of his earlier poems. It was by means of this triple conflation, David-Orpheus-Smart, that emancipation from the constraints of contemporary poetics became possible. In the Seatonian poems Smart began to conceive a poetry of total self-expressiveness; that is to say, a poetry of worship, answering to what he saw as man's supreme function: to glorify God and voice the gratitude of the whole of creation to its maker.

Meanwhile, Smart continued throughout the early 1750s to pour out a stream of minor poems: songs, epigrams, epitaphs, fables, complimentary addresses, verse epistles, and one full-dress satire, *The Hilliad* (1753). This sprightly work, written more or less extempore, was intended to discredit Hill, Smart's enemy in the paper war between Henry Fielding and Hill in which Smart had become embroiled. The point of many of its sallies can now only be recovered with difficulty, but Smart's deft and vivacious handling of personal abuse can still be recognized. Among the shorter poems, the fables were the pieces most highly prized by Smart's contemporaries, and they still wear well, showing a lightness of touch and acuteness of social observation that made eighteenth-century critics put him in the same league as John Gay. Charles Burney in the *Monthly Review* (January 1792) rated him "the most agreeable metrical Fabulist in our language" after Gay, finding that although his versification was less polished and "his apologues in general perhaps less correct" than those of Gay and Edward Moore, nevertheless "in originality, in wit, in humour, the preference seems due to Smart."

In spite of having a wife and family to support, Smart continued as thriftless as ever in the 1750s, spending freely on clothes and entertainment and borrowing from Newbery when he got into difficulties. Hunter describes him as "friendly, affectionate, and liberal to excess," but so regardless of practicalities that according to his wife he often invited company to dinner when there was not enough in the house to provide a meal even for themselves. His prose translation of the works of Horace, undertaken for Newbery in 1755 and published in 1756, brought him a hundred pounds; but Newbery prudently held back all but thirteen pounds for the benefit of Smart's family, a transaction which Smart recalled with passionate indignation many years afterwards. The translation was well received, but to Smart it must have been painful drudgery that brought no personal satisfaction: later he told John Hawkesworth that he was spurred to make his verse translation of Horace (1767) "to supersede the prose translation ... which he said would hurt his memory."

In 1755, also, he and Rolt entered into a ninety-nine-year contract with the publisher Thomas Gardner, binding them to supply material for a new monthly periodical to be called the *Universal Visiter* and prohibiting them from engaging in any similar work as long as the agreement remained in force. The *Universal Visiter* began publication with the January 1756 issue, but Smart's contributions were soon cut short: twice since leaving Cambridge he had suffered bouts of dangerous illness, and in 1756 he had an attack of such severity that his life was despaired of. It has sometimes been assumed that these bouts were mental breakdowns, but such evidence as there is points rather to an acute and recurrent fever of some kind, no doubt accompanied by delirium. Whatever the cause, the third and gravest of the attacks was, by his own account, a turning point in Smart's life which he commemorated with *Hymn to the Supreme Being, on Recovery from a dangerous Fit of Illness* (1756). The poem describes the course of his illness in terms of a spiritual crisis. At the height of his sufferings, he relates, reason, sense, and religious faith all failed him:

> My sick'ning soul was with my blood inflam'd,
> And the celestial image sunk, defac'd and maim'd.

His memory, reviving the sins and follies of his past life, brought him to the point of despair; but then he awoke to the reality of Christ's redeeming grace and forgiveness, "Vengeance divine" was "by penitence supprest," and "soul-rejoicing health" returned. Physical recovery was accompanied by a sense of spiritual regeneration; Christ, restorer of the lame, the sick, and the blind, had performed another miracle:

> He pitying did a second birth bestow
> A birth of joy—not like the first of tears and woe.

Henceforward the poet vowed to consecrate all his acts and abilities to the glorification of God:

> Deeds, thoughts, and words no more his mandates break,
> But to his endless glory work, conceive, and speak.

The hymn is linked with the Seatonian poems on the attributes of the Supreme Being by title and by internal reference. An important difference, however, is that in the hymn Smart at last abandoned Miltonic blank verse in favor of stanzas with a regular metrical pattern and rhyming scheme. He has been described with some justice as dancing in chains in the Seatonian poems; paradoxically, he found greater freedom in the strict measures he adopted in the lyrical poetry of his last decade. The abandonment of blank verse also signaled a more radical shift from Miltonic to Hebraic conceptions of poetry.

The hymn was published in June 1756; less than a year later Smart was admitted to the curable ward of St. Luke's Hospital for Lunatics on Windmill Hill in London. The onset of his breakdown must have been considerably earlier, if Samuel Johnson's recollections are to be taken literally, for, as he reported to James Boswell, Smart's work on the *Universal Visiter* was interrupted by his insanity: "I wrote for some months in 'The Universal Visitor [*sic*],' for poor Smart, while he was mad, not then knowing the terms on which he was engaged to write, and thinking I was doing him good. I hoped his wits would soon return to him. Mine returned to me, and I wrote in 'The Universal Visitor' no longer." It is possible, of course, that Johnson's memory of an episode that occurred almost twenty years earlier conflated Smart's dangerous illness in 1756 with his madness later; but the gap between the two cannot have been more than a matter of months, and there are significant links between the crisis described in the hymn and the form of Smart's insanity. What Smart described in the hymn was a classical conversion experience; the cause of his insanity has been much debated, but contemporary evidence is clear on one point: the form it took was religious mania, with a compulsion to pray in public. Johnson's brisk and charitable comments have often been quoted but bear repetition: "My poor friend Smart shewed the disturbance of his mind, by falling upon his knees, and saying his prayers in the street, or in any other unusual place." And: "I did not think he ought to be shut up. His infirmities were not noxious to society. He insisted on people praying with him; and I'd as lief pray with Kit Smart as any one else. Another charge was, that he did not love clean linen; and I have no passion for it." Hester Lynch Thrale's longer and more circumstantial (but not necessarily more trustworthy) accounts of Smart's madness add detail without materially altering Johnson's assessment. Johnson and Thrale are memorably corroborated by the poet's own account in *Jubilate Agno*: "For I blessed God in St James's Park till I routed all the company. For the officers of the peace are at variance with me, and the watchman smites me with his staff." Hunter attributed Smart's breakdown to a combination of self-neglect and money troubles: "Though the fortune as well as constitution of Mr. Smart required the utmost care, he was equally negligent in the management of both, and his various and repeated embarrassments acting upon an imagination uncommonly fervid, produced temporary alienations of mind; which at last were attended with paroxysms so violent and continued as to render confinement necessary." In the light of modern psychiatric theory, Sir Russell Brain diagnosed Smart's condition as manic-depressive—a verdict that has not subsequently been challenged.

Smart was discharged from St. Luke's, uncured, in 1758 but remained in confinement until 1763, possibly part of the time at home but probably for the last years at a private madhouse in Bethnal Green. It was unquestionably a period of great affliction for him, not least because it involved first temporary and eventually permanent estrangement from his wife. The full details of the breakdown of the marriage are not known, but the outline of what happened seems clear. Entries in *Jubilate Agno* for the late summer of 1759 speak first of "family bickerings and domestic jars," and soon afterward: "For they have seperated me and my bosom, whereas the right comes from setting us together." By this time Anna Maria Smart had moved with her two daughters to Dublin, where she opened a shop. She returned after two years and settled in Reading, where she ran a newspaper for her stepfather, but she seems to have made no attempt to visit her husband throughout the last ten years of his life.

Smart's allusions to Anna Maria in *Jubilate Agno* show conflicting feelings. Twice in 1761 he refers lovingly to her ("God be gracious to my wife," "God be merciful to my wife"), but at the same time he was obsessed by fantasies about being cuckolded, for which no shadow of external evidence has ever been found. References to Moabites (a Puritan term of contempt for Roman Catholics) and "the Moabitish woman" earlier in *Jubilate Agno* may also be significant. After his release, there are no further references to her in his poetry, but an entry in Fanny Burney's journal for 1769 gives a startling indication of the savage resentment he harbored: "he [said that he] knew not if the horrid *old Cat*—as he once politely called his wife, be dead yet or not." Burney's comment on Smart's remark strives for judiciousness: "she had really used him uncommonly ill, even cruelly—nevertheless, it is extreamly shocking to hear him mention a Wife in so unfeeling a manner. And yet, the genius, talents and great merit as is rather generally allowed to Mr. Smart, incline me very much to believe his provocation authorises his hatred—if, after all, any thing can." One understandable ground for grievance would have been that she had sent his daughters to a convent in France a year or two before this reported conversation. On the other hand, Smart's volatile temperament, extravagance, drunkenness, and irresponsibility would always have made him difficult to live with, and the likelihood is that she had the hard choice of choosing between caring for him and safeguarding the welfare of her children.

Despite all the suffering he endured, the "well-nigh sev'n years" (as he counted it) of his incarceration brought forth an astonishing quantity of brilliant and original poetry. Between 1757 and 1763 he wrote *A Song to David*; most if not all of *A Translation of the Psalms of David* and "Hymns and Spiritual Songs for the Fasts and Festivals of the Church of England" (published together in 1765); and the lengthy manuscript of *Jubilate Agno*, the surviving fragments of which, amounting to more than seventeen hundred verses, represent only about a third of what he actually wrote.

Jubilate Agno, even in its fragmentary form, is Smart's "prophetic book": a doxology, evangelical and philosophical manifesto, personal diary, and commonplace book all in one, as well as a remarkable experiment in poetic form. On internal evidence, it appears to have been written over a period of four to five years, from 1758-1759 to 1763. The manuscript, whose existence was not publicly known until 1939, consists of two sets of loose papers, each set containing closely written series of verses all beginning with the same word—*Let* and *For*, respectively. Coincidences of page numbers and dates, together with verbal links between the two sets, suggest that they were intended to be related antiphonally, like the versicles and responses in parts of the Anglican liturgy, or as in Hebrew poetry according to the account given in Robert Lowth's *De Sacra Poesi Hebraeorum* (1753), an influential work with which Smart was familiar. The *Let* verses are invocatory and mostly impersonal, calling on the universal choir of creation to glorify the Lord; the *For* verses add comments, reflections, topical references, and details of Smart's private life and feelings. At the same time, each series of verses is sequentially ordered or linked, thus yielding a complex pattern (not consistently maintained) of vertical and horizontal connections.

The poem is primarily intended as a work of praise and thanksgiving, in accord with

1. Jubilate Agno.

Rejoice in God, O ye Tongues; give the glory to the Lord, and the Lamb.
Nations, and languages, and every Creature, in which is the breath of Life.
Let man and beast appear before him, and magnify his name together.
Let Noah and his company approach the throne of Grace, and do homage to the Ark of their Salvation.
Let Abraham present a Ram, and worship the God of his Redemption.
Let Isaac, the Bridegroom, kneel with his Camels, and bless the hope of his pilgrimage.
Let Jacob, and his speckled Drove adore the good Shepherd of Israel.
Let Esau offer a scape Goat for his seed, and rejoice in the blessing of God his father.
Let Nimrod, the mighty hunter, bind a Leopard to the altar, and consecrate his spear to the Lord.
Let Ishmael dedicate a Tyger, and give praise for the liberty, in which the Lord has let him at large.
Let Balaam appear with an Ass, and bless the Lord his people and his creatures for a reward eternal.
Let Anah, the son of Zibeon, lead a Mule to the temple, and bless God, who amerces the consolation of the creature for the service of Man.
Let Daniel come forth with a Lion, and praise God with all his might through faith in Christ Jesus.
Let Naphtali with an Hind give glory in the goodly words of Thanks-giving.
Let Aaron, the high priest, sanctify a Bull, and let him go free to the Lord and Giver of Life.
Let the Levites of the Lord take the Beavers of the brook alive into the Ark of the Testimony.
Let Eleazar with the Ermine serve the Lord decently and in purity.
Let Ithamar minister with a Chamois, and bless the name of Him, which cloatheth the naked.
Let Gershom with an [Hart] Pygarg bless the name of Him, who feedeth the hungry.
Let Merari praise the wisdom and power of God with the Coney, who scoopeth the rock, and archeth in the sand.
Let Kohath serve with the Sable, and bless God in the ornaments of the Temple.
Let Jehoiada bless God with an Hare, whose mazes are determined for the health of the body and to parry the adversary.
Let Ahitub humble himself with an Ape before Almighty God, who is the maker of variety and pleasantry.
Let Abiathar with a Fox praise the name of the Lord, who ballances craft against strength and skill against number.
Let Moses, the Man of God, bless with a Lizard, in the sweet majesty of good-nature, and the magnanimity of meekness.
Let

First page of Fragment A of Jubilate Agno, *written while Smart was under confinement for mental illness (fMS Eng 719, Houghton Library, Harvard University)*

Smart's belief in the primacy of gratitude: "For there is no invention but the gift of God, and no grace but the grace of gratitude," he declares. Writing in the spirit and rhapsodic cadences of the Psalms and canticles (he calls the work "my MAGNIFICAT"), Smart summons man and beast to "Rejoice in God his name." He envisages himself, the poet, as "the Lord's News-Writer—the scribe-evangelist," spreading the Word in its divine purity ("for I preach the very GOSPEL of CHRIST without comment") and adventuring in the name of the Lord to combat the evil influence of atheistic philosophy and scientific materialism by renewing the spirit of Christian worship in England:

> For I am inquisitive in the Lord, and defend the philosophy of scripture against vain deceit. . . .
> For Newton . . . is more of error than of the truth, but I am of the WORD of GOD. . . .
> For by the grace of God I am the Reviver of ADORATION amongst ENGLISH-MEN.

The magniloquence of this kind of utterance contrasts with the humility and simplicity of other lines: "For I am a little fellow, which is intitled to the great mess by the benevolence of God my father"; "For in my nature I quested for beauty, but God, God hath sent me to sea for pearls." The range of register in *Jubilate Agno* is indeed one of its conspicuous features; corresponding to the sweep of Smart's vision, which sees God glorified as much by the beetle and the cricket ("Let Chalcol praise with the Beetle, whose life is precious in the sight of God, tho his appearance is against him"; "Let Mephibosheth with the Cricket praise the God of chearfulness, hospitality, and gratitude") as by the moon in its horizontal magnitude, or the satellites of the planet Jupiter. The principle underlying this work and all of Smart's religious poetry is that the natural creation manifests the glory of God by virtue of its existence:

> For a man speaks HIMSELF from the crown of his head to the sole of his feet.
> For a LION roars HIMSELF compleat from head to tail.
> For all these things are seen in the spirit which makes the beauty of prayer.

In Smart's belief, as Marcus Walsh observes in *Christopher Smart: Selected Poems* (1979), "every creature worships God simply by being itself, through its peculiar actions and properties. . . . The well-known lines on Smart's cat Jeoffry, far from exemplifying a childlike naivety of vision, are an elaborate demonstration of how each closely observed act may be taken as part of the cat's divine ritual of praise":

> For he is the servant of the Living God duly and daily serving him.
> For at the first glance of the glory of God in the East he worships in his way.
> For is this done by wreathing his body seven times round with elegant quickness.
> For then he leaps up to catch the musk, which is the blessing of God upon his prayer. . . .

—and so on for seventy lines.

These themes of praise and adoration explain Smart's motive but not his design in *Jubilate Agno,* and account for only part of the mélange of ideas which make up this extraordinary work: science, politics, language, national and international affairs, genealogy, and horticulture are only some of the topics explored. The problems of interpretation are formidable: while *Jubilate Agno* evidently represents a synoptic vision of some kind, attempts to find a unified meaning or consistent principle of organization have been persistently balked not only by the fragmentary state of the text but also by the obscurity of many of the allusions, the abrogation of "normal" principles of order and connection, and Smart's condensed style, peculiar syntax, and irreverent wordplay. When it was first published in William Force Stead's edition under the title *Rejoice in the Lamb,* as a linear text with *Let* and *For* verses printed in successive blocks, it was understandably regarded mainly as a fascinating curiosity, at best the incoherent outpourings of a mad genius, although showing remarkable gifts of observation and expression and flashes of spiritual insight. Elizabeth Scott-Montagu, who reviewed Stead's edition in *Nineteenth Century* (June 1939), was exceptional among early critics in her recognition of a powerful and consistent vision behind the seemingly insane disorder of the work. Donald Greene, however, was the first to recognize the far-reaching and subversive implications of Smart's philosophical and scientific ideas, claiming him as "the earliest of the outright rebels against Newtonian and Lockean 'rationalism'" and arguing that his criticism of Newtonianism was as radical as William Blake's and conducted with "rather more philosophic precision."

Since 1954, when the antiphonal structure of *Jubilate Agno* was first demonstrated in W. H.

Bond's edition, few critics have dared to account for its peculiarities as the mere aberrations of a deranged mind; but attempts to find in it an integrated meaning or design still depend on a selective reading of the text. The most persuasive of such attempts so far have been those, such as A. D. Hope's study of Smart's apocalyptic vision, which seek to correlate Smart's theological and cosmological beliefs with his bold speculations about and experiments with language.

Knowledge of Smart's personal life during the seven years of his "jeopardy," as he calls it in *Jubilate Agno*, has to be pieced together from scanty external testimony and revealing glimpses supplied by *Jubilate Agno* itself. At St. Luke's he was under the relatively humane and enlightened care of Dr. William Battie, and at least from 1759 he had access to newspapers and books and was allowed to keep a cat ("For I am possessed of a cat, surpassing in beauty, from whom I take occasion to bless almighty God") and to work in the garden. Although he still referred to himself as a "prisoner," he was thankful that "I am not in a dungeon but am allowed the light of the Sun." When Johnson visited him he found that Smart got exercise by digging in the garden: "Let Pink, house of Pink rejoice with Trigonum a herb used in garlands—the Lord succeed my pink borders," Smart wrote in October 1762. Other entries, however, paint a darker picture. He writes of being "in twelve hardships," refers to some instrument used on him ("For they work me with their harping-irons, which is a barbarous instrument, because I am more unguarded than others"), and is acutely aware of his humiliating status: "for silly fellow! silly fellow! is against me and belongeth neither to me nor my family." He was not altogether forgotten by the outside world, however. In 1759 David Garrick gave a benefit performance of Voltaire's *Mérope* (1743), adapted by Aaron Hill, on Smart's behalf, and several friends used the occasion to publish sympathetic verses about him, lamenting the temporary eclipse of his talents.

A Song to David was almost certainly written while Smart was still in the madhouse. The tirelessly repeated legend, originating from John Langhorne's review in the *Monthly Review* (April 1763), that this poem "was written when the author was denied the use of pen, ink and paper, and was obliged to indent his lines, with the end of a key, upon the wainscot" is manifestly absurd but is probably an accurate indication of its date. The preeminence of *A Song to David* among Smart's works has been virtually undisputed since Browning made it the centerpiece of his poem on Smart in *Parleyings with Certain People of Importance in Their Day* (1887), and until the publication of *Jubilate Agno*, and the reprinting of "Hymns and Spiritual Songs" in 1949, the song continued to figure in popular imagination as the unique phenomenon that Browning described: a sudden and inexplicable outburst of poetic fire from a dusty waste of decent but commonplace verse, the product of a single transfiguring experience. *A Song to David* is still justifiably regarded as Smart's crowning achievement, but affinities in quality as well as theme and expression between it and Smart's other religious verse of the same period are now well recognized. The interpretative possibilities of reading the song in close conjunction with *Jubilate Agno*, however, have not yet been exhausted. The relationship between the two works is that of a crystal to its menstruum: the leading themes and symbols which exist in solution, as it were, in *Jubilate Agno* are transmuted in *A Song to David* into an intricate structure of magnificent symmetry and grace.

In 1936 William Butler Yeats singled out *A Song to David* in the introduction to the *Oxford Book of Modern Verse* as the inaugural poem of the Romantic period, in which man, "passive before a mechanized nature," began to beat against the door of his prison. Even without knowledge of *Jubilate Agno* Yeats recognized that *A Song to David* was more than a religious panegyric of unusual scale and splendor; as Browning also recognized, it was a reaffirmation of spiritual realities in an age of scientific materialism, of the conjunction of nature and supernature in an age of natural theology. The anti-Newtonian principles which Smart hammered out at length and in detail in *Jubilate Agno* are subsumed in *A Song to David* within a harmonious scheme of Christian metaphysics set forth by David, whose celebration of the works of creation is the only true knowledge:

O DAVID, scholar of the Lord!
Such is thy science, whence reward
  And infinite degree;
O strength, O sweetness, lasting ripe!
God's harp thy symbol, and thy type
  The lion and the bee!

In its own time *A Song to David* was received with more perplexity than either admiration or hostility: "a very curious composition, being a strange mixture of *dun obscure* and glowing genius at times," wrote Boswell on 30 July 1763 to

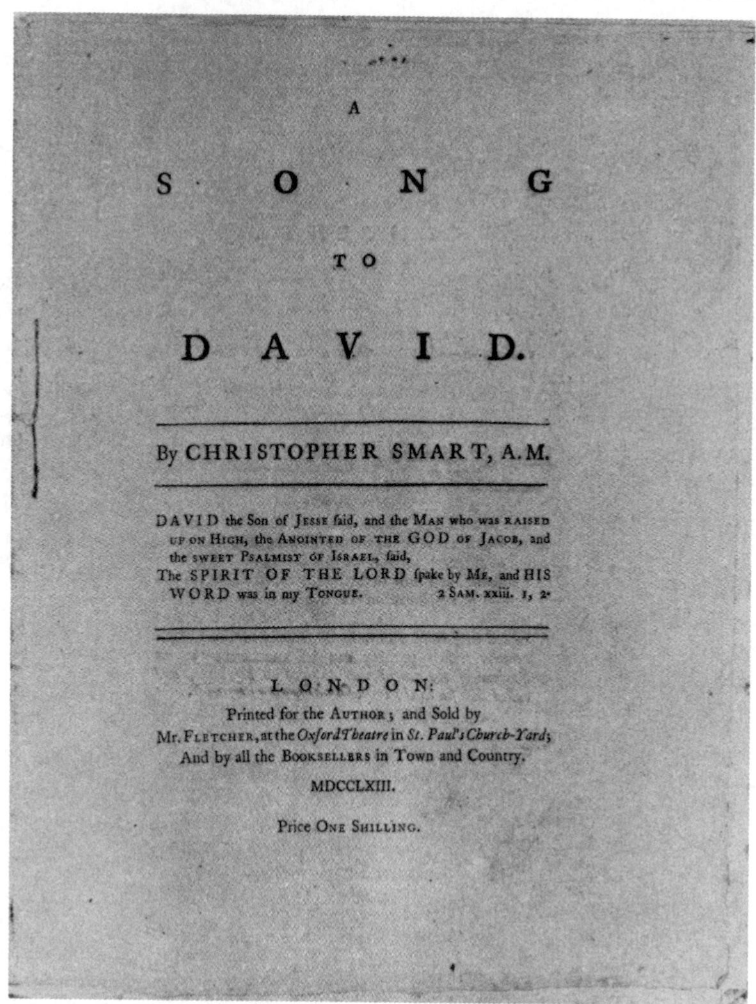

A

SONG

TO

DAVID.

By CHRISTOPHER SMART, A.M.

DAVID the Son of JESSE ſaid, and the MAN who was RAISED UP ON HIGH, the ANOINTED OF THE GOD OF JACOB, and the SWEET PSALMIST OF ISRAEL, ſaid,
The SPIRIT OF THE LORD ſpake by ME, and HIS WORD was in my TONGUE. 2 SAM. xxiii. 1, 2.

LONDON:
Printed for the AUTHOR; and Sold by
Mr. FLETCHER, at the *Oxford Theatre* in *St. Paul's Church-Yard*;
And by all the BOOKSELLERS in Town and Country.
MDCCLXIII.

Price ONE SHILLING.

Title page for the poem that is generally regarded as Smart's crowning achievement (G. Ross Roy Collection, Thomas Cooper Library, University of South Carolina)

a friend, Sir David Dalrymple. Friends and enemies alike discovered traces of Smart's madness in it: "I have seen his Song to David and from thence conclude him as mad as ever," Mason wrote to Gray in June 1763, while nevertheless making strenuous efforts to raise money on Smart's behalf. The *Critical Review* (April 1763) contrived to be censorious and condescending in almost equal measures; it hinted at the impropriety of "a Protestant's offering up either hymns or prayers to the dead," conceding, however, that "great rapture and devotion is discernable in this extatic song" and concluding that it was "a fine piece of ruins." Langhorne in the *Monthly Review* paid it the tribute of a longer and more discriminating examination, noting in many places "a grandeur, a majesty of thought, not without a happiness of expression" but finding it obscure at times and lacking in regularity: "From the sufferings of this ingenious gentleman, we could not but expect the performance before us to be greatly irregular; but we shall certainly characterise it more justly, if we call it irregularly great." In short, contemporary readers regarded as regrettable aberration what modern critics have seen as the daring originality of Smart's assumption of the role of poet-prophet.

In *A Song to David* the process of self-identification with David, the archetypal divine poet, which began with the Seatonian poems, is completed. The poem is both an affirmation and an example of the ideal of poetry represented for Smart by the psalmist, or "Great Author of the Book of Gratitude" as Smart designates him. In eighteenth-century terms, *A Song to David* is generically and qualitatively a "sublime" ode, intended to match what Smart describes as the "prodigious grandeur and genuine majesty" of

David's poetry. Its architectonics, as well as its style and versification, all contribute to this characterization. For example, at the precise arithmetical center of the poem, as Christopher Dennis has shown, stands a sequence of ten stanzas corresponding to the ten-string harp of David, the instrument and symbol of creative power. Far from being "a fine piece of ruins," in fact, the poem is constructed on numerological principles with "exact regularity and method," as Smart claimed in response to his critics in the "Advertisement" to *Poems On several Occasions* (1763). As Butt observes, "the poem is unique amongst the lyrical poems of the century in its expression of religious ecstasy within the confines of the strictest formality."

In Smart's *A Translation of the Psalms of David* (1765), in his "Hymns and Spiritual Songs" (published together with the translation of the Psalms), and in his later poems, David is replaced by Christ as Smart's source of inspiration: "Muse, through Christ the Word, inventive" is invoked in Hymn 3, "Epiphany." From *Jubilate Agno* onward, the concept of *logos*, the creative Word, is fundamental to Smart's poetics. The "Hymns and Spiritual Songs" are second only to *A Song to David* in accomplishment. Intended "for the Fasts and Festivals of the Church of England," they are devotional poems of a kind clearly related to seventeenth-century Anglican tradition but unique in the eighteenth century. In language, imagery, use of formal patterning and lyrical bravura, as well as in the quality of his faith, Smart in these poems is closer to George Herbert, Robert Herrick, and Andrew Marvell than to the hymn writers of his own age. More intimate than *A Song to David*, they are described by Devlin as possessing "a quality all their own, austerely tender," while sharing with the best of Smart's other poems the capacity to express "the flush of enthusiasm . . . with lapidary precision."

The "Hymns and Spiritual Songs" were almost entirely neglected until the twentieth century, although Le Noir must have hoped to gain wider circulation for them when she reprinted several in the second volume of a collection titled *Miscellaneous Poems* (1825-1826), commending their "originality, ardent piety, and true poetic fire" in preference to *A Song to David*, which she thought overrated. While it is broadly true, as Walsh says, that "Smart's *Hymns* are imaginative poetry, hymns only in name, making too few of the inevitable practical compromises to be acceptable in popular congregational use," a few of them have been successfully set to music and included in modern hymnals.

The manuscript of *Jubilate Agno* breaks off abruptly at the end of January 1763, two lines after an entry saying "God be gracious to John Sherrat [*sic*]." Sherratt was a London entrepreneur and self-appointed reformer of private madhouses; Smart may have known him since the early 1750s, when Sherratt was manager of Marylebone Gardens. Sherratt was instrumental in securing Smart's release, as he acknowledges with gratitude in "An Epistle to John Sherratt, Esq." included in the small volume *Poems by Mr. Smart*, which was published in July 1763. On leaving the madhouse Smart took rooms in Park Street, Westminster. There he was visited in October 1764 by Hawkesworth, who wrote to Smart's sister, Margaret Hunter, that he had found Smart comfortably established "with very decent people, in a house most delightfully situated with a terras that overlooks St. James's Park, and a door into it." On Smart's table Hawkesworth saw "a quarto book, in which he had been writing, a prayer book and a Horace," which neatly encapsulates Smart's main preoccupations in his later years. The stigma of insanity had not turned him into a social pariah: as Hawkesworth delicately puts it, he was "by no means considered in any light that makes his company as a gentleman, a scholar, and a genius less desirable." To this year belongs a cheerful verse epistle to Dr. James Nares, the musician, inviting him to dinner and written with all the gaiety and unforced good humor of poems in the same vein composed before Smart's confinement; the epistle was published in the *Universal Museum* in April 1765.

This period was soured, however, by quarrels with his critics and self-imposed alienation from his family. Smart's attitude to Hawkesworth, whom he greeted, Hawkesworth wrote to Smart's sister, "with an ardour of kindness natural to the sensibility of his temper," was in conspicuous contrast to his response to news of his mother and sister, which he received in pointed silence. When told that his sister and brother-in-law would be glad to see Smart at their home in Kent, Hawkesworth reports that "he replied very quick, 'I cannot afford to be idle;' I said he might employ his mind as well in the country as the town, at which he only shook his head."

It is certainly true that Smart was busy at this time. In addition to collecting subscribers, preparing the Psalms and hymns for publication, and seeing *A Song to David* through the press, in

Portrait, traditionally assumed to be of Smart, by an unknown artist (National Portrait Gallery, London)

1763 and 1764 he had three small volumes of poems published and wrote the libretto for an oratorio, *Hannah* (1764), with a score by John Worgan; when Hawkesworth visited him he had completed *A Poetical Translation of the Fables of Phaedrus* (1765) and was already at work on the verse translation of Horace. But the failure of *A Song to David* to win public applause was deeply galling to him, and he reacted angrily in print to his critics, dragging up old grievances with futile indignation.

Smart's three small collections of verse, *Poems by Mr. Smart, Poems On several Occasions,* and *Ode to the Right Honourable the Earl of Northumberland, on his being appointed Lord Lieutenant of Ireland. Presented on the Birth-Day of Lord Warkworth. With some other Pieces* (1764), contain short odes, complimentary addresses, fables, songs, epigrams, and so on. These poems look at first sight like a return to the relatively lighthearted, secular versifying of the 1750s. But almost nothing Smart wrote after 1759 is entirely unaffected by his Christian "rebirth," and in these volumes he seems to have been trying out a new kind of secularized religious poetry. This kind of poetry is most beautifully exemplified by "On a Bed of Guernsey Lilies" (published in *Ode to the Right Honourable the Earl of Northumberland*) in which the light lyrical framework delicately implies a message of Christian hope and reassurance:

Ye beauties! O how great the sum
   Of sweetness that ye bring;
On what a charity ye come
   To bless the latter spring! . . .
We never are deserted quite;
'Tis by succession of delight
   That love supports his reign.

Few of the other poems are quite of this caliber, but Smart's attempts to reconcile secular and Christian ideals in "Munificence and Modesty" and in his panegyrical poems yield a great deal of interest. Smart's critical enemies, however, took their revenge on him by dismissing the books with abuse and contempt, and even the well-disposed, like Langhorne, found his new manner of writing disconcertingly obscure.

Meanwhile, owing to delays in its publication, Smart's *Translation of the Psalms of David* was preceded by a rival version by James Merrick. Smart had the chagrin of seeing his version unfavorably compared to Merrick's; dismissed—perhaps predictably—with contempt by his old enemies in the *Critical Review* and the *Monthly Review*; and ignored by the Church of England, for whose use it had been so carefully prepared. As Walsh notes, Smart's translation was not mere hackwork but "an extraordinarily ambitious attempt to meet a strongly voiced demand for a new Anglican metrical Psalter, for regular use in the divine service." Like his hymns, it was part of his campaign for liturgical reform; like the hymns, also, it expresses a theology which is close to that of the Evangelical wing of the church, stressing salvation through faith rather than works. Walsh points out that among Smart's many additions to the original text of the Psalms, the word *grace* is more frequently introduced than any other. The translation announced itself as *Attempted in the Spirit of Christianity*; such an attempt was not a novelty in itself, but Smart's adaptation of the Psalter to Christian thought, expression, and symbolism is audaciously thorough, making few concessions to the standards of language for congregational singing set by the metrical versions of Thomas Sternhold and John Hopkins (1562) or the *New Version* (1696) by Nahum Tate and Nicholas Brady that were already in use in Anglican services.

Troubles of a more practical kind soon followed. Within three years of Smart's release from the madhouse he was again in danger of imprisonment, this time for debt. In December 1765 he was arrested at the suit of the printer of the Psalms and "must have gone to jail for that very book, from which I was in hopes of ingenuous bread, if it had not been for a kind friend, who cou'd not bear to see my tears," Smart wrote to another friend, Paul Panton, on 10 January 1766. Smart was never again wholly out of trouble over money, in spite of diligent and in part successful efforts on the part of his friends to secure employment or support for him. Hunter says that he was maintained in his last years "partly by his literary occupations, and partly by the generosity of his friends; receiving among other benefactions fifty pounds a year from the Treasury." Fifty pounds a year should have been sufficient to keep Smart in reasonable comfort, but he was incurably improvident. "During the greater part of his life," writes Hunter, "he was wholly inattentive to oeconomy; and by this negligence lost first his fortune and then his credit."

The publication in 1767 of Smart's verse translation of the works of Horace, now recognized as a work of originality, verve, and wit, did nothing to retrieve his fortunes or his reputation in his own time. Only two reviewers took any notice of the work at all. The *Critical Review* (August 1767) gave it half-hearted praise for its occasional felicities, its fastidiousness (giving "an inoffensive turn to all those passages which have a tendency to suggest immodest ideas"), and its scholarly apparatus. The *Political Register* (December 1767) allotted it one word: "Unequal." Thereafter, the translation passed into virtual oblivion until 1950, when Robert Brittain revived interest in it by reprinting a selection of odes and epistles in his edition of Smart's poems.

Horace was an important pattern and influence throughout Smart's career. Several of his youthful odes were modeled on Horace; one of his earliest publications was a vivacious imitation of Satire III, Book I (1750); and as poet and critic Horace remained a constant standard of reference for Smart. It was not the Horatian urbanity, so much admired by poets from Ben Jonson to Pope, that most attracted him, but rather the qualities of Horace's poetic language. In the preface to his verse translation Smart comments on "the lucky risk of the Horatian boldness," explaining that "Horace is not so much an original in respect to his matter and sentiments . . . as to that unrivalled peculiarity of expression, which has excited the admiration of all succeeding ages." By "peculiarity of expression" he means not only that *curiosa felicitas* (studied grace) which critics since Petronius Arbiter have attributed to Horace but especially that quality which he labels *impression*. "The beauty, force and vehemence of *Impression*," he says, is the mark of every great genius, but particularly of lyrical poets; it is "a talent or gift of Almighty God, by which a Genius is impowered to throw an emphasis upon a word or sentence in such wise, that it cannot escape any reader of sheer good sense or true critical sagacity." It would appear from other comments and references of his that Smart was thinking of specific ways in which the poet may arrest or electrify the reader. He apparently had in mind not the use of intrinsically unusual words or grammatical constructions to achieve striking semantic effects but rather what may be achieved by using "ordinary" or "normal" words and constructions in unusual collocations or in startlingly unexpected contexts. In this way words and larger sense-units are invested with something akin to that special "force and violence" which the philosopher David Hume (in *A Treatise of Human Nature* [1739] and other works) attributes to that class of perceptions to which, likewise, he assigns the name *impressions*. It is in ways of this kind that Smart sought to give to his translation, as to all his poetry after 1763, that "unrivalled peculiarity of expression" which he so much admired in Horace.

The last five years of Smart's life were spent in increasing poverty and need: most of his surviving letters after 1766 are concerned with money troubles. When Newbery died in 1767, provisions in his will ensured that none of the money left to Anna Maria Smart should be "subject or liable to the debts power or control of her present husband"; and in 1769 Smart was disappointed in the hope of benefiting from the Durham estate of his cousin, Francis Smart. Help came in small ways—through the exertions of friends in Durham he was made beneficiary of a charitable trust in 1769—but he was reduced at times to begging small sums from those acquaintances whose generosity and patience had not already been exhausted. Charles Burney was one of these; his daughter Fanny mentions in her diary for 12 September 1768 that Smart had sent "a most affecting Epistle to papa, to entreat him to lend him 1/2 a guinea" in 1767; she comments: "How great a pity so clever, so ingenious a man should be reduced to such shocking circumstances." In the same entry she notes a visit from Smart the previous day: "He is extremely grave, and has still great wildness in his manner, looks and voice—'tis impossible to *see* him and *think* of his works, without feeling the utmost pity and concern for him." On another visit, the following year, he presented her with a rose and a courtly compliment: "It was given me, said he, by a fair lady—though not so fair as you." To this period belong also his visits to the hospitable home of Nicholas Kempe, where Smart liked to listen to Kempe's son John playing the flute; in old age John Kempe recalled in the *Gentleman's Magazine* (1823) that "I have often soothed the wanderings of his melancholy by some favorite air; he would shed tears when I played, and generally wrote some lines afterwards." Another friendship that apparently survived was with John Wilkes, for whom Smart composed a birthday ode which was performed with music at the Devil Tavern, Temple Bar, in 1769 (the poem is now lost).

Meanwhile he continued to write energetically, though nothing he produced after 1763 was a success with the public or the critics. The decision of the editor of the posthumous collection of Smart's poems (1791) to exclude the Psalms, hymns, versified parables, translations of Phaedrus and Horace, *A Song to David*, and most of the poems from the small volumes of 1763-1764, on the grounds that they showed "melancholy proofs of the recent estrangement of his mind," accurately reflects the reaction of the public toward Smart's later publications. His second oratorio, *Abimelech* (1768), was performed only once in his lifetime; *The Parables of Our Lord and Saviour Jesus Christ* (1768) was dismissed with derision by the *Monthly Review* (May 1768) and with the faintest of praise by the *Critical Review* (April 1768); while *Hymns, for the Amusement of Children* (1771), his last work, was totally ignored.

By the time *Hymns, for the Amusement of Children* reached the printers, Smart was in prison. He was arrested for debt in April 1770 and committed to the King's Bench Prison, where he remained until his death a year later. His confinement was not onerous: through the good offices of his brother-in-law, Thomas Carnan (publisher of *Hymns, for the Amusement of Children*), he was allowed the "Rules" of the prison, which meant that he had the freedom of St. George's Fields, an area around the prison including shops, public houses, and open ground for walking. Thanks to the ever-loyal Charles Burney he was not totally destitute, for as Fanny Burney records, her father raised a small fund which gave him "a miserable pittance beyond the prison allowance." Even in jail, Smart's affectionate disposition earned him friends among his fellow prisoners. One of these was Mendez Da Costa, clerk of the Royal Society, in prison for fraud, to whose wife Smart addressed a charming verse compliment. Another was James Stephen, the young son of another prisoner, who remembered Smart in his memoirs (1954) as one of "three or four literary characters" who befriended him, lending him books "with a view to the cultivation of my taste." The fullest picture of Smart in prison comes again from Fanny Burney, who notes in her *Memoirs of Dr. Burney* (1832) that he alternated between "partial aberration of intellect, and bacchanalian for-

King's Bench Prison
April [illegible]th 1770.

Dr Sr

After being a fortnight at a spunging house one week at the Marshalsea in the worst of all things, I am this day safely arrived at the King's Bench. — Seven years in Madhouses, eight times arrested in six years, I beg leave to recommend myself to a benevolent & producing friend Yrs affectionately

Christopher Smart.

Letter from Smart to his friend Charles Burney from King's Bench Prison, where Smart was imprisoned for debt in April 1770 and where he died in May 1771 (Pierpont Morgan Library)

getfulness of misfortune," that his piety was sincere, "though fanatical rather than rational," and that his compassion remained constant; she quotes as an example a letter Smart wrote not long before his death to her father, pleading for help for a fellow prisoner "whom I myself have already assisted according to my willing poverty." Smart died on 20 May 1771 after a short illness—"a disorder in his liver," according to Hunter. In a letter written on 25 June, Hunter gave Smart a touching valediction: "I trust he is now at peace; it was not his portion here."

Hymns, for the Amusement of Children was one of three works written for the young in the last phase of Smart's life (the others were the translation of Phaedrus and the versified parables), but it is the only one in which the need for a simplified style to suit such a readership is turned into a positive virtue. As Brittain was among the first to note, in some of the hymns "simplicity of diction" is combined with "the most startlingly accurate arrangement of thought" to achieve a quality similar to that of Blake's *Songs of Innocence* (1789); they speak of a world in which discovery of a lark's nest in a field gives paradisal joy (Hymn 33, "For Saturday"), in which "children in the gall'ries gay, / Shout from each goodly seat," and "my streak'd roses fully, blown, / The sweetness of the Lord make known" (Hymn 25, "Mirth"). The theology of these hymns is in sharp contrast to that of Isaac Watts's *Divine and Moral Songs for Children* (1720), the most successful of earlier attempts of the kind; where Watts's hymns are designed to save children from the dangers of sin, Smart's emphasize the bounteousness of God's blessings on earth and the joyful promise of salvation hereafter.

By the time of his death, Smart's reputation as a poet had suffered a drastic eclipse. From being the pride of Cambridge in his youth—the prize-winning poet with "the sublimest energies of religion" at his command—he sank in estimation into "poor Smart the mad poet," as Thomas Percy described him in a 17 October 1786 letter to Edmond Malone, and thence into comparative neglect until the twentieth century. He became in effect a one-poem author: despite respectful references to some of his other works and occasional reprintings, it was *A Song to David* which kept his name alive. In an undated letter to T. Hall Caine, Dante Gabriel Rossetti pronounced it "the only accomplished poem of the last century"; and the image of Smart as one of the freaks of literary history, an industrious versifier momentarily transformed into a poet of genius, persisted with extraordinary tenacity. Even the publication by Edmund Blunden of some of Smart's hymns, psalms, Horatian translations, and other poems in 1924 caused only a brief flurry of interest, without altering the popular perception of Smart as the author of a solitary masterpiece—an "inestimable jewel buried in an ash-heap," in Edmund Gosse's phrase. The real turning point came with the discovery in 1939 of *Jubilate Agno*, the work which, even more than *A Song to David*, has captured the interest of modern poets—including Allen Ginsberg, Alec Hope, John Heath-Stubbs, Peter Porter, Jeremy Reed, and Wendy Cope—many of whom have paid him the tribute of imitation and parody; while through Benjamin Britten's festival cantata, *Rejoice in the Lamb* (1943), a setting of portions of *Jubilate Agno*, the poetry of Christopher Smart has found a response among many for whom poetry ordinarily has little appeal.

Letters:

The Annotated Letters of Christopher Smart, edited by Betty Rizzo and Robert Mahony (Carbondale & Edwardsville: Southern Illinois University Press, 1991).

Bibliographies:

G. J. Gray, "A Bibliography of the Writings of Christopher Smart, with Biographical References," *Transactions of the Bibliographical Society*, 6 (1903): 269-305;

Robert Mahony and Betty W. Rizzo, *Christopher Smart: An Annotated Bibliography 1743-1983* (New York: Garland, 1984).

Biographies:

Christopher Hunter, "The Life of Christopher Smart," in *The Poems, of the Late Christopher Smart, M.A.*, 2 volumes (Reading: Printed and sold by Smart and Cowslade; and sold by F. Power and Co., London, 1791), I: v-xliii;

K. A. McKenzie, *Christopher Smart, sa vie et ses oeuvres* (Paris: Presses Universitaires de France, 1925);

Edward G. Ainsworth and Charles E. Noyes, *Christopher Smart, a Biographical and Critical Study* (Columbia: University of Missouri, 1943);

Christopher Devlin, *Poor Kit Smart* (London: Hart-Davis, 1961);

Arthur Sherbo, *Christopher Smart, Scholar of the University* (East Lansing: Michigan State University Press, 1967).

References:

Francis D. Adams, "*Jubilate Agno* and the 'Theme of Gratitude,' " *Papers on Language and Literature*, 3 (Summer 1967): 195-209;

Frances E. Anderson, *Christopher Smart* (New York: Twayne, 1974);

James Boswell, *Boswell's Life of Samuel Johnson, Together with Boswell's Journal of a Tour to the Hebrides and Johnson's Diary of a Journey into North Wales*, 6 volumes, edited by George Birkbeck Hill, revised by L. F. Powell (Oxford: Clarendon Press, 1934-1964);

Roland B. Botting, "Christopher Smart in London," *Research Studies of the State College of Washington*, 7 (March 1939): 3-54;

Russell Brain, "Christopher Smart: The Flea That Became an Eagle," in his *Some Reflections on Genius and Other Essays* (London: Pitman, 1960), pp. 113-122;

Frances Burney, *The Early Journals and Letters of Fanny Burney*, 2 volumes, edited by Lars E. Troide (Oxford & New York: Clarendon Press, 1987-1988);

John Butt, *The Mid-Eighteenth Century*, edited and completed by Geoffrey Carnall, volume 9 of *The Oxford History of English Literature* (Oxford: Clarendon Press, 1979);

T. Hall Caine, *Recollections of Dante Gabriel Rossetti* (London: Stock, 1882; Boston: Roberts, 1883), pp. 194-195;

John Chalker, "The Formal Georgic: Philips, Dyer, Smart, Grainger," in his *The English Georgic* (London: Routledge & Kegan Paul, 1969), pp. 34-65;

Gordon Claridge, Ruth Pryor, and Gwen Watkins, "The Powers of Night: Christopher Smart," in their *Sounds from the Bell Jar: Ten Psychotic Authors* (London: Macmillan, 1990), pp. 71-87;

Frances Burney d'Arblay, *Memoirs of Doctor Burney, Arranged from His Own Manuscripts, from Family Papers, and from Personal Recollections*, volume 1 (London: Moxon, 1832), pp. 279-281;

Donald Davie, "Christopher Smart: Some Neglected Poems," *Eighteenth-Century Studies*, 3 (Winter 1969): 242-264;

Davie, "Christopher Smart's Hymns," *P. N. Review*, 17 (November-December 1990): 16-20;

Moira Dearnley, *The Poetry of Christopher Smart* (London: Routledge, 1968);

Christopher M. Dennis, "A Structural Conceit in Smart's *Song to David*," *Review of English Studies*, new series 29 (August 1978): 257-266;

Thomas F. Dillingham, " 'Blest Light: Christopher Smart's Myth of David," in *The David Myth in Western Literature*, edited by Raymond-Jean Frontain and Jan Wojcik (West Lafayette, Ind.: Purdue University Press, 1980), pp. 120-133;

Allan J. Gedalof, "The Rise and Fall of Smart's David," *Philological Quarterly*, 60 (Summer 1981): 369-386;

Gedalof, "Smart's Poetics in *Jubilate Agno*," *English Studies in Canada*, 5 (Fall 1979): 262-274;

Edmund Gosse, "Christopher Smart," *Cambridge Review*, 8 (8 June 1887): 366-368;

Donald J. Greene, "Smart, Berkeley, the Scientists and the Poets," *Journal of the History of Ideas*, 14 (June 1953): 327-352;

Geoffrey Grigson, *Christopher Smart*, Writers and Their Work, no. 136 (London: Longmans, Green, 1961);

Harriet Guest, *A Form of Words: The Religious Poetry of Christopher Smart* (Oxford: Clarendon Press, 1989);

Geoffrey H. Hartman, "Christopher Smart's *Magnificat*: Toward a Theory of Representation," *Journal of English Literary History*, 41 (Fall 1974): 429-454;

A. D. Hope, "The Apocalypse of Christopher Smart," in *Studies in the Eighteenth Century*, edited by R. F. Brissenden (Canberra: Australian National University Press, 1968), pp. 269-284;

Albert J. Kuhn, "Christopher Smart: The Poet as Patriot of the Lord," *Journal of English Literary History*, 30 (June 1963): 121-136;

William A. Kumbier, "Sound and Signification in Christopher Smart's *Jubilate Agno*," *Texas Studies in Literature and Language*, 24 (Fall 1982): 293-312;

David B. Morris, *The Religious Sublime: Christian Poetry and Critical Tradition in Eighteenth-Century Poetry* (Lexington: University Press of Kentucky, 1972);

Claude Rawson, "Christopher Smart," in his *Order from Confusion Sprung* (London: Allen & Unwin, 1985), pp. 372-380;

Marie Roberts, "Christopher Smart," in her *British Poets and Secret Societies* (London: Croom Helm, 1986), pp. 10-51;

Robert D. Saltz, "Reason and Madness: Christopher Smart's Poetic Development," *Southern Humanities Review*, 4 (Winter 1970): 57-68;

Patricia Meyer Spacks, "Christopher Smart: The Mystique of Vision," in her *The Poetry of Vision: Five Eighteenth-Century Poets* (Cambridge, Mass.: Harvard University Press, 1967), pp. 119-164;

James Stephen, *The Memoirs of James Stephen: Written by Himself for the Use of His Children*, edited by Merle M. Bevington (London: Hogarth Press, 1954), pp. 89-90;

Robert Surtees, *The History and Antiquities of the County Palatine of Durham*, volume 4 (London: Printed by and for J. B. Nichols and Son, and Mrs. Andrews, Durham, 1840), pp. 142-144;

R. C. Tennant, "Christopher Smart and *The Whole Duty of Man*," *Eighteenth-Century Studies*, 13 (Fall 1979): 63-78;

Hester Lynch Thrale, *Thraliana: The Diary of Mrs. Hester Lynch Thrale (Later Mrs. Piozzi) 1776-1809*, 2 volumes, edited by Katharine C. Balderston (Oxford: Clarendon Press, 1942);

Arthur Tillotson, ed., *The Percy Letters: The Correspondence of Thomas Percy & Edmond Malone* (Baton Rouge: Louisiana University Press, 1944), pp. 37-38;

Paget Toynbee and Leonard Whibley, eds., *Correspondence of Thomas Gray*, revised by H. W. Starr, 3 volumes (Oxford: Clarendon Press, 1971);

Marcus Walsh, "A Cambridge College Library in the Eighteenth Century: Christopher Smart's Borrowings at Pembroke," *Library*, sixth series 12 (March 1990): 34-49;

Jean Wilkinson, "Three Sets of Religious Poems," *Huntington Library Quarterly*, 36 (May 1973): 203-226;

Karina Williamson, "Christopher Smart's Hymns and Spiritual Songs," *Philological Quarterly*, 38 (October 1959): 413-424;

Williamson, "Smart's Principia: Science and Anti-Science in *Jubilate Agno*," *Review of English Studies*, new series 30 (November 1979): 409-422.

Papers:

Pembroke College Library, Cambridge, has early manuscript copies of six of Christopher Smart's poems, one holograph, and other documents of biographical and bibliographical interest; the Houghton Library at Harvard University holds the manuscript of *Jubilate Agno*; the manuscript of "On Gratitude To the Memory of Mr. Seaton" is in the Berg Collection at the New York Public Library.

Charlotte Smith

(4 May 1749 - 28 October 1806)

Kate Ravin
Emory University

See also the Smith entry in *DLB 39: British Novelists, 1660-1800.*

BOOKS: *Elegiac Sonnets, and Other Essays* (Chichester & London: Printed for J. Dodsley, 1784; enlarged edition, London: Printed for J. Dodsley, H. Gardner, and J. Bew, 1786; Philadelphia: Printed for Thomas Dobson, 1787); enlarged as *Elegiac Sonnets* (London: Printed for T. Cadell, 1789; enlarged edition, London: Printed by R. Noble, for T. Cadell, 1792; Worcester, Mass.: Printed and sold by Isaiah Thomas, and sold by Thomas and Andrews in Boston, 1795; enlarged edition, London: Printed by A. Strahan for T. Cadell; and sold by T. Cadell jun. and W. Davies, 1795; Boston: Printed & sold by William Spotswood, 1795); enlarged as *Elegiac Sonnets, and Other Poems*, 2 volumes (London: Printed for T. Cadell, junior, and W. Davies, 1797);

Emmeline, the Orphan of the Castle: A Novel (4 volumes, London: Printed for T. Cadell, 1788; 2 volumes, Philadelphia: J. Conrad / Baltimore: M. & J. Conrad / Washington: Rapin, Conrad, 1802);

Ethelinde; or, The Recluse of the Lake, 5 volumes (London: Printed for T. Cadell, 1789);

Celestina: A Novel, 4 volumes (London: Printed for T. Cadell, 1791);

Desmond: A Novel, 3 volumes (London: Printed for G. G. J. & J. Robinson, 1792);

The Old Manor House: A Novel, 4 volumes (London: Printed for J. Bell, 1793);

The Emigrants: A Poem, in Two Books (London: Printed for T. Cadell, 1793);

The Wanderings of Warwick (London: Printed for J. Bell, 1794);

The Banished Man: A Novel, 4 volumes (London: Printed for T. Cadell, Jun. & W. Davies, 1794);

Rural Walks: In Dialogues. Intended for the Use of Young Persons, 2 volumes (London: T. Cadell, Jun. & W. Davies, 1795; Philadelphia: From the store of Thomas Stephens, 1795);

Montalbert: A Novel, (3 volumes, London: Printed by S. Low for E. Booker, 1795; 2 volumes, Philadelphia: Printed by George Kline for Mathew Carey, 1800);

A Narrative of the Loss of the Catharine, Venus, and Piedmont Transports, and the Thomas, Golden Grove, and Aeolus Merchant Ships, near Weymouth, on Wednesday the 18th of November Last (London: Printed and sold by Sampson Low; and C. Law, 1796);

Rambles Farther: A Continuation of Rural Walks, in Dialogues. Intended for the Use of Young Persons, 2 volumes (London: Printed for T. Cadell jun. & W. Davies, 1796);

Marchmont: A Novel, 4 volumes (London: Printed by and for Sampson Low, 1796);

Minor Morals, Interspersed with Sketches of Natural History, Historical Anecdotes, and Original Stories, 2 volumes (London: Printed by and for Sampson Low, 1798);

The Young Philosopher: A Novel, 4 volumes (London: Printed for T. Cadell, jun. and W. Davies, 1798);

What Is She?: A Comedy, in Five Acts, as Performed at the Theatre Royal, Covent Garden, attributed to Smith (London: Printed for T. N. Longman & O. Rees, 1799);

The Letters of a Solitary Wanderer: Containing Narratives of Various Description, 5 volumes (volumes 1-3, London: Printed by and for Sampson Low, 1800-1801; volumes 4-5, London: Printed for T. N. Longman & O. Rees, 1802);

Conversations Introducing Poetry: Chiefly on the Subjects of Natural History. For the Use of Children and Young Persons, 2 volumes (London: Printed for J. Johnson, 1804);

The History of England, from the Earliest Records to the Peace of Amiens, in a Series of Letters to a Young Lady at School, 3 volumes, volumes 1

Charlotte Smith (crayon drawing by George Romney, 1792; National Portrait Gallery, London)

and 2 by Smith (London: Printed for Richard Phillips by J. G. Barnard, 1806);

Beachy Head: With Other Poems (London: Printed for the author; and sold by J. Johnson, 1807);

The Natural History of Birds: Intended Chiefly for Young Persons, 2 volumes (London, 1807).

Editions: *The Old Manor House*, edited with introduction by Anne Henry Ehrenpreis (London: Oxford University Press, 1969);

Emmeline: The Orphan of the Castle, edited, with introduction, by Ehrenpreis (London: Oxford University Press, 1971);

Desmond (New York: Garland, 1974);

The Young Philosopher (New York: Garland, 1974);

The Old Manor House, introduction by Janet Todd (London & New York: Pandora Press, 1987);

Marchmont (Las Vegas & Delmar, N.Y.: Scholars' Facsimiles & Reprints, 1989);

Montalbert (Delmar, N.Y.: Scholars' Facsimiles & Reprints, 1989).

TRANSLATIONS: Antoine François Prévost d'Exiles, *Manon Lescaut* (London: Printed for T. Cadell, 1785);

The Romance of Real Life, translated by Smith from François Gayot de Pitaval, *Causes célèbres et interessantes* (3 volumes, London: Printed for T. Cadell, 1787; 1 volume, Philadelphia: Printed by J. Carey, 1799).

Charlotte Smith, whose reputation currently rests on her achievement as a novelist, rose to fame as a poet during the late eighteenth century. Smith has associations with the canonical Romantic poets: her early treatment of the English sonnet influenced both Samuel Taylor Coleridge and John Keats, while William Wordsworth not only experimented with the stanza form of "Saint Monica" (published in *Beachy Head: With Other Poems*, 1807), one of Smith's last poems, but also admired the "true feeling for rural nature" evident in all her work. Smith wrote prolifically, producing three books of poetry, two translations, ten novels, and six works for children. Although she wrote to express intense emotion, Smith was never simply the Shelleyan "nightingale who sits in darkness and sings to cheer its own solitude with sweet sounds"; she wrote to support her family. The early marriage that left Smith with twelve children to feed pushed her first from the landed gentry to London's mercantile sphere and next to its group of published authors. These transitions faced her with both practical hardships and ideological problems. Smith's position as a breadwinning author was consistent with her Christian morality, which denied the value of social position or wealth. Still, her genteel upbringing decreed that ladies could not work for their livings, and convention discouraged women from expressing themselves publicly. When necessity brought Smith to disregard the restrictions on work and self-expression, she wrote poems that aired her grievances at the irresponsibility of her male protectors and the inefficiency of Britain's legal system. But while Smith's frustration steadily mounted, her poems do not grow increasingly bitter. Her three main poetic works—*Elegiac Sonnets, and Other Essays* (1784), *The Emigrants* (1793), and *Beachy Head: With Other Poems*—show a progression from dissatisfaction through rebellion to resignation. The tensions of this poetry, however, complicate the culturally sanctioned position Smith finally assumes.

Charlotte Turner was born on 4 May 1749 to Nicholas and Anna Towers Turner. Her birth took place at their London residence in King's Street, St. James Square, but it was the country, where Charlotte and her two younger siblings spent much of their childhood, that claimed her allegiance. Nicholas Turner's holdings in Sussex and Surrey endowed his children with social position; and Charlotte's privileged childhood led her to expect similar advantages in adult life.

When Charlotte was three years old, Anna Turner died in childbirth. Nicholas mitigated his grief by traveling abroad, leaving his daughters in the care of their maternal aunt, who believed that a young woman's education should culminate in an advantageous marriage. At the age of six Charlotte was sent to school at Chichester; at eight she entered a seminary at Kensington, where she excelled in dancing, drawing, and acting. According to a classmate quoted by Florence May Anna Hilbish, Turner was an avid reader who was "continually composing verses." At twelve Turner entered society, thereby decreasing the amount of attention she could devote to schoolwork. Nicholas Turner had by this time returned to England with depleted resources and soon married a woman who, according to an article in the *Monthly Magazine* (April 1807), although she "exacted much consideration in consequence of her large fortune, had little claim to it from her personal qualities." Charlotte Turner was unlikely to submit to this stepmother's control; thus Nicholas Turner's improvidence and her aunt's urging pushed the girl toward a loveless union. On 23 February 1765, at the age of fifteen, Charlotte Turner married twenty-one-year-old Benjamin Smith. Her groom was the second son of Richard Smith, a West Indian merchant who was also a director of the East India Company in London. If Charlotte embarked on this marriage in hopes of financial security, she was soon, and perpetually, disappointed. Benjamin Smith was selfish, dissolute, violent, and unfaithful. His excesses plunged his family into debt and made them suffer the consequences of default; nonetheless, during their twenty-two-year union, his wife followed him from debtors' prison to the Continent and back to England. Despite the fortitude Charlotte Smith maintained throughout these difficulties, Benjamin's vagaries increased her consciousness of all she had lost when she left her father's protection.

Distress at being transplanted from the Turner residences in Bignor Park, Sussex, and London's aristocratic Westminster district to a second-story flat in Cheapside runs through much of Smith's poetry. "To My Lyre," an uncharacteristically humorous piece written shortly before Charlotte Smith's death and first published in volume 2 of Sir Walter Scott's *Biographical Memoirs of Eminent Novelists, and Other Distinguished Persons* (1843), describes her early feelings of alienation from "Proud city dames with loud shrill clacks, / ('The wealth of nations on their backs . . . ')." This poem allows the bourgeoisie to be "Good sort of people! and well meaners," but Smith adds, "they could not be my congeners, / For I was of a different species." In Benjamin Smith's home Charlotte attended to her querulous, dying mother-in-law, who complained about the girl's deficiencies in housekeeping. Although Charlotte, with characteristic frankness, admitted Mrs. Smith's assessment to be "true enough," she was unwilling either to favor domestic ability over the literary pursuits she enjoyed or to excel in the alternative domain offered by her father-in-law. According to Charlotte Smith's sister, Catherine Anne Dorset, Richard Smith "frequently declared, that such was the readiness of [Charlotte's] pen, that she could expedite more business in an hour from his dictation, than any one of his clerks could perform in a day." As Benjamin continued dissolute, Richard Smith offered Charlotte "a considerable annual allowance, if she would . . . assist him in his business, which he foresaw would be lost to his family after his death." Charlotte declined his proposal, despite her talent in this area. "To My Lyre" reveals both her aptitude for and aversion to commerce: Smith's speaker complains of having been "By early sorrows soon beset, / Annoy'd and wearied past endurance, / With drawbacks, bottomry, insurance, / With samples drawn and tare and tret"; these commercial terms are evidently part of Smith's vocabulary. But the poem's narrator is willing to participate in neither the drudgery nor the diversions of bourgeois society, dismissing City feasts and Lord Mayors' balls as "Scenes that . . . / To my young eyes seem'd gross and sordid." At this juncture Charlotte's class prejudices kept her from participating in London's business world; after Richard Smith's death in 1776, she lost the luxury of such withdrawal. Richard Smith left Charlotte a settlement of about thirty-six thousand pounds to support the seven children Benjamin had to that point fathered, then ignored. This sum would have allowed the Smiths to live (as Charlotte Smith later said in the preface to her novel *The Banished Man* [1794]) "as a *gentleman's family*" if the will's intricacies and a competing claim from one of Richard Smith's male relatives had not resulted in litigation that remained unresolved during the lives of both Charlotte and Benjamin. In the face of these troubles Charlotte turned to writing, first as a vehicle of self-expression and later as a means of income.

In 1783, as a result of his debts, Benjamin Smith was sent to the King's Bench Prison. Leaving their children with her brother, Charlotte shared her husband's seven-month incarceration. Since debtors' wives had access to the outside world, she also fought for his release. She supported her family by selling poems that recalled her childhood in the English countryside as they expressed her current frustration and grief. James Dodsley, the publisher of highest repute, printed them at Smith's expense. Yet he took this minor risk only after the volume had been both approved by and dedicated to William Hayley, the poet noted for his patronage of William Cowper, William Blake, and the painter George Romney. *Elegiac Sonnets, and Other Essays* (1784) was an immediate success and went into a second edition within a year. Subsequently, the book, expanded and revised by Smith, went through nine more editions; its title was changed to *Elegiac Sonnets* in the fourth edition (1786) and to *Elegiac Sonnets, and Other Poems* in the eighth edition (1797). It was also translated into French and Italian. Its popularity testifies to Smith's talent; for according to the *European Magazine* (November 1806), at the time *Elegiac Sonnets, and Other Essays* was published "the town was so nearly satiated with this species of writing, that *the trade* emphatically termed poetry *a drug*." *Elegiac Sonnets, and Other Essays* resolved Smith's financial problems for some time and established her as a legitimate author; it also touched off a debate about sonnet form that was carried on vehemently by some of the period's most eminent writers.

Smith used the preface of *Elegiac Sonnets, and Other Essays* to express discomfort with the limits imposed on her by the sonnet form: "The little poems which are here called Sonnets, have I believe no very just claim to that title: but they consist of fourteen lines, and appear to me no improper vehicle for a single Sentiment." The rhyme schemes of Smith's poems are diverse: some of her sonnets are Shakespearean, one is Petrarchan, another is Spenserian, and the rest are irregular. She defended her deviance from the "legitimate" Italian model on the grounds that "very good judges" had told her "the legitimate Sonnet is ill-calculated for our language." Although Smith's experimentation helped to establish the sonnet's current freedom of form, her preface did not forestall the criticism she anticipated. Perhaps the most virulent opposition came from Anna Seward, a poet who copiously imitated John Milton's Italian-style sonnets. When Smith's poems convinced Seward's correspondent, one Reverend Berwick, that the sonnet need not be merely a light or trivial composition, Seward retorted in a letter of 6 October 1788, using the authority of the seventeenth-century French critic Nicholas Boileau, that " 'Apollo, tired with votaries who assumed the name of poet, on the slight pretense of tagging flimsy rhymes, invented the strict, the rigorous sonnet as a test of skill;'—but it was the legitimate sonnet which Boileau meant, not that facile form of verse which Mrs. Smith has taken, three elegiac stanzas closing with a couplet." Samuel Taylor Coleridge came to Smith's defense in the introduction to a volume of poems by himself and others (1796), explaining that he had deduced the rules for his poems from the work of both Smith and William Lisle Bowles. From them he learned that

William Hayley, a popular poet and patron of William Cowper, William Blake, and the painter George Romney. It was on Hayley's recommendation that the publisher James Dodsley accepted Smith's first book, Elegiac Sonnets, and Other Essays *(portrait by Henry Howard; National Portrait Gallery, London).*

a sonnet ought to be "a small poem, in which some lonely feeling is developed," and that for the most "exquisite" effect "moral sentiments, affections, or feelings, are deduced from, and associated with, the scenery of Nature." Coleridge admitted that the sonnet should be "limited to a *particular* number of lines" but felt that a poet should "consult his own convenience" in regard to rhyme scheme: "Rhymes, many or few, or no rhymes at all—whatever the chastity of his ear may prefer, whatever the rapid expression of his feelings will permit;—all these things are left at his own disposal." Coleridge argued that since poetry should express transient human emotions, confining the English sonnet to the Italian model was to create an unnecessarily "difficult and artificial ... species of composition." He thus dismissed cavils like Seward's: "But the best confutation of such idle rules is to be found in the Sonnets of those who have observed them, in their inverted sentences, their quaint phrases, and incongruous mixture of obsolete and Spenserian words: and when, at last, the thing is toiled and hammered into fit shape, it is in general racked and tortured Prose rather than any thing resembling Poetry."

Smith's work expressed strong emotion, but some readers could not credit her with genuine suffering. In a 9 July 1789 letter to Theophilus Swift, Seward referred to Smith's "everlasting lamentables, which she calls sonnets," as "hackneyed scraps of dismality." A kinder if condescending reviewer in the *Gentleman's Magazine* (April 1786) could not "forbear expressing a hope that the misfortunes [Smith] so often hint[ed] at, [were] all imaginary." Smith's troubles were real, and *Elegiac Sonnets, and Other Essays* allowed her to come to grips with them.

Smith's compositional strategies within her slightly irregular formal limits are fairly consistent. She often begins with an apostrophe to a living person or a personified abstract quality; the next several lines contain description evoked by the person or quality addressed; and in the couplet (or closing lines of the sestets she used alternatively) the speaker explains the bearing the person or quality has on her own life. Smith directs her poems to a variety of people and encompasses a variety of situations, yet through all of them run an attention to nature and a melancholy tone. These sonnets use nature to represent Smith's feelings concretely. In Sonnet XII, "Written at the Sea Shore—October, 1784," for example, Smith's speaker makes explicit the correlation between internal and external conditions: "O'er the dark waves the winds tempestous howl; / The screaming sea-bird quits the troubled sea: / But the wild gloomy scene has charms for me, / And suits the mournful temper of my soul." As these sonnets address class issues, they use nature more subtly to achieve effects of which Smith may not have been fully aware.

Smith wrote *Elegiac Sonnets, and Other Essays* while she was struggling to consolidate a self distinct from the London surroundings that so dissatisfied her. Although in these poems Smith embraces the natural world, she does not identify with all parts of it; and her selective identification reveals her class prejudices. Many of the poems recall her childhood in Sussex. In Sonnet V, which she addresses "To the South Downs," she immediately establishes herself as both a votary of nature and a poet. Smith reminds the hills that as a "happy child," she "wove your bluebells into garlands wild, / And woke your echoes with my artless song." By asserting that her love of nature and poetic vocation preceded her marriage, Smith implies that she is not merely a debtor's wife. This gravitation toward the natural world did not provide Smith with new class allegiances; rather, her idealization of country life betrays her condescension toward rural folk. Sonnets IX, XI, and XXXI contrast the lot of shepherds with that of the poems' speaker. Ostensibly, the shepherds' condition is enviable; Sonnet IX notes a swain "on the turf reclin'd," who "Lies idly gazing" on "the varied clouds which float above." Smith's narrator calls this youth "blest" because he lacks the refinement to suffer as she does: his "rude bosom" has never been "melt[ed]" by those "fine feelings" that trouble "Children of Sentiment and Knowledge born." Throughout this sonnet Smith contrasts her persona with the shepherd: his mind is "idle" and "vacant," hers is busily occupied with problems; he "pours out some tale antique of rural love," she labors over a sonnet of present pain; he is impervious to the deceit or scorn of those above him in society, she suffers from her superiors' contempt. Like many writers of her period Smith endorsed democratic sympathy with the lower class, but her poem reveals anxiety that she might be placed in the same category with a rural laborer—even one of her own creation.

Smith's desire to be acknowledged a child "born" of sentiment and knowledge also surfaces in the literary allusions that provide the impetus for other poems in *Elegiac Sonnets, and Other Essays*. These poems allude to Alexander Pope, Thomas Gray, Edward Young, Milton, and Shakespeare. Such references both helped and hindered Smith; for while the incorporation of canonical texts lent credibility to her work, this appropriation of the "masters" led some contemporaries (including Seward) to charge her with plagiarism. In *Elegiac Sonnets, and Other Essays* Smith not only borrowed lines from male authors but occasionally adopted male voices. The volume contains translations of several Italian sonnets, including four by Petrarch and one by Pietro Metastasio. It also features five poems "supposed to be written by Werther," Johann Wolfgang von Goethe's famous Romantic hero. Since Petrarch's sonnet form was generally accepted as "correct" in the eighteenth century, Smith's translations seem an obvious means of endowing her work with legitimacy; yet her appropriation of these personas also absolved her of the responsibility of speaking in her own voice. Smith may have welcomed such respites from self-revelation since *Elegiac Sonnets, and Other Essays* left her vulnerable to public opinion. The confessional, journalistic style she adopted in most of her poems encouraged readers to equate poet with persona. The translations from the French that Smith produced between 1785 and 1787, conversely, were extended appropriations of male authority that allowed her to use voices with which she could not be identified.

Ironically, Smith relied on these proxies while acting a "masculine" part in the real world. Three months after Benjamin Smith's release from debtors' prison on 2 July 1784, he was again liable for prosecution. This time he chose flight over imprisonment, and Charlotte, by then pregnant with their twelfth child, followed him to Normandy in October. There they spent a miserable winter in an overpriced, dilapidated chateau. To entertain herself and some English friends, Charlotte began to translate the Abbé Prevost's sensational *Manon Lescaut* (1731). Its publication in 1785, after the Smiths' return to England in the spring of that year, was not financially rewarded because contemporary accusations of plagiarism and criticism of the work's "bad" morals forced Smith to withdraw it from circulation. Smith next translated François Gayot de Pitaval's *Causes célèbres et interessantes* (1735-1745). Although the public approved her version, *The Romance of Real Life* (1787), Smith did not find this type of work emotionally satisfying. Moreover, translation was not sufficiently lucrative, since the burden of providing for her eight youngest children belonged solely to Charlotte: in 1787 she separated from Benjamin Smith. Though such action was considered drastic at that time, her decision received, according to Dorset, "the entire approbation of her most dispassionate and judicious friends." Smith and her children settled near Chichester in Sussex, where she turned to writing the novels for which she continues to be known.

Smith produced four novels in the ensuing five years. The first three—*Emmeline, the Orphan of the Castle* (1788), *Ethelinde; or, The Recluse of the Lake* (1789), and *Celestina* (1791)—are sentimental narratives with Gothic elements. In writing these novels, Smith did not abandon poetry completely: *Emmeline*, for example, features sonnets "reflective of her own situation as well as her heroine's," according to Hilbish.

From 1791 to 1793 Smith spent much of her time at the resort town of Brighton. According to Dorset, Smith there "formed acquaintances with some of the most violent advocates of the French Revolution, and unfortunately caught the contagion, though in direct opposition to the principles she had formerly professed, and to those of her family." Her fourth work, *Desmond* (1792), addresses the issue of the revolution. The novel's epistolary form may have given Smith unusual freedom to express herself: she seems to have found authorial security, for example, in having the first volume consist of letters written by male characters. Smith claimed that she had no compunctions about voicing her opinions; in the preface to *Desmond* she asks those who argue that women have no business with politics: "Why not?—Have they no interest in the scenes that are acting around them, in which they have fathers, brothers, husbands, sons, or friends engaged?" Yet even here, Smith's uneasiness with self-expression is evident because she bases a woman's right to speak on the premise that she is related to male political actors. In the preface to a later novel, *The Young Philosopher* (1798), Smith specifically discouraged readers from identifying her sentiments with those of even her "amiable" characters: "I declare . . . against the conclusion, that *I* think either like Glenmorris or Armitage, or any other of my personages."

Desmond was initially lauded by the critics; their praise seems to have encouraged Smith to write *The Emigrants: A Poem in Two Books*, which also addresses the revolution. Despite Smith's assertion that it is "not a party book but a conciliatory book," *The Emigrants* puts forth radical views in the voice of a narrator much like Smith. This work marks Smith's poetic transition from political naïveté to sophistication because, unlike *Elegiac Sonnets, and Other Essays*, it connects effects with causes and focuses on the social institutions responsible for the speaker's misery. Smith dedicated *The Emigrants*, which is set "on the Cliffs to the Eastward of the Town of Brighthelmstone [Brighton] in Sussex," to Cowper because she was influenced by his poem *The Task* (1785) "to attempt, in Blank Verse, a delineation of those interesting objects which happened to excite my attention." These "objects" were the men and women who fled France in the revolution's wake and with whom Smith identified. *The Emigrants* uses descriptions of nature in winter (Book I) and spring (Book II) to suggest the emotions of the French exiles. Smith arranges these characters in contrasting groups that represent religious, domestic, and military life. She then compares the lot of these emigrés with her own condition and asks her English readers to behave compassionately toward the dispossessed wanderers.

The Emigrants has both radical and conservative impulses that suggest the conflict Smith felt at being simultaneously part of England's work force and its gentry. In her radical moments Smith's narrator rebels both against the institutions that caused Smith's poverty in England and against those that led to anarchy in France. The poem attacks England's legal, manorial, and political systems; its main target in France is absolute monarchy. Smith argues against social hierarchy, stating that "the poorest hind, who dies . . . in [God's] fight / Is equal to the imperious Lord, that leads / His disciplin'd destroyers to the field." She also vilifies the politicians who have

Brighthelmstone. Feb. 20th 1793.

Dear Sir

My stay at Eartham was so short, and so much was I occupied during that short time in engaging Mr Hayley's humanity on behalf of some French friends of mine who were likely to be compelled to leave this place & knew not where to find refuge within the distance mark'd by the order of Council – that I was not able to find as much as would suffice to offer you our joint thanks – He assured me that it was his intention to write to you himself in a few days after my departure on Monday last –

I sent the last packet of MMS and a sheet of Letter press that was missing in the 3d Volume on Monday last from London – I trust Mr Rice will receive it so soon as to preclude all possibility of the other Booksellers overtaking him – I troubled you with a short Letter in the packet & shall be greatly oblig'd to you to Let me hear if it was received safe – I am yet more impatient for the French Sonnets. The Old Manor House is not yet publish'd here; It has however been advertis'd as being speedily to be publish'd: but it will be probably quite the end of the Month first – So that as Mr Rice w'd be undoubtedly a fortnight or three weeks before the other Booksellers, I imagine your most obliging wishes in

Letter from Smith to the Reverend Joseph Cooper Walker of Dublin in which she mentions her novel The Old Manor House *and her poem* The Emigrants *(#10808, Henry E. Huntington Library and Art Gallery)*

my favor will not be baffled – Whatever advantage may accrue in consequence of your friendly interposition, I shall be still more obliged to you if you will receive for me & remit to Mr Thomas Watkinson. No 10. Water Street Blackfriars – who is so good as to befriend me in the little money matters I have; & indeed without very great kindness from my friends I know not what would have become of me & my Children this winter.

The Poem which I am about is in Blank verse & is to be entitled "The Emigrants" – Mr Cowper is to correct it under the auspices of Mr Hayley who thinks many parts of the first book which is nearly done, very capital – But indeed I always fear the partiality of his friendship — The Book is to consist of two parts – about a thousand or twelve hundred lines – & will be publish'd here, if I can get peace to finish it, about the beginning of May – It is not a party book but a conciliatory book – & Mr Hayley thinks there is some very good drawing in it.

— Will you forgive this short and incoherent Letter. My Son Charles goes to London tomorrow to see if he can prevail on the Trustees to let him have three hundred pounds to purchase an Ensigncy in some of the new raised companies – as nothing can be more distressing to him & to me, than his being at home witht any plan of Life – I send up by him several letters on business – which I must ~~write~~ in company as the Emigrant

who are yet here some of whom are very agreeable Men, find
some consolation in the society my small book seem affords
them of an evening – The confusion of tongues therefore that I
have around me prevents my adding more at this instant
than a repetition of that gratitude & regard with which I must
ever be Dear Sir your Much oblig'd and most obed Ser.
Charlotte Smith

abused their power: "Ye venal, worthless hirelings of a Court! Ye pamper'd Parasites! whom Britons pay for forging fetters for them." Smith warns these ministers that "if oppress'd too long, / The raging multitude, to madness stung, / Will turn on their oppressors; and no more / By sounding titles and parading forms / Bound like tame victims, will redress themselves!" *The Emigrants* urges the populace not to be deluded by the "worldly grandeur" that often accompanies despotism. Such luxury, Smith explains, "wreathes with silk the iron bonds, / And hides the ugly rivets with her flowers," causing those enslaved to "love the glitter of their chains" and to "forget their weight."

The radical message of *The Emigrants* is not consistent, however, and Smith's class allegiances display themselves in her sympathy for the French nobility. Her speaker pities the Christ-like despot "whose luckless head" bears a "jeweled circlet, lin'd with thorns" and upon whom the crown confers "Hereditary right to rule, unchecked, / Submissive myriads." In a lengthy apostrophe to Marie Antoinette, Smith not only pardons the queen but also holds the mob responsible for royal excesses: "Whate'er thy errors were, / Be they no more remember'd; tho' the rage / Of Party swell'd them to such crimes, as bade / Compassion stifle every sigh that rose / For thy disastrous lot." Smith does more than pity Marie Antoinette: she explicitly identifies with her. "Ah! who knows from sad experience more than I," she asks the queen, "to feel for thy desponding spirit as it sinks / Beneath procrastinated fears for those / More dear to thee than life!" This gesture epitomizes Smith's desire for high social position and her suppression of that desire; for when Smith makes her identification with Marie Antoinette explicit, her point of comparison is not their loss of rank but their culturally sanctioned maternal feelings. *The Emigrants* deplores the regicide, and Smith's conservatism finally predominates. Her solution to the crisis in France is a constitutional monarchy like the one England "boasts." Clearly, Smith's investment in the existing social hierarchy kept her from urging full-scale revolution; but *The Emigrants* represents her most democratic impulses and her most comprehensive poetic attempt to challenge the social structures of England and France.

Those of Smith's contemporaries who did not object to its personal allusions and plaintive tone lauded *The Emigrants*, focusing on Smith's peaceful and ultimately conservative vision. But according to Dorset, as the revolution lost popularity in England Smith's political assertiveness "lost her some friends, and furnished others with an excuse for withholding their interest in favor of her family, and brought a host of *literary ladies* in array against her, armed with all the malignity which envy could inspire!" After *The Emigrants* Smith turned back to writing novels; when she experimented with genre, it was on the safe terrain of books for "young persons."

Many critics consider *The Old Manor House* (1793), which reverts to the sentimental style of her first three narratives and which features subtle delineation of character, Smith's best novel. The novels that followed it—most importantly *The Banished Man, Montalbert* (1795), *Marchmont* (1796), and *The Young Philosopher*—include attacks on the English legal system. The second volume of *Elegiac Sonnets, and Other Poems*, which first appeared in 1797, also features such socially conscious poems as an occasional address "Written for the Benefit of a Distressed Player, Detained at Brighthelmstone for Debt, 1792" and "The Forest Boy," which concludes with an admonition to statesmen who "let loose the demons of war." But while Smith's adult books urged social change, her works for young women dictated absolute adherence to the culture's existing standards of conduct. In the preface to *Rural Walks* (1795), a volume of dialogues designed to "Unite the interest of the novel with the instruction of the schoolbook," Smith explains that her purposes are "To repress discontent," "to check that flippancy of remark, so frequently disgusting in girls of twelve or thirteen," and "to inculcate the necessity of submitting cheerfully to such situations as fortune may throw them into." She also hopes to give her young readers "a taste for the pure pleasures of retirement, and the sublime beauties of Nature." Here Smith implies that an appreciation of nature may enable young women to bear uncomfortable situations, and in the posthumously published *Beachy Head: With Other Poems* nature's sublime beauties help Smith to resign herself to dying without having attained the social status she desired.

In 1795 Smith's daughter Anna Augusta died, and Smith's grief permeates all of her writing thereafter. She traveled to various towns in England, hoping to escape memories of her loss. She held the delay of Richard Smith's bequest responsible for her daughter's death; and while she finally won the legal battle, its resolution came too late to benefit her. About the year 1799 the relative whose claims had been the main impediment to the distribution of Richard Smith's effects agreed to a compromise. Smith knew that the rights of her children would be restored; but the protracted litigation had resulted in the diminution of the original bequest, and even after the earl of Egremont provided Smith with funds to conclude the legal business, delays further prolonged the settlement. Benjamin Smith, who had constantly tried to appropriate his father's estate, died in February 1806, leaving Charlotte free to act as executor of the will. Her declining health would not permit such exertion, however, and the inheritance was not disbursed while she was alive. On 28 October 1806 Smith died in Tilford at the age of fifty-seven.

Aside from the two works published after her death, Smith left few personal effects. *The Natural History of Birds: Intended Chiefly for Young Persons* (1807) continued Smith's didactic project, and her final volume of poetry has similarly instructive content. *Beachy Head: With Other Poems* demonstrates Smith's facility with many kinds of verse. Her most uncharacteristic efforts are rhyming translations of fables from various countries. In her renditions of "The Truant Dove," by Pilpay; "The Lark's Nest," by Aesop; and "Love and Folly," by Jean de La Fontaine, Smith addresses such grave issues as the infidelity of husbands, the necessity of self-reliance, and the blindness of love. But she delivers her message (especially in "The Truant Dove") with wit and humor. More characteristic of Smith are the lyric poems "The Swallow," "Flora," "Studies by the Sea," "The Horologue of the Fields," "A Walk in the Shrubbery," and "Saint Monica," which experiment with different rhyme schemes while they take moral lessons from the book of nature. "Beachy Head" is a loco-descriptive, blank-verse poem that, due to Smith's death, went unfinished. Like Cowper's *The Task*, it uses associations called up by a rural spot to meditate on the world and the poet's place in it. *Beachy Head: With Other Poems* represents Smith's final positions on the issues she had broached in *Elegiac Sonnets* and *The Emigrants*: in these poems she expresses neither the dissatisfaction she had voiced in the former nor the qualified political rebellion she had risked in the latter. Instead, a sense of resignation pervades the book, and Smith's acceptance of her lot is suggested by its recommendation of the values of nature over art, poverty over wealth, and sacrifice over fulfillment. These issues are exemplified in the title poem, yet "Beachy Head" suggests that the resolution to which Smith came was incomplete.

"Beachy Head" insists on the inherent superiority of nature to art, and this dichotomy takes on political as well as aesthetic significance when Smith champions the simplicity of the countryside over the opulence of the court. Contradictions in the poem, however, suggest that Smith's allegiances have not shifted from the aristocracy: the poem applauds the democracy of nature only to impose an aristocratic system on the natural terrain. The narrator compares roses to "velvet robes of regal state / Of richest crimson" and places the heavenly bodies in a class relationship when she describes the "fair [evening] star" as being "Attendant on her queen, the crescent moon." Smith's class allegiances are further revealed by her narrator's relationship to country dwellers.

In *Elegiac Sonnets* Smith had refused to identify with the poor rural folk she described; in *The Emigrants*, she overtly identified with the dispossessed aristocracy. In "Beachy Head" Smith's narrator again distances herself from the "sturdy hind," but the quality that differentiates her from the peasant is intellect rather than the sensibility invoked in *Elegiac Sonnets*. For example, she indulges in a lengthy speculation on why the "strange and foreign forms / Of sea-shells" can be found in the English hills, where "surely the blue Ocean . . . never roll'd its surge." She then contrasts her own intellectual curiosity with the indifference of the peasant, who goes "to his daily task . . . Unheeding such inquiry." In using intellect rather than sensibility, strength rather than weakness, to achieve distance from the rustics, Smith seems to acknowledge the independent, assertive aspects of her personality. But since the poem's moral exemplar is a hermit who sacrifices his life for another and who will be rewarded only in heaven, "Beachy Head" also seems to endorse the self-abnegation required of eighteenth-century women.

The most general contradiction of "Beachy Head" is Smith's continual recommendation of self-denial when self-assertion is apparent in her didactic stance and implicit in the very gesture of literary utterance. Smith's poetry thus reveals the tensions experienced by an eighteenth-century woman who was raised with a genteel ideology and then forced to support a family in a bourgeois, individualist society.

Smith's poetry was generally admired during her lifetime but passed out of fashion after her death. Although Smith considered her true gifts to be poetic, assessments like that of Sir Walter Scott married her to the title "novelist": "while we allow high praise to the sweet and sad effusions of Mrs. Smith's muse, . . . for her invention, . . . her knowledge of the human bosom, her power of natural description, her wit, and her satire, the reader must seek in her prose narratives." Modern feminists are rediscovering Smith's novels and finding them excellent alternatives to canonical feminist texts. Diana Bowstead, for example, writes: "It is difficult to understand why those interested in political, and especially feminist, literature have turned their attention recently so exclusively to Mary Wollstonecraft's clumsy, stridently partisan fiction when there is also Charlotte Smith's decorous and devastating *Desmond* to speak for the times." While Smith's poetry is no less culturally revealing than her prose, twentieth-century critics who have considered Smith as a poet have dwelt on her descriptions of the natural world and have cast her merely as a precursor of the male Romantics. These scholars admit that *The Emigrants* presents, in Bishop C. Hunt's words, "the events of contemporary history unfolding before the poet's very eyes" but assume that Smith's other major poems are devoid of sociopolitical content. Smith's choice of pastoral subject matter was itself political; and although the bulk of Smith's poetry is not overtly radical, critics' refusal to acknowledge its subversive implications suggests how disturbing those implications can be. Smith's compliance does not justify the demands imposed by her culture. Rather, her poems of collusion point toward the injustice of a system that forced women into dependent positions and that encouraged a talented writer like Charlotte Smith to spend her life fighting for a place of passivity in the English gentry, where the glitter of the chains for which she longed could make her forget their weight.

Biographies:

Catherine Anne Dorset, "Charlotte Smith," in *Biographical Memoirs of Eminent Novelists, and Other Distinguished Persons*, 2 volumes, by Sir Walter Scott (Edinburgh: Cadell / London: Houlston & Stoneman, 1843), II: 20-58;

Florence May Anna Hilbish, "Charlotte Smith, Poet and Novelist (1749-1806)," Ph.D. dissertation, University of Pennsylvania, 1941.

References:

Diana Bowstead, "Charlotte Smith's *Desmond*: The Epistolary Novel as Ideological Argument," in *Fetter'd or Free? British Women Novelists, 1670-1815*, edited by Mary Anne Schofield and Cecelia Macheski (Athens: Ohio University Press, 1986), pp. 237-263;

Samuel Egerton Brydges, *Imaginative Biography*, 2 volumes (London: Saunders & Otley, 1834), II: 75-101;

Samuel Taylor Coleridge, Introduction to *Poems on Various Subjects*, by Coleridge, Charles Lamb, and Robert Southey (London: C. G. & J. Robinsons/Bristol: J. Cottle, 1796);

Bishop C. Hunt, Jr., "Wordsworth and Charlotte Smith," *Wordsworth Circle*, 1 (Summer 1970): 85-113;

Roger Lonsdale, ed., *Eighteenth-Century Women Poets: An Oxford Anthology* (Oxford & New York: Oxford University Press, 1989), pp. 365-373;

"Memoirs of Eminent Persons: Memoirs of Charlotte Smith," *Monthly Magazine*, 3 (April 1803): 244-248;

Review of *Sonnets*, by Charlotte Smith, *Gentleman's Magazine*, 54 (April 1786): 333-334;

Sir Walter Scott, *Biographical Memoirs of Eminent Novelists, and Other Distinguished Persons*, 2 volumes (Edinburgh: Cadell / London: Houlston & Stoneman, 1843);

Anna Seward, *Letters of Anna Seward: Written between the Years of 1784 and 1807*, 6 volumes (Edinburgh: Constable, 1811);

George W. Whiting, "Charlotte Smith, Keats, and the Nightingale," *Keats-Shelley Journal*, 12 (Winter 1963): 4-8;

William Wordsworth, *The Prose Works of William Wordsworth*, 3 volumes, edited by Alexander B. Grosart (London: Moxon, 1876), III: 151, 507.

Papers:

The Petworth House Archives in Petworth, Sussex, have letters from Charlotte Smith to the third earl of Egremont or his legal agent, written between 1800 and 1806, as well as letters from other members of Smith's family and legal documents dating from 1773 to 1810. The Beinecke Library of Yale University and the Henry E. Huntington Library and Art Gallery, San Marino, California, have the largest collections of Smith letters in the United States.

Joseph Warton

(April 1722 - 23 February 1800)

David Fairer
University of Leeds

See also the Warton entry in *DLB 104: British Prose Writers, 1660-1800: Second Series.*

BOOKS: *Fashion: An Epistolary Satire to a Friend* (London: Printed for R. Dodsley and sold by T. Cooper, 1742);

The Enthusiast: or, The Lover of Nature (London: Printed for R. Dodsley and sold by M. Cooper, 1744); revised version, in volume 3 of *A Collection of Poems by Several Hands*, edited by Robert Dodsley (London: Printed for R. Dodsley, 1748);

Odes on Various Subjects (London: Printed for R. Dodsley and sold by M. Cooper, 1746; revised, 1747);

Ranelagh House: A Satire in Prose: in the Manner of Monsieur Le Sage, anonymous (London: Printed for W. Owen, 1747);

An Ode, Occasioned by Reading Mr. West's Translation of Pindar (London: Printed for W. Owen, 1749);

An Essay on the Writings and Genius of Pope, anonymous (London: Printed for M. Cooper, 1756); revised as *An Essay on the Genius and Writings of Pope* (London: Printed for R. & J. Dodsley, 1762; revised edition, London: Printed for J. Dodsley, 1772); volume 2 (London: Printed for J. Dodsley, 1782); revised, 2 volumes (London: Printed for J. Dodsley, 1782).

OTHER: *Poems on Several Occasions: By the Reverend Mr. Thomas Warton*, edited, with contributions, by Warton (London: Printed for R. Manby and H. S. Cox, 1748);

Adventurer, nos. 1-140, includes twenty-four numbers signed "Z," by Warton, Thomas Warton, and Jane Warton (London: Printed for J. Payne, 7 November 1752 - 9 March 1754);

The Works of Virgil, 4 volumes, edited, with translations, by Warton and Christopher Pitt (London: Printed for R. Dodsley, 1753);

Sir Philip Sydney's Defence of Poetry, and Observations on Poetry and Eloquence, from the Discoveries of Ben Jonson, edited by Warton (London: Printed for G. G. and J. Robinson, 1787);

The Works of Alexander Pope, 9 volumes, edited by Warton (London: Printed for B. Law, J. Johnson, C. Dilly, G. G. & J. Robinson, J. Nichols, and others, 1797);

The Poetical Works of John Dryden, 4 volumes, edited by Warton and John Warton (London: F. C. & J. Rivington, 1811).

It is common for the brothers Joseph and Thomas Warton to be regarded as a single phenomenon, and to speak of "the Wartons" has a certain justice. They sustained an affectionately close relationship throughout their lives, shared many of the same friends, and helped each other in a variety of critical and poetic projects. It is also convenient for literary history to place them together as "pioneers of Romanticism," primitivists and Gothic enthusiasts who broke away from the "School of [Alexander] Pope" and helped through their critical and poetic writings to reestablish the "native" tradition of Edmund Spenser and John Milton. Joseph and Thomas Warton thought of themselves as pioneers; they attempted consciously to change the taste of the public, and Joseph's *An Essay on the Writings and Genius of Pope* (1756), with its demotion of Pope to the second rank of poets, was in effect complemented by Thomas's *Observations on the Faerie Queene of Spenser* (1754), his recovery in *The History of English Poetry, from the Close of the Eleventh to the Commencement of the Eighteenth Century* (1774-1781) of much older literature, and his edition of the early poems of Milton (1785). Seen from the nineteenth century their work did appear to be part of a single project, and it would be foolish to pretend that their joint influence on taste has been the invention of later scholars.

Although they never collaborated officially, the nature of their cooperation is becoming increasingly clear: Joseph's *Odes on Various Subjects*

Joseph Warton (from a portrait by Sir Joshua Reynolds)

(1746) silently included two of his brother's poems; Thomas assisted with Joseph's *Adventurer* papers (1752-1754), probably writing at least one himself, and saw the essay on Pope through the press at Oxford; Joseph provided material for Thomas's *History of English Poetry*; and they often submitted their poems to each other for approval, suggesting corrections or even supplying additional lines. Perhaps their most significant collaboration was to provide between them at least nineteen poems to eke out the posthumous volume of their father's verse, *Poems on Several Occasions* (1748), which Joseph edited.

Yet to speak of "the Wartons" runs a great risk. The two brothers were as distinctive in character as they were in handwriting: Joseph's writing became increasingly flowing and rapid, full of breathless dashes, while Thomas's became ever more crabbed, scratchy, and laconic; Joseph held the public position of headmaster of Winchester, while Thomas's home was his Oxford College; Joseph was twice married and had children, while Thomas was a confirmed bachelor; Joseph unfailingly charmed the ladies, whereas Thomas unwound among the boys of his brother's school. In their work, too, the emphases are differently placed: the sensational primitivism in *The Enthusiast* (1744) is as characteristic of Joseph as the melancholy nostalgia in the "Ode Written at Vale-Royal Abbey" is of Thomas.

Joseph Warton, the eldest child of Thomas and Elizabeth Richardson Warton, was born at Dunsfold, Surrey, where his maternal grandfather, Joseph Richardson, was rector; he was baptized on 22 April 1722. His father, known to posterity as Thomas Warton the Elder, was at the time professor of poetry at the University of Oxford and in 1723 became vicar of Basingstoke,

Hampshire, and master of the local grammar school. Joseph's early education was therefore in good hands, and in 1736 he was sent to Winchester College, an institution to which he was devoted for the rest of his life. William Collins had entered two years earlier; the friendship that developed between Warton and Collins took a literary turn in October 1739 when they sent some short poems to the prestigious *Gentleman's Magazine*. Their publication attracted favorable notice, and two poetic careers were launched at once.

Warton and Collins were elected to scholarships at New College, Oxford; but no vacancy occurred, and Warton entered the university as a commoner of Oriel College in September 1740. As an undergraduate he developed the tastes he was to exhibit through the rest of his life. He wrote to his father: "I shall read Longinus as long as I live: It is impossible not to catch fire and raptures from his glowing style. The noble causes he gives . . . for the decay of the sublime amongst men, to wit—the love of pleasure, riches, and idleness, would almost make one look down upon the world with contempt." This enthusiastic longing for lost sublimity and contempt for modern luxury marks his early poetry and prose. His first independent publication was a heroic-couplet satire titled *Fashion* (1742); he never acknowledged the poem, and it has never been reprinted. With all the confidence of youth it lashes the modish vices of the day and the malign power of the goddess Fashion; although the satiric portraits lack Pope's subtlety of tone, the young man has obviously steeped himself in Pope's satires as well as those of John Oldham and Edward Young. Warton's later prose satire, *Ranelagh House* (1747), finds similar targets among the fashionable company of that "temple of Luxury."

Warton took his B.A. degree in 1744, was immediately ordained, and became a curate in his father's parish. In that year his single most influential poem, *The Enthusiast*, with its effective evocations of the delights of nature, was published. Warton celebrates a world unfettered by rules, where all art is negative artifice: "Can [the landscape gardener William] Kent design like Nature?" he asks. The greatest painters are outdone by "the thousand-colour'd tulip," and the ancient hero Aeneas is aestheticized into a man who prefers sublime mountain scenery to the classical columns of Rome. "Happy the first of men . . . ," Warton continues, "who in sheltering groves, / Warm caves, and deep-sunk vallies liv'd and lov'd." In spite of its naive moments the poem's blank verse achieves a genuine fervor and momentum, and much has obviously been learned from the best scenic passages in James Thomson's *The Seasons* (1726-1730).

A personal crisis came in September 1745 when Thomas Warton the Elder died, leaving Joseph head of the family. His father left some troublesome debts, and with the seventeen-year-old Thomas studying at Oxford, the family's budget was severely stretched. Their mother retired to the College of Clergymen's Widows at Winchester, and Joseph was left to look for ways of supplementing their income. Plans for publishing his odes by subscription fell through, but by October 1746 Warton decided that it was feasible to bring out a volume of his father's poems in that way ("It would be easy to raise two or three hundred pounds; a very solid argument, in our present situation," Joseph wrote to Thomas on 29 October). Joseph regarded his editorial role as a corrective and creative one. His father's verses were spruced up with reworked phrases and additional lines to bring them more into accord with Joseph Warton's own taste for striking images, so that verses that had originally been close in spirit to those of Matthew Prior (a friend of Thomas Warton the Elder's) at times bear a remarkable resemblance to the work of the trendy young poets of the 1740s whom the publisher Robert Dodsley had taken under his wing. Joseph and Thomas Warton were also writing poems of their own, and their father's *Poems on Several Occasions* became a repository for a considerable number of their pieces. One of the most interesting areas of recent Warton scholarship has been the identification of their anonymous contributions, and the picture is still not complete.

In May 1746 Collins and Warton, who had both been writing odes, showed each other their work and decided to produce a joint collection. But their plans were changed before an advertisement could appear, and their respective volumes were published in December by different publishers. Warton's *Odes on Various Subjects* seems to have hit public taste more surely, since a second edition was called for a month later. Offering his poems as a corrective to established forms, Warton added a challenging preface asserting the primacy of imagination in poetry, and he included the confident declaration: "the following Odes may be look'd upon as an attempt to bring back Poetry into its right channel." As if to evoke his presiding figure at the outset, the volume

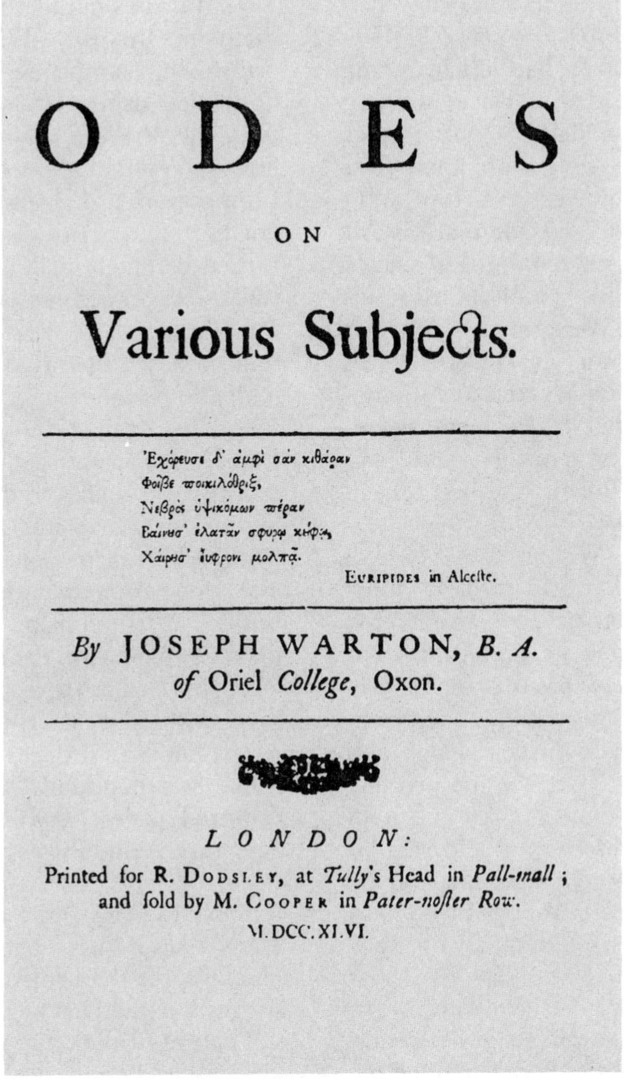

ODES

ON

Various Subjects.

'Εχόρευσε δ' ἀμφὶ σὰν κιθάραν
Φοῖβε ποικιλόθριξ,
Νεβρὸς ὑψικόμων πέραν
Βαίνουσ' ἐλατᾶν σφυρῷ κούφῳ,
Χαίρουσ' εὔφρονι μολπᾷ.

Euripides in Alceste.

By JOSEPH WARTON, *B. A.*
of Oriel *College*, Oxon.

LONDON:
Printed for R. Dodsley, at *Tully's* Head in *Pall-mall*;
and sold by M. Cooper in *Pater-noster Row*.
M.DCC.XLVI.

Title page for Warton's book of poems originally planned as a collaboration with William Collins

opens with "Ode to Fancy," a poem in the octosyllabic rhymes of Milton's *L'Allegro* (1631?); Warton thereby associates his own work with the early Spenserian Milton of the England of Charles I. There are some effectively atmospheric pieces (the odes to Evening, Solitude, and the Nightingale), as well as poems in Warton's more bloodcurdling vein ("To Superstition" and "Against Despair"), and throughout he exploits picturesque personifications. Reading the volume alongside Collins's, Thomas Gray commented in a letter of 27 December 1746 that "each is the half of a considerable Man . . . the first [Warton] has but little Invention, very poetical choice of Expression, and a good Ear, the second, a fine Fancy, model'd upon the Antique, a bad Ear, great Variety of Words and Images with no Choice at all." Gray's distinctions are shrewd and perceptive.

Warton's life became more secure when Charles Paulet, Duke of Bolton, presented him with the rectory of Winslade, Hampshire, in 1747; shortly afterward, on 21 September, Warton married Mary Daman, who lived in the same parish. "Molly" Warton was a good-humored woman whose letters are lively, immediate, and sparkling with gossip, and she was a loving mother to their seven children (Joseph, born in 1749; Anne, born in 1753; Thomas, born in 1754; John, born in 1756; Mary, born in 1758; Charlotte, born in 1761; and Jane, born in 1764). But patronage was an uncertain business, and Warton was considerably embarrassed by an incident in the summer of 1751 when he traveled to France with the duke of Bolton and the duke's longtime mistress, Lavinia Fenton (who had played Polly Peachum in John Gay's *The Beggar's Opera* [1728]). Warton's patron had left his dying wife in England and needed a clergyman on hand to perform an immediate wedding once news of her death came. After more than four months had passed, however, Warton went home. When the duchess died soon afterward Warton asked if he might return, but his chance had gone. The only positive result of this unlikely adventure was that Warton saw the sights of France. But the visit merely confirmed his love of England: his "Verses Written at Montauban in France" (a misnomer for a poem assembled from earlier fragments) is mainly about British liberties and features Boadicea, King Alfred, Magna Charta, and Henry V.

It was in 1753 that Warton came to real prominence in the literary world with his four-volume edition of *The Works of Virgil.* It included Christopher Pitt's translation of *The Aeneid*, but Warton translated the *Eclogues* and *Georgics*, provided a tasteful commentary, and appended critical essays on the pastoral, didactic poetry, and the epic. Visiting London to oversee the printing of these volumes, Warton found himself in the society of his publisher, Dodsley, who held regular literary gatherings at Tully's Head. Soon Warton could count among his friends Young, David Garrick, Joseph Spence, Henry Fielding, and Samuel Johnson.

It was through Johnson that Warton became involved in the *Adventurer*, a twice-weekly periodical published by John Payne and edited by Dr. John Hawkesworth, to which such figures as Bonnell Thornton and George Colman the Elder were contributing. Responsible for the twenty-four papers signed "Z," Warton enlisted his family as helpers: Thomas seems to have coauthored the two-part paper (51 and 57) assessing the claims of Hebrew poetry in terms of Longinian sublimity, and he may have written other pieces; Warton's sister Jane, a governess, was possibly responsible for paper 87 on good breeding. Joseph had included her ode on their father in the 1748 volume, and she blossomed late in life as the anonymous author of a novel, *Peggy and Patty; or, The Sisters of Ashdale* (1783), and a conduct book, *Letters Addressed to Two Young Married Ladies, on the Most Interesting Subjects* (1782). Perhaps the most influential "Z" papers are Joseph's essays on *The Odyssey* (75, 80, 83), which he values more highly than *The Iliad*; *The Tempest* (93, 97); and *King Lear* (113, 116, 122).

Warton's nonliterary career soon took a new direction. In July 1755 he became rector of Tunworth, Hampshire, and in December he was appointed usher, or second master, of Winchester College. Warton was keen to raise the school's literary reputation in both classical and English composition, and in his teaching he stressed the creative and critical approaches to literature rather than mere pedantic book learning. He especially encouraged his pupils in the art of translation as a means of steeping themselves in the style and sentiments of an author. Not surprisingly, he became a much-loved master.

The year 1755 must have been an extremely busy one for Warton. Not only did he move twice, finally settling into the school boardinghouse, but he was also hurriedly writing the work which crowned his literary career. The essay on Pope was being printed at Oxford under the supervision of Thomas, who had to make many editorial decisions while being regularly supplied with copy by post. By October Joseph realized that he had enough material for two volumes and decided to have volume 1 published independently. He pressed on, and two hundred pages of volume 2 were also printed. But work suddenly stopped, and the sheets lay in store for more than twenty-five years before he felt able to bring out a completed second volume. Many reasons have been suggested for Warton's breaking off the project; the most plausible is the suggestion that he was uneasy at the controversial nature of the enterprise for a man in his public position, one with such influential admirers of Pope among his acquaintance as Dodsley, Spence, Young, Johnson, William Warburton, and Lord Lyttelton.

An Essay on the Writings and Genius of Pope was certainly intended to cause a hubbub in the literary world. The publisher, Dodsley, was uneasy about it and kept his name off the title page. Warton, also withholding his name, added a dedication to Young which challenged Pope's preeminence as a poet: "I revere the memory of Pope; I respect and honour his abilities; but I do not think him at the head of his profession." For Warton, Pope excels in the second division of poetry as a writer of a "clear head, and acute understanding" but lacks a mastery of the sublime and pathetic, "the two chief nerves of all genuine poesy"; he also falls short of the "creative and glowing IMAGINATION" which for Warton is the distinguishing mark of a great poet. But the body of the essay is hardly a document of revolu-

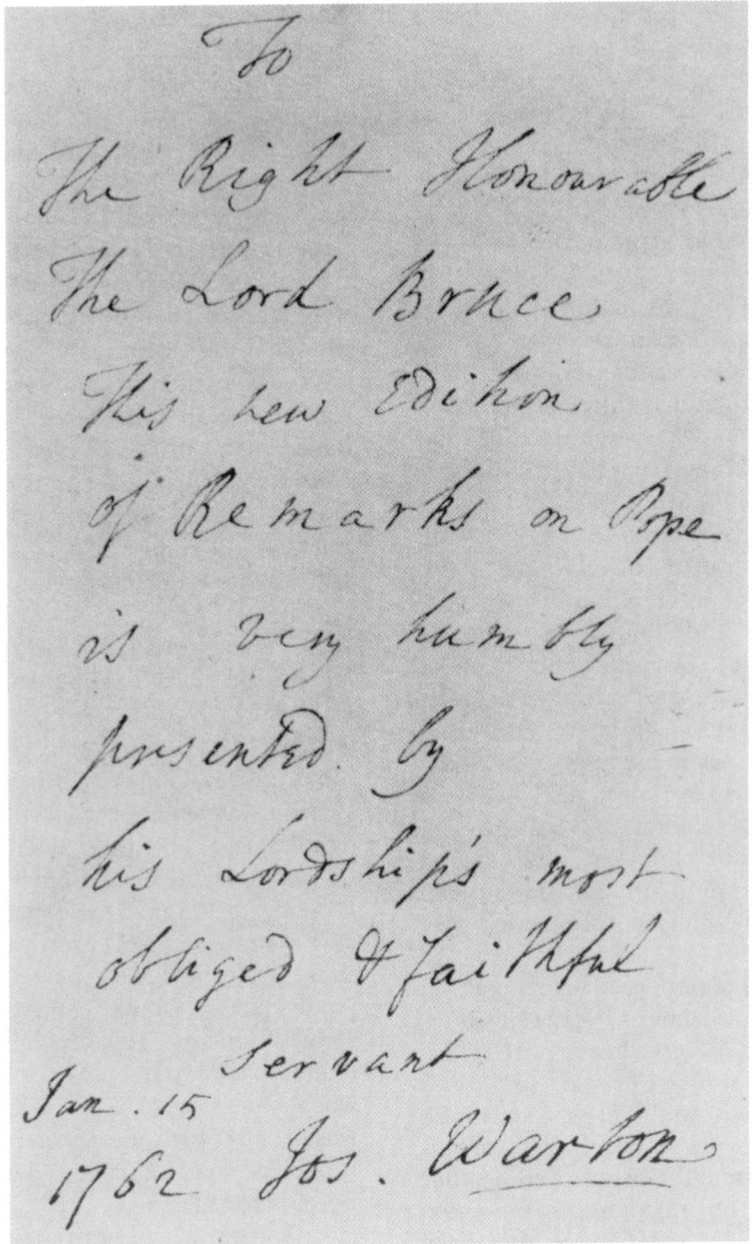

To
The Right Honourable
The Lord Bruce
This new Edition
of Remarks on Pope
is very humbly
presented by
his Lordship's most
obliged & faithful
Servant
Jan. 15
1762 Jos. Warton

Flyleaf inscription in a presentation copy of Warton's An Essay on the Genius and Writings of Pope *(Maggs Bros., catalogue 937, Autumn 1971)*

tion, and Warton has much to say in Pope's praise: *An Essay on Criticism* (1711) is "a masterpiece in its kind," *The Rape of the Lock* (1714) is "the best satire extant." Warton greatly admired *Windsor-Forest* (1713), the "Elegy to the Memory of an Unfortunate Lady," and *Eloisa to Abelard* (1719), the last two being the "only instances" of the pathetic in Pope. Warton's essay is piecemeal and digressive (its method of printing made this lack of structure virtually inevitable), and it often becomes annotatory in approach. But it is clearly the work of a discriminating and knowledgeable critic, and even Johnson, who did not share Warton's aesthetic principles, felt able to refer to it in his "Life of Pope" in *Prefaces, Biographical and Critical, to the Works of the English Poets* (1779-1781) as "a book which teaches how the brow of criticism may be smoothed, and how she may be enabled, with all her severity, to attract and to delight."

The essay sold well, and reviews were generally favorable, but Warton did not have the impulse to complete it. By 1760 he was proposing to Dodsley a project—which never materialized—for a selection of the works of Voltaire. In 1762 a revised edition of the Pope book was published, with the title altered slightly to *An Essay on the Genius and Writings of Pope*; further revisions were made for a 1772 edition. In general however, by 1762 Warton had entered a twenty-year suspension of his literary career.

Warton had received the M.A. from Oxford in 1759. On the resignation of Dr. John Burton in 1766 he was appointed headmaster of Winchester; he gained the B.D. and D.D. from Oxford in 1768. Warton had many women friends and seems to have been particularly relaxed in female company. The death of Molly Warton in 1772 shattered him; but at the end of the following year he married Charlotte Nicholas, who bore him a daughter, Harriet, in 1775. Elizabeth Montague, Hannah More, and Fanny Burney were counted as friends, and Burney's description of Warton presents a "rapturist" of warm feelings and animated conversation with the endearing habit of embracing his acquaintances and enthusing over a poem or picture. Throughout his writings warmth, passion, sublimity, and pathos are the great positives; Warton's literary interests and judgments are often bound up with these qualities, and they are an integral part of his own style.

Warton visited London each Christmas; in 1773 he was elected a member of Johnson's literary group, the Club, where he regularly met men such as Sir Joshua Reynolds, Edmund Burke, George Colman, and Oliver Goldsmith. He also entertained guests at Winchester, including Johnson, Reynolds, and Garrick, and brother Thomas came to stay during vacations from Oxford. In 1778 King George III made an official visit.

As he approached retirement Warton was able to settle down to literary studies once more. In 1787 he produced a combined volume of Sir Philip Sidney's *An Apologie for Poetrie* (1595) and Ben Jonson's *Discoveries* (1640-1641), two texts which were not well known at that date. He had persistent ambitious plans for a history of Hebrew, Greek, Roman, Italian, and French poetry, a project which made little progress although it was regularly advertised; it was probably intended as a complement to Thomas Warton's *History of English Poetry*. On Thomas's death in 1790 Warton engaged to complete his brother's magnum opus; but though he carried off Thomas's papers to Winchester, he seems to have made no progress in the enterprise.

Under Warton's guidance Winchester's reputation as a place of literary endeavor grew. Warton treasured the best examples of verse in English and the classical languages written by his students—some of them still survive among his papers—and he was a benign father figure to them. But discipline was not his forte. There were occasional unfortunate incidents, but none to match the riot of July 1793 when some of the boys seized firearms and were besieged in the college before an audience of thousands. Images of the storming of the Bastille cannot have been far from people's minds, and the scandal was considerable. In the same month Warton moved to Wickham in Hampshire, where he had the living, and resigned shortly afterward from the headmastership.

In retirement at Wickham, Warton turned his thoughts back to Pope. When it had finally appeared in 1782, the second volume of *An Essay on the Genius and Writings of Pope* had aroused some disparaging criticism; but by the 1790s Warton was widely regarded as the leading Pope scholar/critic, and he seemed the ideal person to set about replacing the old Warburton edition of Pope's works (1751). Warton's nine volumes (1797) were a suitable crown for his career; but although he included new letters, poems, and prose pieces (some controversially), his notes were often little advance on his own essay, and many were extracted verbatim from the earlier work. Financially *The Works of Alexander Pope* was a successful enterprise, however, and it is reported that Warton received five hundred pounds for his pains.

Warton's energies appeared undimmed, and with the Pope volumes published he made considerable headway with an edition of the works of John Dryden. At his death on 23 February 1800 two volumes, with notes, were completed, and they were incorporated by his son into a four-volume publication in 1811.

Unlike his brother's, Joseph Warton's career as a poet cannot be said to have extended beyond his twenties: he produced no volume of verse after 1749. But if the critic and editor took over, it is nonetheless clear that there was continuity, that the sensibility of the poet fed the taste of the critic, and the assertive preface to the *Odes on Various Subjects* seems to lead naturally to the project of judging Pope in terms of the Spenser-

Shakespeare-Milton tradition to which that volume allies itself. Warton's consciously pioneering stance as a poet was a practical extension of his interest in literary history, and literary historians have usually valued his work—whether as a prophetic revolutionary (according to Edmund Gosse) or as a transitional, mediating figure (as George Saintsbury contended). In both scenarios a supposed "romantic" movement claims Warton as a seminal voice. But he had less direct influence than did his brother Thomas on the young generation of poets writing at the end of the century, and his poetry and criticism may be best seen as exemplifying mid-century "Sensibility." Since Northrop Frye's identification of an "Age of Sensibility," however, it has been possible to recognize the 1740s as the true revolutionary decade of the eighteenth century, and Warton remains a major figure in this revolution. In John A. Vance's words, "To know Warton's poetry is to capture the growing literary mood of the mid-eighteenth century." Joan Pittock has fittingly made the Warton brothers the focus for her analysis of the developing concept of "taste," and John Sitter has drawn them into the company of novelists and philosophers in his study of the mid-eight eenth century as a period of shifting convictions and crucial artistic choices. It is now understood that *Poems on Several Occasions* is a crucial index of a shift in sensibility, and that the Warton brothers no longer stand in the paternal shadow. Joseph Warton's work in poetry and criticism remains significant, whether in the reassessment of Pope or in the reexamination of the traditional patterns and labels of literary history.

Letters:

"The Correspondence of Joseph Warton," edited by Hugh Reid, doctoral thesis, University of London, 1987.

Bibliography:

John A. Vance, *Joseph and Thomas Warton: An Annotated Bibliography* (New York: Garland, 1983).

Biographies:

John Wooll, *Biographical Memoirs of the Late Revd. Joseph Warton, D.D. . . . To Which Are Added, A Selection from His Works; and a Literary Correspondence Between Eminent Persons* (London: Cadell & Davies, 1806);

Alexander Chalmers, "Joseph Warton," in volume 18 of *The Works of the English Poets*, edited by Chalmers (London: Johnson, 1810), pp. 75-88;

Julia Hysham, "Joseph Warton: A Biographical and Critical Study," Ph.D. dissertation, Columbia University, 1950.

References:

David Fairer, "The Poems of Thomas Warton the Elder?" *Review of English Studies*, new series 26 (August 1975): 287-300; (November 1975): 395-406;

Fairer, "The Poems of Thomas Warton the Elder? —A Postscript," *Review of English Studies*, new series 29 (February 1978): 61-65;

Fairer, "The Writing and Printing of Joseph Warton's *Essay on Pope*," *Studies in Bibliography*, 30 (1977): 211-219;

Arthur Fenner, Jr., "The Wartons 'Romanticize' Their Verse," *Studies in Philology*, 53 (July 1956): 501-508;

Northrop Frye, "Towards Defining an Age of Sensibility," *ELH*, 23 (June 1956): 144-152;

Edmund Gosse, "Two Pioneers of Romanticism: Joseph and Thomas Warton," *Proceedings of the British Academy*, 7 (1915): 145-163;

Philip Mahone Griffith, "Joseph Warton's Criticism of Shakespeare," *Tulane Studies in English*, 14 (1965): 17-27;

Julia Hysham, "Joseph Warton's Reputation as a Poet," *Studies in Romanticism*, 1 (Summer 1962): 220-229;

Paul F. Leedy, "Genres Criticism and the Significance of Warton's Essay on Pope," *Journal of English and Germanic Philology*, 45 (April 1946): 140-146;

Christina le Prevost, "More Unacknowledged Verse by Joseph Warton," *Review of English Studies*, new series 37 (August 1986): 317-347;

William D. MacClintock, *Joseph Warton's Essay on Pope: A History of the Five Editions* (Chapel Hill: University of North Carolina Press, 1933);

Alan D. McKillop, "Shaftesbury in Joseph Warton's *Enthusiast*," *Modern Language Notes*, 70 (May 1955): 337-339;

David B. Morris, "Joseph Warton's Figure of Virtue: Poetic Indirection in *The Enthusiast*," *Philological Quarterly*, 50 (October 1971): 678-683;

Joan Pittock, *The Ascendancy of Taste: The Achievement of Joseph and Thomas Warton* (London: Routledge & Kegan Paul, 1973);

Pittock, Introduction to *Odes on Various Subjects (1746) By Joseph Warton: A Facsimile Reproduction* (Delmar, N.Y.: Scholars' Facsimiles & Reprints, 1977);

Pittock, "Joseph Warton and His Second Volume of the *Essay on Pope*," *Review of English Studies*, new series 18 (August 1967): 264-273;

Arthur H. Scouten, "The Warton Forgeries and the Concept of Preromanticism in English Literature," *Etudes Anglaises*, 40 (October-December 1987): 434-447;

John Sitter, *Literary Loneliness in Mid-Eighteenth-Century England* (Ithaca, N.Y. & London: Cornell University Press, 1982), pp. 120-133;

Paget Toynbee and Leonard Whibley, eds., *The Correspondence of Thomas Gray*, 3 volumes (Oxford: Clarendon Press, 1935); republished, with additions and corrections by Herbert W. Starr (Oxford: Clarendon Press, 1971);

Hoyt Trowbridge, "Joseph Warton on the Imagination," *Modern Philology*, 35 (August 1937): 73-87;

John A. Vance, *Joseph and Thomas Warton* (Boston: Twayne, 1983);

Vance, "The Samuel Johnson-Joseph Warton Friendship," *Johnson Society Transactions* (December 1982): 44-55;

Richard Wendorf, Introduction to *Joseph Warton: Odes on Various Subjects (1746)*, Augustan Reprint Society Publication No. 197 (Los Angeles: William Andrews Clark Memorial Library, University of California, 1979).

Papers:

Three significant collections of Joseph Warton's manuscripts, including correspondence, poetry, and notebooks are in the Bodleian Library, Oxford: the Trinity College Warton papers, the Swann Collection, and the Bodleian's own collections. Winchester College Library has a valuable holding of Wartoniana, and there is also important correspondence in the British Library.

Thomas Warton

(9 January 1728 - 21 May 1790)

David Fairer
University of Leeds

See also the Warton entry in *DLB 104: British Prose Writers, 1660-1800*.

BOOKS: *Five Pastoral Eclogues: The Scenes of which Are Suppos'd to lie among the Shepherds, oppress'd by the War in Germany* (London: Printed for R. Dodsley, 1745);

The Pleasures of Melancholy: A Poem (London: Printed for R. Dodsley and sold by M. Cooper, 1747);

Verses on Miss C-----s and Miss W-----t (London: Printed for W. Owen, 1749);

The Triumph of Isis: A Poem. Occasioned by Isis: An Elegy (London: Printed for W. Owen, 1750);

New-market: A Satire (London: Printed for J. Newbery, 1751);

Ode for Music, as Performed at the Theatre in Oxford, on the Second of July 1751 (Oxford: Printed for R. Clements and J. Barrett; W. Thurlbourne, Cambridge; R. Dodsley, London, 1751);

Observations on the Faerie Queene of Spenser (London: Printed for R. and J. Dodsley and J. Fletcher, Oxford, 1754); revised and enlarged as *Observations on the Fairy Queen of Spenser*, 2 volumes (London: Printed for R. and J. Dodsley and J. Fletcher, Oxford, 1762);

A Description of the City, College, and Cathedral of Winchester (London: Printed for R. Baldwin, sold by T. Burdon, Winchester; B. Collins, Salisbury, 1760);

Mons Catharinae; prope Wintoniam: Poema (London: Printed for R. and J. Dodsley, 1760);

A Companion to the Guide, and a Guide to the Companion: Being a Complete Supplement to All the Accounts of Oxford Hitherto Published (London: Printed for H. Payne, 1760; corrected and enlarged, 1762?);

The Life and Literary Remains of Ralph Bathurst, 2 volumes (London: Printed for R. and J. Dodsley, C. Bathurst, and J. Fletcher, Oxford, 1761);

The Life of Sir Thomas Pope (London: Printed for T. Davies, T. Becket, T. Walters, F. Newbery, and J. Fletcher, Oxford, 1772; enlarged edition, London: Printed for Thomas Cadell, 1780);

The History of English Poetry, from the Close of the Eleventh to the Commencement of the Eighteenth Century, volumes 1-3 (London: Printed for and sold by J. Dodsley, J. Walter, T. Becket, J. Robson, G. Robinson, J. Bew, and Messrs. Fletcher, Oxford, 1774-1781); volume 4, pp. 1-88 (N.p., n.d.);

Poems: A New Edition, with Additions (London: Printed for T. Becket, 1777); revised as *Poems: A New Edition* (London: Printed for T. Becket, 1777; corrected, 1779; corrected and enlarged, London: Printed for G. G. J. & J. Robinson, 1789); greatly enlarged as *Poems on Various Subjects, of Thomas Warton: Now First Collected* (London: Printed for G. G. J. & J. Robinson, 1791);

Specimen of a Parochial History of Oxfordshire (N.p.: Privately printed, 1782); corrected and enlarged as *Specimen of a History of Oxfordshire* (London: Printed for J. Nichols, J. Robson, and C. Dilly; Messrs. Fletchers, D. Prince & J. Cook, Oxford; J. Merrill, Cambridge, 1783); republished as *The History and Antiquities of Kiddington* (London: Nichols, 1815);

An Enquiry into the Authenticity of the Poems Attributed to Thomas Rowley (London: Printed for J. Dodsley & sold by Messrs. Fletchers, Oxford, 1782);

Verses on Sir Joshua Reynolds's Painted Window at New-College Oxford (London: Printed for J. Dodsley & sold by Messrs. Fletchers, Oxford, 1782);

A History of English Poetry: An Unpublished Continuation, edited by Rodney M. Baine, Augustan Reprint Society Publication No. 39 (Los Angeles: William Andrews Clark Memorial Library, 1953).

Thomas Warton (portrait by Sir Joshua Reynolds, by permission of Trinity College, Oxford)

OTHER: Joseph Warton, *Odes on Various Subjects*, contributions by Warton (London: Printed for R. Dodsley, and sold by M. Cooper, 1746; revised, 1747);

Thomas Warton the Elder, *Poems on Several Occasions: By the Reverend Mr. Warton*, edited by Joseph Warton, contributions by Warton (London: Printed for R. Manby and H. S. Cox, 1748);

The Union; or, Select Scots and English Poems, edited by Warton (Edinburgh [i.e., Oxford]: Printed for Archibald Monro and David Murray [i.e., Printed by William Jackson], 1753; London: Printed for R. Baldwin, 1759 [i.e. revised edition, 1760]; revised, 1766);

Inscriptionum Romanarum Metricarum Delectus, edited by Warton (London: Printed for R. & J. Dodsley, 1758);

The Oxford Sausage; or, Select Poetical Pieces, Written by the Most Celebrated Wits of the University of Oxford, edited by Warton (London: Printed for J. Fletcher, 1764; enlarged, 1772);

Anthologiae Graecae à Constantino Cephala Conditae Libri Tres, edited by Warton (Oxford: Printed by the Clarendon Press and sold by Jacob Fletcher; J. Nourse, P. Vaillant, and J. Fletcher, London, 1766);

Theocriti Syracusii Quae Supersunt, 2 volumes, edited by Warton (Oxford: Printed by the Clarendon Press, 1770);

Poems upon Several Occasions, English, Italian, and Latin, with Translations, by John Milton, edited by Warton (London: Printed for J. Dodsley, 1785; revised and enlarged edition, London: Printed for G. G. J. & J. Robinson, 1791).

Edition: *The Poetical Works of the Late Thomas Warton, B.D.*, 2 volumes, edited by Richard

Mant (Oxford: Oxford University Press, 1802).

SELECTED PERIODICAL PUBLICATIONS—UNCOLLECTED: Essays 51 and 57, *Adventurer* (1753), probably coauthored with Joseph Warton;
Essay 33, "Journal of a Senior Fellow," *Idler* (2 December 1758);
Essay 93, "Sam Softly," *Idler* (26 January 1760);
Essay 96, "Hacho, King of Lapland," *Idler* (16 February 1760).

In 1800 Sir Samuel Egerton Brydges (by no means an uncritical admirer of his work) said of Thomas Warton: "Perhaps there was no one, by whose death the literature of England could have sustained a greater chasm." This comment is not an empty encomium but a considered judgment which recognizes the width of Warton's achievement. He was a poet, biographer, humorist, classical scholar, Gothic enthusiast, local historian, literary critic, and editor, and he made a distinct and influential contribution to each field; the gap left by his death could never again be filled by one person.

The future poet laureate was born on 9 January 1728 in the then-small market town of Basingstoke, Hampshire, the younger son of Elizabeth Richardson Warton (daughter of the rector of Dunsfold, Surrey) and Thomas Warton the Elder, headmaster of Basingstoke Grammar School and former fellow of Magdalen College, Oxford, and Oxford professor of poetry. While his elder brother Joseph was sent to Winchester College, Thomas remained at home in Basingstoke under the care of his father. From him Warton gained a thorough knowledge of the classical languages, a fascination for antiquity, a tinge of Jacobitism, and the habit of writing verses. In 1738 he wrote to his older sister, Jane, with a translation from Martial; but a manuscript in the Bodleian Library contains an even earlier poem, "Birds nesting in Dunsfold Orchard," datable by the handwriting to 1735-1736. In his poetic infancy Warton was responding both to the classics and to nature—though his grandfather's orchard is equally the "inchanted Wood" of romance.

Between his matriculation at Trinity College, Oxford, on 16 March 1744 and his appointment to a fellowship in 1752, Warton's poetic output was remarkable. As a seventeen-year-old he made a confident debut on the literary scene with *Five Pastoral Eclogues: The Scenes of Which Are Suppos'd to Lie among the Shepherds, Oppress'd by the War in Germany* (1745). These pastorals, with their startlingly modern setting (soldiers lay waste the shepherds' villages and trample on their sheep), were accompanied by an advertisement praising the simplicity of the ancient writers. Among Warton's papers at Trinity is a draft of this preface which is more overt in its challenge to contemporary taste: "The Author has endeavour'd . . . to imitate that noble simplicity which we find in the ancient Authors, as thinking the Moderns so full of witty conceits, & quaintnesses. But tho' the Moderns have been so successfull in that Kind of writing, The taste of Poetry in England begins to amend. . . ." This statement on literary trends antedates his brother Joseph's similar and better-known declaration in the preface to his *Odes on Various Subjects* (1746).

In the same notebook with a draft of *Five Pastoral Eclogues* he sketched out "An Essay on Romantic Poetry." This tantalizing fragment demonstrates that the undergraduate Warton was not only in touch with the latest trends in poetry but felt able to theorize about them: "The principal use which the ancients made of poetry, as appears by their writings, was to imitate human actions & passions, or intermix here & there descriptions of Nature. Several modern authors have employed a manner of poetry entirely different from this, I mean in imitating the actions of spirits, in describing imaginary Scenes, & making persons of abstracted things, such as Solitude, Innocence, & many others. A Kind of Poetry which perhaps it would not be improper to call a Romantic Kind of Poetry, as it is altogether conceived in the spirit, (tho with more Judgement & less extravagant) & affects the Imagination in the same Manner, with the old Romances." Warton obviously shared his brother's pioneering spirit, and their various statements of 1745-1746 show that they both discerned a shift in poetic taste in the mid 1740s and were determined to exploit it.

Warton's *The Pleasures of Melancholy* was written in 1745 and published two years later; an extended and revised version appeared in Robert Dodsley's 1755 *Collection of Poems*. The opening evokes the figure of Contemplation:

secure, self-blest,
There oft thou listen'st to the wild uproar
Of fleets encount'ring, that in whispers low
Ascends the rocky summit, where thou dwell'st
Remote from man, conversing with the spheres!

This isolated and receptive figure provides an imaginative entry into a series of atmospheric landscapes as the poet explores a world of solitude, darkness, and eerie suggestion. The result is less description than a weaving through words of a contemplative spell, now and again broken by glimpses of a contrasting social world of glitter and artifice. The poem is a deft rondo of moods, undidactic yet argumentative.

During his undergraduate years poetry poured from Warton's pen. He was contributing regularly to Dodsley's *Museum* (1746-1747), and poems by him appeared under the names of both his brother and father. Two pieces were included in Joseph Warton's *Odes on Various Subjects*, the more interesting of which is "Ode to a Gentleman on His Travels through Italy." At least four poems were published as his father's in *Poems on Several Occasions* (1748): "Invocation to a Water-Nymph," which is reminiscent of the songs from John Milton's *Comus* (1634); a short paraphrase of Horace's ode II, 13; "Ode to Taste"; and the most important item, a smooth and accomplished translation of Moschus's "Pastoral on the Death of Bion," again reminiscent of the early Milton ("Wept the mild *Naiads* in their coral Caves; / Nor Echo more from her far-winding Grot / Is heard to sing . . .").

After taking his B.A. in 1747 Warton was elected "Laureate of the Bachelors' Common Room" (amusingly prefiguring his later fame as laureate to George III), a post which carried with it the duty to write a poem on the beauty of the graduates' annual Lady Patroness; his 1747 and 1748 verses (to Miss Cotes and Miss Wilmot) were inscribed in the official book and jointly published in 1749.

Both university and college gave a literary-minded student outlets for the writing of verse, and Warton soon gained a reputation in Oxford. He contributed to the *Student; or, The Oxford and Cambridge Monthly Miscellany* and was probably its Oxford editor. In 1750 he became the toast of the university through his successful defense of Oxford in *The Triumph of Isis*. The previous year *Isis: An Elegy*, by William Mason (a Cambridge man), had seized on a scandalous Jacobite demonstration to attack the university for its morals and its politics. Warton's poetic reply did its job brilliantly, as Mason himself ruefully admitted. *The Triumph of Isis* mingles satire on the pampered clerics of Cambridge with an encomium on Oxford's past, the beauty of its buildings, and the greatness of its poets and statesmen; Oxford's river Isis is personified as a gracious figure reminiscent of Milton's Sabrina. Warton attempts to capture Oxford's magical mixture of water meadows and Gothic architecture, celebrating it as a romantic enclave of idealism away from the sordid money-grubbing and place-seeking of progovernment Cambridge. He even dared to extol William King, the leader of Oxford Jacobitism. King was so impressed that he called at the bookseller's and left five guineas for his anonymous champion.

Warton took his M.A. in 1750. In 1751 his *Ode for Music* was performed by orchestra, chorus, and soloists at the annual commemoration of the university's benefactors in the Sheldonian Theatre. (His friend William Collins's *The Passions* had been similarly honored the previous year.) He was elected a probationary fellow of Trinity in 1752, becoming actual in 1753. This election set the seal on Warton's lifelong devotion to his college and university. He had security, a congenial setting, and his beloved libraries close at hand. He had begun reading in the Bodleian in 1750 and soon discovered the wealth of older literature it contained, both in books and in manuscripts. It has been calculated that in 1753 alone roughly one-ninth of all recorded book orders in the Bodleian were made by him, most being collections of older English literature and especially medieval romances and Elizabethan poetry.

One publication at this time which shows Warton's developing interest in older literature is his anthology of Scottish and English poetry, *The Union* (1753), an unusual collection printed in Oxford with a spoof Edinburgh imprint. It contains a mixture of newer lyric poems (Warton brings together, for example, Thomas Gray's recent *Elegy Written in a Country Churchyard* [1751] with odes to Evening by Collins and by Warton's brother Joseph) and pieces by the older Scottish poets William Dunbar and Sir David Lindsay (he had discovered Lindsay's poems in the Bodleian earlier that year). Warton also included several of his own works, the most important being his longest poem, "Ode on the Approach of Summer" (attributed to "a late member of the university of Aberdeen"). It marks a decisive shift in Warton's middle period, away from the influence of the early Milton toward the rediscovery of the language of natural description and the moods of delight and nostalgia which a landscape might evoke. The long gestation of the poem is revealing. Manuscripts from 1745 show Warton planning a Miltonic diptych of "Summer" and "Winter" (modeled on "L'Allegro" [1631?] and "Il Penseroso" [1632]), but the sketch coalesced into a single poem of 338 lines:

Rustle the breezes lightly borne
O'er deep embattled ears of corn:
Round ancient elm, with humming noise,
Full loud the chaffer-swarms rejoice. . . .

It was Warton's descriptive powers that impressed the critics of the next generation. Nathan Drake praised his fidelity to external nature, Brydges thought that "The Hamlet" combined "the charms of poetry with the accuracy of a naturalist," and a correspondent of the *Gentlemen's Magazine* spoke in 1787 of the "exquisite precision" with which Warton described the countryside around Winslade in Hampshire.

Annotations in his folio edition of the works of Edmund Spenser dating from the early 1750s show that Warton was working toward an edition of the poet. But he eventually adapted his plans and used the annotations in a more extensive way, grouping them under various topics. This project became *Observations on the Faerie Queene of Spenser* (1754), recognized from its publication as a landmark in the writing of English literary history. It showed for the first time the full extent of the influence exerted by medieval romances on the main tradition of English literature; and it was innovatory in its whole critical approach, as Samuel Johnson told Warton in a letter of 16 July 1754: "You have shown to all who shall hereafter attempt the study of our ancient authours the way to success, by directing them to the perusal of the books which those authours had read."

Warton had met Johnson through Joseph Warton, and the two had soon become intimate friends. In the summer of 1754 Johnson stayed with Warton in Oxford (Warton's lively description of this visit was included by James Boswell in *The Life of Samuel Johnson, D.D.* [1791]), and he enjoyed himself so much that he began to think of settling there. Although his own college, Pembroke, cold-shouldered him, Trinity made him feel welcome: "I shall take up my abode at Trinity," he declared. It was largely through Warton's efforts that the university awarded Johnson an M.A. degree in 1755.

In 1756 Warton was elected, like his father before him, to the university professorship of poetry. During his ten-year incumbency he delivered each term a lecture in Latin on the dramatic, epic, lyric, and pastoral poetry of the Greeks. The surviving manuscripts provide a tasteful ramble through Greek literature.

Warton's thirties were a busy and confused time. His various talents led him in different directions, and poetry seems to have slipped into the background. In 1760 alone three works appeared which give some sense of the range of Warton's interests: *A Description of the City, College, and Cathedral of Winchester*, a pocket-sized volume combining historical anecdotes and archaeological details and intended as a guidebook for tourists; a scholarly biographical article on Trinity's founder, Sir Thomas Pope, contributed to the *Biographia Britannica* and eventually expanded into *The Life of Sir Thomas Pope* (1772); and *A Companion to the Guide, and a Guide to the Companion* (1760), a pamphlet which is at the same time a burlesque on, and supplement to, the official Oxford guide.

Another quirky mixture characteristic of Warton is *The Oxford Sausage* (1764), a humorous work of "Taste" whose ingredients were (as the preface says) "*highly seasoned* . . . carefully selected, and happily blended." This delightful and popular anthology of Oxford comic verse includes thirteen of his own pieces; some were reprinted from *Jackson's Oxford Journal*, but six appear in print for the first time here. Warton's comic poetry specializes in burlesque and is a product of Oxford waggery associated especially with the Jelly-Bag Club, a group that met for drink and puns at secret venues around the university. Warton enjoyed what was disapprovingly called "low company," chatting with the bargemen or watching the maneuvers of the local militia. Instead of attending David Garrick's great Stratford Jubilee in 1769 he slipped away to Spithead to see the Russian sailors.

Such activities struck some people as incongruous in a professor who was becoming increasingly respected as a classical scholar: Warton edited a collection of Latin inscriptions (1758) and Constantine Cephalas's *Greek Anthology* (1766), and his substantial edition of Theocritus was published in 1770. As a delegate of the Clarendon Press he was especially concerned with classical editions.

Warton's poetry professorship ended in 1766. He was awarded a B.D. degree in 1767 and came close on two occasions to being appointed Regius Professor of History; but in the end he had to be content with his college and parochial duties. In 1771 the university's chancellor,

Lord Lichfield, presented him with the living of Kiddington, near Woodstock (Warton had been curate of Woodstock since 1755), which helped supplement his stipend; and in the same year he was elected a fellow of the Society of Antiquaries. It must have been a great blow, however, when he failed to be chosen president of Trinity in 1776. By far the most eminent fellow, he had boosted the college's reputation and had written scholarly biographies of both its most celebrated president, Ralph Bathurst (1761), and its founder, Sir Thomas Pope (1772). Perhaps the fellows who voted against him were uneasy about his unconventional character.

By 1776 Warton was also the author of the first volume of his magnum opus, *The History of English Poetry, from the Close of the Eleventh to the Commencement of the Eighteenth Century* (1774-1781). After a century of tentative efforts toward literary history in the guise of anecdotes, catalogues, chronologies, and prefaces, it is Warton who first accepted the challenge of charting the progress of English literature from the Norman Conquest; and he does so in a digressive, unsystematized narrative which encompasses not only poetry but also translation, prose, history, and drama. Clarissa Rinaker's bibliography of printed sources for the history gives a selected list of more than eight hundred titles (many of them foreign), which she admits to be about half the full figure. Warton also used about seven hundred manuscripts, printing for the first time the important lyrics in British Library MS Harley 2253, many extracts from romances, the Bodleian Vernon manuscript, John Gower's *Balades*, and *The Kingis Quair* of James I. He also gave the first full discussion of the origins of the English drama; the first critical survey of the Scottish Chaucerians, Gower, John Lydgate, Thomas Hoccleve, and Stephen Hawes; as well as many selections from the minor poetry of the sixteenth century. It is both a narrative and, in Sir Walter Scott's words, an "immense commonplace-book." Not only Scott but Warton himself found among the rich materials ideas and images for his verse.

Warton never completed the history. Volume three appeared in 1781, but at his death just eleven printed sheets of a fourth volume existed; it is doubtful whether Warton did much sustained work on it after 1782. It is tempting to seek the explanation in Joseph Ritson's *Observations on the Three First Volumes of the History of English Poetry* (1782), an ill-judged and intemperate attack which took delight in exposing Warton's factual errors, confusions, and mistranscriptions. But Ritson's was an isolated voice amid a chorus of approbation and encouragement. It could be that Warton found it less congenial to progress into the seventeenth century, where he would have had to chart the rise of Neoclassical academic criticism and the trend toward courtly elegance and wit.

In any case, Warton was busy with other projects. In 1782 he joined his friends Edmond Malone and George Steevens in engaging in the controversy over Thomas Chatterton's fabrications of poems by "Thomas Rowley." His substantial *An Enquiry into the Authenticity of the Poems Attributed to Thomas Rowley* (1782) showed thoughtfuness and scholarship in a debate which was frequently short of both. Although he found the "Rowley" poems appealing (and gave them lengthy consideration in the history), his experience as a scholar working with historical materials told him that they were not genuine fifteenth-century creations. The following year he published in an enlarged public edition a detailed history of his own parish of Kiddington, designed as a specimen of how a history of Oxfordshire could be built up, parish by parish, by individual local historians. In 1785 Warton's historical scholarship was recognized in his appointment as Oxford's Camden Professor of History, a dignified position but one which made no formal demand other than an inaugural lecture.

Far more pressing on Warton's time was his edition of Milton's shorter poems, a work of thorough scholarship and critical insight which remains useful to this day. He was spurred on to the project by Dr. Johnson's adverse remarks on Milton in his *Prefaces, Biographical and Critical, to the Works of the English Poets* (1779-1781), and some of Warton's notes (particularly those on *Lycidas* [1637]) are direct refutations of Johnson's views. One thing, however, on which the two men could agree was their distaste for Milton's republican politics.

Although literary history was Warton's major concern during his forties and fifties, he continued (unlike his brother) to write poetry. His *Poems: A New Edition, with Additions* (1777) consists of twenty-five pieces—chiefly odes, sonnets, and a few occasional poems—eighteen of which were previously unpublished. Johnson's burlesque of his friend's volume ("Phrase that Time has flung away, / Uncouth Words in Disarray: / Trickt in Antique Ruff and Bonnet, / Ode and Elegy and Sonnet") suggests wrongly that Warton's work is a mere imitation of older forms; it is, rather, a conscious exploration of various poetic voices, and the poems mark a clear break with Warton's work of the 1740s. They have a subtle verbal music, occasional echoes of older bardic invocation, moments of personal meditation and mood-painting, visual images invoking nostalgia and fancy—none of which was likely to appeal to Johnson's reactionary attitude toward the poetry of sensibility. Warton's fascination for the past lies deeper than a mere patina. Of the odes, the companion pieces "The Crusade" and "The Grave of King Arthur" have a bardic fervor and rousing rhythm; quite different are "On the First of April" and "The Hamlet," which celebrate a love of the countryside in a wealth of atmospheric detail, using octosyllabics to subtle effect; the stanzaic ode "The Suicide" has a lurid sublimity which proved popular in its time but has perhaps worn less well.

Probably the most influential poems in the collection are the sonnets, which did much to reestablish the popularity of this distinctive Renaissance form. Warton uses them for meditations on a lost world of the past, a personal bereavement only his imagination can assuage: Stonehenge, Wilton House, Dugdale's *Monasticon*, King Arthur's Round Table at Winchester, and his own "native stream" of the Loddon are some of the contexts for Warton's thoughts on the mind's craving to recapture a lost delight. None speaks more effectively than the Loddon sonnet:

Sweet native stream! those skies and suns so pure
No more return, to chear my evening road!
Yet still one joy remains, that not obscure,
Nor useless, all my vacant days have flow'd,
From youth's gay dawn to manhood's prime mature;
Nor with the Muse's laurel unbestow'd.

Sometimes Warton places the pull of the past in tension with the claims of the present, in a struggle between imagination and reason or judgment. Again the key is to be found in Warton the literary historian, to whom the Elizabethan Age was the most conducive to great poetry. He speaks of it in *The History of English Poetry* as "that period, propitious to the operations of original and true poetry, when the coyness of fancy was not always proof against the approaches of reason, when genius was rather directed than governed by judgement."

Such tensions form the subject of *Verses on Sir Joshua Reynolds's Painted Window at New-College Oxford* (1782), written a few months after Reynolds had proposed his friend for membership in Johnson's literary society, The Club. It is often seen as a recantation by Warton of his renegade delight in the Gothic:

Sudden, the sombrous imagery is fled,
Which late my visionary rapture fed:
Thy powerful hand has broke the Gothic chain,
And brought my bosom back to truth again.

But the victory is won by Decorum and Truth, two of the great principles of Reynolds's discourses on art (1769-1791), and the whole poem is really Warton's graceful compliment to his friend and patron. (On the other hand, when the east end of New College Chapel was uncovered to reveal the original Gothic stonework, one observer reported that "Poor Thomas fetched such sighs as I could not have thought he could breathe.")

Reynolds was indeed a good friend. His 1784 portrait of Warton still looks down on diners in the Senior Common room at Trinity, and it was to him that Warton owed his appointment in 1785 to the poet laureateship, with its twice-yearly duty of composing a formal ode to be set to music for performance at court. His first ode (on the king's birthday in 1785) had to be hurriedly written, leading to merciless mockery in the volume *Probationary Odes* (1785), in which the burlesque offerings of the various "candidates" were placed, with little incongruity, alongside Warton's own. By all accounts, Warton enjoyed the joke. His later laureate odes, however, were effective and dignified, and in them he took the opportunity to explore both historical and descriptive subjects, including the tradition of the laureateship itself. It was generally held that Warton, whose tenure fell between those of William Whitehead and Henry James Pye, raised the reputation of the post at a difficult moment in its history.

In the 1780s Warton gathered around him a band of young poets, many of whom were former schoolboys at Winchester who had come to know him during his stays with his headmaster brother. The best-remembered disciples are three Trinity friends and contemporaries: Henry Headley; William Benwell; and William Lisle Bowles, whose undergraduate sonnets (strongly influenced by his mentor) had a powerful effect on the young Samuel Taylor Coleridge. Sir Herbert Croft wrote to John Nichols on 15 May 1786:

"The magnetism of Tom Warton draws many a youth into rhymes and loose stockings, who had better be thinking of prose and propriety." Warton died on 21 May 1790.

In 1825 Robert Southey wrote of the poetic scene: "If any man may be called the father of the present race, it is Thomas Warton," and he talked of the School of Warton as "the true English school." Such words might shock present-day literary historians, but this reaction would be symptomatic of a general failure to recognize Warton's importance to his age and the representative nature of his various works. He enriched and influenced many fields of endeavor beyond the specialization of English literature—a contribution so wide that it is hard to reassemble and evaluate it. Writers since René Wellek have recognized the "immense historical importance" of *The History of English Poetry*, and J. B. Bamborough has opened up an avenue for assessing Warton's pervasive influence on what is nowadays termed the "first generation of Romantics." For literary scholars, it is perhaps Warton's infusion into English poetry—from *The History of English Poetry* and *Observations on the Faerie Queene of Spenser*—of the sense of a native tradition with complex historical roots which remains his decisive achievement.

Letters:

Clarissa Rinaker, "Twenty-Six Unedited Letters from Thomas Warton to Jonathan Toup, John Price, George Steevens, Isaac Reed, William Mavor, and Edmond Malone," *Journal of English and Germanic Philology*, 14 (1915): 96-118;

"Correspondence of Thomas Warton," *Bodleian Quarterly Record*, 6 (1931): 303-307;

The Correspondence of Thomas Percy and Thomas Warton, edited by M. G. Robinson and Leah Dennis (Baton Rouge: Louisiana State University Press, 1951);

David Fairer, "The Correspondence of Thomas Warton," doctoral thesis, Oxford University, 1975.

Bibliographies:

Clarissa Rinaker, *Thomas Warton: A Biographical and Critical Study*, University of Illinois Studies in Language and Literature, volume 2, no. 1 (Urbana: University of Illinois Press, 1916);

John A. Vance, *Joseph and Thomas Warton: An Annotated Bibliography* (New York: Garland, 1983).

Biographies:

Richard Mant, Memoir of Warton, in *The Poetical Works of the Late Thomas Warton, B.D. . . . Together with Memoirs of His Life and Writings*, 2 volumes (Oxford: Oxford University Press, 1802);

Alexander Chalmers, "Thomas Warton," in *The Works of the English Poets* (London: Johnson, 1810), XVIII: 145-153;

Clarissa Rinaker, *Thomas Warton: A Biographical and Critical Study*, University of Illinois Studies in Language and Literature, volume 2, no. 1 (Urbana: University of Illinois Press, 1916).

References:

J. B. Bamborough, "William Lisle Bowles and the Riparian Muse," in *Essays and Poems Presented to Lord David Cecil*, edited by W. W. Robson (London: Constable, 1970), pp. 93-108;

Samuel Egerton Brydges, *Censura Literaria*, volume 4 (London: Longman, Hurst, Rees & Orme, 1807), p. 275;

R. W. Chapman, ed., *The Letters of Samuel Johnson, with Mrs. Thrale's Genuine Letters to Him*, 3 volumes (Oxford: Clarendon Press, 1952), I:56;

David Fairer, "The Poems of Thomas Warton the Elder?," *Review of English Studies*, new series 26 (August 1975): 287-300; (November 1975): 395-406;

Fairer, "The Origins of Warton's *History of English Poetry*," *Review of English Studies*, new series 32 (February 1981): 37-63;

Arthur Fenner, Jr., "The Wartons 'Romanticize' Their Verse," *Studies in Philology*, 53 (July 1956): 501-508;

Edmund Gosse, "Two Pioneers of Romanticism: Joseph and Thomas Warton," *Proceedings of the British Academy*, 7 (1915): 145-163;

Raymond Dexter Havens, *The Influence of Milton on English Poetry* (Cambridge, Mass.: Harvard University Press, 1922; reprinted, New York: Russell & Russell, 1961), pp. 595-602;

Havens, "Thomas Warton and the Eighteenth-Century Dilemma," *Studies in Philology*, 25 (January 1928): 36-50;

Arthur Johnston, *Enchanted Ground: The Study of Medieval Romance in the Eighteenth Century* (London: Athlone Press, 1964), pp. 100-119;

Lawrence Lipking, *The Ordering of the Arts in Eighteenth-Century England* (Princeton: Princeton University Press, 1970), pp. 352-404;

L. C. Martin, "Thomas Warton and the Early Poems of Milton," *Proceedings of the British Academy*, 20 (1934): 25-43;

Frances Schouler Miller, "The Historic Sense of Thomas Warton, Junior," *ELH*, 5 (March 1938): 71-92;

John Nichols, *Illustrations of the Literary History of the Eighteenth Century*, 8 volumes (London: Printed for the author by Nichols, son, and Bentley, 1817-1858), V: 210;

Ants Oras, *Milton's Editors and Commentators from Patrick Hume to Henry John Todd, 1695-1801*, revised edition (New York: Haskell House, 1967), pp. 17-19, 267-294;

Edward Phillips, *Theatrum Poetarum Anglicanorum*, edited by Samuel Egerton Brydges (Canterbury: Printed by Simmons & Kirkby for J. White, 1800);

Hester Lynch Piozzi, *Thraliana: The Diary of Mrs. Hester Lynch Thrale (Later Mrs. Piozzi) 1776-1809*, 2 volumes, edited by Katherine C. Balderston (Oxford: Clarendon Press, 1942);

Joan Pittock, *The Ascendancy of Taste: The Achievement of Joseph and Thomas Warton* (London: Routledge & Kegan Paul, 1973);

Pittock, "Thomas Warton and the Oxford Chair of Poetry," *English Studies*, 62 (January 1981): 14-33;

Joseph Ritson, *Observations on the Three First Volumes of the History of English Poetry* (London: Printed for J. Stockdale, 1782);

David Nichol Smith, "Thomas Warton's Miscellany: *The Union*," *Review of English Studies*, 19 (July 1943): 263-275;

Smith, "Warton's History of English Poetry," *Proceedings of the British Academy*, 15 (1929), 73-99;

Robert Southey, Review of William Hayley's *Memoirs*, *Quarterly Review*, 31 (March 1825): 263-311;

John A. Vance, *Joseph and Thomas Warton* (Boston: Twayne, 1983);

René Wellek, *The Rise of English Literary History* (Chapel Hill: University of North Carolina Press, 1941), pp. 166-201.

Papers:

Winchester College and Trinity College, Oxford, have some of Thomas Warton's lectures as professor of poetry and manuscripts of three unpublished works: "Observations Critical and Historical, on Castles, Churches, Monasteries, and other Monuments of Antiquity in Various Parts of England" (Winchester); "History of St. Elizabeth's College, Winchester" (Oxford); and an edition of the household expenses of William of Wykeham (Oxford). The Bodleian Library at Oxford and the British Library have the largest holding of Warton correspondence.

William Whitehead

(February 1715 - 14 April 1785)

Gregory G. Kelley
Emory University

See also the Whitehead entry in *DLB 84: Restoration and Eighteenth-Century Dramatists: Second Series.*

BOOKS: *The Green-cloth; or, The Verge of the Court: An Epistle to a Friend,* attributed to Whitehead (London: Noble, 1739);

The Danger of Writing Verse: An Epistle (London: Printed for R. Dodsley & sold by T. Cooper, 1741);

Ann Boleyn to Henry the Eighth: An Epistle (London: Printed for R. Dodsley, sold by M. Cooper, 1743);

Atys and Adrastus: A Tale in the Manner of Dryden's Fables (London: Printed for R. Manby, sold by M. Cooper, 1743);

An Essay on Ridicule (London: Printed for R. Dodsley, 1743);

On Nobility: An Epistle to the Right Hon[ble]*. the Earl of* ****** (London: Printed for R. Dodsley & sold by M. Cooper, 1744);

The Roman Father: A Tragedy, as It Is Acted at the Theatre Royal in Drury-Lane, by His Majesty's Servants, translation and adaptation of Pierre Corneille's *Horace* (London: Printed for R. Dodsley, sold by M. Cooper, 1750);

A Hymn to the Nymph of Bristol Spring (London: Printed for R. Dodsley, sold by M. Cooper, 1751);

Poems on Several Occasions: With the Roman Father, a Tragedy (London: Printed for R. & J. Dodsley, 1754);

Elegies: With an Ode to the Tiber. Written Abroad (London: Printed for R. & J. Dodsley, 1757);

Verses to the People of England (London: Printed for R. & J. Dodsley, sold by M. Cooper, 1758);

The School for Lovers: A Comedy, as It Is Acted at the Theatre Royal in Drury-Lane, translation and adaptation of Bernard le Bovier Fontenelle's *La Testament* (London: Printed for R. & J. Dodsley & sold by J. Hinxman, 1762);

A Charge to the Poets (London: Printed for R. & J. Dodsley & sold by J. Hinxman, 1762);

Orazio: Tragedia del Sig (Florence: Stecchi & Pagani, 1767);

A Trip to Scotland: As It Is Acted at the Theatre Royal in Drury-Lane (London: Printed for J. Dodsley, 1770);

Plays and Poems, 2 volumes (London: Printed for J. Dodsley, 1774);

Variety: A Tale, for Married People (London: Printed for J. Dodsley, 1776);

The Goat's Beard: A Fable, as "Goat" (London: Printed for J. Dodsley, 1777);

*The Court of Adul***y: A Vision* (London: Printed for Smith, 1778);

Poems, edited, with a memoir, by William Mason, published as volume 3 of *Poems and Plays* (London: Printed by A. Ward, sold by J. Robson & W. Clarke, London, and J. Todd, York, 1788);

PLAY PRODUCTIONS: *The Roman Father,* London, Theatre Royal in Drury Lane, 24 February 1750;

Creusa, Queen of Athens, translation and adaptation of Euripides' *Ion,* London, Theatre Royal in Drury Lane, 20 April 1754;

The School for Lovers, London, Theatre Royal in Drury Lane, 10 February 1762;

A Trip to Scotland, London, Theatre Royal in Drury Lane, 6 January 1770.

OTHER: "Observations on the Shield of Aeneas," in volume 3 of *The Works of Virgil, in Latin and English,* 4 volumes, edited by Joseph Warton (London: Printed for Dodsley, 1753), pp. 356-492.

For nearly three decades during the mid eighteenth century—a turbulent time that saw the Seven Years' War, the American Revolution, and the reigns of two controversial kings (George II and George III)—William Whitehead served as poet laureate of England. As a remnant of the earlier Augustan style, Whitehead's verse reflects little of the enormous social changes then evolv-

William Whitehead (engraving from a portrait by R. Wilson)

ing in Europe. If his poems made an inconsequential impression on English literary history, Whitehead did much to repair the dignity of the post of laureate. What had too often for his predecessors been the instrument of a Court party or an organ of flattery became under Whitehead the expression of a generalized patriotism. Poet, playwright, and confidant of nobles, he was well aware of the limitations of his powers. His works ought not to be judged according to standards of greatness to which they do not aspire.

Whitehead was born in Cambridge in 1715; the parish of St. Botolph's records his baptism on 12 February of that year. His father, Richard Whitehead, was the baker for Pembroke Hall of Cambridge University, acquiring some fortune in that position. The elder Whitehead appears to have contributed to the son's taste for fine things; he expended great sums on the adornment of his little estate near Granchester, which for many years was known as "Whitehead's Folly." He did manage to save enough to provide for the liberal education of his two sons—with the help of some aristocratic patronage. Benefiting from the aid of Henry Bromley (later Lord Montfort), high steward of the University of Cambridge, William Whitehead entered Winchester College at the age of fourteen.

At Winchester Whitehead gave the first indications of his literary bent. He acted in the role of Marcia in the school's production of Joseph Addison's *Cato* (1713), but more crucial to the poet's development was his encounter in 1733 with Alexander Pope. Inspecting the college with Pope was Charles Mordaunt, Earl of Peterborough, who offered ten prizes of a guinea each to be awarded for verses to be composed on a subject of Pope's choosing. Pope suggested "Peterborough," and Whitehead won one of the guineas. He was also assigned by Pope the task of translating the first book of his *An Essay on Man* (1733-1734) into Latin, but although he was a good scholar, Whitehead never distinguished himself in Latin composition. Neither the verses on Peterborough nor the translation of Pope's poem survives; but the incident clearly confirmed the young poet's aspiration to literary achievement, and Pope's style would continue to exert a powerful influence throughout his career.

In 1735 Whitehead made application to New College at Oxford, but a lack of influence prevented his entry there. As a result of this disappointment, he instead gained admission at Clare Hall at Cambridge. His father having died, he received a small scholarship available to the orphaned sons of Cambridge tradesmen. Even so, he enrolled with the lowly status of sizar, which originally meant one who pays for his schooling by acting as a servant to wealthier students. Though there is no evidence that such service was actually required of Whitehead, he certainly continued the practice, begun at least as early as Winchester, of cultivating friendships with those whose social rank was superior to his own. "My education rose above my birth," he confesses in his poem "To the Honourable Charles Townsend."

Another early effort shows Whitehead defending himself from the charge of sycophancy to the well-born. In "To the Reverend Mr. Wright" he protests:

> You say I'm dependent; what then?—If I make
> That dependence quite easy to me,
> Say why you should envy my lucky mistake,
> Or why should I wish to be free?

The "secret virtues" of the great attract the poet's attention, he avers, not the "tinsel and plume" of their positions. Comparing his own worth to that of his more influential friends makes Whitehead "sink in confusion bewilder'd." The personal modesty of these lines establishes a keynote for Whitehead, who tends to disarm criticism by discounting his own rather spare talents.

While he was at Cambridge, Whitehead's poems began circulating beyond his immediate group of acquaintances. Most of these works are in heroic couplets, and virtually all reflect the considerable influence of Pope. The best of them are mildly satirical, modest in tone, and limited in scope. The poetic epistle *The Danger of Writing Verse* (1741), for example, attains something of Pope's urbanity, though none of his philosophical depth, as it wryly notes the gap between celestial fire and earthly fame:

> Say, can the bard attempt what's truly great
> Who pants in secret for his future fate?

These lines imply that Whitehead justifies his attachment to the powerful as a security at least for his present fate. *An Essay on Ridicule* (1743) continues in a similar vein his temperate critique of pretension and his equally unruffled vindication of Neoclassical proportion.

On other occasions, however, Whitehead's Cambridge poems depart from the satirical and modulate into a more pathetic key. *Atys and Adrastus* (1743), for example, drawn on a legendary theme from Herodotus, evokes more poignant emotion than do his later attempts at tragic drama. Less successful is the heroic epistle *Ann Boleyn to Henry the Eighth* (1743). Although not devoid of feeling, this slavish imitation of Pope's *Eloisa to Abelard* (1719) can muster but little sympathy for its heroine. Ann's strongest defense, which is not very convincing, is that "fondly wild, by love, by fortunes led," she has excused Henry's crimes and her own.

Whitehead attained the baccalaureate degree in 1739, election to the fellowship of Clare Hall in 1742, and the Master of Arts in 1743. By 1745, however, it became clear to Whitehead that the fellowship alone would not provide him a sufficient living. Moreover, his remaining in that position would have required his taking holy orders, a step for which he considered himself unsuited. William Villiers, Earl of Jersey, offered deliverance in the form of a position as tutor to his son, Viscount Villiers (George Bussy Villiers), and a companion named Stephens. In taking this post Whitehead began an attachment to the earl's family which would last for the rest of his life.

A place in a nobleman's household and the light duties that accompanied it freed Whitehead to pursue his literary inclination steadily, although not very industriously. On 24 February 1750 he attracted the notice of the general public with the performance at Drury Lane of his verse tragedy *The Roman Father.* While it is a no more than competent example of the age's historical, stoic dramas, the play attained considerable success, going through many published editions and holding the stage well into the next century. It was based on Pierre Corneille's *Horace* (1640) and depicted the combat of the Roman Horatii against the Alban Curiatii to protect the liberty of Rome. Despite its title, the dramatic interest of the piece is on the Roman daughter, Horatia, who loves one of the Curiatii brothers. Following the slaying of her lover she goads her victorious brother into killing her, an outcome which required of the poet some rhetorical gyrations. In an epilogue Whitehead reassures the more tender sensibilities in his audience that "There's very little fear the crime should spread."

The play cemented Whitehead's friendship with one of the most influential figures of the day, David Garrick. Actor, playwright, and theatrical impresario, Garrick played the title role in *The Roman Father* and was the recipient of some of Whitehead's more adept complimentary verses. The poem "To Mr. Garrick" demonstrates not only Whitehead's high regard for his sponsor but also the poet's concern that the theater be a vehicle of dignified moral instruction.

Perhaps influenced by his experience with drama in blank verse, Whitehead produced a poem in that meter that unaccountably turned out to be one of his best-known works in his own time, although it is virtually forgotten today. *A Hymn to the Nymph of Bristol Spring* (1751) praises the healthful qualities of English waters in flowing pentameters that contrast favorably with the end-stopped persistence of Whitehead's heroic couplets. The mythological conceit of the poem, however, is only halfhearted and rather ludicrous. Indeed, the work evinces a difficulty for Whitehead in abandoning his earlier satirical mode for the grand, Miltonic style; an amiable strain of self-deprecation recurs. Having dared to praise other rivers than the Avon, the poet makes amends:

> Avonia frowns! and justly may'st thou frown,
> O goddess, on the bard, th'injurious bard,
> Who leaves thy pictur'd scenes, and idly roves
> For foreign beauty to adorn his song.

Judging from the poem's popularity—it was reprinted several times—the public detected no undercutting of the hymn's sincerity. Apparently Whitehead's readership admired the very expatiations that made the bard uneasy.

More characteristic are the humorous tales in iambic tetrameter. Although of uneven merit, some of these retain their appeal. For example, "The Dog" depicts a newly married but unreliable wife who, warned not to ride on the family dog, does just that and earns a bump on the head. The poem ends with a servant speaking the racy lines, "Had Captain Wilkins been forbidden, / Ah master, who had then been ridden?" Several later works in this style, such as *Variety: A Tale, for Married People* (1776) and the fable *The Goat's Beard* (1777) continue this lighthearted and unpretentious inspection of relations between the sexes. Some are less amusing. "A Song for Ranelagh" satirizes, with great prolixity and some self-righteousness, ladies who dress as men to attend masked balls. Nearly always Whitehead limits his sallies to the mildest of human vices and avoids ad hominem attacks.

When, in 1754, Whitehead returned to drama, he again submitted to the fashion for bombastic tragedies on classical themes, a vogue for which his friend Garrick must bear much of the blame. *Creusa, Queen of Athens* represents a significant advancement over the versification and stagecraft of *The Roman Father*, and audiences greeted it with an approbation equal to that of its predecessor. Neither play is likely to be read or watched with much pleasure today. Based on the *Ion* of Euripides, *Creusa* dispenses with such supernatural effects of its source as the intervention of the god Apollo. In doing so, however, Whitehead's play also blunts much of the dramatic effect of the original. While such regularizations of ancient works are viewed today with skepticism, Whitehead's contemporaries, including Horace Walpole, regarded the work highly.

As if to celebrate his theatrical success, Whitehead set out almost immediately with his tutorial charges—who by this time included Viscount Nuneham (George Simon Harcourt), son of the earl of Harcourt (Simon Harcourt)—on a two-year tour of the Continent. Traveling through Germany, Austria, Italy, Switzerland, and the Low Countries, Whitehead composed verses on some of the famous places he and his students visited. On his return to England the resulting volume was published as *Elegies: With an Ode to the Tiber* (1757). These poems, hackneyed and artificial on the whole, do show occasional glimmers of feeling when they address Whitehead's students as "my Villiers" and "noble youth." They have little enough to do with the tombs of Augustus or Marcus Aurelius, but they demonstrate that Whitehead was as proficient, at least technically, in the serious, public poetic forms as he was in the lightweight vers de société.

Even during his absence on the Continent Whitehead had made progress in such governmental stations as were available to poets and tutors. While he was in Italy, Lady Jersey had used her influence to have the duke of Newcastle appoint him to the honorific posts of secretary and registrar of the Order of the Bath. But an even grander assignment awaited only the death in December 1757 of Colley Cibber, the poet laureate. Whitehead's demonstrated competence in various poetic forms was no liability in this case, but nei-

Dame Nature the Goddess, one very bright Day
In strolling thro' Nuneham met Browne by the way;
"And bless me she said with an insolent Sneer,
I wonder that fellow can dare to come here;
What more than I did has your insolence plan'd?
The Lawn, Wood, & Water are all of my Hand;
In my very best manner with Themis's Scales
I lifted the Hills & I scooped out the Vales,
With Sylvan's own umbrage I planted the brow,
And pour'd the rich Thames on the Meadows below."—
I grant it he cried — to your sovereign command
I bow as I ought — Gentle Lady your hand—
The weather's inviting so let us move on,
You know what you did, & now see what I've done.
I with gratitude own you have reason to plead.
That to these happy scenes you were bounteous indeed—
My lovely materials were many & great
(For sometimes you know I'm obliged to create)
But say in return my adorable Dame
To all you see how can you lay a just claim?
Who drew o'er the surface, did you or did I
The smooth flowing outline that steals from the Eye

Manuscript for a poem by Whitehead (JE1034, Henry E. Huntington Library and Art Gallery)

The soft undulations both distant and near
That heave from the Lawns, & yet scarcely appear—
(So bends the ripe harvest the Breezes beneath
As if Earth was in Slumber, & gently took breath)—
Who thin'd, & who group'd & who scatter'd these Trees
Who bade the Slopes fall with that delicate Ease,
Who cast them in shade, & who placed them in light
Who bade them divide & who bade them unite?
The Ridges are melted, the Boundary's gone.
Observe all these Changes, & candidly own
I've cloath'd you when naked, & when overdress'd
Have stripp'd you again to your Boddice & Vest;
Conceal'd every blemish, each beauty display'd
As Reynolds would Picture some exquisite Maid,
Each spirited feature would happily place
And shed o'er the whole inexpressible Grace—
One question remains— up the Green of yon Steep
Who threw the bold Walk with that elegant sweep?
There is little to see till the sumit we gain;—
Nay never draw back you may climb without pain,
And I hope will perceive how each object is caught
And is lost in exactly the point where it ought—

The ground of your Moulding is certainly fine
But the swell of that Knoll, & those openings are mine–
The Prospect wherever beheld must be good,
But has ten times the Charm when you burst from this Wood;
A Wood of my planting"– The Goddess cried "hold
Tis grown very hot, & tis grown very cold"–
She fan'd & she shudder'd, she cough'd & she sneez'd
Inclined to be angry, inclined to be pleased,
Half smiled, & half pouted– then turn'd from the View,
And dropt him a Curtsy, & blushing withdrew–
But soon recollecting her thoughts as she past,
"I may have my revenge on this Fellow at last–
For a lucky conjecture comes into my head,
That (whatéer he has done, or whatéer he has said)
The worlds little malice will balk his design,
Each Fault they'll call His, & each excellence Mine.

W Whitehead

ther was it a requirement. The office of laureate had generally been occupied by poets of at best the second rank, as Cibber's career had attested. It was somewhat unusual, therefore, that when the post was made vacant in 1757 it was first offered to the man popularly viewed as the best living poet, Thomas Gray. In his capacity as lord chamberlain, the duke of Devonshire extended the offer a mere week after Cibber's passing, going so far as to exempt Gray from the obligation of the annual odes. The manner of Gray's refusal provides an instructive instance in how the laureateship was viewed in those days. To William Mason, later Whitehead's biographer as well as his own, Gray wrote: "If any great man would say to me, I make you ratcatcher to his majesty, with a salary of £300 a year and two butts of the finest Malaga; and though it has been usual to catch a mouse or two, . . . yet to you sir, we shall not stand upon these things, I cannot say I should jump at it; nay, if they would drop the very name of the office and call me Sinecure to the King's Majesty, I should still . . . think everybody I saw smelt a rat about me." Shortly after this rebuff the duke of Devonshire submitted to the earl of Jersey's blandishments and appointed Whitehead.

Sharing none of Gray's contempt for the office, Whitehead apparently had no thought of holding the job as a sinecure—if, indeed, that privilege was even extended to one of his moderate fame and talents. Mason suggested that he hire a team of hacks to write the standard annual poems; but, secure in his skill, Whitehead immediately set to work composing the first of the odes on the king's birthday, which, along with odes on the New Year, he produced with unflagging regularity for almost thirty years. None of these poems has found a permanent place in the literary canon. A few of them, however, do possess a certain merit. Whereas earlier laureates had too often served as mere mouthpieces of the ascendant party or fulsome lauders of kingly virtues, Whitehead's odes always support loyalty to country rather than to persons. In an age characterized by seemingly endless and pointless warfare, peace is a frequent theme. A passage from the New Year's ode of 1763 illustrates Whitehead's pacifist inclinations as well as the grandiloquence which was considered excessive even in his own day:

At length th'imperious lord of war
Yields to the fates their ebon car,
And frowning quits his toil;
Dashed from his hand the bleeding spear
Now deigns a happier form to wear,
And peaceful turns the soil.

As is often the case, the satirical attacks on the laureate's productions outnumbered the poems themselves. One assailant who rose a little above the general mass of scurrility was Charles Churchill, who wrote in the third book of *The Ghost* (1763):

Come, METHOD, come in all thy pride,
DULLNESS and WHITEHEAD by thy side,
DULLNESS and METHOD still are one,
And WHITEHEAD is their darling Son.

The laureate took these gibes in good humor and even admitted that "Churchill strings, / Into some motley form his damn'd good things."

A critic who did more lasting damage to Whitehead's fame was Samuel Johnson. Although some years earlier Whitehead had done Dr. Johnson the service of conveying to Lord Chesterfield the plan for the great *Dictionary* (1755), by the 1760s Johnson's gratitude was outweighed by his disdain for the laureate's poems. Unlike nearly every other commentator, Johnson preferred the odes of Whitehead's predecessor. Cibber had been a good actor, a decent playwright, and an admittedly barely passable poet. But James Boswell records Johnson's remark that "Cibber's familiar style was better than that which Whitehead has assumed. *Grand* nonsense is insupportable."

Neither occasional buffets like this one nor the duties of being court poet dampened Whitehead's easygoing temperament. Throughout his tenure as laureate he continued to produce lighter works in the unofficial genres. *A Charge to the Poets* (1762) and "A Pathetic Apology for All Laureates, Past, Present, and to Come" carried on the humorous, preceptive manner he had cultivated as early as *The Danger of Writing Verse*. On 10 February 1762 what is perhaps his finest work, *The School for Lovers*, was produced at Drury Lane. Based on a French original, *Le Testament* (1751) by Bernard le Bovier Fontenelle, this play is too serious to be considered a merely sentimental comedy. An innocent maiden named Caelia has been bequeathed in her father's will to be married to her guardian, the honorable and wealthy country aristocrat Sir John Dorilant. These two must be "schooled" to make the fine distinction between self-interest and the real affection they feel for each other. Much liveliness enters the play through the scheming of Sir John's sister Araminta and Mr. Modely, a character who develops and suffers more than does the usual Fopling Flutter type. The comedy also merits praise in resisting the conventional parceling out of each character in the end to the stereotypically suitable mate.

Some time after this success another member of Dr. Johnson's circle, Oliver Goldsmith, developed an antipathy for Whitehead, though for personal rather than stylistic reasons. In the 1760s Whitehead assisted Garrick at Drury Lane as a reader of new plays. In 1767 Goldsmith brought Garrick his comedy *The Good Natur'd Man* (1768); the impresario suggested a host of changes which Goldsmith found unacceptable and insulting. Garrick called in Whitehead as arbitrator, and in the dispute that followed the poet laureate had to withstand not only Goldsmith's wrath but also that of Joshua Reynolds and Edmund Burke. Between real clashes like this one and satirical sallies like Churchill's, Garrick thought it best to produce Whitehead's farce *A Trip to Scotland* (1770) without identifying its author. In any case, this work was unlikely to augment its creator's fame.

For most of his life Whitehead remained a member of the households of Lords Jersey and Harcourt. Even after the death of the elder Lord Jersey and Whitehead's removal to apartments in London he continued as an intimate to both families. Mason chided him for having "willingly devoted the principal part of his time to the amusement of his patron and patroness," the superannuated Lord and Lady Jersey; but a love of personal ease, not to say indolence, was perhaps Whitehead's chief distinguishing characteristic. That he managed to make his duties light does not disprove his devotion to them. At his quiet death, of natural causes, on 14 April 1785 he was found to have been at work on the King's birthday ode for that year.

A collection of Whitehead's works had been published in 1774, and in 1788 an expanded version was published along with a memoir by Mason. In an age which had its share of rogues and fops, William Whitehead was a man of courtliness and modesty. He knew well that he was no genius, but he developed into a capable and sensible poet. He was, for his time, the ideal poet laureate.

Bibliography:

Carl J. Stratman and others, eds., *Restoration and Eighteenth Century Theatre Research: A Bibliographical Guide, 1900-1968* (Carbondale: Southern Illinois University Press, 1971).

Biographies:

William Mason, "Memoirs," in *Poems*, by Whitehead (London: Printed by A. Ward, sold by J. Robson & W. Clarke, London, and J. Todd, York, 1788);

Alexander Chalmers, "The Life of Whitehead," in *The Works of the English Poets from Chaucer to Cowper*, 21 volumes, edited by Samuel Johnson, with additions by Chalmers (London: Johnson, 1810), XVII: 189-197.

References:

James Boswell, *Boswell's Life of Johnson, Together with Boswell's Journal of a Tour to the Hebrides and Johnson's Diary of a Journey into North Wales*, 6 volumes, edited by George Birkbeck Hill (Oxford: Clarendon Press, 1934-1964), I: 402;

Edmund Kemper Broadus, "William Whitehead," in his *The Laureateship* (London: Oxford University Press at the Clarendon Press, 1921), pp. 135-146;

Alexander Chalmers, "Poems of William Whitehead," in *The Works of the English Poets from Chaucer to Cowper*, 21 volumes, edited by Samuel Johnson, with additions by Chalmers (London: J. Johnson, 1810), XVII: 199-278;

W. Forbes Gray, *The Poets Laureate of England* (London: Pitman, 1914), pp. 167-184;

John Forster, *The Life and Times of Oliver Goldsmith*, second edition, 2 volumes (London: Bradbury & Evans, 1854), II: 60-61;

Walter Hamilton, *The Poets Laureate of England* (London: Stock, 1879), pp. 182-190;

Sir John Hawkins, *The Life of Samuel Johnson, LL.D.*, edited by Bertram H. Davis (New York: Macmillan, 1961), p. 78;

Kenneth Hopkins, *The Poets Laureate* (London: Bodley Head, 1954), pp. 79-91;

Duncan C. Tovey, ed., *Letters of Thomas Gray, Including the Correspondence of Gray and Mason*, 3 volumes (London: Bell, 1909).

John Wolcot
(Peter Pindar)

(circa May 1738 - 14 January 1819)

Lance Bertelsen
University of Texas at Austin

BOOKS: *Persian Love Elegies: To Which Is Added The Nymph of Taurus* (Kingston, Jamaica: From the press of Joseph Thompson and Co., 1773);

The Noble Criketers (Truro, 1778);

A Poetical, Supplicating, Modest and Affecting Epistle to Those Literary Colossuses, the Reviewers (London: Printed for the author and sold by R. Baldwin, 1778);

Lyric Odes, to the Royal Academicians (London: Printed for the author and sold by T. Egerton; Baldwin; and Debrett, 1782; enlarged edition, London: Printed for G. Kearsley; and W. Forster, 1787);

More Lyric Odes, to the Royal Academicians (London: Printed for T. Egerton, 1783);

Lyric Odes, for the Year 1785 (London: Printed and sold by J. Jarvis; J. Debrett; G. Kearsley; and W. Forster, 1785);

The Lousiad: An Heroi-Comic Poem. Canto I (London: Printed and sold by J. Jarvis, 1785; enlarged edition, London: Printed for the author, and sold by W. Forster; by G. Kearsley; and all other booksellers in town and country, 1786; Philadelphia: Reprinted and sold by Daniel Humphreys, 1786);

Farewel Odes: For the Year 1786 (London: Printed for G. Kearsley; and W. Forster, 1786);

A Poetical and Congratulatory Epistle to James Boswell, Esq. on His Journal of a Tour to the Hebrides, with the Celebrated Dr. Johnson (London: Printed for G. Kearsley, 1786);

Bozzy and Piozzi; or, The British Biographers: A Town Eclogue (London: Printed for G. Kearsley, and W. Forster, 1786);

The Lousiad: An Heroi-Comic Poem. Canto II (London: Printed for G. Kearsley, 1787; Philadelphia: Printed for W. Spotswood and Rice & Co., 1789);

Ode upon Ode; or, A Peep at St. James's; or, New-Year's Day; or, What You Will (London: Printed for G. Kearsley, 1787; enlarged, 1787);

An Apologetic Postscript to Ode upon Ode; or, A Peep at St. James's (London: Printed for G. Kearsley, 1787; enlarged, 1788);

Instructions to a Celebrated Laureat; Alias, The Progress of Curiosity; Alias A Birth-day Ode; Alias Mr. Whitbread's Brewhouse (London: Printed for G. Kearsley, 1787; New York: Printed by J. and A. McLean, 1788);

Brother Peter to Brother Tom: An Expostulatory Epistle (London: Printed for G. Kearsley, 1788);

Peter's Pension: A Solemn Epistle to a Sublime Personage (London: Printed for G. Kearsley, 1788);

Peter's Prophecy; or, The President and Poet. Or, An Important Epistle to Sir J. Banks, on the Approaching Election of a President of the Royal Society (London: Printed for G. Kearsley, 1788);

Sir Joseph Banks and the Emperor of Morocco: A Tale (London: Printed for G. Kearsley, 1788);

Expostulatory Odes to a Great Duke, and a Little Lord (London: Printed for G. Kearsley, 1789; Philadelphia: Printed for W. Spotswood, 1790);

Subjects for Painters (London: Printed for G. Kearsley, 1789; Philadelphia: Printed for W. Spotswood, 1790);

A Poetical Epistle to a Falling Minister; also an Imitation of the Twelfth Ode of Horace (London: Printed for G. Kearsley, 1789);

A Benevolent Epistle to Sylvanus Urban, Alias Master John Nichols, Printer, Common-Councilman of Farringdon Ward, and Censor General of Literature (London: Printed for G. Kearsley, 1790);

A Complimentary Epistle to James Bruce, Esq. the Abyssinian Traveller (London: Printed for G. Kearsley, 1790);

Advice to the Future Laureat: An Ode (London: Printed for G. Kearsley, 1790);

A Rowland for an Oliver; or, A Poetical Answer to the Benevolent Epistle of Mr. Peter Pindar. Also the

John Wolcot (National Portrait Gallery, London)

Manuscript Odes, Songs, Letters, &c. &c. of the Above Mr. Peter Pindar, Now First Published by Sylvanus Urban (London: Printed for G. Kearsley, 1790);

The Lousiad: An Heroi-Comic Poem. Canto III (London: Printed for J. Evans, 1791);

Odes to Mr. Paine, Author of "Rights of Man"; on the Intended Celebration of the Downfall of the French Empire, by a Set of British Democrates, on the Fourteenth of July (London: Printed for J. Evans, 1791);

The Remonstrance: To Which Is Added, An Ode to My Ass. Also, The Magpie and Robin, a Tale; An Apology for Kings; and An Address to My Pamphlet (London: Printed for J. Evans, 1791);

The Rights of Kings; or, Loyal Odes to Disloyal Academicians (London: Printed for J. Evans, 1791);

A Commiserating Epistle to James Lowther, Earl of Lonsdale and Lowther, Lord Lieut. and Cust. Rot. of the Counties of Cumberland and Westmoreland (London: Printed for J. Evans, 1791);

A Pair of Lyric Epistles to Lord Macartney and His Ship (London: Printed for H. D. Symonds, 1792);

Odes of Importance, &c. (London: Printed for H. D. Symonds, 1792);

More Money! or, Odes of Instruction to Mr. Pitt: With a Variety of Other Choice Matters (London: Printed for J. Evans, 1792);

The Tears of St. Margaret; also, Odes of Condolence to the High and Mighty Musical Directors, on Their Downfall (London: Printed for H. D. Symonds, 1792);

The Lousiad: An Heroi-Comic Poem. Canto IV (London: Printed for H. D. Symonds, and Robertson and Berry, Edinburgh, 1792);

Odes to Kien Long, the Present Emperor of China; with The Quakers, a Tale; To a Fly, Drowned in a Bowl of Punch; Ode to Macmanus, Townsend, and Jealous, the Thief-Takers (London: Printed for H. D. Symonds, and Robertson and Berry, Edinburgh, 1792);

A Poetical, Serious, and Possibly Impertinent Epistle to the Pope: Also, A Pair of Odes to His Holiness, on His Keeping a Disorderly House; with a Pretty Little Ode to Innocence (London: Printed for T. Evans; and Robertson and Berry, Edinburgh, 1793);

Pindariana; or, Peter's Portfolio: Containing Tale, Fable, Translation, Ode, Elegy, Epigram, Song, Pastoral, Letters. With Extracts from Tragedy, Comedy, Opera, &c. (31 parts, London: Printed by T. Spilsbury and Son, for J. Walker; J. Bell; J. Ladley; and Mr. Jeffrey, 1794-1795; 1 volume, Philadelphia: Printed for B. F. Bache, 1794);

Celebration; or, The Academic Procession to St. James's: An Ode (London: Printed for John Walker, 1794);

Pathetic Odes (London: Printed for John Walker, 1794);

Hair Powder; A Plaintive Epistle to Mr. Pitt (London: Printed for J. Walker; J. Bell; J. Ladley; E. Jeffrey; and Benj. Franklin Bache, Philadelphia, 1795);

The Convention Bill: An Ode (London: Printed for J. Walker; E. Jeffrey; J. Ladley; and J. Bell, 1795);

Liberty's Last Squeak: Containing An Elegiac Ballad, An Ode to an Informer, An Ode to Jurymen, and Crumbs of Comfort for the Grand Informer (London: Printed for J. Walker; J. Ladley; and J. Bell, 1795);

The Royal Tour, and Weymouth Amusements: A Solemn and Reprimanding Epistle to the Laureat. Pitt's Flight to Wimbledon: An Ode (London: Printed for J. Walker; J. Bell; J. Ladley; and E. Jeffrey, 1795);

The Lousiad: Canto V and Last (London: Printed for J. Walker; E. Jeffrey; J. Ladley; and J. Bell, 1795);

The Royal Visit to Exeter: A Poetical Epistle, by John Ploughshare, a Farmer of Morton Hampstead, in the County of Devon. Published by Peter Pindar, Esq. (London: Printed for J. Walker; J. Ladley; and J. Bell, 1795);

One Thousand Seven Hundred and Ninety-Six: A Satire. In Four Dialogues. Dialogue the First and Second (London: Printed for John Walker, 1797);

An Ode to the Livery of London on Their Petition to His Majesty for Kicking out His Worthy Ministers (London: Printed for John Walker, 1797);

Picturesque Views with Poetical Allusions (London, 1797);

Tales of the Hoy: Interspersed with Song, Ode, and Dialogue (London: Printed for W. Richardson, W. West; and W. Clarke, 1798);

Nil Admirari; or, A Smile at a Bishop; Occasioned by an Hyperbolical Eulogy on Miss Hannah More, by Dr. Porteus, in His Late Charge to the Clergy (London: Printed by W. and C. Spilsbury, for West and Hughes, 1799);

Lord Auckland's Triumph; or, The Death of Crim. Con.: A Pair of Prophetic Odes (London: Printed by W. and C. Spilsbury, for West and Hughes, 1800);

Odes to Ins and Outs (London: Printed by W. and C. Spilsbury, for West and Hughes, 1801);

Out at Last! or, The Fallen Minister (London: Printed by W. and C. Spilsbury, for West and Hughes, 1801; Philadelphia: Printed by Thomas S. Manning, 1801);

A Poetical Epistle to Benjamin Count Rumford, Knight of the White Eagle, &c., &c. (London: Printed by W. and C. Spilsbury, for West and Hughes, 1801);

Tears and Smiles: A Miscellaneous Collection of Poems (London: Printed by W. and C. Spilsbury, for West and Hughes, 1801; Philadelphia: Published by J. Conrad & Co.; Baltimore: Published by M. and J. Conrad & Co.; Washington: Rapin, Conrad & Co.; H. Maxwell, printer, 1802);

The Horrors of Bribery: A Penitential Epistle, from Philip Hamilton, Tinman, to the Right Hon. H. Addington. . . . To Which Is Added a Postscript: Containing Sensible Animadversions on Judge Grose's Solemn and Serious Address to the Unfortunate Tinman. Edited by Peter Pindar, Esq. (London: Printed by W. and C. Spilsbury, for T. Dean, 1802);

Pitt and His Statue: An Epistle to the Subscribers. . . . Also, Lord B——and His Motions, &c., &c. (London: Printed by W. and C. Spilsbury, for J. Walker, 1802; Philadelphia: Published by J. Conrad & Co.; Baltimore: M. and J. Conrad Co.; Washington: Rapin, Conrad & Co.; R. Groff, printer, 1802);

The Island of Innocence: A Poetical Epistle to a Friend (London: Printed by W. and C. Spilsbury, for T. Dean, 1802);

The Middlesex Election; or, Poetical Epistles, in the Devonshire Dialect, by Mr. Joseph Budge, in London, to Lord Holle, at Weymouth. Edited by Peter Pindar, Esq. (London: Printed by W. and C. Spilsbury, for J. Walker, 1802);

Great Cry and Little Wool; or, The Squads in an Uproar; or, The Progress of Politics; or, Epistles, Poet-

ical and Picturesque. Written by Toby Scout, Esq. a Member of the Opposition; and Edited by Peter Pindar, Esq., 2 volumes (London: Printed by W. Spilsbury for J. Walker, 1804);

An Instructive Epistle to John Perring, Esqr., Lord Mayor of London: On the Proposal of an Address of Thanks to the Right Hon. Henry Addington, for His Great and Upright Conduct when Prime Minister (London: Printed by C. Spilsbury, for J. Walker, 1804);

Tristia; or, The Sorrows of Peter: Elegies to the King, Lords Grenville, Petty, Erskine, the Bishop of London, Messrs. Fox, Sheridan, &c. (London: Printed by G. Hayden, published by J. Walker, 1806);

One More Peep at the Royal Academy; or, Odes to Academicians, &c. &c. (London: Printed for the author, and sold by J. Walker, 1808);

The Fall of Portugal; or, The Royal Exiles: A Tragedy, in Five Acts (London: Printed for the author, and sold by Longman, Hurst, Rees, Orme, and Walker, 1808);

A Solemn, Sentimental, and Reprobating Epistle to Mrs. Clarke (London: Printed by J. Dean; published by J. Walker; to be had of R. Ryan, 1809);

Epistle the Second to Mrs. Clarke (London: Printed for J. Walker by J. Dean, 1809);

Carleton House Fete; or, The Disappointed Bard: In a Series of Elegies (London: Printed for J. Walker by G. Hayden, 1811);

An Address to be Spoken at the Opening of Drury Lane Theatre by a Landlord in the Character of Peter Puncheon (London, 1813);

A Most Solemn Epistle to the Emperor of China (London: Printed for Walker and Edwards, 1817).

Collections: *The Poetical Works of Peter Pindar, Esq., a Distant Relation to the Poet of Thebes: To Which Are Prefixed, Memoirs and Anecdotes of the Author* (Dublin: Printed by W. Porter for Messieurs Colles, White, Byrne, M'Kenzie, Jones, and Moore, 1789; Philadelphia: Printed for W. Spotswood; Rice & Co., 1789; enlarged, Dublin: Printed by W. Porter for A. Colles, L. White, P. Byrne, J. Jones, and J. Moore, 1791; 2 volumes, Philadelphia: Printed for W. Spotswood, and Rice & Co., 1792);

The Works of Peter Pindar, Esqr., 4 volumes (London: Printed for John Walker, 1794-1796);

The Works of Peter Pindar, Esq., 5 volumes (London: Printed for J. Walker, 1794-1801);

The Works of Peter Pindar, Esq. with a Copious Index (London: Jones, 1824);

Peter Pindar's Poems, selected by P. M. Zall (Columbia: University of South Carolina Press, 1972).

PLAY PRODUCTION: *Nina; or, The Love Distracted Maid*, translated by Wolcot from Nicolas Dalayrac's *Nina*, Covent Garden Theatre, London, 24 April 1787.

OTHER: *Nina; or, The Madness of Love*, translated by Wolcot from *Nina; ou, La folle par amor* (1786), by Nicolas Dalayrac (London: C. Elliot, T. Kay, 1787);

Pilkington's Dictionary of Painters, edited by Wolcot (London, 1799);

The Beauties of English Poetry, 2 volumes, edited by Wolcot (London: Printed for J. Walker, 1804).

As "Peter Pindar," John Wolcot produced an extraordinary quantity of topical verse satires during the late eighteenth and early nineteenth centuries. Taking as his subjects the Royal Academy exhibitions, political events, social scandals, and such notable individuals as Thomas Paine, William Pitt, James Boswell, Sir Joseph Banks, and, most memorably, George III, "Peter Pindar" painted a vivid and often highly amusing picture of his age. At the height of his fame Wolcot commanded a large readership and provoked wildly disparate responses. Robert Burns called him a "delightful fellow, & first favorite of mine." Samuel Taylor Coleridge swore "that my flesh creeps at his name." And William Wordsworth wrote, "[Nicholas] Boileau and [Alexander] Pope and the more redoubted Peter. These are great names."

The date of Wolcot's birth in Dodbrooke, Devonshire, is unknown; but he was baptized in neighboring Kingsbridge on 9 May 1738. The son of Alexander Wolcot, a surgeon, and Mary Ryder Wolcot, John attended Kingsbridge Grammar School until 1751. On the death of his father that year the family moved to Fowey, Cornwall, where Wolcot was placed under the care of his uncle John, a surgeon-apothecary, and two maiden aunts. He later wrote that "he was kept under rigid control by two aunts, who cowed his spirit to such a degree, that though he had been long released from their tyranny, he never should think himself a man."

After attending school at Liskeard and Bodmin he was apprenticed to his uncle, the surgeon-apothecary. In 1761 he completed his apprenticeship and traveled to France. On his return he studied medicine in London for two years before returning to Fowey in 1764. Stories of his romances with local girls abound; he proposed to one Susan Nankivell but was rejected. At his uncle's wish, he finally received his medical degree from the University of Aberdeen on 8 September 1767. Soon thereafter he applied to a distant member of his family, Sir William Trelawney, governor of Jamaica, for a position as his physician, and on 7 August 1768 he departed for Jamaica with the Trelawney entourage.

In Jamaica, Wolcot became a favorite of the governor. On Trelawney's urging and the promise of the living of the parish of St. Anne, worth twelve to fifteen hundred pounds a year, Wolcot returned to England to take holy orders. He was ordained a priest on 24 June 1769. On his return to Jamaica in March 1770 he found the hoped-for living not vacant, but received instead a living of eight hundred pounds per year at Vere. He soon hired a curate and returned to Trelawney's employ. He was appointed physician-general to the cavalry and infantry of the island on 21 May 1770. During this period he wrote a good deal of verse, most in an elegiac vein. "The Nymph of Tauris," an elegy for Trelawney's sister, was published in the 1773 *Annual Register*. On 11 December 1772 Trelawney died, and Wolcot accompanied his widow back to England.

From 1773 to 1779 Wolcot practiced medicine in Truro, Cornwall. During this period his long-held interest in painting and drawing (which had already caused him to make the acquaintance of several British artists, including James Northcote and Richard Wilson) found an object in John Opie, a fifteen-year-old mine carpenter's apprentice. In Opie, Wolcot seems to have discovered not only a fledgling artist of some natural talent but the potential for making a good deal of money. In 1781 the two arrived in London, where Wolcot marketed Opie as an untaught genius—although, as Sir Ellis Waterhouse writes, Wolcot had "fed him on Rembrandt and the Tenebrists, no doubt through the medium of prints. This was done with something of the secrecy that now attends the training of a young racehorse." Wolcot had decided that Opie would specialize in portraiture, and soon the young painter was the rage of London society. This deep involvement in the English art market undoubtedly played a determining role in Wolcot's decision in 1782 to critique the Royal Academy exhibition under the name "Peter Pindar."

By the time of the invention of Peter Pindar, Wolcot had already had three books published: *Persian Love Elegies* (1773) and two verse satires—*The Noble Criketers* (1778) and *A Poetical, Supplicating, Modest and Affecting Epistle to Those Literary Colossuses, the Reviewers* (1778)—none of which attracted much attention. Initially, Peter Pindar's *Lyric Odes, to the Royal Academicians* (1782)—although strikingly original in conception—fared just as badly. Wolcot claimed he lost forty pounds publishing the work. But in subject and approach these odes became the model for Wolcot's subsequent highly popular satires on the Royal Academy, and they went into many editions. The fifteen poems, in varying iambic pentameter and tetrameter, attack the artists for stiff execution (the horse in Sir Joshua Reynolds's potboiler *Col. Tarleton* is like "that Horse / Call'd Trojan, and by Greeks composed of *wood*"); unnatural coloring (in Philip James de Loutherbourg's "Brass Skies, and Golden Hills"); ridiculous subject matter (in Thomas Gainsborough's *Girl with Pigs*), and so forth. Wolcot praises Richard Wilson, George Stubbs, Reynolds, and some of Gainsborough's works, while reserving special scorn for Richard and Maria Cosway, Benjamin West, and several minor painters. But the recurrent theme, and one which pervades Wolcot's work, is the economic element of artistic production. Peter Pindar is fascinated with money, a fascination evident in the epigraph to *Lyric Odes, to the Royal Academicians*:

> Paint and the Men of Canvas fire my Lays,
> Who show their Works for Profit and for Praise;
> Whose pockets know most comfortable Fillings—
> Gaining two *Thousand Pounds* a Year by *Shillings*.

Later in the book he notes that a painter is "more like a Cobler than a Gentleman" who "with scarce more knowledge than these . . . earns a Guinea ev'ry Day with ease."

Wolcot recouped his losses with his next satire, *More Lyric Odes, to the Royal Academicians* (July 1783). The eight odes reiterate many of the strictures (especially on West and the Cosways) of the earlier odes but are particularly interesting for Peter Pindar's description of his poetic process and motivation. "A Desultory way of writing," he calls it, "A hop, and step, and jump, mode of inditing"—a passage that well describes the sponta-

Self-portrait of John Opie, painted in 1785 (National Portrait Gallery, London). Opie was a fifteen-year-old mine carpenter's apprentice in Cornwall when Wolcot discovered him. After art instruction and promotion by Wolcot, Opie became a successful portrait painter in London.

neous, digressive style of these poems. He joins the notions of rapid composition and marketability:

> THUS have I finish'd, for this time,
> My Odes, a little wild and rambling—
> May people bite like Gudgeons at my rhyme!
> I long to see them scrambling—
> Then very soon I'll give 'em more (God willing)
> But this is full sufficient for a *Shilling*
> For such a trifle, *such a heap*!
> Indeed, I sell my Goods too *cheap*.

In June 1785 appeared *Lyric Odes, for the Year 1785*, twenty-three poems containing much the same mixture of ridicule and mock advice as his earlier works. But to pad out his text, Wolcot interpolates a dialogue, an "Ode to Peter Pindar," and other digressions which contribute to the general formlessness of the work. This miscellaneous quality is also evident in his *Farewel Odes: For the Year 1786* (June 1786). Wolcot's last work to address the Royal Academy exhibition was the highly derivative *One More Peep at the Royal Academy* (April 1808).

By 1785 Peter Pindar had become something of a fad, and Wolcot was quick to capitalize on his popularity. Two of his best satires of this period focus on James Boswell and his pretensions as a biographer. *A Poetical and Congratulatory Epistle to James Boswell, Esq. on His Journal of a Tour to the Hebrides, with the Celebrated Dr. Johnson* (April 1786) attacks Boswell's fascination with minutiae and includes a clever prose postscript relating an imaginary visit by Peter to Johnson a few months before the lexicographer's death. When Peter raises the possibility that Boswell will write Johnson's biography, Johnson replies, "Sir, he can-

Portrait of Wolcot by Opie

not mean me so irreparable an injury. Which of us shall die first, is only known to the Great Disposer of events; but were I sure that James Boswell would write *my* Life, I do not know whether I would not anticipate the measure by taking *his*." Peter Pindar's next hit at Boswell—*Bozzy and Piozzi; or, The British Biographers* (1786)—has been called by George Saintsbury "the best thing of its kind ever written." Structured as an argument between Boswell and Hester Thrale Piozzi (whose *Anecdotes of the late Samuel Johnson, LL.D., during the last Twenty Years of His Life* had been published that year), the poem ludicrously highlights the trivial nature of their biographical method. Thus Boswell says:

> While Johnson was in Edinburgh, my Wife,
> To please his palate, studied for her life:
> With every rarity she fill'd her house,
> And gave the Doctor, for his dinner, grouse.

Madame Piozzi counters with her own dinner-table anecdote:

> Dear Doctor Johnson left off Drinks fermented;
> With quarts of chocolate and cream contented:
> Yet often down his throat's prodigious gutter.
> Poor man! he'd pour a flood of melted butter.

In ridiculously recasting "Bozzy's" and Piozzi's anecdotes, Wolcot in effect creates a new text from their texts.

One of Peter Pindar's most popular targets was George III. In 1785 appeared the first canto of *The Lousiad* (1785-1795), a mock-heroic poem based on the true incident of George III's ordering his cook and servants' heads shaved after finding a louse on his dinner plate. The five-canto work chronicles the king's horror at his discovery, his order to the cooks, their "heroic" resistance and petition, the resulting suspense and struggle, and the final shaving. In Canto I, Wolcot discovers one of his truly memorable subjects, the king's rapid, breathless manner of speaking:

"How, how? what, what? what's that, what's that?"
he cries,
With rapid accent, and with staring eyes:
"Look there, look there; what's got into my house?
A Louse, God bless us! Louse, louse, louse, louse,
louse."

George III's well-known foibles—his mundane interests, stumbling speech, poor taste, parsimony, and so forth—were ideal subjects for the topical satirist, and he became one of Peter Pindar's most successful subjects. In poem after poem the monarch is recorded bumbling through his duties and recreations—a likable but ludicrous fellow. Thus, when he visited Samuel Whitbread's brewery, Wolcot "recorded" his conversation in *Instructions to a Celebrated Laureat* (1787):

"Whitbread, d'ye keep a Coach, or job one, pray?
Job, job, that's cheapest; yes, that's best, that's
best.
You put your liveries on the Draymen, hae?
Hae, Whitbread, you have feather'd well your
nest.
What, what's the price now, hae, of all your stock?
But, Whitbread, what's o'clock, pray what's o'clock?"
Now Whitbread inward said, "May I be curst
If I know what to answer first."

Such imaginative fooling and irreverence caught the fancy of the public and earned Wolcot substantial sales. His descriptions of the king played a major role in the popular redefinition of royalty and reflected the shifting mood of the public's relations with George III. In the late 1787 the government appears to have tried to buy him off, but the negotiations came to nothing. In *Peter's Pension* (1788) Wolcot claimed that the government had offered him a pension, but he had declined it. On the other hand, Wolcot tried to curry favor with the Prince of Wales, fulsomely praising him in *Expostulatory Odes to a Great Duke, and a Little Lord* (1789).

During this fecund period Wolcot also wrote for the theater, supplying Covent Garden with a translation of Nicolas Dalayrac's *Nina* (1786) titled *Nina; or, The Love Distracted Maid*, which played on 24 April 1787. Wolcot was fond of music and the stage. He often attended the theater and formed friendships with many actors, musicians, and managers, including George Colman and Joseph Haydn. In 1792 he wrote the libretto for Haydn's *The Storm*.

With the advent of the French Revolution, Peter Pindar turned his pen to politics. In July 1791 the collection of satires *Odes to Mr. Paine, Author of "Rights of Man"* was published. In *The Remonstrance* (October 1791) he rejects the notion that he had joined the king's party just because he attacked Paine; but he nevertheless castigates the revolutionaries. Most of Peter Pindar's many poems dealing with the revolution are in this vein: not so much pro-English as anti-French, not so much promonarchy as antirevolution. Indeed, after the passage of the government's repressive bills against sedition and treason, he spoke out strongly in *Liberty's Last Squeak* (1795) against what he perceived to be the growth of British tyranny.

During the late 1780s and early 1790s Wolcot was at the height of his fame. His satires on scientists (*Sir Joseph Banks and the Emperor of Morocco* [1788]), politicians (*A Poetical Epistle to a Falling Minister* [1789]), authors (*Advice to the Future Laureat* [1790]), George III, Paine, and many others, although rapidly written and uneven in execution, continued to attract a large audience. So successful was he that during the winter of 1793-1794 the London booksellers Robinson, Goulding, and Walker purchased his copyright for an annuity of £250 payable until Wolcot's death.

But success had its price, especially for a man of Wolcot's volatile temperament. He increasingly became the subject of attacks by other writers, one of which led to physical violence and to one of the darkest moments of Wolcot's career. When he satirized the poet Hannah More in *Nil Admirari* (1799), the *Anti-Jacobin Magazine and Review* castigated him as a "monster in human shape" and a "profligate priest whose conversation exhibits a disgusting mixture of obscenity and blasphemy." Thinking, mistakenly, that the author of this piece was William Gifford, Wolcot attacked Gifford's character in a postscript to *Lord Auckland's Triumph* (1800). Gifford replied in *An Epistle to Peter Pindar* (1800). Wolcot wrote a threatening letter to Gifford, who reciprocated. On 18 August 1800 Wolcot found Gifford in Wright's Bookshop and struck him on the head with his cane. Gifford wrestled the cane from Wolcot, beat him with it, and, with the help of the bookseller's assistants, hustled him into the street, throwing his hat and wig after him. This absurd affair achieved immediate notoriety as the "Battle of the Bards" and did substantial damage to both Wolcot's self-esteem and reputation.

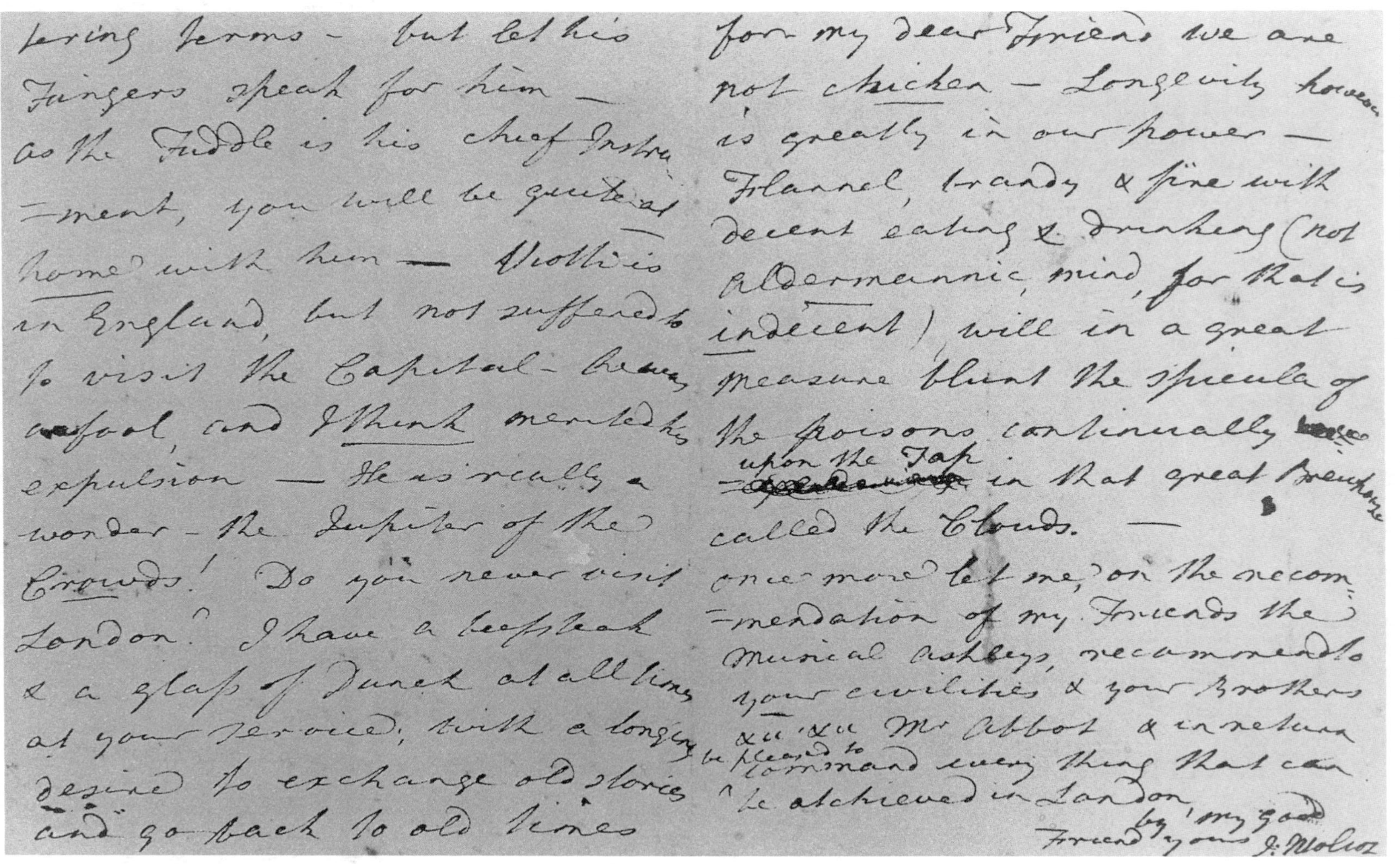

fering Jerons – but let his
Fingers speak for him –
as the Fiddle is his chief Instru-
-ment, you will be quite at
home with him – Viotti is
in England, but not suffered to
to visit the Capital – because
a fool, and I think merited his
expulsion – He is really a
wonder – the Jupiter of the
Crowds! Do you never visit
London? I have a beefsteak
& a glass of Punch at all times
at your service; with a longing
desire to exchange old stories
and go back to old times

for my dear Friend we are
not chicken – Longevity however
is greatly in our power –
Flannel, brandy & fire with
decent eating & drinking (not
Aldermannic, mind, for that is
indecent) will in a great
measure blunt the spicula of
the poisons continually
upon the Tap in that great Brewhouse
called the Clouds. –
once more let me, on the recom-
-mendation of my Friends the
Musical Ashleys, recommend to
your civilities & your Brothers
&c &c Mr Abbot & in return
be pleased to command every thing that can
be achieved in London, my good
Friend by yours J. Wolcot

Third and fourth pages of a letter from Wolcot, dated 11 January 1800, to an unidentified recipient (Pierpont Morgan Library)

Portrait of Wolcot, artist unknown; formerly attributed to Opie (National Portrait Gallery, London)

It seems also to have marked something of a turning point in his poetical fortunes. After 1800, although still regularly having works published, Wolcot began to lose his gift for ludicrous mimicry. His later political poems *Pitt and His Statue* (1802), *The Middlesex Election* (1802), *Great Cry and Little Wool* (1804)—lack the sparkle and bite of his earlier pieces. His *A Solemn, Sentimental, and Reprobating Epistle to Mrs. Clarke* (1809) and *Epistle the Second to Mrs. Clarke* (1809)—dealing with bribery and blackmail charges brought against Mary Ann Clarke, mistress of Frederick, Duke of York—are among Peter Pindar's dullest poems. His last political poem, *Carleton House Fete; or, The Disappointed Bard* (1811), describes the poet's sorrow in having been neither pensioned by the new prince regent nor even invited to the spectacular party given by the prince when he assumed the regency. The tone of resignation summarizes Wolcot's attitude in his final years.

By this time Wolcot must have felt himself a beaten man. In 1807 he had gone through a scandalous and embarrassing trial for allegedly engaging in "criminal conversation" (adultery) with his landlord's wife, the twenty-six-year-old Mrs. Knight; Wolcot's lawyer had argued that he was "upwards of seventy [he was actually sixty-nine], blind, asthmatic, and a very antidote to love," as well as physically incapable of the crime. He was acquitted. By 1811 Wolcot was indeed almost blind. An operation on his right eye in 1814 was unsuccessful, and after this date he had only one more poem published: *A Most Solemn Epistle to the Emperor of China* (1817). In these final years, however, Wolcot remained socially active, seeing his old friends William Godwin, Thomas Rowlandson, and George Morland; dining with William

Hazlitt in 1817; and being introduced to John Keats in 1818. He died on 14 January 1819 and was buried in St. Paul's Covent Garden. By his own wish his coffin was placed touching that of Samuel Butler.

For John Wolcot, poetry was always a commercial venture—one intended first of all to make money. No English poet before him had ever been as open about his opportunistic motivations, and few had ever been so successful. (Wishing to capitalize on his fame, several contemporary writers also used the pseudonym "Peter Pindar.") At his best, he was unsurpassed as a humorous and acute recorder of his times. Kenneth Hopkins calls him "the greatest master of verse caricature in English, perhaps the only one of consequence." Yet his poetry is important not only for its topical panache and brilliant exploitation of popular personalities but also because of its role in the transformation of verse satire. Despite its wide range of specific subjects, Peter Pindar's satire characteristically emphasizes the poet's making of the text and his self-reflexive response to his material. The reader is always, as Thomas Lockwood puts it, "made aware of the subject as the-subject-'Peter'-is-writing-about-in-this-poem." In this respect Wolcot belongs firmly to the tradition of reflexive process satire given early articulation by Charles Churchill and culminating brilliantly with Lord Byron. As Grzegorz Sinko writes, "Wolcot's name emerges as the most significant one in the decades between Churchill and Byron, not merely . . . as an isolated literary fact, but as a link between two generations and, at the same time, as a representative spokesman of his period, which was neither short nor unimportant."

Biography:

Tom Girtin, *Doctor with Two Aunts: A Biography of Peter Pindar* (London: Hutchinson, 1959).

References:

Vincent Carretta, *George III and the Satirists from Hogarth to Byron* (Athens: University of Georgia Press, 1990), pp. 269-273;

William Hazlitt, *Lectures on the English Comic Writers* (London: Taylor & Hessey, 1819);

Kenneth Hopkins, *Portraits in Satire* (London: Barrie, 1958);

Thomas Lockwood, *Post-Augustan Satire: Charles Churchill and Satirical Poetry, 1750-1800* (Seattle: University of Washington Press, 1979);

Theodor Reitterer, *Leben und Werke Peter Pindars (Dr. John Wolcot)* (Vienna & Leipzig: Braumuller, 1900);

Grzegorz Sinko, *John Wolcot and His School: A Chapter in the History of English Satire* (Wroclaw: Prace Wroclawskiego Towarzystwa Naukowego, 1962);

The Trial of Doctor John Wolcot Otherwise Peter Pindar, Esq. for Criminal Conversation with the Wife of Mr. Knight, of the Royal Navy. Before the Right Hon. Lord Ellenborough, in the Court of King's Bench, Westminster; on June the 27th, 1807. To Which Is Added, an Account of the Life of Dr. Wolcot (London: Printed and sold by J. Day, 1807);

Robert L. Vales, *Peter Pindar (John Wolcot)* (New York: Twayne, 1973).

Ann Yearsley

(July 1753 - 8 May 1806)

Donna Landry
University of Southern California

BOOKS: *Poems, on Several Occasions* (London: Printed for T. Cadell, 1785);

Poems on Various Subjects (London: Printed for the author, and sold by G. G. J. & J. Robinson, 1787);

A Poem on the Inhumanity of the Slave-Trade (London: Printed for G. G. J. & J. Robinson, 1788);

Stanzas of Woe, Addressed from the Heart on a Bed of Illness, to Levi Eames, Esq. Late Mayor of the City of Bristol (London: Printed for G. G. J. &. J. Robinson, 1790);

Earl Goodwin: An Historical Play. Performed with General Applause at the Theatre-Royal, Bristol (London: Printed for G. G. J. & J. Robinson, 1791);

The Dispute: Letter to the Public. From the Milkwoman (London: 1791);

Reflections on the Death of Louis XVI (Bristol: Printed for and sold by the author, and by the booksellers of Bristol, Bath, 1793);

Sequel to Reflections on the Death of Louis XVI (Bristol: Printed for and sold by the author, and by the booksellers of Bristol, Bath, 1793);

Catalogue of the Books, Tracts, &c. Contained in Ann Yearsley's Public Library, No. 4, Crescent, Hotwells (Bristol: Printed for the Proprietor, 1793);

An Elegy on Marie Antoinette, of Austria, Ci-Devant Queen Of France: With a Poem on the Last Interview between the King of Poland and Loraski (Bristol: Printed [by J. Rudhall] for and sold by the author, and by the principal booksellers in Bristol, Bath, 1793);

The Royal Captives: A Fragment of Secret History. Copied from an Old Manuscript, 4 volumes (London: Printed for G. G. & J. Robinson, 1795; volumes 1-2, Philadelphia: Printed by William W. Woodward, 1795; volumes 3-4, Philadelphia: Published by Thomas Bradford, 1796);

The Rural Lyre: A Volume of Poems (London: Printed for G. G. & J. Robinson, 1796).

Of all the plebeian female poets of the eighteenth century, Ann Yearsley, the "milkwoman of Bristol," most repays detailed historical study. Her sizable oeuvre, competence across genres, and varied contemporary critical reception give her a strong claim on literary importance as traditionally understood. One can also trace the development of her ideas in relation to political and social events, her increasing radicalization during the French Revolution and its English reception, and her enigmatic but perhaps suggestive silence after 1796. Though she wrote at least one play, *Earl Goodwin* (1791), and a novel, *The Royal Captives* (1795), poetry remained Yearsley's primary medium from her first volume in 1785 to her last in 1796. Yearsley's poetical production is best represented by her three major collections of verse; by a minor volume, *Stanzas of Woe* (1790); and by several singly issued occasional poems, usually of urgently topical significance. If *Poems, on Several Occasions* (1785) documents her first grateful and often self-deprecating experience of patronage through the direct philanthropy of Hannah More and Elizabeth Montagu, *Poems on Various Subjects* (1787) provides ample testimony of her quick and bitter disillusionment with the servility of such clientage and her obsessive desire for self-vindication. Exchanging her exacting female patrons for relative economic independence and the rather distant generosity of Frederick Hervey, Earl of Bristol and bishop of Derry, Yearsley in this second volume becomes aesthetically bolder and more socially critical. Able at last to quit her duties as milkwoman for those of running a somewhat unsuccessful circulating library near Bristol Hot Wells, in the 1790s Yearsley produced accomplished verse that situates her somewhere between civic poet and social dissident. *The Rural Lyre* (1796) marks the end of her literary production and the beginning of her last years of melancholy isolation—a return to obscurity all too common among laboring-class "discoveries" of the period.

Ann Cromartie, the daughter of John Cromartie, a laborer, and Ann Cromartie, a milkwoman, was born on Clifton Hill near Bristol; she was baptized on 15 July 1753 in Clifton Parish Church, according to the parish register. (Yearsley herself, however, appears to have thought that she was born in 1756, the date given in the *Dictionary of National Biography* and followed by most scholars since). According to a correspondent from Clifton writing in the *Gentleman's Magazine* (December 1784), Cromartie's passion for literature was aroused by her mother, who borrowed books from "*her betters*"; and, according to More, who became Yearsley's first patron, it was her brother William who taught her to write. She grew up, like her mother, keeping cows and selling milk from door to door. On 8 June 1774 she married John Yearsley, described by the Clifton correspondent as "of no vice, but of very little capacity." Hoping to enlist her support for Mrs. Yearsley, More wrote to her friend Montagu in August 1784, "and what will excite your compassion for a Woman of *Sentiment*, [she] was sacrificed for *money* at 17 [she was actually twenty] to a silly Man whom she did not like; the Husband had an Estate of near *Six pounds* a year, and the marriage was thought too advantageous to be refused." In the ten years following her marriage Yearsley bore six children, of whom five lived. In early 1784 she was pregnant with her seventh child when the poverty-stricken family, including her aged mother, was evicted from its cottage. Huddled together in a stable and expecting to die of hunger, all except old Mrs. Cromartie were saved when a Mr. Vaughan happened to look into the stable. News of this troubled family reached More through her cook, from whom Ann Yearsley bought kitchen scraps or "hogwash" with which to feed her pig; the cook showed her mistress Yearsley's poems, and in the summer of 1784 Yearsley became the object of More's patronage.

Yearsley's relationship with More, and its acrimonious conclusion, have been the chief means of her entry into the historical record. More's admirers villified Yearsley, and she spent the rest of her public career trying to vindicate herself from charges of ingratitude. The relationship between such a patron and such a client, both strong-willed, seems bound to have eventually foundered on class differences. In such situations, one may well ask how the privileged middle-class reformist is to avoid "patronizing," wounding, and exploiting her protégée and how the laboring-class poet is to use the sisterly literary alliance without sacrificing her dignity and independence when confronted by middle-class propertied confidence, self-righteousness, fear of insurrection, and the authority of "educated" speech.

Reading in Yearsley's poems the "high literary" skill or sense that the century called "genius," so sought after and here so mysteriously acquired, More introduced what she considered the prodigious talent in these "unlettered verses" by means of a prefatory letter to Montagu in *Poems, on Several Occasions*: "All I see of her, raises my opinion of her genius. . . . Confess, dear Madam, that you and I know many a head competently stored with Greek and Latin which cou'd not have produced better Verses. I never met with an Ear more nicely tuned." Promoting the laboring poet does *not* mean, More wrote to Montagu in September 1784, promoting working-class deracination, as had happened with Queen Caroline's patronage of Stephen Duck, the "Thresher Poet," in the 1730s: "I am *utterly* against taking her out of her Station. *Stephen* was an excellent Bard as a *Thrasher*, but as the Court Poet, and Rival of [Alexander] Pope, detestable."

More claimed to have written more than a thousand pages on Yearsley's behalf, soliciting subscriptions and making arrangements with printers; perhaps as much as six hundred pounds was collected and invested by More and Montagu, from which they intended to provide Yearsley with an allowance. More appeared to Yearsley increasingly condescending, and the servility of clientage became unbearable. And once Yearsley insisted on having control of the capital, More would have nothing more to do with her. Yearsley used the money to apprentice her son William to an engraver and to establish a circulating library. Yearsley's account of the affair can be read in the "Narrative" with which she prefaced the fourth edition of *Poems, on Several Occasions* (1786) and her second volume, *Poems on Various Subjects*.

The most insistent strain in Yearsley's verse is that of a struggle for dominance. Yearsley rarely fails to locate herself within the social space of the laboring woman writer—poor, plebeian, and deficient in education and culture. But working within and against the grain of this identity is another sort of authorial consciousness: the striving for a literary freedom from social and sexual constraints through the establishment of a sovereign subject, a self-constituting and imperial

"I" who takes emancipatory pleasure in the imagination and in aesthetic production. This is not quite the "I" of the Wordsworthian egotistical sublime, as John Keats would have it, for the "I" of Yearsley's verse is traversed by struggles and desires unknown to the privileged man and the future poet laureate. But there is in Yearsley's poems something akin to William Wordsworth's command of a landscape and his wish to be reabsorbed into its greenly animate prospects and its natural forces of wind and water that bespeak a power greater than any human one. In a more theoretical sense, the "I" of both her verse and Wordsworth's is the postrevolutionary bourgeois subject whose sense of identity is affirmed through reading and writing. Paradoxically, Yearsley emerges as a self-constituting sovereign subject in verse at the very moment of inscribing herself poetically as "Lactilla," a plebeian craftswoman, a "savage" inspired by the rustic and laboring muse.

In "On Mrs. Montagu," from her first volume, Yearsley both characterizes Lactilla and anticipates the new Romantic landscape poetry, dramatizing a certain reciprocity between nature and mind. This poem shows the failure of ecstatic visionary moments to translate themselves serviceably into textual artifacts, but it preserves something of the fervor and prophetic promise of those moments:

> Oft as I trod my native wilds alone,
> Strong gusts of thought wou'd rise, but rise to die;
> The portals of the swelling soul, ne'er op'd
> By liberal converse, rude ideas strove
> Awhile for vent, but found it not, and died.
> Thus rust the Mind's best powers.

It is through education that the "savage" muse is tamed and the mind's best powers are thoroughly rust-proofed.

Poems, on Several Occasions contains experiments in various traditional poetic genres, including the epistle, the elegy, and the loco-descriptive poem. In "Clifton Hill," the volume's most ambitious effort, Yearsley goes some way toward feminizing the subject matter and the narrational perspective of the traditionally masculine prospect poem. "Clifton Hill" intersperses topographical description with philosophical and social musings in which women are the dominant focus. A brief discourse on the wrongs of female education, for instance, comes between two other, more dramatic, moments of focused female subjectivity: narratives about Yearsley's childhood experiences of graveyard poetry in the company of her mother, whom she mourns and memorializes, and about the tragic history of the mysterious mad Louisa, who sleeps outside until she is institutionalized. Far from being at odds with the natural world, or seeking to dominate or exploit it in accordance with eighteenth-century notions of progress and empire associated with the prospect poem, these female subjects find consolation and safety in the "inhuman" world of natural forces. The "I" of "Clifton Hill" is a migratory one that fuses itself with a variety of perspectives, both human and animal. But Yearsley returns periodically to Lactilla's situation as a working woman for whom winter brings no cessation of labor; cows must be milked and milk sold door-to-door even in the harshest weather:

> . . . half sunk in snow,
> LACTILLA, shivering, tends her fav'rite cow.

Yearsley furnishes the verse-writing milkwoman Lactilla with a certain knowing detachment from the youthful swains and milkmaids for whom the return of spring will bring renewed sensual desire. Reversing the terms of the Freudian dynamic of sublimation, she represents the impulse toward poetry as more fundamental than the sexual impulse. The ardor of the "ruddy swain," inspired by burgeoning vegetation and spring gales, begins as an inarticulate poetical impulse; but lack of education requires that it manifest itself in the pursuit of sexual pleasure:

> The ruddy swain now stalks along the vale,
> And snuffs fresh ardour from the flying gale;
> The landscape rushes on his untaught mind,
> Strong raptures rise, but raptures undefin'd;
> He louder whistles, stretches o'er the green,
> By screaming milk-maids, not unheeded, seen;
> The downcast look ne'er fixes on the swain,
> They dread his eye, retire and gaze again.
> 'Tis mighty Love. . . .

This scene of screaming milkmaids pretending not to notice the young man's presence in spite of his lounging on the green in plain sight, but sneaking the occasional glimpse of him nevertheless, is typical of Yearsley's fresh and skillful rendering of rural social life. There follows a brief discourse on the differences between plebeian and polite rituals of courtship and sexual practice. All this the contemplative Lactilla appears to have put behind her; she merely reports, from an ironi-

Manuscript. Addressed by Mrs Yearsley to a recent widower, with whom she had, had a disagreement.

By all the joys which yet my soul may know!
And all thy pang of complicated woe
I would console thee! — every wish is vain
Thy heart must mourn, nor can I heal thy pain,
Time, and thy Daughters with unceasing care
~~Shall watch thy~~ [illegible] ~~the frequent tear~~
While manly friendship in thy Boys shall prove
How much they owe Thee: and how much they love.
Believe me [illegible], — no flattery tunes my song,
Unaw'd I rove the wilds of life among,
No pow'r subdues me — to no point confin'd
I lash rude folly but I love mankind.
I see Thee now, — not as a Man whose gold
Renders him haughty insolent and bold
But as a Victim at pale Sorrow's shrine
Thy spirit wounded by her shafts like mine.
Bend not to Earth! — O hide the fruitless tear!
Look up! behold thy children claim thy care
For them be reconciled to them return
Lead them to peace and say thou wilt not mourn
To see Thee chearful will their woes beguile
From Thee they'll catch the joy-restoring smile
And while the hymns of filial love arise
Their Mother's Shade shall listen from the skies

Yearsley

10 Sepr Clifton

Poem written by Ann Yearsley on a blank page of her Poems, on Several Occasions *(RB 87116, Henry E. Huntington Library and Art Gallery)*

cal distance, these anthropological observations to an audience for whom they will seem literary novelties. Lactilla's own libidinal investment lies in the emancipatory inspiration offered by the landscape itself, and in her ability to narrate the daily rounds necessitated by her labor. The poet as solitary wanderer was not a new phenomenon, but Yearsley's aestheticization of her labor as a constant source of inspiration was new.

Yearsley's first volume was received enthusiastically. Not only did *Poems, on Several Occasions* go through four editions but the *Monthly Review* (September 1785) found in her best poems "a genius of no uncommon bent, and a fancy pregnant with those images which give to poetry its most captivating power," going on to praise the signs of struggle that were present in the work: "On the whole, these Poems present us with a very striking picture of a vigorous and aspiring genius, struggling with its own feelings. We see an ardent mind exerting itself to throw off every incumbrance that oppresses it, and to burst from the cloud that obscures its lustre." It is ironic that Yearsley could be publicly praised for trying to liberate herself imaginatively at the very moment when the question of upward mobility through access to her subscription money was being so hotly contested. (The *Monthly Review* would give comparable notice to her second volume in 1787 and to her novel in 1795, and the *Critical Review* praised her work as well).

Under the aegis of her new patron, Hervey, *Poems on Various Subjects* demonstrates Yearsley's attempts at self-vindication in the wake of the More controversy, pronounces sharper social criticism than she had previously dared to write, and sometimes displays dazzlingly successful aesthetic experiments. It would seem that Yearsley felt acutely the difference between her own self-representation as Lactilla and More's exploitation of the pathos of her situation. One might go so far as to say that Yearsley repudiated what could be read as class stigma in More's public promotion of her verse and that she ventured to suggest the possibility of a class-free aesthetic interest for her poems. It would be doing Yearsley an injustice to read her only as "a working-class woman poet" in a tokenizing way, for that very condescension was something she seems to have predicted and protested against.

In *Poems on Various Subjects* Yearsley again explores several poetic genres and, perhaps most effectively, exposes the coercive bias perpetuated by certain readings of Scripture and the prohibitions on women's and workers' appropriation of "high literary" culture. "On Jephthah's Vow, Taken in a Literal Sense" draws a connection between the patriarchalism of the Old Testament and the oppressiveness of patriarchy; the poem makes a precise move from the rule of the father per se to the sacrifice of the daughter, mediated by a self-serving notion of "God-the-Father" as *like* the father, the sovereign subject of familial and social relations. The premise of "Addressed to Ignorance, Occasioned by a Gentleman's Desiring the Author never to assume a Knowledge of the Ancients" is Yearsley's having been forbidden to enter the privileged precincts where classical subjects hold sway. "Assum[ing] a Knowledge of the Ancients" would signify, in a poor laboring woman, that she was "getting above herself," putting on airs. Yearsley counters by proving that without recourse to a gentlemanly education she possesses "a Knowledge of the Ancients" sufficient to inform a riotous panorama of classical allusions:

But Zeno, Tibellus, and Socrates grave,
 In the bodies of wan Garreteers,
All tatter'd, cold, hungry, by turns sigh and rave
 At their Publisher's bill of arrears.

. . . .

There's Virgil, the Courtier, with hose out at heel,
 And Hesiod, quite shoeless his foot;
Poor Ovid walks shiv'ring, behind a cart-wheel,
 While Horace cries, "sweep for your soot."

. . . .

But Helen, the Spartan, stands near Charing-Cross,
 Long laces and pins doom'd to cry;
Democritus, Solon, bear baskets of moss,
 While Pliny sells woodcocks hard by.

The most radical suggestion made by Yearsley's comic appropriation of the ancients is that the subject matter of the texts of antiquity cannot be sealed off as an inviolable upper-class preserve but is increasingly open, within a culture of commercial printing, to popular consumption.

The final phase of Yearsley's career was initiated by a furious burst of litigation and published controversy. During the 1789 hay harvest, Yearsley's three sons were horsewhipped by the footman of Levi Eames, the mayor of Bristol—two of them for playing in the mayor's fields, one for "expostulating" with the footman "in a childish manner." Yearsley pressed charges against the footman, but her lawyer advised her to drop the case because he supposed "her purse not to be *quite* so heavy as Mr. Eames's." In June of the following year Yearsley was sitting outside her cottage when Eames's groom chased some children, who were not hers, from the by then former mayor's fields. When the children escaped, he turned on Yearsley so violently that she miscarried later that evening. *Stanzas of Woe*, dedicated ironically to Eames, was her only form of protest. But its publication caused her to lose her commission for an ode on the Magdalen Hospital, a misfortune which she attempted to rectify by publishing *The Dispute: Letter to the Public. From the Milkwoman* (1791).

Such personal sorrow and anger notwithstanding, for the next six years Yearsley attempted to write against the growing tide of reaction that marked the 1790s in England. She expanded her subject matter on several fronts at once, exploring current events abroad, particularly in France, and writing for the first time explicitly about both domestic politics, as in the "Bristol Elegy," and the politics of domesticity, as in "To Mira on the Care of Her Infant." There is much internal evidence in *The Rural Lyre* to support J. M. S. Tompkins's theory that not only "domestic troubles" but Yearsley's identification with "liberal sentiments" brought her career to a premature halt in 1796, because she "could no longer, in this time of growing reaction, expect a fair hearing."

Nevertheless, Yearsley's is a far from programmatic response to current events. Although *Earl Goodwin*, written in 1789, allusively applauds the early stages of the French Revolution as an expression of the will of an oppressed peasantry championed by well-born and educated leaders sympathetic to their plight, the executions of Louis XVI and Marie Antoinette prompted her most direct commentary. As in *A Poem on the Inhumanity of the Slave-Trade* (1788), there is a certain identification with her fellow victims of history, tyranny, and violence. And at moments Yearsley attempts a sublation of the political into the aestheticized body of nature as a substitution for political yearnings gone awry or eternally deferred. In her most Coleridgean moment, in *Stanzas of Woe*, Yearsley simultaneously praises the literal inspiration of the breeze and its analogous properties to human feelings of liberty and strength:

Yet gentle *Air, unseen and ever felt,
To Thee again my invocations rise,
Ah, let me not in burning fevers melt!
But bear at least my spirit thro' the skies.

*This Poem was begun the first morn of the Physician's allowing the air to play through the Author's window.

In her two poems on Louis XVI's execution, written within three weeks of the event, it would seem that liberty resides entirely in natural forces and can be comprehended only imaginatively. In *Reflections on the Death of Louis XVI* (1793) she says:

Ask, ye! where joyous Liberty resorts,
In *France*, in *Spain*, or in *Britannia's* Vale?
O no!—She only with poor Fancy sports
Her richest Dwelling is the passing Gale.

However much in sympathy she might have been with the earlier moments of revolutionary fervor, she has no taste for royal martyrdom; it suggests entirely too much affinity between this supposedly popular rule and the old absolutist tyranny. For her the executions of Louis XVI and Marie Antoinette represent only another instance of needless bloodshed and the shattering of family affections, one of those nearly unrepresentable moments when—as she says in *An Elegy on Marie Antoinette* (1793)—"Hist'ry stands amaz'd."

These urgently topical poems perhaps hold a key to understanding the framing of *The Rural Lyre* three years later, in which Yearsley projects herself as an image of "British Liberty" both in the frontispiece and in several poems—most notably "Brutus: A Fragment," so strongly reminiscent of Pope's unfinished epic on the same theme, which she may have known from Owen Ruffhead's *The Life of Alexander Pope, Esq.* (1769). This volume, her first without an "occasional" or topical title, may have been meant to mark her emergence as a political poet in the bardic sense: the singer of tragic pasts and emancipatory futures whose lyre can both accompany historical struggle and provide touching narratives of the fallen. Her method of entry into these difficult scenes is by way of the domestic relations that may seem to have been relegated to the "private" sphere by the sexual division of labor but so often make themselves visible from a woman's point of view as intrinsic to the workings of the "public" sphere as well—as, indeed, inseparable from it.

Working from the radical republican commonplace that the public order has domestic roots, and that conversely the family may be disrupted by false public values, Yearsley specifies women's possible contributions to a politics that would transform both domestic and public life by collapsing the distinction between them in the interests of greater democracy and participation. Yearsley's poetry in this final phase of her career thus simultaneously attempts to domesticate the political by "bringing it home" and to generate, in a more visionary, utopian, and incompletely articulated sense, a radical democratic politics in which domestic relations, hitherto marginal, are at the center. In this respect Yearsley might be said to anticipate Owenism, with its emphasis on the participation of women, its anticipation of socialism, its advocacy of natural and universal equality, its belief in human perfectibility, its insistence on the mutability of social and political institutions, and its direction toward the future rather than the past.

The Rural Lyre, far from being either a seamlessly Jacobinic or proto-Owenite manifesto, is fraught with contradictory tendencies. Not the least of these contradictions is Yearsley's partial move away from a vocabulary of active class resistance at the very moment when she is striving to articulate a most urgent need for social transformation. And coupled with this partial effacement of class activism is a representation of women that positions Yearsley as close as she ever comes to a politics of domesticity, in which women's power to influence public morality from their hearths and nurseries is celebrated and women's literary and artistic production is both trivialized and presented as a satisfactory substitute for direct political participation. In a sense, the domestication of the political requires that Yearsley put a victimized woman's body at the center of her poems; this is the trope that links works as various as *Earl Goodwin, Stanzas of Woe, An Elegy on Marie Antoinette*, "To Mira, on the Care of Her Infant," and the "Bristol Elegy." The poems of *The Rural Lyre* represent experiments in subject matter as well as style, and a general improvement in Yearsley's poetical accomplishments. Although Tompkins is certainly right to praise this collection as presenting "clear evidence of an advance in style and verse as well as substance," one need not agree with her that Yearsley's use of blank verse and the highly formalized couplet "proves also that in these forms she could never overtake her lack of training," a judgment that suggests failure on Yearsley's part and implies that her silence after 1796 might have been justified. Rather, the increasingly uniform accomplishment of Yearsley's verse in this period, coupled with her use of new and provocative materials, is cause for particular regret that she appears to have published nothing after *The Rural Lyre*.

Advocating female militancy in the service of pacifism, not female passivity in the service of militarism, "To Mira, on the Care of Her Infant" addresses women's domestic power as a potentially peacekeeping force; especially in wartime, while the men are away fighting, women may bring up their children according to more enlightened values. Lactilla, once purveyor of cows' milk, scornfully distances herself from the rebellious laboring woman who nurses for a living:

> I saw the beauteous Caleb t' other day
> Stretch forth his little hand to touch a spray,
> Whilst on the grass his drowsy nurse inhal'd
> The sweets of Nature as her sweets exhal'd:
> But, ere the infant reach'd the playful leaf,
> She pull'd him back—His eyes o'erflow'd with grief;
> He check'd his tears—Her fiercer passions strove,
> She look'd a vulture cow'ring o'er a dove!
> "I'll teach you, brat!" The pretty trembler sigh'd—
> When, with a cruel shake, she hoarsely cried—
> "Your Mother spoils you—every thing you see
> "You covet. It shall ne'er be so with me!"

Lactilla, the figure for the savage laboring-class writer, silently disappears; "coarse" and "furious" nursemaids surface as villains—the return of a repressed, regressive working class. The question of social emancipation becomes confused, is displaced and defused, in the service of vivid representation and the recognition of intractable class differences. Such an impasse between the desire for radical social transformation toward liberty and enlightenment and the seemingly inevitable reproduction of class antagonisms suggests that Yearsley, despite her radicalization, could not push beyond the limits of her historical moment, and thus her visionary politics could not be realized even in verse. Those limits still remain, and the contradictions represented by her last work retain a peculiar urgency today.

According to Robert Southey, when Yearsley died on 8 May 1806 she was in straitened circumstances, never having achieved the leisured gentility to which More appears to have feared she would aspire. That her work has been so little read when it offers such complex aesthetic and intellectual pleasures suggests what can so easily be lost to the historical record or the literary canon through collective "forgetting." And it is this forgetting, this repression of particular struggles and forms of political resistance, that recovering and reading Yearsley's work may help to overcome.

References:

Joseph Cottle, *Early Recollections: Chiefly Relating to the Late Samuel Taylor Coleridge, during His Long Residence at Bristol*, 2 volumes (London: Longman, Rees/Hamilton, Adams, 1837), I: 69-77;

Margaret Doody, *The Daring Muse: Augustan Poetry Reconsidered* (Cambridge: Cambridge University Press, 1985), pp. 130-131, 243;

Moira Ferguson, *First Feminists: British Women Writers 1578-1799* (Bloomington, Ind. & Old Westbury, N.Y.: Indiana University Press & Feminist Press, 1985), pp. 380-397;

Ferguson, "Resistance and Power in the Life and Writings of Ann Yearsley," *The Eighteenth Century: Theory and Interpretation*, 27 (Fall 1986): 247-268;

Mary R. Mahl and Helene Koon, eds., *The Female Spectator: English Women Writers before 1800* (Bloomington, Ind. & Old Westbury, N.Y.: Indiana University Press & Feminist Press, 1977), pp. 277-286;

William Roberts, *Memoirs of the Life and Correspondence of Mrs. Hannah More*, 4 volumes (London: Seeley & Burnside, 1834), I: 361-391; II: 80-81, 223;

Morag Shiach, *Discourse on Popular Culture: Class, Gender and History in the Analysis of Popular Culture* (Oxford: Polity Press, 1989), pp. 45-46, 56-59;

Robert Southey, *The Lives and Works of the Uneducated Poets*, edited by J. S. Childers (London: Milford, 1925), pp. 125-134, 195-198;

Chauncey Brewster Tinker, *Nature's Simple Plan: A Phase of Radical Thought in the Mid-Eighteenth Century* (Princeton: Princeton University Press, 1922), pp. 99-103;

J. M. S. Tompkins, *The Polite Marriage, Etc.: Eighteenth-Century Essays* (Cambridge: Cambridge University Press, 1938), pp. 58-102;

Rayner Unwin, *The Rural Muse: Studies in the Peasant Poetry of England* (London: Allen & Unwin, 1954), pp. 77-81.

Books for Further Reading

Adams, Percy G. *Graces of Harmony: Alliteration, Assonance, and Consonance in Eighteenth-Century British Poetry*. Athens: University of Georgia Press, 1977.

Arthos, John. *The Language of Natural Description in Eighteenth-Century Poetry*. Ann Arbor: University of Michigan Press, 1949.

Bate, Walter Jackson. *The Burden of the Past and the English Poet*. Cambridge, Mass.: Harvard University Press, 1970; London: Chatto & Windus, 1971.

Battestin, Martin C. *The Providence of Wit: Aspects of Form in Augustan Literature and the Arts*. Oxford: Clarendon Press, 1974.

Carretta, Vincent. *The Snarling Muse: Verbal and Visual Political Satire from Pope to Churchill*. Philadelphia: University of Pennsylvania Press, 1983.

Chapin, Chester F. *Personification in Eighteenth-Century English Poetry*. New York: Columbia University Press, 1955.

Clifford, James, ed. *Eighteenth-Century English Literature: Modern Essays in Criticism*. New York: Oxford University Press, 1959.

Damrosch, Leopold, Jr., ed. *Modern Essays on Eighteenth-Century Literature*. New York: Oxford University Press

Davie, Donald. *Articulate Energy: An Inquiry into the Syntax of English Poetry*. London: Routledge & Kegan Paul, 1955.

Davie. *Purity of Diction in English Verse*. London: Chatto & Windus

Davie, ed. *The Late Augustans: Longer Poems of the Later Eighteenth Century*. London: Heinemann, 1958., 1988., 1952.

Doody, Margaret Anne. *The Daring Muse: Augustan Poetry Reconsidered*. New York: Cambridge University Press, 1985.

Edwards, Thomas R. *Imagination and Power: A Study of Poetry on Public Themes*. New York: Oxford University Press, 1971.

Ehrenpreis, Irvin. *Acts of Implication: Suggestion and Covert Meaning in the Works of Dryden, Swift, Pope, and Austen*. Berkeley & Los Angeles: University of California Press, 1980.

Ehrenpreis. *Literary Meaning and Augustan Values*. Charlottesville: University Press of Virginia, 1974.

Engell, James. *The Creative Imagination: Enlightenment to Romanticism*. Cambridge: Harvard University Press, 1981.

Fairchild, H. N. *Religious Trends in English Poetry*, 6 volumes. New York: Columbia University Press, 1939-1968.

Fry, Paul H. *The Poet's Calling in the English Ode*. New Haven: Yale University Press, 1980.

Fussell, Paul. *The Rhetorical World of Augustan Humanism: Ethics and Imagery from Swift to Burke*. Oxford: Clarendon Press, 1965.

Fussell. *Theory of Prosody in Eighteenth-Century England*. New London: Connecticut College, 1954.

Greene, Donald. *The Age of Exuberance: Backgrounds to Eighteenth-Century English Literature*. New York: Random House, 1970.

Griffin, Dustin. *Regaining Paradise: Milton and the Eighteenth Century*. Cambridge: Cambridge University Press, 1986.

Hagstrum, Jean H. *The Sister Arts: The Tradition of Literary Pictorialism and English Poetry from Dryden to Gray*. Chicago: University of Chicago Press, 1958.

Jack, Ian. *Augustan Satire: Intention and Idiom in English Poetry, 1660-1750*. Oxford: Clarendon Press, 1952.

Jackson, Wallace. *The Probable and the Marvelous: Blake, Wordsworth, and the Eighteenth-Century Critical Tradition*. Athens: University of Georgia Press, 1978.

Jones, William Powell. *The Rhetoric of Science: A Study of Scientific Ideas and Imagery in Eighteenth-Century English Poetry*. Berkeley: University of California Press, 1966.

Keener, Frederick M., and Susan E. Lorsch, eds. *Eighteenth-Century Women and the Arts*. New York: Greenwood Press, 1988.

Knapp, Steven. *Personification and the Sublime: Milton to Coleridge*. Cambridge: Harvard University Press, 1985.

Landry, Donna. *The Muses of Resistance: Laboring-Class Women's Poetry in Britain, 1739-96*. Cambridge: Cambridge University Press, 1990.

Lipking, Lawrence I. *The Ordering of the Arts in Eighteenth-Century England*. Princeton: Princeton University Press, 1970.

Mell, Donald C. *English Poetry, 1660-1800: A Guide to Information Sources*. Detroit: Gale Research, 1982.

Mell. *A Poetics of Augustan Elegy: Studies of Poems by Dryden, Pope, Prior, Swift, Gray and Johnson*. Amsterdam: Rodopi, 1974.

Miles, Josephine. *The Continuity of Poetic Language: Studies in English Poetry from the 1540's to the 1940's*. Berkeley: University of California Press, 1951.

Miles. *Eras and Modes in English Poetry*, second edition, revised and enlarged. Berkeley: University of California Press, 1964.

Morris, David B. *The Religious Sublime: Christian Poetry and Critical Tradition in 18th-Century England*. Lexington: University Press of Kentucky, 1972.

Nicolson, Marjorie Hope. *Mountain Gloom and Mountain Glory: The Development of the Aesthetics of the Infinite.* Ithaca, N.Y.: Cornell University Press, 1959.

Nicolson. *Newton Demands the Muse: Newton's Optics and the Eighteenth-Century Poets.* Princeton: Princeton University Press, 1946.

Nokes, David. *Raillery and Rage: A Study of Eighteenth-Century Satire.* Brighton, U.K.: Harvester Press, 1987.

Nokes and Janet Barron. *An Annotated Critical Bibliography of Augustan Poetry.* New York: St. Martin's Press, 1989.

Nussbaum, Felicity A. *The Brink of All We Hate: English Satires on Women, 1660-1750.* Lexington: University Press of Kentucky, 1984.

Piper, William Bowman. *The Heroic Couplet.* Cleveland: Press of Case Western Reserve University, 1969.

Pollak, Ellen. *The Poetics of Sexual Myth: Gender and Ideology in the Verse of Swift and Pope.* Chicago: University of Chicago Press, 1985.

Price, Martin. *To the Palace of Wisdom: Studies in Order and Energy from Dryden to Blake.* Garden City, N.Y.: Doubleday, 1965.

Rawson, Claude Julien. *Order from Confusion Sprung: Studies in Eighteenth-Century Literature from Swift to Cowper.* Boston & London: Allen & Unwin, 1985.

Rothstein, Eric. *Restoration and Eighteenth-Century Poetry, 1660-1780.* Boston: Routledge & Kegan Paul, 1981.

Shuster, George N. *The English Ode from Milton to Keats.* New York: Columbia University Press, 1940.

Sitter, John. *Literary Loneliness in Mid-Eighteenth-Century England.* Ithaca, N.Y.: Cornell University Press, 1982.

Smith, David Nichol. *Some Observations on Eighteenth Century Poetry.* Toronto: University of Toronto Press, 1937.

Spacks, Patricia Meyer. *The Insistence of Horror: Aspects of the Supernatural in Eighteenth-Century Poetry.* Cambridge: Harvard University Press, 1962.

Spacks. *The Poetry of Vision: Five Eighteenth-Century Poets.* Cambridge: Harvard University Press, 1967.

Spector, Robert D. *Backgrounds to Restoration and Eighteenth-Century English Literature: An Annotated Bibliographical Guide to Modern Scholarship.* New York: Greenwood Press, 1989.

Spencer, Jeffry B. *Heroic Nature: Ideal Landscape in English Poetry from Marvell to Thomson.* Evanston, Ill.: Northwestern University Press, 1973.

Sutherland, James R. *A Preface to Eighteenth-Century Poetry.* Oxford: Clarendon Press, 1948; revised edition, London: Oxford University Press, 1963.

Tillotson, Geoffrey. *Augustan Studies.* London: Athlone Press, 1961.

Trickett, Rachel. *The Honest Muse: A Study in Augustan Verse*. Oxford: Clarendon Press, 1967.

Weinbrot, Howard. *Eighteenth-Century Satire: Essays on Text and Context from Dryden to Peter Pindar*. New York: Cambridge University Press, 1988.

Weinbrot. *The Formal Strain: Studies in Augustan Imitation and Satire*. Chicago: University of Chicago Press, 1969.

Williams, Anne. *Prophetic Strain: The Greater Lyric in the Eighteenth Century*. Chicago: University of Chicago Press, 1984.

Contributors

Lance Bertelsen ... *University of Texas at Austin*
Mary Ellen Brown ... *Indiana University*
Garland Cannon ... *Texas A&M University*
David Fairer ... *University of Leeds*
Oliver W. Ferguson ... *Duke University*
Wallace Jackson ... *Duke University*
Jennifer M. Keith ... *Emory University*
Gregory G. Kelley ... *Emory University*
Everard H. King ... *The Memorial University of Newfoundland*
Elizabeth Kraft ... *University of Georgia*
Donna Landry ... *University of Southern California*
Robert Mahony ... *The Catholic University of America*
Alan T. McKenzie ... *Purdue University*
Vincent Newey ... *University of Leicester*
Joan H. Pittock ... *University of Aberdeen*
Kate Ravin ... *Emory University*
John Sitter ... *Emory University*
Patricia Meyer Spacks ... *University of Virginia*
Karina Williamson ... *St. Hilda's College, Oxford, and University of Edinburgh*

Cumulative Index

Dictionary of Literary Biography, Volumes 1-109
Dictionary of Literary Biography Yearbook, 1980-1990
Dictionary of Literary Biography Documentary Series, Volumes 1-8

Cumulative Index

DLB before number: *Dictionary of Literary Biography,* Volumes 1-109
Y before number: *Dictionary of Literary Biography Yearbook,* 1980-1990
DS before number: *Dictionary of Literary Biography Documentary Series,* Volumes 1-8

A

B

C

D

E

F

G

H

I

J

K

L

M

N

O

P

Q

R

S

T

U

V

W

Y

Z

(Continued from front endsheets)

80: *Restoration and Eighteenth-Century Dramatists,* First Series, edited by Paula R. Backscheider (1989)

81: *Austrian Fiction Writers, 1875-1913,* edited by James Hardin and Donald G. Daviau (1989)

82: *Chicano Writers,* First Series, edited by Francisco A. Lomelí and Carl R. Shirley (1989)

83: *French Novelists Since 1960,* edited by Catharine Savage Brosman (1989)

84: *Restoration and Eighteenth-Century Dramatists,* Second Series, edited by Paula R. Backscheider (1989)

85: *Austrian Fiction Writers After 1914,* edited by James Hardin and Donald G. Daviau (1989)

86: *American Short-Story Writers, 1910-1945,* First Series, edited by Bobby Ellen Kimbel (1989)

87: *British Mystery and Thriller Writers Since 1940,* First Series, edited by Bernard Benstock and Thomas F. Staley (1989)

88: *Canadian Writers, 1920-1959,* Second Series, edited by W. H. New (1989)

89: *Restoration and Eighteenth-Century Dramatists,* Third Series, edited by Paula R. Backscheider (1989)

90: *German Writers in the Age of Goethe, 1789-1832,* edited by James Hardin and Christoph E. Schweitzer (1989)

91: *American Magazine Journalists, 1900-1960,* First Series, edited by Sam G. Riley (1990)

92: *Canadian Writers, 1890-1920,* edited by W. H. New (1990)

93: *British Romantic Poets, 1789-1832,* First Series, edited by John R. Greenfield (1990)

94: *German Writers in the Age of Goethe: Sturm und Drang to Classicism,* edited by James Hardin and Christoph E. Schweitzer (1990)

95: *Eighteenth-Century British Poets,* First Series, edited by John Sitter (1990)

96: *British Romantic Poets, 1789-1832,* Second Series, edited by John R. Greenfield (1990)

97: *German Writers from the Enlightenment to Sturm und Drang, 1720-1764,* edited by James Hardin and Christoph E. Schweitzer (1990)

98: *Modern British Essayists,* First Series, edited by Robert Beum (1990)

99: *Canadian Writers Before 1890,* edited by W. H. New (1990)

100: *Modern British Essayists,* Second Series, edited by Robert Beum (1990)

101: *British Prose Writers, 1660-1800,* First Series, edited by Donald T. Siebert (1991)

102: *American Short-Story Writers, 1910-1945,* Second Series, edited by Bobby Ellen Kimbel (1991)

103: *American Literary Biographers,* First Series, edited by Steven Serafin (1991)

104: *British Prose Writers, 1660-1800,* Second Series, edited by Donald T. Siebert (1991)

105: *American Poets Since World War II,* Second Series, edited by R. S. Gwynn (1991)

106: *British Literary Publishing Houses, 1820-1880,* edited by Patricia J. Anderson and Jonathan Rose (1991)

107: *British Romantic Prose Writers, 1789-1832,* First Series, edited by John R. Greenfield (1991)

108: *Twentieth-Century Spanish Poets,* First Series, edited by Michael L. Perna (1991)

109: *Eighteenth-Century British Poets,* Second Series, edited by John Sitter (1991)

Documentary Series

1: *Sherwood Anderson, Willa Cather, John Dos Passos, Theodore Dreiser, F. Scott Fitzgerald, Ernest Hemingway, Sinclair Lewis,* edited by Margaret A. Van Antwerp (1982)

2: *James Gould Cozzens, James T. Farrell, William Faulkner, John O'Hara, John Steinbeck, Thomas Wolfe, Richard Wright,* edited by Margaret A. Van Antwerp (1982)

3: *Saul Bellow, Jack Kerouac, Norman Mailer, Vladimir Nabokov, John Updike, Kurt Vonnegut,* edited by Mary Bruccoli (1983)

4: *Tennessee Williams,* edited by Margaret A. Van Antwerp and Sally Johns (1984)

5: *American Transcendentalists,* edited by Joel Myerson (1988)